More information about this series at https://link.springer.com/bookseries/558

Mounîm El Yacoubi · Eric Granger ·
Pong Chi Yuen · Umapada Pal ·
Nicole Vincent (Eds.)

Pattern Recognition and Artificial Intelligence

Third International Conference, ICPRAI 2022
Paris, France, June 1–3, 2022
Proceedings, Part II

Springer

Editors
Mounîm El Yacoubi
Télécom SudParis
Palaiseau, France

Eric Granger
École de Technologie Supérieure
Montreal, QC, Canada

Pong Chi Yuen
Hong Kong Baptist University
Kowloon, Kowloon, Hong Kong

Umapada Pal
Indian Statistical Institute
Kolkata, India

Nicole Vincent
Université Paris Cité
Paris, France

ISSN 0302-9743 ISSN 1611-3349 (electronic)
Lecture Notes in Computer Science
ISBN 978-3-031-09281-7 ISBN 978-3-031-09282-4 (eBook)
https://doi.org/10.1007/978-3-031-09282-4

This Springer imprint is published by the registered company Springer Nature Switzerland AG
The registered company address is: Gewerbestrasse 11, 6330 Cham, Switzerland

Preface

Welcome to the proceedings of the third International Conference on Pattern Recognition and Artificial Intelligence (ICPRAI 2022), held during June 1–3, 2022 in Paris, France. This conference follows the successful ICPRAI 2018, held in Montréal, Canada, in May 2018 and ICPRAI 2020, held in Zhongshan, China, in October 2020. It was organized by LIPADE (Laboratoire d'Informatique Paris Descartes) at Université Paris Cité with the co-operation of other French universities. The conference was endorsed by the International Association on Pattern Recognition (IAPR) and we hereby thank the organization for this support.

Pattern recognition and artificial intelligence (PRAI) techniques and systems have been applied successfully to solve practical problems in many domains. ICPRAI 2022 brought together numerous scientists from all over the world to present their innovative ideas, report their latest findings, and discuss the fruitful results of research laboratories in up to 43 countries in handwriting recognition, forensic studies, face recognition, medical imaging, deep learning, and classification techniques.

The Organizing Committee of ICPRAI 2022 consisted of well-known experts from all six (habited) continents of the world. The conference invited world-renowned keynote speakers to cover the new PRAI frontiers in depth and in breadth, and we are grateful for their insights. Due to the large number of high-quality papers submitted (a total of 152 submissions were received), the technical program included 81 presentations, as well as four special sessions, related to handwriting and text processing, computer vision and image processing, machine learning and deep networks, medical applications, forensic science and medical diagnosis, features and classification techniques, and various applications. The paper review process was carried out in a very professional way by the Program Committee members. In addition to the rich technical program, the conference also featured practical sessions, to encourage author-editor and inventor-investor interactions, and social events for all conference participants. A pre-conference doctorial consortium took place on May 31, 2022, as a satellite to the main event, offering PhD students the opportunity to present their work and meet senior researchers in their field of interest.

It was a great pleasure to organize this conference including all the above activities, promoting discussions on very innovative pieces of research work and we would like to thank all those involved for a superb technical program and conference proceedings: conference co-chairs, Edwin Hancock and Yuan Y. Tang; special session chairs, Jenny Benois-Pineau and Raphael Lins; and publication chairs, Camille Kurtz and Patrick Wang, along with all the Program Committee members.

We would like to express our gratitude to the numerous committee members who took care of the arrangement local organization, particularly to Florence Cloppet. Special thanks go to local arrangements team of the Université Paris Cité Faculty of Sciences and particularly to the Mathematics and Computer Science departments. All created a very warm and comfortable environment to work in.

Thanks are also due to the organizations listed in the proceedings and those of the organizers of ICPRAI 2022, along with the administration of Université Paris Cité, who gave us strong financial support and support in various forms and means.

Finally, we hope you found this conference to be a rewarding and memorable experience. We hope you enjoyed your stay in Paris.

April 2022

Ching Y. Suen
Nicole Vincent
Mounîm El Yacoubi
Umapada Pal
Eric Granger
Pong Chi Yuen

Organization

ICPRAI 2022 was hosted by Université Paris Cité and organized by LIPADE (Laboratoire d'Informatique Paris Descartes) of Université Paris Cité, France.

Honorary Chair

Ching Y. Suen	Concordia University, Canada

General Chair

Nicole Vincent	Université Paris Cité, France

Conference Chairs

Edwin Hancock	University of York, UK
Yuan Y. Tang	University of Macau, China

Program Chairs

Mounim El Yacoubi	Institut Polytechnique de Paris, France
Umapada Pal	Indian Statistical Institute, India
Eric Granger	École de technologie supérieure, Canada
Pong C. Yuen	Hong Kong Baptist University, China

Special Sessions Chairs

Jenny Benois-Pineau	Université de Bordeaux, France
Raphael Lins	Universidade Federal de Pernambuco, Brazil

Competition Chairs

Jean-Marc Ogier	La Rochelle Université, France
Cheng-Lin Liu	University of Chinese Academy of Sciences, China

Doctoral Consortium

Véronique Eglin	INSA de Lyon, France
Daniel Lopresti	Lehigh University, USA

Organization Chair

Florence Cloppet	Université de Paris, France

Publication Chairs

Camille Kurtz	Université Paris Cité, France
Patrick Wang	Northeastern University, USA

Exhibitions and Industrial Liaison

Alexandre Cornu	IMDS, Canada
Olivier Martinot	Telecom SudParis, France

Publicity Chairs

Jean-Christophe Burie	La Rochelle Université, France
Imran Siddiqi	Bahria University, Pakistan
Michael Blumenstein	University of Technology Sydney, Australia
Rejean Plamondon	Polytechnique Montréal, Canada

Sponsorship Chairs

Laurence Likforman	Telecom Paris, France
Josep Llados	Universitat Autònoma de Barcelona, Spain
Nicola Nobile	Concordia University, Canada

Web

Camille Kurtz	Université Paris Cité, France

Program Committee

Elisa H. Barney Smith	Boise State University, USA
Jenny Benois-Pineau	LaBRI, CNRS, University of Bordeaux, France
Saumik Bhattacharya	IIT Kanpur, India
Michael Blumenstein	University of Technology Sydney, Australia
Jean-Christophe Burie	L3i, La Rochelle Université, France
Sukalpa Chanda	Østfold University College, Norway
Jocelyn Chanussot	Grenoble INP, France
Christophe Charrier	Normandie Université, France
Rama Chellappa	University of Maryland, USA
Farida Cheriet	Polytechnique Montreal, Canada

Florence Cloppet	LIPADE, Université Paris Cité, France
Alberto Del Bimbo	Università degli Studi di Firenze, Italy
Christian Desrosiers	École de technologie supérieure, Canada
Véronique Eglin	LIRIS, INSA de LYON, France
Mounîm A. El Yacoubi	Institut Polytechnique de Paris, France
Gernot Fink	TU Dortmund University, Germany
Andreas Fischer	University of Fribourg, Switzerland
Robert Fisher	University of Edinburgh, UK
Giorgio Fumera	University of Cagliari, Italy
Basilis Gatos	Institute of Informatics and Telecommunications, National Center for Scientific Research, Demokritos, Greece
Eric Granger	École de technologie supérieure, Canada
Edwin Hancock	University of York, UK
Xiaoyi Jiang	University of Münster, Germany
Xiaoyue Jiang	Northwestern Polytechnical University, China
Camille Kurtz	Université Paris Cité, France
Laurence Likforman-Sulem	LTCI, Télécom Paris, Institut Polytechnique de Paris, France
Rafael Lins	Federal University of Pernambuco, Brazil
Cheng-Lin Liu	Institute of Automation, Chinese Academy of Sciences, China
Josep Llados	Universitat Autònoma de Barcelona, Spain
Daniel Lopresti	Lehigh University, USA
Yue Lu	East China Normal University, China
Khoa Luu	Carnegie Mellon University, USA
Angelo Marcelli	Università di Salerno, Italy
Jean Meunier	University of Montreal, Canada
Atul Negi	University of Hyderabad, India
Jean-Marc Ogier	L3i, University of La Rochelle, France
Wataru Ohyama	Saitama Institute of Technology, Japan
Srikanta Pal	Griffith University, Australia
Umapada Pal	Indian Statistical Institute, India
Nicolas Passat	CReSTIC, Université de Reims Champagne-Ardenne, France
Marius Pedersen	Norwegian University of Science and Technology, Norway
Marco Pedersoli	École de technologie supérieure, Canada
Giuseppe Pirlo	University of Bari, Italy
Ajita Rattani	University of Cagliari, Italy
Kaushik Roy	West Bengal State University, India
Partha Pratim Roy	Indian Institute of Technology, India

Su Ruan	Université de Rouen, France
Friedhelm Schwenker	Ulm University, Germany
Imran Siddiqi	Bahria University, Pakistan
Nicolas Thome	Cnam, France
Massimo Tistarelli	University of Sassari, Italy
Seiichi Uchida	Kyushu University, Japan
Nicole Vincent	Universite de Paris, France
Richard Wilson	University of York, UK
Yirui Wu	Hohai University, China
Vera Yashina	Dorodnicyn Computing Center, Russian Academy of Sciences, Russia
Xiao Feng	Northwestern Polytechnical University, China

Keynote Speakers

ICPRAI 2022 was proud to host the following keynote speakers:

Bidyut B. Chaudhuri	Computer Vision & Pattern Recognition Unit, Indian Statistical Institute, India	"Bengali Handwriting Recognition with Transformative Generative Adversarial Net (TGAN)"
Robert B. Fisher	School of Informatics, University of Edinburgh, Scotland, UK	"The TrimBot2020 outdoor gardening robot"
Walter G. Kropatsch	Vienna University of Technology, Austria	"Controlling Topology-Preserving Graph-Pyramid"

Sponsors

Université
Paris Cité

LIPADE
Laboratoire d'Informatique PAris DEscartes

Sciences
Université Paris Cité

IAPR

World Scientific
www.worldscientific.com

international medias
IMDS
data services

IDEMIA

Contents – Part II

Pattern Recognition

Machine Learning

Information Extraction

Contents – Part I

Document

Video – 3D

Feature

Pattern Recognition

PE-former: Pose Estimation Transformer

Paschalis Panteleris[1(✉)] and Antonis Argyros[1,2]

[1] Institute of Computer Science, FORTH, Heraklion, Crete, Greece
{padeler,argyros}@ics.forth.gr
[2] Computer Science Department, University of Crete, Rethimno, Greece
https://www.ics.forth.gr/hccv/

Abstract. Vision transformer architectures have been demonstrated to work very effectively for image classification tasks. Efforts to solve more challenging vision tasks with transformers rely on convolutional backbones for feature extraction. In this paper we investigate the use of a pure transformer architecture (i.e., one with no CNN backbone) for the problem of 2D body pose estimation. We evaluate two ViT architectures on the COCO dataset. We demonstrate that using an encoder-decoder transformer architecture yields state of the art results on this estimation problem.

Keywords: Vision transformers · Human pose estimation

1 Introduction

In recent years, transformers have been gaining ground versus traditional convolutional neural networks in a number of computer vision tasks. The work of Dosovitskiy et al. [3] demonstrated the use of the pure transformer model for image classification. This was followed by a number of recent papers demonstrating improved performance [12], reduced computational requirements [4,14,16,18] or both. All of these pure transformer models are applied only to the task of image classification. For more challenging vision tasks such as 2D human pose estimation, recent methods [7,8,17] use a combination of a convolutional backbone followed by a transformer front-end to achieve similar performance to that of convolutional architectures.

In this work[1], we investigate the use of a pure transformer-based architecture for the task of 2D human pose estimation. More specifically, we focus on single instance, direct coordinate regression of the human body keypoints. We evaluate an encoder-decoder architecture derived from the work of Carion et al. [1]. In our

[1] The research work was supported by the Hellenic Foundation for Research and Innovation (HFRI) under the HFRI PhD Fellowship grant (Fellowship Number: 1592) and by HFRI under the "1st Call for H.F.R.I Research Projects to support Faculty members and Researchers and the procurement of high-cost research equipment", project I.C.Humans, number 91. This work was also partially supported by the NVIDIA "Academic Hardware Grant" program.

M. El Yacoubi et al. (Eds.): ICPRAI 2022, LNCS 13364, pp. 3–14, 2022.
https://doi.org/10.1007/978-3-031-09282-4_1

model we eliminate the need for a convolutional based backbone (a ResNet in the case of [1]) and we replace the encoder part of the transformer with a vision-based [3] transformer encoder. By foregoing with the need of a convolutional backbone, our model is realized by a much simpler architecture.

For the encoder part, we investigate the use of two vision transformer architectures:

- Deit [12]: ViT architecture trained with distillation, which exhibits baseline performance for vision transformers.
- Xcit [4]: Cross-covariance transformers. Xcit reduces the computational requirements by transposing the way ViT operates, i.e., instead of attending on tokens the transformer attends on the token-channels.

When comparing to other regression based methods [7,8] which use a combination of transformers and convolutional backbones, our Deit-based model performs on par with similar sized (in million parameters) models. Moreover, our best model using an Xcit-based encoder achieves state of the art results on the COCO dataset.

We compare our transformer-only architecture with two "baselines". One that uses a ResNet50 as the encoder section and another that uses a ViT (encoder+decoder) feature extractor. The architecture and details of these baselines are discussed in Sect. 3. We demonstrate experimentally that against these baselines, when everything else is kept the same, the transformer encoder improves performance.

Finally, we further improve the performance of our models using unsupervised pre-training, as proposed by Caron et al. [2]. The training results of models that use supervised and unsupervised pre-training are presented in Sect. 4.

In summary, the contributions of our work[2] are the following:

- We propose a novel architecture for 2D human pose estimation that is using vision transformers without the need for a CNN backbone for feature extraction.
- We demonstrate that our proposed architecture outperforms the SOTA on public datasets by as much as 4.4% in AP (compared to [7]).
- We evaluate the performance of different vision transformer encoders for the task of 2D human pose estimation.
- We demonstrate that the unsupervised pretraining of our transformer-based models, improves their performance by 0.5% (for the Xcit model).

2 Related Work

2.1 Vision Transformers

The success of transformers in Natural Language Processing (NLP) has motivated a lot of researchers to adopt transformers for the solution of vision tasks.

[2] Code is available on https://github.com/padeler/PE-former.

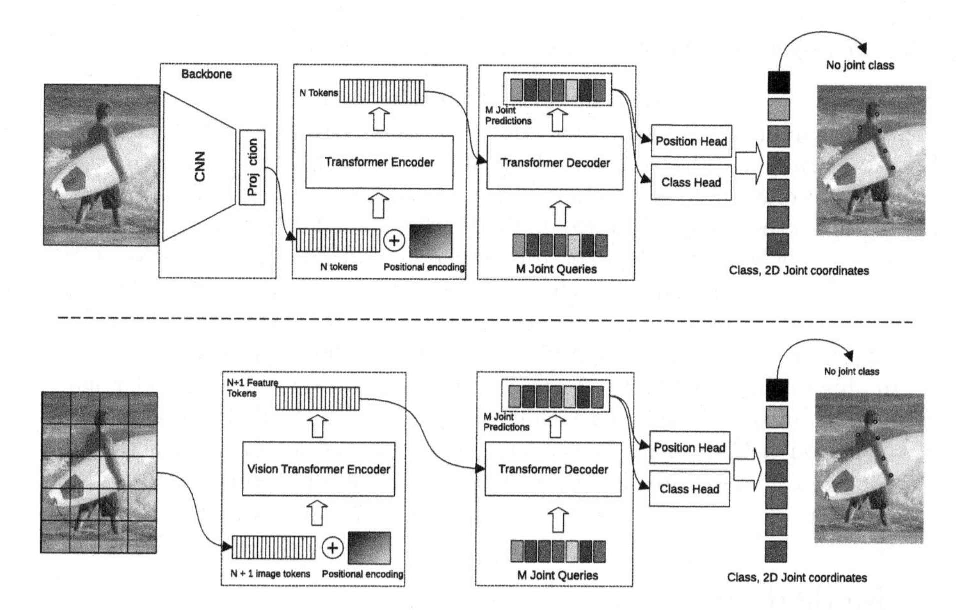

Fig. 1. The DETR model adapted for 2D human pose estimation (top) and our proposed model using Visual transformers (bottom). In our model, the cropped image of a person (bottom left), is split into N tokens of $p \times p$ pixels (typically p is equal to 8 or 16 pixels). The tokens are processed by the transformer encoder (can be Deit or Xcit based). The output feature tokens ($N + 1$ for the class token) are used as the memory tokens in the DETR based transformer decoder. The decoder input is M joint queries. $M = 100$ in our experiments. The Decoder outputs M prediction tokens which are processed by a classification and a regression head (FFNs). The output is 2D joint locations (range $[0, 1]$) and class predictions.

While attention-based mechanisms acting on image features such as the ones produced from a CNN, have been around for many years, only recently, Dosovitskiy et al. [3] demonstrated successfully with ViT the use of transformers for image feature extraction, replacing the use of CNNs for the task of image classification. While the ViT approach is very promising, it still suffers from issues that arise from the quadratic complexity of the attention mechanism and translates to heavy computational and memory requirements. Additionally, the vanilla ViT models and, especially, their larger variants, are very hard to train and require to be trained on huge annotated datasets. Following ViT, many methods [9,14,16,18,19] appeared trying to solve or circumvent these issues while also maintaining SOTA performance [4,12]. In this work, we incorporate two very promising architectures, DEIT [12] and Xcit [4] in our models and evaluate their performance.

2.2 Transformers for Pose Estimation

Attention-based mechanisms have been applied to tackle demanding vision tasks such as 2D human pose estimation. However, these rely on CNN backbones for feature extraction. The addition of an attention mechanism enables methods such as the one proposed by Li et al. [7] to achieve state of the art results, improving on the best CNN based methods such as the HRNet by Sun et al. [11]. However, Li et al. Li et al. [7] base their model and build on an HRNet CNN backbone. Similarly, methods such as TFPose by Mao et al. [8], POET by Stoffl et al. [10] and Transpose by Yang et al. [17], build on a robust CNN backbone and apply the attention mechanism on the extracted image features.

In this work, similarly to [7], we use the transformer-based decoder module and the bipartite matching technique of Carion et al. [1]. However, instead of relying on a CNN backbone or encoder for image features extraction, we introduce an architecture that directly uses the output features from a vision transformer.

3 Method

As shown in Fig. 1 (bottom row), our architecture consists of two major components: A Visual Transformer encoder, and a Transformer decoder. The input image is initially converted into tokens following the ViT paradigm. A position embedding [13] is used to help retain the patch-location information. The tokens and the position embedding are used as input to transformer encoder. The transformed tokens are used as the memory [1] input of the transformer decoder. The inputs of the decoder are M learned queries. For each query the network produces a joint prediction. The output tokens from the transformer decoder are passed through two heads. The heads are feed forward neural networks (FFNs) following the architecture of DETR. The first is a classification head used to predict the joint type (i.e., class) of each query. The second is a regression head that predicts the normalized coordinates in the range $[0, 1]$ of the joint in the input image. Predictions that do not correspond to joints are mapped to a "non object" class.

In Sect. 3.1 we discuss the details of our encoder module and we present the architecture of the various encoders that we examined. In Sect. 3.2 we present the details of the decoder module which is derived from the DETR decoder. Finally, in Sect. 3.3, we discuss the training techniques and hyperparameters used for the experiments.

3.1 Transformer Encoder

Dosovitskiy et al. [3] proposed the use of image patches which, in the case of ViT, have a size of 16×16. This approach of splitting the image into patches is adopted by all the vision transformer methods that appeared since ViT. In general, an input image of dimensions $W \times H$ pixels, is split into $n \times m$ patches, each of which is a square block of $p \times p$ pixels. These patches are flattened into vectors (tokens) and are subsequently passed through the transformer [13] layers. The self-attention mechanism operates on an input matrix $X \in R^{N \times d}$, where N is the number of tokens. Each token has d dimensions. The input X is linearly projected to queries, keys and values (Q, K, V). Keys and values are used to compute an attention map

$$A(K, Q) = Softmax(QK^T/\sqrt{d}).$$

The results of the self-attention mechanism is the weighted sum of the values V with the attention map:

$$Attention(Q, K, V) = A(K, Q)V.$$

The computational complexity of this original self-attention mechanism scales quadratically with N, due to pairwise interactions between all N elements. The use of image patches in ViT instead of pixels makes the use of self-attention tractable, but the quadratic complexity still remains an issue.

In addition to the tokens created from the image patches, a vision transformer also has an extra (learned) token. This token, usually called the CLS token, is used to generate the final prediction when the transformer is trained for a classification task. The transformed tokens at the output of the encoder have the same number of channels as the input. In our model, the output tokens of the encoder transformer including the CLS token are used as the "memory" input of the decoder transformer.

DeiT Encoder: Touvron et al. [12] proposed a training methodology for the ViT architecture that enables efficient training of the vision transformer without the use of huge datasets. The proposed methodology enabled DeiT models to surpass the accuracy of the ViT baseline, while training just on the ImageNet dataset. They further improved on that by proposing a distillation strategy that yielded accuracy similar to that of the best convolutional models. Our DeiT encoder uses the *DeiT-S* model architecture. For our experiments, the encoders are initialized using either the weights provided by the DeiT authors (DeiT-S, trained with distillation at 224 × 224) of the weights provided by the Dino authors. For our experiments we use two versions of the DeiT-S model, both trained with input sizes of 224 × 224 pixels:

1. the DeiT-S variant trained with distillation and
2. the DeiT-S trained using the unsupervised methodology of Dino.

Xcit Encoder: El-Nouby et al. [4] recently proposed the Xcit transformer. In this approach they transpose the encoder architecture. Attention happens between the channels of the tokens rather than between the tokens themselves. The proposed attention mechanism is complemented by blocks that enable "local patch interations", enabling the exchange of information between neighboring tokens on the image plane.

The Xcit transformer scales linearly with the size of patches since the memory and computation expensive operation of attention is applied to the channels which are fixed in size. This characteristic of Xcit enables training with larger input image sizes and more patches. In our experiments we use the *Xcit-Small-12* variant of the model which corresponds roughly to the *DeiT-S* variant of the DeiT architecture. Similar to the DeiT (Sect. 3.1) encoder we use pre-trained weights for this encoder. The weights are obtained with

1. supervised training on the ImageNet and
2. with the unsupervised methodology of Dino.

Resnet Encoder: In order to verify the positive impact of our proposed attention-based encoder we implemented a third type of encoder, this time using Resnet50 [6] as the architecture. The 50-layer variant was selected because it has a similar number of parameters as the examined transformer-based encoders.

The Resnet encoder replaces the "Visual Transformer Encoder" block shown in Fig. 1. Following the DETR implementation we use a 1×1 convolution to project the output features of the Resnet to the number of channels expected by the decoder. Subsequently we unroll each feature channel to a vector. These vectors are passed as the memory tokens to the decoder. The Resnet50 encoder is used to experimentally validate the positive effect of using vision transformers (DEIT or Xcit) versus a conventional convolutional encoder.

VAB (ViT as Backbone): Related work that tackles pose estimation with transformers typically uses a convolutional backbone to extract image features. This model architecture is shown on the top row of Fig. 1. The features created by the CNN backbone are flattened and used as input tokens to a transformer front-end. In this model the transformer consists of an encoder and a decoder block.

For our experiments we replace the CNN backbone for a visual transformer. The vision transformer outputs feature tokens which are subsequently processed by the (unchanged) transformer encoder-decoder block. We call this modification VAB for "ViT as Backbone". The VAB approach is closer in spirit to contemporary methods for pose estimation replacing only the CNN backbone with ViT. However it is larger in number of parameters and requires more computational resources than its CNN-based counterparts. In our experiments we use the DeiT-S as the visual transformer backbone.

3.2 Transformer Decoder

We adapt the decoder block of DETR and use it in our model. A number of learned queries are used to predict joint locations. Predictions that do not correspond to a joint are mapped to the "non-object" class. Following the work of Li et al. [7] we use $M = 100$ queries for all our models. Adding more queries does not improve the result, while having queries equal to the number of expected joints (i.e., 17 for the COCO dataset) gives slightly worse results.

Bipartite graph matching is used at training time to map the regressed joints to the ground truth annotations. In contrast to the DETR decoder, our decoder is configured to regress to 2D keypoints rather than object bounding boxes. This translates to regressing 2 scalar values (x, y) in the range of $[0, 1]$ for each joint. In all our experiments we used a decoder with 6 layers which achieves a good performance balance. Adding more layers to the decoder gives slightly improved results at a cost of more parameters and higher computational and memory requirements.

3.3 Training

We use AdamW to train our models with a weight decay of $1e-4$. For all our experiments we use pretrained encoders while the decoder weights are randomly initialized. The pretrained weights used are noted in each experiment. The learning rate for the encoder is set to $1e-5$ and for the decoder to $1e-4$. The learning rate drops by a factor of 10 after the first 50 epochs and the models are trained for a total of 80 epochs. For all our models we use a batch size of 42.

For data augmentation we follow the approach of Xiao et al. [15]. According to this we apply a random scaling in the range $[0.7, 1.3]$, a random rotation in the range ($[-40°, 40°]$) and a random flip to the image crop. We found experimentally that the jitter, blur and solarization used by [1] for the object detection task were not helpful in our 2D human pose estimation problem, so these operations were not used.

4 Experiments

We compare against two other regression based methods [7,8] for single instance 2D human pose estimation. Both of these methods use a convolutional backbone and an attention mechanism derived from the DETR decoder to regress to the 2D keypoints of a human in the input image crop.

4.1 Evaluation Methodology

We train and evaluate our models on the COCO val dataset. We use the detection results from a person detector with AP 50.2 on the COCO Val2017 set. Following standard practice [7,15] we use flip test and average the results from the original and flipped images. Unless otherwise noted, the methods we compare against use the same evaluation techniques.

4.2 Comparison with SOTA

As shown in Table 1, our architecture performs on par or surpasses methods that use CNN backbones for the same task. Using the DEIT encoder requires more

Table 1. A comparison of transformer based methods for 2D body pose estimation with direct regression. Both TFPose [8] and PRTR [7] models use a Resnet50 for backbone. The dataset is COCO2017-Val. Flip test is used on all methods. The decoder depth for all models is 6. Note: the code for TFPose [8] is not available and the model is not provided by the authors, so the number of parameters is unknown. In our work the "-Dino" suffix denotes the use of unsupervised pretraining, Xcit refers to Xcit-small-12, and Deit refers to Deit-small.

Method	Input size	#Parameters	AP	AR
TFPose	192×256	–	71.0	–
TFPose	288×384	–	72.4	–
PRTR	288×384	41.5M	68.2	76
PRTR	384×512	41.5M	71.0	78
OURS-Deit-dino-p8	192×256	36.4M	70.6	78.1
OURS-Xcit-p16	288×384	40.6M	70.2	77.4
OURS-Xcit-dino-p16	288×384	40.6M	70.7	77.9
OURS-Xcit-dino-p8	192×256	40.5M	71.6	78.7
OURS-Xcit-dino-p8	288×384	40.5M	72.6	79.4

memory and CPU resources although the number of parameters is relatively low. Due to the increased requirements, we limit our comparison tests of DEIT to 192×256 resolution for patch sizes of 8×8 pixels.

Our DEIT variant scores just 0.4% lower than TFPose[3] for input 192×256. However, it outperforms PRTR @ 288×384, despite the higher input resolution and the greater number of parameters ($5.1M$) of the later.

Due to its reduced computational and memory requirements, our Xcit variant can be trained to higher resolutions and, thus, larger number of input tokens. We train networks at 192×256 and 288×384 input resolutions for the 16×16 and 8×8 patch sizes. Our Xcit based models outperform both the TFPose and PRTR networks at their corresponding resolutions, while having the same number of parameters as PRTR.

Overall, patch size of 8×8 pixels and resolutions of 288×384 yield the best performance. In fact, our Xcit-based network (Xcit-dino-p8) at 288×384 outperforms the PRTR trained at the same resolution by 4.4% in AP and 3.4% in AR and even outperforms PRTR at resolution 384×512 by 1.6% in AP. However, experiments of the Xcit variant at even higher resolutions (384×512) did not show any significant improvements.

4.3 Transformer vs CNN vs VAB Encoders

We evaluate the performance of a transformer based encoder (Deit, Xcit) versus a CNN (Resnet50) based encoder and a VAB model. The networks are trained on

[3] We contacted the authors of TFPose for additional information to use in our comparison, such as number of parameters and AR scores but got no response.

Table 2. Encoder Comparison. Deit vs Xcit vs resnet50 vs VAB. For all experiments the patch size is set to 16×16 pixels. Input resolution is 192×256. All Networks are trained and evaluated on the COCO val dataset. Deit performs worse while also having the smallest number of parameters. Xcit is the best performing overall, however it also has 10% more parameters than Deit.

Method	#Parameters	AP	AR
Resnet50-PE-former	39.0M	63.4	72.2
VAB	47.4M	63.2	72.6
Deit	36.4M	62.2	71.6
Xcit	40.6M	66.2	74.6

Table 3. Comparison of Unsupervised Dino weight init. Patch size is set to 16 and input size is 192×256. Dino networks are identical but initialized with the weights of networks trained with the dino unsupervised methodology. Networks are trained and evaluated on the COCO val dataset. Interestingly, the Resnet50 variant does not show the same improvements as the attention-based encoders with unsupervised pre-training.

Method	# Parameters	AP	AR
Deit	36.4M	62.2	71.6
Dino Deit	36.4M	66.7	75.0
Xcit	40.6M	66.2	74.6
Dino Xcit	40.6M	68.0	76.1
Resnet50-PE-former	39.0M	63.4	72.2
Dino Resnet50-PE-former	39.0M	61.0	70.1

COCO and evaluated on the COCO2017-val. For all the encoders, the imagenet pretrained weights are used. The results are shown in Table 2. The networks are trained with an input resolution of 192×256 and patch size of 16×16 pixels. Apart from replacing the encoders, the rest of the model (decoder) and training hyperparameters are kept the same.

As expected, VAB is the largest network with the highest memory and computational requirements. However, it performs on par with the Resnet50 variant. The Resnet variant despite having almost the same number of parameters as Xcit, requires less memory and computational resources during training and inference. Still, it under-performs compared to Xcit by 2.8% in AP and 2.4% in AR. The Deit variant performs a bit worse (1.2% in AP) than Resnet but it is also smaller by $2.6M$ parameters.

Xcit exhibits the best overall performance with a lead of 2.8% in AP and 2.4% in AR over the Resnet50 variant.

4.4 Unsupervised Pre-training

All the models presented in Sect. 3 use pre-trained weights for the encoder part, while the decoder's weights are randomly initialized. We use the weights as they are provided by the authors of each architecture Deit[4], Xcit[5]). Additionally, we evaluate the use of weights[6] created using unsupervised learning [2]. More specifically, we evaluate using the Deit, Xcit and Resnet50 encoders.

Table 3 presents the obtained results. For the purposes of our evaluation we train two Deit (deit-small) and two Xcit (xcit-small-12) variants. For all variants, input resolution of 192×256 and patch size is set to 16×16. All hyper-parameters are kept the same. We initialize the encoders of the Dino variants using weights acquired with unsupervised learning on Imagenet. In contrast, the normal variants start with encoders initialized with weights acquired with supervised learning on Imagenet. For both Deit and Xcit we observe significant improvement on the performance. However, the amount of improvement drops as the overall performance of the network gets higher (see the entries of Table 1 for *OURS-Xcit-p16* and *OURS-Xcit-dino-p16*).

As the authors of [2] hypothesise, we believe that this improvement stems from having the dino-trained model learn a different embedding than the supervised variant. The model is focusing only on the salient parts of the image (i.e., the person) and is not miss-guided by annotation biases and errors that affect the supervised approach. This hypotheses is further supported by the recent work of He et al. [5] on unsupervised learning using masked autoencoders.

Interestingly, our CNN based encoder (Resnet50) does not benefit from the unsupervised pretraining. The resnet50-PE-former-dino pretrained with the DINO weights, yields worse results than the supervised variant (resnet50-PE-former). This result hints to a fundamentally different way the transformer-based methods learn about salient image parts: When training a CNN, interactions are local on each layer (i.e., depend on the size of the convolutional kernel). On the other hand, vision transformers such as Xcit and Deit, allow for long-range interactions. Long range interactions enable the exchange of information between areas in the image that are far apart. For DINO the implicit task during training is to identify salient parts in an image. As a consequence long range interactions help the network reason about larger objects (i.e., a person).

For models with the transformer based encoders (deit, xcit), it is possible that further fine tuning such as pre-training on the same resolution as the final network or pre-training on a person dataset (i.e. COCO-person) instead of imagenet, could further boost the final gains. However these tasks are beyond the scope of this work and are left for future work.

[4] https://github.com/facebookresearch/deit.
[5] https://github.com/facebookresearch/xcit.
[6] https://github.com/facebookresearch/dino.

5 Conclusions

We presented a novel encoder-decoder architecture using only transformers that achieves SOTA results for the task for single instance 2D human pose estimation. We evaluated two very promising ViT variants as our encoders: Xcit and Deit. We verified the positive impact of our transformer based encoder-decoder by comparing with modified versions of our model with a CNN-encoder and a VAB variant. Out model using the Xcit based encoder, performs best both in accuracy and resource requirements, outperforming contemporary methods by as mach as 4.4% in AP on the COCO-val dataset. Our Deit based encoder variant is on par with methods using CNN based backbones for patch sizes of 8×8 pixels. Furthermore, we demonstrate that using unsupervised pretraining can improve performance, especially for larger patch sizes (i.e., 16×16).

Attention-based models look promising for a range of vision tasks. It is conceivable that, with further improvements on the architectures or the training methodologies, these models will dethrone the older CNN-based architectures both in accuracy and resource requirements.

References

1. Carion, N., Massa, F., Synnaeve, G., Usunier, N., Kirillov, A., Zagoruyko, S.: End-to-end object detection with transformers. In: Vedaldi, A., Bischof, H., Brox, T., Frahm, J.-M. (eds.) ECCV 2020. LNCS, vol. 12346, pp. 213–229. Springer, Cham (2020). https://doi.org/10.1007/978-3-030-58452-8_13
2. Caron, M., et al.: Emerging properties in self-supervised vision transformers. arXiv preprint arXiv:2104.14294 (2021)
3. Dosovitskiy, A., et al.: An image is worth 16 × 16 words: transformers for image recognition at scale. arXiv preprint arXiv:2010.11929 (2020)
4. El-Nouby, A., et al.: Xcit: cross-covariance image transformers. arXiv preprint arXiv:2106.09681 (2021)
5. He, K., Chen, X., Xie, S., Li, Y., Dollár, P., Girshick, R.: Masked autoencoders are scalable vision learners. arXiv preprint arXiv:2111.06377 (2021)
6. He, K., Zhang, X., Ren, S., Sun, J.: Deep residual learning for image recognition. In: Proceedings of the IEEE Conference on Computer Vision and Pattern Recognition, pp. 770–778 (2016)
7. Li, K., Wang, S., Zhang, X., Xu, Y., Xu, W., Tu, Z.: Pose recognition with cascade transformers. In: Proceedings of the IEEE/CVF Conference on Computer Vision and Pattern Recognition, pp. 1944–1953 (2021)
8. Mao, W., Ge, Y., Shen, C., Tian, Z., Wang, X., Wang, Z.: Tfpose: direct human pose estimation with transformers. arXiv preprint arXiv:2103.15320 (2021)
9. Mehta, S., Rastegari, M.: Mobilevit: light-weight, general-purpose, and mobile-friendly vision transformer. arXiv preprint arXiv:2110.02178 (2021)
10. Stoffl, L., Vidal, M., Mathis, A.: End-to-end trainable multi-instance pose estimation with transformers. arXiv preprint arXiv:2103.12115 (2021)
11. Sun, K., Xiao, B., Liu, D., Wang, J.: Deep high-resolution representation learning for human pose estimation. In: Proceedings of the IEEE/CVF Conference on Computer Vision and Pattern Recognition, pp. 5693–5703 (2019)

12. Touvron, H., Cord, M., Douze, M., Massa, F., Sablayrolles, A., Jégou, H.: Training data-efficient image transformers & distillation through attention. In: International Conference on Machine Learning, pp. 10347–10357. PMLR (2021)
13. Vaswani, A., et al.: Attention is all you need. In: Advances in Neural Information Processing Systems, pp. 5998–6008 (2017)
14. Wang, S., Li, B.Z., Khabsa, M., Fang, H., Ma, H.: Linformer: self-attention with linear complexity. arXiv preprint arXiv:2006.04768 (2020)
15. Xiao, B., Wu, H., Wei, Y.: Simple baselines for human pose estimation and tracking. In: European Conference on Computer Vision (ECCV) (2018)
16. Xiong, Y., et al.: Nystr\" omformer: A nystr\" om-based algorithm for approximating self-attention. arXiv preprint arXiv:2102.03902 (2021)
17. Yang, S., Quan, Z., Nie, M., Yang, W.: Transpose: keypoint localization via transformer. In: Proceedings of the IEEE/CVF International Conference on Computer Vision, pp. 11802–11812 (2021)
18. Yuan, L., et al.: Tokens-to-token VIT: training vision transformers from scratch on imagenet. arXiv preprint arXiv:2101.11986 (2021)
19. Zhang, Z., Zhang, H., Zhao, L., Chen, T., Pfister, T.: Aggregating nested transformers. arXiv preprint arXiv:2105.12723 (2021)

ConDense: Multiple Additional Dense Layers with Fine-Grained Fully-Connected Layer Optimisation for Fingerprint Recognition

Dane Lang and Dustin van der Haar(✉)

University of Johannesburg, Auckland Park, Gauteng, South Africa
201042463@student.uj.ac.za, dvanderhaar@uj.ac.za

Abstract. Fingerprint recognition is now a common, well known and generally accepted form of biometric authentication. The popularity of fingerprint recognition also makes it the focus of many studies which aim to constantly improve the technology in terms of factors such as accuracy and speed. This study sets out to create fingerprint recognition architectures which improve upon pre-trained architectures - named ConDense - that provide stronger if not comparable accuracy in comparison to related works on the authentication/identification task. Each of these ConDense architectures are tested against databases 1A, 2A, 3A provided by FVC 2006. The ConDense architectures presented in this study performed well across the varying image qualities in the given databases, with the lowest EERs achieved by this study's architectures being 1.385% (DB1A), 0.041% (DB2A) and 0.871% (DB3A). In comparison to related works, the architectures presented in this study performed the best in terms of EER against DB1A, and DB3A. The lowest EER for DB2A reported by a related work was 0.00%.

Keywords: Fingerprint recognition · Convolutional Neural Networks · Transfer learning

1 Problem Background

Fingerprint recognition is now a common, well known and generally accepted form of biometric authentication, an example of which can be seen in modern mobile devices which allow for the authentication of their users through scanning a fingerprint [11]. The popularity of fingerprint recognition also makes it the focus of many studies which aim to constantly improve the technology in terms of factors such as accuracy and speed. This study set out to accomplish two objectives. 1) Create a fingerprint authentication approach, which performs on a comparable if not higher level than related implementations when testing against the study's selected dataset, FVC 2006. 2) Perform a comparison of related fingerprint recognition approaches in order to find the most suitable candidate for use in a fingerprint recognition-based solution. This was enabled

M. El Yacoubi et al. (Eds.): ICPRAI 2022, LNCS 13364, pp. 15–27, 2022.
https://doi.org/10.1007/978-3-031-09282-4_2

by the use of the FVC 2006 [2] competition's fingerprint database which was used to provide a means of evaluating this study's approaches as well as serve to provide other solutions to compare this study's approaches against. Each of the architectures created in this study build additional dense layers on top of pre-trained architectures to improve performance over the base architectures. Few other works evaluate the effect of additional dense layers on CNNs, leading to this approach being named ConDense. The contributions of this study are:

- Results which show that the CNN architectures produced in this study, when tested against FVC 2006's databases DB1A and DB3A, score the lowest EERs when compared against a range of related works from FVC2006's commencement up to modern works.
- A study which shows that optimising the fully connected layers of a CNN can improve the performance of that CNN in terms of EER, ranging from the highest found increase of 60% to the highest reduction of 48%.
- An ablation study which shows that slower learning rates, higher dense layer sizes, and lower dropout percentages result in lower CNN EERs.

In Sect. 2 this paper will first provide an overview of related works. These range from modern implementations to those from the initial FVC 2006 competition. Section 3 provides a high level description of the approach that was used to set up the architectures used in this study. This is followed by the results in Sects. 4, 5 and 6 which detail the architectures created for this study as well as a comparison with the found related work. This paper closes with Sect. 7 which provides a summary of its results.

2 Related Work

A number or related studies on improving fingerprint matching have been performed that uses the FVC 2006's fingerprint databases. This section provides a discussion on these studies. Each which use subsets of the databases provided by FVC 2006 to test their architectures. The results posted by these studies will then be used to compare against the performance of the three architectures presented by this paper.

Priesnitz, Huesmann, Rathgeb, Buchmann and Busch [11] presented a COVID-19 inspired approach to touchless fingerprint recognition. Their approach relies on a mobile device to capture an image of a subject's fingers which run through a series of pre-processing steps which include Otsu's thresholding and a number of processes which isolate each finger's fingertip. One of the databases they tested their solution against was FVC 2006's DB2A where they scored an equal error rate (EER) of 0.15% [11].

He, Liu and Xiang [6] developed an architecture that consisted of two high-level stages: Image alignment through a spatial transformer and image matching via a deep residual network (ResNet). The spacial transformer the authors developed was named AlignNet and was used to allow for rotation invariance in their architecture. The images generated by AlignNet used their ResNet implementation which classified them as either genuine or impostor matches. The authors tested their database against DB1A of FVC 2006 and reported an EER of 3.587% [6].

Sanchez-Fernandez, Romero, Peralta, Medina-Perez, Saeys, Herrera and Tabik [13] created a latent fingerprint identification system - ALFI - which utilised parallelism to quickly process large fingerprint databases. Their study used minutiae-based feature extraction and matching approaches for fingerprint identification. The relevant FVC 2006 databases against which the authors tested their approach are DB2A and DB3A where they scored EERs of 0.48% and 3.70% respectively [13].

Kaggwa, Ngubiri and Tushabe [7] performed a study which compared the results of three separate approaches for feature extraction and matching:

- Minutiae based
- Gabor Filter based
- Combined Feature Level and Score Level Gabor Filter based

The authors' combined feature level and score level gabor filter based approach performed the best in their study, outperforming each of the other approaches in all experiments. The authors begin by using Gabor feature extraction to obtain a set of Gabor features which are then structured into column vectors. These column vectors are then used in "random feature level fusion" [7] before matching. These extracted features are then fed into the matching process, which consists of two steps. Their approach first determines the Euclidean distance between the extracted features to obtain matching scores, followed by score level fusion using the Max Rule [7]. The authors performed their experiments in six permutation sets against DB2A of FVC 2006. The best EER they obtained was in set two, which was 0.00%.

Wahby Shalaby and Omair Ahmad [15] proposed a scheme named "Multilevel Structural Technique for Fingerprint Recognition" (MSFR). In MSFR, fingerprint images are first broken down into a set smaller images that make up the original whole image. The features extracted from these smaller images and the features of the complete image are then used to build a template. The resulting template is then used in the scheme's matching process, which takes into account the features of both the small images and the complete image when matching against another template. The authors tested MSFR against DB1 of FVC 2006 and reported an EER of 5.21%.

Khazaei and Mohades [8] built an approach which makes use of Voronoi diagrams to perform fingerprint matching. Their approach involves first preprocessing images by applying a Gabor filter and skeletonisation to input fingerprint images. Feature extraction is performed on the pre-processed images and Voronoi diagrams are built from the extracted features. The Voronoi diagrams are used to determine central cells which are then provided to a matching algorithm for comparison. The authors tested their approach against databases 1A, 2A and 3A of FVC 2006 and obtained EERs of 2.8% (DB1A), 3.65% (DB2A) and 1.15% (DB3A).

Lastly, the organisers of FVC 2006 posted the results of their competition which included the top three algorithms by EER in both their open and light categories. In the open category, the best performing algorithms for each database scored 5.564% (DB1), 0.021% (DB2) and 1.534% (DB3). The best performing algorithms for the light category scored 5.356% (DB1), 0.148% (DB2) and 1.634% (DB3).

3 Methods

This study aims to use deep learning to provide an improved approach to fingerprint classification in terms of accuracy. Instead of attempting to build a new architecture from the ground up, a solution was created which makes use of the advances made by already existing CNN architectures which provide solutions to similar problems. The three architectures that were selected are Xception [3], Inception V3 [14] and ResNet 152 V2 [5] for their small memory footprint and high base accuracy. Each of these three architectures will form the base of our CNN architectures, after which additional fully connected layers are added to explore their effect on improving the accuracy of the pre-trained architectures. The name selected for the approach of introducing the higher complexity fully connected layers is ConDense, which will be provided as a suffix for each pre-trained architecture's name wherever these modified architectures are used. Sections 4, 5 and 6 provide an overview of our experiments and our results.

4 Experiment Data

Biometric authentication is an ever-evolving field where over time the need for improvements in areas such as accuracy, efficiency and cost effectiveness are a driving force behind advances. The drive for such improvements lead to the creation of datasets and competitions that aid in developing and testing potential advances in biometric authentication. In the case of fingerprint biometrics, an example of these is the Fingerprint Verification Competition whose first edition was run in the year 2000 [9]. This section provides an overview of FVC 2006 the latest iteration outside of FVC-onGoing, whose fingerprint database are used in training and testing the Convolutional Neural Network architectures presented in this paper. FVC 2006 was selected due to its good variety of fingerprint images captured for databases one through three and its continued relevance in evaluating the performance of modern fingerprint recognition solutions [1,6,12,13].

Table 1. The differences between fingerprint capturing/generation technologies and image dimensions in the databases provided by FVC 2006 [2]

Database	Technology	Image dimensions (pixels)
DB1	Electric Field Sensor	96×96
DB2	Optical Sensor	400×560
DB3	Thermal Sweeping Sensor	400×500
DB4	Synthetic Fingerprint Generator	288×384

The most recent FVC outside of the current ongoing online initiation occurred in 2006 and made available four fingerprint databases. The fingerprints for these databases were each captured using different technologies which in turn produced images whose resolution differed per database [2,4]. Databases one to four are suffixed with the letters A and B e.g. "DB1A" and "DB1B". The databases suffixed with A contained 12 samples from each of 120 subjects and those suffixed with B contained 12 samples from each of 10 subjects. A summary of the differences of each database is given in Table 1 and examples of the samples captured for each database can be seen in Fig. 1.

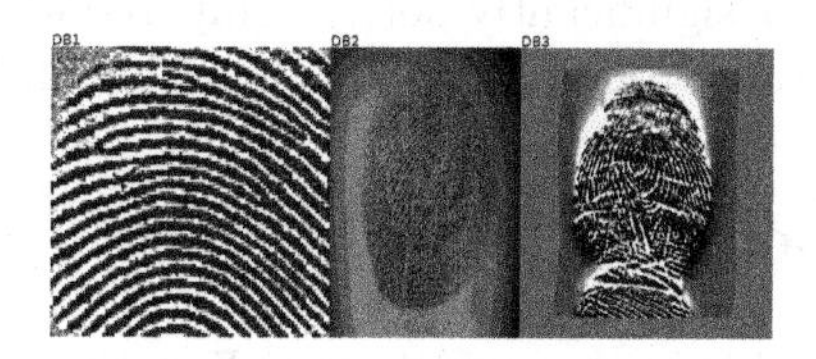

Fig. 1. The differences between fingerprint images in the databases provided by FVC 2006 [2]

To aid in evaluating the performance of the Xception-ConDense, Inception-ConDense and ResNet-ConDense architectures that were produced for this study, the three non-synthetic fingerprint databases were selected for use in training and evaluation. The use of the FVC 2006 databases allows for the derivation of performance metrics and their subsequent comparison against related studies which have also utilised the same databases. In addition this also allows for a comparison of performance for each of the architectures presented in this paper when running against different databases to show how the different image capturing methods and dimensions potentially affect performance. Lastly, the varying sensors and fidelities allow for a good evaluation of fingerprint recognition algorithms.

Using FVC 2006 gives access to the four fingerprint databases which were provided to the competition's contestants. For the purposes of the greater study under which this one falls - which would only make use of non-synthetic fingerprints - only databases DB1, DB2 and DB3 are used. Each of the fingerprint images provided in the databases is in greyscale.

DB1 provides the smallest of the fingerprint images provided for FVC 2006. The images were captured using a AuthenTec Electric Field Sensors and are 96×96 pixels in size [2]. DB1A provides fingerprints for 140 subjects with 12 samples per subject. DB1B provides 12 samples for 10 subjects. The size difference between images provided in FVC 2006 can be seen in Fig. 1. Architectures presented in FVC 2006 tended to perform the poorest in terms of EER when tested against this database, potentially due to the relatively small size and low detail of the images. The lowest EER on DB1 was reported as 5.564% (open category).

Fingerprint images from DB2 are the largest in terms of image size of those provided by the competition. The images from DB2 are 400×560 pixels and were captured by a BiometriKa Optical Sensor [2]. As with DB1, DB2A provides images for 140 subjects with 12 samples each and DB2B provides 10 subjects with 12 samples per subject. FVC 2006 architectures performed the best when using DB2 with the lowest EER reported as 0.021% (open category).

Lastly, in terms of size the images from DB3 fit between those of DB1 and DB2. Images from DB3 are 400×500 pixels and were captured by a Atmel Thermal Sweeping Sensor [2]. Once again, DB3A provided 12 samples for each subject, and DB3B provided 12 samples for 10 subjects. Performance of architectures against DB3 was significantly better compared to those running against DB1, with the best of these (open category) reporting an EER of 1.534%.

5 Experiment Setup

When training the architectures which use Xception-ConDense, Inception-ConDense and ResNet-ConDense, there are two stages: The first is pre-processing where fingerprint images are modified in accordance with requirements from each pre-trained architecture. The second is where the pre-processed images are fed into each of the architectures for training.

Pre-processing, as mentioned above, is the first step in the two-part process. Here a number of modifications to the FVC 2006 fingerprint images are required before they can be passed to each CNN architecture for training/testing. When training, the first 10 of the 12 samples for each subject in any given database are used, giving a 83%:17% split. The remaining two for each subject are then used for testing.

By their nature, the greyscale images provided by the FVC 2006 databases are single-channel images. The pre-trained architectures that are used in this study were trained using ImageNet weights that require three-channel images. To compensate for this, the grey channel of each FVC 2006 image is duplicated twice to create a three-channel image.

The new three-channel image is then fed into a architecture-specific pre-processing function, where Xception-ConDense, Inception-ConDense and ResNet-ConDense each provide their own means of pre-processing images. These pre-processed images are then resized to the dimensions of the images that were used to originally train the architectures. The sizes used are 299×299 (Xception-ConDense), 299×299 (Inception-ConDense) and 224×224 (ResNet-ConDense).

After pre-processing is complete, these pre-processed images are provided to each of the architectures in turn for use in training. First, the ground truth labels for each image is established for use in the training process. These are then used to guide each architecture in terms of making correct classifications.

The structure of each of this study's architecture, can be seen in Fig. 2. The initial layer is the input layer, whose shape is set to the dimensions of the images based on each pre-trained architecture's specific sizes. These input layers then lead into their respective pre-trained architectures. After the pre-trained

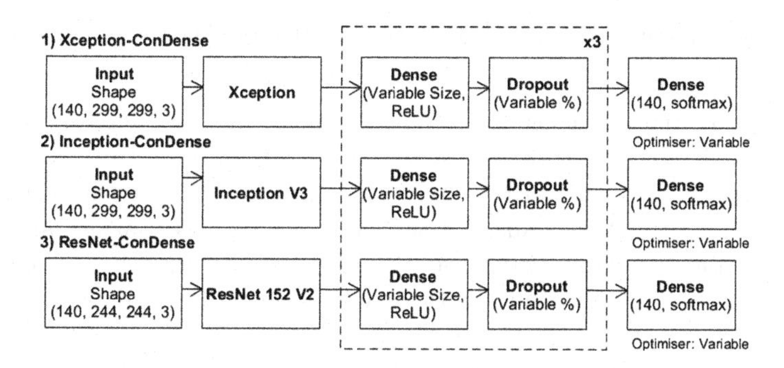

Fig. 2. Overview of classifier architectures for Xception-ConDense (1), Inception-ConDense (2) and ResNet-ConDense (3) architectures.

architecture layers, the structure for each architecture is largely the same. Three sets of a combination of a fully connected (Dense) layer and a dropout layer are then added. The dense layers have an output size which varies by the database to which it is applied with Rectified Linear Unit (ReLU) being the activation function in each case. The dropout layers are each set to a percentage which varies by the database to which it is applied. The final layer in each of the architectures is a dense layer set to the number of subjects that are used to train the model, which is 140. The activation function for the final layer is softmax.

6 Experiment Results

6.1 Ablation Study

The base architectures are initialised using a number of hyperparameters that govern training and certain aspects of our architecture layers. The hyperparameters that were focused on in this study were learning rate, optimiser, dense layer size and dropout percentage used in the architecture with the options for each shown below:

- Learning Rate - 0.01, 0.001 and 0.0001.
- Optimiser - Adam and SGD.
- Dense layer size - 256, 512, 1024 and 2048.
- Dropout - 0.1, 0.2, 0.3, 0.4 and 0.5.

Keras Tuner [10] was used to find the optimal hyperparameter per architecture/database combination. The hyperparameters that were identified for each combination are shown in Table 2. Table 2 shows that in most cases, lower learning rates, higher denser layer sizes, and lower dropout are needed to achieve lower EERs.

Table 2. Hyperparameters used for each combination of ConDense architecture and FVC 2006 database.

ConDense architecture	Inception			Exception			ResNet		
FVC 2006 Database	1A	2A	3A	1A	2A	3A	1A	2A	3A
Learning Rate	0.0001	0.0001	0.0001	0.0001	0.0001	0.01	0.0001	0.0001	0.01
Optimiser	Adam	Adam	Adam	Adam	Adam	SGD	Adam	Adam	SGD
Dense Layer Size	2048	2048	2048	1024	2048	1024	2048	1024	2048
Dropout	0.1	0.1	0.5	0.2	0.1	0.1	0.1	0.2	0.2

6.2 Architecture Performance

The first set of results were obtained by testing the architectures against DB1A of FVC 2006. Of the three architectures, the one that resulted in the lowest EER was the Inception-ConDense architecture with an EER of 1.522%. This was followed by ResNet-ConDense and Xception-ConDense with EERs of 1.778% and 1.829% respectively.

The Inception-ConDense architecture's higher EER is evident from the Receiver Operating Characteristic (ROC) curve generated for the three architectures, shown in Fig. 3, where the Inception-ConDense architecture's true positive rate (TPR) reaches the highest peak at 95% before seeing a large increase in false positive rate (FPR) starting at 2.5%. The Precision-Recall curve given in Fig. 4 shows that the precision of each of the architectures noticeably begin to decrease as recall reaches 0.4. The Xception-ConDense architecture has the highest area under the curve (AUC) with 0.824.

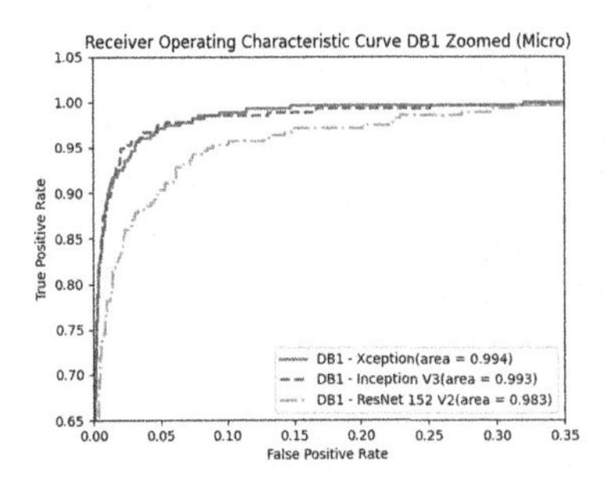

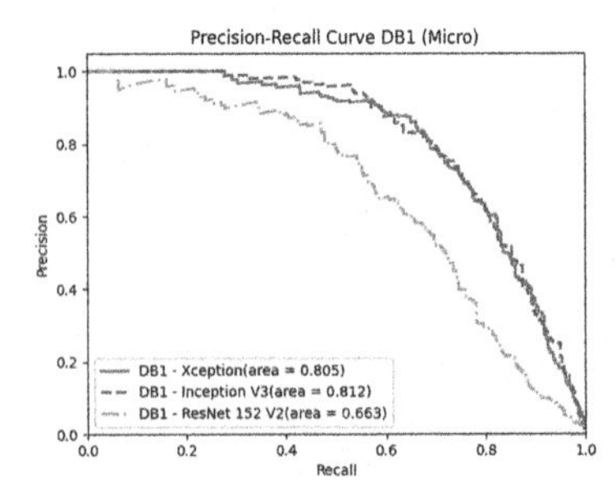

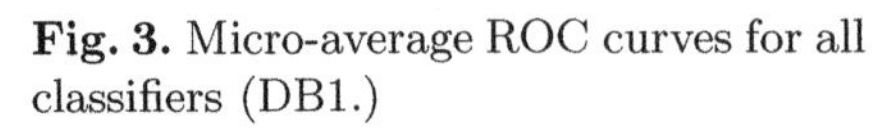

Fig. 3. Micro-average ROC curves for all classifiers (DB1.)

Fig. 4. Micro-average precision-recall curves for all classifiers (DB1.)

For the second set of results, each of the architectures were tested against DB2A of FVC 2006. In this category each of the architectures performed considerably better than in their test against DB1A. The top architecture was Xception-ConDense which scored an EER of 0.041%. The Inception-ConDense and ResNet-ConDense architectures scored 0.103% and 0.144% respectively.

In this category's ROC curve shown in Fig. 5, the Xception-ConDense architecture's FPR begins noticeably increasing at a TPR of 97.5%. The large change in FPR begins rising from 0.5%. The Precision-Recall curve given in Fig. 6, shows that each of the architectures begin losing precision at approximately 75% recall, but the Xception-ConDense architecture maintains the highest precision before a significant drop until a recall of 80% is achieved. At this point the precision is still above 95% precision.

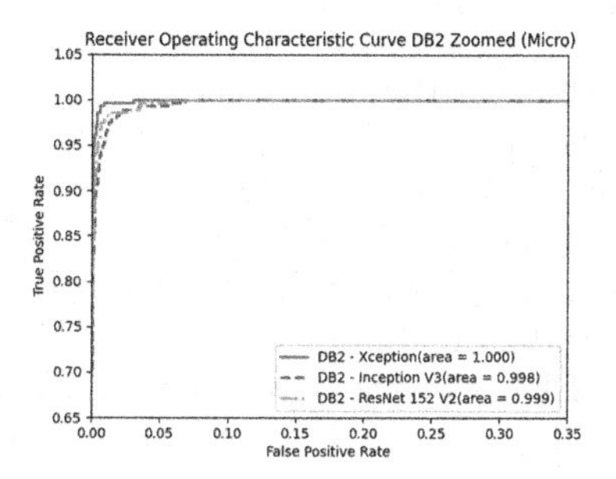

Fig. 5. Micro-average ROC curves for all classifiers (DB2.)

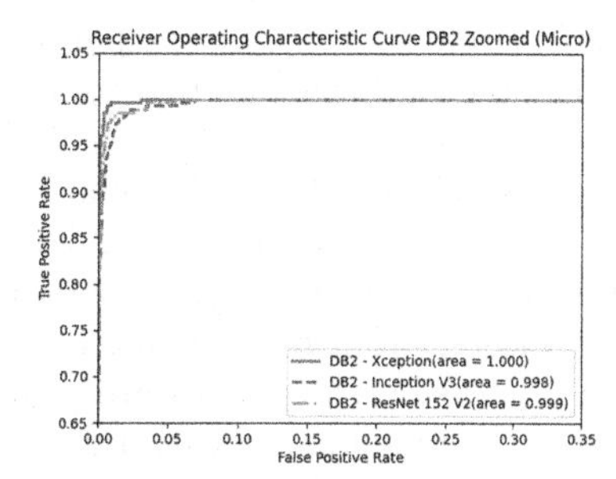

Fig. 6. Micro-average precision-recall curves for all classifiers (DB2.)

The last set of results were obtained were from testing the architectures against DB3A of FVC 2006. The top performing architecture for this set of tests was once again Xception-ConDense. Here the architecture achieved an EER of 0.953%. Inception-ConDense and ResNet-ConDense performed considerably worse with EERs of 1.711% and 2.592% respectively. In broader terms all the architectures performed worse in the tests against DB3 compared to those of DB2.

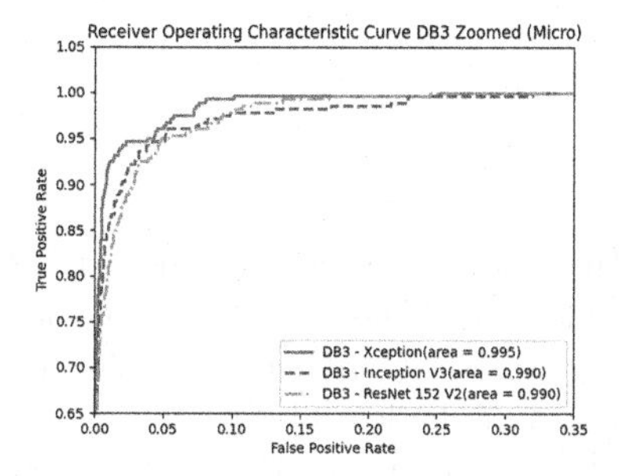

Fig. 7. Micro-average ROC curves for all classifiers (DB3.)

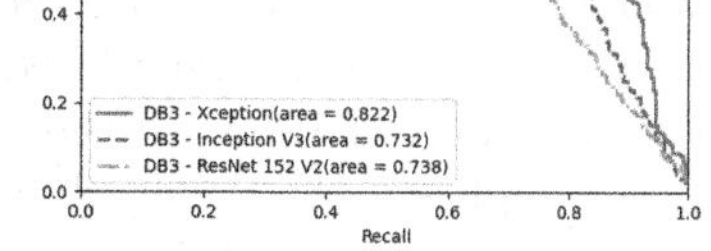

Fig. 8. Micro-average precision-recall curves for all classifiers (DB3.)

Considering the ROC curve shown in Fig. 7, all of the architectures begin showing a large increase in FPR at just below 95% TPR. The best performing of these, the Xception-ConDense architecture, reaches approximately a 95%

TPR with a FPR of 4%. The Precision-Recall curve shown in Fig. 8 shows that the Inception-ConDense and ResNet-ConDense architectures start seeing a decline at approximately 27% recall where the same drop is seen for Xception-ConDense at 44% recall. The Xception-ConDense architecture reaches 60% Recall at approximately 95% precision before seeing a steep decline in recall.

6.3 Comparison to Related Work

This section provides a comparison of the performance of the architectures against the performance reported by the authors of the studies under Sect. 2. The differences in performance will be discussed with reference to the EERs obtained by each of the different architectures. Each of the studies listed under Sect. 2 conducted their tests against subsets of the databases provided by FVC 2006. As a result only a small number of them have used all the databases that were selected from FVC 2006 for use in this study. In addition, where the EERs for ConDense architectures are provided the EERs for their base architectures are also provided along with the percentage change in EER that resulted from the addition of multiple dense layers.

Table 3. Comparison of the performance of related work and this paper's ConDense architectures when trained and tested against DB1.

Method (DB1)	EER %	Non-ConDense EER %	Change %
Xception-ConDense	**1.385**	2.079	34
Inception-ConDense	1.390	1.4825	6
ResNet-ConDense	2.697	1.8191	−48
Khazaei and Mohades [8]	2.8		
He, Liu and Xiang [6]	3.587		
Wahby Shalaby and Omair Ahmad [15]	5.21		
FVC 2006 Light [2]	5.356		
FVC 2006 Open [2]	5.564		

When testing against DB1, the architectures scored the lowest three EERs when compared against the related work. The lowest of the three was Xception-ConDense with 1.385%, with the highest being ResNet-ConDense with 2.697%. The next highest was the work of Khazaei and Mohades [8] with 2.8%. The results show a significant improvement in EER compared to the best original FVC 2006 open and light category results which were both above 5% [2]. The comparison of the DB1 results to all relevant related works can be seeing in Table 3.

The next set of results are those for DB2. Here the work of Kaggwa, Ngubiri and Tushabe scored the lowest EER of 0.00% [7]. This was followed by FVC 2006's best open category result which was 0.021% [2]. These are directly followed by Xception-ConDense with an EER of 0.041%. The full comparison of results for DB2 can be seen in Table 4.

Table 4. Comparison of the performance of related work and this paper's ConDense architectures when trained and tested against DB2.

Method (DB2)	EER %	Non-ConDense EER %	Change %
Kaggwa, Ngubiri and Tushabe [7]	**0.00**		
FVC 2006 Open [2]	0.021		
Xception-ConDense	0.041	0.092	56
FVC 2006 Light [2]	0.148		
Priesnitz et al. [11]	0.15		
Inception-ConDense	0.167	0.121	−38
Sanchez-Fernandez et al. [13]	0.48		
ResNet-ConDense	0.193	0.493	61
Khazaei and Mohades [8]	3.65		

The final set of results are those for DB3. Here the Xception-ConDense architecture achieved the lowest EER of 0.871%. The second and third lowest EERs were reported by Khazaei and Mohades and ResNet-ConDense with EERs of 1.15% [8] and 1.449% respectively. The full comparison of these results can be seen in Table 5.

The results of the study show that across all three databases, the introduction of additional dense layers improved the performance of their base architectures in 2/3 of the cases. The most significant improvement is seen for ResNet-ConDense in Table 4 with an improvement of 61% with the highest reduction in Table 3 for ResNet-ConDense with −48%.

The authors of this study endeavoured to find any relevant studies for performance comparisons. The results of this study are reported to the best of the authors' knowledge. When looking at past and present results for DB1 and DB3, it can be seen that these categories are the most challenging of the three databases that FVC 2006 provided. The architectures attained the lowest EERs in these categories, showing significant improvements when compared against related work. The Xception-ConDense architecture performed consistently well, where it placed in the top three architectures in all of the tests against the FVC 2006 databases. This study set out to build CNN architectures which provide improved accuracy when compared to existing approaches. The performance of the architectures' created in this study when testing against DB1 and DB3 shows that study was successful in achieving that goal.

Table 5. Comparison of the performance of related work and this paper's ConDense architectures when trained and tested against DB3.

Method (DB3)	EER %	Non-ConDense EER %	Change %
Xception-ConDense	**0.871**	1.202	28
Khazaei and Mohades [8]	1.15		
ResNet-ConDense	1.449	2.980	51
FVC 2006 Open [2]	1.534		
FVC 2006 Light [2]	1.634		
Inception-ConDense	1.745	1.647	−6
Sanchez-Fernandez et al. [13]	3.70		

7 Conclusion

This study set out to accomplish two objectives. 1) Create a fingerprint authentication approach which performs on a comparable if not higher level than related implementations when testing against the study's selected dataset, FVC 2006. 2) Perform a comparison of related fingerprint recognition approaches in order to find the most suitable candidate for use in a fingerprint recognition-based solution. The results when testing against the FVC 2006 database in Sect. 6 show that for DB1A, the Xception-ConDense architecture had the lowest EER of 1.385%. For DB2A, the solution from Kaggwa, Ngubiri and Tushabe [7] performed the best with an EER of 0.00%. Lastly, for DB3A the Xception-ConDense pipeline scored the lowest EER of 0.871%. Our implementations for DB1A and DB3A satisfy our first objective where, to the best of our knowledge, we could not find approaches that score lower EERs against those databases. We satisfy our second objective with our comparison for DB2A, where we identified Kaggwa, Ngubiri and Tushabe's approach as the lowest scoring approach [7]. Lastly, this study has shown that - while further study is required to determine the cause - the addition of more complex fully-connected layers to the base pre-trained architectures resulted in solutions which produce the lowest EERs in two of the three categories against which they were evaluated.

References

1. Agarwal, D., Garima, Bansal, A.: A utility of ridge contour points in minutiae-based fingerprint matching. In: Chaki, N., Pejas, J., Devarakonda, N., Rao Kovvur, R.M. (eds.) ICCIDE 2020, pp. 273–286. Springer, Singapore (2021). https://doi.org/10.1007/978-981-15-8767-2_24
2. Cappelli, R., Ferrara, M., Franco, A., Maltoni, D.: Fingerprint verification competition 2006. Biometric Technol. Today **15**(7), 7–9 (2007)
3. Chollet, F.: Xception: deep learning with depthwise separable convolutions. CoRR abs/1610.02357 (2016). http://arxiv.org/abs/1610.02357

4. Fierrez, J., Ortega-Garcia, J., Torre-Toledano, D., Gonzalez-Rodriguez, J.: BioSec baseline corpus: a multimodal biometric database. Pattern Recogn. **40**(4), 1389–1392 (2007)
5. He, K., Zhang, X., Ren, S., Sun, J.: Identity mappings in deep residual networks. CoRR abs/1603.05027 (2016). http://arxiv.org/abs/1603.05027
6. He, Z., Liu, E., Xiang, Z.: Partial fingerprint verification via spatial transformer networks. In: 2020 IEEE International Joint Conference on Biometrics (IJCB), pp. 1–10 (2020)
7. Kaggwa, F., Ngubiri, J., Tushabe, F.: Combined feature level and score level fusion Gabor filter-based multiple enrollment fingerprint recognition. In: 2016 International Conference on Signal Processing, Communication, Power and Embedded System (SCOPES), pp. 159–165 (2016)
8. Khazaei, H., Mohades, A.: Fingerprint matching algorithm based on Voronoi diagram. In: 2008 International Conference on Computational Sciences and Its Applications, pp. 433–440 (2008)
9. Maio, D., Maltoni, D., Cappelli, R., Wayman, J., Jain, A.: FVC 2000: fingerprint verification competition. IEEE Trans. Pattern Anal. Mach. Intell. **24**(3), 402–412 (2002)
10. O'Malley, T., et al.: Kerastuner (2019). https://github.com/keras-team/keras-tuner
11. Priesnitz, J., Huesmann, R., Rathgeb, C., Buchmann, N., Busch, C.: Mobile touchless fingerprint recognition: implementation, performance and usability aspects. Sensors **22**, 792 (2021)
12. Sabir, M., Khan, T., Arshad, M., Munawar, S.: Reducing computational complexity in fingerprint matching. Turk. J. Electr. Eng. Comput. Sci. **28**, 2538–2551 (2020)
13. Sanchez-Fernandez, A.J., et al.: Asynchronous processing for latent fingerprint identification on heterogeneous CPU-GPU systems. IEEE Access **8**, 124236–124253 (2020)
14. Szegedy, C., Vanhoucke, V., Ioffe, S., Shlens, J., Wojna, Z.: Rethinking the inception architecture for computer vision. CoRR abs/1512.00567 (2015). http://arxiv.org/abs/1512.00567
15. Wahby Shalaby, M., Omair Ahmad, M.: A multilevel structural technique for fingerprint representation and matching. Sig. Process. **93**(1), 56–69 (2013)

A Sensor-Independent Multimodal Fusion Scheme for Human Activity Recognition

Anastasios Alexiadis(✉), Alexandros Nizamis, Dimitrios Giakoumis, Konstantinos Votis, and Dimitrios Tzovaras

Centre for Research and Technology Hellas, Information Technologies Institute (CERTH/ITI), 6km Charilaou-Thermi, Thessaloniki, Greece
{talex,alnizami,dgiakoum,kvotis,Dimitrios.Tzovaras}@iti.gr

Abstract. Human Activity Recognition is a field that provides the fundamentals for Ambient Intelligence and Assisted Living Applications. Multimodal methods for Human Activity Recognition utilize different sensors and *fuse* them together to provide higher-accuracy results. These methods require data for all sensors employed to operate with. In this work we present a sensor-independent, in regards to the number of sensors used, scheme for designing multimodal methods that operate when sensor-data are missing. Furthermore, we present a data augmentation method that increases the fusion model's accuracy (up to 11% increases) when operating with missing sensor-data. The proposed method's effectiveness is evaluated on the ExtraSensory dataset, which contains over 300,000 samples from 60 users, collected from smartphones and smartwatches. In addition, the methods are evaluated for different number of sensors used at the same time. However, the max number of sensors must be known beforehand.

Keywords: Automatic Human Activity Recognition · Multimodal fusion · Sensor fusion · Sensor-independent fusion

1 Introduction

Automatic Human Activity Recognition (HAR) is a field that constitutes the fundamentals of Ambient Intelligence (Aml) and Assisted Living Applications (AAL). It comprises the challenges of recognizing and understanding human activities and their context which are the basic pre-requisites for integrating human-aware machine decision capabilities. Human Activity Recognition can be performed using static sensors (e.g., mounted video camera [22]) or wearable sensors (e.g., smart watch or other wearable sensors [15]) or by combining both.

There is a plethora of methods to perform human activity recognition [17]. The main categories are (i) unimodal and (ii) multimodal human activity recognition methods, according to the type of sensor they employ. Unimodal methods utilize data from a single modality, such as audio signal. These methods can be categorized into (i) space-time, (ii) stochastic, (iii) rule-based and (iv) shape-based methods. On the other hand Multimodal methods combine features from

M. El Yacoubi et al. (Eds.): ICPRAI 2022, LNCS 13364, pp. 28–39, 2022.
https://doi.org/10.1007/978-3-031-09282-4_3

different sources (such as combining features from audio sensors with features from video sensors) [19] and can be categorized to: (i) affective, (ii) behavioral and (iii) social networking methods.

In this work we present a sensor-independent fusion method in respect to the number of sensors utilized. In addition to this, we introduce a data augmentation method that augments the collected data with sub-sets of utilized sensor data per observation, and apply these methods to fuse unimodal models for the ExtranSensory dataset [16]. This dataset served as a test-case for our proposed methods. Our methods can be used with any model that fuses a number of unimodal models for a set of sensors. The ExtraSensory dataset contains over 300,000 examples from 60 users of diverse ethnic backgrounds, collected from smartphones and smartwatches. It includes heterogeneous measurements from a variety of wearable sensors (i.e., accelerometer, gyroscope, magnometer, watch compass, audio etc.). Not all the sensors were available at all times, some phones did not have some sensors, whereas in other cases sensors were sometimes unavailable.

The remainder of the paper is structured as follows: A brief review of the related work is presented in the next section. Afterwards we present our methods for sensor-independent (in respect to the number of sensors) fusion and for data augmentation. We evaluate our methods on a set of experiments and discuss the results. Finally, we conclude the paper and present our directions for future work.

2 Related Work

In the recent years due to the rise of IoT devices and smart living environments, a lot of research has been conducted related to human activity recognition and many methods have been developed and applied. In introduction section is mentioned that the methods are distinguished in five major categories, space-time, stochastic, rule-based, shape-based and multimodal methods. In this chapter, we are presenting a brief literature review related to multimodal methods for human activity recognition in order to place our work in the current state-of-the-art and to indicate innovation and contribution of our work in the field.

As an event or action can be described by different types of data and features that provide more and useful information, several multimodal methods for human activity recognition are based on fusion techniques [4]. In [12] the multimodal fusion for human activity detection is further classified in data and feature fusion methods. In [19] a decision fusion method is also considered. The latter is not a direct fusion scheme as it firstly applies separate classifiers to obtain probability scores and combines them for final decision making [7,21]. Since the current work is considered as a more direct type of fusion, the relevant works in this section are presented based on data and feature methods classification. Data fusion aims to increase accuracy, robustness and reliability of a system devoted to human activity recognition as this type of fusion involves integration of data collected by multiple mobile and wearable sensor devices. The work of [20] introduces a deep learning framework named DeepSense, targeting to overcome noise and feature customization challenges in order to increase recognition accuracy. The framework exploits interactions among different sensory modalities by integrating convolutional and recurrent neural networks to sensors. To the same aim [13] proposes a deep learning framework for activity recognition based on convolutional and LSTM recurrent units. The framework is suitable for multimodal wearable sensors as it can perform sensor fusion naturally without requiring expert knowledge in designing features. In [14] the authors introduce an activity recognition system to be used for elderly people monitoring. The system collects and combines data from sensors such as state sensors at doors, movement sensors in rooms and sensors attached to appliances or furniture pieces. However, the activity recognition is enabled just by using some multiple Hidden Markov Models (HMMs). A combination of HMMs and neural networks for multi-sensor fusion for human daily activity recognition has been introduced in [23]. The solution was based on wearable sensors and tested in a robot-assisted living system for elderly people environment. Other similar approaches such as [10] are based on information fusion of features extracted from experimental data collected by different sensors, such as a depth camera, an accelerometer and a micro-Doppler radar. The authors create combinations of the aforementioned sensors data for classification of the activity. They found that the addition of more sensors was continuously improving the accuracy of classification. In particular, the authors have measured the accuracy of quadratic-kernel SVM classifier and of an Ensemble classifier.

In order to further increase the accuracy and to improve performance of activity recognition systems some fusion methods at the features level have been developed in previous years. Feature fusion techniques enable the combination of features extracted from sensor data with machine learning algorithms. This type of fusion is used in the current work as well. Regarding the sensors used for activity recognition they are lay on various categories such as (a) 3D sensors [1,9,18] for recognising activities such as walking, running or sitting, (b) thermal cameras [3,11] for household activity recognition and (c) event cameras [8] for event-based activity detection or even activity tracking applications [2]. In [6] a multimodal feature-level fusion approach for robust human action recognition was proposed. The approach utilizes data from multiple sensors such as depth sensor, RGB camera, and wearable inertial sensors. The recognition framework was tested on a publicly available dataset including over 25 different human actions. For training and testing the proposed fusion model, SVM classifiers and K-nearest neighbor were used. The authors observed that better results were produced by using more sensors in the fusion. However, the achieved accuracy improvement had some significant loses (over 10%) in terms of performance comparing to fusion approaches with less sensors combinations. In another approach [19] a human action recognition with multimodal feature selection and fusion based on videos was introduced. The authors extracted both audio and visual features from a public dataset/video and used them as input for a set of SVM classifiers. The outputs were fused to obtain a final classification score through fuzzy integral and two-layer SVM. The authors observed that audio context is more useful than visual one but the audio is not always helpful for some actions due to its high diversity. Recently, in [5] the authors proposed an intelligent sensor fusion strategy for activity recognition in body sensor networks that very often have uncertain or even incomplete data. Their approach was based on the Dezert-Smarandache theory. In this, as training dataset they employed kernel density estimation (KDE)-based models for sensors readings and they selected the best discriminative model of them. A testing dataset was also used in order to calculate basic belief assignments based on KDE models for each activity. Finally, the calculated belief assignments were combined with redistribution rules for final decision-making. The authors concluded that their approach outperformed state-of-the-art methods in accuracy, as it was tested and compared in two public datasets.

In this work, a novel feature fusion method that provides high accuracy and robustness in the human activity recognition, in comparison to aforementioned data fusion techniques, is introduced. Furthermore, the introduced approach provides a fusion method that is sensor-independent, in terms of sensors' number. Opposite to other fusion approaches that were introduced in the previous paragraph, our approach does not require to recreate the fusion model in the case that less sensors are available. Another improvement that the method introduces in comparison with the above-mentioned fusion methods, is the data augmentation technique that was applied. This technique augments the collected data with sub-sets of utilized sensor data per observation. By adding combinations of existing sensor data the amount of the available data is increased, so the method's accuracy with regards to human activity recognition is increased as well.

3 Methods

Seven unimodal classifiers were given, which are considered as black boxes for the scope of this paper, where each one classifies human daily activities according to a specific sensor from the ExtraSensory dataseset. Each classifier applies to one of the following sensors:

- Watch Accelerometer (WA)
- Watch Compass (WC)
- Phone Accelerometer (PA)
- Phone Gyroscope (PG)
- Phone Magnet (PM)
- Phone State (PS)
- Audio (A)

In Table 1 the F1 scores of the seven classifiers in regards to their respective test sets (which are sub-sets of the test set containing only the observations that contain data for their respective sensors) are presented. A dash "–" denotes that there were no observations of the respective sensor for that class. There are 16 daily activity classes. Each of the seven classifiers contains a 32-node dense layer followed by a softmax layer at their end.

Table 1. Unimodal classifiers F1-scores

Classes	WA F1	WC F1	PA F1	PG F1	PM F1	PS F1	A F1
SITTING-TOILET	0.23	0.0	0.0	0.0	0.0	0.08	0.13
SITTING-EATING	0.7	0.38	0.064	0.0	0.0	0.26	0.42
STANDING-COOKING	0.09	0.0	0.0	0.13	0.13	0.0	0.33
SITTING-WATCHING TV	0.05	0.0	0.67	0.57	0.57	0.72	0.83
LYING DOWN-WATCHING TV	0.63	0.0	0.28	0.18	0.18	0.37	0.58
STANDING-EATING	0.24	0.49	0.47	0.22	0.22	0.62	0.69
STANDING-CLEANING	0.63	0.0	0.4	0.19	0.19	0.69	0.77
WALKING-EATING	0.43	0.0	0.27	0.38	0.38	0.43	0.6
STANDING-WATCHING TV	0.33	0.46	0.3	0.27	0.27	0.54	0.59
STANDING-TOILET	0.29	0.31	0.59	0.5	0.5	0.7	0.79
WALKING-WATCHING TV	0.49	0.0	0.1	0.08	0.08	–	0.63
WALKING-COOKING	0.42	0.0	0.39	0.11	0.11	0.37	0.51
SITTING-COOKING	0.59	0.0	0.35	0.38	0.38	0.67	0.68
WALKING-CLEANING	0.05	0.0	0.19	0.1	0.1	0.11	0.48
LYING DOWN-EATING	0.16	0.0	0.62	0.58	0.58	0.24	0.73
SITTING-CLEANING	0.15	0.0	0.0	0.0	0.0	0.16	0.27
Accuracy	0.55	0.4	0.5	0.45	0.45	0.65	0.74
Macro avg	0.34	0.1	0.29	0.23	0.23	0.4	0.57
Weighted avg	0.55	0.34	0.52	0.43	0.43	0.64	0.75

3.1 Sensor Independent Fusion Model

For the fusion model a feed-forward Artificial Neural Network was used. The softmax layer for each unimodal model was discarded so when simulating each of the models we obtain a feature vector of length 32 (the output of the penultimate layer of the unimodal models). These feature vectors provide the inputs to their respective unimodal models' softmax layers, and thus contain the activity information extracted from the data before being converted to a probability distribution by the softmax layer. Each unimodal model is simulated using its design features from observations of its respective sensor.

The input layer is defined with a length of 32 multiplied by the number of sensors. To provide sensor independence in respect to the number of sensors used we add a binary vector to the input layer of the network with length equal to the number of sensors. So for our specific case the input layer has a size of $32 \cdot 7 + 7 = 231$.

$$F_{s1_1} F_{s1_2} ... F_{s1_{32}} ... F_{s7_1} F_{s7_2} ... F_{s7_{32}} ... F_{acts7}, F_{acts6} ... F_{acts1}$$

The diagram above illustrates the input layer of the fusion model. F_{s1_1} denotes the first feature of the first sensor, $F_{s1_{32}}$ denotes the last feature of the first sensor, whereas F_{acts1} denotes the binary feature that actives/deactivates

Algorithm 1. Create Fusion model training set

procedure CREATE_DATASET($train, feature\_sensors, unimodal\_models, sensors$)
$T \leftarrow [0]_{len(train) \times 32 \cdot len(sensors) + len(sensors)}$ {Matrix of zeros}
for each sensor k ranging from 0 to $len(sensors) - 1$ **do**
  $train\_s \leftarrow train[feature\_sensors[sensors[k]]]$
  $train\_sn \leftarrow train\_s.dropna()$
  $idxs \leftarrow train\_sn.index$
  $feature\_matrix \leftarrow simulate\_model(unimodal\_models[sensors[k]], train\_sn)$
  for each observation i ranging from 0 to $len(T) - 1$ **do**
    if $i \in idxs$ **then**
      $T[i, T.no\_of\_cols - k - 1] \leftarrow 1$
    end if
  end for
  for each observation i ranging from 0 to $len(feature\_matrix) - 1$ **do**
    $T[idxs[i], k \cdot 32 : (k+1) \cdot 32] \leftarrow feature\_matrix[i]$
  end for
end for
return T

sensor 1 input for the fusion model. When F_{acts1} is set to 0, the features corresponding to sensor 1 input, that is the features from F_{s1_1} to $F_{s1_{32}}$ are set to 0 too. When F_{acts1} is set to 1, the input features corresponding to sensor 1 on the input of the fusion model are set to the 32 values of the feature vector which is the output of the respective unimodal model for sensor 1. In a similar manner we set the other sensor inputs. The fusion model performs feature-level fusion.

Algorithm 1 computes the dataset for training the fusion model. It is given the training set (*train*) containing the features for all sensors, a dictionary (*feature_sensors*) with mappings of the form $sensor\_name \rightarrow [feature\_indeces]$, for each sensor providing the indices for each sensor's features in the training set, a dictionary of the unimodal models (*unimodal_models*) of the form $sensor\_name \rightarrow model$ and a list of the sensor names (*sensors*). For each observation in the training set, the feature vectors of the unimodal models are computed, in the cases when there are data available for their respective sensors, and the activating feature for these sensors is set to 1. When data is missing for a sensor, the respective features for that sensor are set to 0, as well as the activating feature.

3.2 Data Augmentation Method

A data augmentation method was designed and implemented based on the following premise: The dataset can be expanded by adding more observations with all possible subsets of activated sensors from the sensors containing data, in each observation of the original dataset. As an example, consider the case of adding more data based on a single observation, where only five of the seven sensors are utilized. The following combinations are available with only the five sensors activated:

Algorithm 2. Data augmentation method

procedure AUGMENT_DATA($data, Y, no\_of\_sensors, C$)
$aug\_data \leftarrow ()$ {Empty Sequence}
$aug\_Y \leftarrow ()$ {Empty Sequence}
$sensor\_ids \leftarrow \{z : \exists n \in \mathbb{Z}$ such that $z = 0 + 1 \times n$, and $z \in [0, no\_of\_sensors - 1)\}$
for each observation i ranging from 0 to $len(data) - 1$ **do**
  $sources\_used \leftarrow \sum_{x=data.no\_of\_cols-no\_of\_sensors}^{data.no\_of\_cols} data[i, x]$
  for each sensor k ranging from $no\_of\_sensors - 1$ to 0 in steps of -1 **do**
    if $k < sources\_used$ **then**
      if $k < C$ **then**
        break
      end if
      $v \leftarrow \binom{sensor\_ids}{k}$ {k-length tuples with no repetition}
      for l ranging from 0 to $len(v) - 1$ **do**
        $OBV \leftarrow [0]_{data.no\_of\_cols}$ {Vector of zeros}
        for m ranging from 0 to $len(v[l]) - 1$ **do**
          $OBV[v[l][m] \cdot 32 : (v[l][m]+1) \cdot 32] \leftarrow data[i, v[l][m] \cdot 32 : (v[l][m]+1) \cdot 32]$
          $OBV[data.no\_of\_cols - v[l][m] - 1] \leftarrow 1$
        end for
        $aug\_data \leftarrow aug\_data^\frown(OBV)$ {Sequence Concatenation}
        $aug\_Y \leftarrow aug\_Y^\frown(Y[i])$
      end for
    else
      $aug\_data \leftarrow aug\_data^\frown(data[i, :])$
      $aug\_Y \leftarrow aug\_Y^\frown(Y[i])$
    end if
  end for
end for
return $as\_matrix(aug\_data), as\_vector(aug\_Y)$

```
[('s1', 's2', 's3', 's4', 's5'),
 ('s1', 's2', 's3', 's4', 's6'),
 ...,
 ('s2', 's4', 's5', 's6', 's7'),
 ('s3', 's4', 's5', 's6', 's7')]
```

For each of these cases we know the target activity, it holds the same label as the original observation which contains data for all sensors, so we can augment the dataset with a new observation per case, where data is provided for the respective sensors above and the features of the missing sensor data, as well as their respective activation features, are set to 0 in the fusion model training set.

The proposed method starts with k equals the activated sensors of each observation and loops, decreasing the number of used sensors by 1 in each iteration and computes the combinations, that is the k-length tuples with no repetition for each value of k until $k < C$ where C is a constant defining the minimum number of sensors that can be utilized. No interpolation or estimation techniques are performed to augment the dataset, the labels for the generated data are already known as well as the sensor data used for the new observations are the feature vectors computed by the unimodal models for the measured sensor data.

Algorithm 2 augments the dataset based on the above method. It is given the dataset for the fusion model (*data*), which is computed using Algorithm 1, the vector of labels containing the class for each observation (Y), the number of sensors ($no\_of\_sensors$) and the constant C, defining the minimum number of sensors utilized for the augmented dataset. For each observation in the training set, all $k - tuple$ combinations without repetition are computed, ranging from k equal to the number of activated sensors down to C.

4 Evaluation

To evaluate the proposed methods a set of experiments was devised to investigate the fusion model's improvement of F1-score per class, for the whole test set, as well as specific sub-sets of the test-set split according to the number of sensors used per observation. The dataset was split 70%–30% into a train and a test set. The resulting train and test sets were the ones used to train and test the unimodal models. The training set was farther split 80%–20% during training for the final train and validation sets. The fusion model was trained using the Adam optimizer with $lr = 0.001$, using a $batch\_size = 64$ for 200 epochs using early-stopping with $patience = 50$ for validation accuracy, while reducing the learning rate when the validation accuracy has stopped improving using $factor = 0.1, patience = 2$. The training set was shuffled for the training process.

Table 2. Fusion Model with no data augmentation in training/validation sets, no data augmentation in test set. Xs F1 denotes F1 scores for X sensors, Xs S denotes support

Classes	2s F1	2s S	3s F1	3s S	4s F1	4s S	5s F1	5s S	6s F1	6s S	7s F1	7s S	As F1	As S
SITTING-TOILET	0.50	2	0.50	2	0.84	22	0.82	145	0.69	64	0.67	18	0.38	17
SITTING-EATING	0.90	14	0.67	4	0.70	18	0.89	69	0.52	9	0.94	154	0.55	30
STANDING-COOKING	0.67	2	1.00	2	0.51	17	0.00	1	0.71	104	0.71	12	0.55	14
SITTING-WATCHING TV	–	–	0.80	4	0.83	47	0.87	611	0.50	2	0.43	7	0.87	2294
LYING DOWN-WATCHING TV	0.92	6	0.89	4	0.44	4	0.71	119	0.85	137	0.59	59	0.70	228
STANDING-EATING	0.97	18	0.95	30	0.50	8	0.85	328	0.65	51	0.70	90	0.78	479
STANDING-CLEANING	–	–	–	–	0.83	5	0.25	3	0.53	9	0.88	942	0.89	401
WALKING-EATING	–	–	–	–	0.67	2	0.59	15	0.86	588	0.65	27	0.73	523
STANDING-WATCHING TV	–	–	–	–	0.00	1	0.77	22	0.76	76	0.89	830	0.68	227
STANDING-TOILET	0.00	1	1.00	2	0.88	109	0.72	61	0.83	340	0.72	234	0.86	1522
WALKING-WATCHING TV	–	–	0.67	3	0.38	9	0.75	104	0.73	117	–	–	0.70	209
WALKING-COOKING	–	–	–	–	0.00	1	0.84	26	0.50	3	0.78	208	0.72	80
SITTING-COOKING	–	–	–	–	–	–	0.50	1	0.81	36	0.73	60	0.74	59
WALKING-CLEANING	–	–	–	–	0.67	3	0.67	13	0.76	29	0.87	44	0.52	57
LYING DOWN-EATING	–	–	–	–	–	–	0.64	59	0.67	5	0.60	23	0.79	96
SITTING-CLEANING	–	–	–	–	–	–	–	–	0.51	35	0.46	8	0.58	9
Accuracy	0.88	43	0.88	51	0.77	246	0.82	1577	0.80	1605	0.84	2716	0.82	6245
Macro avg	0.66	43	0.81	51	0.56	246	0.66	1577	0.68	1605	0.71	2716	0.69	6245
Weighted avg	0.88	43	0.88	51	0.78	246	0.82	1577	0.80	1605	0.84	2716	0.82	6245

Table 3. Fusion Model with no data augmentation in training/validation sets, with data augmentation in test set. Xs F1 denotes F1 scores for X sensors, Xs S denotes support

Classes	2s F1	2s S	3s F1	3s S	4s F1	4s S	5s F1	5s S	6s F1	6s S	7s F1	7s S	As F1	As S
SITTING-TOILET	0.08	357	0.10	595	0.14	595	0.22	337	0.54	135	0.63	18	0.14	1949
SITTING-EATING	0.19	630	0.25	1050	0.34	1050	0.81	6180	0.90	1215	0.92	154	0.32	3453
STANDING-COOKING	0.24	294	0.32	490	0.40	490	0.56	294	0.68	86	0.80	12	0.40	1666
SITTING-WATCHING TV	0.65	47894	0.73	78780	0.79	75044	0.82	32741	0.23	58	0.32	7	0.75	242583
LYING DOWN-WATCHING TV	0.36	4748	0.46	7808	0.54	7533	0.59	3295	0.85	7182	0.60	59	0.49	24168
STANDING-EATING	0.50	10059	0.59	16765	0.66	16017	0.68	6697	0.73	1560	0.71	90	0.62	51306
STANDING-CLEANING	0.46	8040	0.61	13234	0.73	12618	0.47	570	0.67	694	0.88	942	0.64	41442
WALKING-EATING	0.41	10943	0.50	18099	0.56	16497	0.62	7490	0.87	6150	0.68	27	0.52	55018
STANDING-WATCHING TV	0.40	4626	0.49	7632	0.57	7494	0.55	2414	0.67	1755	0.90	830	0.51	22690
STANDING-TOILET	0.57	31899	0.67	53029	0.75	52447	0.81	24898	0.58	464	0.71	234	0.70	169256
WALKING-WATCHING TV	0.38	4327	0.48	7142	0.56	6834	0.64	2915	0.68	496	–	–	0.52	21776
WALKING-COOKING	0.19	1680	0.28	2800	0.40	2732	0.51	1198	0.57	218	0.76	208	0.32	8655
SITTING-COOKING	0.41	1239	0.51	2065	0.59	1895	0.59	614	0.83	344	0.71	60	0.53	6002
WALKING-CLEANING	0.21	1197	0.28	1995	0.35	1961	0.40	916	0.63	166	0.84	44	0.31	6168
LYING DOWN-EATING	0.50	2016	0.59	3360	0.68	3326	0.78	1695	0.37	91	0.62	23	0.64	10785
SITTING-CLEANING	0.06	189	0.10	247	0.14	143	0.18	64	0.11	3	0.43	8	0.10	646
Accuracy	0.53	130138	0.63	215091	0.70	206676	0.76	92318	0.81	20617	0.84	2716	0.65	667563
Macro avg	0.35	130138	0.43	215091	0.51	206676	0.58	92318	0.62	20617	0.70	2716	0.47	667563
Weighted avg	0.54	130138	0.63	215091	0.70	206676	0.76	92318	0.81	20617	0.84	2716	0.66	667563

Table 4. Fusion Model with data augmentation in training/validation sets, with data augmentation in test set. Xs F1 denotes F1 scores for X sensors, Xs S denotes support

Classes	2s F1	2s S	3s F1	3s S	4s F1	4s S	5s F1	5s S	6s F1	6s S	7s F1	7s S	As F1	As S
SITTING-TOILET	0.13	357	0.19	595	0.23	595	0.31	337	0.60	135	0.63	18	0.21	1949
SITTING-EATING	0.31	630	0.39	1050	0.46	1050	0.86	6180	0.91	1215	0.93	154	0.43	3453
STANDING-COOKING	0.44	294	0.53	490	0.61	490	0.71	294	0.80	86	0.86	12	0.57	1666
SITTING-WATCHING TV	0.72	47894	0.78	78780	0.82	75044	0.85	32741	0.29	58	0.44	7	0.79	242583
LYING DOWN-WATCHING TV	0.45	4748	0.54	7808	0.60	7533	0.64	3295	0.87	7182	0.60	59	0.56	24168
STANDING-EATING	0.59	10059	0.66	16765	0.69	16017	0.71	6697	0.74	1560	0.71	90	0.66	51306
STANDING-CLEANING	0.65	8040	0.75	13234	0.81	12618	0.56	570	0.68	694	0.89	942	0.77	41442
WALKING-EATING	0.48	10943	0.57	18099	0.62	16497	0.66	7490	0.89	6150	0.59	27	0.58	55018
STANDING-WATCHING TV	0.45	4626	0.54	7632	0.61	7494	0.57	2414	0.69	1755	0.91	830	0.55	22690
STANDING-TOILET	0.69	31899	0.76	53029	0.81	52447	0.85	24898	0.58	464	0.72	234	0.78	169256
WALKING-WATCHING TV	0.49	4327	0.57	7142	0.63	6834	0.71	2915	0.73	496	–	–	0.60	21776
WALKING-COOKING	0.38	1680	0.49	2800	0.57	2732	0.59	1198	0.58	218	0.76	208	0.51	8655
SITTING-COOKING	0.60	1239	0.67	2065	0.72	1895	0.68	614	0.86	344	0.76	60	0.67	6002
WALKING-CLEANING	0.24	1197	0.29	1995	0.32	1961	0.32	916	0.72	166	0.91	44	0.29	6168
LYING DOWN-EATING	0.66	2016	0.72	3360	0.76	3326	0.82	1695	0.31	91	0.76	23	0.74	10785
SITTING-CLEANING	0.35	189	0.41	247	0.39	143	0.35	64	0.21	3	0.33	8	0.38	646
Accuracy	0.64	130138	0.71	215091	0.76	206676	0.79	92318	0.83	20617	0.85	2716	0.72	667563
Macro avg	0.48	130138	0.55	215091	0.60	206676	0.64	92318	0.65	20617	0.72	2716	0.57	667563
Weighted avg	0.63	130138	0.71	215091	0.75	206676	0.79	92318	0.83	20617	0.85	2716	0.72	667563

Table 2 presents the results for these experiments. The F1 columns denote the F-1 scores per number of sensors used, whereas the S columns denote the corresponding samples provided in the test set (*support* metric), e.g., *3s F1*, denotes the F1-scores for the sub-set holding the observations which utilized data from exactly 3 sensors, whereas *3s S* denotes the number of samples provided for that sub-set (*support*). *As* denotes that the whole test-set was used (*all sensor data*). The resulting model provided an accuracy of 82% on the whole test set, whereas the sub-set containing the observations which hold data for all 7 sensors provided an accuracy of 84%. There were fewer observations that provided data

Table 5. Fusion Model with data augmentation in training/validation sets, no data augmentation in test set. Xs F1 denotes F1 scores for X sensors, Xs S denotes support

Classes	2s F1	2s S	3s F1	3s S	4s F1	4s S	5s F1	5s S	6s F1	6s S	7s F1	7s S	As F1	As S
SITTING-TOILET	0.80	2	0.80	2	0.86	22	0.80	145	0.63	64	0.60	18	0.31	17
SITTING-EATING	0.86	14	0.67	4	0.73	18	0.83	69	0.60	9	0.93	154	0.52	30
STANDING-COOKING	0.80	2	1.00	2	0.55	17	0.00	1	0.68	104	0.73	12	0.57	14
SITTING-WATCHING TV	–	–	0.89	4	0.76	47	0.87	611	0.44	2	0.50	7	0.88	2294
LYING DOWN-WATCHING TV	1.00	6	0.75	4	0.43	4	0.67	119	0.85	137	0.63	59	0.66	228
STANDING-EATING	0.97	18	0.95	30	0.43	8	0.84	328	0.64	51	0.68	90	0.76	479
STANDING-CLEANING	–	–	–	–	0.67	5	0.00	3	0.33	9	0.89	942	0.88	401
WALKING-EATING	–	–	–	–	0.57	2	0.56	15	0.87	588	0.62	27	0.70	523
STANDING-WATCHING TV	–	–	–	–	0.00	1	0.78	22	0.74	76	0.91	830	0.72	227
STANDING-TOILET	0.00	1	0.80	2	0.84	109	0.69	61	0.83	340	0.70	234	0.87	1522
WALKING-WATCHING TV	–	–	0.67	3	0.29	9	0.82	104	0.71	117	–	–	0.68	209
WALKING-COOKING	–	–	–	–	0.00	1	0.84	26	0.67	3	0.76	208	0.73	80
SITTING-COOKING	–	–	–	–	–	–	1.00	1	0.80	36	0.74	60	0.74	59
WALKING-CLEANING	–	–	–	–	0.67	3	0.60	13	0.82	29	0.89	44	0.48	57
LYING DOWN-EATING	–	–	–	–	–	–	0.60	59	0.55	5	0.69	23	0.80	96
SITTING-CLEANING	–	–	–	–	–	–	–	–	0.46	35	0.43	8	0.78	9
Accuracy	0.91	43	0.88	51	0.74	246	0.81	1577	0.80	1605	0.85	2716	0.82	6245
Macro avg	0.74	43	0.82	51	0.52	246	0.66	1577	0.66	1605	0.71	2716	0.69	6245
Weighted avg	0.90	43	0.88	51	0.74	246	0.81	1577	0.80	1605	0.84	2716	0.82	6245

for less than 5 sensors, according to the support metrics. The classes with larger sample sizes (e.g., *SITTING-WATCHING TV* and *STANDING-TOILET*) had accuracy scores of at least 86%, whereas on the opposite spectrum classes with too few samples (e.g., *SITTING-TOILET* and *STANDING-COOKING*) had low scores of 38% and 55% respectively denoting balancing issues between the classes.

The next set of experiments investigates the proposed data augmentation's method performance. In Table 3 we present the result of the experiments with the test set augmented with a value of $C = 2$ by using Algorithm 2. In Table 4 both the training/validation sets are augmented with a value of $C = 2$, as well as the test set. Finally in Table 5 only training and validation sets are augmented with a value of $C = 2$. As there are more combinations of 2-sensor data than 3-sensor data, and 3-sensor data than 4-sensor data etc., in Table 3 we can observe a sharp drop on the accuracy of the new augmented data set, as it drops to 65%, whereas the accuracy on the sub-set containing data for all 7-sensors remains at 84%. In Table 4 we observe an increase of total accuracy to 72%. When providing data for at least 4 sensors the accuracy is higher, 76% for 4-sensor observations, 79% for 5-sensor observations and 83% for 6-sensor observations. The largest increase of performance was 11% for 2-sensor observations. Notice that according to Table 1 the sensor unimodal models do not perform equally. From this premise it follows logically that not all sensor sub-sets will perform equally (especially the 2 sensor sub-sets). In Table 5 we can observe that the fusion model trained using the augmented training and validation sets performs equally to the non-augmented one on the original test set with an accuracy score of 82%. Its 2-sensor accuracy is higher though (91% versus 88% when trained without the proposed data augmentation method).

5 Conclusions and Future Work

In this work, we proposed a sensor-independent fusion method in respect to the number of sensors utilized for Automatic Human Activity Recognition. It utilizes feature-level fusion. This method allows the design of fusion models that can operate with fewer data sources than the ones the model was designed to operate on. However, the max number of sensors must be known beforehand.

Furthermore, to increase the fusion model's performance when operating on observations with fewer sensor data we proposed a data augmentation method that uses no interpolation or estimation techniques to augment the dataset. Instead it generates all possible combinations of utilized sensors for recorded observations, with a minimum number of sensor data required defined by a constant. The results showed an increase in all sub-sets of the test set, split according to the number of sensors used per observation, indicating the method's effectiveness.

For the future we will investigate class balancing methods to improve the scores for classes with fewer samples. Moreover, we will also investigate the individual sensor contributions to the results, as well as the accuracy differences between different combinations of sensors totaling to the same number, e.g., what is the difference of accuracy when using 3-sensor data between *Audio, Watch Compass, Phone Magnet* and *Phone State, Watch Accelerometer, Phone Accelerometer*. The goal is to generate a general method of evaluating a sensor's performance in the fusion model, while the unimodal models for the sensors are considered as black boxes.

Acknowledgments. The research work was supported by the Hellenic Foundation for Research and Innovation (H.F.R.I.) under the "First Call for H.F.R.I. Research Projects to support Faculty members and Researchers and the procurement of high-cost research equipment grant" (Project Name: ACTIVE, Project Number: HFRI-FM17-2271).

References

1. Aggarwal, J.K., Xia, L.: Human activity recognition from 3d data: a review. Pattern Recogn. Lett. **48**, 70–80 (2014)
2. Barrios-Avilés, J., Iakymchuk, T., Samaniego, J., Medus, L.D., Rosado-Muñoz, A.: Movement detection with event-based cameras: comparison with frame-based cameras in robot object tracking using powerlink communication. Electronics **7**(11), 304 (2018)
3. Batchuluun, G., Nguyen, D.T., Pham, T.D., Park, C., Park, K.R.: Action recognition from thermal videos. IEEE Access **7**, 103893–103917 (2019)
4. Chandrasekaran, B., Gangadhar, S., Conrad, J.M.: A survey of multisensor fusion techniques, architectures and methodologies. In: SoutheastCon 2017, pp. 1–8. IEEE (2017)
5. Dong, Y., Li, X., Dezert, J., Khyam, M.O., Noor-A-Rahim, M., Ge, S.S.: Dezert-Smarandache theory-based fusion for human activity recognition in body sensor networks. IEEE Trans. Industr. Inf. **16**(11), 7138–7149 (2020)

6. Ehatisham-Ul-Haq, M.: Robust human activity recognition using multimodal feature-level fusion. IEEE Access **7**, 60736–60751 (2019)
7. Grabisch, M., Raufaste, E.: An empirical study of statistical properties of the Choquet and Sugeno integrals. IEEE Trans. Fuzzy Syst. **16**(4), 839–850 (2008)
8. Innocenti, S.U., Becattini, F., Pernici, F., Del Bimbo, A.: Temporal binary representation for event-based action recognition. In: 2020 25th International Conference on Pattern Recognition (ICPR), pp. 10426–10432. IEEE (2021)
9. Lee, Y.-S., Cho, S.-B.: Activity recognition using hierarchical hidden Markov models on a smartphone with 3d accelerometer. In: Corchado, E., Kurzyński, M., Woźniak, M. (eds.) HAIS 2011. LNCS (LNAI), vol. 6678, pp. 460–467. Springer, Heidelberg (2011). https://doi.org/10.1007/978-3-642-21219-2_58
10. Li, H., et al.: Multisensor data fusion for human activities classification and fall detection. In: 2017 IEEE SENSORS, pp. 1–3. IEEE (2017)
11. Naik, K., Pandit, T., Naik, N., Shah, P.: Activity recognition in residential spaces with internet of things devices and thermal imaging. Sensors **21**(3), 988 (2021)
12. Nweke, H.F., Teh, Y.W., Mujtaba, G., Al-Garadi, M.A.: Data fusion and multiple classifier systems for human activity detection and health monitoring: review and open research directions. Inf. Fusion **46**, 147–170 (2019)
13. Ordóñez, F.J., Roggen, D.: Deep convolutional and LSTM recurrent neural networks for multimodal wearable activity recognition. Sensors **16**(1), 115 (2016)
14. Sebestyen, G., Stoica, I., Hangan, A.: Human activity recognition and monitoring for elderly people. In: 2016 IEEE 12th International Conference on Intelligent Computer Communication and Processing (ICCP), pp. 341–347. IEEE (2016)
15. Uddin, M.Z., Soylu, A.: Human activity recognition using wearable sensors, discriminant analysis, and long short-term memory-based neural structured learning. Sci. Rep. **11**(1), 16455 (2021)
16. Vaizman, Y., Ellis, K., Lanckriet, G.: Recognizing detailed human context in the wild from smartphones and smartwatches. IEEE Pervasive Comput. **16**(4), 62–74 (2017). https://doi.org/10.1109/MPRV.2017.3971131
17. Vrigkas, M., Nikou, C., Kakadiaris, I.A.: A review of human activity recognition methods. Front. Robot. AI **2**, 28 (2015). https://doi.org/10.3389/frobt.2015.00028
18. Wang, L., Huynh, D.Q., Koniusz, P.: A comparative review of recent kinect-based action recognition algorithms. IEEE Trans. Image Process. **29**, 15–28 (2019)
19. Wu, Q., Wang, Z., Deng, F., Chi, Z., Feng, D.D.: Realistic human action recognition with multimodal feature selection and fusion. IEEE Trans. Syst. Man Cybern. Syst. **43**(4), 875–885 (2013). https://doi.org/10.1109/TSMCA.2012.2226575
20. Yao, S., Hu, S., Zhao, Y., Zhang, A., Abdelzaher, T.: DeepSense: a unified deep learning framework for time-series mobile sensing data processing. In: Proceedings of the 26th International Conference on World Wide Web, pp. 351–360 (2017)
21. Zeng, Z., Zhang, Z., Pianfetti, B., Tu, J., Huang, T.S.: Audio-visual affect recognition in activation-evaluation space. In: 2005 IEEE International Conference on Multimedia and Expo, p. 4. IEEE (2005)
22. Zhang, S., Wei, Z., Nie, J., Huang, L., Wang, S., Li, Z.: A review on human activity recognition using vision-based method. J. Healthc. Eng. **2017**, 3090343 (2017)
23. Zhu, C., Sheng, W.: Multi-sensor fusion for human daily activity recognition in robot-assisted living. In: Proceedings of the 4th ACM/IEEE International Conference on Human Robot Interaction, pp. 303–304 (2009)

Comparative Study of Activation Functions and Their Impact on the YOLOv5 Object Detection Model

John Doherty[1(✉)], Bryan Gardiner[1], Emmett Kerr[1], Nazmul Siddique[1], and Sunilkumar S. Manvi[2]

[1] Intelligent Systems Research Centre, Ulster University, Northland Road, Derry BT48 7JL, United Kingdom
{doherty-j92,b.gardiner,ep.kerr,nh.siddique}@ulster.ac.uk

[2] School of Computer Science and Engineering, REVA University, Karnataka 560064, India
Ssmanvi@reva.edu.in

Abstract. Object detection is an important aspect of computer vision research, involving determining the location and class of objects within a scene. For an object detection system to run in real-time, it is vital to minimise the computational costs while maintaining an acceptably high accuracy. In a Convolutional Neural Network (CNN) there is a direct correlation between the accuracy and the computational cost incurred by increasing the number of layers. Activation functions play a key role in a CNN to utilise nonlinearity to help balance the computational cost and accuracy. In this paper, a series of improvements are proposed to the state-of-the-art one-stage real-time object detection model, YOLOv5, providing the capability to enhance the overall performance. The validity of replacing the current activation function in YOLOv5, Swish, with a variety of alternative activation functions was investigated to aid in improving the accuracy and lowering the computational costs associated with visual object detection. This research demonstrates the various improvements in accuracy and performance that are achievable by appropriately selecting a suitable activation function to use in YOLOv5, including ACON, FReLU and Hardswish. The improved YOLOv5 model was verified utilising transfer learning on the German Traffic Sign Detection Benchmark (GTSDB) achieving state-of-the-art performance.

Keywords: Activation function · Deep learning · Object detection · YOLO

1 Introduction

Since the launch of the Microsoft Common Objects in Context (MSCOCO) dataset in 2015, many research teams have been striving to achieve state-of-the-art object detection performance on this dataset. Many researchers have used Convolutional Neural Network (CNN) based object detectors. These detectors can be separated into one-stage and two-stage detectors. Two-stage visual object detection models have seen a vast improvement in accuracy, however, much of this comes at the cost of increased inference time. For

M. El Yacoubi et al. (Eds.): ICPRAI 2022, LNCS 13364, pp. 40–52, 2022.
https://doi.org/10.1007/978-3-031-09282-4_4

a system to be capable of running in real-time, it is vital that computational costs are minimised while ensuring that the accuracy is not severely impacted. To enable this, a recent rise has been seen in the development and usage of CNN-based one-stage object detection models [1]. These one-stage object detection models can achieve impressive accuracy, rivalling that of some two-stage object detectors, while running with substantially lower computational costs. This allows for these one-stage object detectors to run at incredible speeds on standard computer hardware or embedded systems [2]. While developing these one-stage object detection models, an extremely wide variety of activation functions have been utilised [3–5].

Activation functions are utilised in deep learning networks to enable the transformation of a weighted input signal to an output signal, which in turn enables the transfer of this output signal to the next layer in the network. The prediction accuracy of a deep learning network relies heavily on a variety of factors, two of the most important are the number of layers within the network, and the activation function used [6]. The ideal number of layers that should be utilised as well as the specific activation function that should be chosen varies based on the application of the network. Adding additional layers to a deep learning network may positively impact its performance, but it will do so at great cost to computational time [7]. To offset the increase in computational time, it is an option to alter the activation function to achieve improved performance.

An activation function creates a differentiator between a deep learning network and a linear regression model. If a deep learning network has no activation function, the predicted output will be proportional to the provided input [8]; similarly, if a linear activation function is utilised, the output will be similar to the input, with the addition of some small error. A non-linear activation function enables a deep network to take full advantage of its ability to learn from noisy data, such as the errors present in real-world input data [9]; in a CNN, this can be seen as a non-linear activation function being applied after each convolutional layer, with the activation function converting the output from the convolutional layer into a suitable input for the next layer in a non-linear manner. This change is one of the key reasons deep learning networks have seen such widespread adoption in object detection, as the use of non-linear activation functions can allow for quicker interpretation of complex data without the need of adding additional hidden layers, helping to keep computational costs as low as possible.

In 2016, Redmon et al. [10] proposed the YOLO algorithm. YOLO, or *You Only Look Once*, has went through many iterations, through to YOLOv5 in 2020 [11]. This paper modifies the most modern, accurate and extremely efficient YOLOv5 providing an improved model which will enhance accuracy and reduce inference time and will be made available for use in many real-time object detection tasks. This is achieved by introducing a variety of state-of-the-art activation functions which are applied to a create a novel version of YOLOv5. The improved YOLOv5 models are then trained and tested on MSCOCO proposing a selection of models which outperform the standard implementation. The top performing models are then trained and tested on the German Traffic Sign Detection Benchmark (GTSDB) dataset achieving state-of-the-art performance for a real-time object detection method.

The remainder of this paper is organised as follows. Section 2 includes a brief overview of CNN architectures for general object detection followed by traffic sign object detection, while Sect. 3 discusses the architecture of YOLOv5 in detail, while also outlining the various activation functions that have been used throughout the experiments. Section 4 features details of the experimental work, alongside the analysis of the experimental results, while Sect. 5 concludes the paper and discusses the direction of future work.

2 Related Work

As previously discussed, CNN-based object detection models can be divided into a variety of categories, including one-stage, two-stage, anchor-based and anchor-free detectors. For the purpose of this research, focus will be placed on one-stage detectors as they achieve a good balance of inference time and computational overhead.

Feng et al. [12] proposed a task-aligned one-stage object detection model (TOOD) which utilises a task-aligned head and learning mechanism, aiming to provide balance between the classification and localisation tasks within object detection - TOOD achieves a Mean Average Precision (mAP) at 0.5 of 60.0 on MSCOCO.

Fully Convolutional One-Stage (FCOS) is a one-stage object detector which solves object detection in a per-pixel prediction fashion [13]. This network eliminates the need of anchor boxes, vastly reducing computational costs. FCOS achieved a peak mAP at 0.5 of 64.1 on MSCOCO.

Chen et al. [14] proposed a Location-Aware Multi-Dilation (LAMD) module, which embeds spatial information from the head into the classifier, which improves robustness to the shifting of bounding boxes. They successfully implemented LAMD into state-of-the-art one-stage object detectors and improved the performance of ResNet-50 mAP at 0.5 on MSCOCO from 55.0 to 59.7.

You Only Look Once (YOLO) is a family of object detectors which have pushed the envelope for performance of one-stage object detectors. YOLO revolutionized the one-stage object detection method, by only giving an image one full forward pass through a single neural network prior to classification [10]. YOLO splits the input image into a $s \times s$ grid pattern, with each grid cell being responsible for predicting bounding boxes and confidence scores for objects. YOLO features a variety of advantages when compared to other one-stage object detectors, including the utilisation of global context, as the network evaluates the entire image at test time, along with speed that is an order of magnitude faster than other comparable one-stage object detectors [15].

CNN-based object detection models have been used for a wide variety of tasks, but an increasingly popular task is real-time traffic sign detection due to the increase into research surrounding autonomous driving.

Zhu et al. [16] proposed a novel labelled traffic sign detection dataset consisting of over 100,000 images with 30,000 traffic-sign instances gathered from Tencent Street Views, called the Tsinghua-Tencent 100k (TT100K). They also designed an end-to-end CNN-based object detector which achieved 88% accuracy in traffic sign detection in TT100K, compared to Fast R-CNN which achieved 50% accuracy. The TT100K dataset features a few problems, including extreme class imbalance, along with 100,000 images, with only 10,000 of those containing a traffic sign, meaning 90% of the dataset are background images.

Zhang et al. [17] utilised a YOLOv3 based approach to achieve real-time detection on small traffic signs. Their model utilised data augmentation, mainly through image mixup. Alongside this, they also used a multi-scale spatial pyramid pooling block in Darknet53 to learn object features more comprehensively. While training the model on the TT100K dataset. They achieved a mAP of 86% in detection while running at 23.81 FPS.

Liang et al. [18] developed a two-stage network which utilises a deep feature pyramid architecture with lateral connections, along with a densely connected CNN to strengthen the feature transmission, leading to more accurate classification with less parameters. They achieved 95% Area Under Precision-Recall Curve (AUC) on traffic sign detection from the GTSDB, and 82%–100% Accuracy across multiple TT100K classes, approximately a 10%–15% improvement from Faster R-CNN in the same task.

Wang et al. [19] proposed a traffic sign detection method which utilises histogram of oriented gradient and a "coarse-to-fine" sliding window scheme to achieve high recall and precision ratios, while also being robust to adverse situations including back lighting, occlusion and low quality.

3 Methodology

3.1 YOLOv5 Network Architecture

As YOLOv5 is yet to have a published peer-reviewed scientific paper from the creator, the YOLOv5 GitHub page has served as the main source of information to date regarding the model [11]. The network structure of YOLOv5, presented in Fig. 1, can be described as follows:

- The backbone is a modified version of the original DarkNet [10] architecture used across the family of YOLO models. The version in YOLOv5 has been written in Python and modified to utilise Cross-Stage-Partial-Connections (CSP). This is based on the utilisation of CSPs in YOLOv4 [20]. The backbone receives input images with a $640 \times 640 \times 3$ resolution. This input is transformed into a $320 \times 320 \times 12$ feature map, followed by a convolutional operation of 32 kernels, becoming a $320 \times 320 \times 32$ feature map.
- The neck is a modified Path Aggregation Network (PANet). The PANet is utilised to generate feature pyramids at multiple scales to enhance the model's ability to detect and recognise objects of varying sizes [21].
- The head is a standardised YOLO head. It takes inputs at 3 scales (8, 16, 32), which enables it to detect small, medium, and large objects respectively. Previous single scale heads have been tested on YOLOv5 and perform worse than the current implementation.

There are a few features specific to YOLOv5 which help improve its performance over previous iterations, including the use of the BottleneckCSP module which performs feature extractions on the feature map, as well as the use of mosaic data augmentation and auto learning bounding box anchors. When compared with other large-scale CNNs, this module can help reduce gradient information duplication in the optimisation process

[22]. YOLOv5 has been noted to achieve similar or even higher accuracy at a lower computational cost when compared to YOLOv4 [23], while YOLOv4 achieved a ~10% higher mAP than YOLOv3 [24].

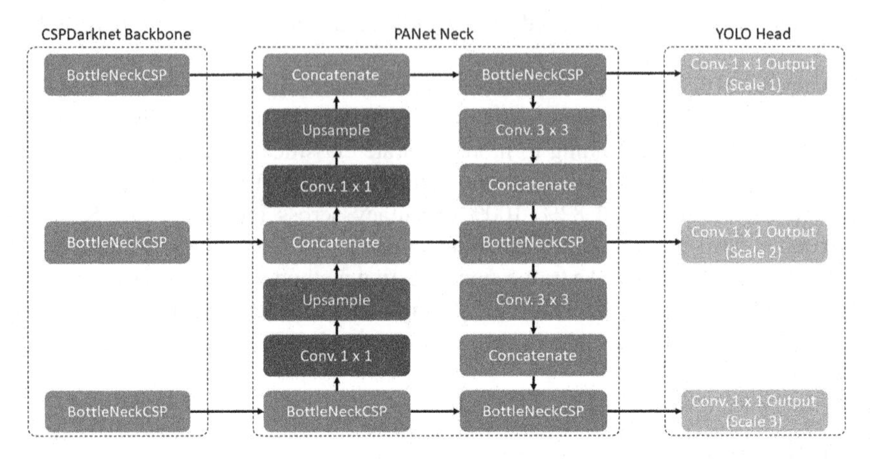

Fig. 1. YOLOv5 network structure

3.2 Activation Functions

There are a wide range of potential activation functions to choose from when attempting to create the most optimal object detector. As YOLOv5 is a one-stage detector with a large focus placed on computational efficiency, it is believed that the best activation functions to evaluate are those which will have a minimal impact on computational cost while simultaneously increasing accuracy.

In its default configuration, YOLOv5 uses the Swish activation function [25]. Swish can be best described as an activation function which nonlinearly interpolates between a standard linear function and the ReLU activation function [26]. Swish is generally viewed as a best-of-both-worlds scenario between a linear and a more complex non-linear activation function. It has been noted that Swish improves performance on ImageNet when compared to the ReLU and Sigmoid functions [27].

A Sigmoid activation function, sometimes referred to as a squashing function is much more complex than a linear activation function due to its use of an exponential term which causes increased computational cost, while also being much better at learning nonlinearity in patterns in wide datasets. A Sigmoid function has some major drawbacks, including sharp damp gradients during backpropagation from deeper hidden layers, along with gradient saturation and slow convergence [28].

The LeakyReLU activation function is an improved version of the ReLU [29] activation function. Whereas ReLU is a piecewise linear function that outputs the input directly if positive, otherwise, outputting zero, LeakyReLU provides a small positive slope for negative values [30]. This alleviates the dying ReLU problem, where nodes within a deep network are inactive and only output 0 for any input. LeakyReLU often performs on par or slightly better than ReLU [31].

The Flexible Rectified Linear Units (FReLU) activation function is a modified version of the ReLU activation function, where the rectified point of ReLU is redesigned as a learnable parameter [32]. FReLU tends to converge on a negative value, improving the expressiveness and performance while being no more computationally expensive than the original ReLU or LeakyReLU.

Hardswish is a modified version of the Swish activation function. Hardswish replaces the more computationally expensive sigmoid section of the Swish activation function with a piecewise linear analogue section [33], making Hardswish less computationally expensive than Swish while maintaining a similar accuracy.

Activate or Not (ACON) modifies the Maxout [34] activation function in a similar manner as to how Swish modifies ReLU. ACON has a dynamic non-linear degree with a switching factor that decays to zero as the non-linear function becomes linear. ACON has been noted to improve performance in ImageNet when compared to Swish and ReLU [35].

Mish is inspired by Swish, and uses the Self-Gating property where the non-modulated input it multiplied by the output of the non-linear function of the input [36]. Mish has shown improvements in both final accuracy and stability when compared with ReLU and Swish [37].

The mathematical functions and ranges of each activation function are represented in Table 1.

Table 1. Further activation function information

Activation function	Mathematical definition	Range (x)
Swish	$f(x) = x * \left(1 + \mathrm{e}^{-x}\right)^{-1}$	$-0.28, +\infty$
Sigmoid	$f(x) = \frac{1}{1+\mathrm{e}^{-x}}$	$0, +1$
LeakyReLU	$f(x) = \begin{cases} 0.01x \; if\,(x < 0) \\ x \quad\; if\,(x \geq 0) \end{cases}$	$-\infty, +\infty$
FreLU	$f(x) = \begin{cases} x + b_L \; if\,(x > 0) \\ b_L \quad\; if\,(x \leq 0) \end{cases}$	$-\infty, +\infty$
Hardswish	$f(x) = \begin{cases} 0 & if\,(x \leq -3) \\ x & if\,(x \geq +3) \\ x \cdot \frac{x+3}{6} & otherwise \end{cases}$	$-1, +\infty$
ACON	$f(x) = (P_1 - P_2)x \cdot \sigma(\beta(P_1 - P_2)x) + P_2x$	$-\infty, +\infty$
Mish	$f(x) = \frac{\mathrm{e}^x \omega}{\delta^2}$	$-0.31, +\infty$

4 Experiments

4.1 Datasets

The experiments are conducted using two separate datasets. Firstly, the models are trained from scratch on the MSCOCO dataset. MSCOCO features over 328,000 images across 80 classes with an extremely wide range of images, alongside annotations for object detection including bounding boxes and per-instance segmentation masks.

The second dataset is the German Traffic Sign object detection dataset (GTSDB) containing 900 images across four classes; mandatory, danger, prohibitory and other. Each image in the dataset is fully annotated with bounding boxes and per-instance segmentation masks and is originally split into 600 training images and 300 evaluation images. As GTSDB is not natively supported by YOLOv5 due to the annotation type used, a pre-processing step of converting its annotations to a format which YOLOv5 requires was completed. During this, the dataset split was also changes to 80% training, 10% testing and 10% validation.

4.2 YOLOv5 Model Selection

YOLOv5 features four models: YOLOv5s, YOLOv5m, YOLOv5l, YOLOv5x. These models all include the core features of YOLOv5 but feature an increasing number of BottleneckCSP modules and hyperparameters, increasing both accuracy and inference time. The advertised inference time and mAP on the COCO test-dev dataset can be seen in Table 2.

Table 2. Comparison of YOLO models [11]

Model	Input size	mAP 0.5:0.95	mAP 0.5	Speed (ms)
YOLOv5s	640 × 640	36.7	55.4	2.0
YOLOv5m	640 × 640	44.5	63.1	2.7
YOLOv5l	640 × 640	48.2	66.9	3.8
YOLOv5s	640 × 640	50.4	68.8	6.1

Based on this, it was decided to utilise the YOLOv5l model as the basis for the object detection model as it is believed it has the best balance of accuracy to inference time.

4.3 Experimental Setup

The experiments feature a two-pronged approach. Initially, MSCOCO is utilised as the training dataset and the various YOLOv5 models are trained from scratch with modified activation functions. An activation function comparative analysis is conducted, comparing vital factors in performance including inference and training time, along with

Precision, Recall, also known as True Positive Rate (TPR) and equivalent to the inverse of the False Positive Rate (FPR), and mAP. Following this, the top performing models are used to complete a series of transfer learning experiments to determine which achieves the best performance on the GTSDB dataset.

4.4 Activation Function Comparative Analysis

A number of experiments were conducted using the YOLOv5 models with modified activation functions. Firstly, the models were trained on the MSCOCO dataset for a set number of 1000 epochs; this training occurred with default YOLOv5 dataset augmentation, with the resolution of each training image augmented from the original 640 × 480 pixels to 640 × 640 pixels. This is required as the default configuration of YOLOv5 expects a 640 × 640 input to map correctly to the three scaled outputs. Each experiment was run on the Kelvin2 Cluster, which is a part of the Northern Ireland High Performance Computing (NI-HPC) cluster [38]. The experiments were carried out on an Nvidia Tesla V100 graphics card with 32 GB of VRAM, along with 4 cores of an AMD EPYC 7702 64-Core Processor, acting as 8 data loaders, and a batch size of 32 (with the exception of ACON, requiring a batch size of 16 to fit into the 32 GB VRAM limit). It was found that the peak performance of each activation function occurred at different points in the training cycle, so the results for the peak performance have been shown, and the epoch this performance was achieved at has been noted; along with the time taken per epoch (in minutes). The results from these various experiments can be seen in Table 3.

Table 3. Experimental results from training from scratch on MSCOCO with modified activation functions on YOLOv5l

Activation function	Epoch	Precision	Recall	mAP 0.5	mAP 0.5:0.95	Inference speed (ms)	Time per epoch (min)	Total training time (hours)
Swish	274	0.706	0.602	0.648	0.452	6.8	35	159.8
ACON	272	0.694	0.611	0.650	0.456	10.5	110	498.7
FReLU	437	0.729	0.604	0.658	0.459	9.0	45	327.8
Hardswish	465	0.712	0.603	0.649	0.456	6.5	22	170.5
LeakyReLU	472	0.726	0.591	0.646	0.450	6.7	25	197.7
Mish	341	0.658	0.544	0.578	0.393	6.9	10	56.8
Sigmoid	799	0.724	0.583	0.633	0.439	6.7	24	319.6

Upon analysis of the obtained results, both Hardswish and LeakyReLU either match or exceed the default Swish activation function (in terms of mAP) while maintaining a similar inference time and reduced training time while some others, namely FReLU and ACON, achieve an extremely higher mAP at the cost of some computational overhead during both inference and training.

From these results it has been noted that FReLU is the best performer, achieving the highest Precision at 0.729, mAP 0.5 at 0.658 and mAP 0.5:0.95 at 0.459, while losing to ACON in Recall which scored 0.610. A close runner up to FReLU and ACON is Hardswish, achieving a Precision of 0.712, Recall of 0.602, mAP 0.5 of 0.649 and mAP 0.5:0.95 of 0.459. This is a drop of only 0.017, 0.001, 0.009 and 0.003 respectively, achieving the same training and inference time as the default Swish activation function.

While these results demonstrate improvement on the current state-of-the-art, it is important to note that FReLU took 45 min per epoch, almost double that of Swish, while also running 2.2 ms slower per image, equating to a real-world performance drop of 36 FPS. It is also important to note that each activation function performed similarly from a computational standpoint with the exception of FReLU and ACON. This is to be expected as these are much more complex activation functions which require greater computational overhead to utilise. Surprisingly, Mish completed each epoch in only 10 min, while still taking 6.9 ms per image.

It is vital to consider the combination of both the number of epochs required for an activation function to achieve its best performance, along with the time taken for each epoch to be completed. ACON achieves peak performance at only 272 epochs, but with each epoch taking over 110 min this equates to a real-world training time of almost 500 h, while FReLU requires 437 epochs at 45 min each, which is over 327 h of training. Hardswish achieves peak performance at 465 epochs, with each epoch only taking 25 min, meaning this is only 194 h of training, under half of the training time required for ACON and around 2/3 of the time required for FReLU.

For this reason, it is recommended that when aiming for the best balance of training time and performance, the Hardswish activation function should be selected to replace the standard Swish activation function in the YOLOv5l model, as Hardswish achieves better precision, recall, mAP 0.5 and mAP 0.5:0.95 for a marginal training time increase and slightly lower computational cost at run-time.

If a peak in accuracy is required while still being able to run in real-time, the recommendation is to select FReLU as the desired activation function. FReLU achieves the highest precision, mAP 0.5 and mAP 0.5:0.95 out of all tested activation functions, while still running at over 110 FPS.

4.5 Model Verification Using Transfer Learning

Following from the previous experiments and to verify the proposed models, further experiments were completed to investigate which YOLOv5 model will achieve the best performance on the GTSDB dataset. Transfer learning was utilised as GTSDB is a small dataset which is not well suited to full training from scratch. These experiments were completed on the same hardware and settings as previously used.

The fully trained Swish, FReLU and Hardswish models from the previous experiments were used as the basis for transfer learning. Using the weights generated from the previous experiment, two independent training sessions for each set of weights were created. Firstly, each model was trained with the first 24 layers frozen, leaving only the final fully connected layer unfrozen. This should provide the quickest training time, at the cost of some accuracy. Following this, the same initial weights were reused, and the experiment was repeated, but only the first 10 layers representing the backbone were frozen; this should slightly increase the training time but provide substantially higher accuracy. The results from the transfer learning experiment are presented in Table 4.

Table 4. Experimental results from transfer learning on GTSDB with modified activation functions on YOLOv5l

Activation function	Precision	Recall	mAP 0.5	mAP 0.5:0.95	Speed (ms)
10 layers frozen					
Swish	0.956	0.894	0.937	0.773	9.6
FReLU	0.950	0.915	0.944	0.774	13.0
Hardswish	0.972	0.937	0.960	0.801	9.4
24 layers frozen					
Swish	0.641	0.391	0.478	0.308	9.6
FReLU	0.600	0.555	0.579	0.406	12.8
Hardswish	0.650	0.346	0.455	0.266	9.9

The results from the transfer learning experiments show that impressive results can be achieved with minimal training. Each model took around 50–200 epochs to achieve their top performance, with each epoch taking between 3 and 5 s. The exact time per epoch or number of epochs for each result was not noted as they are within the margin of error, and peak performance can be achieved in a matter of minutes.

Some key observations can be made from the analysis of these results; firstly, the performance from freezing only the initial 10 layers is vastly superior to the performance of freezing all layers other than the final layer. This is to be expected, as the GTSDB dataset is quite small at only 900 images, and extremely different than the original MSCOCO dataset the network is pretrained on.

Secondly, similar comparisons to the original experiment on MSCOCO can be drawn. Both FReLU and Hardswish outperform Swish in mAP 0.5 and 0.5:0.95, while Hardswish has a marginally lower inference time, and FReLU has a significantly higher inference time. In contrast to the original experiment, Hardswish performs higher than FReLU across the board while running over 3 ms quicker per image.

The results from Hardswish with the first 10 layers frozen are state-of-the-art for the GTSDB dataset, outperforming previous examples such as Rajendran et al. [39] achieving a 0.922 mAP 0.5 at 100 ms per image on a modified YOLOv3 network.

The results presented are key in showing the improvements in accuracy that can be gained by improving the existing YOLOv5 model through changing the activation function with a choice of suggested activation functions. The improved YOLOv5 model achieves a higher accuracy than current state-of-the-art GTSDB models outlined in Sect. 2.

5 Conclusion

In this paper an in-depth analysis of the effects of changing the existing Activation Function in the YOLOv5 object detection model was completed. The experimental results show that a significant improvement in mAP can be found by replacing the standard Swish activation function with a variety of others, including FReLU, ACON and Hardswish. This work was expanded, showing the potential application of the improved YOLOv5l models on the task of real-time traffic sign object detection. This paper demonstrates the improvements in performance than be achieved by using a synergistic strategy focusing on activation function and transfer learning balance. Future work will focus on further improvements to YOLOv5, including modifying model structure, potentially replacing the PANet neck, as well as improving the top performing YOLOv5l models through further hyperparameter tuning utilising a genetic algorithm.

References

1. Sultana, F., Sufian, A., Dutta, P.: A review of object detection models based on convolutional neural network. In: Advances in Intelligent Systems and Computing, pp. 1–16 (2020)
2. Soviany, P., Ionescu, R.T.: Optimizing the trade-off between single-stage and two-stage deep object detectors using image difficulty prediction. In: 20th International Symposium on Symbolic and Numeric Algorithms for Scientific Computing, SYNASC (2018)
3. Hou, Q., Xing, J.: KSSD: single-stage multi-object detection algorithm with higher accuracy. IET Image Process. **14**(15), 3651–3661 (2020). https://doi.org/10.1049/iet-ipr.2020.0077
4. Kim, S., Kim, H.: Zero-centered fixed-point quantization with iterative retraining for deep convolutional neural network-based object detectors. IEEE Access **9**, 20828–20839 (2021). https://doi.org/10.1109/ACCESS.2021.3054879
5. Shakarami, A., Menhaj, M.B., Mahdavi-Hormat, A., Tarrah, H.: A fast and yet efficient YOLOv3 for blood cell detection. Biomed. Sig. Process. Control **66**, 102495 (2021). https://doi.org/10.1016/j.bspc.2021.102495
6. Goyal, M., Goyal, R., Reddy, P.V., Lall, B.: Activation functions. In: Pedrycz, W., Chen, S.-M. (eds.) Deep Learning: Algorithms and Applications. SCI, vol. 865, pp. 1–30. Springer, Cham (2020). https://doi.org/10.1007/978-3-030-31760-7_1
7. Patel, S., Patel, A.: Object detection with convolutional neural networks. In: Joshi, A., Khosravy, M., Gupta, N. (eds.) Machine Learning for Predictive Analysis. LNNS, vol. 141, pp. 529–539. Springer, Singapore (2021). https://doi.org/10.1007/978-981-15-7106-0_52
8. Goodfellow, I., Bengio, Y., Courville, A.: Deep Learning. MIT Press (2016)
9. Li, S., Chen, S., Liu, B.: Accelerating a recurrent neural network to finite-time convergence for solving time-varying Sylvester equation by using a sign-bi-power activation function. Neural Process. Lett. **37**, 189–205 (2013). https://doi.org/10.1007/s11063-012-9241-1
10. Redmon, J., Divvala, S., Girshick, R., Farhadi, A.: You only look once: unified, real-time object detection. In: IEEE Conference on Computer Vision and Pattern Recognition (CVPR), pp. 779–788. IEEE (2016)
11. Jocher, G.: YOLOv5 Github. https://github.com/ultralytics/yolov5
12. Feng, C., Zhong, Y., Gao, Y., Scott, M., Huang, W.: TOOD: task-aligned one-stage object detection. In: IEEE/CVF International Conference on Computer Vision, pp. 3510–3519 (2021)
13. Tian, Z., Shen, C., Chen, H., He, T.: FCOS: fully convolutional one-stage object detection. In: IEEE/CVF International Conference on Computer Vision (ICCV), pp. 9626–9635. IEEE (2019)

14. Chen, Q., Wang, P., Cheng, A., Wang, W., Zhang, Y., Cheng, J.: Robust one-stage object detection with location-aware classifiers. Pattern Recogn. **105**, 107334 (2020). https://doi.org/10.1016/j.patcog.2020.107334
15. Hui, J.: Real-time Object Detection with YOLO, YOLOv2 and now YOLOv3. https://jonathan-hui.medium.com/real-time-object-detection-with-yolo-yolov2-28b1b93e2088
16. Zhu, Z., Liang, D., Zhang, S., Huang, X., Li, B., Hu, S.: Traffic-sign detection and classification in the wild. In: IEEE Conference on Computer Vision and Pattern Recognition (CVPR), pp. 2110–2118 (2016)
17. Zhang, H., et al.: Real-time detection method for small traffic signs based on Yolov3. IEEE Access **8**, 64145–64156 (2020). https://doi.org/10.1109/ACCESS.2020.2984554
18. Liang, Z., Shao, J., Zhang, D., Gao, L.: Traffic sign detection and recognition based on pyramidal convolutional networks. Neural Comput. Appl. **32**(11), 6533–6543 (2019). https://doi.org/10.1007/s00521-019-04086-z
19. Wang, G., Ren, G., Wu, Z., Zhao, Y., Jiang, L.: A robust, coarse-to-fine traffic sign detection method. In: International Joint Conference on Neural Networks (IJCNN), pp. 1–5. IEEE (2013)
20. Bochkovskiy, A., Wang, C.-Y., Liao, H.-Y.M.: YOLOv4: optimal speed and accuracy of object detection. arXiv (2020)
21. Liu, S., Qi, L., Qin, H., Shi, J., Jia, J.: Path aggregation network for instance segmentation. In: IEEE/CVF Conference on Computer Vision and Pattern Recognition, pp. 8759–8768. IEEE (2018)
22. Tan, S., Lu, G., Jiang, Z., Huang, L.: Improved YOLOv5 network model and application in safety helmet detection. In: IEEE International Conference on Intelligence and Safety for Robotics (ISR), pp. 330–333. (2021)
23. Nelson, J.: YOLOv5 is here: state-of-the-art object detection at 140 FPS. https://blog.roboflow.com/yolov5-is-here/. Accessed 11 Dec 2021
24. Ampadu, H.: Yolov3 and Yolov4 in object detection. https://ai-pool.com/a/s/yolov3-and-yolov4-in-object-detection
25. Solawetz, J., Nelson, J.: YOLOv5 improvement strategy. https://blog.roboflow.com/how-to-train-yolov5-on-a-custom-dataset/. Accessed 10 Dec 2021
26. Ramachandran, P., Zoph, N., Le, Q. V.: Searching for activation functions. In: 6th International Conference on Learning Representations, ICLR 2018 - Workshop Track Proceedings (2018)
27. Ye, A.: Swish: booting ReLU from the activation function throne. https://towardsdatascience.com/swish-booting-relu-from-the-activation-function-throne-78f87e5ab6eb. Accessed 13 Dec 2021
28. Nwankpa, C., Ijomah, W., Gachagan, A., Marshall, S.: Activation Functions: Comparison of trends in Practice and Research for Deep Learning (2018)
29. Shen, F., Gan, R., Zeng, G.: Weighted residuals for very deep networks. In: 3rd International Conference on Systems and Informatics (ICSAI), pp. 936–941 (2016)
30. Xu, J., Li, Z., Du, B., Zhang, M., Liu, J.: Reluplex made more practical: leaky ReLU. In: IEEE Symposium on Computers and Communications (ISCC), pp. 1–7 (2020)
31. Khalid, M., Baber, J., Kasi, M.K., Bakhtyar, M., Devi, V., Sheikh, N.: Empirical evaluation of activation functions in deep convolution neural network for facial expression recognition. In: 43rd International Conference on Telecommunications and Signal Processing (TSP), pp. 204–207 (2020)
32. Qiu, S., Xu, X., Cai, B.: FReLU: flexible rectified linear units for improving convolutional neural networks. In: 24th International Conference on Pattern Recognition (ICPR), pp. 1223–1228 (2018)
33. Howard, A., et al.: Searching for MobileNetV3. In: IEEE/CVF International Conference on Computer Vision (ICCV), pp. 1314–1324. IEEE (2019)

34. Castaneda, G., Morris, P., Khoshgoftaar, T.M.: Evaluation of maxout activations in deep learning across several big data domains. J. Big Data **6**(1), 1–35 (2019). https://doi.org/10.1186/s40537-019-0233-0
35. Ma, N., Zhang, X., Liu, M., Sun, J.: Activate or not: learning customized activation (2020)
36. Misra, D.: Mish: a self regularized non-monotonic activation function (2019)
37. Wright, L.: Meet Mish—new state of the art AI activation function. The successor to ReLU? https://lessw.medium.com/meet-mish-new-state-of-the-art-ai-activation-function-the-successor-to-relu-846a6d93471f. Accessed 09 December 2021
38. Northern Ireland High Performance Computing. https://www.ni-hpc.ac.uk/about/
39. Rajendran, S.P., Shine, L., Pradeep, R., Vijayaraghavan, S.: Real-time traffic sign recognition using YOLOv3 based detector. In: International Conference on Computing, Communication and Networking Technologies, ICCCNT (2019)

Application of A* to the Generalized Constrained Longest Common Subsequence Problem with Many Pattern Strings

Marko Djukanovic[1(✉)], Dragan Matic[1], Christian Blum[2], and Aleksandar Kartelj[3]

[1] Faculty of Natural Sciences and Mathematics, University of Banjaluka, Banjaluka, Bosnia and Herzegovina
{marko.djukanovic,dragan.matic}@pmf.unibl.org
[2] Artificial Intelligence Research Institute (IIIA-CSIC), Campus UAB, Bellaterra, Spain
christian.blum@iiia.csic.es
[3] Faculty of Mathematics, University of Belgrade, Beograd, Serbia

Abstract. This paper considers the constrained longest common subsequence problem with an arbitrary set of input strings and an arbitrary set of pattern strings as input. The problem has applications, for example, in computational biology, serving as a measure of similarity among different molecules that are characterized by common putative structures. We develop an exact A* search to solve it. Our A* search is compared to the only existing competitor from the literature, an AUTOMATON approach. The results show that A* is very efficient for real-world benchmarks, finding provenly optimal solutions in run times that are an order of magnitude lower than the ones of the competitor. Even some of the large-scale real-world instances were solved to optimality by A* search.

1 Introduction

The longest common subsequence (LCS) problem is a prominent string problem. Given is a set of input strings $S = \{s_1, \ldots, s_m\}$, where each s_i consists of letters from a finite alphabet Σ, the goal is to find a string of maximal length that is a common subsequence of all input strings. Even though the problem is easily stated, it is challenging to solve, as it is known to be $\mathcal{NP}$–hard for an arbitrary number ($m > 1$) of input strings [20]. Solutions to LCS problems are commonly used as similarity measures in evolutionary microbiology and computational biology. Identifying LCS solutions to biological sequences (DNA, RNA, or protein sequences) plays a significant role in the field of sequence alignment and pattern discovery. LCS solutions may also serve for the discovery of structural or evolutionary relationships among the inputs sequences [22]. The related literature offers numerous variants of the original LCS problem, arising from practical applications. They are generally obtained by adding further constraints

M. El Yacoubi et al. (Eds.): ICPRAI 2022, LNCS 13364, pp. 53–64, 2022.
https://doi.org/10.1007/978-3-031-09282-4_5

and requirements to the original LCS problem. These variants include, but are not limited to, the longest common palindromic subsequence problem [3], the repetition–free longest common subsequence problem [1], and the arc–preserving longest common subsequence problem [17].

Another variant, the constrained longest common subsequence (CLCS) problem [24], requires a single pattern string p in addition to the set S of m input strings as input. The aim of the CLCS problem is to find a LCS s^* of all strings in S that contains p as a subsequence. This problem is $\mathcal{NP}$–hard as it includes the basic LCS problem as a special case when $p = \epsilon$, where ϵ is the empty string. In practical applications, however, considering more than one pattern string seems often to be required. As an example consider Tang et al. [23], in which `RNase` sequences were aligned with the restriction that each of the three active-site residues `His`(H), `Lyn`(K), and `His`(H) has to be a subsequence of any valid solution. Another example from the biological context concerns [21], in which a large set of real bacterial RNA sequences is considered, under the restriction that solutions must contain 15 different patterns (the so-called *contig primer structures*). Therefore, a generalized version of the CLCS problem, called GCLCS (or (m, k)–CLCS), with arbitrary large sets of input strings and pattern strings was considered in [8]. The GCLCS problem is formally defined as follows. Given a set of $m > 1$ input strings ($S = \{s_1, \ldots, s_m\}$) and a set of $k \geq 1$ pattern strings ($P = \{p_1, \ldots, p_k\}$) the task is to find a sequence s of maximum length that fulfills the following two conditions: (1) s is a subsequence of each string $s_i \in S$, and (2) each pattern $p_j \in P$ is a subsequence of s. Any sequence that fulfills these two conditions is a *feasible solution.*

Related Work. The basic LCS problem has been tackled both by a wide range of exact and approximate approaches. For a fixed number of m input strings, the LCS problem is polynomially solvable by dynamic programming (DP) [15] which runs in $O(n^m)$ time, where n is the length of the longest input string. However, with increasing n and/or m, the application of DP quickly turns unpractical. In addition to DP, various parallel exact approaches were proposed. An example is the one from [19] called FAST_LCS. This algorithm is based on the use of a so-called successors table data structure, utilizing the pruning operations to reduce the overall computational effort. Quick-DP was introduced in [25] based on a fast divide-and-conquer technique. More recently, the Top_MLCS algorithm was proposed in [18], based on a directed acyclic layered-graph model. The most recent exact approach is A* [11]. This approach outperforms the other algorithms in terms of memory consumption, running time, and the number of benchmark instances solved to optimality. However, exact approaches are still quite limited and can only solve small LCS instances (up to $m = 10$ and $n = 100$), and their main bottleneck is an excessive memory consumption. Concerning larger LCS problem instances, research has mostly been focused on heuristic approaches. Among various different metaheuristic approaches, the generalized beam search approach from [9] is currently the state-of-the-art heuristic approach.

The CLCS problem with two input strings ($m = 2$) and one pattern string ($k = 1$) was well studied over the last two decades. Several efficient exact approaches were proposed, including dynamic programming, sparse dynamic programming, and a bit-parallel algorithm [4,5,24]. As in the case of the LCS problem, the current state-of-the-art approach for the CLCS problem is A* [7]. In particular, A* has a run time which is about one order of magnitude lower than the one of the second-best approach. In [6], this A* search was adapted to the more general CLCS variant with an arbitrary number of $m \in \mathbb{N}$ input strings. The algorithm was shown to scale well from small to medium sized instances and, in some cases of a long pattern string, even to larger instances.

Finally, concerning the GCLCS problem, it is known that no approximation algorithm can exist [14]. Moreover, the GCLCS problem with $m = 2$ input strings and an arbitrary number of pattern strings is $\mathcal{NP}$-hard, which can be proven by reduction from the 3-SAT problem. This implies that the GCLCS problem, as a generalization of the latter variant of the CLCS problem, is also $\mathcal{NP}$-hard. In [8] it was even proved that finding any feasible solution to the GCLCS problem is $\mathcal{NP}$–complete. In the same paper, the authors proposed various heuristic approaches, such as a greedy search, a beam search and a hybrid of variable neighbourhood search and beam search. The efficiency of these approaches was studied along the following two lines: finding a feasible solution and finding high-quality solutions. However, concerning exact algorithms, the related literature only offers the Automaton approach from [12] which runs in $O(|\Sigma|(\mathcal{R} + m) + nm + |\Sigma|\mathcal{R}n^k)$ time complexity, where $\mathcal{R}$ is the size of the resulting subsequence automaton which, in the worst case scenario, is $O(n^m)$.

Our Contributions. Due to the success of A* for related problems and due to the lack of exact approaches for the general GCLCS problem, we develop an A* search approach that employs a problem-specific node filtering technique as one of its main features. Note that our A* differs from the A* approach for the CLCS problem with only one pattern string in several aspects: (1) the search is based on a different search framework, which implies the utilization of different data structures in order to obtain an efficient search process, and (2) it employs a problem-specific node filtering technique. The quality of our approach is analysed on a wide range of benchmark instances, in comparison to the Automaton approach from the literature.

We emphasise that A* search and the Automaton approach are built upon different methodologies. The Automaton approach is fully constructive. It builts numerous automata along the way: common subsequence automaton, an intersection automaton, and finally a maximum length automaton, from which the optimal solution can be derived. On the other hand, our A* search is an informed search that generates its nodes on the fly. It is using a heuristic rule to expand the most promising nodes at each iteration, with the hope of reaching a complete node as soon as possible. Note that in contrast to the Automaton approach, which provides useful information only when the maximum length automaton is generated, our A* search method is able to provide a dual bound on the optimal solution at each iteration.

The rest of the paper is organized as follows. In Sect. 2 we describe the state graph for the GCLCS problem. Section 3 is reserved to present our A* search approach. The experimental evaluation is provided in Sect. 4, while Sect. 5 offers conclusions and outlines future work.

2 The State Graph for GCLCS Problem

For a string s and $1 \leq x \leq y \leq |s|$, let $s[x,y] = s[x] \cdots s[y]$ be the contiguous (sub)string which starts at index x and ends at index y. If $x > y$, $s[x,y]$ is the empty string ε. By convention, the first index of a string s is always 1. By $|s|_\mathtt{a}$ we denote the number of occurrences of letter $\mathtt{a} \in \Sigma$ in string s. Given a position vector $\vec{\theta}$, $S[\vec{\theta}] := \{s_i[\theta_i, |s_i|] \mid i = 1, \ldots, m\}$ is the set of suffix input strings starting from the positions of $\vec{\theta}$. Similarly, given $\vec{\lambda} = (\lambda_1, \ldots, \lambda_k)$, $1 \leq \lambda_j \leq |p_j| + 1$ for $j = 1, \ldots, k$, denotes a *position vector* concerning the set of pattern strings P, and $P[\vec{\lambda}] := \{p_j[\lambda_j, |p_j|] \mid j = 1, \ldots, k\}$ is the set of pattern suffix strings starting at the positions of $\vec{\lambda}$.

Preprocessing Data Structures. We make extensive use of the following data structures constructed during preprocessing in order to establish an efficient search. For each $i = 1, \ldots, m$, $l = 1, \ldots, |s_i|$, and $c \in \Sigma$, $\mathtt{Succ}[i, x, \mathtt{c}]$ stores the minimal index y such that (1) $x \geq y$ and (2) $s_i[y] = \mathtt{c}$, that is, the position of the next occurrence of letter $\mathtt{c}$ in string s_i starting from position x. If no such letter $\mathtt{c}$ exists in s_i, then $\mathtt{Succ}[i, x, \mathtt{c}] := -1$. This data structure can be built in $O(m \cdot n \cdot |\Sigma|)$ time. Further, table $\mathtt{Embed}[i, x, j]$ for all $i = 1, \ldots, m$, $j = 1, \ldots, k$, and $x = 1, \ldots, |p_j| + 1$ stores the right-most (highest) position y of s_i such that $p_j[x, |p_j|]$ is a subsequence of $s_i[y, |s_i|]$. Note that when $x = |p_j| + 1$ it follows that $p_j[x, |p_j|] = \varepsilon$. In this case $\mathtt{Embed}[i, x, j]$ is set to $|s_i| + 1$.

The State Graph. In this section we describe the state graph for the GCLCS problem in the form of a rooted, directed, acyclic graph. In particular, the state graph consists of nodes $v = (\vec{\theta^v}, \vec{\lambda^v}, l^v)$, where

- $\vec{\theta^v}$ is a position vector regarding the input strings;
- $\vec{\lambda^v}$ is a position vector regarding the pattern strings;
- l^v is the length of a partial solution that induces node v as explained in the following.

We say that a partial solution s_v induces a node $v = (\vec{\theta^v}, \vec{\lambda^v}, l^v)$ as follows.

- Position vector $\vec{\theta^v}$ is defined such that $s_i[1, \theta^v_i - 1]$ is the shortest possible prefix string of s_i of which s_v is a subsequence, for all $i = 1, \ldots, m$.
- Position vector $\vec{\lambda^v}$ is defined such that $p_j[1, \lambda^v_j - 1]$ is the longest possible prefix string of p_j which is a subsequence of s_v, for all $j = 1, \ldots, k$.
- $l^v := |s_v|$

Note that such a node v may represent several different partial solutions. The root node of the state graph is $r = ((1, \ldots, 1), (1, \ldots, 1), 0)$, induced by the empty partial solution ε, where $0 = |\varepsilon|$. By Σ^{nd}_v we denote the set of *non-dominated letters* that can be used to extend any of the partial solutions represented by a node v. The term *extending a partial solution* refers hereby to appending a (suitable) letter to the end of the respective partial solution that induces node v. The way of deriving this set of letters (Σ^{nd}_v) is described as follows. A letter $\mathtt{c}$ belongs to the set $\Sigma_v \supseteq \Sigma^{\text{nd}}_v$ iff the following two conditions are fulfilled:

1. Letter c appears in each of the suffix strings $s_i[\theta_i^v, |s_i|]$, $i = 1, \ldots, m$.
2. Let $I_{cov} := \{j \in \{1, \ldots, k\} \mid \lambda_j^v \leq |p_j| \wedge p_j[\lambda_j^v] = \mathtt{c}\}$ and $I_{ncov} := \{1, \ldots, k\} \setminus I_{cov}$. For all $i = 1, \ldots, m$, the following must hold:
   - For all $j \in I_{cov}$ it holds that $\theta_i + \mathtt{Succ}[i, \theta_i^v, \mathtt{c}] + 1 \leq \mathtt{Embed}[i, \lambda_j^v + 1, \mathtt{c}]$;
   - For all $j \in I_{ncov}$ it holds that $\theta_i^v + \mathtt{Succ}[i, \theta_i^v, \mathtt{c}] + 1 \leq \mathtt{Embed}[i, \lambda_j^v, \mathtt{c}]$.

Note that Condition 1 may be checked in $O(m)$ time, whereas Condition 2 may be checked in $O(km)$ time. The set Σ_v is further reduced by removing dominated letters. We say that letter $\mathtt{a} \in \Sigma$ *dominates* letter $\mathtt{b} \in \Sigma$ iff $Succ[i, \theta_i^v, \mathtt{a}] \leq Succ[i, \theta_i^v, \mathtt{b}]$, for all $i = 1, \ldots, m$. By removing dominated letters from Σ_v, we finally obtain set Σ_v^{nd}. Now, for each letter $\mathtt{c} \in \Sigma_v^{\mathrm{nd}}$, a successor node w of v is generated in the following way.

- $\theta_i^w \leftarrow \mathtt{Succ}[i, \theta_i^v, \mathtt{c}] + 1$, for all $i = 1, \ldots, m$;
- If $p_j[\lambda_j^v] = \mathtt{c}$ then $\lambda_j^w \leftarrow \lambda_j^v + 1$; $\lambda_j^w \leftarrow \lambda_j^v$ otherwise;
- $l^w \leftarrow l^v + 1$.

Moreover, a directed arc vw is added from node v to node w and is labeled with letter c, that is, $\ell(vv') = \mathtt{c}$.

We call a node v *non-extensible* if $\Sigma_v^{\mathrm{nd}} = \emptyset$. Moreover, it is *feasible* iff $\lambda_j^v = |p_i| + 1$, for all $j = 1, \ldots, k$, which means that the respective solution contains all pattern strings as subsequences. A longest path (in terms of the number of arcs) from the root node to a non-extensible and feasible node represents an optimal solution to respective problem instance. An example of the state graph of an GCLCS problem instance is shown in Fig. 1. In general, it is infeasible to produce the whole state graph before running an algorithm. Instead, the state graph is discovered step-by-step and searched on the fly. In the next section, based on the above state graph description, we develop an A* search algorithm for the GCLCS problem.

3 A* Search for the GCLCS Problem

We make use of the previously explained state graph for defining an A* search approach. A* was introduced as a general concept by Hart et al. [16]. Since then it has been successfully applied to numerous hard optimization problems that can be phrased in terms of finding a best path in a graph. A* search is an informed search as it utilizes a heuristic as guidance. It works in a best-first-search manner by always expanding a most promising not-yet-expanded node. In order to evaluate nodes v we make use of a function $f(v) = g(v) + h(v)$ where (1) $g(v)$ represents the length of the longest path from the root node to node v; and (2) $h(v)$ represents an estimation of the length of the longest path from v to a *goal node*, a node that is feasible and non-extensible. Note that $h()$ is a dual bound. In this work we set $h() = \mathrm{UB}()$, where $\mathrm{UB}()$ calculates the tightest LCS upper bound known from literature; see [2,9,25] for details.

In the following, we introduce the data structures necessary to make A* an efficient graph search approach in the context of GCLCS problem. In essence, A* search maintains two sets of nodes:

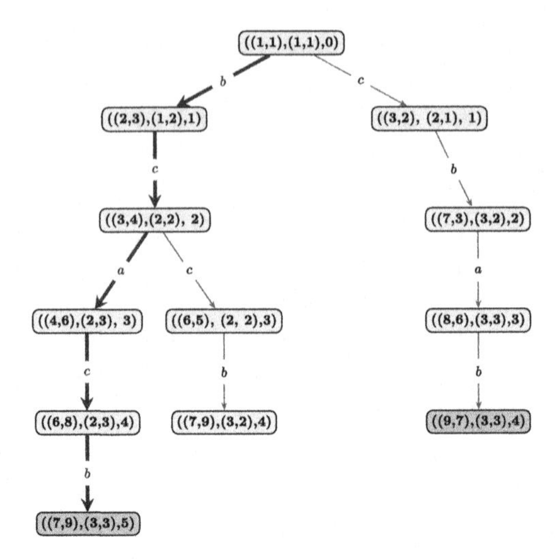

Fig. 1. The full state graph for GCLCS instance ($S = \{s_1 = \texttt{bcaacbad}, s_2 = \texttt{cbccadcb}\}$, $P = \{\texttt{cb}, \texttt{ba}\}$, $\Sigma = \{\texttt{a}, \texttt{b}, \texttt{c}, \texttt{d}\}$). It contains three non-extensible solutions. Two of them (marked by light-gray color) correspond to a feasible solution. Solution $s = \texttt{bcacb}$ is optimal. It is represented by node $v = (\vec{\theta^v} = (7,9),\ \vec{\lambda}^v = (3,3),\ l^v = 5)$. The corresponding path is displayed in blue. (Color figure online)

- The set of all nodes encountered during the search is realized by means of a hash map N. Each key $(\vec{\theta}^v, \vec{\lambda}^v)$ of N is mapped to the length of the currently longest path found from the root node to node v. The two position vectors together define a node v as previously described. Note again that there may exist more than one such path to the same node and, thus, the same node may represent several (partial) solutions, which helps saving memory and computational effort.
- The set of discovered, but not-yet-expanded (open) nodes $Q \subseteq N$. This set is realized by means of a priority queue whose nodes are prioritized according to their f-values; nodes with higher f-values are preferred.

With the help of these two sets, the required queries can be efficiently resolved. For example, the question if there was already a node encountered during the search defined by position vectors $\vec{\theta}$ and $\vec{\lambda}$ can be determined in constant time. Moreover, the node with the highest priority—that is, the one with the highest f-value—can be retrieved from Q in constant time. Note that after such a node-retrieval, Q must be reorganized. This process can efficiently be done in $O(\log(|Q|))$ time.

The pseudo-code of our A* search is given in Algorithm 1. Data structures N and Q are initialized with the root node r. At each iteration, the algorithm retrieves a highest-priority node v from queue Q. Then, it is first checked if v corresponds to a feasible, non-extensible solution. If so, the search is terminated since a proven optimal solution has been found. Otherwise, the upper bound $\mathrm{UB}(v)$ of v is calculated and—in case $\mathrm{UB}(v) \geq l^v + \max\{|p_i| - \lambda_i^v + 1 \mid i =$

Algorithm 1. A* search for the GCLCS problem.

Data structures: N, the hash map containing the generated combinations of position vectors $\vec{\theta}$ and $\vec{\lambda}$; $N[\vec{\theta}, \vec{\lambda}]$ holds the length of the currently longest path for this combination; Q, priority queue with all open nodes
Create root node $r = ((1, \ldots, 1), (1, \ldots, 1), 0)$
$\vec{\theta}^r \leftarrow (1, \ldots, 1)$ (length m), $\vec{\lambda}^r \leftarrow (1, \ldots, 1)$ (length k)
$N[(\vec{\theta}^r, \vec{\lambda}^r] \leftarrow 0$
$Q \leftarrow \{r\}$
while *time* $\wedge$ *memory limit* are not exceeded $\wedge$ $Q \neq \emptyset$ **do**
  $v \leftarrow Q.pop()$
  if $\mathrm{UB}(v) \geq l^v + \max\{|P_i| - \lambda_i^v + 1 \mid i = 1, \ldots, k\}$ **then**
    Determine Σ_v^{nd} (non-dominated letters)
    if $\Sigma_v^{\mathrm{nd}} = \emptyset$ **then**
      Derive the solution s represented by v
      if s is a feasible non-extensible solution **then return** provenly optimal solution s **end if**
    else
      for $c \in \Sigma_v^{\mathrm{nd}}$ **do**
        Generate node v' from node v via extension by letter c
        if $(\vec{\theta}^{v'}, \vec{\lambda}^{v'}) \in N$ **then**
          if $N[(\vec{\theta}^{v'}, \vec{\lambda}^{v'})] < l^{v'}$ **then** // a better path found
            $N[(\vec{\theta}^{v'}, \vec{\lambda}^{v'})] \leftarrow l^{v'}$
            Update priority value of node v in Q
          end if
        else // a new node
          $f_{v'} \leftarrow l^{v'} + \mathrm{UB}(v')$
          Insert v' into Q with priority value $f_{v'}$
          Insert v' into N
        end if
      end for
    end if
  end if
end while
return empty solution ε

$1, \ldots, k\}$—node v is expanded with all possible letters from Σ_v^{nd} as explained in Sect. 2. Further, for each generated child node v' of node v, it is checked if N already contains a corresponding key $(\vec{\theta}^{v'}, \vec{\lambda}^{v'})$. If not, v' is added to N and Q. Otherwise, it is checked if a longer path than the currently known one from the root node to node v' was discovered. If this is the case, the value of the corresponding key in N is updated accordingly, node v' is added in Q and the outdated entry is removed from Q. The above steps are repeated until either (1) an optimal solution is found as described above, or (2) Q becomes empty or (3) the memory or time limit is exceeded.

From a theoretical perspective, A* possesses some important characteristics. First, function h is *consistent*, that is, it never underestimates the length of the longest path from any node to a goal node (i.e., the optimum of the corresponding subproblem). This implies that a provenly optimal solution is found when the node retrieved from Q is a goal node. Second, the utilized upper bound UB is *monotonic*, which means that the difference in the values for any pair of parent/child nodes is never smaller that the weight of the respective arc, i.e., one in our case. As a consequence, no re-expansions of already expanded nodes are required during the search. Thus, a minimum number of node expansions is performed in order to find an optimal solution, concerning all search approaches that rely on the same state graph and the same heuristic guidance.

A search time complexity.* The number of visited nodes is bounded by $O(n^{m+k})$. Concerning the time complexity of lines 7–28 of Algorithm 1, operation *pop*() is executed in constant time. Subsequently, a necessary rearrangement of p.q. Q is executed in $O(\log(|Q|)) = O(\log(n^{m+k})) = O((m+k)\log(n))$ time. Line 9, for generating set Σ_v^{nd}, takes $O(|\Sigma|(m+km)) + O(|\Sigma|^2 m)$ time. Lines 14–26 are executed in $O(|\Sigma|(m+k+\log(|Q|))) = O(|\Sigma|(m+k+(m+k)\log(n)))$ time. Thus, the overall time complexity of A* search is equal to $O(n^{m+k}(((|\Sigma|+1)(m+k)\log(n) + |\Sigma|((|\Sigma|+k+2)m+k)))$.

4 Experimental Evaluation

For the experimental evaluation we consider, apart from our A* approach, the AUTOMATON approach from [12]. A* was implemented in C++ using GCC 7.4 for compilation, and the experiments were conducted on a machine with an Intel Xeon E5-2640 processor with 2.40 GHz and a memory limit of 16 GB. Note that the implementation of the AUTOMATON approach was adapted to use the same amount of memory (16 Gb) as A*. Moreover, both algorithms were tested on the same machine. The maximal CPU time allowed for each run of both algorithms was set to 180 min.

Benchmark Instances. The following three benchmark sets were used. Benchmark RANDOM contains ten randomly generated instances per each combination of the following parameters: $m \in \{2, 5, 10\}$, $k \in \{2, 5, 10\}$, $p \in \{20, 50\}$, $|\Sigma| \in \{2, 20\}$ and $n = 100$. In total, RANDOM consists of 360 problem instances. As a reminder, m refers to the number of input strings, k to the number of pattern strings, and $|\Sigma|$ to the alphabet size. Moreover, p refers to the fraction between n and the length of the pattern strings (all pattern strings are of equal length $n = 100$). The second benchmark set REAL is composed of 12,681 bacterial 16S rRNA gene sequences. The whole set is divided into 49 classes (i.e., instances), where each class contains the sequences from one bacterial phylum. More detailed information about each class can be found in [8]. The third benchmark set (called FARHANA-REAL) was used for the evaluation of AUTOMATON in [12]. It consists of real-world instances generated on the basis of the NCBI database (see Table 2). This set contains 32 instances subdivided into the following four groups: `Rnase`, `Protease`, `Kinase`, and `Globin`. This division is made on the basis of a different set of pattern strings for each group. In particular,

Table 1. Results for instances from benchmark set RANDOM

(a) Instances with $|\Sigma| = 2$

Instance group			A*			AUTOMATON		
m	p	k	$\overline{\lvert s\rvert}$	$\overline{t[s]}$	$opt[\%]$	$\overline{\lvert s\rvert}$	$\overline{t[s]}$	$opt[\%]$
10	20	10	51.2	133.29	80	0.0	–	0
10	20	2	0.0	–	0	0.0	–	0
10	20	5	11.7	72.66	20	0.0	–	0
10	50	10	11.8	28.35	20	0.0	–	0
10	50	2	0.0	–	0	0.0	–	0
10	50	5	11.9	67.80	20	0.0	–	0
2	20	10	82.3	0.02	100	82.3	12.01	100
2	20	2	78.2	0.06	100	78.2	2.74	100
2	20	5	79.3	0.06	100	79.3	6.21	100
2	50	10	78.5	0.05	100	78.5	11.88	100
2	50	2	77.6	0.07	100	77.6	2.82	100
2	50	5	78.4	0.06	100	78.4	6.25	100
5	20	10	69.3	54.64	100	0.0	–	0
5	20	2	64.0	39.51	100	0.0	–	0
5	20	5	65.5	47.67	100	0.0	–	0
5	50	10	58.5	77.23	90	0.0	–	0
5	50	2	64.6	37.38	100	0.0	–	0
5	50	5	57.4	137.19	90	0.0	–	0

(b) Instances with $|\Sigma| = 20$

Instance group			A*			AUTOMATON		
m	p	k	$\overline{\lvert s\rvert}$	$\overline{t[s]}$	$opt[\%]$	$\overline{\lvert s\rvert}$	$\overline{t[s]}$	$opt[\%]$
10	20	10	50.0	0.03	100	0.0	–	0
10	20	2	10.6	0.16	100	0.0	–	0
10	20	5	25.0	0.05	100	0.0	–	0
10	50	10	20.0	0.13	100	0.0	–	0
10	50	2	7.7	0.10	100	0.0	–	0
10	50	5	10.6	0.15	100	0.0	–	0
2	20	10	53.1	0.01	100	5.2	141.37	10
2	20	2	31.8	0.60	100	31.8	3.09	100
2	20	5	36.4	5.05	100	36.4	8.18	100
2	50	10	35.2	0.25	100	35.2	21.14	100
2	50	2	32.7	0.06	100	32.7	3.06	100
2	50	5	33.2	0.07	100	33.2	7.28	100
5	20	10	50.0	0.02	100	4.1	53.87	10
5	20	2	13.7	2.13	100	13.7	6.12	100
5	20	5	25.1	0.21	100	25.1	11.37	100
5	50	10	20.4	2.81	100	20.4	20.56	100
5	50	2	12.7	1.24	100	12.7	6.11	100
5	50	5	13.4	2.50	100	13.4	10.64	100

in the case of `Rnase` the set of pattern strings is {`H`, `K`, `HKSH`, `HKSTH`}; for group `Protease` it is {`P`, `L`, `DGTG`, `IIGL`}; for the group `Kinase` it is {`G`, `KEL`, `DFG`, `PEDR`}; and for group `Globin` it is {`P`, `KF`, `HGLSLH`, `LVLA`}. Apart from these four groups, there is one additional problem instance called `Input100` with $m = 100$ input strings of different lengths (ranging from 41 to 100) and having only one pattern string of length one, which is `S`.

Results for Benchmark Set RANDOM. Tables 1 and 2 report the results of the two competitors on RANDOM and FARHANA-REAL benchmarks, respectively. The first block of columns shows the name of the respective instance group, together with the number of instances in that group. The following three columns are reserved for the results of A* search. The first column provides the average solution quality delivered upon termination ($\overline{t}[s]$). The second one shows the average running time, for those instances/runs for which an optimal solution could be found ($\overline{t}[\mathrm{s}]$). Finally, the third column indicates the percentage of instances for which an optimal solution was found ($opt[\%]$). The last three table columns report the results of AUTOMATON in the following way: the average solution quality ($\overline{|s|}$), the average running time ($\overline{t}[\mathrm{s}]$) and the percentage of instances solved to optimality ($opt[\%]$).

Concerning instances $|\Sigma| = 2$, Table 1a allows the following observations. A* was able to solve almost all instances (118 out of 120 problem instances) with $m \leq 5$ to optimality. In contrast, the AUTOMATON approach was successful only for the instances with $m = 2$. Concerning the instances with $m = 10$, 16 out of 60 instances were solved by A* and none by the AUTOMATON approach. Finally, concerning the computation times for those instances for which both

Table 2. Results for the real-world benchmark set FARHANA-REAL from [12].

Instance group	#inst	A*			AUTOMATON		
		$\overline{\lvert s\rvert}$	$\bar{t}$[s]	*opt*[%]	$\overline{\lvert s\rvert}$	$\bar{t}$[s]	*opt*[%]
`Rnase`	3	68.33	0.12	100	68.33	4.78	100
`Protease`	15	55.60	0.70	100	55.60	4.71	100
`Kinase`	3	111.00	0.10	100	111.00	13.40	100
`Globin`	10	84.10	0.11	100	84.10	7.80	100
`Input100`	1	2.00	0.06	100	2.00	48.38	100

approaches were successful in finding an optimal solution, A* search is the clear winner exhibiting computation times about two orders of magnitude lower than those of AUTOMATON (around 100 times faster). The following observations can be made from Table 1b (for the instances with $|\Sigma| = 20$). First, A* was able to solve all instances (180 out of 180 problem instances) to optimality. The AUTOMATON approach was competitive on the instances with $m \leq 5$ by solving 102 out of 120 instances, but none of the instances with $m = 10$ were solved. Second, the running times of A* (limited to those instances which both algorithm could solve) appear to be much shorter than those of AUTOMATON.

Results for Benchmark Set REAL. A* was able to solve four (out of 49) real-world problem instances to proven optimality. This is quite notable since similar problems for real-world instances are rarely solved to optimality in the literature. Moreover, in three out of four cases, A* requires only a fraction of a second to prove optimality. In particular, instance Aminicenantes (result: 1365) was solved in 11.51 s, instance Atribacteria (result: 1499) in 0.12 s, instance Ignavibacteriae (result: 1354) in 0.12 s, and instance WPS-1 (result: 1358) in 0.1 s. In contrast, AUTOMATON was not able to deliver any optimal solutions since it was—in all cases—running out of time. This is because AUTOMATON was not able to finish its intermediate step of constructing the intersection automaton within the given time limit. Finally, for the instances not solved by A*, the reason of not doing so, was memory limit exceeding.

Results for Benchmark Set FARHANA-REAL*; see Table* 2. The following observations can be made. First, both algorithms were able to find optimal solutions for all 32 instances. Second, in comparison to AUTOMATON, A* required substantially less time; about an order of magnitude less. Finally, for the largest instance (*Input100*), the runtime is more than 500 times in favor of A*.

5 Conclusions and Future Work

In this paper we presented an A* approach for solving the generalized longest common subsequence problem with an arbitrary number of pattern strings. Our algorithm utilizes a problem-specific node filtering technique in order to exclude suboptimal solutions from the search. The experimental evaluation shows that A* is efficient in solving all instances with two input strings based on rather small alphabet sizes (up to four) to optimality. Moreover, A* search is also well-suited for instances with shorter input strings (up to $n = 100$), even when there is a larger number of patterns given as input. In comparison to the exact AUTOMATON approach from the literature, it turns out that A* can find proven optimal solutions in an order of magnitude faster than AUTOMATON when applied to real-world instances.

In the future work it seems promising to focus on developing tight upper bounds for the GCLCS problem and utilizing them in our A* approach. Concerning anytime algorithms based on A* [10], it would be interesting to obtain heuristic solutions in combination with dual bounds for large-sized instances (when classical A* search fails to prove optimality due to time or memory restrictions). Moreover, studying problems related to the GCLCS problem, such as the restricted LCS problem [13], might be a promising research direction.

Acknowledgements. Christian Blum was funded by project CI-SUSTAIN of the Spanish Ministry of Science and Innovation (PID2019-104156GB-I00). Dragan Matić is partially supported by Ministry for Scientific and Technological Development, Higher Education and Information Society, Government of Republic of Srpska, B&H under the Project "Development of artificial intelligence methods for solving computer biology problems".

References

1. Adi, S.S.: Repetition-free longest common subsequence. Discr. Appl. Math. **158**(12), 1315–1324 (2010)
2. Blum, C., Blesa, M.J., López-Ibáñez, M.: Beam search for the longest common subsequence problem. Comput. Oper. Res. **36**(12), 3178–3186 (2009)
3. Chowdhury, S.R., Hasan, M., Iqbal, S., Rahman, M.S.: Computing a longest common palindromic subsequence. Fund. Inform. **129**(4), 329–340 (2014)
4. Deorowicz, S.: Bit-parallel algorithm for the constrained longest common subsequence problem. Fund. Inform. **99**(4), 409–433 (2010)
5. Deorowicz, S., Obstój, J.: Constrained longest common subsequence computing algorithms in practice. Comput. Inf. **29**(3), 427–445 (2012)
6. Djukanovic, M., Berger, C., Raidl, G.R., Blum, C.: On solving a generalized constrained longest common subsequence problem. In: Olenev, N., Evtushenko, Y., Khachay, M., Malkova, V. (eds.) OPTIMA 2020. LNCS, vol. 12422, pp. 55–70. Springer, Cham (2020). https://doi.org/10.1007/978-3-030-62867-3_5
7. Djukanovic, M., Berger, C., Raidl, G.R., Blum, C.: An A* search algorithm for the constrained longest common subsequence problem. Inf. Process. Lett. **166**, 106041 (2021)
8. Djukanovic, M., Kartelj, A., Matic, D., Grbic, M., Blum, C., Raidl, G.: Graph search and variable neighborhood search for finding constrained longest common subsequences in artificial and real gene sequences. Technical report AC-TR-21-008 (2021)

9. Djukanovic, M., Raidl, G.R., Blum, C.: A beam search for the longest common subsequence problem guided by a novel approximate expected length calculation. In: Nicosia, G., Pardalos, P., Umeton, R., Giuffrida, G., Sciacca, V. (eds.) LOD 2019. LNCS, vol. 11943, pp. 154–167. Springer, Cham (2019). https://doi.org/10.1007/978-3-030-37599-7_14
10. Djukanovic, M., Raidl, G.R., Blum, C.: Anytime algorithms for the longest common palindromic subsequence problem. Comput. Oper. Res. **114**, 104827 (2020)
11. Djukanovic, M., Raidl, G.R., Blum, C.: Finding longest common subsequences: new anytime A* search results. Appl. Soft Comput. **95**, 106499 (2020)
12. Farhana, E., Rahman, M.S.: Constrained sequence analysis algorithms in computational biology. Inf. Sci. **295**, 247–257 (2015)
13. Gotthilf, Z., Hermelin, D., Landau, G.M., Lewenstein, M.: Restricted LCS. In: Chavez, E., Lonardi, S. (eds.) SPIRE 2010. LNCS, vol. 6393, pp. 250–257. Springer, Heidelberg (2010). https://doi.org/10.1007/978-3-642-16321-0_26
14. Gotthilf, Z., Hermelin, D., Lewenstein, M.: Constrained LCS: hardness and approximation. In: Ferragina, P., Landau, G.M. (eds.) CPM 2008. LNCS, vol. 5029, pp. 255–262. Springer, Heidelberg (2008). https://doi.org/10.1007/978-3-540-69068-9_24
15. Gusfield, D.: Algorithms on Strings, Trees and Sequences: Computer Science and Computational Biology. Cambridge University Press (1997)
16. Hart, P.E., Nilsson, N.J., Raphael, B.: A formal basis for the heuristic determination of minimum cost paths. IEEE Trans. Syst. Sci. Cybern. **4**(2), 100–107 (1968)
17. Jiang, T., Lin, G., Ma, B., Zhang, K.: The longest common subsequence problem for arc-annotated sequences. J. Discrete Algorithms **2**(2), 257–270 (2004)
18. Li, Y., Wang, Y., Zhang, Z., Wang, Y., Ma, D., Huang, J.: A novel fast and memory efficient parallel MLCS algorithm for long and large-scale sequences alignments. In: Proceedings of the 32nd International Conference on Data Engineering, ICDE 2019, pp. 1170–1181 (2016)
19. Liu, W., Chen, L.: A fast longest common subsequence algorithm for biosequences alignment. In: Li, D. (ed.) CCTA 2007. TIFIP, vol. 258, pp. 61–69. Springer, Boston (2008). https://doi.org/10.1007/978-0-387-77251-6_8
20. Maier, D.: The complexity of some problems on subsequences and supersequences. J. ACM **25**(2), 322–336 (1978)
21. Martínez-Porchas, M., Vargas-Albores, F.: An efficient strategy using k-mers to analyse 16s rRNA sequences. Heliyon **3**(7), e00370 (2017)
22. Mount, D.W.: Bioinformatics: Sequence and Genome Analysis, 2nd edn. Cold Spring Harbour Laboratory Press, Cold Spring Harbour (2004)
23. Tang, C.Y.: Constrained multiple sequence alignment tool development and its application to RNase family alignment. J. Bioinf. Comput. Biol. **01**(02), 267–287 (2003)
24. Tsai, Y.-T.: The constrained longest common subsequence problem. Inf. Process. Lett. **88**(4), 173–176 (2003)
25. Wang, Q., Korkin, D., Shang, Y.: A fast multiple longest common subsequence (MLCS) algorithm. IEEE Trans. Knowl. Data Eng. **23**(3), 321–334 (2011)

Robot Path Planning Method Based on Improved Grey Wolf Optimizer

Yilin Su[1], Yongsheng Li[2(✉)], Lina Ge[2], and Minjun Dai[1]

[1] College of Electronic Information, Guangxi University for Nationalities, Nanning 530006, Guangxi, China

[2] School of Artificial Intelligence, Guangxi University for Nationalities, Nanning 530006, Guangxi, China

lyshlh@163.com

Abstract. Aiming at the shortcomings of the classical grey wolf optimizer in solving the path planning problem of mobile robots, such as low search efficiency and broken line turning, this paper proposes an improved Grey Wolf Optimizer based on dynamic programming to apply to robot path planning. In the process of initial population generation, ant colony optimization is introduced to generate feasible paths, and the idea of random walk, sine function and logarithmic function is used to optimize the wolf group algorithm, balance the global and local exploration capabilities, and improve the search efficiency. At the same time, dynamic programming and B-spline curve are introduced to trim redundant path points and smooth turning angles. Simulation results show that the algorithm can efficiently avoid obstacles in various path planning environments. It has the characteristics of short time-consuming, good optimization effect, smooth corner and not easy to fall into local optimization. It is an efficient algorithm for solving robot path planning problems.

Keywords: Grey Wolf Optimizer · Dynamic programming · Random walk · Ant colony optimization · B-spline

1 Introduction

Mobile robot path planning [1], is that the robot plans a safe travel route by itself based on its own sensor's perception of the environment, and at the same time completes the task efficiently. The mobile robot needs to plan a path from the initial position to the target position in the work scene. The path should meet a series of requirements such as short path, high efficiency and high safety, and must be able to avoid static and dynamic obstacles along the way [2].

Mobile robot path planning technology can be roughly divided into swarm intelligent bionic algorithms, artificial intelligence-based algorithms, geometric model-based algorithms, and local obstacle avoidance algorithms. At present, a large number of swarm intelligent bionic algorithms have been applied to the path planning of mobile robots. [3] Intelligent search algorithm heuristic intelligent search method is mainly based on

M. El Yacoubi et al. (Eds.): ICPRAI 2022, LNCS 13364, pp. 65–77, 2022.
https://doi.org/10.1007/978-3-031-09282-4_6

natural body algorithm, mainly Ant Colony Optimization (ACO) [4], Particle Swarm Optimization (PSO) [5], Genetic Algorithm (GA) [6], Grey Wolf Optimizer (GWO) [7] etc. In literature [8], ant colony optimization and particle swarm optimization algorithm are fused to obtain the global optimal path through the ant colony optimization. The improved particle swarm algorithm finds the optimal solution in the global range and takes it as the initial pheromone of ants, improving the ability of the algorithm to find the optimal solution. Literature [9] proposed an improved crossover operator to solve the genetic algorithm path planning problem in a static environment; Literature [10] adopts a method of introducing position-order coding, and introduces random single point insertion operator and multi-point insertion operator in the iterative process, so as to achieve the optimal solution when the maximum number of iterations is reached through secondary search.

In view of the disadvantages of low search efficiency and broken line turning in the path planning of mobile robots, this paper studies an improved Grey wolf optimizer based on dynamic programming applied to the robot path planning. In the process of generating initial population, ant colony optimization is introduced to generate feasible paths; then, the path generated by wolf pack algorithm with sine function and logarithm function optimization is used to expand the search range and accelerate the convergence speed of the algorithm, so as to approach the optimal path with a greater probability; finally introduce dynamic programming and B-spline curve to trim Redundant path points and smooth corners.

2 Grey Wolf Optimizer

Grey Wolf Optimizer (GWO) is a new heuristic swarm intelligence method proposed by Mirjalili et al. in 2014. The method is simple, easy to use, flexible and extensible. In the GWO, regarding each individual in the population as a solution, define the wolves corresponding to the current optimal solution, optimal solution, and sub-optimal solution as α, β, and γ wolves, respectively. The rest of the individuals define ω wolves, which is the lowest individual, and ω obeys According to the orders of other high-level gray wolves, hunting operations were carried out according to relevant instructions [11].

In the process of preying on prey by gray wolf populations, their predatory behavior is defined as follows:

$$D = \left|C^* X_p(t) - X(t)\right| \tag{1}$$

$$X(t+1) = X_p(t) - A * D \tag{2}$$

In Eq. (1), D represents the distance between individual Wolf and prey. Formula (2) is the updating formula of individual positions of wolves: $X_p(t)$ represents the position of prey of the t generation; X(t) represents the positions of individuals in the t-generation Wolf tribe. A and C are coefficients, and the calculation formula is as follows:

$$a = 2 - \frac{2^* process}{Max\_iter} \tag{3}$$

$$A = 2a * r_1 \tag{4}$$

$$C = 2r_1 \tag{5}$$

Among them: iter is the number of iterations, Max_iter is the maximum number of iterations; $r_1, r_2 \in [0,1]$. When the gray wolf captures its prey (when it is close to the target), the position update of the individual gray wolf is determined based on the positions of the three wolves. The mathematical model is as follows:

$$D_i^j(t) = \left|C * X_i^j(t) - X^j(t)\right| \tag{6}$$

$$X_m^j(t) = X_i^j(t) - A * D_i^j(t),\ m = 1, 2, 3 \tag{7}$$

$$X(t+1) = \frac{1}{3} * \sum X_m(t) \tag{8}$$

Among them: $D_i^j(t)$ represents the distance between the wolf individual of the t generation and the wolf individual i(i = α, β, γ); Eqs. (6)–(8) define the step length and direction of ω wolves moving to α, β and γ wolves respectively. Formula (8) represents a new generation of gray Wolf individuals after location updating.

3 An Improved GWO Based on Random Walk and Dynamic Programming (RWDPGWO) to Solve the Robot Path Planning Problem

3.1 The Two Algorithms are Mixed to Quickly Find the Initial Path

GWO has strong random search ability, which enables it to find the optimal solution with a large probability. However, due to the lack of sufficient information communication between artificial wolves, the global nature of the algorithm is not high and the algorithm is too scattered, which leads to its slow iteration speed [12]. Ant colony optimization has strong robustness and positive feedback, and is good at solving combinatorial optimization problems. However, the positive feedback mechanism of ant colony optimization is easy to lead to further enhancement of pheromone on the better path and make it fall into local optimal. Therefore, this paper proposes a hybrid ant colony optimization and grey wolf optimizer. The algorithm introduces the ant colony optimization to draw a feasible path direction, and then uses the grey wolf optimizer to iteratively optimize. The hybrid algorithm has both the high robustness of the ant colony and the high randomness of the wolf colony. It can find a feasible and better path stably, and it can also jump out of the local optimum.

Use the ant colony optimization to initialize the gray wolf position X(t) and calculate the fitness value Fit(t). After the ant colony optimization iteration is completed, the initial path and path length are generated, namely the initial gray wolf position X(t) and fitness value Fit(t) is as follows:

$$\text{Fit(t)} = \min\{D_l(k)\} \tag{9}$$

$$X(t) = ROUT_l(k) \tag{10}$$

$ROUT_l(k)$ is the path with the shortest path length among paths generated by k iterations, that is, its path length is equal to $\min\{D_l(k)\}$.

3.2 Random Walk Nonlinear Adjustment Step Size Factor to Improve Search Efficiency

The convergence factor α and the step size A_i in grey wolf optimizer directly affect the performance of grey wolf optimizer, more suitable for the convergence factor of the problem and more suitable for the changing requirements of the step, can help the algorithm converge faster to find the optimal solution. [13] The random walk model is a mathematical statistical model. It consists of a series of trajectories, each of which is random. It can be used to represent the irregular form of change, just like a random process record formed by a person who takes random steps after drinking.

The convergence factor α linearly decreasing strategy and a single random step size in the original algorithm cannot reflect the actual optimization process, so the convergence factor α and the step size A_i adopt the non-linear change strategy of random walk. This article adds random walk thought, trigonometric function and logarithmic function on the basis of the original algorithm. The improvement ideas of grey wolf optimizer are as follows:

Adjust the convergence factor a to make the gray wolf population coordinate between global and local search, so a In the early stage of optimization, it should be reduced at a faster speed, and in the later stage of optimization, it should be reduced at a slower speed, balanced algorithm for exploration and mining capabilities, combined with the number of iterations ($\frac{iter}{Max\_iter}$), as the number of times increases, a gradually decreases, and the search area is gradually concentrated to the area where the optimal solution is most likely to appear, improving the search efficiency. The logarithmic function has the characteristics of rapid change in the early stage and gradually gentler in the later stage. Therefore, the logarithmic function ln() is added to the formula (3), so that the convergence factor a presents a steep, non-linear convergence change in the early stage and gentle late stage, and the improved formula (11) is generated as follows:

$$a = 2 - 2 * \ln\left(1 + \left(\frac{iter}{Max_{iter}}\right)^{\frac{1}{2}}\right) \tag{11}$$

Using the mathematical properties of the sine function, balancing the ability of the algorithm to explore globally and locally in the search process, increase the fluctuation interval, and use it to regulate the non-linear changes in the interval, adding the sine function to the formula (4) obtains the formula (13). In order to coordinate with the improved sine function, the single coefficient of formula (5) is changed to π multiplied by a set of random numbers to obtain Formula (16), so that its search area is transformed into a random irregular belt region to improve the search efficiency. Based on Formula (6)–(8) and combined with the improved formula (11)–(13), the individual position updating formula and step size change formula are updated into Formula (14) (15):

$$C_i = \left(2r_{1,i} - 1\right) * \pi \tag{12}$$

$$A_i = r_{2,i} * \sin(C_i) + A_i \tag{13}$$

$$D_i = |A_i * X_i(t) - X(t)| \tag{14}$$

$$X_i(t+1) = X_i(t) + a * D_i \tag{15}$$

where $r_{1,i} \in [0, 1]$, $r_{2,i} \in [0, 1]$; π is Pi, $i = \alpha, \beta, \gamma$.

3.3 Improve Search Strategy Based on DP Algorithm Idea

Dynamic programming (DP) is a method used in mathematics, computer science and economics to solve complex problems by dividing the original problem into relatively simple subproblems. The basic idea is to divide a given problem into several subproblems, solve all the subproblems, and then merge the solutions of the subproblems to get a solution to the original problem. [14] For waypoints $x_j(t) \in X(t), X(t) = \{x_j(t)\}$, modelled on the dynamic programming-the largest sub-segment and algorithm optimization path selection, find the longest distance d_t from $x_j(t)$, the connection between $x_j(t)$ and $x_{j+d_t}(t)$ does not pass through obstacles.

Formula (16) and (17) are the optimization formula of the path point with the maximum distance from the selected point, formula (16) is the objective function, formula (17) is the constraint condition, and formula (18) is the specific of formula (17) content:

$$\max\ d_t \tag{16}$$

$$\text{s.t check}\left(x_j(t), x_{j+d_t}(t)\right) = 0 \tag{17}$$

$$\text{check}(X(t), X(t+d_t)) = \begin{cases} 1, \text{ Connect}\left(x_j(t), x_{j+d_t}(t)\right)\text{through obstacles} \\ 0, \text{ otherwise} \end{cases} \tag{18}$$

Among them, check() is a judgment function used to judge whether the connection of $X(t), X(t+d_t)$ passes through obstacles. After finding d_t, remove $X(t), X(t+d_t)$ from the path A new path is generated between the path points, and the formula (19) Pos is the optimized path point set:

$$Pos = \left\{x_j(t), x_{j+d_t}(t)\right\}, j = 1, 2, \ldots.. \tag{19}$$

3.4 Use Spline Curve B-spline Curve to Optimize the Path

If the robot uses broken line to turn, it not only increases the loss of the robot and has a low safety factor, but also is not suitable for the hardware operation of the robot. Therefore, b-spline curve is used to plan the optimal walking route of the robot, which not only smoothes the corner, but also shortens the path length. Based on the shortest path found by the improved grey wolf optimizer, the quasi-uniform B-spline curve is used to optimize the smooth path. The calculation formula of the quasi-uniform B-spline curve algorithm is as shown in formula (20):

$$p(u) = [P_0 P_1 \ldots..P_n] \begin{bmatrix} B_{0,k}(u) \\ \vdots \\ B_{n,k}(u) \end{bmatrix} = \sum_{i=1}^{n} P_i B_{i,k}(u) \tag{20}$$

Formula (21) is the calculation formula for the coordinate points of the B-spline curve, where Pi is the control point, that is, the node on the original path. k is the order, which controls the generation of arcs by several nodes.

$$B_{i,k}(u) = \begin{cases} \begin{cases} 1, u_i \le u \le u_{i+1} \\ 0, \text{other} \end{cases} \\ \frac{u-u_i}{u_{i+k}-u_i} B_{i,k-1}(u) + \frac{u_{i+k}-u}{u_{i+k}-u_{i+1}} B_{i+1,k-1}(u), k > 2 \end{cases} \tag{21}$$

$$[u_0, u_1 \ldots u_k, u_{k+1}, \ldots, u_{n+k}] \tag{22}$$

Formula (21) is the node vector, which is a set of non-decreasing sequence, the head and tail values are generally defined as 0 and 1, in the quasi-uniform B-spline curve, the nodes at both ends have the repeatability k. In formula (21), u_i is a certain continuously changing value of the node vector, and $u_i \in [0, 1]$.

Because the requirements for the turning angle and obstacle distance of the path are different under different maps and conditions, the order of the B-spline curve is set to be adaptive. On the premise that the conditions are met, k starts to decrease from the higher order until the smooth path generated does not pass through obstacles. The calculation formula is as shown in formula (23) (24):

$$\text{flag} = \text{judge}(\text{B}_{\text{i,k}}) = \begin{cases} 0, \text{ passing obstacles} \\ 1, \text{ not passing obstacles} \end{cases} \tag{23}$$

$$k = \begin{cases} k, & \text{flag} = 0 \\ k-1, & \text{flag} = 1 \end{cases} \tag{24}$$

The path optimized by the B-spline curve has a smoother curve and solves the polyline turning problem that is common in path planning. At the same time, the optimized path has a better effect than the original path.

3.5 Algorithm Flow

The algorithm first uses the ant colony algorithm to initialize the gray wolf position X(t), and calculates the fitness value Fit(t), then finds out the α wolf, β wolf, and γ wolf in the gray wolf group, and calculates the convergence factor a. Using the formula (19), calculate the distance D_i between the gray wolf individual X(t) and the α wolf, β wolf, and γ wolf respectively, then calculate $X_i(t)$ according to D_i, and then use $X_i(t)$ to find the optimized path $X_i(t+1)$. Repeat the above steps until the current path fitness value does not change within 2 iteration intervals or reaches the maximum number of iterations. Finally, use the DP algorithm to optimize the found path, and use the B-spline curve to smooth the path. Specifically The algorithm flow is as follows (Fig. 1):

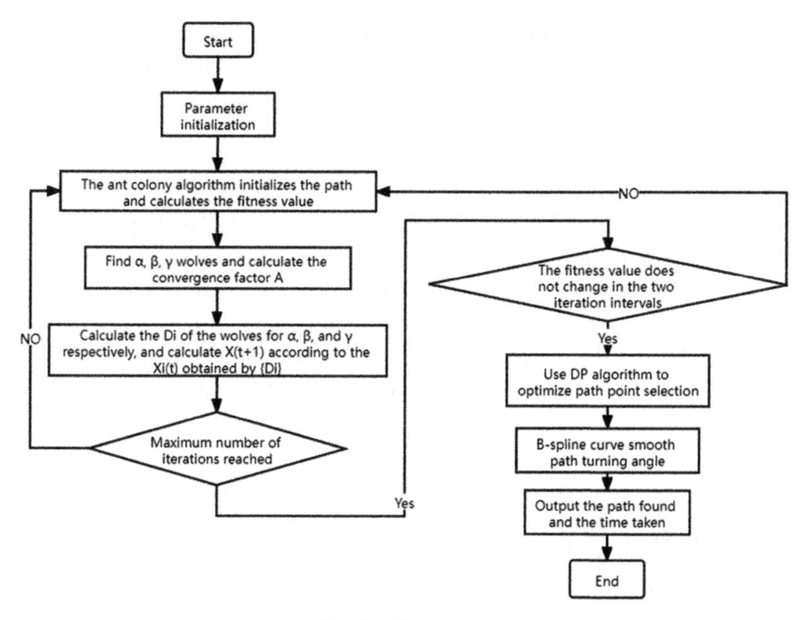

Fig. 1. Flowchart.

4 Simulation

In order to verify the performance of the RWDPGWO, this paper has done a lot of simulation experiments, and the experimental results also verify that the improved algorithm proposed in this paper has faster convergence speed and stronger global optimization ability. The operating environment of the experiment is: Windows7 64bit; software version: Matlab R2018a; processor: Inter(R) Core(TM) i5-5200U; processor frequency: 2.20 GHz; memory capacity: 4 GB. The simulation experiment is carried out in a 20 * 20 grid simulation environment, and the size of each independent grid is set to 1 * 1, and the mobile robot is adaptive to the distance each time it moves. In order to verify the efficiency of this algorithm, simulation experiments were carried out by running this algorithm and other algorithms in different environments.

Through experimental verification, if $M > 15$ or $k > 2$ is selected, the effect of initializing the path is not significantly improved, but the time spent is significantly increased; if $M < 15$ or $k < 2$ is selected, the time is not significantly reduced but the effect of initializing the path is significantly reduced. Therefore, the number of ants in the RWDPGWO is set to 15, and the number of iterations of the ant colony optimization is set to 2.

4.1 Comparison of RWDPGWO and GWO Simulation

Figure 2 shows the optimal path found by the RWDPGWO and the GWO in the grid environment of Fig. 2, where GWO takes the number of parameter individuals $M = 20$ and the maximum number of iterations Max_iter = 20. It can be seen from the figure that the path of the RWDPGWO is smooth, with few turns, and the forward direction is the end direction. The path of the GWO has many turns. And the forward direction is repeated, which shows that compared with the GWO, the RWDPGWO has a better path planning effect.

Figure 3 is the convergence diagram of the two algorithms in the environment shown in Fig. 2. Table 1 shows the path planning results of RWDPGWO and GWO in the environment shown in Fig. 2. It can be seen from Table 1 that RWDPGWO finds the cubic optimal solution ten times, and the optimal solution is 27.7905. The optimal solution found by GWO is 30.6274, RWDPGWO is 2.8369 better than GWO. At the same time, it can be seen from Table 1 that the running time of RWDPGWO is shorter than that of GWO, and the convergence speed is faster, and GWO does not converge to the optimal value. In terms of time and quality, the performance of RWDPGWO is better (Table 1).

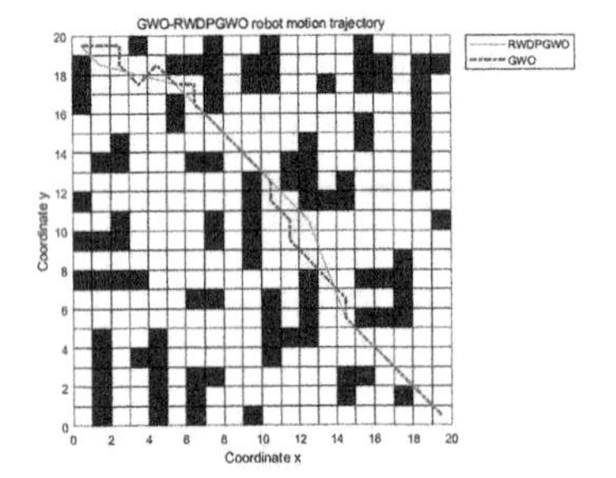

Fig. 2. Path comparison between RWDPGWO and classical GWO

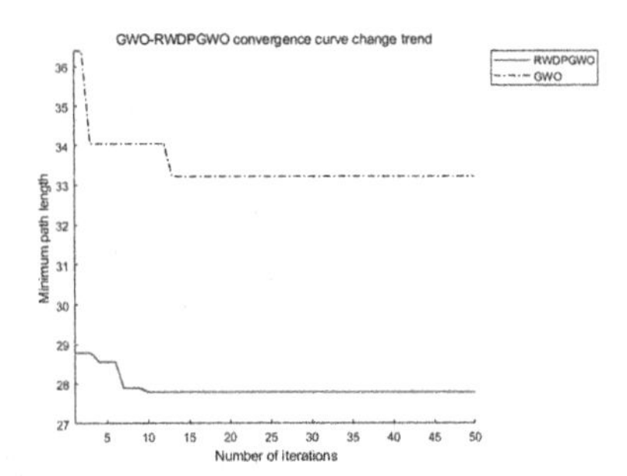

Fig. 3. Comparison of convergence trend of RWDPGWO and classical GWO

Table 1. Comparison of the shortest path length of the proposed algorithm and the GWO.

Serial number	RWDPGWO		GWO	
	Path length	Convergence time/s	Path length	Convergence time/s
1	27.7905	2.4175	30.6274	23.6422
2	27.9258	8.7857	32.0416	23.7972
3	27.9011	8.4258	31.7990	24.7061
4	27.9258	10.8577	34.6274	23.6862
5	27.9824	4.8817	33.2131	24.7377
6	27.7905	5.9732	34.0416	23.7995
7	28.0592	3.5650	33.2132	24.6539
8	27.9824	4.8817	34.0416	23.6771
9	27.7905	10.5847	33.4558	24.9598
10	28.0760	5.8907	33.7990	23.5628

4.2 Comparison of RWDPGWO with GA and PSO

In order to further verify the effectiveness of the RWDPGWO, two intelligent optimization algorithms, GA and PSO, are selected for simulation test comparison to verify the superiority of the algorithm performance in this paper.

Figures 4 and 5 are the comparison of the paths planned by RWDPGWO and GA in the environment of Fig. 4 and the comparison of the convergence trend in the environment of Fig. 4, where the GA parameters are: crossover probability pc = 0.8, mutation probability pm = 0.2, population number NP = 200, maximum evolutionary algebra max_gen = 100. It can be clearly found that the algorithm in this paper converges faster and the path is shorter.

As can be seen from the simulation test data in Table 2, in the environment of Fig. 4, the optimal path found by RWDPGWO is 30.3449. Compared with the optimal path found by genetic algorithm 31.5563, the optimal path found by RWDPGWO is better than 1.2114, and the optimal path found by RWDPGWO within a few iterations. It is shown that RWDPGWO has faster searching speed than GA.

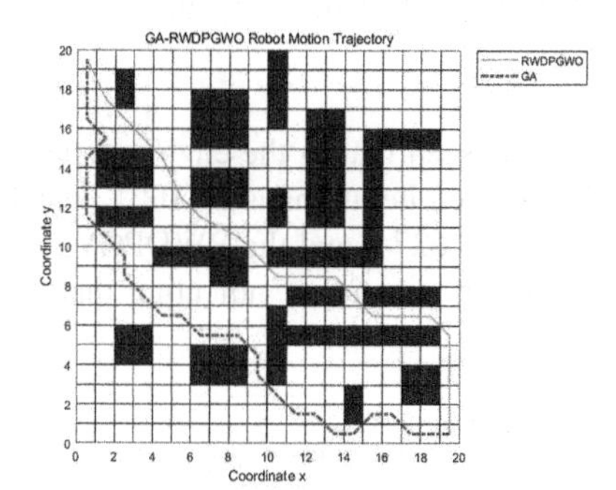

Fig. 4. Path comparison between RWDPGWO and GA

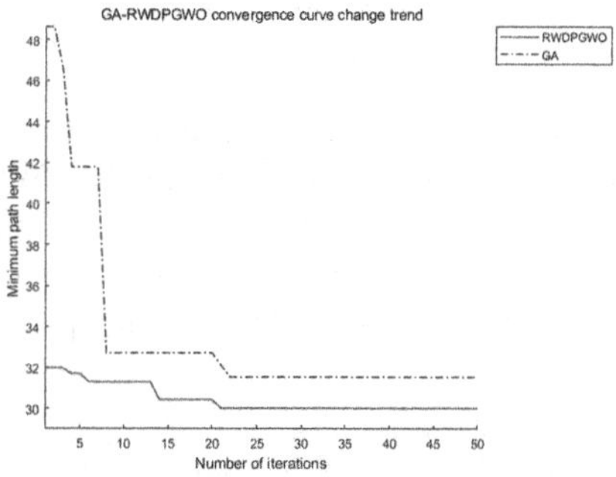

Fig. 5. Comparison of the convergence trend of RWDPGWO and GA

Figures 6 and 7 are the comparison of the paths planned by the RWDPGWO and PSO in the environment of Fig. 6 and the comparison of the convergence trend in the environment of Fig. 6, where the parameters of the PSO are: cognitive coefficient c1 = 0.5, social learning coefficient c2 = 0.7, population size Popsize = 20, inertia coefficient w = 0.95. It can be clearly seen that the path optimized by the RWDPGWO is better than PSO in terms of length and turning smoothness, and the initial value of the path length is much lower than that of PSO.

Table 2. Comparison of RWDPGWO and GWO with ten simulations.

Serial number	RWDPGWO			GA		
	Path length	Convergence time/s	Convergence iterations	Path length	Convergence time/s	Convergence iterations
1	30.3449	11.4138	10	31.5563	20.9132	39
2	30.3582	3.4677	3	31.5563	25. 4546	23
3	30.6275	9.0789	7	32.1421	23. 4432	38
4	30.7763	6.7969	6	31.5563	19.4728	25
5	30.6913	3.4133	3	32.3848	30.9056	70
6	30.7758	12.5939	11	33.2132	26.9903	40
7	30.8034	11.4129	10	32.3848	19.8132	8
8	30.8133	2.1556	2	33.213	22.8453	32
9	30.6719	6.7960	6	33.2132	20.9763	36
10	30.6631	12.0783	10	33.2132	20.9763	36

From the simulation test data in Table 3, it can be seen that in the environment of Fig. 6, the optimal path found by the RWDPGWO for ten iterations is 27.1001, which is 1.5173 better than the optimal path found by PSO 28.6274, and the RWDPGWO is less. The optimal path was found within the number of iterations, indicating that the RWDPGWO has better optimization performance.

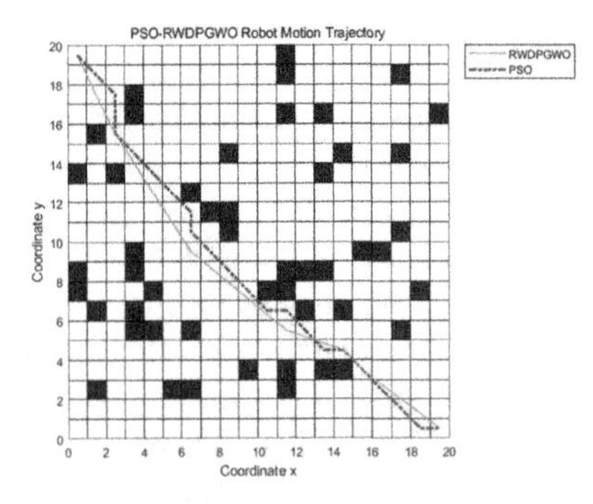

Fig. 6. Path comparison between RWDPGWO and PSO

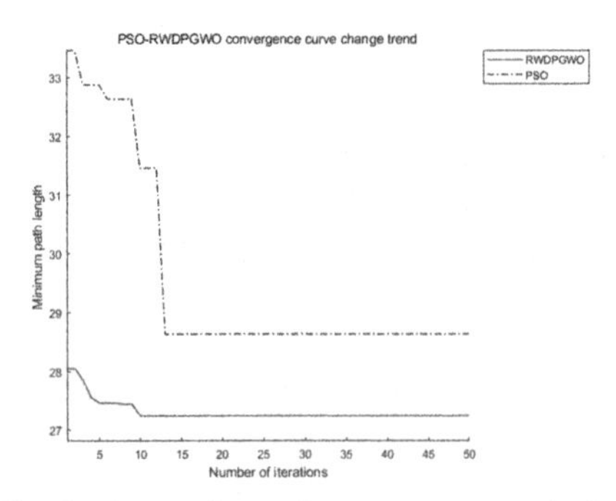

Fig. 7. Comparison of convergence trend of RWDPGWO and PSO

4.3 Comparison of RWDPGWO and Various Improved ACO

ACO is an intelligent bionic optimization algorithm inspired by the foraging behavior characteristics of ant population in nature. [15] Literature [16] and literature [17] are improved ACO applied to path planning.

Table 3. Comparison of ten simulation data of RWDPGWO and GWO particle swarm algorithm.

Serial number	RWDPGWO			PSO		
	Path length	Convergence time/s	Convergence iterations	Path length	Convergence time/s	Convergence iterations
1	27.1001	16.3974	16	32.6274	3.710998	17
2	27.2185	15.3918	15	28.6274	4.487097	20
3	27.2296	9.1748	9	31.2132	4.302588	19
4	27.2296	12.4484	12	28.6274	3.862517	18
5	27.2940	7.1877	7	30.0416	3.687252	16
6	27.1001	1.1626	1	30.6274	3.784927	18
7	27.3370	10.465	10	28.6274	3.748565	18
8	27.1001	5.2375	5	31.4558	4.001684	19
9	27.3458	3.0827	3	30.0416	3.862848	18
10	27.1001	16.3974	16	32.6274	3.710998	17

Figures 8, 9 and 10 are the comparison diagrams between the optimal path trajectory planned by literature [16], literature [17], and ACO and RWDPGWO, in which the parameters of ACO: the number of ants M = 80, the pheromone Concentration A = 1, heuristic factor B = 8, information evaporation coefficient Rho = 0.4, pheromone enhancement coefficient Q = 1. Obviously, the optimal path planned by RWDPGWO is shorter, takes less time, and the path is more smooth.

From the simulation test data in Table 4, it can be seen that in the environment of Fig. 10, the path and time spent by RWDPGWO are better than those in literature [16], literature [17] and ACO, which shows that the RWDPGWO has strong application significance (Table 4).

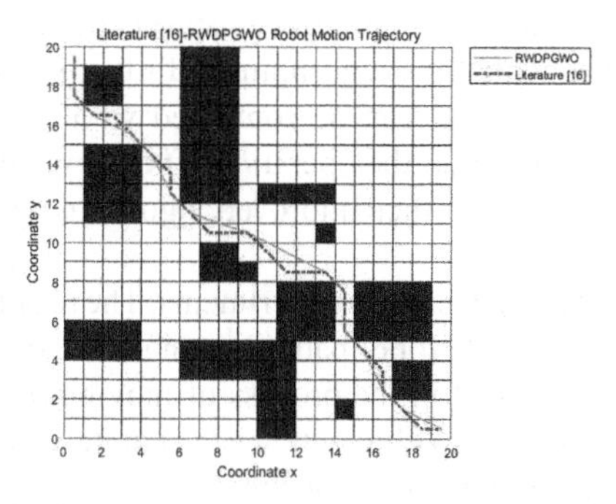

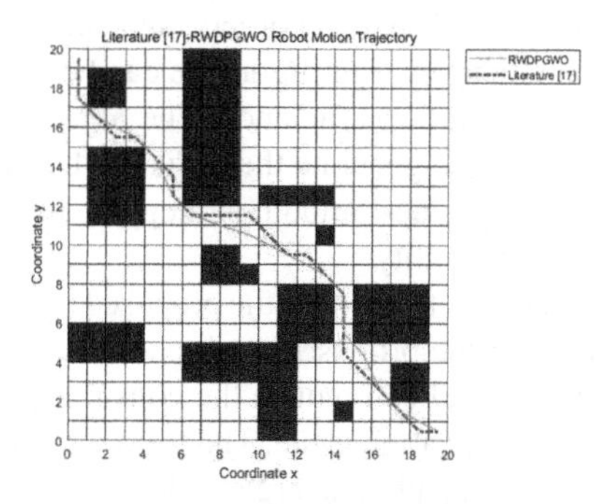

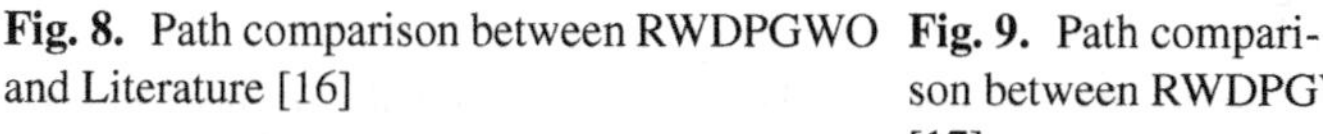

Fig. 8. Path comparison between RWDPGWO and Literature [16]

Fig. 9. Path comparison between RWDPGWO and Literature [17]

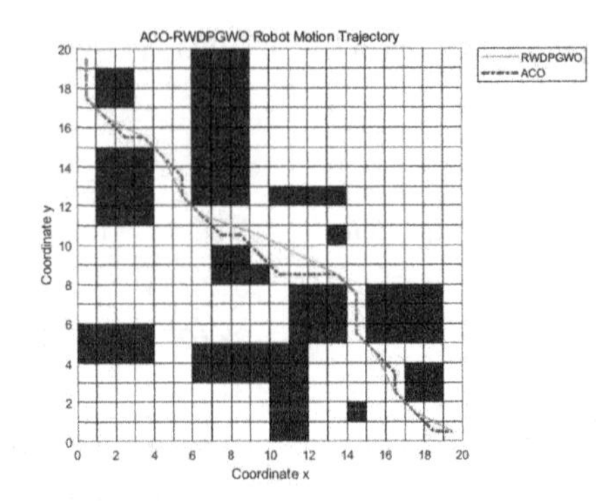

Fig. 10. Path comparison between RWDPGWO and ACO

Table 4. Algorithm simulation data comparison.

Optimization	Optimal path length	The number of convergence iterations	Spend time/s
RWDPGWO	28.87	12	16.47
Literature [16]	30.5	30	18.9
Literature [17]	30.38	6	–
Ant Colony Optimization	30.38	15	17.2

5 Conclusion

In robotics research, path planning has always been one of the research hotspots that has received wide attention. [18] Simulation experiments in different scale and complexity environments show that this algorithm is greatly improved compared with wolf swarm algorithm and other improved algorithms, effectively reduces the path length and the number of redundant corners, and speeds up the iterative convergence speed and operation efficiency This algorithm can be combined with other algorithms to further speed up the operation efficiency. The algorithm in this paper can be combined with other algorithms to generate the initial path to further speed up the operation efficiency. The proposed Prune- Smooth strategy is also applicable to other Improved algorithm with strong scalability.

The effectiveness of the proposed method is verified through experiments. The results show that the proposed method can better complete the robot path planning, save time and cost, and can reduce the consumption of the robot in the process of moving, Has strong application value. The follow-up will study how to efficiently and accurately find the optimal path in a large-scale and complex environment reasonably.

Acknowledgement. This work was supported by National Natural Science Foundation of China (No. 61862007, No. 61866003).

References

1. Hossain, M.A., Ferdous, I.: Autonomous robot path planning in dynamic environment using a new optimization technique inspired by Bacterial Foraging technique. Robot. Auton. Syst. **64**, 137–141 (2014)
2. Lin, H., Xiang, D., Ouyang, J., Lan, X.: A survey of research on path planning algorithms for mobile robots. Comput. Eng. Appl. **57**(18), 38–48 (2021)
3. Zhu, D., Yan, M.: Overview of mobile robot path planning technology. Control Decis. **7**, 7 (2010)
4. Zhang, Y., Wang, C., Xia, X., et al.: Path planning of robot based on improved ant colony optimization (2011)
5. Mo, H., Xu, L.: Research of biogeography particle swarm optimization for robot path planning. Neurocomputing **148**, 91–99 (2015)
6. Alajlan, M., Koubaa, A., Chaari, I., et al.: Global path planning for mobile robots in large-scale grid environments using genetic algorithms. In: 2013 International Conference on Individual and Collective Behaviors in Robotics (ICBR). IEEE (2013)
7. Tsai, P.-W., Nguyen, T.-T., Dao, T.-K.: Robot path planning optimization based on multi-objective grey wolf optimizer. In: Pan, J.-S., Lin, J.C.-W., Wang, C.-H., Jiang, X.H. (eds.) ICGEC 2016. AISC, vol. 536, pp. 166–173. Springer, Cham (2017). https://doi.org/10.1007/978-3-319-48490-7_20
8. Han, Y., Xu, Y., Zhou, J.: Robot path planning based on particle swarm optimization and ant colony fusion algorithm. Modular Mach. Tool Automatic Process. Technol. **552**(02), 47–50 (2020). https://doi.org/10.13462/j.cnki.mmtamt
9. Lamini, C., Benhlima, S., Elbekri, A.: Genetic algorithm based approach for autonomous mobile robot path planning. Procedia Comput. Sci. **127**, 180–189 (2018)
10. Huang, H., Ren, Z., Wei, J.: Improved wolf pack algorithm to solve traveling salesman problem. Comput. Appl. Res. **36**(12), 4 (2019)
11. Mirjalili, S., Mirjalili, S.M., Lewis, A.: Grey wolf optimizer. Adv. Eng. Softw. **69**(3), 46–61 (2014)
12. Liu, J., Wei, X., Huang, H.: An improved grey wolf optimization algorithm and its application in path planning. IEEE Access **9**, 121944–121956 (2021). https://doi.org/10.1109/ACCESS.3108973.2021
13. Pearson, K.: The problem of the random walk. Nature **72**(1865), 294 (1905)
14. Zhang, H., Zhang, X., Luo, Y., et al.: Overview of adaptive dynamic programming. Acta Automatica Sinica **4**, 303–311 (2013)
15. Jiang, C., Fu, J., Liu, W.: Research on vehicle routing planning based on adaptive ant colony and particle swarm optimization algorithm. Int. J. Intell. Transp. Syst. Res. **19**(6), 83–91 (2020)
16. Cao, X., Wang, Z., Feng, J., Zha, M., Wang, Y.: Research on robot global path planning based on improved ant colony optimization. Comput. Eng. Sci. **42**(03), 564–570 (2020)
17. Li, Z., Zhao, Q.: Mobile robot path planning based on artificial potential field ant colony optimization. In: Electronics Optics and Control, pp. 1–8, 26 November 2021
18. Han, X., Dun, X., Lin, Z.: Optimization and simulation of robot movement path based on A* improved algorithm. Comput. Simul. **38**(2), 5 (2021)

Space-Time Memory Networks for Multi-person Skeleton Body Part Detection

Rémi Dufour[1(✉)], Cyril Meurie[1,2(✉)], Olivier Lézoray[1,3(✉)], and Ankur Mahtani[1(✉)]

[1] FCS Railenium, 59300 Famars, France
{remi.dufour,ankur.mahtani}@railenium.eu
[2] Univ Gustave Eiffel, COSYS-LEOST, 59650 Villeneuve d'Ascq, France
cyril.meurie@univ-eiffel.f
[3] Normandie Univ, UNICAEN, ENSICAEN, CNRS, GREYC, Caen, France
olivier.lezoray@ensicaen.fr

Abstract. Deep CNNs have recently led to new standards in all fields of computer vision with specialized architectures for most challenges, including Video Object Segmentation and Pose Tracking. We extend Space-Time Memory Networks for the simultaneous detection of multiple object parts. This enables the detection of human body parts for multiple persons in videos. Results in terms of F1-score are satisfactory (a score of 47.6 with the best configuration evaluated on PoseTrack18 datatset) and encouraging for follow-up work.

Keywords: Space Time Memory Networks · Skeleton body part detection · Pose tracking

1 Introduction

Autonomous transportation systems, in particular autonomous cars and trains, have recently received much interest. To reach a high level grade of automation, many specific challenges need to be addressed. For autonomous trains, without any staff on board, both surveillance and security have to be performed automatically with cameras coupled with adequate computer vision algorithms. In this context, pose detection and tracking is a basic requirement of camera surveillance, that many other applications can use as input (action recognition, people counting, free seat detection, etc.). DeepPose [17] was the first Deep Neural Network (DNN) architecture for pose estimation, formulating it as a joint regression problem. Many works have extended it in several directions [2,6,18]. Rapidly, the challenging case of multi-person pose estimation has emerged where the number of persons to have their pose estimated is unknown. This is performed with either top-down or bottom-up approaches [8]. The former detects humans at a large scale and locates skeleton key-points at a smaller scale. The latter detects skeleton key-points first and skeletons parts are built from them. Bottom-up methods

M. El Yacoubi et al. (Eds.): ICPRAI 2022, LNCS 13364, pp. 78–90, 2022.
https://doi.org/10.1007/978-3-031-09282-4_7

have better scaling properties which makes them more suitable for surveillance tasks. Recently, Cao *et al.* have proposed [4] a bottom-up multi-stage refinement DNN trained with intermediate supervision. Their approach produces two outputs: body key-point parts' confidence maps and Part Affinity Fields (PAFs) that are vector fields indicating both the confidence and direction of a limb that links two body key-point parts. This approach has been extended in [10] with the use of Part Intensity Fields (PIFs). All these advances were made possible with the advent of new large scale datasets and benchmarks such as MC-COCO and PoseTrack [1,11]. Once the humans' pose skeletons have been extracted, they have to be tracked along video frames. As for pose estimation, they can be divided into top-down [7,13,19] and bottom-up [5,9,16] approaches. Top-down approaches use a person detector to obtain bounding boxes in which poses are estimated, and then track poses across time. Bottom-up approaches produce confidence maps to detect each body parts, and then group the key-points in frames (people skeletons) and across time. Raaj *et al.* have proposed an extension of PAFs with a temporal dimension, called Spatio-Temporal Affinity Fields (STAF) [16], by performing pose tracking and key-point matching across frames. Doering *et al.* [5] followed a similar direction. They built a siamese network encoding two consecutive frames to obtain belief maps, PAFs and Temporal Flow Fields (TFF) to track key-points among frames. Jin *et al.* [9] used a SpatialNet to produce key-point heat maps and key-points embeddings to group the proposals together into human pose proposals, and then used a TemporalNet to perform temporal grouping. These methods use frame-to-frame matching and do not maintain a long term memory of previous frames and estimated poses, even if this could be beneficial for performance during long surveillance tasks. At the same time, object tracking algorithms that incorporate a memory have recently been proposed within the domain of Video Object Segmentation (VOS) [15]. VOS takes a segmentation map of an object for the first frame of a video and aims at performing the segmentation for the other frames. The Space-Time Memory Networks (STM) [14] approach has recently made a breakthrough in VOS. Using the flexible memory networks system [12], it can make use of an arbitrary number of past images and predict the object segmentation in the current frame, only being limited by available memory. Pre-trained on synthetic sequences created from multiple image datasets, and then fine-tuned on video datasets such as Youtube-VOS [20] and DAVIS-2017 [15], it achieved state of the art performance when considering both quality and speed of tracking. However, maintaining a long term memory of skeleton parts along the frames of a video has still not been investigated even if this could be beneficial for performance during long surveillance tasks. In this paper, we investigate a new system for online multi-person skeleton body part detection in videos by adapting the STM architecture [14] for long-term tracking. In contrast to existing methods, our approach uses a memory of previous frames and estimated skeletons parts. This system could be integrated within most pose tracking systems by replacing its skeleton body part detection.

The paper is organized as follows. Section 2 presents our adapted STM architecture and dedicated training strategy. Section 3 presents experiments that establish the ability of STM to detect skeleton body parts and provides results with our proposed network architecture. Last section concludes.

2 STM Multi-person Skeleton Body Part Detection

2.1 STM Architecture

The original STM architecture is one of the fastest running algorithms when it comes to single object VOS. It is also suited for the VOS task on the DAVIS-2017 dataset, in which the videos contain at most a few objects to track. It is illustrated in Fig. 1 and described in detail in [14]. Nevertheless, the STM architecture is not built to scale up easily to any number of objects, as each object has to be processed independently with a dedicated STM. This causes slower processing times and larger memory requirements when the number of objects to track increases. In this paper, we propose an adaptation of STM for detecting skeleton key-points and edges.

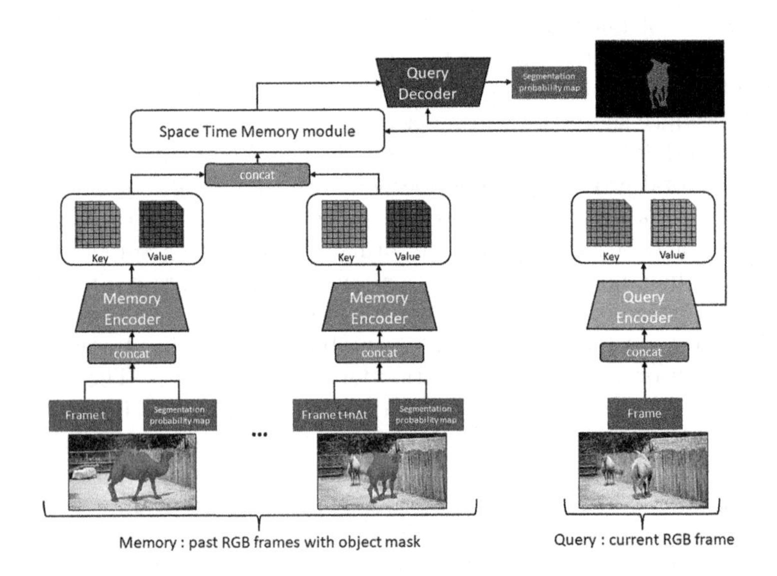

Fig. 1. Original STM architecture.

2.2 STM-skeletons Architecture

In order to adapt the STM architecture for multi-person skeleton body part detection, we have made several modifications to the original STM architecture so that several skeletons can be processed within a single inference. First, to be efficient, the proposed architecture must be able to produce several outputs in contrast to STM that produces only one segmentation map. Second, as we want to detect and track skeletons parts, we have to represent them by specific channels. This new

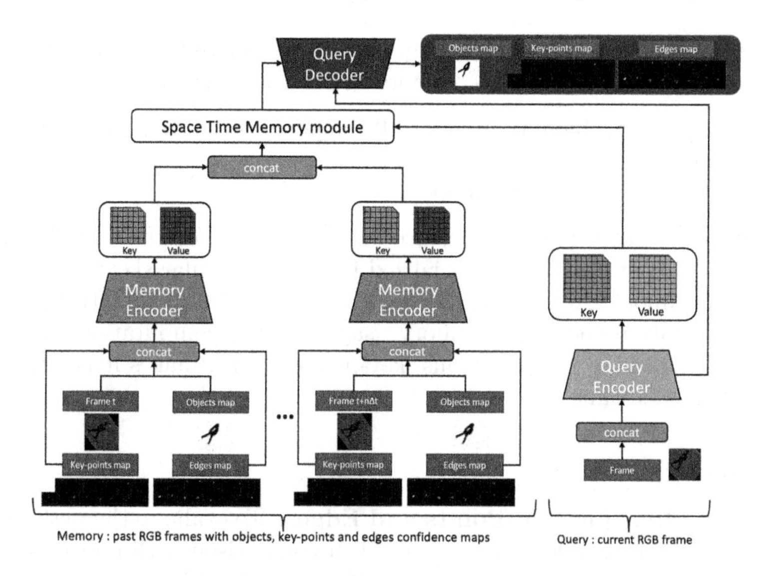

Fig. 2. Our proposed STM-skeletons architecture.

architecture is illustrated in Fig. 2. The first modifications do concern the encoder inputs. The classical STM takes an RGB frame and its segmentation probability map as concatenated inputs. The proposed architecture, called STM-skeletons, represents skeletons by both their key-points and the edges joining two key-points. The skeleton key-points and edges are each represented in dedicated confidence maps: one per skeleton key-point for all persons and one per skeleton edge for all persons. The value provides the belief that a skeleton key-point or edge of one person (among all those that appear) is present at this pixel. Therefore, we consider four different kinds of inputs that are concatenated:

- The input RGB frame (as in STM),
- A segmentation probability map for all the persons that appear in the frame (it was for only one person in the original STM),
- N_K confidence maps that represent the probability of occurence of a given skeleton key-point for all the persons,
- N_E confidence maps that represent the probability of occurence of a given skeleton edge for all the persons.

The confidence maps for the edges do not contain any orientation information as in PAFs [4] and are more likely to be called as Part Affinity Maps (PAMs). With such a modification, the encoder can deal with the simultaneous encoding of the skeleton key-points and edges of several persons. This makes the STM-skeletons model more suitable for tracking multi-person key-points and edges. As for the original STM, for the memory encoder, the input channels can either be given from a ground-truth or estimated from previous predictions. The memory encoder has its first layer of the backbone ResNet modified to be adapted to the new dimensionality of the input. For the decoder, a similar configuration to STM is kept, except for the last layer that now produces several prediction maps instead of a single one (that was a segmentation map). Therefore, the last layer produces:s

- A segmentation probability map for all the persons that appear in the frame,
- N_K skeleton key-point confidence maps,
- N_E skeleton edge confidence maps.

This new architecture slightly sacrifices the generality of the trained model. Indeed, each output channel is specialized for one particular skeleton key-point or edge, and cannot be reused to track another person' key-points. However, this change drastically reduces the memory usage and the computation time when detecting and tracking many persons' key-points, which makes it necessary for real-world and real-time usage.

2.3 Training

Confidence Maps for Key-Points and Edges. To evaluate the performance during the training, the loss function needs a comparison with a ground-truth. We construct it in a similar manner to [4]. The ground truth confidence maps are constructed from ground truth key-points and edges. For a body part key-point j in a given skeleton k at location $x_{j,k} \in \mathbb{R}^2$, the value of the key-point confidence map $S_{j,k}$ at pixel location p is $S_{j,k}(p) = exp\left(\frac{\|p-x_{j,k}\|}{\sigma}\right)$ where σ controls the spread of the peak around the key-point. We proceed similarly for edges $E_{i,j,k}$ joining two key-points i and j in the skeleton k and generate a spread along the edge line and its extremities. The predicted confidence maps of key-points or edges are aggregated with a max operator. Ground-truth are obtained from two well know datasets: MS-COCO [11] and PoseTrack18 [1].

Hyper-parameters and Tuning. Training is done using one Nvidia Tesla V100 GPU with a batch size of 1. The used optimizer is Adam, with a learning rate of 10^{-6}. The considered losses are the MSE, the Pearson Correlation Coefficient and the Focal losses [3]. The official weights (obtained from a pre-training on several image datasets and fine-tuned on DAVIS 2017 as in [14]) are used for initialization of both STM and STM-skeletons. For the later only the layers in common with the original STM architecture are initialized with the official weights. Moreover, for all experiments the batch normalization layers are disabled as in [14].

Pre-training on Synthetic Data. The PoseTrack18 dataset features a large amount of video sequences, but the diversity of persons and contexts are inferior to large-scale image datasets such as MS-COCO. In order to leverage the large quantity of images in MS-COCO key-points for pose tracking, we created synthetic video sequences from singular images. A given sample image is translated, rotated, scaled, sheared at random N times in a cumulative way for the creation of a sequence of N frames (see Fig. 3). In the rest of the paper, pre-trainings have a duration of 5 epochs on the MS-COCO_Train set.

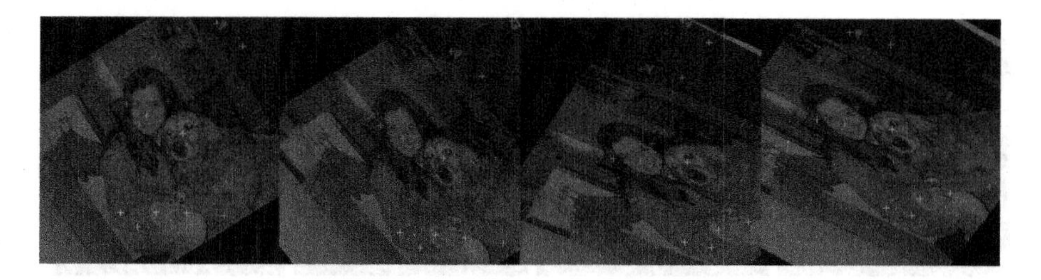

Fig. 3. Synthetic sequence created from a single image from MS-COCO key-points.

Fine-Tuning on Real Video Sequences. We fine-tune our models on the PoseTrack18_Train set that contains real video sequences. Training samples are created by choosing a video at random, and then taking a subset of N frames in the video sequence, keeping their ordering. We consider 30 epochs for the fine-tuning training schedule.

Data Augmentation for Refinement. For the long-term tracking, the algorithm needs to be able to correct the mistakes it can have made in the previous memorized frames in order to be able to "refine" them. Ideally, its prediction at frame T should be better than its prediction at frame $T-1$. However, the samples shown to the model during training contain ground-truth annotations, which do not feature many mistakes. In order to prepare the model to deal with these mistakes, we conceived a method similar to [6]. It consists in implementing a data augmentation scheme for refinement, where during the construction of the key-point and edge confidence maps for the memory frames, random transformations are applied. These transformations are: i) small random displacement of the ground truth key-points positions (called jitter), ii) randomization of the size, shape and orientation of the key-points' or edges' Gaussian peaks (called rand), iii) Key-points or edges false positives added to the confidence maps (called baits), iv) Randomization of the intensity of the Gaussian peaks by multiplication with a random factor in the interval $[0,1]$ (called dull_clouds). This data augmentation scheme is illustrated in Fig. 4. In Sect. 3 we will examine the impact of these options on tracking performance.

Cyclic Training. When being used for long-term tracking, the memorization mode of our model will take as input the prediction it has made for the previous frames. However, in the normal training procedure, the confidence maps that are shown to the model are created from the ground-truth annotations. This difference between the way it is trained and the way it is meant to be used for long-term tracking might lead to worse performance. We therefore created a specific training procedure that we call "cyclic". In the latter, for a sample sequence, the model is initialized by memorizing the ground truth annotation for the first few frames, and then, for the last few frames, detects the skeletons' parts independently, based on the memory of its own predictions. In this procedure,

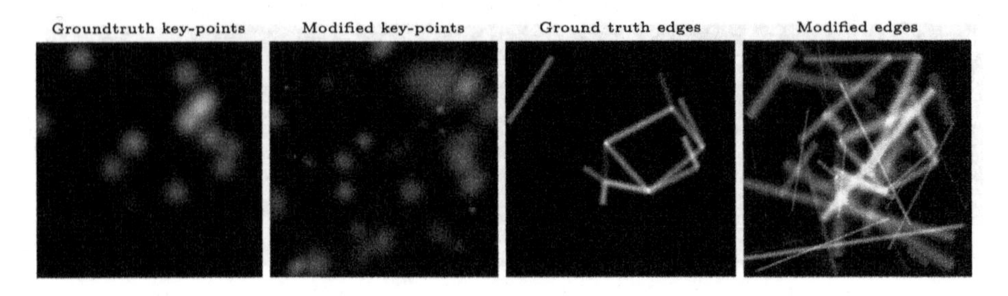

Fig. 4. Confidence maps for skeleton key-points and edges before and after data augmentation. Each key-point or edge type is shown in a particular color.

the model can produce predictions for multiple frames, therefore the training loss is the sum of the loss of each prediction.

3 Results

In this section, we experimentally show that STM architecture, without modification, can be used for the task of detecting and tracking skeleton body parts. These experiments also enable to compare different training parameters and procedures and to define the best ones. The metrics used for these experiments are precision, recall and F1-score. We can not use, at this stage, MOTA and mAP metrics generally used for a complete tracking system because we propose in this paper a component of such a system. Then, we provide results with our proposed architecture better adapted for the multi-person case. When we refer to validation datasets, these have not been used during training.

3.1 Video Skeleton Segmentation

First, we aim at showing the ability of STM to detect and track several people skeletons simultaneously. The object probability map that STM takes as input for memory frames (and produces as output for query frames) is considered to be a map that provides the belief for a pixel to belong to the skeleton of one person with possibly several persons' skeletons in the image. The STM was not intended for that as it was designed for segmenting a *single* object. As the output we want to predict is not binary (in contrast to the classical STM that outputs a binary segmentation map), we examine the impact of different loss functions on the performance: the Pearson Correlation Coefficient (CC) and focal losses (see [3] for an overview of these losses). The training procedure is the following. From the official STM weights, we do a pre-training on the synthetic MS-COCO videos (detailed in the previous section). We evaluate the trained model on the validation subset of MS-COCO key-points. We initialize the tracking with a ground truth for the first frame, and use STM to obtain the skeletons confidence map for the rest of the video sequences. We binarize the predictions with a threshold of 0.5 and compute classical performance metrics: precision, recall, and F1-score. Table 1 presents the quantitative results. We can notice that the different losses functions led to similar results with a small advantage to the focal loss in terms of F1-score. We therefore keep the focal loss for our next experiments. On the synthetic MS-COCO_Validation the skeletons are mostly well detected. This shows that the STM architecture is able to process confidence maps instead of segmentation masks. The pre-trained model has then been used as is on the PoseTrack18_Validation. As expected the results are worse, as it was not fine-tuned on PoseTrack18_Train, but as shown in Fig. 5 the predictions results are good nevertheless, even if not very precisely located. This validates the interest of STM for detection tasks instead of segmentation.

Table 1. STM performances for producing a multi-person skeleton confidence map.

	Precision	Recall	F1-score
	MS-COCO_Validation		
CC-loss	**80.7**	64.6	71.8
MSE loss	79.1	67.4	72.8
Focal loss	77.8	**70.8**	**74.1**
	PoseTrack18_Validation		
CC-loss	**48.0**	26.7	34.3
MSE loss	46.8	27.5	34.6
Focal loss	44.3	**32.1**	**37.2**

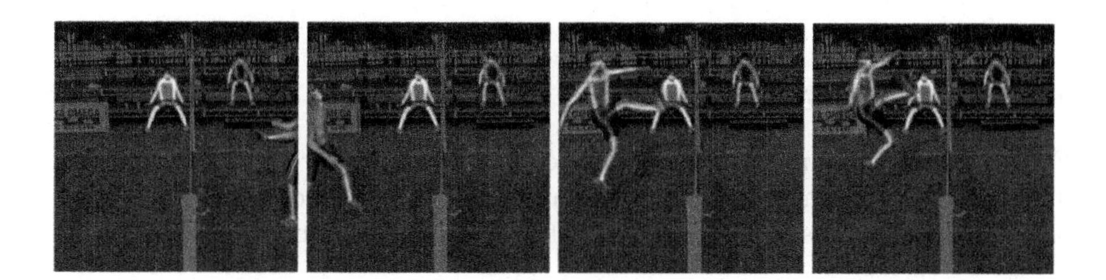

Fig. 5. STM detection results for producing a multi-person skeleton confidence map.

3.2 Video Skeleton Edge Prediction

Second, we now consider our proposed STM-skeletons architecture but to predict only edge skeleton confidence maps (i.e., the N_K confidence maps are discarded). The aim of this experiment is to show that the modification that we propose enables to detect different skeleton parts instead of a single skeleton confidence map. In addition, this will enable us to perform a fine-tuning of the model on PoseTrack18_Train. We ran multiple pre-training and fine-tuning and evaluated the resulting models on MS-COCO_Validation, and PoseTrack18_Validation.

Table 2 presents the quantitative results. Figure 6 shows some detection results, where every skeleton edge is assigned a particular color. On MS-COCO the results are better than with the original STM (in the first experiment) and shows the benefit of our approach of multi-person multi-part detection. On Pose-Track18, fine-tuning the model provides some improvement but the results are still low. This shows that the training of our model, especially for long and difficult sequences, such as these of PoseTrack18 needs a more carefully designed training.

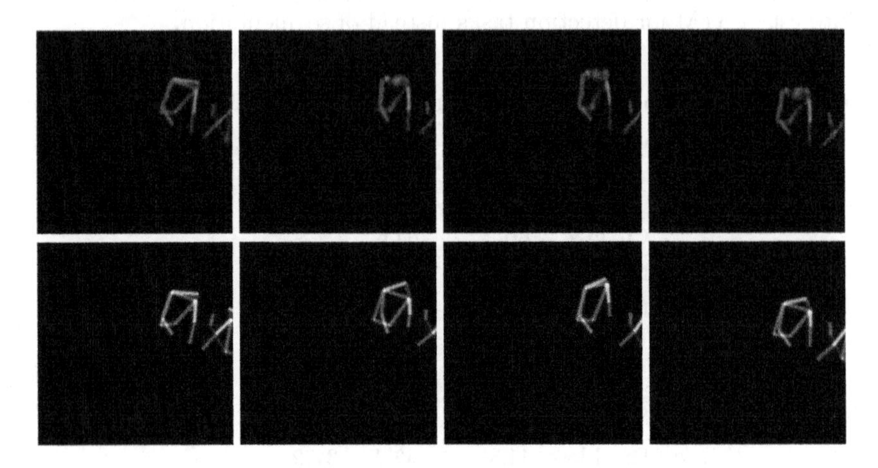

Fig. 6. Edges skeleton detection results by STM-skeletons. Top row: prediction, Bottom row: ground truth.

3.3 Video Pose Estimation

For this third experiment, we investigate more deeply different training procedures and data augmentation options for STM-skeletons to enhance the results on PoseTrack18. This time we consider the full STM-skeletons architecture that

Table 2. Proposed STM-skeletons performances for detecting multi-person edges' skeleton confidence maps.

	Precision	Recall	F1-score
	MS-COCO_Validation		
Focal loss pre-trained	88.1	**74.3**	**80.7**
Focal loss fine-tuned 30 epochs	**88.5**	65.1	75.0
	PoseTrack18_Validation		
Focal loss pre-trained	**35.2**	16.1	22.1
Focal loss fine-tuned 30 epochs	29.0	**31.2**	**30.1**

predicts both key-points and edges. We analyze the impact of different choices of training configurations, and different options for data augmentation as presented in Sect. 2.3. The models are pre-trained during 5 epochs on MS-COCO key-points, and fine-tuned during 50 epochs on PoseTrack18_Train. The evaluation is done on PoseTrack18_Validation and we use for this a dedicated metric more suited to evaluate the accuracy of the key-points prediction. We match every key-point with its closest corresponding prediction, and consider it as a True Positive if the prediction is within a radius of 10 pixels from the ground truth. Edges are not considered in the evaluation results. Results are shown in Table 3. Several data augmentation configurations are considered and each checkmark tells which one is considered. We also look at the influence of fine-tuning. When comparing the same configurations, before and after fine-tuning, we notice a systematic improvement, this shows the importance of fine-tuning on the real video sequences from PoseTrack18_Train. If we compare Configurations 1 and 2 with the others, we can see that cyclic training provides a significant improvement, and on its own is almost enough to replace data augmentation. This shows that it is important to perform memorization not only with the ground truth but also with predictions. The augmentations rand, baits, and jitter can be considered as useful options that show a consistent improvement, in particular when cyclic training is disabled. These options are required to obtain the best performance measured in terms of F1-score, obtained after fine-tuning with Configuration 5.

Table 3. Performances of STM-skeletons with different pre-training procedures, and different data augmentation options.

	Cyclic	rand	baits	jitter	dull_clouds	Precision	Recall	F1-score
Without fine-tuning						PoseTrack18_Validation		
Configuration 1						**82,6**	6.1	11.4
Configuration 2		✓	✓	✓		57.4	25.9	35.7
Configuration 3	✓					67.3	25.7	37.2
Configuration 4	✓	✓				46.9	28.2	35.2
Configuration 5	✓	✓	✓	✓		52.1	**31.0**	**38.9**
Configuration 6	✓	✓	✓	✓	✓	48.7	27.3	35.0
With fine-tuning						PoseTrack18_Validation		
Configuration 1						**81.3**	17.9	29.4
Configuration 2		✓	✓	✓		73.1	31.8	44.4
Configuration 3	✓					70.9	35.0	46.8
Configuration 4	✓	✓				62.3	**36.4**	46.0
Configuration 5	✓	✓	✓	✓		69.8	36.2	**47.6**
Configuration 6	✓	✓	✓	✓	✓	69.8	32.2	44.0

The precision, recall and F1-score are good aggregate metrics to compare the performance of different training procedures, however, they do not inform us on whether the differences are in long-term or short-term tracking. In order to make sure that our training procedure is advantageous for long term tracking, we compare in Fig. 7 the evolution of recall scores over time, on sequences from PoseTrack18_Validation. We can see that the differences in the first few frames are negligible, and that they increase over time. This shows that fine-tuning on PoseTrack18_Train and cyclic training improve long-term rather than short-term tracking performance.

Finally, to obtain better detection results, the proposed multi-person skeleton body part detection has to be included within a complete tracking system as in [4] where the detection is processed with non-maximum suppression, body part detection association and skeleton matching across frames. This will obviously further enhance the predictions our architecture gives.

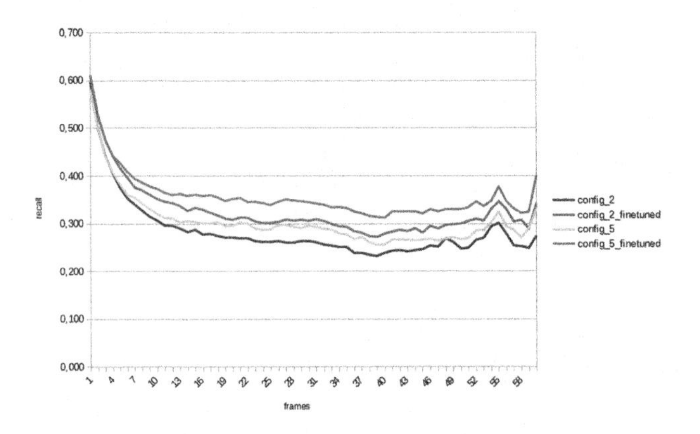

Fig. 7. Evolution of recall over time depending on model training configuration.

4 Conclusion

We have proposed a new algorithm for multi-person skeleton body part detection. Building up on the recent Video Object Segmentation architecture called Space-Time Memory Networks, we have modified it so that it is adapted to multi-person skeletons key-points and edge prediction. We have designed a two-stage pre-training/fine-tuning procedure for this architecture that aims at improving the capacities of the model. In addition we use a specific data augmentation and a cyclic training scheme. The impact of these different elements has been evaluated on the PoseTrack18 dataset. While at this stage the results cannot yet be compared to the state-of-the-art of skeleton pose estimation in videos (as several additional steps for filtering and matching have to be done), we have shown that our method can be interesting. In particular, in contrast to existing approaches, the proposed architecture can make use of a long-term memory.

Acknowledgments. This research work contributes to the french collaborative project TASV (autonomous passengers service train), with SNCF, Alstom Crespin, Thales, Bosch, and SpirOps. It was carried out in the framework of FCS Railenium, Famars and co-financed by the European Union with the European Regional Development Fund (Hauts-de-France region).

References

1. Andriluka, M., et al.: PoseTrack: a benchmark for human pose estimation and tracking. In: CVPR, pp. 5167–5176 (2018)
2. Belagiannis, V., Zisserman, A.: Recurrent human pose estimation. In: FG, pp. 468–475 (2017)
3. Bruckert, A., Tavakoli, H.R., Liu, Z., Christie, M., Meur, O.L.: Deep saliency models?: the quest for the loss function. Neurocomputing **453**, 693–704 (2021)
4. Cao, Z., Hidalgo Martinez, G., Simon, T., Wei, S., Sheikh, Y.A.: OpenPose: realtime multi-person 2D pose estimation using part affinity fields. IEEE Trans. Pattern Anal. Mach. Intell. **43**(1), 172–186 (2019)
5. Doering, A., Iqbal, U., Gall, J.: JointFlow: temporal flow fields for multi person pose estimation. In: BMVC, pp. 261–272 (2018)
6. Fieraru, M., Khoreva, A., Pishchulin, L., Schiele, B.: Learning to refine human pose estimation. In: CVPR, pp. 318–327 (2018)
7. Girdhar, R., Gkioxari, G., Torresani, L., Paluri, M., Tran, D.: Detect-and-track: efficient pose estimation in videos. In: CVPR, pp. 350–359 (2018)
8. Insafutdinov, E., Pishchulin, L., Andres, B., Andriluka, M., Schiele, B.: DeeperCut: a deeper, stronger, and faster multi-person pose estimation model. In: Leibe, B., Matas, J., Sebe, N., Welling, M. (eds.) ECCV 2016. LNCS, vol. 9910, pp. 34–50. Springer, Cham (2016). https://doi.org/10.1007/978-3-319-46466-4_3
9. Jin, S., Liu, W., Ouyang, W., Qian, C.: Multi-person articulated tracking with spatial and temporal embeddings. In: CVPR, pp. 5657–5666 (2019)
10. Kreiss, S., Bertoni, L., Alahi, A.: PifPaf: composite fields for human pose estimation. In: CVPR, pp. 11977–11986 (2019)
11. Lin, T.-Y., et al.: Microsoft COCO: common objects in context. In: Fleet, D., Pajdla, T., Schiele, B., Tuytelaars, T. (eds.) ECCV 2014. LNCS, vol. 8693, pp. 740–755. Springer, Cham (2014). https://doi.org/10.1007/978-3-319-10602-1_48
12. Miller, A., Fisch, A., Dodge, J., Karimi, A.H., Bordes, A., Weston, J.: Key-value memory networks for directly reading documents. In: EMNLP, pp. 1400–1409 (2016)
13. Ning, G., Huang, H.: LightTrack: a generic framework for online top-down human pose tracking. In: CVPR, pp. 4456–4465 (2020)
14. Oh, S.W., Lee, J.Y., Xu, N., Kim, S.J.: Video object segmentation using spacetime memory networks. In: ICCV, pp. 9225–9234 (2019)
15. Pont-Tuset, J., Perazzi, F., Caelles, S., Arbeláez, P., Sorkine-Hornung, A., Van Gool, L.: The 2017 Davis challenge on video object segmentation. arXiv:1704.00675 (2017)
16. Raaj, Y., Idrees, H., Hidalgo, G., Sheikh, Y.: Efficient online multi-person 2D pose tracking with recurrent spatio-temporal affinity fields. In: CVPR, pp. 4620–4628 (2019)
17. Toshev, A., Szegedy, C.: DeepPose: human pose estimation via deep neural networks. In: CVPR, pp. 1653–1660 (2014)

18. Wei, S.E., Ramakrishna, V., Kanade, T., Sheikh, Y.: Convolutional pose machines. In: CVPR, pp. 4724–4732 (2016)
19. Xiu, Y., Li, J., Wang, H., Fang, Y., Lu, C.: Pose flow: efficient online pose tracking. In: BMVC, pp. 53–64 (2018)
20. Xu, N., et al.: Youtube-VOS: A large-scale video object segmentation benchmark. arXiv:1809.03327 (2018)

Lip-Based Identification Using YOLOR

Wardah Farrukh and Dustin van der Haar(✉)

Academy of Computer Science and Software Engineering, University of Johannesburg, Cnr University Road and Kingsway Avenue, Johannesburg 2006, South Africa
dvanderhaar@uj.ac.za

Abstract. In recent years, the exploitation of lip prints for biometric identification has gained much attention from the research community, with most of the efforts devoted to establishing that the physiological characteristic of the lip is discriminative and unique. Up until now research in this area has employed more classical feature engineering-based approaches and results that have been achieved are still not comparable with those yielded by more commonly used biometric characteristics. Furthermore, the field of lip detection is still an ongoing topic of research due to its many challenges which hinders the success of lip detection techniques. This work will determine the viability of newer methods on the task of lip detection and identification through the application of newer deep learning methods which is an apparent gap in this area. In this study YOLOR is applied on samples of faces from the CFD dataset to effectively achieve lip detection and identification. The results obtained are promising with a mAP of 99.5% and a precision and recall score of 67% and 99%, respectively.

Keywords: Deep learning · YOLOR · Lip detection · Lip identification

1 Introduction

It is widely acknowledged that traditional methods of authentication such as passwords are not the most effective means of authentication, leading to an increased attention of biometric recognition [1]. Replacing traditional methods with a biometric trait has many advantages; it cannot be lost, forgotten, stolen, or disclosed [1]. Currently, biometric recognition systems are applied in many real-life scenarios ranging from border control to unlocking mobile devices. Although various biometric traits have achieved state-of-the-art results, such as fingerprint and face, research is still carried out in this area to design novel biometric systems, based on other biometric traits, which may possess useful properties not available in mainstream solutions [2]. One such trait that has gained attention recently is the human lip. Its uniqueness has been confirmed by Tsuchihashi and Suzuki [3] due to the grooves present on the surface of the lip. Furthermore, previous research that has been undertaken in this field has proven that lip prints can be used to recognise individuals [4]. However, research within this area is still in its early stages and has relied on traditional machine learning methods thus far to achieve recognition. Biometric recognition has now shifted from hand-crafted features to deep learning architectures and have achieved state-of-art results for fingerprint,

M. El Yacoubi et al. (Eds.): ICPRAI 2022, LNCS 13364, pp. 91–101, 2022.
https://doi.org/10.1007/978-3-031-09282-4_8

face, and iris recognition [6] as well as many others. To date lip-based recognition has not gained much deep learning-based research, especially compared to other biometric traits. More importantly, previous research into lip-based recognition is inconsistent with results reported on small or private datasets, and different metrics making comparison difficult [7]. Therefore, novel approaches are required for lip-based recognition, in order to evaluate whether the recognition rates are comparable with those achieved through other well-established biometric traits.

With the rapid development of artificial intelligence (AI), deep learning architectures have become popular for object detection because they can identify and process data efficiently. Therefore, it is worthwhile to explore how these architectures will perform in the realm of lip-based recognition. Furthermore, lip detection remains an ongoing topic of research which originates from numerous applications such as speaker verification or standalone lip-based biometric systems. Automating the process of lip detection and recognition is quite a difficult task in computer vision due to the variation amongst humans and environmental conditions [8]. Taking the above aspects into account, this paper investigates the effectiveness of employing deep learning techniques to detect the lips and process lip prints for biometric identification. The aim of this paper is to advance the field forward by applying an end-to-end deep learning technique to improve the performance of lip-based identification. The main contributions of this paper are as follows:

- We have prepared ground truth labels on a publicly available dataset (Chicago Face Dataset) which can be used for lip segmentation and recognition.
- We have proposed a modified YOLOR model on the CFD to achieve lip-based identification.
- The paper provides an up-to-date comprehensive review on lip segmentation. We have expanded on the technological challenges and provided a thorough summary of the current research status.

The remainder of the paper is organised as follows. Section 2 discusses the literature study with a problem background in Sect. 2.1 and similar work conducted in Sect. 2.2. The architecture adopted and the experiment setup are outlined in Sect. 3. The results of the current study are highlighted in Sect. 4, followed by a discussion of the obtained results in Sect. 5. Conclusions are eventually drawn in Sect. 6.

2 Literature Study

2.1 Problem Background

From published literature [4, 6], it can be seen that lip-based recognition is not a well-researched area. More importantly, lip-based recognition works are mostly based on hand-crafted features. Many of the hand-crafted features are based on edges (SIFT [9], LBP [10], Sobel and Canny [11]), or are derived from the transfer domain such as Gabor wavelets [12]. Once the feature or feature representation is extracted, it is fed into the classifier to perform recognition. According to Minaee et al. [6] numerous challenges arise in hand-crafted features for biometric recognition. For instance, it would take a considerable number of experiments to find the best classical method for a certain biometric. Furthermore, many of the traditional methods are based on a multi-class support vector machine (SVM) trained in a one-vs-one fashion, which does not scale well when the number of classes is extensive [6]. Therefore, more sophisticated, and state-of-the-art methods are needed to consolidate the research on lip biometrics. Since biometric recognition has shifted from classical models to deep learning models, it is worthwhile to explore how lip-based identification will perform using state state-of-the-art methods. This would involve automating the process of lip detection and identification. According to Hassanat et al. [8], lip detection is an automatic process used to localize the lips in digital images. This is a crucial area of research because it is a fundamental step in many applications such as lip-reading applications, face recognition, facial expression recognition, and lip-based biometric systems [8]. However, there are still many challenges to overcome in the field of lip detection [7, 8]. The lips comprise a very small part of the face and therefore, algorithms such as Faster R-CNN and YOLO require more processing time which greatly affects its speed at which it can make predictions [13]. Datasets are also often private [7] and do not have a balance of ethnicities, thus making it difficult to compare results. Additionally, low colour contrast between the lip and face regions, diversity of lip shape and the presence of facial hair and poor lighting conditions hinder the success of algorithms for lip detection [8]. Although lip detection techniques have been proposed, there is a significant room for further improvement in lip detection and identification.

2.2 Similar Work

Several image segmentation techniques have been proposed over the years. However, due to the low chromatic and luminance contrast between the lips and the skin, only a few of these techniques have been applied to the task of lip detection [14]. As a result, a variety of methods for detecting lips in colored images have been proposed, which can be divided into three categories: color-based, model-based, and hybrid-based techniques [14, 15].

Colour-Based Approach

Color-based approaches employ a preset color filter capable of distinguishing between lip and non-lip pixels within a specific color space [15] and can segment the lip with good results when there is a high color contrast. For example, Chang et al. [16] used chromaticity thresholding to segment the lips by identifying skin regions in the image. Sadeghi et al. [17] proposed a Gaussian mixture model of RGB values using a modified version of the predictive validation technique. Another traditional approach proposed by Shemshaki et al. [18] uses chromatic and *YCbCr* colour spaces to detect the skin and lip pixel values. However, the approach adopted by Xinjun et al. [19] is slightly more flexible where they design colour filters consisting of both RGB and *YUV* components. These filters effectively threshold the pixels based on a colour ratio. Beaumesnil and Luthon [20] propose using k-means clustering on the *U* channel from the *LUX* colour space to classify pixels as either lips or face. Skodras et al. [21] improve this method by using k-means clustering to automatically adapt the number of clusters. Rohani et al. [22] use fuzzy c-means clustering with preassigned number of clusters. FCM clustering is applied to each transformed image along with *b* components of the *CIELAB* colour space. Cheung et al. [23] build on this by initialising an excess number of clusters, which are then reduced by merging clusters with coincident centroids. In more recent approaches, the power of neural networks is exploited to perform lip detection. Hassanat et al. [8] use colour spaces to classify pixels as lips or non-lips using artificial neural networks. More recently, Guan et al. [24] proposed a new fuzzy deep neural network that integrates fuzzy units and traditional convolutional units. The convolutional units are used to extract features while the fuzzy logic modules are used to provide segmentation results with an end-to-end training scheme.

Although colour-based approaches are computationally inexpensive and allow rapid detection of the target region, Wang et al. [25] discourage approaches that rely solely on colour information due to the low contrast between the lips and skin. Additionally, colour-based techniques are highly sensitive to variations in illumination and camera orientations [14]. Gritzman [14] also states that some authors have also expressed concerns that the resulting segmentation is often noisy.

Model-Based Approach

Model-based approaches use previous knowledge of the lip contour to build a lip model and can be quite robust [15, 24]. The mostly widely used lip models are the active contour model (ACM), the active shape model (ASM), and the active appearance model (AAM). Model-based techniques are usually invariant to rotation, transformation, and illumination [15]. Liew et al. [26] used a deformable geometric model to identify the lip shape. The model enables prior knowledge about the lips' expected shape, and it describes different shape variations. In 2014, Sangve and Mule [27] did not only use colour spaces for lip detection like the aforementioned methods, but also introduced person recognition based on the lips. They did this by combining the region of interest with the AAM, ASM, and point distribution model (PDM). More recently in 2018, Lu and Liu [28] proposed a localised active contour model-based method using two initial contours in a combined color space to segment the lip region.

Lip models provide geometric constraints for the final lip shape and reduce the influence caused by false edges to a certain extent. However, research [29] has shown that lip-model-based approaches depend on good initialisation and are still sensitive to noise boundaries caused by various backgrounds such as mustache and teeth.

Hybrid Approach

Hybrid approaches are often combined with colour-based techniques and model-based techniques. By utilising a hybrid approach, the computational complexity of model-based techniques is reduced by using colour-based techniques to obtain a quick estimation of the lip region [14, 15]. Sensitivity to illumination and noisy segmentation of colour-based techniques is reduced by the smoothness and shape constraints of model-based techniques [14]. For example, Werda et al. [30] proposed a hybrid technique for lip Point Of Interest localisation using colour information to locate the mouth in the first stage, and a geometric model to extract the shape of the lip in the second stage. Similarly, Mok et al. [31] proposed to segment the lips by first transforming the RGB image to the *CIELAB* colour space, thereafter, applying a fuzzy clustering method incorporating a shape function to obtain a rough estimation. An ASM is matched to the lips for accurate detection of lip contours. Tian et al. [32] presented a lip tracking method by combining lip shape, colour and motion information. The shape of the lip is modelled using two parabolas. The colour information of the lips and the skin is modelled as a Gaussian mixture.

Based on previous works discussed above, the existing lip detection techniques achieve good segmentation results to a certain extent. Research demonstrates that state-of-the-art deep learning-based approaches are not yet introduced to the field of lip detection and recognition. With the rapid development of AI, deep neural networks have excelled in image processing and computer vision [6], providing a promising direction for solving the difficulties in lip detection.

3 Experiment Setup

3.1 Dataset Selection

Extracting visual features related to lip-based identification requires an accurate extraction of the lip. Therefore, selecting an appropriate dataset is crucial to the development of the study. Some datasets have a very low resolution with poor visibility of lip patterns, while other sets have few ethnicities and the results from these datasets would not be effective. Therefore, the Chicago Face Database (CFD) [34] is employed for the current study. The CFD consists of high-resolution images of 597 male and female samples of different ethnicities. Each sample is represented with a neutral expression image and a subset of the samples are also represented with happy (open and closed mouth), angry, and fearful expressions. The CFD is particularly suited since it includes self-identified Asian, Black, Latino and White ethnicities of different ages. Currently, the CFD has limited data in terms of the number of samples per individual. Therefore, to overcome this drawback data augmentation is applied to artificially increase the data in the dataset. The methods used for data augmentation include the following modifications to the original image: horizontal flip, a rotation and an increase and decrease in brightness. Geometric transformations are helpful for positional biases present in the dataset [33]. Furthermore, altering the brightness of the original image is important because in real-life scenarios dramatic image variations arise from changes in illumination.

3.2 Proposed Architecture

YOLO is an effective state-of-the-art object recognition algorithm which uses convolutional neural networks to detect objects. As the name suggests, the algorithm only requires a single forward propagation through the neural network to detect objects. Therefore, the prediction is done in a single algorithm run in the entire image. Over the last 5 years, the YOLO algorithm has progressed and updated to various variants such as YOLOv3, YOLOv4, YOLOv5 and the most recent, YOLOR.

YOLOR ("You Only Learn One Representation") is the latest evolution of the YOLO models introduced by Wang et al. [35]. YOLOR pretrains an implicit knowledge network with all of the tasks present in the dataset, namely object detection, instance segmentation, keypoint detection, image caption, multi-label image classification, and long tail object recognition [35]. The concept of YOLOR is based on using implicit and explicit knowledge in conjunction with each other. According to Wang et al. [35] explicit knowledge is provided to neural networks by providing thoroughly annotated image datasets or clear metadata. For neural networks, however, implicit knowledge is obtained by features in the deeper layers. The authors have combined both explicit and implicit learning in a unified network. This unified network creates a unified representation to serve a variety of tasks at once. There are three processes by which this architecture is made functional: space reduction, kernel space alignment and more functions [35]. When implicit knowledge is introduced to the neural network that was already trained with explicit knowledge, the network benefits the performance of various tasks [35]. This novel approach propels YOLOR to the state-of-the-art for object detection in the speed/accuracy tradeoff landscape. Therefore, it is employed for the current study (Fig. 1).

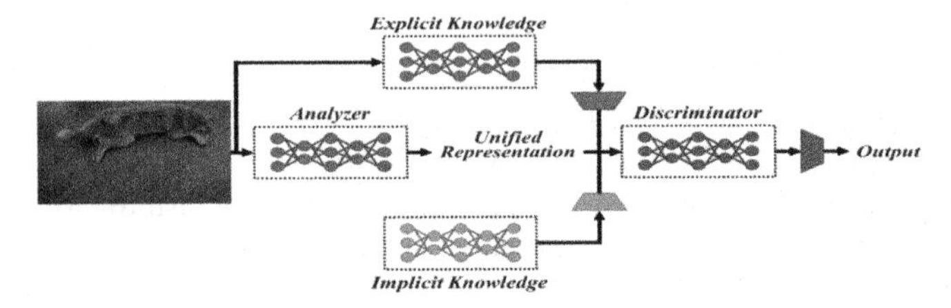

Fig. 1. YOLOR concept with implicit and explicit knowledge [35]

For the current study, the classification head for lip recognition has been modified by keeping only one fully connected layer with neurons equal to the number of samples in the training database. Since all YOLO anchor boxes are auto-learned in YOLOv5 (anchor box auto-learning has been integrated), the anchor boxes are modified using the YOLOv5 anchor box parameters which can be seen below:

Anchor box: [10,13, 16,23, 30,33] [30,61, 62,45, 59,119] [116,90, 156,198, 373,326].

Furthermore, the learning rate is set to 0.001 with Adam as the learning optimizer. The size of the input images has been modified to 448 × 448. The momentum is set to 0.937 with a decay of 0.0005. Lastly, the number of epochs chosen to train the model is set to 100 with a batch size of 8. Lastly, the benchmark parameters that will be used to assess the performance of the proposed model include mAP, Precision, Recall and a Precision × Recall (PR) Curve. Although facial landmarks detectors from D-lib can be used to detect and segment the specific region it is worthwhile to explore how end-to-end deep learning algorithms perform on object detection tasks due to the new era of machine learning.

An ablation study is commonly used to examine the model's stability and performance after removing or changing different layers and hyper-parameters. When these components in a model's architecture are changed, the network's performance can be identical, increased, or decreased. Generally, accuracy can be improved by experimenting with various hyper-parameters such as optimizer, learning rates, loss functions, and batch sizes. In this regard, two case studies are conducted and the findings are analyzed. The results indicate that overall detection rate has increased, demonstrating the utility of this technique in the current study. The results of this ablation study are shown in Table 1.

Table 1. Ablation study by optimizing parameters and anchor box

	Hyper-parameter optimization	Anchor box optimization	Result (%) (mAP)
Unmodified YOLOR	Default	Default	93%
Modified YOLOR	Yes	Yes	99.5%

4 Results

Essentially, the training procedure consisted of 100 epochs where the dataset was split into 80% for training, 10% for validation and 10% for training. The fundamental and first step of the lip biometric system is to detect the lip within the image frame. This step is crucial and must be accurate as this affects the system's overall performance. Using all the predictions for detecting the lips within the images a smooth precision × recall curve was built. The PR curve for the model during testing is shown Fig. 2 and the mAP graph is represented in Fig. 4. From Fig. 2 and Fig. 4 it is evident that the model achieved excellent results in terms of detecting the lip region with a mAP of 99.5%. Figure 4 shows the results of mAP for the different epochs obtained on the dataset with the YOLOR model.

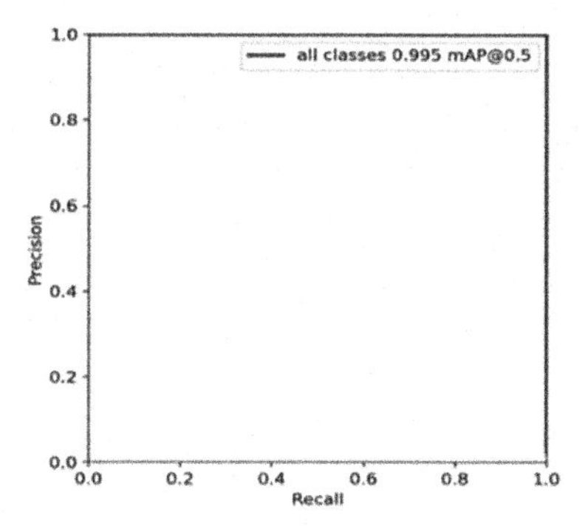

Fig. 2. Precision × Recall Curve of YOLOR model with a mAP of 0.995

Precision is a ratio between the number of positive results and the number of positive results predicted by the classifier. With regards to precision, it is evident that it increases and decreases as the number of epochs progress until it finally stabilises. The overall precision achieved is 67% while the overall recall obtained is 99% which is represented in Fig. 4. Based on these results, the model has a slightly lower precision in comparison to the total recall. This indicates that although the model is classifying most of the samples correctly, it has a few false positives and some prediction noise. This could be due to the changes in illumination and rotations of the images. After the models were trained, they were tested against images that had not been used during training. Figure 3 represents the detections (localization and classification of the samples) made by the YOLOR model after training. It is evident that those images which were augmented by applying brightness and darkness transformations with rotations received a lower identification rate than the original images. With regards to the actual identification of the different samples in the dataset, the original images received an identification rate of 0.8 or higher which indicates the model's potential in identifying the samples correctly. Although the results achieved for the augmented images are low in comparison to the original images, the brightness and darkness transformations are beneficial for the model to adapt to different illumination situations. Similarly, the rotation transformations are quite favourable for improving the robustness of the model.

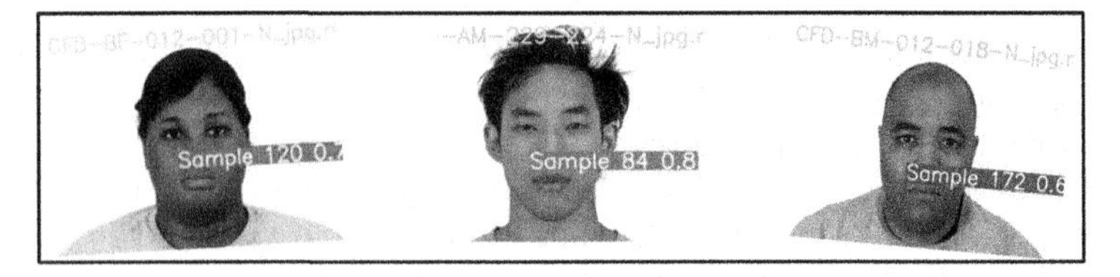

Fig. 3. Predictions made by the YOLOR model

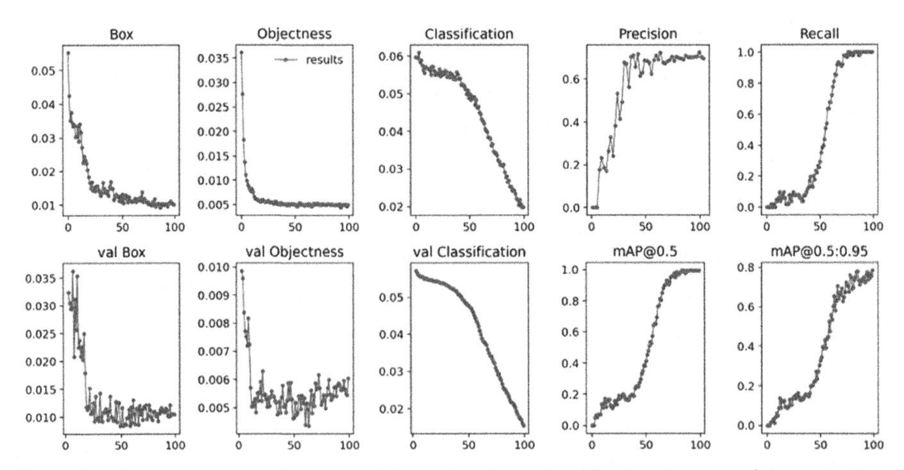

Fig. 4. Lip Recognition results obtained including loss, classification loss, precision, recall and mAP for 100 epochs

5 Discussion

This work presented a deep learning architecture to detect (localize and classify) lips from within an image frame. Based on the results discussed above, this model, as demonstrated in Figs. 4 and 6, was well balanced between precision and recall and had a good confidence rate in its predictions. Additionally, this model also ensured a precision rate higher than 60% and a recall rate near 100%. Furthermore, the model was able to ideally detect the lips with an average mAP of 99.5% and identified most of the samples with an identification rate of 0.8, thus highlighting its potential in the field of lip-based recognition. The results can be compared to similar work discussed in Sect. 2.2 where various algorithms and techniques were used to detect the lip. Based on the results it is evident that that an end-to-end deep learning technique produced a better accuracy in detecting the lip. Furthermore, it is noticeable that lip-based recognition in a short stretch of time will achieve recognition rates comparable to well-established modalities.

It is evident from previous works that more traditional feature engineering-based approaches have been used for the task of lip detection. Although good segmentation results were achieved, these approaches are discouraged [25] and have certain limitations. Deep learning-based approaches in this context are advantageous since they do not rely solely on colour information and are not sensitive to noise boundaries due to the annotation of images. Furthermore, it provides an end-to-end learning scheme thereby completely automating the process of region selection, feature extraction and classification. Due to its powerful learning ability and advantages in dealing with occlusions, transformations and backgrounds, deep learning-based object detection has the potential to contribute to the field of lip detection and recognition.

6 Conclusion

The goal of the proposed work was to train a dataset using a deep learning architecture that can perform end-to-end lip-based identification. This study has employed a state-of-the-art deep learning architecture i.e., YOLOR to perform object detection and exhibited promising results. The average mAP obtained is 99.5% which indicates the model's potential in efficiently detecting the lips. A precision score of 67% and a recall score 99% is achieved by the respective model. The results of this experiment further demonstrate that the YOLOR model can provide high classification accuracy. An overview of the study indicates that deep learning architectures have potential for lip-based recognition. Previous work has demonstrated that traditional methods were mostly used to detect the lips and it highlighted that very little work has been done on lip-based recognition using deep learning architectures. This study has therefore fulfilled the apparent gap in this domain by not only using a deep learning architecture but one of the most recent architectures. The lip biometric has fewer research compared to other popular biometrics. It is relatively new and hence offers many research possibilities. Therefore, there are still many gaps in this area that can be researched and explored. One of the evident gaps within this domain is unconstrained lip recognition. Lip-based recognition has not been explored in the unconstrained environment. Therefore, there is a need to explore the power of deep learning-based methods to develop effective and efficient lip recognition methods in real-life scenarios.

References

1. Boonkrong, S.: Authentication and Access Control: Practical Cryptography Methods and Tools, vol. 11844, pp. 405–417. Apress (2021)
2. Kamboj, A., Rani, R., Nigam, A.: A comprehensive survey and deep learning-based approach for human recognition using ear biometric. Vis. Comput. (2021)
3. Tsuchihashi, Y., Suzuki, T.: Studies on personal identification by means of lip prints. Forensic Sci. **3**, 233–248 (1974)
4. Sandhya, S., Fernandes, R.: Lip print: an emerging biometrics technology - a review. In: 2017 IEEE International Conference on Computational Intelligence and Computing Research (ICCIC), pp. 1–5 (2017)
5. Choras, M.: Lips recognition for biometrics. Adv. Biometrics, 1260–1269 (2009)
6. Minaee, S., Abdolrashidi, A., Su, H., Bennamoun, M., Zhang, D.: Biometrics recognition using deep learning: a survey (2019)
7. Bebis, G., et al. (eds.): Advances in Visual Computing, vol. 11845. Springer, Cham (2019). https://doi.org/10.1007/978-3-030-33723-0
8. Hassanat, A., Alkasassbeh, M., Al-Awadi, M., Alhasanat, E.: Colour-based lips segmentation method using artificial neural networks. In: IEEE Information and Communication Systems (ICICS), Amman (2015)
9. Bakshi, S., Raman, R., Sa, P.: Lip pattern recognition based on local feature extraction. In: 2011 Annual IEEE India Conference (INDICON), India (2011)
10. Sandhya, S., Fernandes, R., Sapna, S., Rodrigues, A.: Comparative analysis of machine learning algorithms for Lip print. Evol. Intell. (2021)
11. Bandyopadhyay, S.K., Arunkumar, S., Bhattacharjee, S.: Feature extraction of human lip prints. J. Current Comput. Sci. Technol. **2**(1), 1–8 (2012)
12. Niu, B., Sun, J., Ding, Y.: Lip print recognition using Gabor and LBP features. DEStech Trans. Comput. Sci. Eng. (2017)
13. Fessel, K.: 5 significant object detection challenges and solutions. Medium (2021). https://towardsdatascience.com/5-significant-object-detection-challenges-and-solutions-924cb09de9dd
14. Gritzman, A.D.: Adaptive Threshold Optimisation for Colour-based Lip Segmentation in Automatic Lip-Reading Systems. University of the Witwatersrand, Johannesburg (2016)
15. Saeed, U., Dugelay, J.L.: Combining edge detection and region segmentation for lip contour extraction. In: Articulated Motion and Deformable Objects, 6th International Conference, Port d'Andratx (2010)
16. Chang, T., Huang, T., Novak, C.: Facial feature extraction from color images. In: Proceedings of the 12th IAPR International Conference on Pattern Recognition, Computer Vision and Image Processing, Israel (1994)
17. Sadeghi, M., Kittler, J., Messer, K.: Modelling and segmentation of lip area in face images. Proc. IEE Conf. Vis. Image Sig. Process. **149**(3), 179–184 (2002)
18. Shemshaki, M., Amjadifard, R.: Lip segmentation using geometrical model of color distribution. In: 7th IEEE Iranian Machine Vision and Image Processing (2011)
19. Xinjun, M.A., Hongqiao, Z.: Lip segmentation algorithm based on bi-color space. In: Proceedings of the 34th Chinese Control Conference, Hangzhou (2015)
20. Beaumesnil, B., Luthon, F.: Real time tracking for 3d realistic lip animation. Pattern Recogn. **1**, 219–222 (2006)
21. Skodras, E., Fakotakis, N.: An unconstrained method for lip detection in color images. In: Acoustics, Speech and Signal Processing (ICASSP), pp. 1013–1016 (2011)
22. Rohani, R., Alizadeh, S., Sobhanmanesh, F., Boostani, R.: Lip segmentation in color images. Innov. Inf. Technol., 747–750 (2008)

23. Cheung, Y., Li, M., Cao, X., You, X.: Lip segmentation under MAP-MRF framework with automatic selection of local observation scale and number of segments. IEEE Trans. Image Process. **23**(8), 3397–3411 (2014)
24. Guan, C., Wang, S., Liew, A.W.-C.: Lip image segmentation based on a fuzzy convolutional neural network. IEEE Trans. Fuzzy Syst. **28**(7), 1242–1251 (2020)
25. Wang, S., Liew, A., Lau, W., Leung, S.: Lip region segmentation with complex background. In: Visual Speech Recognition: Lip Segmentation and Mapping: Lip Segmentation and Mapping, p. 150 (2009)
26. Liew, A.W.C., Leung, S.H., Lau, W.H.: Lip contour extraction from color images using a deformable model. Pattern Recogn. **35**, 2949–2962 (2002)
27. Sangve, S., Mule, N.: Lip recognition for authentication and security. IOSR J. Comput. Eng. **16**(3), 18–23 (2014)
28. Lu, Y., Liu, Q.: Lip segmentation using automatic selected initial contours based on localized active contour model. EURASIP J. Image Video Process. (2018)
29. Cheung, Y.M., Li, M., Cao, X.C., You, X.G.: Lip segmentation under MAP-MRF framework with automatic selection of local observation scaleand number of segments. IEEE Trans. Image Process. **23**(8), 3397–3411 (2014)
30. Werda, S., Mahdi, W., Hamadou, A.B.: Colour and geometric based model for lip localisation: application for lip-reading system. In: 14th International Conference on Image Analysis and Processing, pp. 9–14 (2007)
31. Mok, L.L., Lau, W.H. Leung, S.H., Wang, S.L., Yan, H.: Person authentication using ASM based lip shape and intensity information. In: 2004 International Conference on Image Processing, vol. 1, pp. 561–564 (2001)
32. Kanade, T., Cohn, J.F.: Robust lip tracking by combining shape, color and motion. In: 4th Asian Conference on Computer Vision, pp. 1040–1045 (2000)
33. Johnston, B., Chazal, P.D.: A review of image-based automatic facial landmark identification techniques. EURASIP J. Image Video Process. (2018)
34. Ma, D., Wittenbrink, B.: The Chicago face database: a free stimulus set of faces and norming data. Behav. Res. Methods **47**, 1122–1135 (2015)
35. Wang, C.-Y., Yeh, I.-H., Liao, H.-Y.M.: You only learn one representation: unified network for multiple tasks (2021)

Parallel $\mathcal{O}(log(n))$ Computation of the Adjacency of Connected Components

Majid Banaeyan(✉) and Walter G. Kropatsch

TU Wien, Pattern Recognition and Image Processing Group 193/03, Vienna, Austria
{majid,krw}@prip.tuwien.ac.at

Abstract. Connected Component Labeling (CCL) is a fundamental task in pattern recognition and image processing algorithms. It groups the pixels into regions, such that adjacent pixels have the same label while pixels belonging to distinct regions have different labels. The common linear-time raster scan CCL techniques have a complexity of $\mathcal{O}(image - size)$ in a 2D binary image. To speed up the procedure of the CCL, the paper proposes a new irregular graph pyramid. To construct this pyramid, we use a new formalism [1] that introduces an order of the pixels in the base grid to detect the redundant edges through the hierarchical structure. These redundant edges, unlike the usual methods of constructing the irregular pyramid, are removed before contracting the edges. This not only simplifies the construction processes but may decrease memory consumption by approximately half. To perform the CCL task efficiently the proposed parallel algorithm reduces the complexity to $\mathcal{O}(log(n))$ where the n is the diameter of the largest connected component in the image. In addition, using an efficient combinatorial structure the topological properties of the connected components including adjacency of CCs, multi-boundaries and inclusions are preserved. Finally, the mathematical proofs provide fully parallel implementations and lead to efficient results in comparison with the state-of-the-art.

Keywords: Connected Component Labeling · Irregular graph pyramid · Parallel processing · Combinatorial map · Pattern recognition

1 Introduction

Connected Component Labeling (CCL) is used in analysing binary images as a basic task [16]. Given as input a binary image, its values distinguish between background (zero) or foreground (one) regions. After this, a region is **connected** if all pairs of pixels are connected by a chain of neighbors. They may be multiple regions with value zero and multiple regions with value one. CCL assigns a unique label to each different region. In general, the CCL algorithms divide into

Supported by Pattern Recognition Image Processing (PRIP) group, Vienna, Austria.

M. El Yacoubi et al. (Eds.): ICPRAI 2022, LNCS 13364, pp. 102–113, 2022.
https://doi.org/10.1007/978-3-031-09282-4_9

two main categories [11] based on label-propagation [10] or label-equivalence-resolving [12]. All of these approaches are linear and a pixel usually is visited in the raster-scan search. In other words, such algorithms may differ from one-scan or two-scan searching through the entire image, but all of them are in the order of image size, $\mathcal{O}(MN)$ in a $M \times N$-sized (2D) binary image. Recently, the algorithm proposed in [3] uses a pyramid structure for the CCL. However, because of the linear propagation of the labels, it is linear as well.

In contrast, In this study, the proposed Parallel Pyramidal Connected Component (//ACC[1]) method reduces the complexity impressively to the logarithmic order of the diameter of the largest connected component in the image. To this aim, we employ a new formalism in [1] to recognize the redundant edges in the pyramid. Removing these redundant edges *before* contracting the edges, not only is performed in parallel but may decrease memory consumption by half in comparison with efficient pyramids [17].

To construct the irregular pyramid, the **R**emove **t**hen **C**ontract (RtC) algorithm is proposed. The proposed algorithm speeds up the labeling task which makes it more efficient to be used in various application areas of machine learning and artificial intelligence such as document analysis and object recognition [15].

1.1 Motivations and Notations

Irregular pyramids are a stack of successively reduced graphs where each graph is constructed from the graph below by selecting a specific subset of vertices and edges. For generation of irregular pyramids, two basic operations on graphs are needed: edge contraction and edge removal. The former contracts an edge $e = (v, w)$, identifies v and w and removes the edge. All edges that were incident to the joined vertices will be incident to the resulting vertex after the operation. The latter removes an edge from the graph, without changing the number of vertices or affecting the incidence relationships of other edges. Note that in this study for preserving topology the self-loops are not contractable. In each level of the pyramid, the vertices and edges disappearing in level above are called *non-surviving* and those appearing in the upper level *surviving* ones.

Definition 1 (Contraction Kernel (CK). *A contraction kernel is a spanning tree of the connected component with the surviving vertex as its root.*

Each contraction kernel is a tree including one surviving vertex and the remaining non-surviving vertices of the CC.

A ***plane*** graph is a graph embedded in the plane such that its edges intersect only at their endpoints [18]. In plane graph there are connected spaces between edges and vertices and every such connected area of the plane is called a *face*. The *degree* of the face is the number of edges bounding the face. In addition a face bounded by a cycle is called an *empty face*. In a non-empty face traversing the boundary would require to visit vertices or edges twice.

[1] It is pronounced pac where the // and A stand for parallel and pyramidal.

There are different structures to build the irregular pyramid such as simple graphs [7], dual multi-graphs [13] and combinatorial maps (CM) [6]. The simple graph cannot distinguish some topological configurations (inclusions and multiple adjacency) [14]. The problem with dual graphs is that they cannot unambiguously represent a region enclosed in another one on a local level [7]. Therefore, in this paper the CM is used which not only resolves the mentioned problems but also can be extended to higher dimensions (nD).

A **combinatorial pyramid** is a hierarchy of successively reduced combinatorial maps [6]. A combinatorial map (CM) is similar to a graph but explicitly stores the orientation of edges around each vertex. To this aim, a permutation, σ, is defined encoding consecutive edges around a same vertex while turning counterclockwise. The clockwise orientation is denoted by σ^{-1}. In the CM each edge divides into two half-edges. Each half-edge is called a *dart* and the α is an *involution* providing a one-to-one mapping between consecutive darts forming the same edge such that $\alpha(\alpha(d)) = d$.

Figure 1 left, shows a set of 8 adjacent darts with their σ relations in a face of degree 4. In the middle, it shows the encoding of the darts. For instance, consider $e = (1, 2)$ where $\alpha(1) = 2$, $\alpha(2) = 1$, $\sigma(1) = 5$. In this paper, we assign an odd number to the left-side dart of a horizontal edge while assigning an even number to its right-side dart. Similarly, we assign an odd number to the up-side dart of a vertical edge while assigning an even number to its down-side dart. The d_{odd} indicates an odd dart and the d_{even} indicates an even dart (Fig. 1 right).

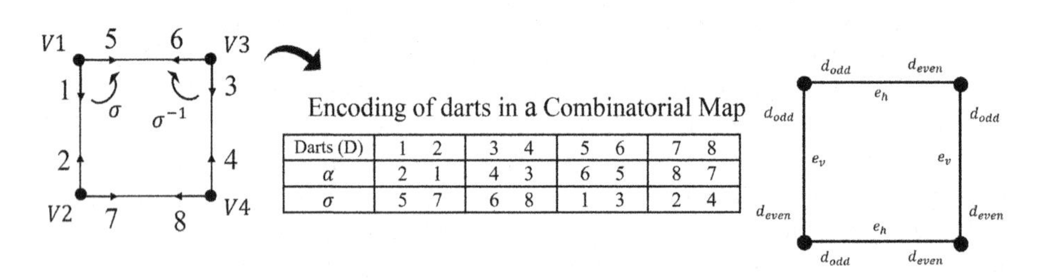

Darts (D)	1	2	3	4	5	6	7	8
α	2	1	4	3	6	5	8	7
σ	5	7	6	8	1	3	2	4

Fig. 1. Combinatorial map [1]

2 The RtC Algorithm for Pyramid Construction

In the original irregular pyramids [7] selected edges are first contracted. Edge contraction has the main advantage to preserve the connectivity. But it has a side effect to produce multiple edges and self-loops. Some of these edges are necessary to properly describe topological relations like inclusions and multiple connections between the same vertices. However, many of them are not necessary and hence called *redundant*. Redundant edges are removed through the simplification procedure after the contractions. However, in the proposed **R**emove **t**hen **C**ontract (**RtC**) algorithm, the redundant edges are removed *before* the contractions and in a parallel way. To this aim, the RtC introduces a new formalism to define the redundant edges (Sect. 2.3). Since the RtC is used for the CCL task, the input is a binary image where the 4-connectivity between pixels is assumed because the 8-connectivity would not create a plane graph.

2.1 Edge Classification

Consider the neighborhood graph $G(V, E)$ of a binary image P where the vertices V correspond to the pixels P and the edges E connect two vertices if the corresponding pixels are 4-neighbors. Let the gray-value of vertex $g(v) = g(p)$ where $p \in P$ is a pixel in image corresponding to vertex v. Let $contrast(e)$ be an attribute of an edge $e(u, v)$ where $u, v \in V$ and $contrast(e) = |g(u) - g(v)|$. Since we are working with binary images, the pixels (and corresponding vertices can) have only two gray values 0 and 1. Similarly the edge contrast can have only two possible values 0 and 1. The edges in the neighborhood graph can be classified into the following two categories:

Definition 2 (Zero-edge) *An edge is a zero-edge iff the contrast between its two endpoints is zero. The zero-edge is denoted by* e_0.

Definition 3 (One-edge) *An edge is a one-edge iff the contrast between its two endpoints is one. The one-edge is denoted by* e_1.

The set of edges classified as zero-edge is denoted as E_0 and the set of edges classified as one-edge is denoted as E_1. The edge set $E = E_0 \cup E_1$.

A connected component consists of E_0 and E_1 connects different CCs together. Thus, the proposed algorithm for doing the labeling task, only considers E_0 as the candidates of the selection of the CK. Figure 2 shows a binary image with its corresponding neighborhood graph. Edges E_0 are black while E_1 are red.

2.2 Selecting the Contraction Kernel

The way a CK is selected has a main role in detecting the redundant edges in the neighborhood graph. To this purpose, a total order defined over the indices of vertices. Consider the binary image has M rows and N columns such that $(1, 1)$ is the coordinate of the pixel at the upper-left corner and (M, N) at the lower-right corner. An index $Idx(.,.)$ of each vertex is defined:

$$Idx : [1, M] \times [1, N] \mapsto [1, M \cdot N] \subset \mathbb{N} \tag{1}$$

$$Idx(r, c) = (c - 1) \cdot M + r \tag{2}$$

where r and c are the row and column of the pixel(v), respectively. Since the set of integers is totally ordered each vertex has a unique index. The important property of such totally ordered set is that every subset has exactly one minimum and one maximum member (integer number). This property provides a unique orientation between non-surviving and surviving vertices. Consider a non-surviving vertex v. In order to find the surviving vertex, v_s, an incident

e_0 must be found in its neighborhood. Such a neighborhood $\mathcal{N}(v)$ is defined as follows [1]:

$$\mathcal{N}(v) = \{v\} \cup \{w \in V | e_0 = (v, w) \in E_0\} \tag{3}$$

if such neighborhood exists ($|\mathcal{N}(v)| > 1$) the surviving vertex is:

$$v_s = \text{argmax}\{Idx(v_s)| \ v_s \in \mathcal{N}(v), |\mathcal{N}(v)| > 1\} \tag{4}$$

Definition 4 (Orientation of a e_0). *A $e_0 = (v, w) \in E_0$ is oriented from v to w if w has the largest index among the neighbors, $Idx(w) = \max\{Idx(u)|u \in \mathcal{N}(v)\}$. All edges to the other neighbors remain non-oriented.*

Based on the definition above, a chain of oriented edges connects each non-surviving vertex to its corresponding survivor vertex. In Fig. 2 the oriented edges are represented by an arrow over each e_0. The surviving vertices (4, 12, 15), are presented by a green circle around each one.

In this paper, vertices surrounded by only $e_1 \in E_1$ are ***isolated vertices***. The isolated vertices will not be contracted through the construction process and they survive until the top of the pyramid. In the Fig. 2 the isolated vertices are 10 and 16 indicated by a blue circle.

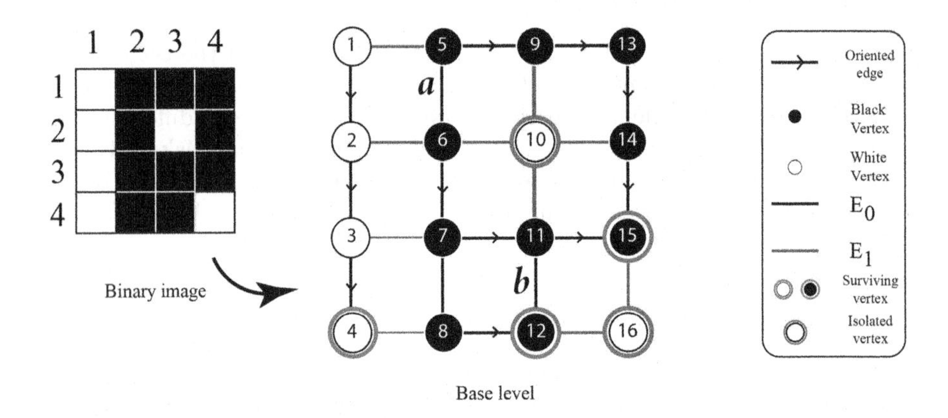

Fig. 2. The neighborhood graph of a 4 by 4 binary image.

2.3 Redundant Edges

In [1], redundant edges are investigated in details. To construct the irregular pyramid based on the RtC algorithm, first, the redundant edges are defined.

Definition 5 (Redundant-Edge (RE)). *In an empty face, the non-oriented edge incident to the vertex with lowest Idx is redundant iff:*

- *The empty face is bounded by only non-oriented edges with the same contrast value.*

– *The empty face is bounded by non-oriented edges with the same contrast value and oriented edges.*

Proposition 1. *The upper bound of the maximum number of redundant edges (REs) is equal to half of the edges of the grid at base level.*

Proof. Can be found in [1]. □

Since edges classify into E_0 and E_1, the Redundant Edges (REs) are partitioned into *Redundant Zero-Edges* (RE_0) and *Redundant One-Edges* (RE_1) as well:

$$RE = RE_0 \dot{\cup} RE_1 \tag{5}$$

Removing RE and contracting the selected CKs at the base level, result in building the first level of the pyramid. To build the upper levels, the CKs are selected and then are contracted until there is no edge remaining for contraction. At this point, the pyramid reaches to its top level and the RtC algorithm is terminated.

In Fig. 3, different levels of the pyramid are shown. At the base level, the RE_0 is shown by a black dashed-line and the RE_1 are shown by red dashed-lines. Furthermore, the Region Adjacency Graph (RAG) of the middle and top level are illustrated. The RAG at top of the pyramid represents the connections between four different connected components. Using the combinatorial map structure, the **inclusion** relation is preserved as it is represented by the loop **a** around the vertex 10. Additionally, the structure preserves the **multiple boundaries** as it is shown by two different edges between vertices 4 and 15 with different paths of vertices (4-3-2-1-5-9-13-14-15 and 4-8-12-11-15) from the base level.

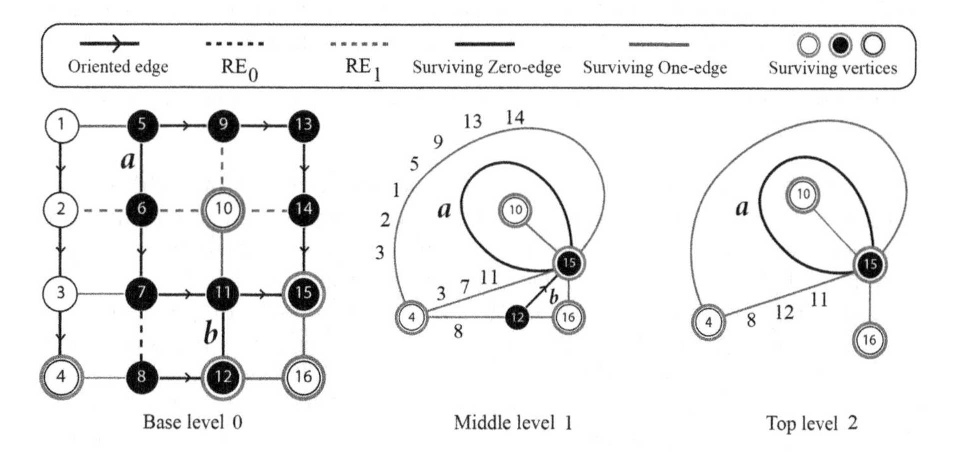

Fig. 3. Binary irregular pyramid. (Color figure online)

2.4 Parallel Pyramidal Connected Component (//ACC)

The goal of connected component labeling is to assign a unique label to the vertices of a CC at the base level. Given a binary image as an input, first the corresponding pyramid is built by the RtC. At the top of the constructed pyramid, the RAG presents connected components (CCs) and the connectivity relations. Each CC is represented by one surviving vertex. The range of vertices between 1 to $M.N$ is kept. For each vertex a label as a new attribute is initialized. A surviving vertex at the top uses its index Idx as its unique label. To propagate down, each non-surviving vertex below the top level checks its parent and fills the label with the label of the parent. By reaching to the base level all the vertices receive their labels and the labeling task is finished. Since the CCL task is performed using the pyramid structure and in parallel, we call it **P**arallel **P**yramidal **C**onnected **C**omponent (//**ACC**).

3 Parallel Complexity

In this section the parallel complexity of the proposed //ACC algorithm is investigated. Whenever we talk about complexity, it is always assumed parallel complexity. The size of the binary input image is $M \times N$. Therefore, the indices of the vertices and the neighborhood relations of the edges are known. Note that such indexing is available *before* constructing the pyramid and in off-line processes. The edge classification and selection of the CKs are both performed locally over a vertex and its neighborhoods and therefore in parallel.

To remove the redundant edges (RE), a dependency between edges is considered. We define such dependency relation to detect a set of redundant edges where by simultaneously removing, the combinatorial structure is not harmed. Therefore, first a set of dependent darts is defined as follows:

Definition 6 (Dependent Darts). *All darts of a σ-orbit sharing an endpoint are dependent darts.*

Afterwards, by using the corresponding edge of each dart, $e = (d, \alpha(d))$, the set of dependent darts leads to the set of **dependent edges**. As a consequence, two edges not sharing an endpoint are independent. In this way, the only case of the dependency between RE occurs when the RE share an endpoint.

In the grid at the base level the RE may be horizontally or vertically connected and therefore are not independent. However, consider a horizontal edge in an odd row of the grid. This edge is independent to all other horizontal edges of other odd rows. Similarly, a vertical edge in an odd column is independent to all other vertical edges of other odd columns. Such independency occurs between edges in even rows and even columns as well. Figure 4.a , represents the set of independent edges at the base. Thus, all the edges in grid are classified into four independent set of edges.

As a result, removing all edge belong to each independent set (1, 2, 3 or 4), occurs simultaneously. This means, all the RE are removed in only four steps where each step has the complexity $\mathcal{O}(1)$. Therefore removing the redundant edges is performed in parallel.

The disjoint sub-trees of a CK do not share any edges and therefore their contractions are performed in parallel. The challenging task is how to contract edges inside a tree of a CK in parallel? To this aim, we introduce two methods, one only for the base and the other for the remaining levels of the pyramid.

Contractions at the Base Level: Note that the diameter of a CK is the length of the largest path in the CK.

Proposition 2. *The complexity of contracting a CK has a logarithmic bound as follow:*

$$log_2(\delta(CK)) \leq complexity \quad of \quad contracting \quad a \quad CK \leq log_3(\delta(CK)) \quad (6)$$

where the $\delta(CK)$ *is the diameter of the CK of the largest connected component in the image.*

Proof. Based on (4), the maximum diameter of an oriented sub-tree graph corresponding to a $M \times N$ image is equal to $M + N - 1$. We consider a line sequence of edges with its length equal to this diameter. Next, the numbers from 0 to $M + N - 2$ are assigned to the vertices of the line sequence. By choosing the survivor vertices at $3n+1$ ($n \in \{0, 1, 2, [(M+N-2)/3]\}$), adjacent non-survivors ($3n$ and $3n + 2$) are contracted to this survivor (Fig. 4.b). Since each survivor belongs to a CK with the diameter at most 2, a line sequence consists of $3k$ vertices where $k \in \{1, 2, 3, ...\}$, needs only $log_3(3k)$ steps to select the survivors. The worst case occurs when the length of the line sequence is 4 and therefore, two steps ($log_2(4)$) are required for selecting the survivors. □

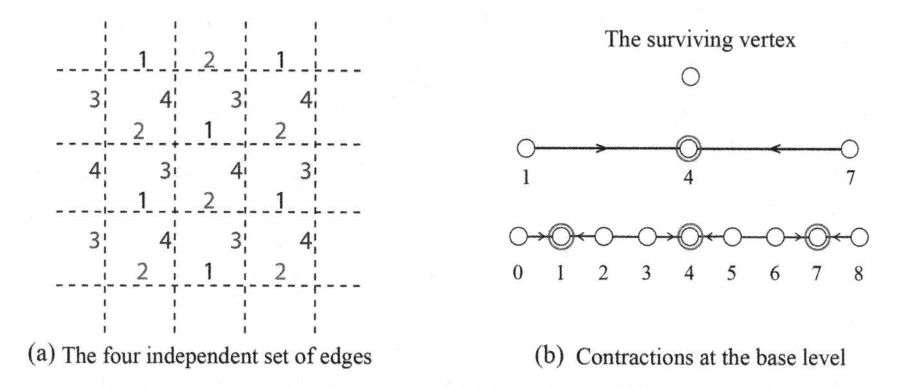

Fig. 4. Independent edge sets [1], and contractions at the base

Contractions at Upper Levels: Based on (4), all remaining non-oriented E_0 are vertical edges at the base level (Fig. 5.b). The E_0 of two different CCs are disjointed and therefore they are independent. The E_0 of a CC may have at the worst case the $N-1$ vertical non-oriented edges in the neighborhood graph of the M by N binary image (CC1 in Fig. 5.b). These non-oriented edges receives their orientations at the next level ($L=1$) through the procedure of selecting the CKs and create a line of oriented edges. Such the line sequence of oriented E_0 are contracted in $\mathcal{O}(log_2(N-1))$ as visually is encoded in Fig. 5.c.

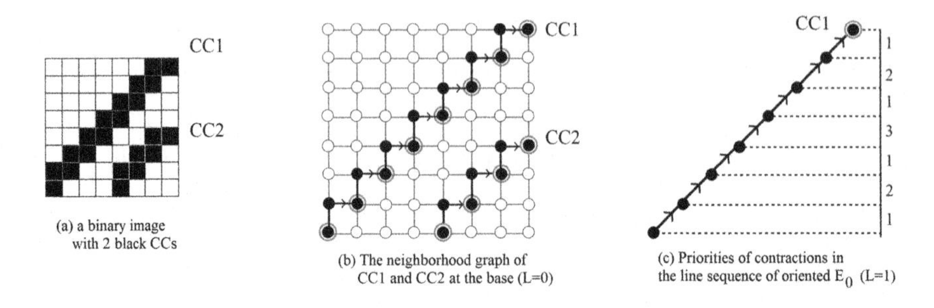

Fig. 5. Priorities of contractions at level 1

4 Comparisons and Results

Simulations use MATLAB software and execute over CPU with AMD Ryzen 7 2700X, 3.7 GHz. The YACCLAB [9] benchmark was used for evaluating the proposed algorithm. The algorithm is executed over 89 random, 128 MRI and 128 finger-print images from this benchmark. Table 1 shows the results.

Table 1. Results over images of different categories from (YACCLAB[9]).

Database type	Random images	MRI images	Finger-print images
Size of the image	128 × 128	256 × 256	300 × 300
Redundant edges (average)	27.66%	46.49%	46.05%
Redundant edges (worst case)	23.18%	44.42%	42.50%
Number of connected components	2192	691	543
Execution time (ms) (in average)	0.098	1.643	2.317
Execution time (ms) (worst case)	0.127	2.973	3.518

The average percentage of the redundant edges (RE) over each category is represented. For example in the finger-print images, about 45% of the edges are redundant while they are all removed in parallel. Moreover, the number of connected components and the average time in each category are shown. The category of Random Images consist of only small objects. It means the diameter of a CK of the largest connected component of these small objects is negligible in compare to the diameter of the image. Therefore the complexity is near to the $O(1)$. Essentially, the worst case occurs when the size of an object is as large as the whole image. In such the case, the complexity is equal to the logarithmic of the diameter of the image.

The inclusion relationship (hole) is one of the important topological information between connected components. The implementation of the proposed labeling //ACC, not only performs the labeling task, but also provides the number of inclusions between connected components. Furthermore, the simulations represent the adjacency and multi-adjacency of CCs. Such valuable topological information are missing in usual CCL algorithms. Figure 6 shows the CCL over a binary mitochondria image. The corresponding graph of the base level and categories of the edges are illustrated. The image consists of 9 connected component where the inclusion number is 7. In addition, the number of different edges for the mitochondria image are compared. The experimental results show approximately half of the edges in this image are RE.

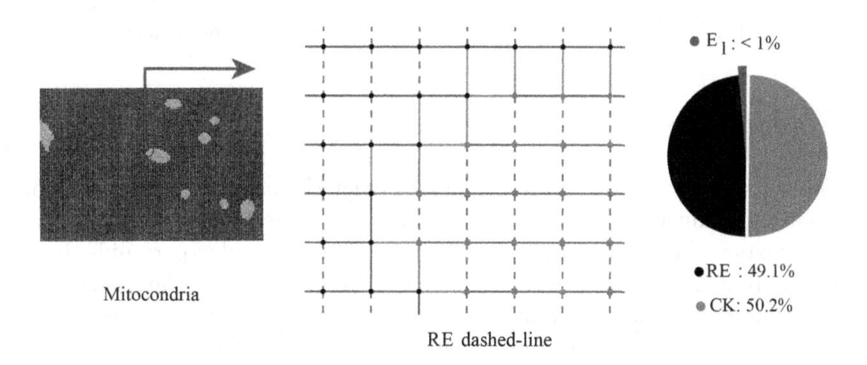

Fig. 6. A binary mitochondria image from [9]. Number of CCs is 9. The number of inclusions (holes) is 7. The RE are almost half of the edges.

Figure 7 shows the execution time of the //ACC algorithm over different image-sizes and compares it with the state-of-the-art methods from [5]. Although for small images the efficient algorithms in [5] are executed in higher speeds the //ACC with its logarithmic complexity reaches to the faster labeling results for big data, i.e., images larger than one million pixels.

Removing the RE not only speeds up the execution, but also decreases the memory consumption. The comparison is done with the originally proposed canonical represented [17] that also is used in [2,4,8]. In canonical representation, the minimum storage required to store the structure is equal to the number of darts i.e. twice the number of edges. By using the proposed RtC method, we eliminate the edges that are structurally redundant and consequently reduce the storage space of darts. Since the upper bound of the maximum number of RE is equal to half of the edges, the memory consumption of the proposed algorithm may decrease approximately by half.

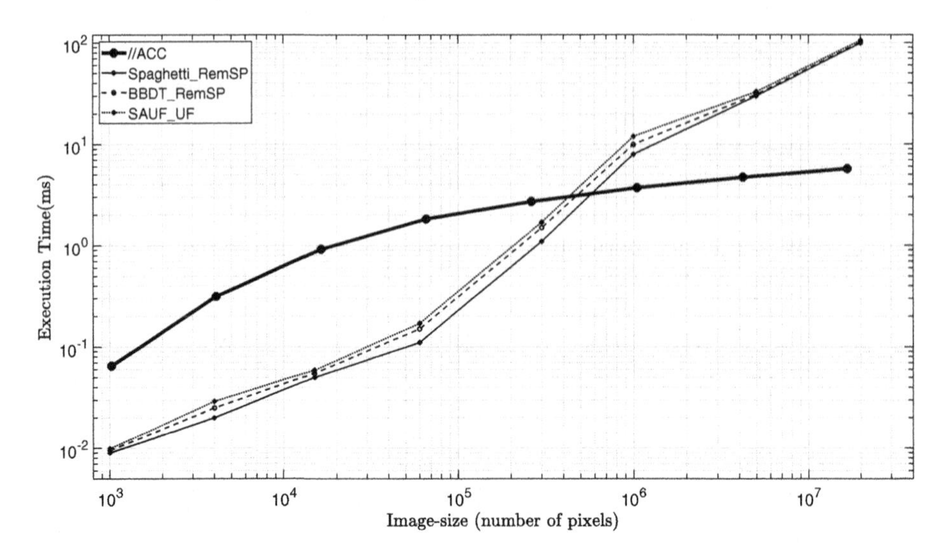

Fig. 7. Illustration of the execution time (ms) over different image-sizes

5 Conclusions

The paper presented a new approach to construct the irregular graph pyramids such that the connected component labeling can be performed in parallel and therefore faster. Unlike the usual construction of the irregular pyramids, in this paper, the redundant edges were removed in parallel *before* the contractions while they used to be removed after contractions and in a sequential order. The experimental results show that nearly half of the edges are removed as redundant edges that decreases the memory consumption to half of the combinatorial map of the base level of the pyramid. The logarithmic complexity of the algorithm speeds up the execution and suits it particularly for large images. In addition, the proposed method provides additional topological information such as inclusion and multi-boundaries. Moreover, what we proved it seems to be true for general graphs. Finally, using the combinatorial structure the proposed connected component labeling method can be extended to higher dimensions (nD) and to multi-label segmented images.

References

1. Banaeyan, M., Batavia, D., Kropatsch, W.G.: Removing redundancies in binary images. In: International Conference on Intelligent Systems and Patterns Recognition (ISPR), Hammamet, Tunisia, 24–25 March. Springer, Heidelberg (2022). (in print)
2. Banaeyan, M., Huber, H., Kropatsch, W.G., Barth, R.: A novel concept for smart camera image stitching. In: Čehovin, L., Mandeljc, R., Štruc, V. (eds.) Proceedings of the 21st Computer Vision Winter Workshop 2016, pp. 1–9 (2016)

3. Banaeyan, M., Kropatsch, W.G.: Pyramidal connected component labeling by irregular graph pyramid. In: 2021 5th International Conference on Pattern Recognition and Image Analysis (IPRIA), pp. 1–5 (2021)
4. Batavia, D., Gonzalez-Diaz, R., Kropatsch, W.G.: Image = Structure + Few colors. In: Torsello, A., Rossi, L., Pelillo, M., Biggio, B., Robles-Kelly, A. (eds.) S+SSPR 2021. LNCS, vol. 12644, pp. 365–375. Springer, Cham (2021). https://doi.org/10.1007/978-3-030-73973-7_35
5. Bolelli, F., Allegretti, S., Baraldi, L., Grana, C.: Spaghetti labeling: directed acyclic graphs for block-based connected components labeling. IEEE Trans. Image Process. **29**, 1999–2012 (2020)
6. Brun, L., Kropatsch, W.: Combinatorial pyramids. In: Proceedings of International Conference on Image Processing, vol. 2, pp. II-33. IEEE (2003)
7. Brun, L., Kropatsch, W.G.: Hierarchical graph encodings. In: Lézoray, O., Grady, L. (eds.) Image Processing and Analysis with Graphs: Theory and Practice, pp. 305–349. CRC Press (2012)
8. Cerman, M., Janusch, I., Gonzalez-Diaz, R., Kropatsch, W.G.: Topology-based image segmentation using LBP pyramids. Mach. Vis. Appl. **27**(8), 1161–1174 (2016). https://doi.org/10.1007/s00138-016-0795-1
9. Grana, C., Bolelli, F., Baraldi, L., Vezzani, R.: YACCLAB - yet another connected components labeling benchmark. In: 2016 23rd International Conference on Pattern Recognition (ICPR), pp. 3109–3114. Springer, Heidelberg (2016)
10. He, L., Chao, Y., Suzuki, K.: Two efficient label-equivalence-based connected-component labeling algorithms for 3D binary images. IEEE Trans. Image Process. **20**(8), 2122–2134 (2011)
11. He, L., Ren, X., Gao, Q., Zhao, X., Yao, B., Chao, Y.: The connected-component labeling problem: a review of state-of-the-art algorithms. Pattern Recogn. **70**, 25–43 (2017)
12. Hernandez-Belmonte, U.H., Ayala-Ramirez, V., Sanchez-Yanez, R.E.: A comparative review of two-pass connected component labeling algorithms. In: Batyrshin, I., Sidorov, G. (eds.) MICAI 2011. LNCS (LNAI), vol. 7095, pp. 452–462. Springer, Heidelberg (2011). https://doi.org/10.1007/978-3-642-25330-0_40
13. Kropatsch, W.G.: Building irregular pyramids by dual graph contraction. IEE-Proc. Vis. Image Signal Process. **142**(No. 6), 366–374 (1995)
14. Kropatsch, W.G., Macho, H.: Finding the structure of connected components using dual irregular pyramids. In: Cinquième Colloque DGCI, pp. 147–158. LLAIC1, Université d'Auvergne, ISBN 2-87663-040-0 (1995)
15. Qin, H., El Yacoubi, M.A.: End-to-end generative adversarial network for palm-vein recognition. In: Lu, Y., Vincent, N., Yuen, P.C., Zheng, W.-S., Cheriet, F., Suen, C.Y. (eds.) ICPRAI 2020. LNCS, vol. 12068, pp. 714–724. Springer, Cham (2020). https://doi.org/10.1007/978-3-030-59830-3_62
16. Shapiro, L.G.: Connected component labeling and adjacency graph construction. Mach. Intell. Pattern Recogn. **19**, 1–30 (1996)
17. Torres, F., Kropatsch, W.G.: Canonical encoding of the combinatorial pyramid. In: Proceedings of the 19th Computer Vision Winter Workshop, pp. 118–125 (2014)
18. Trudeau, R.: Introduction to Graph Theory. Dover Books on Mathematics (1993)

Encoding Sensors' Data into Images to Improve the Activity Recognition in Post Stroke Rehabilitation Assessment

Issam Boukhennoufa[1](✉), Xiaojun Zhai[1], Victor Utti[2], Jo Jackson[2], and Klaus D. McDonald-Maier[1]

[1] School of Computer Science and Electronic Engineering, University of Essex, Colchester, UK
ib20472@essex.ac.uk

[2] School of Sport, Rehabilitation and Exercise Sciences, University of Essex, Colchester, UK

Abstract. It is of vital importance to accurately monitor post-stroke and one common way is to use wearable sensors to collect data and apply Convolutional Neural Networks (CNNs) to process it. In this paper a pipeline for TS classification is evaluated on a complex dataset which comprises 18 different ADLs collected from inertial measurement units sensors. The pipeline involves imaging the segmented TS data by employing three encoding techniques namely: Gramian Summation Angular Fields (GASF), Gramian Difference Angular Fields (GADF) and Markov Transition Fields (MKV). These encoding techniques were originally designed for univariate time-series, one contribution of this work is to propose a way to adapt it to multivariate TS by imaging each axis of the sensors separately and fusing them together to create multi-channel images. Another limitation comes from the fact that the resulting image size equals the sequence length of the original TS, we tackle this by employing a linear interpolation on the TS sequence to increase or decrease it. A comparison of the performance accuracy with respect to the employed encoding technique and the image size has been done. Results showed that GASF and GADF performed better than MTF encoding, besides fusing the images together and increasing the image size to a certain limit improved the accuracy from 87.5% for the state-of-the-art results to 91.5%.

Keywords: Stroke rehabilitation · Human activity recognition · CNN · Image fusion

1 Introduction

Stroke is a global public health issue with around 17 million person in the world affected annually [10]. If not fatal, stroke can lead to temporary or permanent sensory-motor impairments [15] that negatively impact the execution of Activities of Daily-Living (ADLs) [17]. Consequently, almost one post-stroke survivor over two encounters limitations in ADLs [8]. The limitations resulting from these

M. El Yacoubi et al. (Eds.): ICPRAI 2022, LNCS 13364, pp. 114–123, 2022.
https://doi.org/10.1007/978-3-031-09282-4_10

impairments are of high concern among survivors and therapy professionals. Indeed, research work has shown strong correlations between the completion of ADLs, the quality of life of the patients [14] and the risk of re-hospitalisation [13]. ADLs, are the basic tasks of every-day's life involving walking, sitting down, standing up, toileting, folding clothes, practising physical exercises ... etc. [23]. They are defined as tasks that comprise dynamic spatio-temporal harmonisation of the limbs. Therefore, measurement of the ADLs is critical to acquire pertinent clinical data, making designing effective monitoring tools important for tailoring post-stroke rehabilitation [9].

In this context, Human activity recognition (HAR) offers an interesting solution towards the monitoring of ADLs. HAR is a broad field of study that aims to identify specific movement of a person based on information collected from sensors [20]. The sensor data may be remotely recorded from devices like cameras, radars and force plates or locally recorded using Wearable Sensors (WS) which are increasingly being used due to their unobtrusiveness, low cost and high portability. Numerous WS based HAR systems have been developed, some using Inertial Measurement Units (IMU) only that combine accelerometers to collect the linear acceleration and gyroscopes that collect the angular turning rates of the monitored object. Other studies interfaced IMUs with external biological sensors to acquire additional information when measuring posture or movement, like Electromyography (EMG) to measure the muscular activity, Flex sensors to measure the amount of deflection or bending while griping objects and insole pressure sensors to measure the force exercised by the feet while performing the activities [4].

The most challenging task of WS-based HAR using data in a real time scenario is to get an accurate and reliable information of the patient's activities and behaviors. To do so, many approaches have been investigated, ranging from a conventional signal processing modelling approach that seeks a mathematical relationship between an activity and the different modelling parameters, to Machine Learning (ML) algorithms, that extract pertinent features to allow the model to differentiate and recognise the different activities [1,6,7], to more recently Deep Learning (DL) algorithms that can automatically extract features and learn to distinguish between the activities [1,12,16]. Signal processing and conventional ML algorithms, require domain expertise in order to engineer relevant features while deep learning algorithms can work on raw data and requires less domain knowledge.

DL algorithms and especially Convolutional Neural Networks (CNNs) accomplished outstanding performance in the computer-vision field [18] and are starting to outperform traditional ML techniques in HAR. Inspired by these results, numerous methods have been utilised in order to take advantage of the CNN based DL models. Compared to images that are the main input structure of the CNN based computer vision models, Time Series (TS) data from WSs has a sequential time-dependent arrangement [5]. In case the data from the sensor varies only on a single axis it is known to be a univariate TS, while if it varies on multiple axes, it is known as multivariate TS. One method to have a CNN-TS classification model is to segment the TS sequential data into multiple chunks using a sliding window, and then feed these resulting chunks to a 1 Dimension (1D) Kernel CNN model. Whereas, an alternative way is to encode the TS data chucks into images, and then feed the resulting images into 2 Dimension (2D) Kernel CNN model (computer vision models).

In this paper, each individual axis of the sensors is first encoded into an image, after that the images are fused together to form multi-channel images. In case of a single tri-axial sensor, the resulting image would be 3-channel, like a RGB image. In case of two tri-axial sensors, the image would be 6-channels. The images are then fed to XResnet18 with an input shape that matches the structure of the fed images.

In addition, the resulting images' sizes from these encoding techniques are fixed by the TS sequence length limiting the image size if the chosen window is small. This is something that has been addressed in this work. A linear interpolation is applied on the original TS sequence to generate new data-points without changing the data structure. This allowed to up-sample the data and permitted to increase the accuracy further. There are other methods to increase the image size utilised in computer vision like padding zeros on the edges, but these methods do not add relevant information in a HAR context.

The paper is organised as follows, Sect. 2 describes the dataset, Sect. 3 shows the results on the 2D models and comparison of our results with other works on the same dataset. Section 4 concludes the paper.

2 Dataset Description and Preparation

In this paper the WISDM Smartphone and Smartwatch Activity and Biometrics Dataset [22] was utilised. This dataset was actualised in late 2019. It includes diverse and complex ADL and this makes it a good candidate for evaluating the algorithms. It consists of 18 activities (Table 1) performed by 51 different participants for three minutes. Two Inertial measurement unit (IMU) sensors (triaxial accelerometer and triaxial gyroscope) from a smartwatch and a smartphone were utilised respectively to collect the data. The smartwatch was mounted on the participant's dominant hand, and the smartphone placed on the waist, with each using a frequency 20 Hz. Hierarchically, the dataset is divided into two folders, phone and watch, each folder is sub-divided into two sub-folders accelerometer and gyroscope, each containing 51 files corresponding to the different participants IDs. Each file contains the following information: subject-ID, activity-code (character between 'A' and 'S' no 'N' that identifies the activity), timestamp, x, y, z sensors' readings (i.e. accelerometer or gyroscope).

Table 1 shows the different activities involved and their labels.

3 Encoding Pipeline

In this section we will discuss our proposed approach, the images of the different sensors' axis are fused together and image sizes are increased using a linear interpolation technique. The resulting images are then fed to a 2 dimension CNN based model.

Table 1. Dataset activities and their labels.

Activity orientation	Activities
Non-hand-oriented activities	Walking (A), Jogging (B), Stairs (C), Sitting (D), Standing (E), Kicking (M)
Hand-oriented activities (Eating)	Eating soup (H), Eating chips (I), Eating pasta (J), Drinking (K), Eating sandwich (L)
Hand-oriented activities (General)	Typing (F), Playing catch (O), Dribbling (P), Writing (Q), Clapping (R), Brushing teeth (G), Folding clothes (S)

3.1 Encoding Techniques

Three encoding techniques proposed by in [21] are utilised in this paper namely the Gramian Angular Summation Field (GASF), Gramian Angular Difference Field (GADF) and MKV.

GMAF. GMAF is an encoding technique that transforms TS data into images, it uses the polar coordinates representation of the data presented in a matrix-form called the Gramian matrix. Each element of this matrix is either the addition (GASF) of the cosines of the polar-angles or the difference (GADF) of their sines. This mapping maintains the temporal-dependency of the TS, the time increases as the position shifts from the top left to the bottom right. Due to this feature, the polar-coordinates can be reverted back to the original TS data by its transformation principle.

The steps to encode the TS data into images using GAF are given bellow:

- First data should be re-scaled to the range [0,1] (or [−1,1]) using the linear normalisation equation.
- After that, the data is mapped into its polar coordinates representation.
- Finally we either sum (GASF) or differentiate (GADF) the cosines or the sines respectively of the polar angles in order to build the Gramian matrix. Details are given in [2].

Markov Transition Fields. The Markov Transition Field (MKV) is given as follows:

$$M = \begin{bmatrix} w_{ij|x_1 \in q_i, x_1 \in q_j} & \cdots & w_{ij|x_1 \in q_i, x_n \in q_j} \\ w_{ij|x_2 \in q_i, x_1 \in q_j} & \cdots & w_{ij|x_2 \in q_i, x_n \in q_j} \\ \vdots & \ddots & \vdots \\ w_{ij|x_n \in q_i, x_1 \in q_j} & \cdots & w_{ij|x_n \in q_i, x_n \in q_j} \end{bmatrix} \tag{1}$$

A $Q \times Q$ Markov transition matrix (W) is built by dividing the data (magnitude) into Q quantile bins. The quantile bins that contain the data at time stamp i and j (temporal axis) are q_i and q_j ($q \in [1, Q]$). M_{ij} denotes the transition

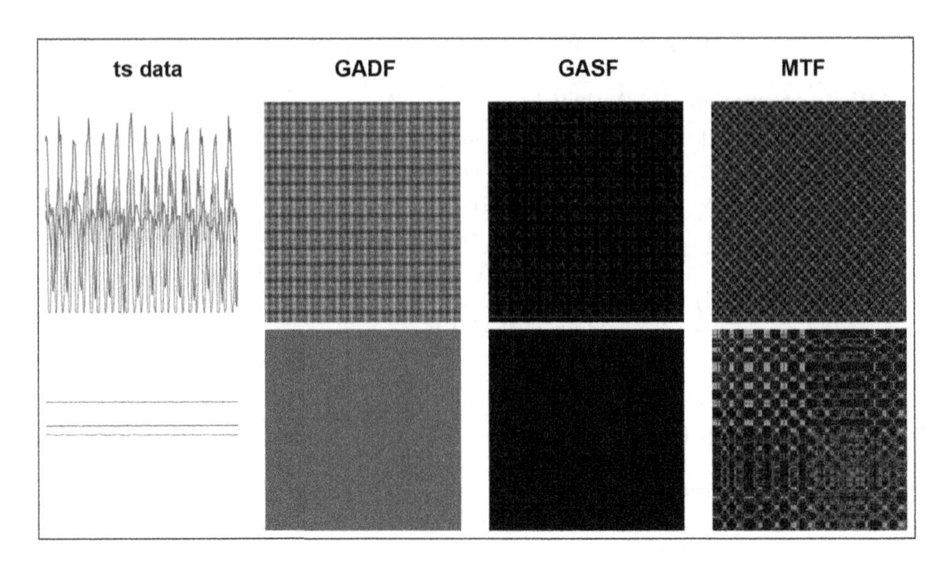

Fig. 1. The TS data from accelerometer and the different corresponding encoded images for jogging at the top and standing soup at the bottom.

probability of $q_i \rightarrow q_j$. That is, the matrix W which contains the transition probability on the magnitude axis is spread out into the MKV matrix by considering the corresponding temporal positions.

By assigning the probability from the quantile at time step i to the quantile at time step j at each pixel M_{ij}, the MKV M actually encodes the multi-span transition probabilities of the TS. $M_{i,j||i-j|=k}$ denotes the transition probability between the points with time interval k. For example, $M_{ij|j-i=1}$ illustrates the transition process along the time axis with a skip step. The main diagonal M_{ii}, which is a special case when $k = 0$ captures the probability from each quantile to itself (the self-transition probability) at time step i. To make the image size manageable and computation more efficient, The MKV size is reduced by averaging the pixels in each non-overlapping $m \times m$ patch with the blurring kernel $\{\frac{1}{m^2}\}_{m\times m}$. That is, the transition probabilities are aggregated in each sub-sequence of length m together. To the contrary to the GMAF, This mapping does not maintain the temporal-dependency of the TS.

3.2 Image Fusion and Interpolation

The TS windows are encoded into images using the previously described encoding techniques, images resulting from different axes are fused together to create multiple channel images. A linear interpolation is used before that in order to either up-sample or down-sample the images' sizes.

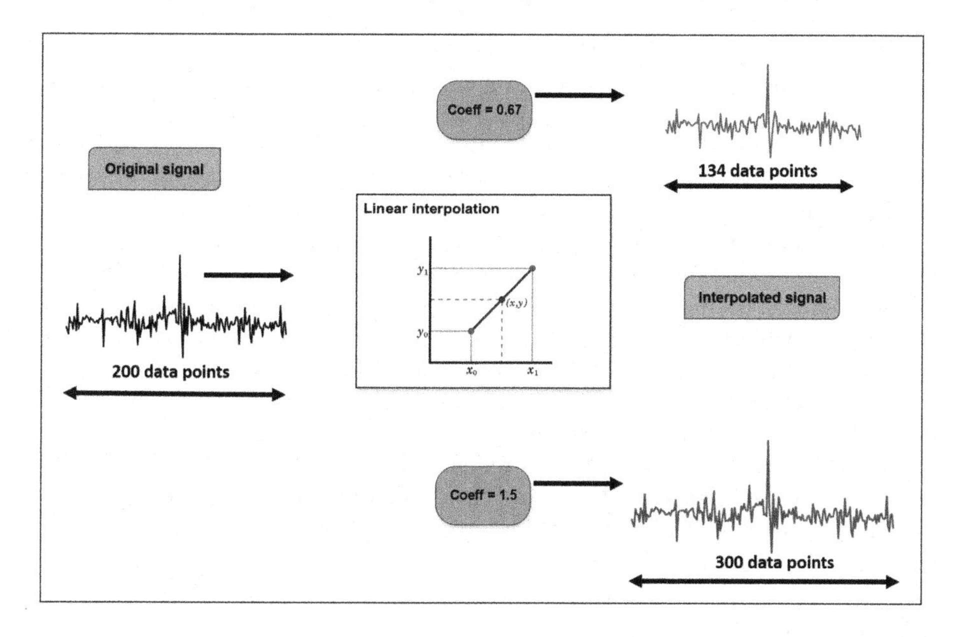

Fig. 2. Linear interpolation of Imu data.

Image Fusion. These encoding techniques described in Sect. 3.1 transform univariate TS windows into single-channel images whose size equals that of the window-length. In this work, the window size is 200, subsequently the resulting images are 200 × 200. In case of multivariate TS, as it is in this work, each sensor's axis is encoded into images. For acceleration or gyroscope only data, the three axis $(x - y - z)$ are transformed into three-channel images, meaning, the resulting images for the different axis corresponding to the same window are fused together to create three-channel images (A 3 × 200 window generates 3 × 200 × 200 images). In case of the combination of the two sensors, six-channel images are generated by fusing the images for each axis (a 6 × 200 window generates 6 × 200 × 200 images).

Figure 1 illustrates two windows of data corresponding to three axis acceleration data for jogging activity and standing activity and the corresponding GASF, GADF, MKV.

A limitation when using these three encoding techniques is that the resulting images size is set by the window length of the TS data. Sometimes changing the image size would improve classification accuracy, or speed up the training. In this work, an additional layer of pre-processing is done on the TS data to change its size before encoding it into images using linear interpolation.

Linear Interpolation. Linear interpolation is a technique to fit a curve using linear-polynomials to generate new data points within the interval of a discrete-set of already known data points. It has been used in this work to over-sample windows of data to increase the size of the windows by adding new points. Another approach would have been to increase the window size when segmenting the dataset, but that would decrease the number of the resulting windows, hence reducing the dataset size. In addition, as stated earlier, in this work the same window used in other works has been chosen in order to have an objective performance comparison.

If the two known points are given by the coordinates (x_0, y_0) and (x_1, y_1), the linear interpolation is the straight line between these points. In this work, an interpolation coefficient (Coeff) is defined, which is a parameter that controls the factor at which resulting data length (rdl) is increased from the original data length (odl): $Coeff = rdl \div odl$. For example, a coeff of 2 would yield to doubling the data points of the window. The added data points are homogeneously spread along the window in order not to affect the data distribution.

A Coeff in the range [0, 1] means reducing the window length, for example, a coeff of 0.5 would yield to decreasing the data points of the window by half.

Figure 2 describes the coeff-based interpolation used in this work before constructing the images.

3.3 Experimental Results

Only the data from the watch sensors are considered, data from the phone are not included because the sensor placement on the waist did not capture relevant information for hand oriented activities, thus yielding to a bad classification performance. The dataset has been segmented into 10 s chunks corresponding to 200 readings using non-overlapping windows. This window-length has been chosen in order to compare with the original paper results and other works that used this dataset. Every segment of data is labeled with the most recurring corresponding activity. Data are normalised and re-scaled to the range $[-1, 1]$. After that, a linear interpolation is done on the windows either to up-sample or down-sample the data-windows as described in Sect. 3.2 to see the effect of either increasing or decreasing the image size. The sizes chosen are: 50, 100, 200 (no interpolation), 300, 400, 500. After that the associated windows for each sensor are encoded using three encoding techniques described in Sect. 3.1. The resulting images for the different axes are fused together to create 3-channel images when the source is gyroscope only or accelerometer only, or 6-channel images for their combination as explained in Sect. 3.2.

The dataset is decomposed into training and validation using a 75%–25% split. Many classification models have been investigated and the Xresnet18 [11] was finally selected because it performed best without transfer learning. Xresnet is the popular Resnet [19] architectures with three different tweaks on the residual blocks. The accelerometer, gyroscope data and their combination from the watch are encoded into different sized images as explained in Sect. 3.3 and then fed to the XResnet18 model. The resulting validation accuracies are given Table 2, representing the accuracy for each encoding technique for each sensor per image size. From these results we notice numerous points:

Table 2. Accuracies per image size for the different encoding techniques

Sensor	Encoding	50	100	200	300	400	500
ACC	GADF	75.11327	82.8838	85.775	86.3878	87.4496	86.8796
	GASF	85.3897	85.5596	86.3028	88.0017	88.9573	88.1504
	MKV	38.0123	59.2483	73.2003	74.4653	76.237	75.4301
GYRO	GADF	69.473	78.3815	82.9524	84.2814	86.1418	85.3349
	GASF	70.0093	78.6847	**82.416**	**86.1473**	86.3003	85.4934
	MKV	50.1435	62.1398	69.0065	73.6358	77.1659	76.359
Watch	GADF	77.8624	83.9086	86.646	87.9552	88.4551	87.6482
	GASF	82.6232	84.5275	**89.0502**	**91.4544**	88.3361	87.5292
	MKV	49.0597	70.7451	78.6479	81.6234	82.421	81.6141

- Fusing the images significantly increased accuracy to 91.5% for the combined sensors, GASF encoding 300 image size.
- The GASF is the best performing encoding technique, it performs slightly better than GADF for all the sensors and sizes.
- MKV is the worst performing encoding, it performs worse than all the models.
- Up-sample Interpolation of the data increased the classification accuracy for almost all the models until a $Coeff \approx 2$ e.g. It increased the accuracy for the GASF-200-watch from 89.1% to 91.5% for GASF-300-watch, and 82.9% for the GADF-200-gyro to 86.1% for GADF-400-gyro.
- Increasing Coeff further than 2, led the performance accuracy to decrease in all models.
- Down-sample interpolation improves the accuracy from the TS models in [3] from for some models, a Coeff of 0.5 performed better for example in the GASF-100-ACC, GADF-100-watch, and GASF-100-watch. Only a single model with a Coeff of 0.25, i.e. the GASF-50-ACC performed better than the TS model. Down-sample interpolation can be useful, when a performance accuracy improvement is sought, and keeping also a balance with the computation complexity.
- 6-channel images resulting from fusing all the sensors performed better than the 3-channel images from the individual sensors.

4 Conclusion

In this paper we surveyed the segmented TS data were transformed into images using three different encoding techniques namely GASF, GADF and MKV. Images resulting from the different axes of the sensors were fused together to create multiple channels images. To increase the images' sizes, a linear interpolation is performed on the data windows to generate new data points. These different encoding techniques, and different images' sizes are compared to find the optimal performing configuration and see how these different parameters affect the classification performance. Increasing the images sizes using the linear interpolation increases the classification accuracy up to a factor of 2, after that the performance decreases. In addition, decreasing the image sizes from the original window length improves the accuracy of the performance when compared with TS models, this can give balance between a good performance and computation complexity. Besides, fusing images improves the accuracy from 83% for the 1D models to 91.5% in case of GASF encoding and 300 size images. MKV encoding does not perform very well when compared with other encoding techniques.

Acknowledgements. This work is supported by the UK Engineering and Physical Sciences Research Council (EPSRC) through grants EP/R02572X/1, EP/P017487/1, EP/V000462/1, EP/X52590X/1 and EP/V034111/1.

References

1. Bobin, M., Amroun, H., Boukalle, M., Anastassova, M., Ammi, M.: Smart cup to monitor stroke patients activities during everyday life. In: 2018 IEEE International Conference on Internet of Things (iThings) and IEEE Green Computing and Communications (GreenCom) and IEEE Cyber, Physical and Social Computing (CPSCom) and IEEE Smart Data (SmartData), pp. 189–195. IEEE (2018)
2. Boukhennoufa, I., Zhai, X., McDonald-Maier, K.D., Utti, V., Jackson, J.: Improving the activity recognition using GMAF and transfer learning in post-stroke rehabilitation assessment. In: 2021 IEEE 19th World Symposium on Applied Machine Intelligence and Informatics (SAMI), pp. 000391–000398. IEEE (2021)
3. Boukhennoufa, I., Zhai, X., Utti, V., Jackson, J., McDonald-Maier, K.D.: A comprehensive evaluation of state-of-the-art time-series deep learning models for activity-recognition in post-stroke rehabilitation assessment. In: 2021 43rd Annual International Conference of the IEEE Engineering in Medicine & Biology Society (EMBC), pp. 2242–2247. IEEE (2021)
4. Boukhennoufa, I., Zhai, X., Utti, V., Jackson, J., McDonald-Maier, K.D.: Wearable sensors and machine learning in post-stroke rehabilitation assessment: A systematic review. Biomedical Signal Processing and Control 71, 103197 (2022)
5. Brillinger, D.R.: Time Series: Data Analysis and Theory. SIAM (2001)
6. Capela, N.A., Lemaire, E.D., Baddour, N.: Feature selection for wearable smartphone-based human activity recognition with able bodied, elderly, and stroke patients. PLoS ONE **10**(4), e0124414 (2015)
7. Chaeibakhsh, S., Phillips, E., Buchanan, A., Wade, E.: Upper extremity post-stroke motion quality estimation with decision trees and bagging forests. In: 2016 38th Annual International Conference of the IEEE Engineering in Medicine and Biology Society (EMBC), pp. 4585–4588. IEEE (2016)
8. Crichton, S.L., Bray, B.D., McKevitt, C., Rudd, A.G., Wolfe, C.D.: Patient outcomes up to 15 years after stroke: survival, disability, quality of life, cognition and mental health. J. Neurol. Neurosurg. Psychiatry **87**(10), 1091–1098 (2016)
9. Centers for Disease Control and Prevention: Outpatient rehabilitation among stroke survivors-21 states and the district of Columbia, 2005. MMWR Morb. Mortal Wkly Rep. **56**(20), 504–507 (2007)
10. Feigin, V.L., et al.: Global and regional burden of stroke during 1990–2010: findings from the global burden of disease study 2010. Lancet **383**(9913), 245–255 (2014)

11. He, T., Zhang, Z., Zhang, H., Zhang, Z., Xie, J., Li, M.: Bag of tricks for image classification with convolutional neural networks. In: Proceedings of the IEEE/CVF Conference on Computer Vision and Pattern Recognition, pp. 558–567 (2019)
12. Kaku, A., Parnandi, A., Venkatesan, A., Pandit, N., Schambra, H., Fernandez-Granda, C.: Towards data-driven stroke rehabilitation via wearable sensors and deep learning. arXiv preprint arXiv:2004.08297 (2020)
13. Mast, B.T., Azar, A.R., MacNeill, S.E., Lichtenberg, P.A.: Depression and activities of daily living predict rehospitalization within 6 months of discharge from geriatric rehabilitation. Rehabil. Psychol. **49**(3), 219 (2004)
14. Mayo, N.E., Wood-Dauphinee, S., Côte, R., Durcan, L., Carlton, J.: Activity, participation, and quality of life 6 months poststroke. Arch. Phys. Med. Rehabil. **83**(8), 1035–1042 (2002)
15. Pound, P., Gompertz, P., Ebrahim, S.: Illness in the context of older age: the case of stroke. Sociol. Health Illn. **20**(4), 489–506 (1998)
16. Quinn, T.J., Langhorne, P., Stott, D.J.: Barthel index for stroke trials: development, properties, and application. Stroke **42**(4), 1146–1151 (2011)
17. Shamay, N.S., William, T.W., Patrick, K.W., Philip, T.T., Jefferry, W.C.: Sensorimotor impairments of paretic upper limb correlates with activities of daily living in subjects with chronic stroke. S. Afr. J. Physiother. **67**(1), 9–16 (2011)
18. Simonyan, K., Zisserman, A.: Very deep convolutional networks for large-scale image recognition. arXiv preprint arXiv:1409.1556 (2014)
19. Szegedy, C., Ioffe, S., Vanhoucke, V., Alemi, A.: Inception-v4, inception-ResNet and the impact of residual connections on learning. In: Proceedings of the AAAI Conference on Artificial Intelligence, vol. 31 (2017)
20. Vrigkas, M., Nikou, C., Kakadiaris, I.A.: A review of human activity recognition methods. Front. Robot. AI **2**, 28 (2015)
21. Wang, Z., Oates, T.: Encoding time series as images for visual inspection and classification using tiled convolutional neural networks. In: Workshops at the Twenty-Ninth AAAI Conference on Artificial Intelligence, vol. 1 (2015)
22. Weiss, G.M.: WISDM smartphone and smartwatch activity and biometrics dataset. UCI Machine Learning Repository (2019)
23. Wiener, J.M., Hanley, R.J., Clark, R., Van Nostrand, J.F.: Measuring the activities of daily living: Comparisons across national surveys. J. Gerontol. **45**(6), S229–S237 (1990)

Momentum Residual Embedding with Angular Marginal Loss for Plant Pathogen Biometrics

Shitala Prasad[1(✉)], Pankaj Pratap Singh[2], and Piyush Kumar[3]

[1] Visual Intelligence, I2R, A*Star, Singapore, Singapore
shitala@ieee.org

[2] Computer Science and Engineering, CIT Kokrajhar, Kokrajhar, India
pankajp.singh@cit.ac.in

[3] Computer Science and Engineering, NIT Patna, Patna, India
piyush.cs@nitp.ac.in

Abstract. Plant diseases are a considerable threat in the agriculture sector and therefore, early detection and diagnosis of these diseases are very essential. In this paper, we have proposed a deep learning approach for plant leaf disease detection that utilizes momentum residual neural network to optimized the learning space. Further, the feature is tuned to additive angular margin to get the prime leaf disease discriminative representation. The proposed model has been extensively trained and tested on two publicly available Tomato and PlantVillage leaf disease datasets and achieved a *top-1* accuracy of 99.51% and 97.16%, respectively. The proposed approach shows its superiority over the existing methodologies and sets a new benchmark for these two considered datasets.

Keywords: Plant leaf disease identification · Deep learning · Angular marginal embedding · ResNet · Momentum

1 Introduction

Agriculture has been of the major source of income for the majority of people in many developing countries like India. The commercialization in field of agriculture has greatly affected our environment and the agro-based companies are now coming up with several new techniques that help them to increase the yield. To list down one of the biggest concerns in the field of agriculture is the disease detection. Early stage pathogen detection not only helps in preventing the widespread of disease among other plants but also assist farmers to spray right pesticides on time [18]. This averts the substantial economic losses. The impact of plant illness ranges from mild manifestation to the destruction of complete plantations. According to the fact from FAO,[1] the estimated annually crop production loss due to pest is between 20% to 40% globally. This costs a global economy loss of around $220B and invasive insects around US$70B.

Plant enhancement and protection is a major concern and several new measures and technological improvements [18]. There are numerous emerging trends and bio-solutions for sustainable crop protection and identify crop diseases at the early stage.

[1] [Online]: http://www.fao.org/news/story/en/item/1187738/icode/.

M. El Yacoubi et al. (Eds.): ICPRAI 2022, LNCS 13364, pp. 124–136, 2022.
https://doi.org/10.1007/978-3-031-09282-4_11

If pathogens are identified earliest, precautionary measures can be taken to prevent the spread of diseases to other parts of the plant and minimize it's growth to crop field. As a best solution, visual intelligence can replace the expert botanist in future to increase the assistance level in farming because availability of experts are not always feasible. Such visual technology along with mobile computing will be the future of farming and can be the third eye of a farmer [21].

In today's digital world, deep learning (DL) is playing the major role in mimicking human's intelligence for visual information. It combines image analysis with mathematical equations for resulting in very high accuracy. DL is now applied in various fields like object detection [17,27], biometrics [6], biomedical image classification [11] and agro-field [13]. In field of agriculture, DL is mainly aimed for plant species identification and disease recognition [2,3,15]. In computer vision (CV), deep convolutional neural network (CNN) is considered as the best DL method for visual challenges. Deep CNNs such as AlexNet [14], GoogLeNet [25], ResNet [26] *etc.* are being used for the detection and classification of plant leaf pathogens.

As the basic requirement of CNN, the models are heavily depends on huge training dataset. Generally, CNN models show a great improvement in results and has high generalizability on the sufficiently large datasets. The datasets that are presently available for plant pathogens typically not enough for the diverse conditions in agriculture, which is a basic necessity for making high accuracy models. If the dataset is very tiny, the CNN models may over-fit and performs badly on real environment data. Hence, diverse data augmentation techniques are being used to enhance the dataset [1]. Thus, previous research were limited to hand-crafted features for plant leaf disease identification [16,19,24,31].

In past few years, due to DL's requirement an increase in agricultural datasets are seen and researchers started exploring CNN to obtain a exponential improvement in results. Thus, in this paper we introduced angular marginal loss in momentum residual embedding for plant leaf disease identification to accurately recognition the pathogens at the earliest stage as possible. For this a strong generalization approach is needed which in our case is resolved *via* a MomentumNet [23]. We investigated the momentum hyper-parameters in ResNet for plant pathogen diagnostic. The proposed approach set a new state-of-the-art method in two publicly available datasets: Tomato Leaf Disease[2] and PlantVillage Leaf Disease[3]. The major contribution of this paper is three fold: (1) proposed a simple yet powerful angular marginal momentum residual embedding for plant leaf disease diagnosis, (2) explored the momentum in residual space for disease identification and (3) performed an extensive experiments on public datasets and set a new state-of-th-art benchmark.

The paper is organized in the following manner: Sect. 2 contains the related work about the existing methods in field of agriculture, Sect. 3 presents the proposed methodology, which includes momentum ResNet model description and the implementation details, Sect. 4 consists of summary of datasets used in this paper, followed by the experimental setup and their results. Lastly, we conclude the paper in Sect. 5.

[2] [Online]: https://www.kaggle.com/kaustubhb999/tomatoleaf.

[3] [Online]: https://www.kaggle.com/soumiknafiul/plantvillage-dataset-labeled.

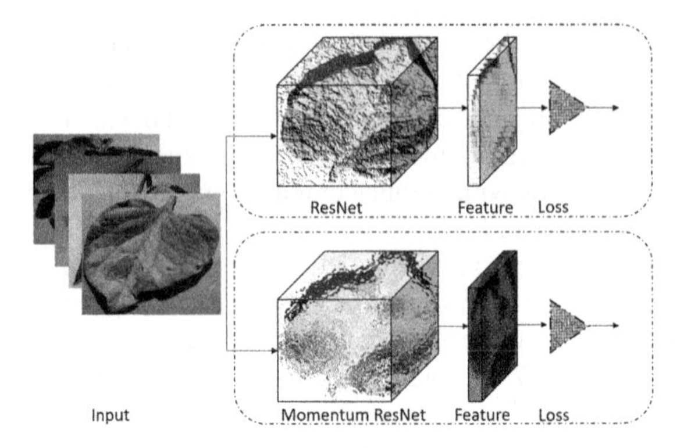

Fig. 1. The overall block diagram of the proposed method.

2 Related Work

With improvements in living standards, we increasingly having higher expectations for the quality of our daily vegetations. However, the fruits and vegetables that we consume are susceptible to diseases, insects, or improper post-harvest treatment during production, planting, storage, transportation, *etc*. This reduces both the edible and the economic values of horticultural products when damage occurs. Therefore, quality or disease detection in agricultural products is currently a challenging and hot field. In more recent studies, DL methods combined with RGB images have been widely employed as effective and non-invasive disease detection approaches to tackle practical problems such as post-harvest grading classification. Compared to traditional machine-learning approaches, DL have been applied to analyse and process image data directly and have been proven to be a better classifier.

As mentioned earlier, in agriculture plant diseases cause havoc resulting in huge economic loss and thus researchers are putting enormous efforts to check on these infections. In 2017, Prasad *et al.* used simple CNN methods to compare plant leaf species identification [20] with traditional hand-crafted methods. Akila and Deepan [4] used Faster R-CNN [22] for plant leaf disease detection and classification. Popular deep CNN models like region-based fully convolutional network (R-FCN), Single Shot Detector (SSD), You Only Look Once (YOLO) and ResNet are very common in plant disease detection and classification. Their are several data augmentation techniques like image rotations, perspective and affine transformations.

In [9], Fuentes *et al.* have proposed a disease detection system that is capable of distinguishing nine sorts of maladies and bugs in tomato plants with a mAP of 83% with VGG-16 backbone. While with ResNet-50 the same detector achieved 75.37% mAP. On the other hand, when SSD was used with ResNet-50, the mAP hit 82.53% and with R-FCN it's 85.98%. Zhang *et al.* distinguish eight types of tomato leaf illness by using a simple transfer learning concept [30]. The deep models they use were AlexNet, GoogLeNet and ResNet to achieved 97.28% accuracy on PlantVillage dataset. Elhassouny and Smarandache have proposed mobile app to classify nine different diseases of tomato by using light weight MobileNet [8]. They achieved 90.3% accuracy on

PlantVillage dataset for the disease classification. Whereas, Widiyanto *et al.* achieved 96.6% accuracy to distinguish our types of tomato leaf disease along with healthy leave [28].

In [12], Karthik *et al.* used two deep learning architectures on PlantVillage dataset to detect three diseases in tomato plants. The first model was a feed-forward residual network and the second model includes an attention mechanism along with residual net. They achieve highest accuracy of 98% with attention-based residual CNN. On contrary, Agarwal *et al.* have developed a simple three layer CNN model with two fully connected layers to detect ten types of leaves of tomato including healthy leaf to achieve an overall accuracy of 91.2% [3].

Using simple transfer learning Altuntas and Kocamaz achieved 96.99% PlantVillage dataset [5]. In [2], Abbas *et al.* have proposed a DL method for tomato leaf disease identification by utilizing conditional generative adversarial network (C-GAN) to generate synthetic leaf images. They used DenseNet-121 to train on synthetic and real plant leaf images for classification. They achieved 99.51% accuracy for five classes on publicly available PlantVillage dataset.

For further literature, you can follow Yang and Yong (2021) which reviewed several technical methods in field of horticulture [29].

3 Research Methodology

In this section, we detail the proposed methodology and the loss functions used in this paper followed by the training and implementation details. An overall block diagram of the proposed method is shown in Fig. 1.

3.1 Backbone Network

A residual neural network, in short ResNet, is a CNN architecture that helps to build deeper neural network by utilizing the key concept of skip connections or shortcuts to jump over layers [10]. This skipping helps in build deeper network layers without falling into the problem of vanishing gradients. There are different versions of ResNet which is mainly defined by the their depth. To create a residual block, we add a shortcut to the main path in the plain neural network, as shown in the Fig. 2a. Mathematically it can be represented as:

$$x_{n_1} = x_n + F(x_n) \tag{1}$$

In ResNet, we use identity block when both input and output activation dimensions are the same while convolution block is used when they are of different dimensions. That is, the residual blocks can be of two main types depending up on the input and output dimensions. Thus, it is widely used in CV tasks with promising results. As a backbone to the proposed task, we used ResNet-18 which has roughly 11 million training parameters.

In DL, back-propagation is used for optimizing deep architectures which eventually requires to store activation values of each layer during the evaluation of the network. This introduces a constrain on the amount of memory usage in respect to the depth of deep architectures. Thus, to further optimize the plant pathogen identification we used momentum ResNet, discussed in next sub-section.

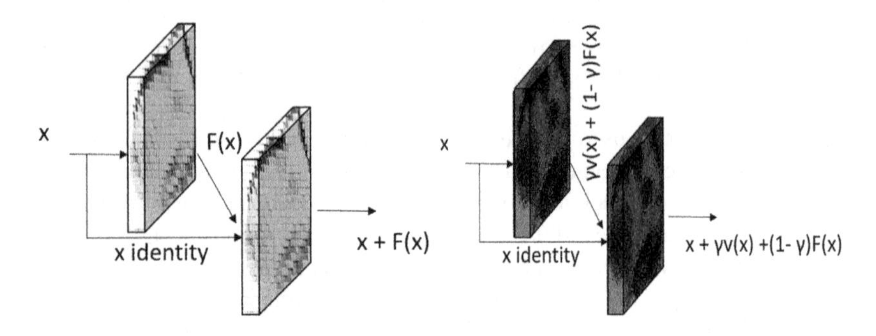

Fig. 2. The basic comparison of: (a) ResNet and (b) momentum ResNet.

3.2 Momentum

As introduced by Sander *et al.*, the momentum residual neural networks (Momentum ResNets) is a simple modification of the ResNet on forward rule [23]. This modification, without any constraint on its architecture, is perfectly invertible. The basic conceptual difference between ResNet and MomentumNet is shown in Fig. 2.

$$v_{n+1} = \gamma v_n + (1-\gamma)F(x_n) \tag{2}$$

$$x_{n_1} = x_n + v_{n+1} \tag{3}$$

where, $F(.)$ is the parametric function, v is the velocity and γ is the momentum term which ranges between zero to one.

Sarder *et al.* theoretically showed that MomentumNet are easily used in the learning to optimize setting, where other reversible models fail to converge [23]. The parameter γ controls how much a MomentumNet diverges from a standard ResNet and also the amount of memory saving. If it is closer to zero, MomemntumNet is closer to ResNets and will save less memory. Whereas, higher the momentum, the higher the memory is saved. Following the settings, in our experiments, we choose $\gamma = 0.9$ which is also the best performer in our use case (see the experiment section).

3.3 Loss Function

Inspired by ArcFace performance in face recognition [7], we adopted it for our plant pathogen diagnosis too. An additive angular margin loss designed on the *softmax* loss is used in this paper. It actually adds a margin penalty m between I_i and Wyi based on the feature and weight normalization. This simultaneously enhances the intra-class compactness and inter-class discrepancy [7].

$$\mathcal{L} = -\frac{1}{N}\sum_{i=1}^{N}\log\frac{e^{s(cos(\theta_{y_i}+m))}}{e^{s(cos(\theta_{y_i}+m))}+\sum_{j=1,j\neq y_i}^{n}e^{cos(\theta_j)}} \tag{4}$$

where N is the number of data samples and y_i is the output corresponding to i-th sample. For additional elaboration, refer ArcFace by Deng *et al.* [7].

For leaf disease recognition, we used cross-entropy loss $\mathcal{L}$ which is defined as:

$$\mathcal{L}(p_i) = -\log p_i \tag{5}$$

where, p_i is the probability computed using *softmax* and i is the class.

3.4 Training and Implementation

All the experiments were conducted in PyTorch[4] and used a standard Adam optimizer with learning rate $\Lambda = 0.001$, batch size, $b = 64$ and weight decay $w = 0.0005$. The input image size is set to 224 for all the experiments. The 20% of training set was used for validation while training. The network is trained for 10 epochs to learning pathogens pattern, see the details in next Section. Note, each experiments were performed three times and then the results are averaged.

4 Experimental Results

In this section, we evaluate the proposed approach on two publicly plant leaf disease datasets for recognition and perform rigorous experiments to validate our hypothesis on different state-of-the-art methods.

4.1 Datasets Description

In this paper we considered two different types of plant leaf datasets for our experiments: (1) Tomato leaf disease and (2) PlantVillage leaf disease. The sample images from these two datasets are shown in Fig. 3.

Tomato Leaf Disease Dataset. This dataset consists of nine different tomato leaf diseases and one healthy class. In total this dataset has ten classes with 1000 each for training and 100 for testing. The diseases it includes are: Tomato mosaic virus, Target Spot, Bacterial spot, Tomato Yellow Leaf Curl Virus, Late blight, Leaf Mold, Early blight, Spidermites Two-spotted spider mite, Tomato healthy and Septoria leaf spot. The resolution is 256×256 for all images in the dataset.

PalntVillage Leaf Disease Dataset. This dataset is a recreated of the original, downloaded from Kaggel. It includes five plant species with healthy and diseased leaf images. The species that are consideration in this dataset are apple (scab, black rot, rust and healthy), corn (cercospora leaf spot, common rust, healthy and northern leaf blight), grape (black rot, esca black measles, healthy and leaf blight), potato (early blight and late blight) and tomato (bacterial spot, late blight, septoria leaf spot, target spot and mosaic virus) which in total contains 31,397 images. In total we have 25 classes in this dataset among which 20 are diseased and five are healthy leaves. Each class have at least 100 images to train and 126 images for testing. The resolution of PlantVillage dataset is also 256×256.

[4] PyTorch [online]: https://pytorch.org/.

Fig. 3. Samples images (row-wise): (a) Tomato leaf diseases and (b) PlantVillage leaf diseases.

Table 1. Comparison with state-of-the-art methods in Tomato leaf disease dataset. *Results are quoted from [2], – means results are not reported by the authors and **is from Kaggle.

Methods	Accuracy (%)		#Parameters
	Top-1	*Top-2*	
DenseNet121 [2]	94.34	–	7.2M
DenseNet121 + Synthetic images [2]	<u>97.11</u>	–	7.2M
VGG19* [2]	89.60	–	144M
ResNet-50* [2]	76.90	–	23.9M
MobileNet* [2]	91.90	–	3.4M
DenseNet-201 [2]	93.71	–	≈20M
EfficientNet-B4**	95.23	–	17.9M
ResNet-18 *our*	97.85	99.90	11.4M
Momentum ResNet-18 *our*	**99.51**	**100**	11.4M

Table 2. Comparison with state-of-the-art methods on PlantVillage leaf disease dataset. *Results are quoted from the paper and – means results are not reported.

Methods	Accuracy %)		#Parameters
	Top-1	*Top-2*	
MobileNet* [3]	63.75	–	3.4M
VGG16* [3]	77.20	–	138M
InceptionV3* [3]	63.40	–	23.9M
ToLeD* [3]	<u>91.2</u>	–	≈2M
ResNet-18 *our*	96.38	100	11.4M
Momentum ResNet-18 *our*	**97.41**	**100**	11.4M

4.2 Results and Comparison

As discussed in previous sections, we used two different types of datasets for our experiments and compare it with the state-of-the-art methods. Table 1 shows a detailed comparison on Tomato leaf disease dataset and is observed that the proposed angular marginal loss in momentum ResNet embedding outperforms the state-of-the-art methods by a margin of 2.4% in *top-1* accuracy. The methods reported in [2], are all deep models and the second best performer is the DenseNet-121 which achieves 97.11% accuracy when trained with synthetic dataset. This increase in training dataset increases the overall training cost compared to our proposed approach. An author from Kaggle also used EfficientNet-b4 for disease identification and achieved 95.23% top accuracy.[5] The proposed angular marginal feature in momentum residual embedding optimizes the leaf pathogen representation and discriminate them with high accuracy (Table 1).

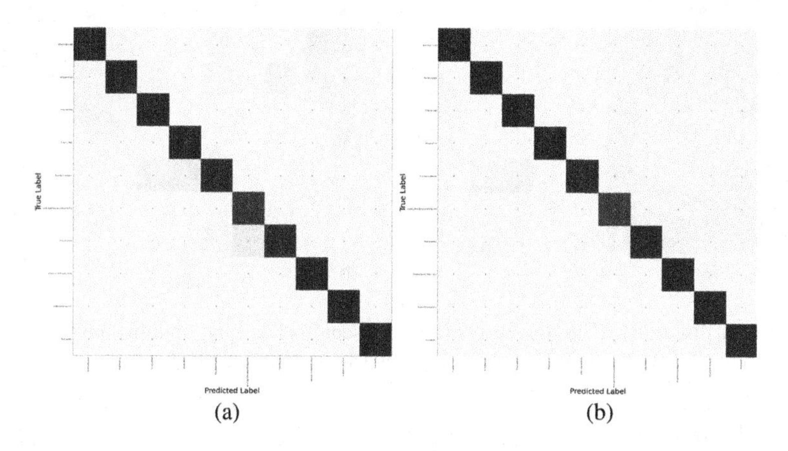

Fig. 4. Confusion matrix for Tomato leaf dataset: (a) ResNet-18, (b) momentum ResNet-18. Zoom to 400% for better visualization.

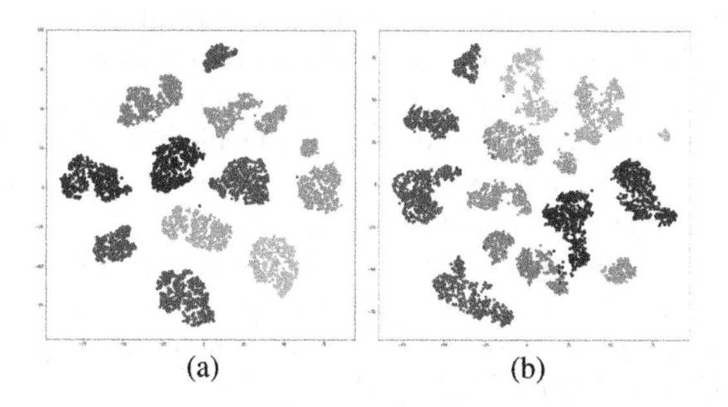

Fig. 5. Embedding space for Tomato leaf dataset: (a) momentum ResNet-18 and (b) ResNet-18. Zoom to 400% for better visualization.

[5] [Online]:https://www.kaggle.com/balasubramaniamv/tomato-leaf-efficient-net-b4.

Table 2 shows comparison on the second considered dataset where the proposed approach reached 97.41% with momentum ResNet-18 backbone. On contrary, the second best result with ResNet-18, we achieved 96.38% *top-1* accuracy and 100% *top-2* accuracy. As state-of-the-art method, ToLeD [3] accomplished 91.20% accuracy which is 6.21% lower than our proposed method. The best results are shown in bold in Tables 1 and 2.

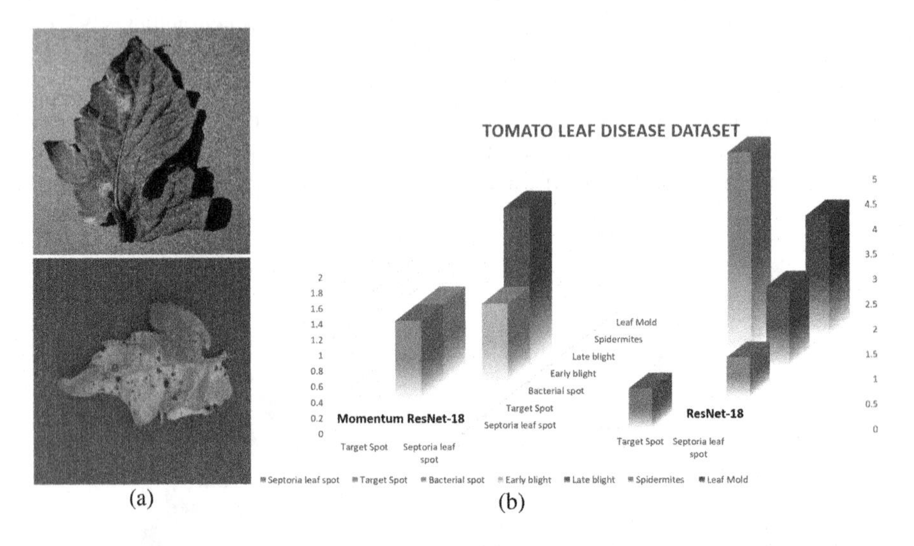

Fig. 6. Tomato diseased leaf: (a) target spot (top) and septoria leaf spot (bottom) and (b) confusion distribution for ResNet-18 and momentum ResNet-18. Zoom to see the details.

4.3 Qualitative Analysis

Other than the quantitative analysis of the proposed method, we also performed qualitatively analysed on our outputs. Figure 4 shows a confusion matrix for backbone ResNet-18 and momentum ResNet-18 for Tomato leaf disease dataset. According to these confusion matrices, the proposed model is additionally confident and is confused only with tomato's target sport and leaf spot (Fig. 6). Therefore, we explore the detail of these two diseases and Fig. 6b shows the exact number of miss-match distribution. Further, we show another qualitative analysis for incorrect predictions of Tomato leaf diseases in Fig. 7. There are total 22 disease samples that are miss-diagnosed using ResNet-18 backbone while only 5 in case of momentum ResNet-18.

Further, the embedding space for Tomato leaf dataset are shown in Fig. 5 to clearly discriminate different classes in momentum ResNet-18 (Fig. 5a) and ResNet-18 (Fig. 5b). As we see, the inter-class distance in momentum ResNet-18 is much higher and easily separable compared to ResNet-18.

4.4 Ablation Study

To pool a better understanding of modules in the proposed approach for plant leaf disease diagnosis, we conduct capacious ablation experiments to examine the role of momentum ResNet. As illustrated in Table 3, we evaluate the performance of several training settings on the Tomato leaf disease dataset with ResNet-18 backbone. By applying the momentum ResNet-18 with pre-trained model, we set up a strong benchmark of 99.51% *top-1* accuracy, which is significantly better than ResNet-181 without momentum (97.85%) and without pre-trained (97.25%). There is a clear 1.66% improvement by simply adding a momentum concept to the existing network without any additional computational cost. In comparison to these, the baseline model, *i.e.*, ResNet-18 without angular margin, momentum and pre-trained weights, it achieves *top-1* accuracy 95.01% and *top-2* accuracy 98.00%.

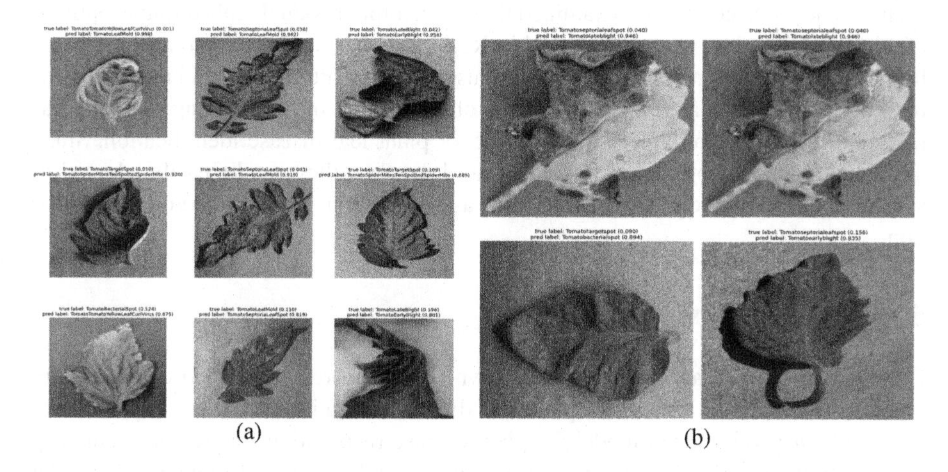

Fig. 7. Incorrect prediction on Tomato leaf dataset: (a) ResNet-18 and (b) momentum ResNet-18. Zoom to see the details.

Table 3. Ablation study on Tomato leaf disease dataset with ResNet-18.

Settings	Angular	Momentum	Pre-trained	Accuracy (%)	
				Top-1	*Top-2*
ResNet-18 (*baseline*)	×	×	×	95.01	98.00
ResNet-18	✓	✓	×	97.25	99.90
ResNet-18	✓	×	✓	97.85	99.00
ResNet-18	✓	✓	✓	**99.51**	**100**

Table 4. Ablation study for various μ on PlantVillage leaf disease dataset.

Momentum ResNet-18	$\mu = 0.1$	$\mu = 0.2$	$\mu = 0.4$	$\mu = 0.6$	$\mu = 0.8$	$\mu = 0.9$	$\mu = 1.0$
Top-1	86.45	87.22	97.20	96.83	97.20	**97.41**	97.04
Top-2	99.00	99.38	100	99.96	100	**100**	99.96

Secondly, we examined the momentum parameter in momentum ResNet-18 for plant leaf disease diagnosis. Table 4 shows the detailed experimental results by varying the momentum from 0.1 to 1. Noticeably, the best performing momentum for pant leaf disease discrimination is $\mu = 0.9$.

4.5 Discussion

In this sub-section, we summarized the experimental results and analyse them as per our claims. Based on previous sub-sections, for plant leaf disease diagnosis task complex residual architecture is the best choice as they can represent the features more uniquely (Table 1 and 2). Secondly, we examined that momentum residual embedding is optimal (Table 3). The major boost is observed in ResNet-18 backbone compared to the baseline method when angular marginal loss is used in momentum residual embedding for both the considered datasets. Thirdly, it is observed that the embedding with angular marginal feature performances much better for plant leaf disease identification. Since all feature vectors proposed in this paper are learnable, they can be easily adopted to several other multimedia applications such as recognition, retrieval and/or categorization.

5 Conclusion and Future Works

Deep learning-based approaches have shown promising results in filed of agriculture and thus we explored it more for plant leaf disease recognition. In this study, we have proposed yet another deep model for plant disease recognition for five different crop species. In the proposed approach, we introduce angular marginal momentum ResNet embedding to optimize the learning space and increase the performance in terms of *top-1* and *top-2* accuracy. The proposed model is simple and easy to train, compared to other state-of-the-art methods, and outperforms at $\mu = 0.9$. The proposed method set up a new benchmark on these two publicly available datasets that are considered in this paper. For future work, we would further like to work on light-weight angular momentum residual embeddings.

Acknowledgement. This work is carried out at Computer Science and Engineering, CIT Kokrajhar, India and would like to thank all individuals of the department. Also a special thanks to Google Research for Colaboratory (Colab) which allows to combine deep learning codes along with images, HTML, LaTeX and more, in a single document.

References

1. Abayomi-Alli, O.O., Damaševičius, R., Misra, S., Maskeliūnas, R.: Cassava disease recognition from low-quality images using enhanced data augmentation model and deep learning. Expert Syst. **38**, e12746 (2021)
2. Abbas, A., Jain, S., Gour, M., Vankudothu, S.: Tomato plant disease detection using transfer learning with C-GAN synthetic images. CEA **187**, 106279 (2021)
3. Agarwal, M., Singh, A., Arjaria, S., Sinha, A., Gupta, S.: ToLeD: tomato leaf disease detection using convolution neural network. Procedia Comput. Sci. **167**, 293–301 (2020)

4. Akila, M., Deepan, P.: Detection and classification of plant leaf diseases by using deep learning algorithm. IJERT **6**(07), 1–5 (2018)
5. Altuntaş, Y., Kocamaz, F.: Deep feature extraction for detection of tomato plant diseases and pests based on leaf images. Celal Bayar Univ. J. Sci. **17**(2), 145–157 (2021)
6. Chai, T., Prasad, S., Wang, S.: Boosting palmprint identification with gender information using DeepNet. Futur. Gener. Comput. Syst. **99**, 41–53 (2019)
7. Deng, J., Guo, J., Xue, N., Zafeiriou, S.: ArcFace: additive angular margin loss for deep face recognition. In: CVPR, pp. 4690–4699 (2019)
8. Elhassouny, A., Smarandache, F.: Smart mobile application to recognize tomato leaf diseases using Convolutional Neural Networks. In: IEEE ICCSRE, pp. 1–4 (2019)
9. Fuentes, A., Yoon, S., Kim, S.C., Park, D.S.: A robust deep-learning-based detector for real-time tomato plant diseases and pests recognition. Sensors **17**(9), 2022 (2017)
10. He, K., Zhang, X., Ren, S., Sun, J.: Deep residual learning for image recognition. In: CVPR, pp. 770–778 (2016)
11. Inés, A., Domínguez, C., Heras, J., Mata, E., Pascual, V.: Biomedical image classification made easier thanks to transfer and semi-supervised learning. Comput. Methods Programs Biomed. **198**, 105782 (2021)
12. Karthik, R., Hariharan, M., Anand, S., Mathikshara, P., Johnson, A., Menaka, R.: Attention embedded residual CNN for disease detection in tomato leaves. Appl. Soft Comput. **86**, 105933 (2020)
13. Li, Y., Yang, J.: Meta-learning baselines and database for few-shot classification in agriculture. CEA **182**, 106055 (2021)
14. Matin, M.M.H., Khatun, A., Moazzam, M.G., Uddin, M.S., et al.: An efficient disease detection technique of rice leaf using AlexNet. J. Comput. Commun. **8**(12), 49 (2020)
15. Nandhini, S., Ashokkumar, K.: Improved crossover based monarch butterfly optimization for tomato leaf disease classification using convolutional neural network. Multimedia Tools Appl. **80**(12), 18583–18610 (2021). https://doi.org/10.1007/s11042-021-10599-4
16. Pinki, F.T., Khatun, N., Islam, S.M.: Content based paddy leaf disease recognition and remedy prediction using support vector machine. In: 2017 ICCIT, pp. 1–5. IEEE (2017)
17. Prasad, S., Kong, A.W.K.: Using object information for spotting text. In: ECCV, pp. 540–557 (2018)
18. Prasad, S., Peddoju, S.K., Ghosh, D.: AgroMobile: a cloud-based framework for agriculturists on mobile platform. IJAST **59**, 41–52 (2013)
19. Prasad, S., Peddoju, S.K., Ghosh, D.: Multi-resolution mobile vision system for plant leaf disease diagnosis. SIViP **10**(2), 379–388 (2015). https://doi.org/10.1007/s11760-015-0751-y
20. Prasad, S., Peddoju, S.K., Ghosh, D.: Efficient plant leaf representations: a comparative study. In: IEEE TENCON, pp. 1175–1180 (2017)
21. Prasad, S., Peddoju, S.K., Ghosh, D.: Agriculture as a service. IEEE Potentials **40**(6), 34–43 (2021). https://doi.org/10.1109/MPOT.2015.2496327
22. Ren, S., He, K., Girshick, R., Sun, J.: Faster R-CNN: towards real-time object detection with region proposal networks. ANIPS **28**, 91–99 (2015)
23. Sander, M.E., Ablin, P., Blondel, M., Peyré, G.: Momentum residual neural networks. arXiv preprint arXiv:2102.07870 (2021)
24. Tian, J., Hu, Q., Ma, X., Han, M.: An improved KPCA/GA-SVM classification model for plant leaf disease recognition. J. CIS **8**(18), 7737–7745 (2012)
25. Trivedi, J., Shamnani, Y., Gajjar, R.: Plant leaf disease detection using machine learning. In: Gupta, S., Sarvaiya, J.N. (eds.) ET2ECN 2020. CCIS, vol. 1214, pp. 267–276. Springer, Singapore (2020). https://doi.org/10.1007/978-981-15-7219-7_23

26. Wang, C., Ni, P., Cao, M.: Research on crop disease recognition based on multi-branch ResNet-18. In: Journal of Physics: Conference Series, vol. 1961, p. 012009. IOP Publishing (2021)
27. Wang, W., Lai, Q., Fu, H., Shen, J., Ling, H., Yang, R.: Salient object detection in the deep learning era: an in-depth survey. IEEE Trans. PAMI **44**(6), 3239–3259 (2021)
28. Widiyanto, S., Fitrianto, R., Wardani, D.T.: Implementation of convolutional neural network method for classification of diseases in tomato leaves. In: IEEE ICIC, pp. 1–5 (2019)
29. Yang, B., Xu, Y.: Applications of deep-learning approaches in horticultural research: a review. Horticult. Res. **8**(1), 1–31 (2021)
30. Zhang, K., Wu, Q., Liu, A., Meng, X.: Can deep learning identify tomato leaf disease? Adv. Multimedia **2018**, 1–10 (2018)
31. Zhang, S., Huang, W., Zhang, C.: Three-channel convolutional neural networks for vegetable leaf disease recognition. Cogn. Syst. Res. **53**, 31–41 (2019)

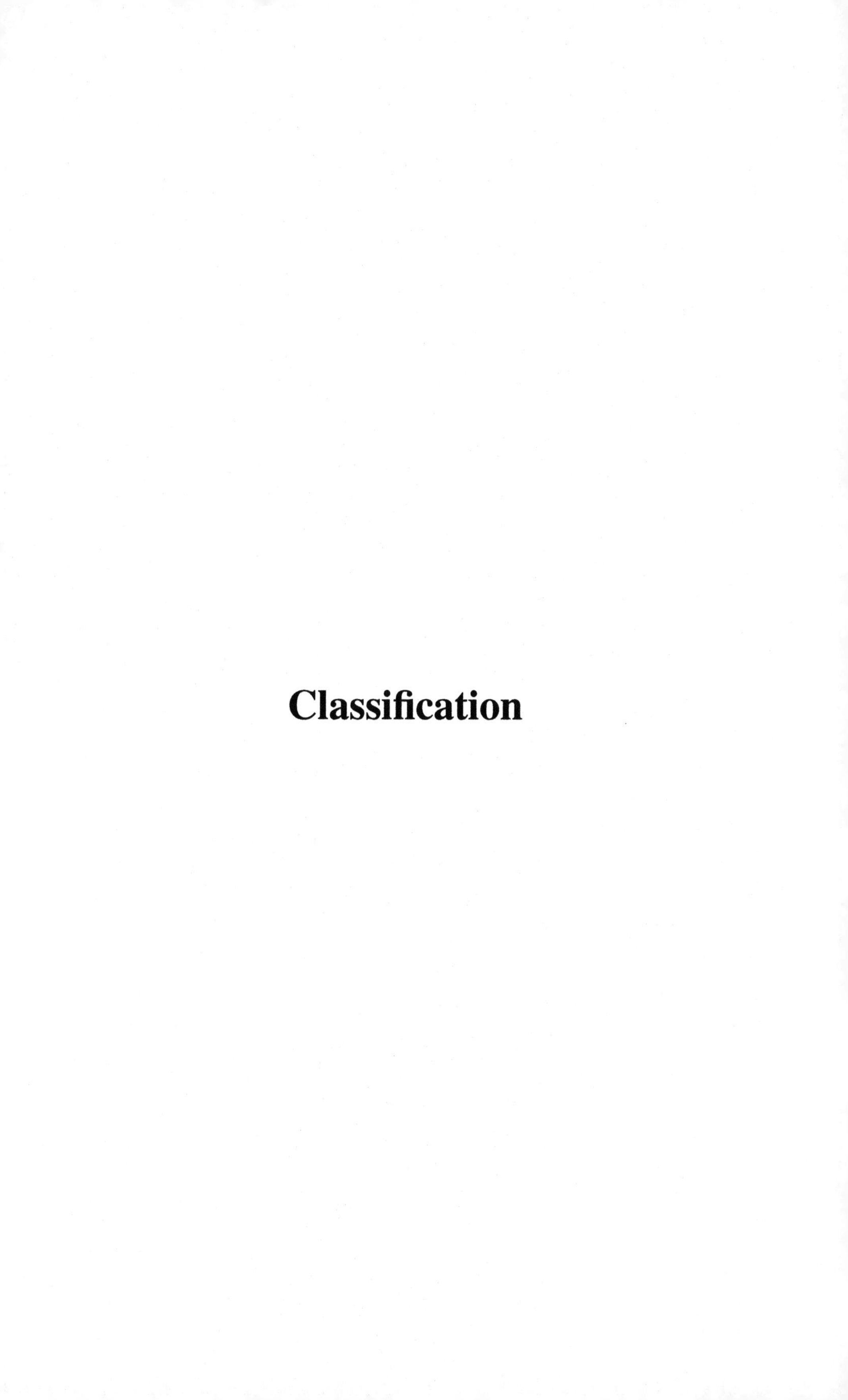

Classification

Hierarchical Approach for the Classification of Multi-class Skin Lesions Based on Deep Convolutional Neural Networks

Samia Benyahia[1], Boudjelal Meftah[2(✉)], and Olivier Lézoray[3]

[1] Department of Computer Science, Faculty of Exact Sciences, University of Mascara, Mascara, Algeria
benyahia.samia@univ-mascara.dz

[2] LRSBG Laboratory, University of Mascara, Mascara, Algeria
boudjelal.meftah@univ-mascara.dz

[3] Normandie Université, UNICAEN, ENSICAEN, CNRS, GREYC, Caen, France

Abstract. Skin lesion is one of the most critical challenges nowadays due to the difficulty of distinguishing a benign lesion from a malignant one. Melanoma represents a malignant melanocytic type of cancer among the most dangerous ones. In contrast, basal cell carcinoma and squamous cell carcinoma represent no malignant melanocytic types of cancer that threaten many human lives. Fortunately, there is some possibility of a cure it if is detected early and well treated. Currently, dermatologists use a hierarchical visual categorization of the lesion or skin biopsy for the diagnostic of skin lesion types. However, computer-aided detection methods can be more accurate, faster, and less expensive than human based techniques. We propose to combine both strategies to develop an efficient skin lesion classification model: the hierarchical organization accredited by dermatologists and a deep learning architecture. In this work, we propose a new hierarchical model for detecting various types of skin lesions based on the combination of several models of convolutional neural networks, where each model is specialized to some types of skin lesion according to the taxonomy. The obtained results highlight the benefits of addressing the classification of different skin lesions with CNNs in such a hierarchically structured way.

Keywords: Classification · Convolutional neural networks · Hierarchical diagnosis · Skin lesion diagnosis

1 Introduction

Human skin represents the most significant organ covering the body. The skin acts as a huge sensor packed with nerves to keep the brain in touch with the outside world. At the same time, it helps regulate body temperature and damaging sunlight, additionally allowing us free movement, and protecting us from

M. El Yacoubi et al. (Eds.): ICPRAI 2022, LNCS 13364, pp. 139–149, 2022.
https://doi.org/10.1007/978-3-031-09282-4_12

microbes. Human skin is made up of three layers: epidermis, dermis, and hypodermis. The epidermis that represents the outermost layer of the skin and consists mainly of cells called keratinocytes. The dermis is beneath the epidermis and consists of tough connective tissue and hair follicles. Then, the hypodermis, the deeper subcutaneous tissue, consists of fat and connective tissue. The melanin pigmentation of existing mesodermal cells can absorb UV radiations and cause cancers capable of spreading to other organs. Skin cancer is considered as one of the most diagnosed cancer in the world, and its diagnosis in a precise time is an essential health requirement. However, every misdiagnosis of skin cancer can lead to the death of a patient. Dermatologists experts declare that if the cancer is early diagnosed and followed by an appropriate treatment, they can avoid the patient's death and therefore improve global healthcare. Due to the difficulty of analyzing skin images and detecting cancer with traditional medical techniques such as the ABCD rule or the 7 point list, various other methods have been proposed.

In recent years, we have witnessed an extensive use of Convolution Neural Networks (CNN), that have outperformed other conventional machine learning approaches. CNNs reduce the need of manually handcrafting features by learning highly discriminative features while being trained in an end-to-end supervised way. Several CNN models have been successfully used for the identification of skin cancer lesions with higher efficiency in a reasonable time. We review some of them in the sequel.

Sara Atito et al. [1] proposed a deep learning method for skin lesion classification by fusing and fine-tuning an ensemble of three pre-trained deep learning architectures (Xception, Inception ResNet-V2, and NasNetLarge) using the ISIC2019 database and achieved an accuracy of 93.70%.

Pacheco et al. [2] proposed an ensemble of thirteen different convolutional neural networks (CNN) for diagnosing eight skin lesions using ISIC 2019 and achieved an accuracy of 89.7%. The test data represents only 10% of the dataset with an ensemble of the best three models based on the balanced accuracy.

Gessert et al. [3] proposed a deep learning method for skin lesion classification with an ensemble of CNNs including EfficientNets, SENet, and ResNeXt WSL, with a multiple model input resolutions and a search strategy. The proposed ensemble achieved an accuracy of 63.6% in the ISIC 2019 challenge test dataset.

Kassem et al. [4] proposed a deep learning method for classifying eight different skin lesions based on the modified GoogleNet architecture by adding more filters to each layer using ISIC 2019 and a multiclass SVM. They achieved an accuracy of 94.92%.

To et al. [5] proposed a multi-step approach to the problem of classification of skin cancer detection. They divided the task into many smaller sub-tasks easier to treat using several CNNs, Inception Resnet, Exception Net, and EfficientNet with data normalization and a dedicated loss functions. The proposed approach achieved an accuracy of 56.3% on the ISIC 2019 challenge test dataset.

Pollastri et al. [6] proposed a classification model based on the ensembling of two baseline models. Each baseline model contains different CNNs such as ResNet-152, DenseNet-201 and SeResNext-101, SeResNext-50, and SeNet-154. They employed data augmentation techniques to training the model, and achieved an accuracy of 59.3% on the ISIC 2019 challenge test dataset.

With the impressive growth of deep networks, this paper investigates the ability of commonly pre-trained convolutional neural network architectures to diagnose various dermoscopic skin lesions by improving diagnosis with multiple CNN organized into a hierarchical tree, and each one performs individually a decision for a specific type of skin lesion. Unlike the end-to-end model used in most state-of-art approaches, we propose a hierarchical approach to classify eight types of skin lesions using ResNet and DenseNet convolutional neural networks on the ISIC 2019 dataset. This choice is justified by a subsequent work done on a set of machine learning classifiers. We have found that ResNet and DenseNet give better accuracy [7].

The rest of the paper is structured as follows. Section 2 focuses on the methodology adopted for the classification task and describes the various pretrained CNN we used. Section 3 describes the experimental results. The last Section provides the conclusion of this study.

2 Methodology

The overall steps of our proposed model are shown in Fig. 1. In the first step, we divide the dermoscopic image dataset into two parts: the first represents the training data, and the second represents the testing data. The training phase is composed of five independent CNNs organized into a hierarchical tree, and each one performs individually a decision for a specialized and specific type of skin lesion.

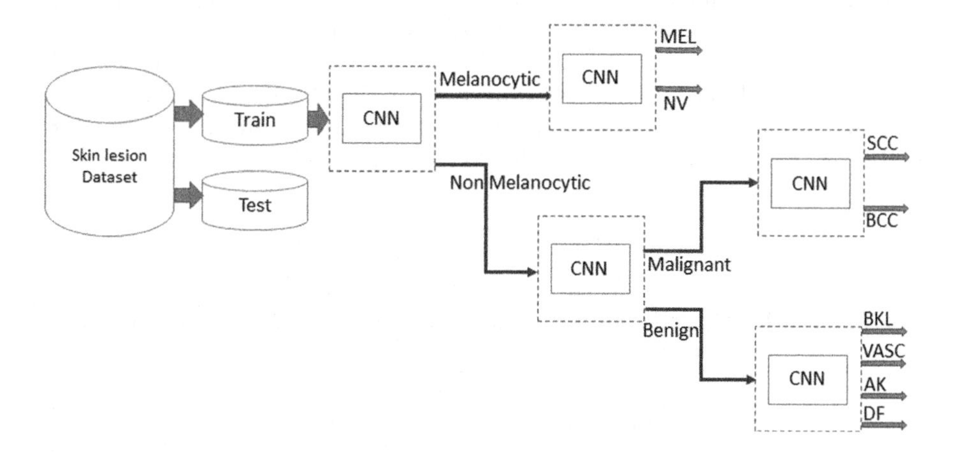

Fig. 1. Proposed method's flowchart

The first CNN is used for distinguishing between melanocytic and non-melanocytic lesions. Identified Melanocytic lesions are injected into the second CNN to distinguish between melanocytic malignant (Melanoma) and melanocytic benign (Nevus). Contrariwise, identified non-melanocytic lesions are fed to the third CNN to distinguish between non-melanocytic malignant and non-melanocytic benign lesions. The fourth CNN receives non-melanocytic malignant lesions as input and distinguishes Squamous cell Carcinoma (SCC) from Basal carcinoma (BCC).

Finally, the fifth CNN acquires non-melanocytic benign as input and distinguishes Dermatofibroma (DF), vascular lesion (VASC), actinic keratosis (AK), Benign keratosis (BKL). Once the training phase is finished we evaluate the model with a test dataset.

2.1 Convolutional Neural Networks

In recent years, deep Convolutional Neural Networks (CNN) have enabled many breakthroughs for different applications in the domain of dermoscopy image analysis. It was used as a feature extractor directly from images or for the classification and segmentation tasks [8–11], with various architectures (LeNet, AlexNet, VGGNet, ResNet, DenseNet, GoogLeNet...etc.). A CNN can be trained from scratch, used from pre-trained architectures initially trained on vast datasets, or fine-tuned for the problem under study. In this work, we tackled the skin lesion classification problem by using two of the most accurate pre-trained CNNs among the top-ranked architectures of the ImageNet Large Scale Visual Recognition Challenge (ILSVRC) [12]: ResNet and DenseNet.

ResNet is a convolutional neural network architecture proposed by He et al. in 2015 [13]. They are characterized by residual blocks that introduce skip connections between layers where each layer feeds into the following layer (Fig. 2). ResNet architecture contains 3 × 3 convolutions, global average pooling, and max-pooling layers, residual blocks, batch normalization layers followed by a fully connected layer, and finally a softmax for the classification. The ResNet architecture comes with several variations with different numbers of layers such as ResNet18, ResNet34, ResNet50, ResNet101, and ResNet152.

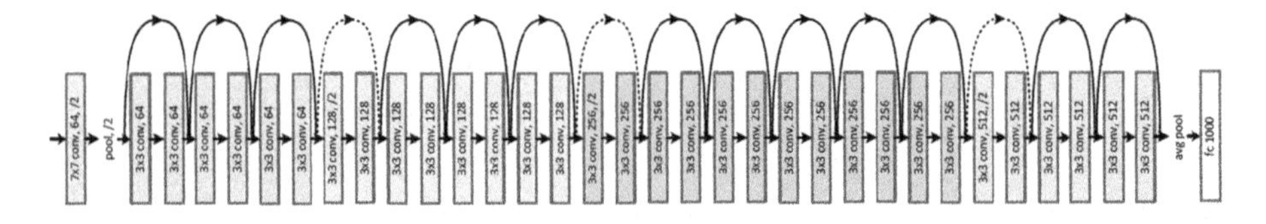

Fig. 2. ResNet architecture [13].

DenseNet is a convolutional neural network architecture proposed by Huang et al. in 2016 [14]. It introduces shortcut connections, where the concept consists of dense blocks linked by transition layers. Each dense block is composed of convolution layers (Fig. 3). It is connected to all prior layers, and all feature maps from previous layers are passed to all subsequent layers in the same block. The DenseNet architecture contains a convolution filter, global average pooling and max-pooling layers, transition layers, dense blocks followed by fully connected layers, and finally a softmax for the classification. The DenseNet architecture comes with several variations with different numbers of layers such as DensNet-121, DensNet-169, DensNet-201, and DensNet-246.

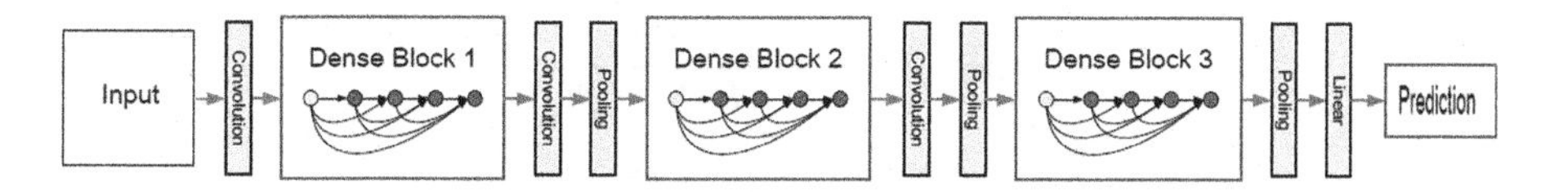

Fig. 3. DenseNet architecture [14].

3 Experimental Results and Discussion

3.1 Dataset

The ISIC 2019 dataset was provided from the International Skin Imaging Collaboration (ISIC) Archive [15–17] as part of the ISIC 2019 challenge, which maintains an archive of dermoscopic images. This dataset is divided into eight classes: Melanoma (MEL); Melanocytic nevus (NV); Basal cell carcinoma (BCC); Actinic keratosis (AK); Benign keratosis (BKL); Dermatofibroma (DF); Vascular lesion (VASC); Squamous cell carcinoma (SCC). Figure 4 shows some samples from the ISIC 2019 dataset.

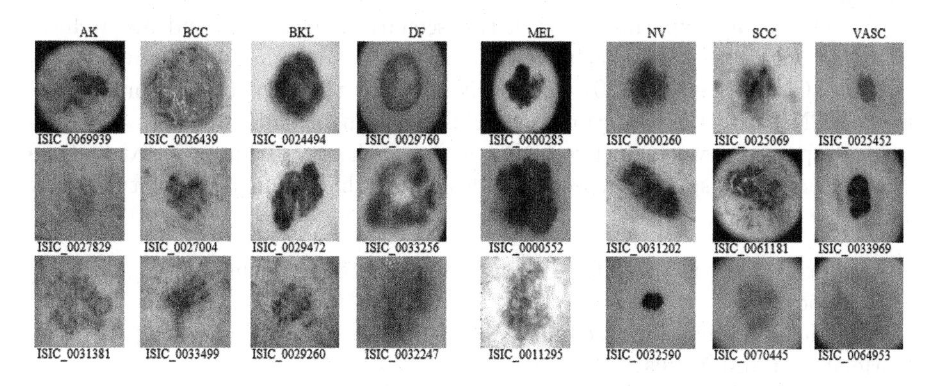

Fig. 4. Samples from ISC 2019 dataset.

3.2 Evaluation Metrics

The evaluation of the proposed model is computed using different performance metrics: accuracy, sensitivity, specificity, and precision, as defined below.

$$Accuracy = \frac{(TP + TN)}{(TP + FP + FN + TN)} \tag{1}$$

$$Sensitivity = \frac{TP}{(TP + FN)} \tag{2}$$

$$Specificity = \frac{TN}{(FP + TN)} \tag{3}$$

$$Precision = \frac{TP}{(TP + FP)} \tag{4}$$

where TP, FP, FN, TN refer to true positive, false positive, false negative, and true negative respectively.

3.3 Results and Discussion

Several experiments have been conducted with the ISIC 2019 dataset. The dataset was divided into three separated parts: 80%, 10%, and 10%, respectively for the training, validation, and testing datasets. We specify that no data pre-processing has been done. All experiments were trained with the same training dataset and tested with the same test dataset.

All experiments were performed on a desktop computer equipped with a Core i9 processor, and 32 GB RAM carried on NVIDIA GTX1080ti GPU card. CNNs are trained and evaluated using Python 3.6.10, Keras 2.2.4 [18] and a tensorflow backend 1.14 [19].

We carried out experiments with two scenarios: sequential and hierarchical classification approaches. Each scenario is tested without data augmentation with two CNNs: DenseNet201 and ResNet50. For the sequential approach, we use the CNN directly to perform the classification in end-to-end. In the hierarchical approach, we train five CNNs where each one performs individually a classification for a specific type of skin lesion in a hierarchically structured way such that:

- The first CNN is used for distinguishing between melanocytic and non-melanocytic
- For Melanocytic, the second CNN is used for distinguishing between Melanoma and Nevus
- For non Melanocyt, the third CNN is used to distinguish between non-melanocytic malignant and non-melanocytic benign
- For non Melanocyt malignant, the fourth CNN is used to distinguish between Squamous cell Carcinoma and Basal carcinoma

- For non Melanocyt benign, the fifth CNN is used to distinguish between Dermatofibroma, vascular lesion, actinic keratosis and benign keratosis.

Table 1 depicts the performance results obtained for classifying the ISIC 2019 dataset into eight classes with ResNet50 and DenseNet201 for both sequential and hierarchical architectures without augmentation. Through the obtained results from Table 1, we can observe that the proposed hierarchical model achieves the best results as compared to the sequential model for both architectures DenseNet201 and ResNet50. On the other side, we find that the DenseNet201 model provides the best results as compared to ResNet50.

Table 1. Summary of results obtained with sequential and hierarchical Resnet50 and DenseNet201 architectures.

Metric	Sequential ResNet50	Hierarchical ResNet50	Sequential DenseNet201	Hierarchical DenseNet201
Accuracy	64.03%	77.69%	66.69%	**79.43%**
Sensitivity	37.33%	**76.60%**	38.21%	76.37%
Specificity	94.32%	95.83%	94.40%	**95.89%**
Precision	35.14%	66.35%	35.86%	**69.14%**

The dataset used in this work is extremely unbalanced. There are many more samples in some classes than in others. For example, as shown in Table 2, NV contains 12875 samples versus DF having only 239 samples. Table 2 shows the distribution of all the samples for each class in the dataset.

Table 2. Distribution of ISIC 2019 samples for each class.

Diagnostic class	Description	Number of images	Percentage of images
NV	Melanocytic nevus	12875	50.83%
MEL	Melanoma	4522	17.85%
BCC	Basal cell carcinoma	3323	13.14%
SCC	Squamous cell carcinoma	628	2.48%
DF	Dermatofibroma	239	0.94%
VASC	Vascular lesion	253	1.00%
AK	Actinic keratosis	867	3.42%
BKL	Benign keratosis	2624	10.36%

The popular procedure employed to deal with this issue is to artificially augment the less frequent classes by augmenting the data with different ratios for different classes, or to decrease the most frequent classes by upsampling and downsampling or both. In this work, we use both upsampling and downsampling before feeding the images to the networks. The training data was also augmented using the following transformations: rotations, zooming, shearing, Flips (top-bottom, left-right), and skew-left-right, contrasting. Examples can be seen in Fig. 5.

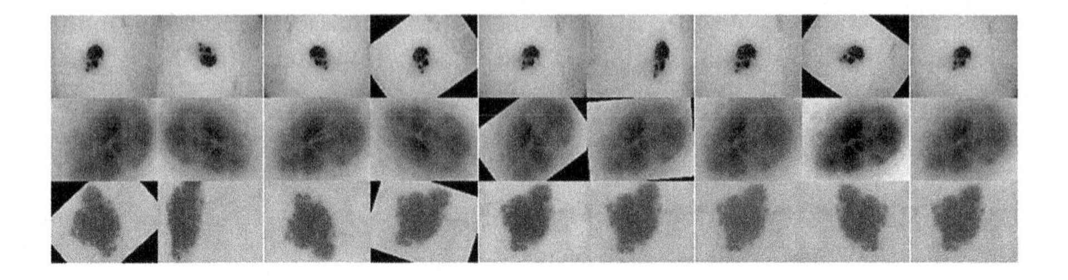

Fig. 5. The different types of data augmentation we have considered.

Table 3 depicts the results obtained for classifying the ISIC 2019 dataset into eight classes with ResNet50 and DenseNet201 for both sequential and hierarchical architectures with augmentation.

Table 3. Summary of results obtained with sequential and hierarchical ResNet50 and DenseNet201 architectures with data augmentation.

Metric	Sequential ResNet50	Hierarchical ResNet50	Sequential DensNet201	Hierarchical DensNet201
Accuracy	77.81%	78.91%	74.37%	**81.11%**
Sensitivity	71.52%	67.43%	**73.12%**	70.59%
Specificity	95,84%	95,88%	95.34%	**96.06%**
Precision	63.43%	61.29%	60.96%	**67.70%**

Through the evaluation and results obtained from Tables 3 and 1, we can notice that data augmentation improves the accuracy for all models either sequential or hierarchical. Figures 6 and 7 present a visualization of the performance metrics obtained with DenseNet201 and ResNet50 respectively for sequential and hierarchical approaches.

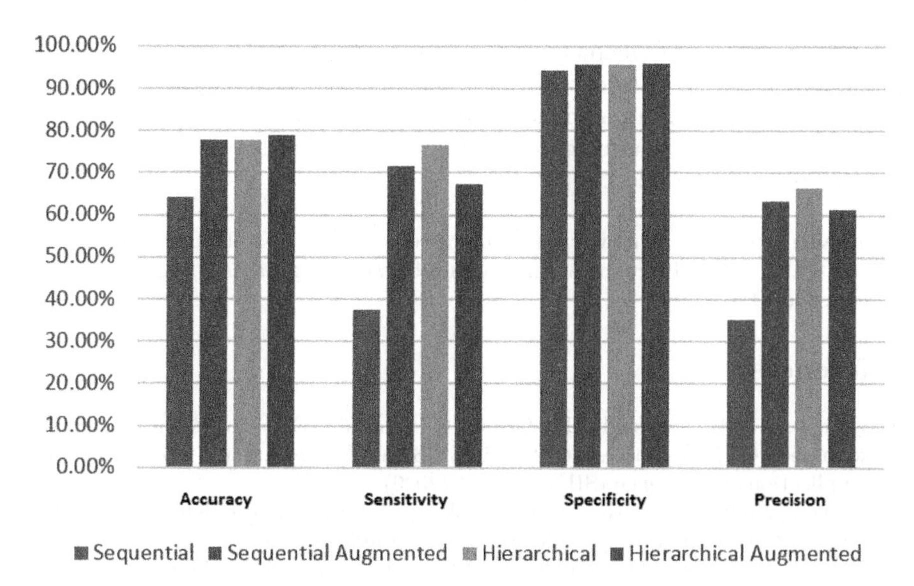

Fig. 6. Summary of results obtained with DenseNet201.

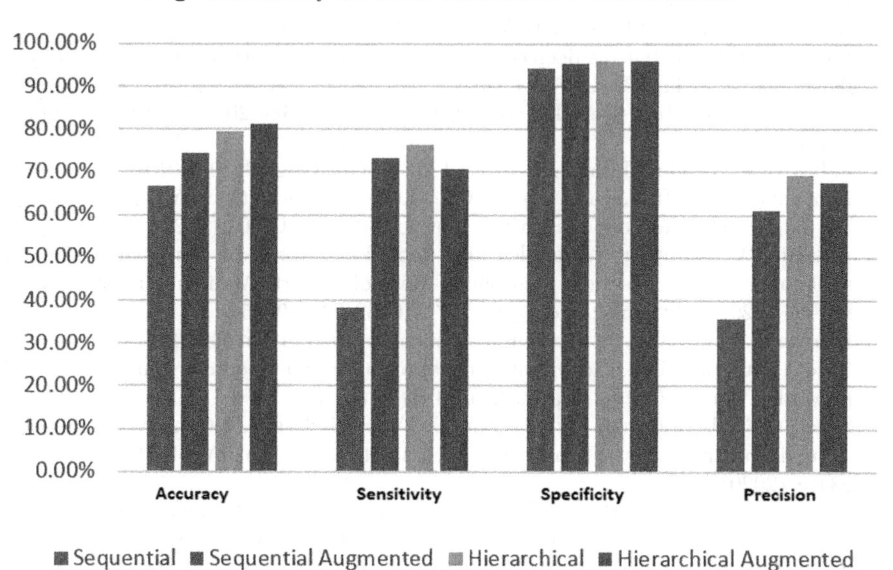

Fig. 7. Summary of results obtained with ResNet50.

4 Conclusion

This paper has presented a structured hierarchical classification for multi-class skin lesions based on a deep convolutional neural network system. Further, we presented comparative studies between the proposed hierarchical model and a sequential model using different CNN architectures: Resnet50 and DenseNet201. In this study, the results obtained exhibit that the hierarchically structured classification based on a distinction between melanocytic and non-melanocytic followed by a hierarchical diagnosis of the other classes leads to better results than the sequential models.

Acknowledgements. This work was completed as part of the Hubert Curien Partnership (PHC) TASSILI cooperation program between Algeria and France under the project code 19MDU212.

References

1. Ahmed, S.A.A., Yanikoğlu, B., Göksu, O., Aptoula, E.: Skin lesion classification with deep CNN ensembles. In: 28th IEEE Signal Processing and Communications Applications Conference (SIU), pp. 1–4 (2020)
2. Pacheco Andre G.C., Ali, A., Trappenberg, T.: Skin cancer detection based on deep learning and entropy to detect outlier samples (2019)
3. Gessert, N., Nielsen, M., Shaikh, M., Werner, R., Schlaefer, A.: Skin lesion classification using ensembles of multi-resolution EfficientNets with metadata. MethodsX **7**, 100864 (2020)
4. Kassem, M.A., Khalid, M.H., Mohamed, M.F.: Skin lesions classification into eight classes for ISIC 2019 using deep convolutional neural network and transfer learning. IEEE Access **8**, 114822–114832 (2020)
5. To, T.D., et al.: Multi-step skin cancer classification. ISIC 2019 Challenge Submission (2019)
6. Pollastri, F., et al.: AImageLab-PRHLT. ISIC Challenge 2019 (2019)
7. Benyahia, S., Meftah, B., Lézoray, O.: Multi-features extraction based on deep learning for skin lesion classification. Tissue Cell **74**, 101701 (2022)
8. Adegun, A., Viriri, S.: Deep learning techniques for skin lesion analysis and melanoma cancer detection: a survey of state-of-the-art. Artif. Intell. Rev. **54**(2), 811–841 (2020). https://doi.org/10.1007/s10462-020-09865-y
9. Benyahia, S., Meftah, B.: Automatic diagnosis system for classification, segmentation, detection and tracking of Skin lesion based on Deep convolutional neural networks. Models Optim. Math. Anal. J. **6**(1) (2018)
10. Saket, C.S., Tembhurne, J.V., Diwan, T.: A multi-class skin Cancer classification using deep convolutional neural networks. Multimedia Tools Appl. **79**(39), 28477–28498 (2020)
11. Khushboo, M., Elahi, H., Ayub, A., Frezza, F., Rizzi, A.: Cancer diagnosis using deep learning: a bibliographic review. Cancers **11**(9), 1235 (2019)
12. Olga, R., et al.: ImageNet large scale visual recognition challenge. Int. J. Comput. Vision **115**(3), 211–252 (2015)
13. He, K., Zhang, X., Ren, S., Sun, J.: Deep residual learning for image recognition. In: IEEE Conference on Computer Vision and Pattern Recognition (CVPR), pp. 770–778 (2016)
14. Huang, G., Liu, Z., Weinberger, K.Q.: Densely connected convolutional networks. In: IEEE Conference on Computer Vision and Pattern Recognition (CVPR), pp. 2261–2269 (2017)
15. Tschandl, P., Rosendahl, C., Kittler, H.: The HAM10000 dataset, a large collection of multi-source dermatoscopic images of common pigmented skin lesions. Sci. Data **5**, 180161 (2018)

16. Codella, N.C.F., et al.: Skin Lesion Analysis Toward Melanoma Detection: A Challenge 2017 International Symposium on Biomedical Imaging (ISBI), International Skin Imaging Collaboration (ISIC) (2017)
17. Combalia, M., et al.: BCN20000: Dermoscopic Lesions in the Wild (2019)
18. Chollet, F., et al.: Keras (2015). https://github.com/fchollet/keras
19. Abadi, M., et al.: TensorFlow: a system for large-scale machine learning. In: 12th fUSENIXg Symposium on Operating Systems Design and Implementation (fOSDIg 16), pp. 265–283 (2016)

The FreshPRINCE: A Simple Transformation Based Pipeline Time Series Classifier

Matthew Middlehurst(✉) and Anthony Bagnall

School of Computing Sciences, University of East Anglia, Norwich, UK
M.Middlehurst@uea.ac.uk

Abstract. There have recently been significant advances in the accuracy of algorithms proposed for time series classification (TSC). However, a commonly asked question by real world practitioners and data scientists less familiar with the research topic, is whether the complexity of the algorithms considered state of the art is really necessary. Many times the first approach suggested is a simple pipeline of summary statistics or other time series feature extraction approaches such as TSFresh, which in itself is a sensible question; in publications on TSC algorithms generalised for multiple problem types, we rarely see these approaches considered or compared against. We experiment with basic feature extractors using vector based classifiers shown to be effective with continuous attributes in current state-of-the-art time series classifiers. We test these approaches on the UCR time series dataset archive, looking to see if TSC literature has overlooked the effectiveness of these approaches. We find that a pipeline of TSFresh followed by a rotation forest classifier, which we name FreshPRINCE, performs best. It is not state of the art, but it is significantly more accurate than nearest neighbour with dynamic time warping, and represents a reasonable benchmark for future comparison.

Keywords: Time series classification · Transformation based classification · Time series pipeline

1 Introduction

A wide range of complex algorithms for time series classification (TSC) have been proposed. These include ensembles of deep neural networks [14], heterogeneous meta-ensembles build on different representations [22], homogeneous ensembles with embedded representations [26] and randomised kernels [10]. The majority of these algorithms rely on some form of transformation: features that in some way model the discriminatory time characteristics are extracted and used in the classification process. These features are often very complex, and usually embedded in the classifiers in complicated ways. For example, the Temporal Dictionary Ensemble (TDE) [19] is centred around the Symbolic Fourier Approximation (SFA) [25] transformation. The transform itself simply discretises the series into

M. El Yacoubi et al. (Eds.): ICPRAI 2022, LNCS 13364, pp. 150–161, 2022.
https://doi.org/10.1007/978-3-031-09282-4_13

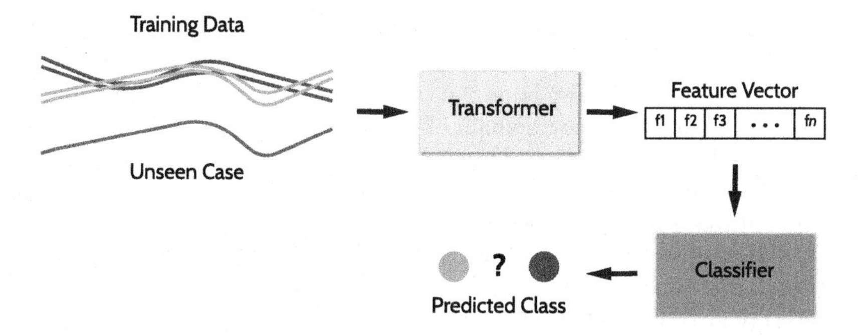

Fig. 1. Visualisation of a simple pipeline algorithm for TSC. Could using standard transformers and vector based classifiers be as good as state of the art TSC algorithms?

a set of words using a sliding window. However, just performing the transform does not lead to an algorithm that is competitive in accuracy. TDE also employs a spacial pyramid, uses bi-gram frequency, a bespoke distance function and a Gaussian process based parameter setting mechanism. The complexity increases further if the data is multivariate, containing multiple time series per case.

Researchers not directly involved in TSC algorithm research, and data scientists in particular, often ask the not unreasonable question of whether these complicated representations are really necessary to get a good classifier. They wonder whether a simple pipeline using standard feature extractors, as illustrated in Fig. 1 would not in fact be at least as good as complicated classifiers claiming to be state of the art? Clearly, the answer will not be the same for all problems, and the detailed answer depends on what level of accuracy is deemed sufficient for a particular application. However, we can address the hypothesis of whether, on average, a standard pipeline of transformation plus classifier performs as well as bespoke benchmarks and state of the art. Specifically, we compare a range of pipeline combinations of off the shelf unsupervised time series transformers with commonly used vector based classifiers to the current state of the art in TSC as described in [22]. In Sect. 2 we describe the transformers and classifiers used in our pipeline experiments, and give a brief overview of the state of the art in TSC. In Sect. 3 we describe our experimental structure, and in Sect. 4 we present our findings. Finally, in Sect. 5 we draw our conclusions and summarise what we have learnt from this study.

2 Background

TSC algorithms tend to follow one of three structures. The simplest involves single pipelines such as that described in Sect. 1, where the transformation is either supervised (e.g. Shapelet Transform Classifier [6]) or unsupervised (e.g. ROCKET [10]). These algorithms tend to involve an over-produce and select strategy: a huge number of features are created, and the classifier is left to determine which are most useful. The transform can remove time dependency, e.g. by calculating summary features. We call this type series-to-vector transformations. Alternatively, they may be series-to-series, transforming into an alternative time series representation where we hope the task becomes more easily tractable (e.g. transforming to the frequency domain of the series).

The second transformation based design pattern involves ensembles of pipelines, where each base pipeline consists of making repeated, different, transforms and using a homogeneous base classifier (e.g. Canonical Interval Forest [21]). These ensembles can also be heterogeneous, collating the classifications from transformation pipelines and ensembles of differing representations of the time series (e.g. HIVE-COTE [22]).

The third common pattern involves transformations embedded inside a classifier structure. An example of this is a decision tree: where the data is transformed, or a distance measure is applied prior to any splitting criteria at each node (e.g. TS-CHIEF [26]).

2.1 State of the Art for TSC

The state-of-the art for TSC consists of one classifier from each of the structures described, as well as a deep learning approach.

The Random Convolutional Kernel Transform (ROCKET) [10] is a transform designed for classification. It generates a large number of parameterised convolutional kernels, used as part of a pipeline alongside a linear classifier. Kernels are randomly initialised with respect to the following parameters: the kernel length; a vector of weights; a bias term added to the result of the convolution operation; the dilation to define the spread of the kernel weights over the input instance; and padding for the input series at the start and end. Each kernel is convoluted with an instance through a sliding window dot-product producing an output vector, extracting only two values: the max value and the proportion of positive values. These are concatenated into a feature vector for all kernels.

The Time Series Combination of Heterogeneous and Integrated Embedding Forest (TS-CHIEF) [26] is a homogeneous ensemble where hybrid features are embedded in tree nodes rather than modularised through separate classifiers. The trees in the TS-CHIEF ensemble embed distance measures, dictionary based histograms and spectral features. At each node, a number of splitting criteria from each of these representations are considered. These splits use randomly initialised parameters to help maintain diversity in the ensemble.

InceptionTime [14] is the only deep learning approach we are aware of which achieves state-of-the-art accuracy for TSC. InceptionTime builds on a residual network (ResNet), the prior best network for TSC [13]. The network is composed of two blocks of three Inception modules [27] each, as opposed to the three blocks of three traditional convolutional layers in ResNet. These blocks maintain residual connections, and are followed by global average pooling and softmax layers as before. InceptionTime creates an ensemble of networks with randomly initialised weightings.

The Hierarchical Vote Collective of Transform Ensembles, HIVE-COTE 1.0 (HC1) [2], alongside the three algorithms above, are not significantly different to each other in terms of accuracy. Additionally, all are significantly more accurate on average than the best performing algorithms from the bake off comparison of time series classifiers five years prior [3].

The second release of HIVE-COTE, **HIVE-COTE 2.0 (HC2)** [22] is a heterogeneous ensemble of four classifiers built on four different base representations. HC2 is the only algorithm we are aware of which performs significantly better than the four algorithms above. In HC2, three new classifiers are introduced, with only the Shapelet Transform Classifier (STC) [5] retained from HC1. TDE [19] replaces the Contractable Bag-of-SFA-Symbols (cBOSS) [20]. The Diverse Representation Canonical Interval Forest (DrCIF) replaces both Time Series Forest (TSF) [12] and the Random Interval Spectral Ensemble (RISE) [17] for the interval and frequency representations. An ensemble of ROCKET [10] classifiers called the Arsenal is introduced as a new convolutional/shapelet based approach. Estimation of test accuracy via cross-validation is replaced by an adapted form of out-of-bag error, although the final model is still built using all training data.

2.2 Unsupervised Time Series Transformations

Time Series Feature Extraction based on Scalable Hypothesis Tests (TSFresh) [8] is a collection of just under 800 features[1] extracted from time series data. TSFresh is very popular with the data science community, and is frequently proposed as a good transform for classification. The **Highly Comparative Time Series Analysis (*hctsa*)** [15] toolbox can create over 7700 features[2] for exploratory time series analysis. Alongside basic statistics of time series values, *hctsa* includes features based on linear correlations, trends and entropy. Features from various time series domains such as wavelets, information theory and forecasting among others are also present. Both TSFresh and *hctsa* cover similar domains, extracting masses of summary features from the time series. Some of these extracted features will be similar, with differently paramaterised variations of the same feature included if applicable.

The Canonical Time Series Characteristics (catch22) [18] are 22 features chosen to be the most discriminatory of the full *hctsa* [15] set. This was determined by an evaluation over the UCR datasets. The *hctsa* features were initially pruned, removing those which are sensitive to mean and variance and any which could not be calculated on over 80% of the UCR datasets. A feature evaluation was then performed based on predictive performance. Any features which performed below a threshold were removed. For the remaining features, a hierarchical clustering was performed on the correlation matrix to remove redundancy. From each of the 22 clusters formed, a single feature was selected, taking into account balanced accuracy, computational efficiency and interpretability.

[1] https://tsfresh.readthedocs.io/en/latest/text/list_of_features.html.

[2] https://hctsa-users.gitbook.io/hctsa-manual/list-of-included-code-files.

Like the *hctsa* set it was extracted from, the catch22 features cover a wide range of feature concepts.

Time Series Intervals are used in the interval based representation of TSC algorithms. Classifiers from this representation extract multiple phase-dependent subseries to extract discriminatory features from. Classifiers from this representation include TSF [12] and the Canonical Interval Forest (CIF) [21]. Both of these algorithms select intervals with a random length and position, extracting summary features from the resulting subseries and concatenating the output of each. This interval selection and feature extraction process can itself be used as an unsupervised transformation.

Generalised Signatures [23] are a set of feature extraction techniques, primarily for multivariate time series based on rough path theory. We specifically look at the generalised signature method [23] and the accompanying canonical signature pipeline. Signatures are collections of ordered cross-moments. The pipeline begins by applying two augmentations by default. The basepoint augmentation simply adds a zero at the beginning of the time series, making the signature sensitive to translations of the time series. The time augmentation adds the series timestamps as an extra coordinate to guarantee each signature is unique and obtain information about the parameterisation of the time series. A hierarchical dyadic window is run over the series, with the signature transform being applied to each window. The output for each window is then concatenated into a feature vector.

3 Experimental Structure

We perform our experiments on 112 equal length datasets with no missing values from the UCR time series archive [9]. We resample each dataset randomly 30 times in a stratified manner, with the first resample being the original train-test split from the archive. Each algorithm and dataset resample are seeded using the fold index to ensure reproducibility.

The transformations used in our experiments can be found in the Python `sktime`[3] package. Each transformer was built and saved to file, with the process being timed for our timing experiments. The classification portion of our pipelines, and the TSC algorithms used in our comparison, were run using the Java `tsml`[4] toolkit implementations. An exception for this is the deep learning approach InceptionTime, which we use the `sktime` companion package `sktime-dl`[5] to run.

To compare our results for multiple classifiers over multiple datasets we use critical difference diagrams [11]. We replace the post-hoc Nemenyi test with a comparison of all classifiers using pairwise Wilcoxon signed-rank tests, and cliques formed using the Holm correction as recommended in [4,16].

[3] https://github.com/alan-turing-institute/sktime.
[4] https://github.com/uea-machine-learning/tsml.
[5] https://github.com/sktime/sktime-dl.

We create pipelines primarily using the transformations described in Sect. 2.2, with the exception of the *hctsa* feature set, which required too much processing time and memory to be run in our timeframe. In addition to these transformations, we also include two benchmark transformations: Principal Component Analysis (PCA) and seven basic summary statistics. The seven statistics we use are the mean, median, standard deviation, minimum, maximum and the quantiles at 25% and 75%. PCA and basic summary statistics are the simplest transformations available, and perhaps one of the simplest approaches one could take towards TSC, alongside building classifiers on the raw time series and one-nearest-neighbour classification with Euclidean distance.

Our random interval transformation experiments extract 100 randomly selected intervals per dataset. We form two random interval pipelines, one extracting our basic summary statistics from each interval (RandInterval) and the other extracting the Catch22 features (RandIntC22).

For the classifier portion of our pipelines, we test three different vector based classifiers. Rotation Forest (RotF) [24] is the classifier of choice for the STC pipeline, and has shown to be significantly better than other popular approaches on problems only containing continuous attributes [1]. Extreme Gradient Boosting (XGBoost) [7] of Kaggle fame is our second classifier option. Our third option is a ridge regression classifiers with cross-validation to select parameters (RidgeCV), the better performing linear classifier suggested for the ROCKET pipeline [10].

4 Results

We structure our results to answer four specific questions:

1. Which transformation is best given a specific classifier?
2. Which classifier is best, given a specific transform?
3. How do the pipeline classifiers compare to standard benchmarks?
4. How do the pipeline classifiers compare to state-of-the-art?

Figures 2 show the relative performance of difference transforms for our three base classifiers. We include for reference our two baseline classifiers, Rotation Forest (RotF) built on the raw time series and 1-nearest neighbour using dynamic time warping with a tuned window size (DTWCV).

The pattern of results is similar for all three classifiers: TSFresh and RandIntC22 are ranked top for all three classifiers. Both are significantly higher ranked than all the other transforms, and both baseline classifiers, except for the case of TSFresh with a ridge classifier. Summary statistics is always the worst approach and PCA, Catch22, Signatures are no better than, or worse than, the benchmark classifiers. RandomIntervals is significantly better than the benchmarks with rotation forest. There is an anomaly when drawing cliques (RotF and DTW are not always in the same clique despite there being no significant difference in all experiments, as it is impossible to draw accurately), but the initial indications are clear: TSFresh and RandIntC22 are the best performing

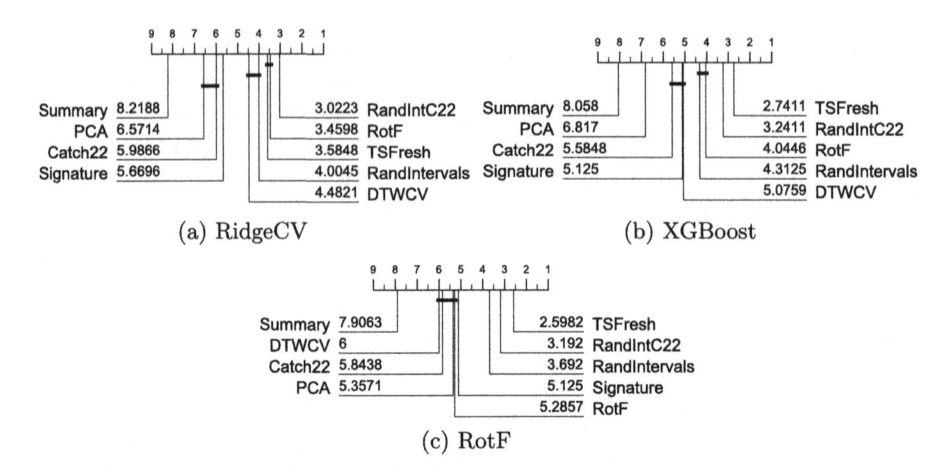

Fig. 2. Relative rank performance of seven transforms used in a simple pipeline with a linear ridge classifier (a), XGBoost (b) and rotation forest (c). TSFresh and RandInt22 are significantly better than all other transforms with most base classifiers.

techniques and, with the possible exception of RandomIntervals, the others do not outperform the standard benchmarks, and are therefore of less interest. We investigate the relative performance of classifiers by comparing the two best transforms (TSFresh and RandIntC22) in combination with the three classifiers. Figure 3 shows that RotF is significantly better than RidgeCV and XGBoost for both transforms. This supports the argument made in [1] that rotation forest is the best classifier for problems with all continuous attributes. Figures 4 show the pairwise scatter plots for four pairs of pipelines. Figures (a), (b) and (c) show the difference in accuracies on the archive for both TSFresh and RandIntC22 using each of our base classifiers. Figure (d) compares our best performing pipeline, TSFresh with rotation forest, to the next best, TSFresh pipeline using XGBoost.

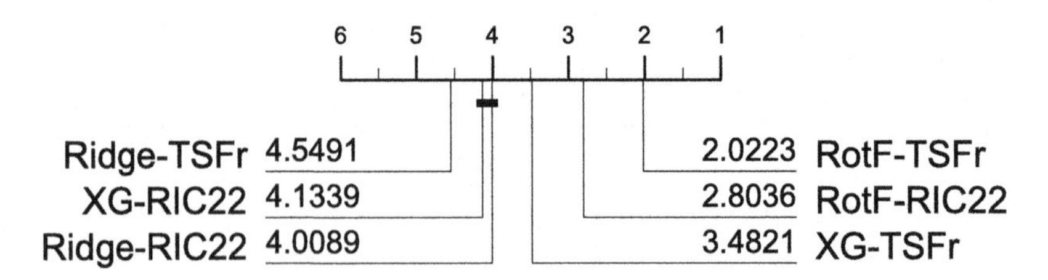

Fig. 3. Relative performance of three classifiers Rotation Forest, XBoost and RidgeCV (prefixes RotF, XG and Ridge) with two transforms TSFresh and RandIntCatch22 (suffix TSFr and RIC22). RotF is significantly better than the other classifiers, and RotF with TSFresh is the best overall combination.

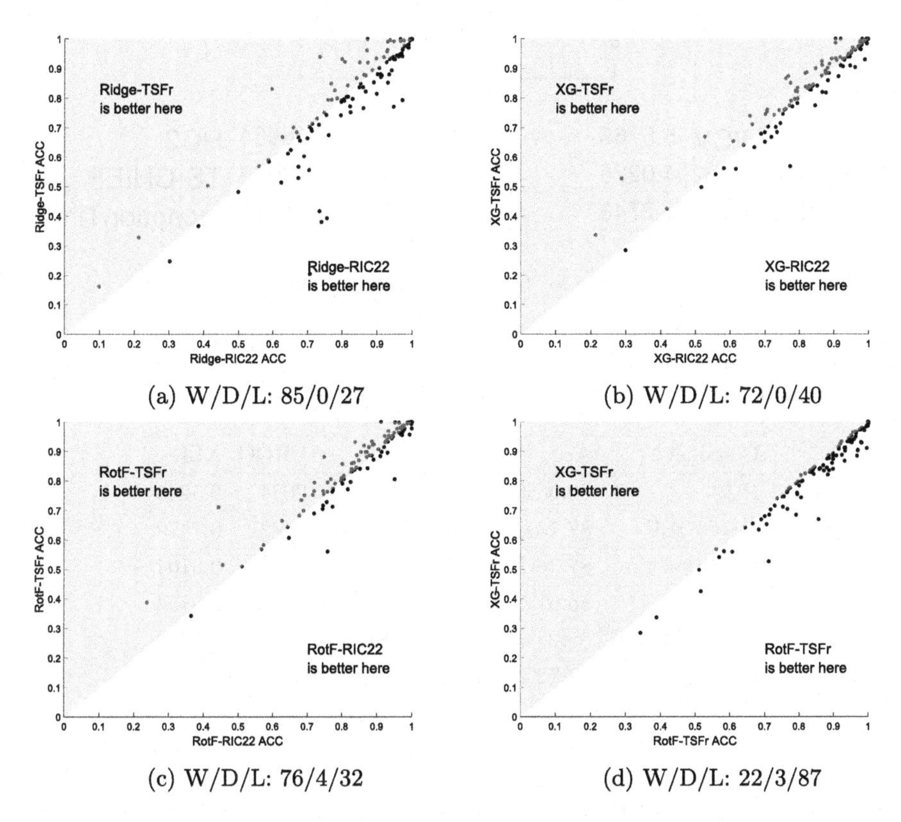

(a) W/D/L: 85/0/27

(b) W/D/L: 72/0/40

(c) W/D/L: 76/4/32

(d) W/D/L: 22/3/87

Fig. 4. Pairwise scatter plots for TSFresh vs RandIntC22 with (a) RidgeCV, (b) XGBoost and (c) rotation forest, and (d) the scatter plot of using TSFresh with XGBoost with TSFresh. (a), (b) and (c) demonstrate the superiority of TSFresh over RandIntC22. (d) shows that rotation forest significantly outperforms XGBoost.

Our primary finding is that the pipeline of TSFresh and rotation forest is, on average, the highest ranked and the most accurate simple pipeline approach for classifying data from the UCR archive. We feel the approach deserves a name better than RotF-TSFr. Hence, we call it the FreshPRINCE (Fresh Pipeline with RotatIoN forest Classifier). We investigate classification performance of the FreshPRINCE against the current and previous state of the art. Figure 5 shows FreshPRINCE against the very latest state of the art, HIVE-COTEv2.0 (HC2), the previously best performing algorithms, InceptionTime, TS-CHIEF and ROCKET and the popular benchmark, DTWCV. Figure 5 shows that FreshPRINCE does not achieve SOTA, but it does perform better than the popular benchmark 1-NN with DTW (DTWCV). Table 1 presents the summary performance measures averaged over all data. FreshPRINCE is approximately 6.5% more accurate than DTWCV, but on average 1.4% and 3.8% less accurate than ROCKET and HC2.

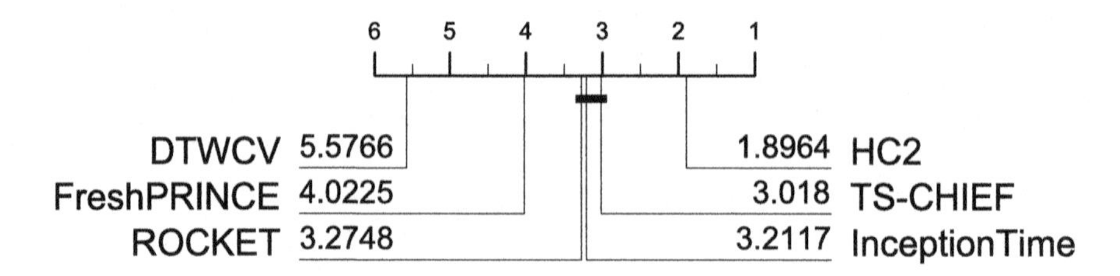

Fig. 5. Critical difference plot for FreshPRINCE against SOTA and DTW.

Table 1. Summary performance statistics averaged over 112 UCR datasets. Test set accuracy (Acc), balanced accuracy (BalAcc), F1 statistic (F1), Area under the receiver operator curve (AUROC) and negative log likelihood (NLL).

Classifier	Acc	BalAcc	F1	AUROC	NLL
HC2	89.06%	86.85%	0.8575	0.9684	0.5245
TS-CHIEF	87.73%	85.80%	0.8475	0.9592	0.7479
InceptionTime	87.36%	85.67%	0.8443	0.9583	0.6104
ROCKET	86.61%	84.58%	0.8339	0.9536	1.5754
FreshPRINCE	85.22%	82.98%	0.8168	0.9565	0.7230
DTWCV	77.72%	76.10%	0.7449	0.7860	1.4796

Table 2 displays the run times for generating the results summarised in Fig. 5 and Table 1. The FreshPRINCE is not as fast as the ROCKET classifier, but is still faster than then other SOTA TSC algorithms.

Table 2. Classifier runtimes, Average (Minutes), Total (Hours), Max (Hours).

	DTWCV	FreshPRINCE	Rocket	InceptionTime	TS-CHIEF	HC2
Average	13.9545	10.5905	1.52939	46.3823	544.7552	182.844
Total	26.0485	19.7689	2.85461	86.5802	1016.8751	341.3084
Max	7.3248	3.856	0.4301	7.1093	166.7567	54.9177

We believe that, given the simplicity of the pipeline approach, the FreshPRINCE pipeline should be a benchmark against which new algorithms should be compared. If the claimed merits of an approach are primarily its accuracy, then we believe it should achieve significantly better accuracy than the simple approach of a TSFresh transform followed by a rotation forest classifier.

4.1 Implementation and Reproduction of Results

Given that we suggest FreshPRINCE as a benchmark classifier for new comparisons, we also provide resources for using it as such. We include our results for

FreshPRINCE on the 112 UCR datasets used in this experiment on the time series classification web page.[6] For experiments outside the UCR archive, we have implemented the pipeline in the Python *sktime* package. The most commonly used machine learning package for Python, *sklearn*, does not contain a rotation forest implementation. As such, we also include an implementation of the algorithm in *sktime*.

Listings 1.1 displays the process for running FreshPRINCE using the *sktime* package, loading data from its .ts file forma.

```
from sktime.utils.data_io import
    load_from_tsfile_to_dataframe as load_ts
from sktime.classification.feature_based import
    FreshPRINCE

if __name__ == "__main__":
    # Load dataset
    trainX, trainY = load_ts("../Data/data_TRAIN.ts")
    testX, testY = load_ts("../Data/data_TEST.ts")

    # Create classifier and build on training data
    fresh_prince = FreshPRINCE()
    fresh_prince.fit(trainX, trainY)

    # Find accuracy on testing data
    accuracy = fresh_prince.score(testX, testY)
```

Listing 1.1. Running the FreshPRINCE pipeline in Python using *sktime*.

FreshPRINCE can also be run using a *sklearn* pipeline, using the *sktime* TSFresh transformer and rotation forest implementations, as shown in Listing 1.2.

```
    fresh_prince = Pipeline([
            (
                "transform",
                TSFreshFeatureExtractor(
                    default_fc_parameters="comprehensive"),
            ),
            ("classifier", RotationForest()),
        ])
```

Listing 1.2. Forming the FreshPRINCE pipeline in Python using *sktime* components and the *sklearn* Pipeline framework.

5 Conclusion

We have tested a commonly held belief that a simple pipeline of transformation and standard classifier is a useful approach for time series classification. We have found that there is some merit in this opinion: simple transformations such

[6] http://www.timeseriesclassification.com/results.php.

as PCA or summary stats are not effective, but more complex transformations such as TSFresh and random intervals with the Catch22 features do achieve a respectable level of accuracy on average. They are significantly worse than state of the art in 2021 and 2020, but significantly better than the state from 10 years ago (DTWCV). We suggest the best performing pipeline, a combination of TSFresh and rotation forest we call FreshPRINCE for brevity, be used more commonly as a TSC benchmark.

Acknowledgements. This work is supported by the UK Engineering and Physical Sciences Research Council (EPSRC) iCASE award T206188 sponsored by British Telecom. The experiments were carried out on the High Performance Computing Cluster supported by the Research and Specialist Computing Support service at the University of East Anglia.

References

1. Bagnall, A., Bostrom, A., Cawley, G., Flynn, M., Large, J., Lines, J.: Is rotation forest the best classifier for problems with continuous features? ArXiv e-prints arXiv:1809.06705 (2018)
2. Bagnall, A., Flynn, M., Large, J., Lines, J., Middlehurst, M.: On the usage and performance of HIVE-COTE v1.0. In: Proceedings of the 5th Workshop on Advances Analytics and Learning on Temporal Data. Lecture Notes in Artificial Intelligence, vol. 12588 (2020)
3. Bagnall, A., Lines, J., Bostrom, A., Large, J., Keogh, E.: The great time series classification bake off: a review and experimental evaluation of recent algorithmic advances. Data Min. Knowl. Disc. **31**(3), 606–660 (2016). https://doi.org/10.1007/s10618-016-0483-9
4. Benavoli, A., Corani, G., Mangili, F.: Should we really use post-hoc tests based on mean-ranks? J. Mach. Learn. Res. **17**, 1–10 (2016)
5. Bostrom, A., Bagnall, A.: Binary Shapelet transform for multiclass time series classification. In: Madria, S., Hara, T. (eds.) DaWaK 2015. LNCS, vol. 9263, pp. 257–269. Springer, Cham (2015). https://doi.org/10.1007/978-3-319-22729-0_20
6. Bostrom, A., Bagnall, A.: Binary Shapelet transform for multiclass time series classification. In: Hameurlain, A., Küng, J., Wagner, R., Madria, S., Hara, T. (eds.) Transactions on Large-Scale Data- and Knowledge-Centered Systems XXXII. LNCS, vol. 10420, pp. 24–46. Springer, Heidelberg (2017). https://doi.org/10.1007/978-3-662-55608-5_2
7. Chen, T.: XGBoost: a scalable tree boosting system. In: Proceedings of 22nd ACM SIGKDD International Conference on Knowledge Discovery and Data Mining (2016)
8. Christ, M., Braun, N., Neuffer, J., Kempa-Liehr, A.W.: Time series feature extraction on basis of scalable hypothesis tests (tsfresh-a Python package). Neurocomputing **307**, 72–77 (2018)
9. Dau, H., et al.: The UCR time series archive. IEEE/CAA J. Autom. Sin. **6**(6), 1293–1305 (2019)
10. Dempster, A., Petitjean, F., Webb, G.: ROCKET: exceptionally fast and accurate time series classification using random convolutional kernels. Data Min. Knowl. Disc. **34**, 1454–1495 (2020)

11. Demšar, J.: Statistical comparisons of classifiers over multiple data sets. J. Mach. Learn. Res. **7**, 1–30 (2006)
12. Deng, H., Runger, G., Tuv, E., Vladimir, M.: A time series forest for classification and feature extraction. Inf. Sci. **239**, 142–153 (2013)
13. Ismail Fawaz, H., Forestier, G., Weber, J., Idoumghar, L., Muller, P.-A.: Deep learning for time series classification: a review. Data Min. Knowl. Disc. **33**(4), 917–963 (2019). https://doi.org/10.1007/s10618-019-00619-1
14. Fawaz, H., et al.: InceptionTime: finding AlexNet for time series classification. Data Min. Knowl. Disc. **34**(6), 1936–1962 (2020)
15. Fulcher, B., Jones, N.: hctsa: a computational framework for automated time-series phenotyping using massive feature extraction. Cell Syst. **5**(5), 527–531 (2017)
16. García, S., Herrera, F.: An extension on "statistical comparisons of classifiers over multiple data sets" for all pairwise comparisons. J. Mach. Learn. Res. **9**, 2677–2694 (2008)
17. Lines, J., Taylor, S., Bagnall, A.: Time series classification with HIVE-COTE: the hierarchical vote collective of transformation-based ensembles. ACM Trans. Knowl. Disc. Data **12**(5), 1–36 (2018)
18. Lubba, C., Sethi, S., Knaute, P., Schultz, S., Fulcher, B., Jones, N.: catch22: CAnonical Time-series CHaracteristics. Data Min. Knowl. Disc. **33**(6), 1821–1852 (2019)
19. Middlehurst, M., Large, J., Cawley, G., Bagnall, A.: The Temporal Dictionary Ensemble (TDE) classifier for time series classification. In: Hutter, F., Kersting, K., Lijffijt, J., Valera, I. (eds.) ECML PKDD 2020. LNCS (LNAI), vol. 12457, pp. 660–676. Springer, Cham (2021). https://doi.org/10.1007/978-3-030-67658-2_38
20. Middlehurst, M., Vickers, W., Bagnall, A.: Scalable dictionary classifiers for time series classification. In: Yin, H., Camacho, D., Tino, P., Tallón-Ballesteros, A.J., Menezes, R., Allmendinger, R. (eds.) IDEAL 2019. LNCS, vol. 11871, pp. 11–19. Springer, Cham (2019). https://doi.org/10.1007/978-3-030-33607-3_2
21. Middlehurst, M., Large, J., Bagnall, A.: The canonical interval forest (CIF) classifier for time series classification. In: 2020 IEEE International Conference on Big Data (Big Data), pp. 188–195. IEEE (2020)
22. Middlehurst, M., Large, J., Flynn, M., Lines, J., Bostrom, A., Bagnall, A.: HIVE-COTE 2.0: a new meta ensemble for time series classification. Mach. Learn. **110**(11), 3211–3243 (2021). https://doi.org/10.1007/s10994-021-06057-9
23. Morrill, J., Fermanian, A., Kidger, P., Lyons, T.: A generalised signature method for multivariate time series feature extraction. arXiv preprint arXiv:2006.00873 (2020)
24. Rodriguez, J., Kuncheva, L., Alonso, C.: Rotation forest: a new classifier ensemble method. IEEE Trans. Pattern Anal. Mach. Intell. **28**(10), 1619–1630 (2006)
25. Schäfer, P., Högqvist, M.: SFA: a symbolic Fourier approximation and index for similarity search in high dimensional datasets. In: Proceedings of the 15th International Conference on Extending Database Technology, pp. 516–527 (2012)
26. Shifaz, A., Pelletier, C., Petitjean, F., Webb, G.I.: TS-CHIEF: a scalable and accurate forest algorithm for time series classification. Data Min. Knowl. Disc. **34**(3), 742–775 (2020). https://doi.org/10.1007/s10618-020-00679-8
27. Szegedy, C., et al.: Going deeper with convolutions. In: Proceeding of the IEEE Conference on Computer Vision and Pattern Recognition, June 2015

Robust Detection of Conversational Groups Using a Voting Scheme and a Memory Process

Victor Fortier[1], Isabelle Bloch[1](✉), and Catherine Pélachaud[2]

[1] Sorbonne Université, CNRS, LIP6, Paris, France
victor.fortier@etu.sorbonne-universite.fr,
isabelle.bloch@sorbonne-universite.fr
[2] CNRS, ISIR, Sorbonne Université, Paris, France
catherine.pelachaud@sorbonne-universite.fr

Abstract. Studies in human-human interaction have introduced the concept of F-formation to describe the spatial organization of participants during social interaction. This paper aims at detecting such F-formations in images of video sequences. The proposed approach combines a voting scheme in the visual field of each participant and a memory process to make the detection in each frame robust to small, irrelevant changes of participant's behavior. Results on the MatchNMingle data set demonstrate the good performances of this approach.

Keywords: F-formation · Clustering · Temporal regularity

1 Introduction

Participants during social interaction place themselves in certain spatial formations, so as to see each other and respect social and cultural distancing [4]. They can face each other, be side by side... Their position and behavior such as body orientation and gaze behavior can indicate a great quantity of information; they can reveal information about their level of engagement, their focus of interest but also the quality of their relationship, their degree of intimacy, to name a few [1]. Participants' position and behavior evolve continuously to accommodate others' behaviors and to obey to some socio-cultural norms. A group can be defined as an entity where individuals are spatially close, and each member is able to see and know the other members. Group members perform a common, shared activity by interacting socially. People can be simply gathered spatially (e.g. people in a queue), doing an action together but do not interact together (e.g. watching a film at the cinema) or discussing together on a given topic. Studies in human-human interaction have introduced the concept of F-formation [8] that defines three zones: O-space, P-space and R-space. The O-space corresponds to

This work was partly supported by the chair of I. Bloch in Artificial Intelligence (Sorbonne Université and SCAI).

M. El Yacoubi et al. (Eds.): ICPRAI 2022, LNCS 13364, pp. 162–173, 2022.
https://doi.org/10.1007/978-3-031-09282-4_14

the convex space between the participants of a group; the P-space corresponds to the belt where the participants are; and the R-space is the space outside the participants.

Lately computational models have been designed to detect if individuals form a group and what is its formation based on proxemics and behaviors [2]. Further analysis can be pursued to characterize the dynamics of the social interaction between participants. Such models can then be used to drive the behaviors of robots when interacting with humans.

The aim of our study is to detect, analyze and understand social interactions from images and videos, in order to build computational models of social interactions. We focus on free-standing conversational groups with limited size (typically 2–6 persons) that are discussing with each other [9].

To this aim, we rely on the existing database MatchNMingle [2]. This database contains videos of group interaction that have been annotated at different levels (activity, speaking, laughing, non-verbal behavior). As a first step, we detect group formations using still images and consider only two visual cues, namely distance and gaze direction. The proposed approach is based on a voting procedure to find the O-spaces and the groups. It does not require any heavy learning method. Moreover, a new feature of the approach is that the detection in still images is made more robust by exploiting the temporal information in the video sequence.

Related work is briefly summarized in Sect. 2, the proposed approach is described in Sect. 3, and results on the MatchNMingle data set [2] are provided in Sect. 4.

2 Related Work

One of the pioneering methods to detect F-formations from images is called the “Hough Voting for F-formations”, which constructs a Hough accumulator and where groups are extracted from it by searching for local maxima [3]. The method reduces the detection of F-formations to that of O-spaces. An O-space corresponds to the intersection of the visual fields of its participants. Thus, the method models each individual's field of attention by drawing many samples from a 2D Gaussian distribution centered at some distance from its position and respecting its orientation. Each sample corresponds to a vote that remains to be aggregated in the Hough accumulator. Finally, the local maxima correspond to the positions that received votes from most of the individuals in the scene. That is, they correspond to the positions of the O-space centers and thus to the searched F-formations. Further studies applied the paradigm of the voting process in a Hough space [12,13]. Later on, the same authors proposed an approach based on graph-cut to optimize an objective function defined from the probability of the assignment of participants to groups, under minimum description length constraint to limit the number of clusters [14]. These authors also addressed detection in videos using a game-theoretic approach [16]. With respect to the static approach, this approach includes an additional fusion step over a sequence. However groups are fixed in time. Other fusion approaches have been proposed, with the same drawback. To account for evolution over time, tracking methods have been used, but this is out of the scope of this paper.

Hung and Kröse [7] proposed to model the interactions between individuals as a graph. The analysis of the graph gives information on group formations. The authors defined the "Dominants Sets for F-formations" method that sees F-formations as entities where the affinity (probability of interaction) between all members of a group is higher than that between a member of the group and an individual outside the group. This definition is closed to the dominant set problem which is known to be an NP-complete problem. The dominant sets of a graph are subsets of vertices of a graph for which any of its vertices is either a leaf, or is connected by an edge to an element [5]. A group can be viewed as an undirected graph where each vertex corresponds to an individual and edges are weighted. A weight on an edge corresponds to the affinity between individuals linked by the edge. It is estimated from their body positions and orientations. The dominant sets can be detected by optimization methods that provide an approximate solution to determine the groups in a scene.

Lately, Thompson and colleagues [15] applied to dominant sets a message-passing Graph Neural Network (GNN) to predict how individuals are grouped together. This approach requires a lot of data and annotations, so as to train properly the network. Other methods based on neural network and deep learning have similar strong requirements, and are out of the scope of this paper.

The approach we propose is lighter as only a very limited learning step is required to set parameters once for all, and the whole method has a low complexity. Moreover, we exploit the temporal information to improve the detection in each frame, providing a better regularity over time, including the short changes in position or gaze direction, while keeping the meaningful changes (i.e. not assuming that the groups are fixed over time).

3 Proposed Approach: Multiple Votes and Exploiting Temporal Information

3.1 Voting in Each Frame

The main idea of the proposed approach is to detect F-formations by identifying the O-spaces of each group. To this end, we use the position, orientation and field of view of each person to model "votes" for a O-space center, drawn from uniform distributions in the field of view.

More precisely, let (x_i, y_i) denote the position of person (or participant) i in the image, and θ_i her orientation. Her field of view is defined as a cone of aperture $\alpha \in [0, 2\pi]$, truncated at a minimal radius $\gamma d_{\max}$ and a maximal radius $\beta d_{\max}$ where γ and β are parameters in $[0, 1]$, with $\gamma \leq \beta$, and $d_{\max}$ the maximal distance on the scene (in practice the length of the image diagonal). Each vote provides a potential O-space center (x_i^k, y_i^k), $k \leq n_s$, where n_s denotes the number of samples, defined as:

$$x_i^k = x_i + d^k \cos \theta_i^k \tag{1}$$
$$y_i^k = y_i + d^k \sin \theta_i^k \tag{2}$$

where $d^k \sim U([\gamma d_{\max}, \beta d_{\max}])$ and $\theta_i^k \sim U([\theta_i - \frac{\alpha}{2}, \theta_i + \frac{\alpha}{2}])$.

If the votes of two persons are close to each other, this means that the persons are close to each other and in a spatial configuration that allows for interaction. Otherwise, they are either too far from each other or not looking at each other, or not looking at a common region of space. Relevant O-spaces (and thus, F-formations) can therefore be identified by clustering the votes according to the Euclidean distance. Since the number of clusters is not known, a simple idea consists in applying any clustering method (e.g. K-means), with different numbers of clusters, and choosing the best one. To this end, we propose to define a score of a clustering based on the silhouette, measuring the similarity of a vote with the cluster it belongs to (mean distance to the other votes in the cluster), and its dissimilarity with the other clusters (smallest mean distance to the votes in the other clusters) [11]. The scores for each vote are then averaged for a cluster, and then for all the clusters, thus providing a global score for a given clustering. The clustering with the highest global score is finally chosen. Each person i is then assigned to the cluster containing the majority of her votes. All persons assigned to the same cluster belong to the same F-formation.

The principle of the proposed approach is illustrated in Fig. 1.

To fasten the computation, a simplified approach consists in setting $\alpha = 0$, and $\gamma = \beta$, which means that the field of view of each person is reduced to one point, corresponding to a unique vote for this person. However, this is a strong limitation with respect to the human perception, which impacts the results, as will be shown in Sect. 4.

3.2 Increasing Robustness by Taking into Account Temporal Memory

Instead of applying the previous approach in a static way, where each frame is processed independently, we now propose to exploit the dynamics of videos. The underlying hypothesis is that F-formations are usually quite stable over time, with a few changes from time to time, where some persons can leave a group to join another one. Moreover, small changes for instance in a person's body orientation or gaze direction, during a very short time, do not imply that this person has left the group. To model this behavior, we propose a method inspired by the work in [10]. We define a memory process, where two persons i and j in a group increase progressively their interaction (learning process) while forgetting progressively their interaction when they are no more in the same group (forgetting process). In particular, if a person briefly looks in another direction (or towards another F-formation) and rapidly returns to looking at her partners of her initial F-formation, this change of behavior will not be considered as changing group, thus increasing the stability of the detected F-formations. More formally, the memory process at time t and during a time interval Δt is modeled as:

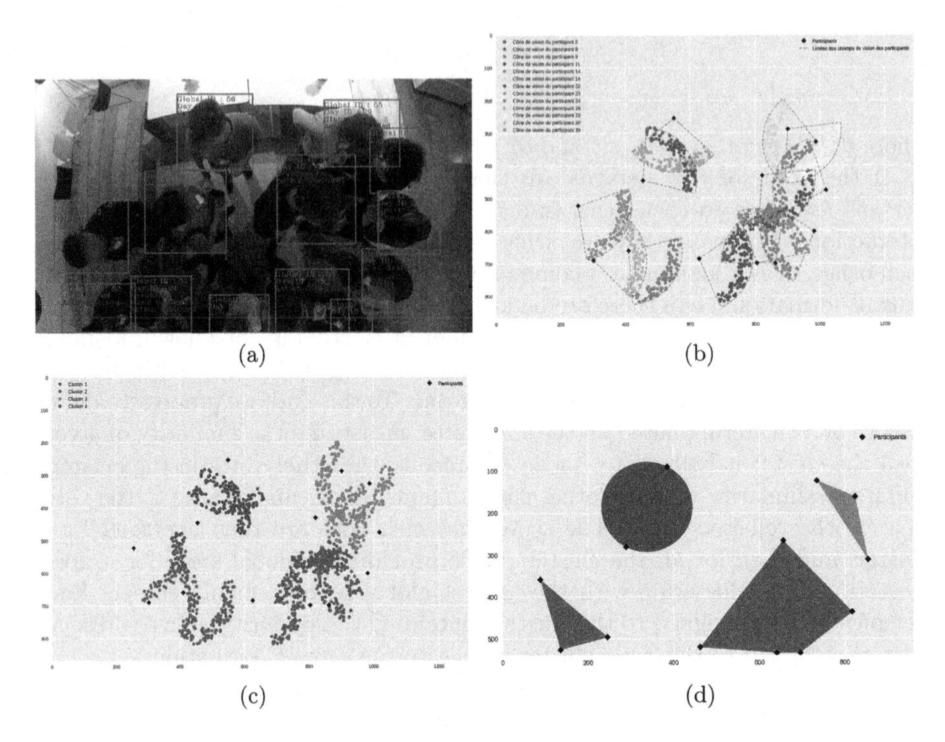

Fig. 1. Illustration of the identification of F-formations: (a) original image, (b) votes within the field of view, (c) clustering of the votes, and (d) obtained F-formations.

$$M_{i,j}(t+\Delta t) = \begin{cases} (1-\frac{\Delta t}{\tau_l})M_{i,j}(t) + \frac{\Delta t}{\tau_l} & \text{if } i \text{ and } j \text{ belong to the same group} \\ (1-\frac{\Delta t}{\tau_f})M_{i,j}(t) & \text{otherwise} \end{cases} \tag{3}$$

where τ_l is the learning rate and τ_f the forgetting rate. They are not necessarily equal, and if the learning process is considered faster than the forgetting process, then we will choose $\tau_l < \tau_f$. The process is initialized by setting $M_{i,j} = 0$ for all i and j, $i \neq j$. The time interval Δt is typically defined from the step s between frames to be analyzed and the video frequency f (e.g. $\Delta t = s/f$). For instance, to analyze every 20th frame in a video (such as in the Mingle base) with 20 frames per second, then we can set $\Delta t = 1$. Figure 2 illustrates two different behaviors of a person's memory with respect to a second person.

Two persons i and j are considered to interact at time t if $M_{i,j}(t)$ is above some threshold value (0.5 in our experiments). A graph is then defined, where vertices are the persons present in the scene and there is an edge between i and j if the corresponding persons do interact. Groups are then obtained by selecting

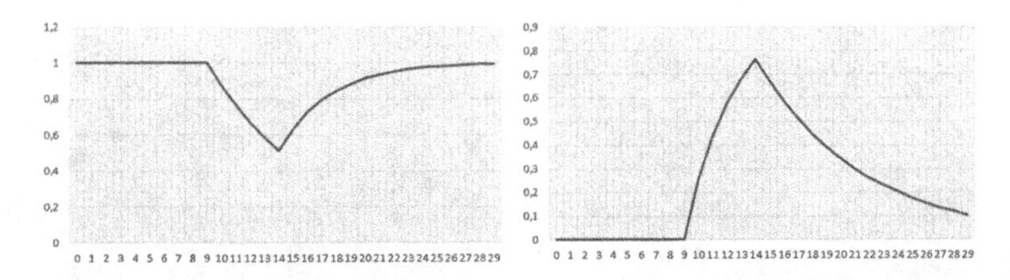

Fig. 2. Examples of the evolution of the memory in time. Left: a person knows a second person, then moves to another group and progressively forgets the second person, then joins the group again, and so "re-learns" the second person. Right: no interaction between two persons, then progressive learning, and then forgetting again.

the maximal cliques in the graph. An example is illustrated in Fig. 3. Note that a person can belong to several groups.

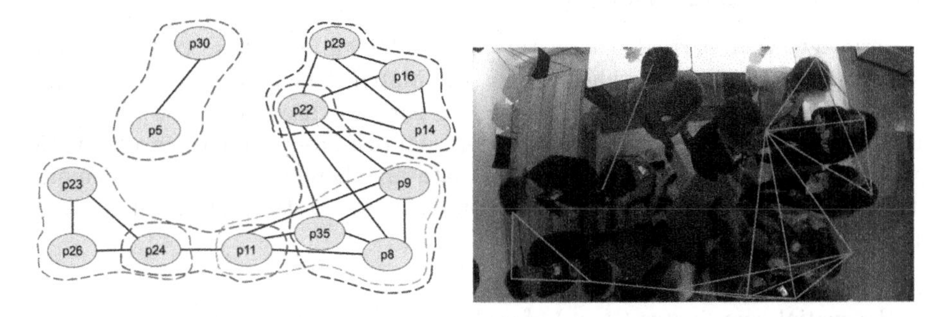

Fig. 3. Left: graph where vertices are persons and edges represent their interactions, and maximal cliques. Right: edges of the graph superimposed on the image.

Now, to restrict the groups to F-formations where one person can belong to only one of them, as is the case in the ground-truth of the Mingle data base, a last assignment step is required. The membership of person i to a group C_k at time t is defined as:

$$\mu(i,k,t) = \frac{1}{|C_k| - 1} \sum_{j \in C_k, j \neq i} M_{i,j}(t) \tag{4}$$

and the assignment is then $\arg\max_k \mu(i,k,t)$. A result is illustrated in Fig. 4. The comparison with the static approach, using only the information from this particular frame, without using the memory from frame to frame, shows a better consistency in the result when using the memory process, and better matches with the ground truth. In particular persons unassigned in the static mode are now correctly assigned to a group, and wrong assignments are also corrected.

Fig. 4. Left: final result, after maximal cliques detection and assignment of each person to one group. Right: result on the same frame, but without using the memory process.

4 Experiments and Results

4.1 MatchNMingle Data Set

Experiments were carried out on the MatchNMingle data base [2]. This data base consists of "speed-dating" videos (the Match data base), and of cocktail videos (the Mingle data base). This second part was used here. Several videos show participants moving freely in space, from one group to another one, with potentially complex interactions. These data are therefore relevant to demonstrate the usefulness of the proposed approach. Annotations are available and include:

- the list of participants;
- the spatial coordinates (x_i, y_i) of each participant i in each frame;
- the head orientation θ_i^{head} and body orientation θ_i^{body} of each participant in each frame;
- the coordinates $(x_1, y_1), (x_2, y_2)$ of the diagonal points of the bounding box of each participant in each frame;
- the F-formations, where each F-formation is defined as the set of its participants, its starting frame and its ending frame.

In our experiments, we used the position of the participants and the head orientation ($\theta_i = \theta_i^{head}$) as input data (see Sect. 3), and infer the F-formations.

4.2 Evaluation Criteria

The obtained F-formations can be compared to the ground-truth (provided as annotations with the data set). This amounts to compare two clusterings of the same data. A common measure to this end is the adjusted rand index (ARI) [6], which allows comparing two partitions of the same data, with potentially different cardinalities. This index takes values in $[-1, 1]$, and two partitions are considered as approximately similar if the index is higher than 0.5.

Let F_t denotes the partition (i.e. the set of F-formations) obtained in frame t of a video, and G_t the corresponding ground-truth. We denote by $ARI(F_t, G_t)$

the adjusted rand index comparing F_t and G_t. Averaging over all processed frames ($t = 1...T$) leads to a global score $EC = \frac{1}{T}\sum_{t=1}^{T} ARI(F_t, G_t)$, which should be as close to 1 as possible.

4.3 Parameter Setting

In our experiments, we set the number of samples in the voting procedure to $n_s = 100$. The field of view is parametrized by the aperture α, and the coefficients β and γ defining the truncation in terms of distance. According to the human perception, the maximum angle of vision is $\frac{2\pi}{3}$, and we performed experiments with $\alpha \in \{0, \frac{\pi}{6}, \frac{\pi}{3}, \frac{\pi}{2}, \frac{2\pi}{3}\}$. The parameter β defines the maximal distance $\beta d_{\max}$ at which votes can occur. In our experiments, $d_{\max}$ was set to the length of the image diagonal, and we limited β to 0.25 so as not to allow for votes that are too far away. Experiments were performed with $\beta \in \{0.05, 0.10, 0.15, 0.20, 0.25\}$, and γ is defined as $\gamma = (1 - \gamma')\beta$, where $\gamma' \in \{0, 0.25, 0.75, 1\}$, with the constraint $\gamma \leq \beta$. The choice of particular values of these three parameters was done using a small part of the data base (every 20th frames in a sequence of 5000 frames in one of the videos of the Mingle data base). All the values were tested, and the ones providing the best EC values (computed over these frames only) were chosen. An example of the EC values obtained for $\alpha = \pi/2$ is illustrated in Fig. 5. Similar tests were also performed for other values of α. Although this is a greedy approach, it is performed only once, and the number of parameters combinations to test remains limited. Then the obtained optimal parameters were fixed for all other frames and all videos. Finally, all experiments have been performed with parameters $\alpha = \pi/2, \beta = 0.15, \gamma = 0.11$. An example of the corresponding visual field is illustrated in Fig. 6. To illustrate the usefulness of the visual field and the votes, results are also compared with $\alpha = 0, \beta = \gamma = 0.1$, i.e. each participant votes for only one point, the center of the O-space.

In the clustering procedure, the number of clusters varies from 2 to n_p, where n_p denotes the number of persons in the scene. The parameters of the memory process are set as follows in our experiments: $\Delta t = 1$, $\tau_l = 3$ and $\tau_f = 8$.

4.4 Results

Qualitative results have been illustrated in Sect. 3, and demonstrate the improvement brought by the memory process over a purely static, frame by frame, approach. In this section, we propose a quantitative evaluation.

Figure 7 illustrates, on a sequence of one of the videos, the ARI values computed using:

1. a simple method, where only the distance between two persons is used to decide whether there should be grouped into a F-formation. This is performed by determining the connected components of a graph where vertices represent participants, and two vertices are linked by an edge if the distance between the corresponding participants is less than $\beta d_{\max}$. This method is obviously too simple, as shown by the low ARI values, below 0.5 most of the time, and is no longer considered in the remaining of our evaluation;

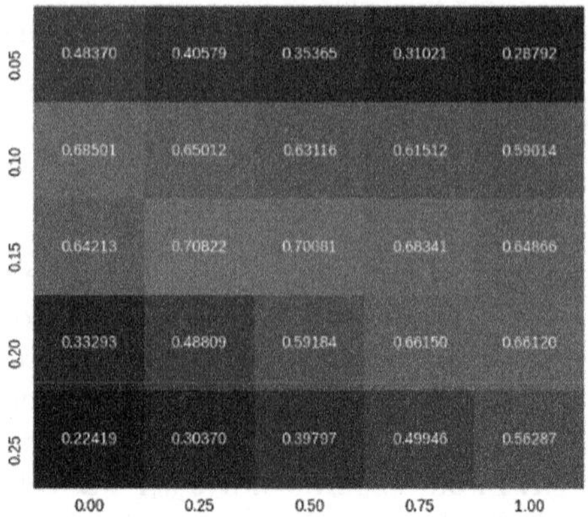

	0.00	0.25	0.50	0.75	1.00
0.05	0.48370	0.40579	0.35365	0.31021	0.28792
0.10	0.68501	0.65012	0.63116	0.61512	0.59014
0.15	0.64213	0.70822	0.70081	0.68341	0.64866
0.20	0.33293	0.48809	0.59184	0.66150	0.66120
0.25	0.22419	0.30370	0.39797	0.49946	0.56287

Fig. 5. *EC* values obtained on the frames used for training, for $\alpha = \pi/2$, and different values of β (ordinate) and $\gamma' = 1 - \gamma/\beta$ (abscissa). The highest score is obtained for $\beta = 0.15, \gamma' = 0.25$ (i.e. $\gamma = 0.11$).

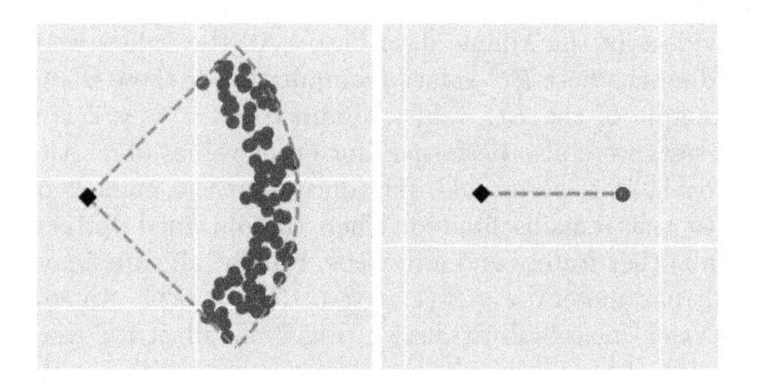

Fig. 6. Left: example of a visual field, in which votes are drawn, for the final parameter setting $\alpha = \pi/2, \beta = 0.15, \gamma = 0.11$. Right: vote for only one point, the center of the O-space, corresponding to $\alpha = 0, \beta = \gamma = 0.1$.

2. method 2: our proposed method, using distance and angle, but simplified by using parameters $\alpha = 0, \beta = \gamma$, i.e. each participant votes for only one point (center of the O-space). This shows a clear improvement over the previous naive approach;
3. method 3: our proposed method where several votes are drawn in the visual field. The results are even better, both in terms of ARI values and regularity of the detections. The method is also less sensitive to orientation due to the use of the visual field.

One can notice a few bad detections, e.g. frame 3940, where the ARI values are 0.27 for methods 2 and 3. This is improved by the memory process, as demonstrated next. The overall scores over the considered frames for the three methods are $EC_1 = 0.3, EC_2 = 0.76, EC_3 = 0.81$, respectively.

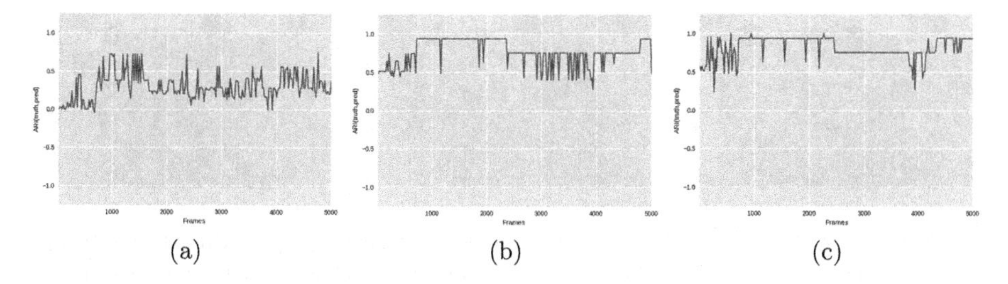

Fig. 7. Comparison of the ARI values on a sequence of frames of one of the Mingle videos. (a) Only distance is used (global score $EC_1 = 0.3$). (b) Distance and angle are used, with only one vote per participant ($EC_2 = 0.76$). (c) Proposed voting method, where each participant votes several times in her visual field ($EC_3 = 0.81$).

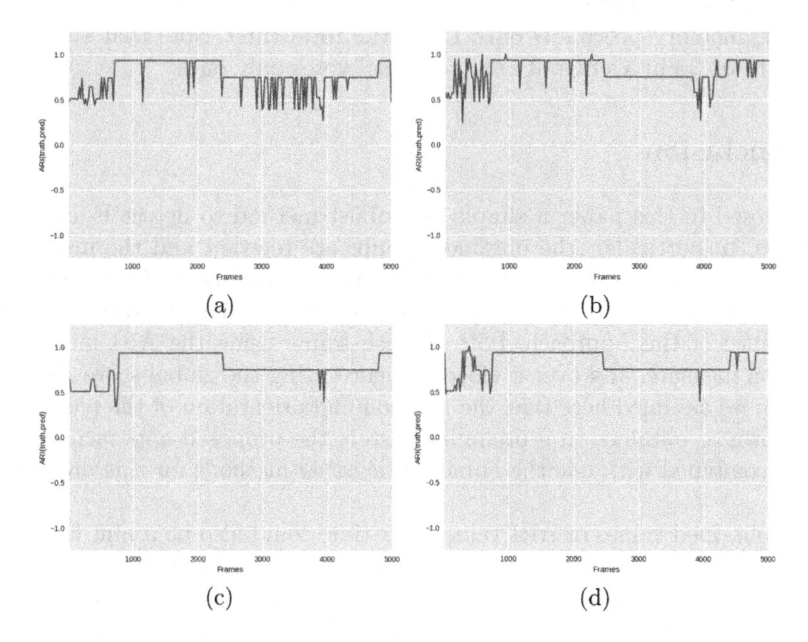

Fig. 8. (a) Method 2 (only one vote per participant) without memory, $EC_2 = 0.76$. (b) Method 3 (several votes in the visual field) without memory, $EC_3 = 0.81$. (c) Method 2 with memory process, $EC_2 = 0.78$. (d) Method 3 with memory process, $EC_3 = 0.82$.

Figure 8 compares the results for methods 2 and 3, without and with the memory process. Without the memory process, the global scores are $EC_2 = 0.76, EC_3 = 0.81$, while with the memory process they are $EC_2 = 0.78, EC_3 = 0.82$. This shows a slight improvement of the detection of F-formations, and a high improvement of the temporal regularity, which better matches what is intuitively expected in such scenarios. The results also confirm the superiority of the proposed method as described in Sect. 3, enhanced with the memory process to increase robustness to brief, non significant changes of head orientation.

Fig. 9. Excerpt of frames 720, 740, 760 in a video from the Mingle data set, exhibiting changes in the F-formations, correctly detected by the analysis of ARI values over time.

Without any specific code optimization, the computation time is 1.5 s in average on a standard computer, and most of the time is spent on the clustering part. The memory process is only 1% of the total time. Note that the time is reduced to 0.23 s in average if any individual votes only once.

5 Conclusion

We proposed in this paper a simple yet robust method to detect F-formations in images. In particular, the obtained groups are relevant and the influence of brief changes of position or gaze direction, which do not mean changes of group, is reduced thanks to a memory process. The results demonstrated the good performance of this approach, both in each frame using the ARI index as an evaluation measure, and over a video sequence using the global score EC.

While we assumed here that the position and orientation of the participants were known or obtained in a preliminary step, the proposed approach could be directly combined with one the numerous existing methods for this preliminary step.

The obtained values of ARI values over time could also be a hint for change detection, using graphs such as the one in Fig. 8 (d). Lower ARI values indicate changes in the F-formations. As an example, frames 720, 740 and 760, illustrated in Fig. 9, show such changes. The stability of the F-formations along time can be evaluated by $SC = \frac{1}{t_2-t_1}\sum_{t=t_1}^{t_2-1} ARI(F_t, F_{t+1})$, which will be close to 1 if the F-formations do not evolve much from t_1 to t_2 (i.e. always the same groups of discussion). This can help detecting in which time interval significant changes occur. A deeper analysis is left for future work.

Acknowledgments. The experiments in this paper used the MatchNMingle Dataset made available by the Delft University of Technology, Delft, The Netherlands [2].

References

1. Beebe, S.A., Masterson, J.T.: Communicating in Small Groups. Pearson Education, Boston (2003)

2. Cabrera-Quiros, L., Demetriou, A., Gedik, E., van der Meij, L., Hung, H.: The MatchNMingle dataset: a novel multi-sensor resource for the analysis of social interactions and group dynamics in-the-wild during free-standing conversations and speed dates. IEEE Trans. Affect. Comput. **12**(1), 113–130 (2018)
3. Cristani, M., et al.: Social interaction discovery by statistical analysis of F-formations. In: British Machine Vision Conference, vol. 2, p. 4 (2011)
4. Hall, E.T.: The Hidden Dimension, Reprint. Anchor Books, New York (1990)
5. Hu, S., et al.: A hybrid framework combining genetic algorithm with iterated local search for the dominating tree problem. Mathematics **7**(4), 359 (2019)
6. Hubert, L., Arabie, P.: Comparing partitions. J. Classif. **2**, 193–218 (1985)
7. Hung, H., Kröse, B.: Detecting F-formations as dominant sets. In: 13th International Conference on Multimodal Interfaces, pp. 231–238 (2011)
8. Kendon, A.: Conducting Interaction: Patterns of Behavior in Focused Encounters, vol. 7. Cambridge University Press, Cambridge (1990)
9. Mohammadi, S., Setti, F., Perina, A., Cristani, M., Murino, V.: Groups and crowds: behaviour analysis of people aggregations. In: International Joint Conference on Computer Vision, Imaging and Computer Graphics, pp. 3–32 (2017)
10. Ramírez, O.A.I., Varni, G., Andries, M., Chetouani, M., Chatila, R.: Modeling the dynamics of individual behaviors for group detection in crowds using low-level features. In: 25th IEEE International Symposium on Robot and Human Interactive Communication (RO-MAN), pp. 1104–1111 (2016)
11. Rousseeuw, P.J.: Silhouettes: a graphical aid to the interpretation and validation of cluster analysis. J. Comput. Appl. Math. **20**, 53–65 (1987)
12. Setti, F., Hung, H., Cristani, M.: Group detection in still images by F-formation modeling: A comparative study. In: 14th International Workshop on Image Analysis for Multimedia Interactive Services (WIAMIS), pp. 1–4. IEEE (2013)
13. Setti, F., Lanz, O., Ferrario, R., Murino, V., Cristani, M.: Multi-scale F-formation discovery for group detection. In: 2013 IEEE International Conference on Image Processing, pp. 3547–3551 (2013)
14. Setti, F., Russell, C., Bassetti, C., Cristani, M.: F-formation detection: individuating free-standing conversational groups in images. PLoS ONE **10**(5), e0123783 (2015)
15. Thompson, S., Gupta, A., Gupta, A.W., Chen, A., Vázquez, M.: Conversational group detection with graph neural networks. In: International Conference on Multimodal Interaction, pp. 248–252 (2021)
16. Vascon, S., et al.: Detecting conversational groups in images and sequences: a robust game-theoretic approach. Comput. Vis. Image Underst. **143**, 11–24 (2016)

Fusing AutoML Models: A Case Study in Medical Image Classification

Melissa Dale(✉), Arun Ross, and Erik M. Shapiro

Michigan State University, East Lansing, MI 48824, USA
dalemeli@msu.edu

Abstract. Automated Machine Learning (AutoML) tools are being increasingly used by researchers to solve a large number of pattern recognition tasks. A typical AutoML tool efficiently evaluates the performance of classifiers (e.g., SVM, Neural Network, Decision Tree, etc.) on an input dataset and determines the best performing classifier, along with the corresponding optimized parameters. In this work, we explore the use of a fusion scheme to combine the outputs of multiple classifier models generated and optimized by an AutoML tool known as Auto Tuned Models (ATM). We show that this approach provides a flexible framework that can be successfully applied to a wide variety of medical image classification tasks. Because each individual classification model is optimized for the given dataset, regardless of the size of the dataset, there is no requirement to identify and transfer knowledge from other domains. We generate up to 3,600 models for each dataset and explore the efficiency of fusion on subsets of models, as well as present two methods to automatically sort the classifier models for fusion. Experiments conducted on three medical imaging datasets, viz., stem cell, brain tumor and prostate cancer, convey the benefits of the proposed fusion scheme in improving classification accuracy.

Keywords: AutoML · Score fusion · MRI Classification

1 Introduction

A classical pattern recognition system maps input data (e.g., an image) to an output label referred to as a class (e.g., "face" or "bicycle" or "stem-cell"). This mapping is accomplished using a classifier such as a neural network or a support vector machine, with each classifier having a number of tunable parameters. Determining the best classifier and the associated optimized parameters for a given pattern recognition task is often relegated to a trial-and-error approach that can be both laborious and sub-optimal. Further, a classification model (i.e., a classifier along with its parameters) that is optimal on one dataset may not work well on other datasets.

To address this issue, there is a need for developing techniques that can *automatically* determine the best classifier for a given dataset. Over the years, a suite of such automated machine learning (AutoML) tools have been created and shown to have the ability to surpass the state of the art performances of previously hand-selected models. One such tool, Auto Tuned Models (ATM), not only surpassed performance of human-tuned models on 30% of 420 datasets in OpenML, but also completed this work in 1/100th of the time [21].

M. El Yacoubi et al. (Eds.): ICPRAI 2022, LNCS 13364, pp. 174–185, 2022.
https://doi.org/10.1007/978-3-031-09282-4_15

These tools have the ability to produce many different optimized classifier models based on different classifier types and different parameter combinations. In this work, we explore the possibility of combining multiple classifier models generated by an AutoML tool in order to further improve classification accuracy. The fusion scheme is tested on three medical imaging datasets corresponding to stem cell detection, brain tumor classification and prostate cancer classification.

Medical image classification is often challenging due to the costs of the imaging machines, the required expertise to annotate images, and patient privacy laws. These challenges often result in limited data availability which can restrict the ability to train deep neural networks, which often require large annotated datasets. Adaptations to deep neural networks such as transfer learning [4] or self-supervised learning techniques [11] have been proposed to address these challenges. However, these approaches rely on the ability to appropriately select an existing architecture or the creation of custom image transformations. Thus, the use of classification techniques that do not require copious amounts of annotated training data can be pertinent in such cases (Fig. 1).

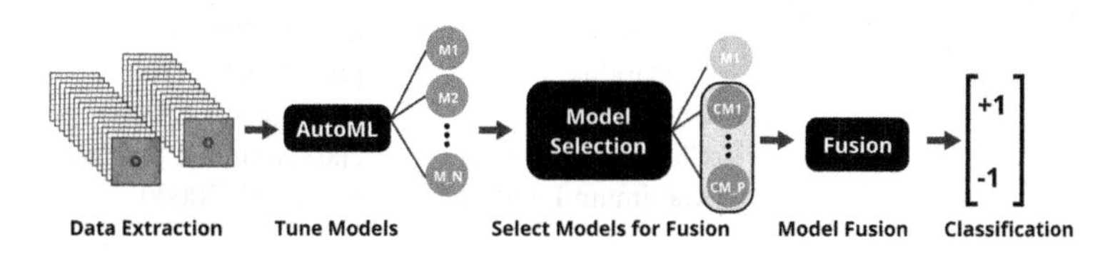

Fig. 1. Overview of proposed approach beginning with curating the dataset, producing candidate classifier models and choosing a subset of models for score fusion.

2 Background

We define a **classifier** as the type of classification algorithm, such as K-Nearest Neighbors (KNN), support vector machine (SVM), or multiple-layered perceptron (MLP). Once a classifier's parameters have been set, either by human intuition or via an AutoML tool, the resulting instance is referred to as a **classifier model** (see Table 1).

2.1 Pattern Recognition with AutoML

Given labeled data, a supervised classifier learns a model that can accurately map the input data to the correct output class label. The performance of a model depends on many factors such as the amount of training data available, the balance of data across classes, and the distribution of the data itself. A classifier model that performs well on a given dataset may not achieve the same performance on a different dataset for the same task.

Software packages used to generate these models have started to offer automated methods for classifier selection and parameter tuning. These methods are referred to as **automated machine learning (AutoML)** tools, and have provided a way to intelligently find classifier models optimized for specific datasets [12]. Popular AutoML tools include Auto-WEKA [14], Auto-Sklearn [10], and TPOT (Tree-based Pipeline Optimization Tool for Automating Data Science) [19]. In this work, we utilized a recently developed AutoML tool known as Auto Tuned Models (ATM) [21]. We choose ATM for its ability to tune models in parallel, as well as the ability to archive all the generated models.

ATM is constructed with Python's SciKit-Learn, and allows the same classifiers that are supported in SciKit-Learn. An example of the SVM classifier, its parameters, and the resulting tuned model are given in Table 1.

Table 1. Example of a classifier, parameters of the classifier, and values of these parameters. A **classifier model** denotes a classifier with fixed parameter values.

Classifier	Parameters	Model
Support vector machine (SVM)	C	'C': 0.032573723204237015
	Kernel	'kernel': 'linear'
	Probability	'probability': True
	Cache Size	'cache_size': 15000
	Class Weight	'class_weight': 'balanced'
	Maximum Iterations	'max_iter': 50000

The above approaches focus on classical pattern recognition approaches. Newer AutoML tools such as Auto-DeepLab [17] and Auto-Keras [13] focus on tuning deep learning models. However, we do not focus on the latter set of tools as our goal is to demonstrate how simple classification models, trained on small-sized datasets, can be judiciously selected and combined to improve classification performance in the context of medical image classification.

2.2 Fusion

An AutoML tool typically outputs multiple classifier models, including the one with the highest accuracy on the training set. While one model may have the highest accuracy, is it possible to leverage multiple models to achieve higher performance? Combining multiple sources of information to improve performance is generally referred to as **fusion**, and there are multiple levels at which fusion can be performed. This includes fusion at the raw data level [8], feature level, score level [20], rank level [20], and decision level [16].

This work considers fusion of multiple classifier models generated by ATM at the score level. Since this technique relies only on the score reported, it is possible to use this approach without knowledge of the features used to produce the score. In this work, the score generally denotes the confidence of each classifier model when it renders an output class label based on the input feature vector.

There are many approaches to fusion, such as the simple sum rule where scores are averaged [20]. The fusion in this paper is performed with an SVM, where the scores from multiple models are input to an SVM which then maps this score vector to an output class or label. The question we raise is the following: how do we determine the models whose scores have to be fused?

3 Datasets

Three different medical imaging datasets are utilized in this work. These datasets include stem cells, brain tumors, and prostate cancer grade classifications for magnetic resonance imaging (MRI) scans. In our analysis, the MRI scans are comprised of a stack of 16-bit tiff images. These images are generated from DICOM (Digital Imaging and Communications in Medicine standard), a common file format generated by medical imaging machines such as MRIs.

3.1 MSU Stem Cell Dataset

Afridi et al. created a dataset of 6 *in vivo* MRI scans of rat brains that were hand-labeled for stem cells by radiologists [1,2]. This dataset was generated from 2 different MRI machines of varying field strengths, and is intended to evaluate the generalizability and robustness of potential stem cell detection algorithms. Each scan is composed of 16-bit tiff images (Fig. 2, left), which radiologists manually reviewed to identify and label stem cells. Once a stem cell is identified, a 9×9 pixel patch is extracted around the stem cell (Fig. 2, right).

Using handcrafted features and Bayesian Classifiers, Afridi et al. [1] obtained an AUC accuracy of 89.1%. They were able to further improve performance using a CNN-based approach that incorporated the information about the time radiologists spent identifying stem cells (referred to as Labeling Latency). This approach achieved an accuracy of 94.6% [2]. For our analysis, we divide the labeled data into 80% training and 20% testing. This is summarized in Table 2 (Figs. 3).

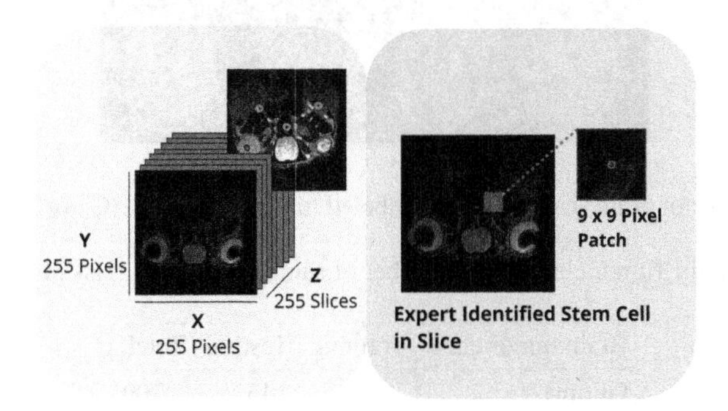

Fig. 2. Visualization of a labeled MRI scan with stem cells marked in green (left). Extracting patches containing identified stem cells, forming the stem-cell patches (right). (Color figure online)

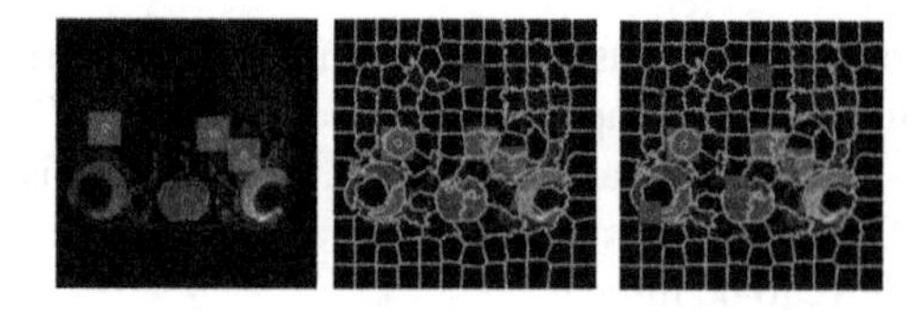

Fig. 3. Non-stem cell patch extraction: After all stem cells have been identified (left), super-pixels are calculated (center) and super-pixels are randomly selected such that there is no overlap with stem-cell patches (right).

Table 2. Number of samples for each class in the training, testing, and entire stem-cell dataset

Stem cell detection	Training	Testing	Total
Stem cell	31,910	8,067	39,977
Non-stem cell	31,976	7,905	39,881
TOTAL	**63,886**	**15,972**	**79,858**

3.2 Brain Tumor Classification

Cheng et al. [6] generated a dataset comprised of brain scans of 233 patients with identified tumors. Figure 4 provides examples of four slices (top) and the annotated tumors (bottom). In addition to the manually segmented tumor masks (highlighted in yellow on the bottom row), we display the bounding box surrounding the tumors in red. Three types of tumors are identified: Glioma, Meningioma, and Pituitary. Table 3 gives the breakdown of the 3,064 MRI slices. For our analysis, we divide the labeled data into 80% training and 20% testing. This is summarized in Table 3.

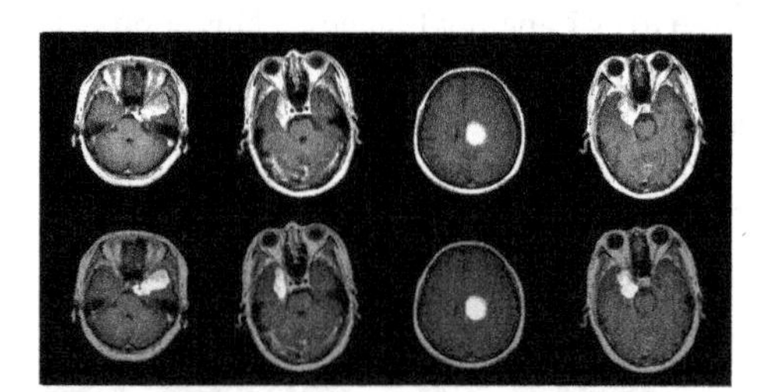

Fig. 4. Example of brain scans (top) and labeled tumors (bottom). (Color figure online)

Table 3. Brain Tumor classes and number of samples for each class in the dataset

Brain tumor class	Training	Testing	Total
Glioma	566	143	709
Meningioma	1,141	290	1,431
Pituitary	744	180	924
TOTAL	**2,451**	**613**	**3,064**

The authors of this dataset explored classification of tumors through region augmentation by including the segmented tumor and the regions surrounding it [7]. They obtained a classification accuracy of 82.3%. Afshar et al. further improved classification performance to 86.56% by designing a Capsule Network [3]. In our work, however, we only use the segmented tumor without surrounding pixels for classification.

3.3 Prostate Cancer Classification

The American Association of Physicists in Medicine, the International Society for Optics and Photonics, and the National Cancer Institute collaborated to create the PROSTATEx Challenges for classifying the aggressiveness of prostate cancer [5]. The PROSTATEx challenge dataset provides information for 182 subjects. This information includes multiple MRI scans with multiple weighting agents, and a cancer diagnosis based on Gleason Score grouping. A low Gleason score indicates small, well formed and uniform glands, i.e., mostly normal cells. A high score indicates irregular sizes, glands, or masses (abnormal cells). These scores are categorized into 5 groups defined in Table 4. Additionally, a set of KTrans images (a measure of capillary permeability is provided for each patient. This data is already divided into training and test sets. The best results of this competition was an AUC accuracy score of 95% (https://prostatex.grand-challenge.org/evaluation/results/) (Fig. 5).

Table 4. Grade grouping of the Gleason Scores and number of samples for each group in the dataset

Grade group	Training samples	Testing samples
Grade group 1 (Gleason score < 6)	9	4
Grade group 2 (Gleason score 3 + 4 = 7)	2,405	236
Grade group 3 (Gleason score 4 + 3 = 7)	1,063	28
Grade group 4 (Gleason score 4 + 4 = 8; 3 + 5 = 8; 5 + 3 = 8)	304	8
Grade group 5 (Gleason scores 9–10)	88	4
TOTAL	**3,869**	**280**

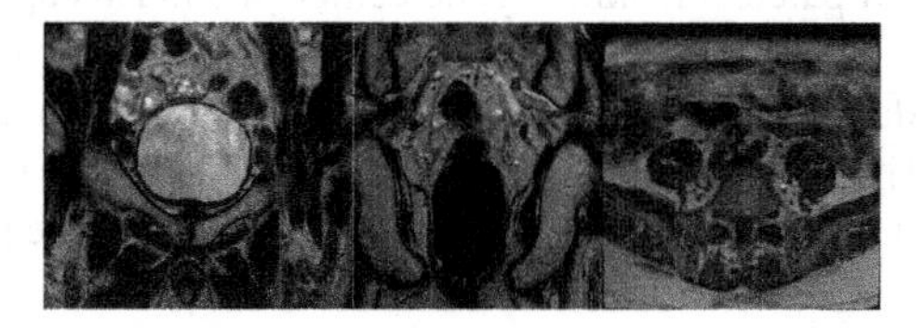

Fig. 5. Examples of prostate scans from the PROSTATEx Challenge dataset.

4 Proposed Approach

The contribution of this work is the principled use of fusion to combine the multiple classifier models produced by an AutoML tool such as ATM. Questions we explore include which data representations to use, how many models are necessary to fuse, and how to select models for fusion. In this section, the proposed approach is described in detail. The proposed approach implements the following steps:

1. **Extract Data**: For each of the datasets described in Sect. 2, image patches are extracted from the MRI scan and given a class label.
2. **Form Feature-Sets**: While the pixels in a patch can be directly used as raw input to ATM, we also consider alternate inputs where a patch is subjected to different feature extraction techniques via texture descriptors. These alternate representations along with the original patch representation are referred to as Feature-Sets.
3. **Generate Models with ATM**: ATM [21] generates multiple classifier models from the training set of extracted patches and the corresponding feature-sets.
4. **Collect Model Scores**: Test patches are given as input to the models to obtain a score (described later in Sect. 4.4).
5. **Perform Fusion**: The scores of multiple classifier models are fused using an SVM classifier.

For the rest of this section, let m_{ijk} represent the ith model pertaining to the jth classifier tuned on the kth feature-set ($i \in Z$, $j \in J$, $k \in K$), and let FM represent the subset of models to be used in fusion. Here, K represents the feature-sets (raw, scaled, HOG, LBP, LBP-Uniform, LBP-Rotation Invariant), and J represents the collection of classifiers (Logistic Regression, Support Vector Machine, Linear Classifier with Stochastic Gradient Descent, Decision Tree, Extra Trees, Random Forest, Gaussian Naive Bayes, Multinomial Naive Bayes, Bernoulli Naive Bayes, Gaussian Process, Passive Aggressive, K Nearest Neighbors, Multi-Layer Perceptron).

4.1 Data Extraction

For the stem cell dataset, we use the same method proposed by Afridi et al. [2] to extract image patches. We center patches around regions of interest (stem cell and non-stem cell), as shown in Fig. 2. The resulting patches are 9×9 pixels.

For the brain tumor dataset, we first find the smallest width and also the smallest height of all the bounding boxes within the dataset. This worked out to be 14 pixels on both dimensions. We then locate the center pixel of the tumor's bounding box, and extract a 14×14 pixel patch surrounding the center pixel. This approach ensures that the patches contain only tumor information and nothing of the surrounding brain tissue.

For the prostate dataset, locations of legions were provided in the same manner as the stem cell data. That is, an expert identified point-of-interest is labeled within an MRI scan. We extract a 15×15 pixel patch of the slice around the point of interest.

4.2 Data Descriptors Through Feature-Sets

In addition to the raw pixel values within the patches, scaled pixel intensities and texture descriptors are also considered. These methods produce the following feature-sets: Raw pixel intensities (in the range [0, 65,535]), Scaled Intensities (in the range of [0, 255]), Histogram of Oriented Gradients (HOG) [9], DAISY feature descriptors [22], and Local Binary Pattern (Classical, Rotation-Invariant, Uniform) [18].

4.3 Model Generation

Once all the feature-sets are generated, the labeled training data for each feature-set in K is run through ATM. We set ATM's model budget, B, to 600 models for each feature-set in K. With $|K| = 6$, this means ATM produces up to 3,600 tuned models. Since the number of tuned models is very large, we would like a principled manner to form a subset of candidate models, FM, that will reliably improve performance while efficiently selecting only the models necessary to achieve good results. This selection process is described in Sect. 4.5.

4.4 Model Scores

Given an input feature-set, each tuned classifier model predicts an output class label. Additionally, each model produces a score, which in many cases, corresponds to a probability value. For example, a multi layered perceptron (MLP) model classifies the input data by using a softmax score, which is the probability that the input data belongs to class y. If scores are not readily available from a tuned model, other representations of prediction strengths are used to estimate a score. To obtain scores for the KNN classifier, for example, we average the Euclidean distance of the K neighbors. The smaller the distance, the stronger the evidence is that the point is correctly classified. For the Extra Trees and Random Forest classifiers, the score denotes the percentage of trees that correctly classify the sample, and for the singular decision tree, the score corresponds to the percentage of nodes in agreement.

4.5 Model Selection for Fusion

With so many optimized models generated, a question arises. Should all models be included in fusion? It is possible that several optimized models are only slight variations of a dominant classifier's parameters, resulting in redundant score data and biased classification predictions. Before we propose methods to automatically select models for fusion, we first explore various methods to partitioning the models to form subset FM and address potential bias.

Forming FM: The first obvious method to subsetting M into FM is to select the top n models reporting the highest classification accuracy (**Top**). This approach is straightforward and is effective at drastically cutting the size of M. However, as before, we find that if a certain classifier performs particularly well on a dataset, a large portion of the n models in FM will belong to the same classifier and make similar classification errors. Therefore, we next explore forming FM by partitioning M based on the classifier type (**CS**), the feature-set (**FS**), and the classifier-feature-set combination (**CFS**). To form FM, we select the highest performing model from each partition. For example, in the CS stratification approach we select the model with the highest reported AUC accuracy for each classifier type. Lastly, we form FM by considering every optimized model produced by ATM ($FM == M$). In summary, the following are the approaches we apply to form FM: **Top**, **CS**, **FS**, **CFS**, and the entire set of models.

Once the models in FM have been identified using one of the aforementioned methods, the next step is to design an algorithm to effectively select the minimal number of classifier models to fuse. Intelligently selecting models for fusion begins with deciding which model best complements the models already selected for fusion. To facilitate this, we compute the pair-wise score correlation between all pairs of candidate models. Typically, combining models which are least correlated can be beneficial [15]. In this work, we develop two techniques for selecting models to fuse. In both approaches, we start with the best performing model generated by ATM and then use pairwise correlation value to guide model selection. Then, we compare the performance of these two approaches, examining how the accuracy and efficiency are impacted by the number of models fused.

Static Selection: The first selected model is the best model produced by ATM. The remainder of the models in FM that are not selected form the unselected model set. The next model chosen is the unselected model with the least correlation to the last selected model. This process is repeated until there are no more unselected models and the selection is complete. By using the Pearson correlation between models' scores across training samples in order to select models, we are selecting models whose scores contain new information not captured by the previously selected models.

Algorithm 1. Static Selection

DECLARE: $Selected \leftarrow$ ARRAY[0:2] of $sorted(FM)$
DECLARE: $NotSelected \leftarrow ARRAY[2:n]$ of $sorted(FM)$
while length of NotSelected > 1 **do**
  $corrs \leftarrow pearson(Selected, NotSelected)$
  $Selected$ insert $min(corrs)$ Model
  $NotSelected$ remove $min(corrs)$ Model
end while

Dynamic Selection: We next explore sorting models by dynamically updating the correlation values after selecting a new model for fusion. Once the first 2 candidate models are selected as described in the static sort above, we immediately fuse the selected models to obtain a new model with the new set of fused scores. We update the correlation coefficients with the unselected models to account for the scores from the newly fused model. This selection method is dynamic and allows for the flexibility to select the next model based on the current models already selected for fusion.

Algorithm 2. Dynamic Selection

DECLARE: $Selected \leftarrow$ ARRAY[0:2] of $sorted(FM)$
DECLARE: $Fused \leftarrow Fused(Selected)$
DECLARE: $NotSelected \leftarrow ARRAY[2:n]$ of $sorted(FM)$
while length of NotSelected > 1 **do**
  $corrs \leftarrow pearson(Selected, NotSelected)$
  $Selected$ insert $min(corrs)$ Model
  $NotSelected$ remove $min(corrs)$ Model
  $Fused \leftarrow fuse(Selected)$
  $NotSelected$ insert $Fused$ Model
end while

5 Results and Analysis

The proposed method is able to improve the AUC accuracies, both over any individual AutoML generated model and over the previous state-of-the-art accuracies described in Sect. 3. We focus on the Prostate and Brain datasets, as ATM produced significantly optimized models for the Stem Cell dataset with individual AUC accuracies over 99%. While no single stratification approach universally performed the best, we find that using a stratification approach reports higher AUC accuracies than *randomly* selecting the same number of models (repeated 5 times), as shown in Table 5, with the class-feature stratification (CFS) technique providing the best results with the fewest models for the prostate dataset, and selecting models from the top-performing stratification (TOP) provides the best results for the brain dataset. Figure 6 shows how the AUC accuracies change as models are added to the fusion.

Table 5. Summary of the best accuracies (%) achieved through fusion compared to previous published performances. Entries in parenthesis indicate number of models fused and the stratification approach. Note, ATM produced models which achieve strong results and so fusing additional models are not considered.

	Brain tumor	Prostate	Stem cell
Previous accuracy	86.56 [3]	95.00 [5]	94.6 [2]
SVM fusion: proposed model selection	**100 (27, TOP)**	**100 (124, CFS)**	**99.8 (1)**
SVM fusion: random model selection	91.45 ± 0.5889 (27)	99.16 ± 0.0004 (124)	71.43 (1)

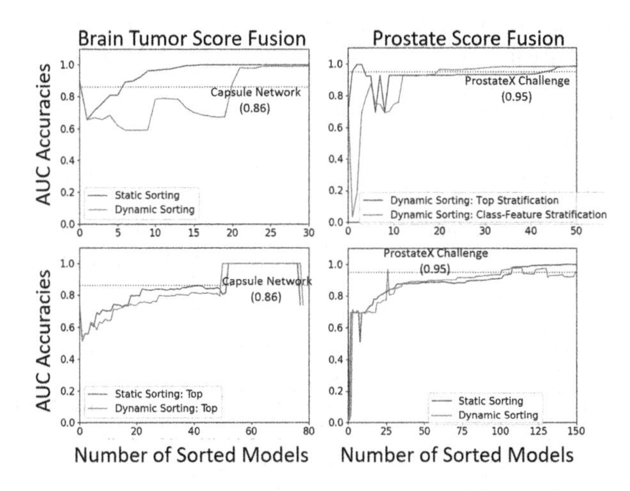

Fig. 6. Plots illustrating the changes in accuracy as increasing number of models are included for fusion. Left: Brain dataset, Right: Prostate dataset.

6 Summary

We applied score fusion to combine multiple classification models generated by an AutoML tool to produce improved accuracy on three medical imaging datasets. Further, we developed two methods to select models for fusion based on Pearson's correlation coefficient. This case study focused on medical image datasets, and obtained several classification models via an AutoML tool (ATM) to fuse together. We observe that fusing models improves the accuracy beyond the best individual classification model produced by ATM, and that the highest accuracy achieved through fusion of these models surpasses the accuracy of even deep learning approaches. Furthermore, these results are achieved with small training data sizes without auxiliary information, such as labeling behavior or pixels surrounding the area of interest. This underscores the importance of judiciously selecting models for fusion in order to improve classification accuracy.

References

1. Afridi, M.J., Liu, X., Shapiro, E., Ross, A.: Automatic in vivo cell detection in MRI. In: Navab, N., Hornegger, J., Wells, W.M., Frangi, A.F. (eds.) MICCAI 2015. LNCS, vol. 9351, pp. 391–399. Springer, Cham (2015). https://doi.org/10.1007/978-3-319-24574-4_47
2. Afridi, M.J., Ross, A., Shapiro, E.M.: L-CNN: exploiting labeling latency in a CNN learning framework. In: Pattern Recognition (ICPR), pp. 2156–2161 (2016)
3. Afshar, P., Mohammadi, A., Plataniotis, K.N.: Brain tumor type classification via capsule networks. In: 25th IEEE International Conference on Image Processing (ICIP), pp. 3129–3133 (2018)
4. Alzubaidi, L., et al.: Novel transfer learning approach for medical imaging with limited labeled data. Cancers **13**(7), 1590 (2021)
5. Armato, S.G., et al.: PROSTATEx challenges for computerized classification of prostate lesions from multiparametric magnetic resonance images. J. Med. Imaging **5**(4), 044501 (2018)
6. Cheng, J.: Brain Tumor Dataset, April 2017. https://doi.org/10.6084/m9.figshare.1512427.v5. https://figshare.com/articles/brain_tumor_dataset/1512427/5
7. Cheng, J., et al.: Enhanced performance of brain tumor classification via tumor region augmentation and partition. PLoS ONE **10**(10), e0140381 (2015)
8. Chitroub, S.: Classifier combination and score level fusion: concepts and practical aspects. Int. J. Image Data Fusion **1**(2), 113–135 (2010). https://doi.org/10.1080/19479830903561944
9. Dalal, N., Triggs, B.: Histograms of oriented gradients for human detection. In: IEEE Computer Society Conference on Computer Vision and Pattern Recognition, vol. 1, pp. 886–893 (2005)
10. Feurer, M., et al.: Efficient and robust automated machine learning. In: Advances in Neural Information Processing Systems, pp. 2962–2970. Curran Associates, Inc. (2015)
11. Ghesu, F.C., et al.: Self-supervised learning from 100 million medical images (2022)
12. Hutter, F., Kotthoff, L., Vanschoren, J.: Automated Machine Learning: Methods, Systems, Challenges. Springer, Cham (2019). https://doi.org/10.1007/978-3-030-05318-5
13. Jin, H., Song, Q., Hu, X.: Auto-keras: efficient neural architecture search with network morphism. arXiv preprint arXiv:1806.10282 (2018)

14. Kotthoff, L., Thornton, C., Hoos, H.H., Hutter, F., Leyton-Brown, K.: Auto-WEKA: automatic model selection and hyperparameter optimization in WEKA. In: Hutter, F., Kotthoff, L., Vanschoren, J. (eds.) Automated Machine Learning. TSSCML, pp. 81–95. Springer, Cham (2019). https://doi.org/10.1007/978-3-030-05318-5_4
15. Kuncheva, L.I., Whitaker, C.J.: Measures of diversity in classifier ensembles and their relationship with the ensemble accuracy. Mach. Learn. **51**(2), 181–207 (2003)
16. Lam, L., Suen, S.: Application of majority voting to pattern recognition: an analysis of its behavior and performance. IEEE Trans. Syst. Man Cybern. Part A Syst. Hum. **27**(5), 553–568 (1997)
17. Liu, C., et al.: Auto-deeplab: hierarchical neural architecture search for semantic image segmentation. In: Proceedings of the IEEE Conference on Computer Vision and Pattern Recognition, pp. 82–92 (2019)
18. Ojala, T., Pietikainen, M., Maenpaa, T.: Multiresolution gray-scale and rotation invariant texture classification with local binary patterns. IEEE Trans. Pattern Anal. Mach. Intell. **24**(7), 971–987 (2002)
19. Olson, R.S., et al.: Automating biomedical data science through tree-based pipeline optimization. In: Squillero, G., Burelli, P. (eds.) EvoApplications 2016. LNCS, vol. 9597, pp. 123–137. Springer, Cham (2016). https://doi.org/10.1007/978-3-319-31204-0_9
20. Ross, A.A., Nandakumar, K., Jain, A.K.: Handbook of Multibiometrics. Springer, Boston (2006). https://doi.org/10.1007/0-387-33123-9
21. Swearingen, T., et al.: ATM: A distributed, collaborative, scalable system for automated machine learning. In: IEEE International Conference on Big Data, Boston, MA, USA, 11–14 December, pp. 151–162 (2017). https://doi.org/10.1109/BigData.2017.8257923
22. Tola, E., Lepetit, V., Fua, P.: Daisy: an efficient dense descriptor applied to wide-baseline stereo. IEEE Trans. Pattern Anal. Mach. Intell. **32**(5), 815–830 (2010)

Ordinal Classification and Regression Techniques for Distinguishing Neutrophilic Cell Maturity Stages in Human Bone Marrow

Philipp Gräbel[1(✉)], Martina Crysandt[2], Barbara M. Klinkhammer[3], Peter Boor[3], Tim H. Brümmendorf[2], and Dorit Merhof[1]

[1] Institute of Imaging and Computer Vision, RWTH Aachen University, Aachen, Germany
{graebel,merhof}@lfb.rwth-aachen.de

[2] Department of Hematology, Oncology, Hemostaseology and Stem Cell Transplantation, University Hospital RWTH Aachen University, Aachen, Germany

[3] Institute of Pathology, University Hospital RWTH Aachen University, Aachen, Germany

Abstract. An automated classification of hematopoietic cells in bone marrow whole slide images would be very beneficial to the workflow of diagnosing diseases such as leukemia. However, the large number of cell types and particularly their continuous maturation process makes this task challenging: the boundaries of cell type classes in this process are fuzzy, leading to inter-rater disagreement and noisy annotations. The data qualifies as *ordinal data*, as the order of classes is well defined. However, a sensible "distance" between them is difficult to establish.

In this work, we propose several classification and regression techniques for ordinal data, which alter the encoding of network output and ground-truth. For classification, we propose using the Gray code or decreasing weights. For regression, we propose encodings inspired by biological properties or characteristics of the dataset. We analyze their performance on a challenging dataset with neutrophilic granulocytes from human bone marrow microscopy images. We show that for a sensible evaluation, it is of utmost importance to take into account the relation between cell types as well as the annotation noise. The proposed methods are straight-forward to implement with any neural network and outperform common classification and regression methods.

Keywords: Ordinal classification · Regression · Cell classification

This work was supported by the German Research Foundation (DFG) through the grants SFB/TRR57, SFB/TRR219, BO3755/6-1. The authors would like to thank Reinhild Herwartz and Melanie Baumann for their efforts in sample preparation and annotation.

M. El Yacoubi et al. (Eds.): ICPRAI 2022, LNCS 13364, pp. 186–195, 2022.
https://doi.org/10.1007/978-3-031-09282-4_16

1 Introduction

For the diagnosis of hematopoietic diseases such as leukemia it is necessary to analyze bone marrow samples in addition to peripheral blood. The major advantage of bone marrow analysis is a more detailed insight into hematopoiesis, the cell-forming process. The ratio of immature to mature granulocytes is of major importance, particularly for the detection of chronic myelogenous leukemia. While the process of maturation is a mostly continuous process, hematologists define five classes of granulocytes subsequent to the immature blast stage: promyelocytes, myelocytes, metamyelocytes, band granulocytes and segmented granulocytes. In theory, these maturity stages are well defined. However, manual class assignment by experts is fuzzy at transition stages which results in noisy labels. Inter-rater disagreement between adjacent classes can be observed. This refers not only to the annotations used in training but also to the desired predictions, which hampers a valid, automated evaluation.

Given the described continuous maturation process with transitions between classes and the resulting inter-rater disagreement between adjacent maturity stages, classification may not be the best option. While annotations are typically given as one of five maturity stages – and predictions ought to follow the same format – network optimization could be performed as a regression task. Formulated as regression, the task lies in predicting the maturity stage as a number, instead of a class. As the order of maturity stages is known without an obvious distance metric between those stages, this problem falls into the category of ordinal classification or regression.

The field of regression is a common research area, including some research which takes ordinal data into account. Also ordinal regression and classification have been researched extensively for generic classifiers [6]. Straight-forward approaches in this context, such as assigning regression targets or misclassification costs, can be transferred to deep learning. Other deep learning approaches require extensive changes to the network architecture and/or training process, for example, through pairwise comparisons [9].

In the field of hematopoietic cell classification from bone marrow microscopy images, the relationship between different classes is usually ignored. Song et al. [12, 13] work with bone marrow images but only distinguish between the erythroid and myeloid cell. The maturity grade within individual lineages is not further considered. Choi et al. [3] use a VGG architecture [11] to distinguish between different maturity stages within these two lineages. They treat most classes independently, but refine the prediction of the two most mature neutrophilic cells with a second VGG network. Preliminary experiments on our dataset showed, however, that this network architecture is outperformed by using a DenseNet [5]. Chandradevan et al. [2] perform a simple classification using a VGG network. All aforementioned methods do not perform an analysis on the relationship between adjacent maturity stages and do not take this knowledge into account for training and prediction.

Contribution

In this work, we propose and investigate several strategies to improve common classification and regression techniques in the case of ordinal data and justify the need for those by providing a multi-rater data analysis of the given dataset. These straight-forward techniques are based on an established classification architecture and require minimal changes to the final linear layer and the class encoding. They achieve improved results in the case of classification and regression of neutrophilic granulocytes in human bone marrow microscopy images in an evaluation on multi-rater data.

2 Materials and Methods

2.1 Image Data

The data is obtained from human bone marrow samples as a purely retrospective, pseudonymized analysis under the Helsinki Declaration of 1975/2000 with written informed consent of all patients. Each sample is stained using the standardized Pappenheim staining procedure [1]. Image acquisition is performed with a whole slide scanner using 63× magnification and automatic immersion oiling. From each sample, relevant regions are selected using a lower magnification overview scan. In each region, cell positions are first proposed by an object detection network and then manually corrected. Each cell is annotated by two medical experts, who have agreed on the cell type. This annotated label is later referred to as an *MTA*-label and it forms the ground truth in all training processes. Examples are shown in Fig. 1.

In this work, the focus lies on predicting maturity stages. To this end, patches that are centered around individual cells of the neutrophilic granulopoiesis are extracted. In total, this results in 4301 cells from six classes: blast, promyelocyte, myelocyte, metamyelocyte, band granulocyte and segmented granulocyte. Of these, 767 cells have been annotated by additional different experts (two to three medical experts, with one annotation as mentioned above). If one expert declares a cell to be one of the considered cell types, while another assigns a completely different cell lineage, this is denoted by the cell type *other*.

Inter-rater Analysis. A comparison between two of the raters highlights the characteristics of inter-rater variability with respect to the maturity progression. Ignoring the *other* class, they agreed on the maturity stage in 65.3% of all cases. In 96.6% of all cases, however, they only differed by, at most, one stage. Apart from a single case, the remainder is, at most, two stages apart.

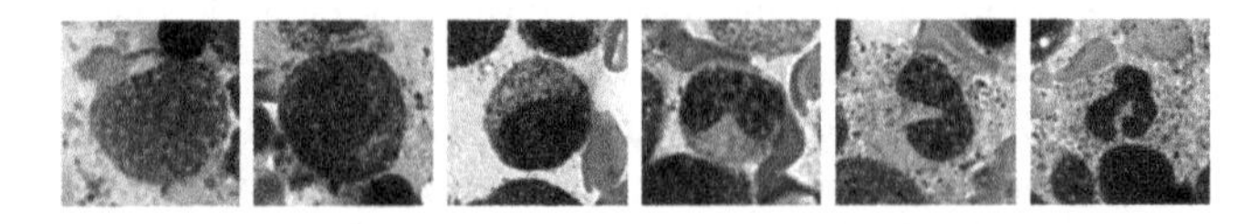

Fig. 1. One example for every cell type, which corresponds to a single maturity stage. From left to right: blast, promyelocyte, myelocyte, metamyelocyte, band granulocyte and segmented granulocyte.

This highlights the importance of a) using methods that not only consider absolute labels but also consider the data as ordinal and b) a multi-rater evaluation. When not taking the ordinality of this data into account, the ground truth provided by a single expert (or even multiple experts working together on a single annotation) could be considered wrong by a second expert in almost a third of all cases. This could lead to undesirable effects in training by putting a focus on "false" predictions that would actually be considered as correct by another rater.

Due to the necessary amount of manual work by medical experts, it is often impossible to obtain a complete multi-rater dataset for training. Instead, we propose strategies to include the ordinality of data into the training on a single-rater dataset. Nevertheless, the evaluation needs to be performed on multi-rater data, in order to get an indication of the actual success of such techniques.

2.2 Classification Techniques

Classification using convolutional neural networks is commonly performed using the Cross-Entropy Loss on the softmax output of the network. However, this loss treats all classes independently – the relationship between adjacent maturity stages can not be modeled using this loss. This can be mitigated by adapting the optimization target, which is usually a one-hot encoded vector representing the ground truth class. We propose two alternative ground truth encodings which are based on (1) declining weights and (2) on the Gray code to incorporate the biological dependencies into the target vector. Both methods are applied by computing the binary cross-entropy loss on a sigmoidal activation of the network output.

According to the taxonomy of Gutiérrez et al. [6], these approaches are similar to *cost-sensitive classification* techniques. They differ, however, in the encoding, which in this work is specifically designed to work with a typical deep learning architecture and the corresponding loss functions.

Declining Weights. Instead of using the one-hot encoding to represent a class (e.g. $[0, 0, 1, 0, 0, 0]$ to represent the myelocyte), we propose an encoding that additionally assigns a smaller number to adjacent classes. Specifically, each class c is represented based on the distance to the ground truth class c_{gt} using $w_{\text{dec}}^{|c-c_{\text{gt}}|}$. The distance here refers to the number of cell types between a class (inclusive) and the ground truth class (exclusive), such that adjacent classes have a distance of 1). For instance, with $w_{\text{dec}} = \frac{1}{2}$ and $c_{\text{gt}} = 2$ (myelocyte), this yields $[\frac{1}{4}, \frac{1}{2}, 1, \frac{1}{2}, \frac{1}{4}, \frac{1}{8}]$ as an encoding. Consequently, mis-classifications between adjacent classes yield lower losses than mis-classifications between distant classes.

Compared to similar ordinal classification techniques [8], we encode the relationship between classes not as a *cost* but as an *acceptability* measure.

Gray Code. As another alternative to one-hot encoding, we propose utilizing the *Reflected Binary Code* (RBC), also known as the Gray code [4]. This code has

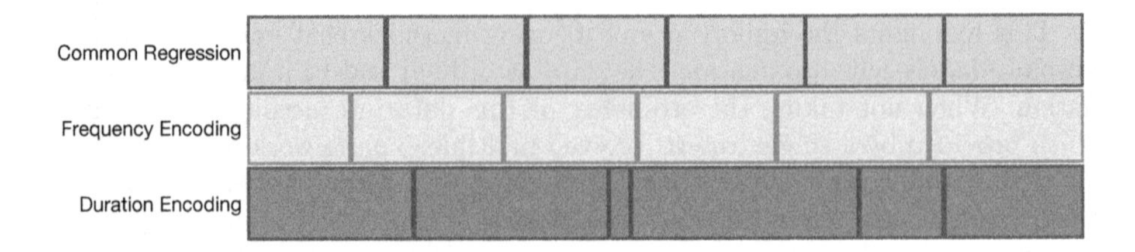

Fig. 2. Target intervals for regression techniques.

the advantage of differing only in one bit in the encoding of adjacent numbers. This encoding allows the representation of n classes in $\lceil \log n \rceil$ bits. Due to the property of RBC, adjacent classes have similar encodings. For the six classes in this dataset, the first six of the eight possible encodings with the required three bits are used. For instance, a myelocyte ($c = 2$) is encoded as $\text{RBC}(c) = [0, 1, 1]$. Again, this code results in lower losses if adjacent classes are mis-classified.

2.3 Regression Techniques

Regression techniques predict a continuous number (in this case correlating to the grade of maturity) instead of a class. The simplest implementation of regression would be to assign an integer number (0–5) to each class. Since the order of the classes is known but the distance is not, we propose using domain knowledge to obtain a more suitable encoding. We propose using either the cell frequencies or biological knowledge about the cell types.

In addition to the established regression technique, we design specific targets for the given use-case. These are not encoded as scalars, as is commonly done, but as intervals. We further investigate different ways of sampling training values from these intervals as well as handling predictions in correctly predicted intervals.

Both proposed intervals are illustrated in Fig. 2.

Frequency-Based Regression. This method utilizes the number of samples per class to obtain a more suitable encoding. More precisely, we compute for each class c a value $f_c = \log \frac{n_c}{\bar{n}}$ based on the number of samples of that class n_c and the average number of samples of all classes $\bar{n}$. In this case, this results in the values $[0.74, 1.09, 0.95, 1.00, 1.09, 1.12]$. Each class c is assigned to a range determined by the cumulative sum to $[\sum_{i<c} f_i, \sum_{i \leq c} f_i]$, which starts at 0 for $c = 0$ and is unlimited for the last class. In order to determine a label in training, we either draw a number at random from this range or use the center.

This encoding ensures that classes with fewer samples are mapped to a smaller range of values.

Stage Duration. During the maturation process, cells at each stage take a specific amount of time to develop. According to the literature, typical times are

24, 28, 3, 33, 12 and 20 h for each stage, respectively. These numbers can be used in a similar way as the numbers f_c from the previous section. Ranges can be defined in the same way and training labels can be drawn at random from the range or fixed to the center.

This encoding ensures that classes with shorter duration in the bone marrow are mapped to a smaller range of values.

Loss Computation. In both frequency-based and duration-based encoding, each cell type is represented by an interval of numbers. We analyze four different options on defining a loss for the training process. First, we use the Mean-Squared-Error (MSE) loss between prediction and the mean of the ground truth interval. Second, we use MSE loss between prediction and a randomly drawn number from within the ground truth interval. Furthermore, we use the same two options but set the loss to 0 if the prediction lies within the correct interval.

2.4 Experimental Setup

The base network architecture is a DenseNet-121 [7] pre-trained on ImageNet [10], which showed excellent results in similar tasks [5]. We train with a batch size of 64 with image patches of size $224 \times 224\,\text{px}^2$ normalized to zero mean and unit variance with respect to the ImageNet data. Training is performed to a maximum of 256 epochs and stopped early if the validation score has not improved for 128 epochs. For the final evaluation on the test set, we use the network from the epoch with the highest validation score, which is the macro F1-score. In total, we train the network in five-fold cross-validation (four sets for training, one set for validation). Each trained network is evaluated on the previously excluded part of the dataset with annotations by multiple experts.

For the evaluation, we derive three different measures (*any*, *most* and *MTA*) based on the F1-score which differ in the matching between prediction and the ground truth labels. *Any* results in a true positive if the prediction matches any of the ground truth labels. *Most* results in a true positive only if the prediction matches the most frequent ground truth label (or any of the most frequent ground truth labels in case of a tie). *MTA* results in a true positive only if the prediction matches the label from the team of *MTA*s who also annotated the training and validation datasets. Labels by other experts are ignored in this evaluation mode.

Next to common classification (denoted as *CLF* in Fig. 3) and regression (*REG*), we evaluate the presented methods in different configurations. For classification-based methods, we evaluate the Gray Code method (*RBC*) and the Declining weights method (d_w) with weights $w \in [0.1, 0.2, 0.5]$. For the regression-based methods, we evaluate both frequency-based (f) and duration-based (t) regression. For each of these, we evaluate choosing the labels as mean (denoted by μ as index) or random (r). We further test whether it is beneficial to set the loss to zero if the predicted number falls into the correct interval. The *other* label does not contribute to the loss if it is encountered during training. It

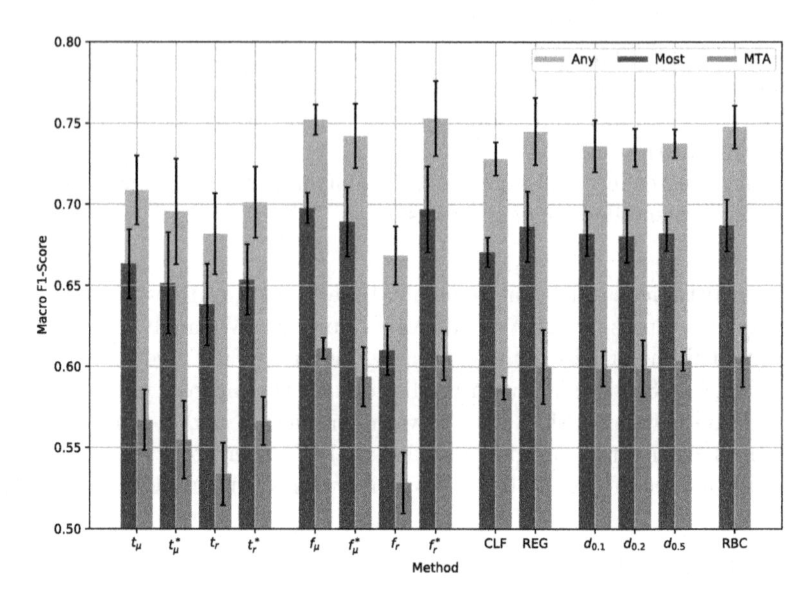

Fig. 3. Resulting F1-Scores (y-axis) for the various methods (x-axis). t refers to duration-based regression, f to frequency-based regression, with μ indicating choosing the mean as a label, and r indicating random drawing. An asterix (*) means that the loss is set to zero if the interval is correctly predicted. *CLF* and *REG* refer to common classification and regression, respectively. d_w denotes the Declining weights and *RBC* the Gray Code method. Colors denote different evaluation metrics as described in Sect. 2.4.

is further ignored in the evaluation (even though false predictions of *other* are still counted as false negatives).

3 Results

Figure 3 shows the evaluation in terms of F1-scores for each method. For all methods, the F1-Score using *most*-matching is higher than *MTA*-matching. In the following, differences in F1-score are given in percentage points (p.p.) rather than percentage.

In terms of common classification and regression methods, regression performs better with increases of 1.7, 1.6 and 1.3 for *any*, *most* and *MTA*-matching, respectively. While the Declining weights method yields better results than common classification (improvements of 1.0, 1.2, 1.6), scores are slightly lower (by 0.7, 0.2, 0.6) compared to common regression. There are only minor differences for different weights. The Gray Code method, however, slightly exceed the common regression scores as well (by 0.3, 0.1, 0.6).

Of the regression methods, frequency-based regression performs generally better than duration-based regression, with the exception of random drawing without setting the loss to zero in the correct interval. For both methods, random drawing performs better with setting the loss to zero if the prediction lies in the correct interval. Whereas, using the mean performs better if the loss is not set to zero. Depending on the matching, two or three of the frequency-based regression methods outperform common classification and regression. The largest improvement (of 0.7, 1.2, 1.1) to common regression can be observed for frequency-based regression using the mean.

4 Discussion

The results highlight properties of the data as well as the ordinal classification and regression techniques.

The fact that generally higher scores are achieved for *most* rather than for *MTA*-matching indicates that cases exist, in which two raters contradict the *MTA* annotation. The former is used as a ground truth for training and would be used for evaluation if no multi-rater annotations were available. This highlights the importance of taking the inter-rater variability into account both for evaluation and for training. For evaluation, differences of approximately 0.15 in terms of macro F1-Score can be observed in the evaluation of this scenario. A correct and medically relevant interpretation of results and, consequently, of the quality of newly developed methods needs to take this into account. However, trends between evaluation metrics are generally similar such that using only the *MTA*-label as an approximation is a valid choice for comparison between methods. In future work, the inter-rater disagreement ought also to be reflected in the training process.

The importance of taking the ordinal nature of the data into account is further supported by performance differences between common regression and classification. Without further adaption to the data, regression already outperforms common classification by taking the order of classes into account.

Regarding ordinal classification techniques, both approaches presented improve results compared to common classification. The Declining weights method, however, does not reach the performance of common regression. It is furthermore interesting to note that the choice of weights in the evaluated range only has a negligible influence on the results. Even a small weight of $w = 0.1$ already performs consistently better than common classification. A larger weight results in smaller variance between folds and very slight F1-Score improvements. The Gray Code method performs better compared to both common classification and regression. Furthermore, the variance of the results is slightly lower than with regression. Both approaches can easily be transferred to other classification tasks with ordinal data and require no restructuring of the network backbone.

Of the two regression techniques, frequency-based regression generally yields superior results. This can, in part, be explained by the comparatively short duration of cells in the third maturity stage, which may lead to predictive difficulties using duration-based regression. Furthermore, the variation of interval lengths is much larger than in the frequency-based approach. In both approaches, setting the loss to zero within the correct predicted interval is beneficial if random labels are drawn, but not if the mean is used. While the mean "pulls" the prediction towards the interval center, this is not the case for randomly chosen labels, which even fluctuate for each sample in every epoch. Frequency-based regression outperforms all other approaches in both random sampling and interval mean. The latter achieves this with lower variance, which makes it the most superior method. Frequency-based regression can also be easily transferred to other applications of ordinal classification, as no external domain knowledge but rather a property of the dataset itself is used.

The methods presented are easily applicable to other applications with ordinal data and adapting them to an established network architecture is straight-forward. Taking ordinality into account is particularly beneficial for mitigating inter-rater variability: inter-rater disagreement is usually of lower severity (i.e., "off-by-one" disagreements are most likely). By directly incorporating and minimizing the severity of mis-classifications into the training process through ordinal methods, the network becomes capable of learning a similar behavior. While this does not necessarily increase measures such as the F-score (which treats all mis-classifications the same when not working with a multi-rater dataset, as used in this work), it improves the clinical soundness of results. It also becomes easily possible to identify "borderline-cases", either by regression values close to class thresholds or through the softmax values for the predicted classes, and validate them in a post-processing step.

Compared to the non-public data reported in related works, the dataset described in this paper is more challenging. Whereas Song et al. [12,13] only differentiate between two lineages, we focus explicitly on the maturity progression within those lineages. The dataset by Choi et al. [3] includes these classes but does not include labels from multiple independent raters (only a label confirmation by a second rater).

Even though they evaluate the most commonly considered cell classes, the image data by Chandradevan et al. [2] is selected to be as simple as possible for classification. This makes the applicability of this dataset in real world clinical applications doubtful.

5 Conclusion

We proposed and evaluated several methods for the handling of ordinal data using various encodings for different regression and classification techniques. All methods are straight-forward to implement without any changes to the network backbone. We show that several of these techniques, particularly Gray Code based classification and frequency-based regression, improve ordinal classification results on a challenging hematopoietic cell dataset. This is supported by an analysis on a dataset annotated by multiple experts. This study highlights the importance of taking into account dependencies between classes and noisy labels between adjacent classes.

References

1. Binder, T., Diem, H., Fuchs, R., Gutensohn, K., Nebe, T.: Pappenheim stain: description of a hematological standard stain - history, chemistry, procedure, artifacts and problem solutions. J. Lab. Med. **36**(5), 293–309 (2012)
2. Chandradevan, R., et al.: Machine-based detection and classification for bone marrow aspirate differential counts: initial development focusing on nonneoplastic cells. Lab. Invest. **100**(1), 98–109 (2019)
3. Choi, J.W., et al.: White blood cell differential count of maturation stages in bone marrow smear using dual-stage convolutional neural networks. PLoS ONE **12**(12), e0189259 (2017)
4. Frank, G.: Pulse code communication. US Patent 2,632,058, 17 Mar 1953
5. Gräbel, P., et al.: Systematic analysis and automated search of hyper-parameters for cell classifier training. In: IEEE International Symposium on Biomedical Imaging (ISBI) (2020)
6. Gutiérrez, P.A., Perez-Ortiz, M., Sanchez-Monedero, J., Fernandez-Navarro, F., Hervas-Martinez, C.: Ordinal regression methods: survey and experimental study. IEEE Trans. Knowl. Data Eng. **28**(1), 127–146 (2015)
7. Huang, G., Liu, Z., Van Der Maaten, L., Weinberger, K.Q.: Densely connected convolutional networks. In: Proceedings of the IEEE Conference on Computer Vision and Pattern Recognition, pp. 4700–4708 (2017)
8. Kotsiantis, S.B., Pintelas, P.E.: A cost sensitive technique for ordinal classification problems. In: Vouros, G.A., Panayiotopoulos, T. (eds.) SETN 2004. LNCS (LNAI), vol. 3025, pp. 220–229. Springer, Heidelberg (2004). https://doi.org/10.1007/978-3-540-24674-9_24
9. Liu, Y., Kong, A.W.K., Goh, C.K.: A constrained deep neural network for ordinal regression. In: Proceedings of the IEEE Conference on Computer Vision and Pattern Recognition, pp. 831–839 (2018)
10. Russakovsky, O., et al.: ImageNet large scale visual recognition challenge. Int. J. Comput. Vision **115**(3), 211–252 (2015)
11. Simonyan, K., Zisserman, A.: Very deep convolutional networks for large-scale image recognition. arXiv preprint arXiv:1409.1556 (2014)
12. Song, T.H., Sanchez, V., ElDaly, H., Rajpoot, N.: Simultaneous cell detection and classification in bone marrow histology images. IEEE J. Biomed. Health Inform. **23**, 1469–1476 (2018)
13. Song, T.H., Sanchez, V., Eldaly, H., Rajpoot, N.M.: Hybrid deep autoencoder with curvature gaussian for detection of various types of cells in bone marrow trephine biopsy images. In: 2017 IEEE 14th International Symposium on Biomedical Imaging (ISBI 2017), pp. 1040–1043. IEEE (2017)

Towards Automated Monitoring of Parkinson's Disease Following Drug Treatment

Amir Dehsarvi(✉), Jennifer Kay South Palomares, and Stephen Leslie Smith

University of York, York YO10 5DD, UK
amir.dehsarvi@york.ac.uk

Abstract. This paper reports an automated approach to the clinical monitoring of Parkinson's disease (PD) by applying Evolutionary Algorithms (EAs) to resting-state functional magnetic imaging (rs-fMRI) data. The novel application of EAs to both map and predict the functional connectivity is considered in patients receiving the drug Modafinil versus placebo. Specifically, Cartesian Genetic Programming (CGP) was used to classify Dynamic Causal Modeling (DCM) analysis and timeseries. Results were validated with two other commonly used classification methods (Artificial Neural Networks and Support Vector Machines) using k-fold cross-validation. Across DCM and timeseries analyses, findings revealed maximum accuracies of 74.57% for CGP. In addition to its comparable performance relative to other techniques, CGP's "open-box" properties offer the possibility of decoding the classifier more easily than in the other methods. The findings support the applicability of both DCM analyses for classification and CGP as a novel classification technique for brain imaging data with medical implications for medication monitoring.

Keywords: Evolutionary algorithms · Cartesian Genetic Programming · Classification · Parkinson's disease · Resting-state fMRI · Dynamic Causal Modeling

1 Introduction

By 2050, 16% of people globally will be over age 65, an increase from 9% in 2019 [1]. Cognitive decline associated with ageing is the leading cause of non-communicable diseases, such as Parkinson's disease (PD) [2], which occurs in 0.1–0.2% of the population and in 1–2% over 60 years of age [3]. This paper reports a new method of monitoring PD using evolutionary algorithms (EAs).

Approximately half of PD patients report fatigue-related symptoms, for which Modafinil (Provigil) is prescribed [4] to enhance fatigue, attention, and memory. Regular monitoring is necessary to ensure patients are administered appropriate levels of medication, given their changing symptomology (and medication side effects). Hence, this research proposes a technique for accurate monitoring of PD using Evolutionary Algorithms (EAs) on rs-fMRI data for participants prescribed Modafinil.

M. El Yacoubi et al. (Eds.): ICPRAI 2022, LNCS 13364, pp. 196–207, 2022.
https://doi.org/10.1007/978-3-031-09282-4_17

1.1 Learning Algorithms

Machine learning algorithms are becoming increasingly relevant for monitoring early stages of cognitive decline, providing enhanced reliability and efficiency in disease classification, including PD patients [5]. EAs are optimizing algorithms derived from Darwinian evolutionary theory. Cartesian Genetic Programming (CGP) is a subtype of EAs that evolves directed acyclic computational structures of nodes. Recurrent CGP (RCGP) is an extension of CGP that includes cyclic or feedback connections. The application of CGP and RCGP to neuroimaging data (including rs-fMRI, as per this research) has not been explored and potentially presents a novel and relevant tool for disease monitoring. EAs combined with an expressive dynamical representation enable researchers to examine a large variety of classifiers and, hence, they can be a crucial and valuable tool. These classifiers extend the current knowledge in the field given that they are efficient in detecting trends without the use of expert knowledge, leading to findings that may not have otherwise been identified. Whilst these classifiers are a relevant tool in guiding and/or supporting a medical diagnosis or disease management, any monitoring solutions require a clinician to outline possible biological foundations of these solutions.

1.2 rs-fMRI Data

Resting-state functional magnetic imaging (rs-fMRI) involves exploring the functional activity in the brain when the participant is at rest (as opposed to performing a specific task in the scanner). There is a broad literature on rs-fMRI [6], including research examining the classification of participant groups or brain states using functional connectivity. rs-fMRI enables researchers to examine questions that are not suited to task-related fMRI paradigms, focusing on changes in functional connectivity [7] and facilitating the concurrent exploration of multiple cortical circuits. Confounding variables (e.g., between participant variance in task performance) are also reduced as participants are at rest [8]. Rest activation is linked to minimum of ten functional resting state networks [6], such as the Default Mode Network (DMN) [9], among others. DMN is typically examined when conducting rs-fMRI research and, therefore, it is explored in the current study. Abnormal patterns of activation can be investigated using functional connectivity, nevertheless, causal influences (effective connectivity, i.e., the causal impact of one neuronal system on another) cannot be determined [10]. Dynamic Causal Modeling (DCM), in contrast, is derived from a neuronal model of coupled neuronal states and enables investigation of the effective connectivity underlying functional connectivity via nonlinear designs to detect a generative model of measured neural activity [10]. The current research applies EAs, specifically CGP and RCGP, for the classification of rs-fMRI in PD using DCM and timeseries analyses. Findings are validated via two typically used classification techniques (Artificial Neural Networks, ANN, and Support Vector Machines, SVM) including via *k*-fold cross-validation (CV).

2 Methods

2.1 Overview

This research involved the analysis of rs-fMRI data taken from OpenfMRI database (accession number: ds000133; [11]), in which healthy young adults were administered a single dose of 100 mg of Modafinil (versus not). The activity of the resting state networks and the functional connectivity were examined, and this data was subjected to classification to explore the physiological impact of Modafinil by applying EAs, specifically CGP and Recurrent CGP (RCGP), for the classification of rs-fMRI using DCM and timeseries analyses. The OpenfMRI dataset used in this experiment is heavily class-imbalanced, with many more control participant records relative to participant records administered Modafinil. Hence, this research explored the applicability of classification methods to class-imbalanced data, with implications for the transferability of medical research based on limited and imbalanced sample sizes.

2.2 Participants

Twenty-six male participants were tested (age range: 25–35 years). Participants were right-handed, with similar educational level, and no history of psychiatric, neurological or medical conditions. The participants provided written consent and the study was approved by the ethics committee of University of Chieti (PROT 2008/09 COET on 14/10/2009) and conducted in accordance with the Helsinki Declaration.

2.3 Procedure

Participants were told to consume their normal amount of nicotine and caffeine and to refrain from consuming alcohol 12 h prior to the study. Participants were administered Modafinil (100 mg) or placebo. The study was double blind and both the Modafinil and placebo pills looked identical. Following consumption of the drug, participants were given a rs-fMRI scan. Data from all participants were processed and separated into their corresponding treatment groups. Data from one control participant was excluded, as this data was too poor quality to be analyzed. Pre-session data was also categorized as placebo/control as this research only examines the effect of Modafinil on brain functionality. The Modafinil group contains 39 participants: 13 participants tested in one session with three runs. The control group contains 111 participants: 12 participants tested in two sessions with three runs plus 13 participants tested in one session with three runs.

2.4 rs-fMRI Acquisition

rs-fMRI BOLD data was separated in three runs (duration: 4 min each) and then high resolution T1 anatomical images were acquired. Participants were instructed to focus on the center of a grey screen that was projected on an LCD screen, viewed via a mirror located over the participant's head. The participant's head was placed in an eight-channel coil with foam padding to reduce involuntary head movements. BOLD functional imaging was performed with a Philips Achieva 3T Scanner (Philips Medical Systems,

Best, The Netherlands), using T2*-weighted echo planar imaging (EPI) free induction decay (FID) sequences and applying the following parameters: Echo Time (TE) 35 ms, matrix size 66×66, Field of View (FoV) 256 mm, in-plane voxel size 464 mm, flip angle 75°, slice thickness 4 mm and no gaps. 140 functional volumes consisting of 30 transaxial slices were acquired per run with a volume Repetition Time (TR) of 1671 ms. High resolution structural images were acquired at the end of the three rs-fMRI runs through a 3D MPRAGE sequence employing the following parameters: sagittal, matrix 256×256, FoV 256 mm, slice thickness 1 mm, no gaps, in-plane voxel size 1 mm $\times$ 1 mm, flip angle 12°, TR = 9.7 ms and TE = 4 ms [12].

2.5 Imaging Data Analysis

Preprocessing. The imaging data analyses were conducted with CONN (version 17.c) [13] and SPM12 (version 6906 - Wellcome Department of Imaging Neuroscience, London, UK) [14] software packages based on MATLAB. Preprocessing included 4D NIFTI import, 4D to 3D NIFTI conversion, and decrease of spatial distortion via the Field Map toolbox in SPM12. Anatomical data was segmented and both anatomical and functional data were normalized. All the functional images were motion corrected and coregistered to participants' own high-resolution anatomical image. The participants' anatomical images were normalized to the standard T1 template in the MNI space, as provided by SPM12. Subsequently, the normalization parameters of each participant were applied to the functional images to normalize all the functional images into the MNI space. The EPI data was unwarped (using field-map images) to compensate for the magnetic field inhomogeneities, realigned to correct for motion, and slice-time corrected to the middle slice. The normalization parameters from the T1 stream were then applied to warp the functional images into MNI space. All the functional images were spatially smoothed using a Gaussian kernel with 8 mm FWHM [15] to account for inter-participant variability while maintaining a relatively high spatial resolution. Linear and quadratic detrending of the fMRI signal was applied, which involved covarying out WM and CSF signal. WM and CSF signals were predicted for each volume from the mean value of WM and CSF masks, derived by thresholding SPM's tissue probability maps at 0.5. The data was bandpass filtered (0.008–0.1 Hz).

Processing

Timeseries. Functional connectivity in DMN is well studied. Hence, this research took as regions of interest (nodes) the most commonly reported four major parts of DMN, as shown in Fig. 1: medial prefrontal cortex (mPFC, centered at 3, 54, −2), posterior cingulate cortex (PCC, centered at 0, −52, 26), left inferior parietal cortex (LIPC, centered at −50, −63, 32), and right inferior parietal cortex (RIPC, centered at 48, −69, 35). For each participant, the volumes of interest were defined as spheres centered at the coordinates outlined above with an 8 mm radius and with a mask threshold of 0.5. The first eigenvectors were extracted after removing the effect of head motion and low frequency drift. This vector is stored for each region as timeseries.

Dynamic Causal Modeling (DCM). The spectral DCM analyses were conducted using the DCM12 implemented in SPM12. The regions of interest of DCM analyses were

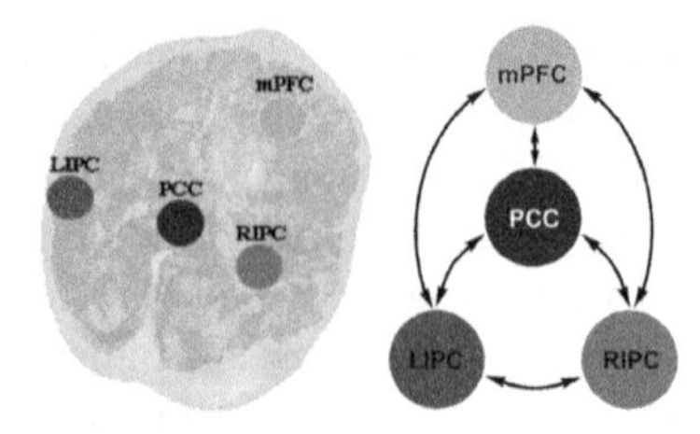

Fig. 1. The four DMN regions of interest used in this research

defined according to the peak of the DMN independent component maps, as presented in Fig. 1. The fundamental aim of this DCM analysis was to examine the endogenous/intrinsic effective connectivity and to investigate the causal interactions across these regions. The modelled low frequency fluctuations were set as key inputs to all four nodes, and different models were defined by considering a full connection for all nodes. Expected posterior model probabilities and exceedance probabilities were computed. The intrinsic connectivity parameters (16 values that were stored in DCM.Ep.A matrix, all parameters of intrinsic/effective connectivity [10]) from each participant were subjected to classification using CGP.

2.6 Cartesian Genetic Programming

CGP [16] is a form of GP [17], that encodes computational structures as generic cyclic/acyclic graphs. For this research, a new cross platform open source CGP library [18] was used since it can evolve symbolic expressions, Boolean logic circuits, and ANN, and it can be extended to diverse research areas. The CGP library enables the control of evolutionary parameters and the application of custom evolutionary stages.

Classification. To have equal class representation, data from each class was divided randomly into subsets of 70% (training), 15% (validation), and 15% (test). The geometry of the programs in the population (chromosomes) has fifty nodes with a function set of four mathematical operations ($+$, $-$, $\times$, $\div$), multiple inputs (according to the datasets), and one output (class 1 for Modafinil participant group, class 0 for the control participant group). At each generation, the fittest chromosome is selected, and the next generation is formed with its mutated versions (mutation rate $= 0.1$). Evolution stops when 15000 iterations are reached. To obtain statistical significance, the classification was done in 10 runs for each combination of inputs and the accuracy was averaged over the runs. The results (the winning chromosome, the networks, and the accuracy values) were stored for each run individually.

Classification of Timeseries. rs-fMRI is a widespread tool for exploring the functionality of the brain, using volume timeseries data. These scans contain abundant data; hence, obtaining relevant and useful data from raw scans (i.e., high dimensional datasets) can be difficult. Machine learning algorithms provide various tools that create datasets with less dimensions and more useful data, although challenges persist regarding how to select relevant data and how to maintain the interpretability of this data. This can result in losing important properties of the raw data, although dealing with such a large number of features can be computationally expensive and very time consuming.

In the current experiment, the RCGP algorithm is used to classify the features that appeared across time in participant scans. The number of timeseries values is 145, i.e., for each of the four regions in the DMN, there is a vector of 145 values. Analyzing/classifying the timeseries values was conducted in three different ways in terms of inputs to the classifier:

1. The timeseries values for each region separately were used as inputs to the classifier, to classify with 145 features per region (relating to DMN regions: LIPC, RIPC, PCC, and mPFC) and per participant.
2. The timeseries values together in four columns (one per region) were used as inputs to the classifier to classify the data with four columns (corresponding to the four DMN regions) of 145 features per participant.
3. The timeseries values inserted together in one column were used as inputs to the classifier to classify the data with 580 features in one vector for each participant. The order of inputting the timeseries values for each DMN region to form the final vector was consistent between participants.

Classification was completed in 10 runs per combination of inputs and the mean across the runs was calculated. The same inputs were used to classify the data using ANN and SVM in MATLAB for comparison/validation. RCGP was used with 10% probability for the recurrent connections. See Fig. 2 for a complete pipeline of the data preprocessing and processing.

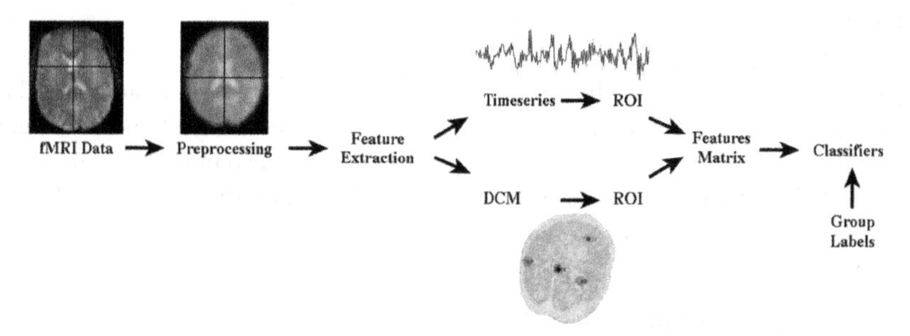

Fig. 2. Data analysis pipeline used in this research

Classification of DCM. The classification was run in the CGP Library with 16 inputs (all the DCM values sorted by region and presented as only one vector for each participant). To facilitate comparison, the classification with data from the same participant records was run using ANN and SVM, both run in MATLAB.

2.7 Adaptive Synthetic Sampling

ADASYN [19] was used to generate synthetic data leading to balanced class-distributions for the training set. Nevertheless, a limitation of generating synthetic balanced data is that it is applied only to the training sets. The classifier trained for CV is a different classifier with a different accuracy level than that used in the classification part. Therefore, classification accuracy for the validation and test sets is typically reduced. Indeed, the development of accurate classifiers that can be applied to heavily class-imbalanced data with the objective of detecting a minority class (e.g., PD patients) are required. The Modafinil group contained 39 participant records and the control group contained 111 participant records, resulting in highly imbalanced data. Hence, ADASYN was used to make the data balanced. After the process, the minor group for each combination (in the training set) had a higher number of records, which made the data balanced for cross-validation. The validation and test sets were kept the same.

2.8 *k*-Fold Cross-Validation

10-fold CV was used to evaluate the classification accuracy using an unbiased estimate of the generalization accuracy [22]. Advantages of CV include generating of independent test sets with improved reliability. With *10*-fold CV, typically one (of *10*) subset is the test set and remaining nine subsets are training sets. These sets are then rotated so that each set is used to test the data once. One repetition of the *10*-fold CV does not produce sufficient classification accuracies for comparison, therefore, *10*-fold CV is repeated 10 independent times and the mean accuracy over all *10* trials is calculated.

3 Results

This study examined the classification of 39 participant records administered Modafinil versus 111 control participant records. The analysis (classification) focused on organizing features to be used as inputs to the classifier in CGP and also in RCGP, implemented using the CGP Library. To validate the results, the analysis/classification was additionally completed using ANN and SVM, both in MATLAB.

3.1 Classification of Timeseries

Initially, the timeseries values for each region were used as inputs to the classifier individually. Therefore, the data was classified with 145 features from each region per participant. The same procedure was completed separately for each DMN region (PCC, mPFC, RIPC, and LIPC). Then, the timeseries values were used as inputs to the classifier to classify the data in four columns (relating to the four DMN regions) of 145 features per participant. Finally, the timeseries values together in one column were used as inputs to the classifier to classify the data with 580 features in one vector for each participant. The results after 10 runs for each combination were averaged and are summarized in Table 1. The classification was also done using ANN and SVM. For SVM, only the training and test sets were considered for classification.

Table 1. Classification accuracy rates for the timeseries values

		Training % (*SD*)	Validation % (*SD*)	Test % (*SD*)
Classification accuracy rates for each DMN region				
PCC	RCGP	73.75 (*2.98*)	75.52 (*1.59*)	74.28 (*1.22*)
	ANN	83.74 (*7.78*)	73.48 (*12.88*)	72.18 (*8.01*)
	SVM	100 (*0*)	NA	73.81 (*0.50*)
mPFC	RCGP	71.88 (*5.00*)	74.80 (*1.57*)	73.52 (*1.38*)
	ANN	78.07 (*9.02*)	71.75 (*9.90*)	64.78 (*9.93*)
	SVM	100 (*0*)	NA	74.00 (*0.46*)
RIPC	RCGP	74.40 (*2.96*)	76.51 (*2.57*)	71.26 (*5.94*)
	ANN	81.92 (*7.63*)	72.18 (*7.46*)	70.00 (*8.06*)
	SVM	100 (*0*)	NA	73.71 (*0.49*)
LIPC	RCGP	72.79 (*3.52*)	74.79 (*1.55*)	72.53 (*3.22*)
	ANN	85.88 (*10.20*)	70.88 (*11.96*)	70.45 (*8.65*)
	SVM	100 (*0*)	NA	73.90 (*0.49*)
Classification accuracy rates for all the DMN regions (4 inputs)				
	RCGP	73.63 (*2.11*)	75.92 (*2.16*)	73.99 (*2.94*)
	ANN	73.83 (*0.17*)	74.49 (*0.67*)	74.24 (*0.49*)
	SVM	74.25 (*0.05*)	NA	73.95 (*0.05*)
Classification accuracy rates for all the DMN regions (1 input)				
	RCGP	74.68 (*1.60*)	76.55 (*2.82*)	74.57 (*1.82*)
	ANN	73.97 (*0.13*)	74.11 (*0.37*)	74.01 (*0.45*)
	SVM	74.00 (*0.00*)	NA	74.00 (*0.00*)

The Modafinil group was successfully classified from the control group with a maximum accuracy of 74.57% using RCGP (minimum accuracy: 71.26%). The results from the other two classification techniques (ANN and SVM) validated this finding as they were comparable: 64.78–74.24% for ANN and SVM in all the different combinations of inputs. Unlike for the DCM analyses, mixed ANOVAs were not conducted to evaluate the correspondence between participant group and timeseries features, given that there were 580 features per participant, which would not be interpretable.

3.2 Classification of Dynamic Causal Modeling (DCM)

Classification using the CGP Library was executed with 16 inputs (all the DCM values sorted by region and presented as one vector for each participant) and 1 output (class 1 for the Modafinil group and class 0 for the control group). The results were then averaged over 10 runs and are presented in Table 2. The classification was done using ANN and SVM. For SVM, only the training and test sets were considered for classification.

Table 2. Classification accuracy rates for DCM values

	Training % (*SD*)	Validation % (*SD*)	Test % (*SD*)
CGP	75.63 (*7.13*)	80.35 (*6.18*)	73.89 (*7.70*)
ANN	79.99 (*5.57*)	73.93 (*7.94*)	67.39 (*6.57*)
SVM	73.81 (*0.50*)	NA	73.81 (*0.50*)

The Modafinil group was successfully classified from the control group with 73.89% accuracy using CGP. The results from the other two classification methods (ANN and SVM) validated this finding as they were comparable: 67.39% for ANN and 73.81% for SVM. A sample of the CGP classification network generated is shown in Fig. 3 and reflects one of the benefits of CGP in terms of providing a white box solution, which is not easily achieved with ANN and SVM classification methods. Such networks and their respective mathematical expressions are very complex and often difficult to interpret but potentially provide useful information.

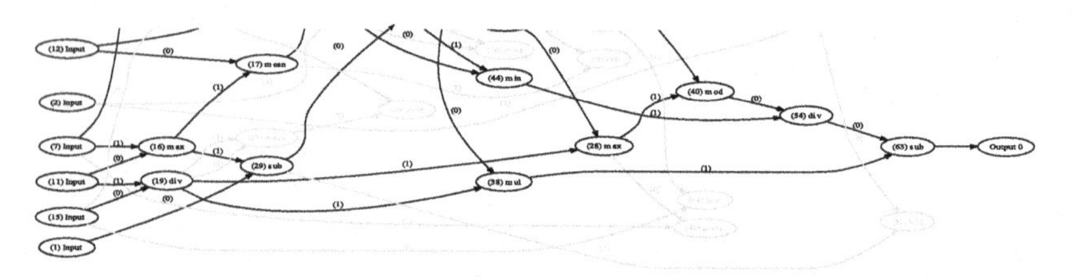

Fig. 3. A sample of the CGP classification tree for the classification of Modafinil vs. control

To evaluate the correspondence between participant group and DCM features, a mixed 2 × 16 ANOVA between the participant group (Modafinil and control) and DCM features (16 inputs per participant) was conducted. A Greenhouse-Geisser correction was used as the model violated sphericity. The ANOVA revealed a significant main effect of DCM features $\left(F(4.39, 210.64) = 228.90, MSE = 2.71, p < .001, \eta_p^2 = .83\right)$. There was no significant interaction effect between participant group and DCM features $\left(F(4.39, 210.64) = 0.83, MSE = 0.01, p = .516, \eta_p^2 = .02\right)$ and no significant main effect of group $\left(F(1, 48) = 1.12, MSE = 0.00, p = .294, \eta_p^2 = .02\right)$. This main effect of features represents the key finding as it indicates that the features in general are essential, whereas information on participant group per se is not.

3.3 *k*-Fold Cross-Validation

To evaluate the performance of the classifier, *k*-fold CV was conducted on all the different combinations of inputs for both DCM and timeseries values.

Cross-Validation for RCGP for Timeseries. The inputs were divided into 10 folds with 80% of the data for training, 10% for validation, and 10% for test. After the artificial data samples were synthesized for the minor class in the training set, CV was repeated for 10 runs and the results were averaged, see Table 3. Findings indicated that the Modafinil group were successfully classified from the control group with a maximum accuracy of 63.13% using RCGP in CV (minimum accuracy: 51.67%).

Table 3. Cross-validation results for the timeseries values

		Training % (*SD*)	Validation % (*SD*)	Test % (*SD*)
Classification accuracy rates for each DMN region				
PCC	RCGP	58.74 (*5.37*)	70.36 (*0.83*)	63.13 (*2.86*)
mPFC	RCGP	57.01 (*5.13*)	67.26 (*3.52*)	58.69 (*3.99*)
RIPC	RCGP	55.14 (*4.91*)	68.51 (*4.04*)	58.09 (*5.80*)
LIPC	RCGP	56.97 (*4.41*)	70.05 (*2.41*)	58.09 (*4.31*)
Classification accuracy rates for all the DMN regions (4 inputs)				
	RCGP	44.63 (*5.99*)	71.74 (*10.16*)	51.67 (*8.30*)
Classification accuracy rates for all the DMN regions (1 input)				
	RCGP	60.21 (*3.59*)	69.86 (*2.53*)	60.73 (*3.96*)

Cross-Validation for CGP for DCM. The inputs were divided into 10 folds with 80% of the data used for training, 10% for validation, and 10% for test. After the artificial data samples were synthesized for the minor class in the training set, CV was repeated for 10 runs and the results averaged. Findings revealed that the Modafinil group were successfully classified from the control group with 59.55% accuracy using CGP in CV.

4 Conclusion

In this paper CGP was used for timeseries and DCM analyses, and the findings validated with two other widely used classification techniques (ANN and SVM) and using *k*-fold CV. ADASYN was used to balance the data before performing CV, providing a more equal class distribution within the training set. Findings revealed a maximum classification accuracy of 75%. An important finding was that there was almost no difference in the classification accuracies between timeseries and DCM data. CGP provided equivalent performance accuracy when compared with ANN and SVM classification methods. A key question for future research is whether CGP is relevant for the classification of PD patients (rather than healthy participants, as per the current research) administered Modafinil relative to non-medicated PD patients with fatigue.

A key aspect of this research was the application of a dynamical method of classification (RCGP). CGP has been previously used in the classification of biomedical data but not brain imaging data. This research applied CGP to rs-fMRI data, a timely approach given that fMRI is a non-invasive method that generates images with high spatial resolution and good temporal resolution, and it is widely used in medical facilities.

This research used a novel approach, applying classification to DCM data. Findings revealed that DCM data for classification provided comparable accuracy across all three classifiers, relative to timeseries data, which is surprising as other research has revealed that classification often provides better accuracies with raw unprocessed data. Timeseries data is raw fMRI data and includes over 100 features. In contract, DCM data is processed, representing the effective connectivity (the causal effect) of one neuronal region on another and, in this case, contained only 16 features. These findings underscore the relevance of DCM data for classification, even though this data is processed and contains much less features relative to timeseries data.

Following *k*-fold CV, classification accuracy for timeseries values decreased to 52–63% and for DCM values accuracy was reduced to 60%. This is because of the heavily class-imbalanced data containing 39 Modafinil records and 111 control participant records, yet, standard classification methods typically assume balanced class distributions. Imbalanced data significantly reduces classification accuracy given that the classifier cannot be trained efficiently to distinguish the differences between features in the two classes. A widely used solution involves modifying the data to obtain a sample with balanced class distributions, which often increases the overall classification accuracy compared to the original imbalanced sample. Nevertheless, this solution is not perfect given that the balanced data is only used in the training set, which compromises the accuracy in the validation and test sets as the classifier that was trained for the CV is a different classifier with a different accuracy level than that used in the classification part. The fact that findings revealed accuracies of approximately up to 75% in the classification of Modafinil timeseries and DCM data speaks to the robustness of CGP as a classification method, even for highly imbalanced data as in this research.

References

1. United Nations: "GLOBAL ISSUES: Ageing, United Nations, 24 January 2022. https://www.un.org/en/global-issues/ageing. Accessed 24 Jan 2022
2. Levy, G.: The relationship of Parkinson disease with aging. Arch. Neurol. **64**(9), 1242–1246 (2007). https://doi.org/10.1001/archneur.64.9.1242
3. Nussbaum, R.L., Ellis, C.E.: Alzheimer's disease and Parkinson's disease. N. Engl. J. Med. **348**(14), 1356–1364 (2003). https://doi.org/10.1056/NEJM2003ra020003
4. Elbers, R.G., Berendse, H.W., Kwakkel, G.: Treatment of fatigue in Parkinson disease. JAMA **315**(21), 2340 (2016). https://doi.org/10.1001/jama.2016.5260
5. Lones, M.A., Alty, J.E., Duggan-Carter, P., Turner, A.J., Jamieson, D.R.S., Smith, S.L.: Classification and characterisation of movement patterns during levodopa therapy for Parkinson's disease. In: Proceedings of the 2014 Conference Companion on Genetic and Evolutionary Computation Companion - GECCO Comp 2014, pp. 1321–1328 (2014). https://doi.org/10.1145/2598394.2609852
6. Damoiseaux, J.S., Greicius, M.D.: Greater than the sum of its parts: a review of studies combining structural connectivity and resting-state functional connectivity. Brain Struct. Funct. **213**(6), 525–533 (2009). https://doi.org/10.1007/s00429-009-0208-6

7. Buckner, R.L., Andrews-Hanna, J.R., Schacter, D.L.: The brain's default network: anatomy, function, and relevance to disease. Ann. N. Y. Acad. Sci. **1124**, 1–38 (2008). https://doi.org/10.1196/annals.1440.011
8. Ferreira, L.K., Busatto, G.F.: Resting-state functional connectivity in normal brain aging. Neurosci. Biobehav. Rev. **37**(3), 384–400 (2013). https://doi.org/10.1016/j.neubiorev.2013.01.017
9. Raichle, M.E., MacLeod, A.M., Snyder, A.Z., Powers, W.J., Gusnard, D.A., Shulman, G.L.: A default mode of brain function. Proc. Natl. Acad. Sci. U.S.A. **98**(2), 676–682 (2001). https://doi.org/10.1073/pnas.98.2.676
10. Friston, K.J., Kahan, J., Biswal, B.B., Razi, A.: A DCM for resting state fMRI. Neuroimage **94**, 396–407 (2014). https://doi.org/10.1016/j.neuroimage.2013.12.009
11. Cera, N., Tartaro, A., Sensi, S.L.: Modafinil alters intrinsic functional connectivity of the right posterior insula: a pharmacological resting state fMRI study. PLoS ONE **9**(9), 1–12 (2014). https://doi.org/10.1371/journal.pone.0107145
12. Esposito, R., et al.: Acute effects of modafinil on brain resting state networks in young healthy subjects. PLoS ONE **8**(7), 1 (2013). https://doi.org/10.1371/journal.pone.0069224
13. Whitfield-Gabrieli, S., Nieto-Castanon, A.: Conn: a functional connectivity toolbox for correlated and anticorrelated brain networks. Brain Connectivity **2**(3), 125–141 (2012). https://doi.org/10.1089/brain.2012.0073
14. Friston, K.J., Penny, W.D., Ashburner, J., Kiebel, S.J., Nichols, T.: Statistical Parametric Mapping: The Analysis of Funtional Brain Images, 1st ed. Elsevier/Academic Press (2006)
15. Razi, A., Kahan, J., Rees, G., Friston, K.J.: Construct validation of a DCM for resting state fMRI. Neuroimage **106**, 1–14 (2015). https://doi.org/10.1016/j.neuroimage.2014.11.027
16. Miller, J.F., Thomson, P.: Cartesian genetic programming. In: Proceedings of the Third European Conference on Genetic Programming (EuroGP), vol. 1820, pp. 121–132 (2000)
17. Banzhaf, W., Nordin, P., Keller, R.R.E., Francone, F.F.D.: Genetic Programming: An Introduction, vol. 1. Morgan Kaufmann San Francisco, San Francisco (1998)
18. Turner, A.J., Miller, J.F.: Introducing a cross platform open source Cartesian Genetic Programming library. Genet. Program Evolvable Mach. **16**(1), 83–91 (2014). https://doi.org/10.1007/s10710-014-9233-1
19. He, H., Bai, Y., Garcia, E.A., Li, S.: ADASYN: adaptive synthetic sampling approach for imbalanced learning. In: 2008 IEEE International Joint Conference on Neural Networks, pp. 1322–1328, June 2008. https://doi.org/10.1109/IJCNN.2008.4633969
20. Kohavi, R.: A study of cross-validation and bootstrap for accuracy estimation and model selection. In: The International Joint Conference on Artificial Intelligence (IJCAI), vol. 14, no. 2, pp. 1137–1145 (1995)

A Hierarchical Prototypical Network for Few-Shot Remote Sensing Scene Classification

Manal Hamzaoui(✉), Laetitia Chapel, Minh-Tan Pham, and Sébastien Lefèvre

Université Bretagne-Sud, IRISA UMR 6074, 56000 Vannes, France
{manal.hamzaoui,laetitia.chapel,minh-tan.pham,
sebastien.lefevre}@univ-ubs.fr

Abstract. Few-shot learning (FSL) aims at making predictions based on a limited number of labeled samples. It is a hot topic in many fields such as natural language processing, computer vision and more recently, remote sensing. In this work, we focus on few-shot remote sensing scene classification which aims to recognize unseen scene categories at training stage from few or even a single labeled sample at test stage. Although considerable progress has been achieved in this topic, less attention has been paid to leveraging the prior structural knowledge. In this paper, we learn transferable visual features by introducing the class hierarchy which encodes the semantic relationship between the classes. We build on a prototypical network and we define *hierarchical prototypes* that allow us to encode the different levels of the hierarchy. Experiments conducted on the remote sensing NWPU-RESISC45 dataset demonstrate that the proposed hierarchical prototypical network acts as a regularizer and leads to better performance than the original network in the context of few-shot remote sensing scene classification.

Keywords: Few-shot learning · Class hierarchy · Scene classification · Remote sensing

1 Introduction

Scene classification is an important research topic in remote sensing which aims to automatically assign a specific semantic category to each remote sensing scene image. Deep learning frameworks have been applied to this problem and have achieved outstanding performance on most remote sensing image scene classification (RSISC) datasets. They essentially extract end-to-end features from images using deep neural networks such as Auto-Encoders [6] and Convolutional Neural Networks (CNN) [14]. However, most of supervised deep remote sensing scene classification algorithms are "data-hungry" as they require a large amount of labeled data for training. When the labeled data are insufficient, there would be an obvious over-fitting and irrelevant extracted features, leading to a degradation of classification performance. However, obtaining labeled samples may be tough as it is labor-intensive, time-consuming and may need strong human expertise.

M. El Yacoubi et al. (Eds.): ICPRAI 2022, LNCS 13364, pp. 208–220, 2022.
https://doi.org/10.1007/978-3-031-09282-4_18

Inspired by the human ability to learn new abstract concepts from very few, or even one, examples and to generalize quickly to new instances [15], few-shot learning (FSL) was introduced as one of the alternative ways to deal with the "data-hungry" issue. FSL methods can be divided into three categories [18]: metric learning, meta-learning and transfer learning. Metric learning methods learn a distance function that brings samples from the same category as close as possible in the feature space while pushing samples from other categories as far away as possible. As for meta-learning, also known as learning to learn, it is the most common approach in FSL, which efficiently optimizes the model parameters to new tasks. Transfer learning aims at using the knowledge gained from relevant tasks towards new tasks , *e.g.* fine-tuning the pre-trained models is a powerful transfer method.

Recently, the combination of meta-learning and metric learning has been one of the most studied approaches in FSL for natural image classification [17,20] and for remote sensing scene classification [22]. First, based on meta-learning, these approaches construct tasks with few labeled samples, which enhances the generalization performance of the model for new tasks. Then, the similarity between image features is measured to make predictions. Some of related methods include relation network [19], classical matching network [20] and prototypical network [17].

In addition to the sparsity of labeled data, it may be more challenging to classify remote sensing data than natural images. Indeed, remote sensing scene images may present confusing visual similarity between different classes. The large intra-class variation may even exceed the inter-class variance, thus similar semantic classes may present significant visual dissimilarity [5]. Another challenge is that remote sensing images are top-down views and contain inevitably many objects that are not relevant to the semantic class of the scene [10]. Yet, this characteristic could be very useful in multi-label or hierarchical classification tasks where several levels of semantic granularity are considered.

In the recent years, many approaches were proposed to tackle the problem of few-shot remote sensing scene classification (FSRSSC). In [9], the authors adopted the attention mechanism to delve into the inter-channel and inter-spatial relationships to discover discriminative regions in the remote sensing scene images. The authors in [3] used a Siamese-prototype network with prototype self-calibration and inter-calibration to learn more discriminative prototypes. In [22], the authors introduced a pre-training step on the base data to provide better initialization of the feature extractor and performed the few-shot remote sensing scene classification using cosine distance metric. However, to the best our knowledge, the majority of these methods have focused only on visual scene information to improve feature representations without considering semantic knowledge that may exist within these classes. Yet this type of semantic knowledge about classes, which can consist of attributes, word embeddings or even a knowledge graph (e.g. WordNet [13]), is commonly used in zero-shot learning (ZSL) and increasingly in few-shot natural images classification approaches.

Semantic knowledge is not a novelty in ZSL, since this task can not be accomplished without such knowledge. However, in FSL, this semantic knowledge has hardly been used until recently. [2] proposed the TriNet to tackle the "1-shot" task by synthesizing the instance features from the semantic space which is given by the label embeddings. In [21], the authors proposed a method called Semantic Guided Attention (SEGA) mechanism which leverages semantic knowledge to guide the visual perception in learning the discriminative visual features of each class. Most of these FSL approaches that introduce semantic knowledge involve the text modality . However, few attention has been paid to knowledge transfer based on the class hierarchy which is either built using text modality as in [8] or already predefined as in [11]. In [8], the authors proposed a hierarchical image recognition approach by performing Softmax optimization on all levels of the class hierarchy. This allows learning transferable visual features through this class hierarchy which encodes semantic relationships between seen and unseen classes. In [11], a class hierarchy was introduced to address the multi-class FSL problem. The authors proposed a "memory-augmented hierarchical-classification network (MahiNet)" model which leverages the hierarchy as prior knowledge to train a coarse-to-fine classifier where each coarse class can cover multiple finer classes.

According to [11], FSL with knowledge transfer can be accomplished independently of an additional modality such as text and yields competitive performances, when the class hierarchy is known or easily obtained, which fits well with our research interests. This class hierarchy has been successfully applied to traditional supervised learning tasks. It can be introduced in the learning process according to three approaches [1]: a label-embeddings approach, a hierarchical loss or hierarchical architectures. In label-embeddings approach, a mapping function is used to encode class relationship information and associate it to class representations such as *soft-labels* [1]. Hierarchical loss-based methods adjust the loss to be optimized by assigning a higher penalty to predictions that are distant from the true label in the class hierarchy, such as *hierarchical cross-entropy* loss [1]. As for hierarchical networks, they introduce the class hierarchy into the classifier architecture without necessarily changing the loss function, allowing them to make super-class predictions at early layers and fine predictions at later layers.

The remote sensing classes can be easily arranged in a hierarchical structure following well-known organizations such as Corine Land Cover (CLC), the European Nature Information System (EUNIS) habitat classification scheme or other structures such as done in [12] where they propose a hierarchical organization of the scene classes of the PatternNet [25] remote sensing scene dataset.

In this work, we rely on the semantic knowledge associated with scene classes through their hierarchical organization. We build on prototypical networks to define a hierarchical variant: in a nutshell, hierarchical prototypes are attached to each level of the hierarchy, allowing us to first consider high-level aggregated information before making a fine prediction. We show on a remote sensing dataset that it acts as a regularizer, giving better performances not only at the top nodes of the hierarchy, but also at the leaf classes. We also show that it performs better than *soft-labels* [1] that we introduce for the first time (to our knowledge) in a remote sensing few-shot learning context.

The remainder of our paper is organized as follows. In Sect. 2, we provide some details about FSL and prototypical networks. Section 3 presents in depth the proposed method. We describe the experimental setup and the obtained results in Sect. 4. Conclusion and future works are given in Sect. 5.

2 Few-Shot Classification with Prototype Learning

2.1 Problem Formulation of the FSL

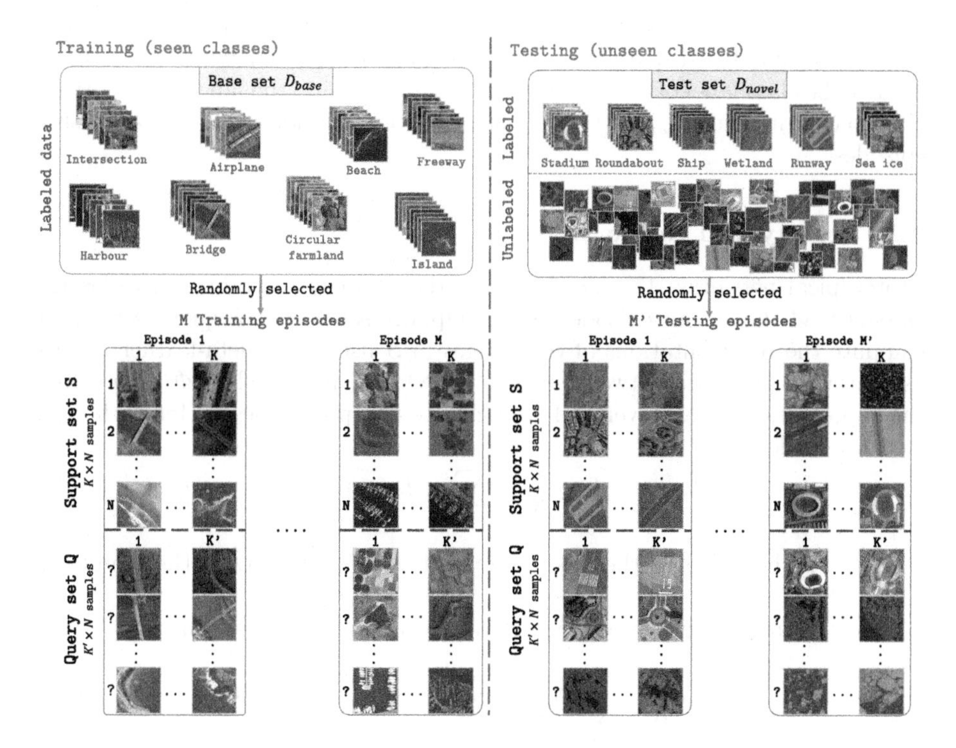

Fig. 1. Illustration of N-way K-shot classification episodes. The left side shows the M episodes of the training step; each episode consists of $N \times K$ support samples and $N \times K'$ query samples. The testing step is similarly defined on M' episodes, as shown on the right.

In few-shot classification, we assume that we have two sets, a large labeled training set, referred to as the base set D_{base}, and a test set with few labeled images per class, the novel set D_{novel}. The classes that constitute the base and novel sets, denoted C_{base} and C_{novel} respectively, are disjoint $C_{base} \cap C_{novel} = \emptyset$. To mimic the sparsity of the test data in the training stage, we adopt the N-way K-shot strategy (an episodic learning strategy) used in various FSL studies [17, 20], in which N refers to the number of classes and K (usually set to 1 or 5) is the number of labeled images per classes during a training/testing episode. For each episode, we randomly sample a subset of N classes out of C_{base} during training and out of C_{novel} during testing, which we denote C_e, to construct the episode support set S and the episode query set Q. During a training episode, we randomly sample K labeled images from D_{base} for each class $c \in C_e$, resulting in the episode support set $S = \{(x_i, y_i)\}_{i=1}^{N\times K}$, where x_i is an image and $y_i \in C_e$ its corresponding label. Similarly for the episode query set Q, K' labeled images are sampled from the base set D_{base} for each class $c \in C_e$, resulting in $Q = \{(x_q, y_q)\}_{q=1}^{N\times K'}$. In this training step, the support set S and the query set Q are used to learn the model that projects the input images into the feature space. The testing step is also carried out with the same episodic strategy where we have an unlabeled query set Q (drawn from D_{novel}) for which we want to predict the class label of each query sample $x_q \in Q$ using the labeled support set S (also drawn from D_{novel}). Figure 1 shows a visualization of the N-way K-shot episodes.

2.2 Prototypical Networks

Prototypical networks [17] adopt an episodic strategy to train a meta-learner classifier $\mathcal{M}$. Given an episode with a support set S and a query set Q, we compute the representations of the images in S using the meta-learner feature extractor f_Φ (a neural network such as CNN) parameterized by Φ. Thereafter, the representations are averaged to compute the prototypes p^c for each class $c \in C_e$ as follows:

$$p^c = \frac{1}{K} \sum_{(x_i, y_i) \in S^c} f_\Phi(x_i) \tag{1}$$

where S^c is the subset of the episode support set S that contains the samples of class $c \in C_e$.

To optimize the feature extractor f_Φ, we minimize the loss function:

$$\mathcal{L} = -\frac{1}{N \times K'} \sum_{c \in C_e} \sum_{(x_q, y_q) \in Q^c} \log p_\Phi(y_q = c \mid x_q) \tag{2}$$

where Q^c is the subset of the episode query set Q that contains the samples of class c, $p_\Phi(y_q = c \mid x_q)$ is the probability of predicting a query sample $(x_q, y_q) \in Q$ as class c and is given as:

$$p_\Phi(y_q = c|x_q) = \frac{\exp(-d(f_\Phi(x_q), p^c))}{\sum_{c' \in C_e} \exp(-d(f_\Phi(x_q), p^{c'}))} \tag{3}$$

where $d(.)$ represents a certain distance measurement, such as the Euclidean distance [17] or the Cosine distance [22].

3 A Hierarchical Prototypical Network for Few-Shot Image Classification

3.1 Overall Framework

We propose a meta-learning framework whose complete pipeline is illustrated in Fig. 2 to solve the few-shot problem when a hierarchy that describes the organization between the classes is available. We train a meta-learner classifier $\mathcal{M}$ by adopting an episodic training strategy. During training stage, using the support set S, we compute N prototypes $\mathcal{P} = \{p^c\}_{c \in C_e}$ for each class in the current task (episode) and N_h hierarchical prototypes for their super-classes. The query features are then compared to both the scene and the hierarchical prototypes, allowing us to compute an episodic error at different levels of the class hierarchy $\mathcal{H}$ to be minimized and used to finetune the parameters Φ of the feature extractor f_Φ. At testing stage, the parameters Φ of the feature extractor f_Φ are fixed and the meta-learner classifier $\mathcal{M}$ is evaluated on a set of episodes sampled from the novel classes in D_{novel}.

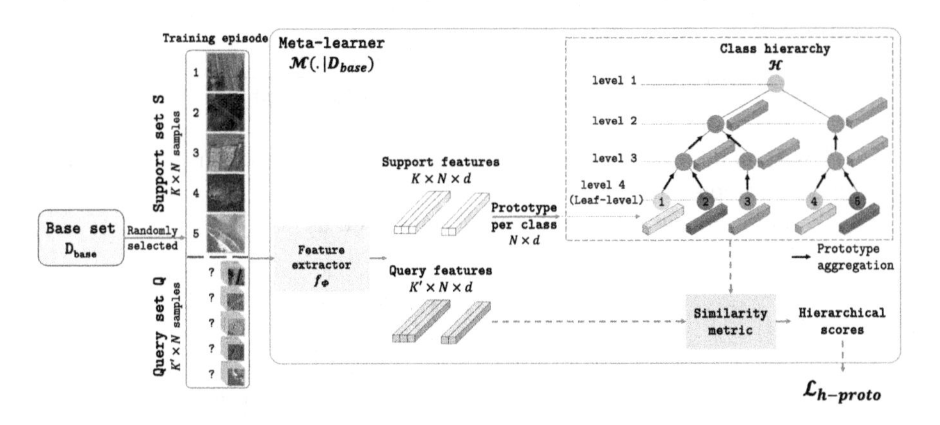

Fig. 2. Overall framework of the proposed hierarchical prototypical network for few-shot image classification. In this example (one-shot), $N = 5$, $N_h = 5$, $K = 1$, $K' > 1$ (usually set to 15).

3.2 Hierarchical Prototypical Network

Some works have already attempted to introduce the class hierarchy knowledge into the few-shot classification process. In [8], the authors suggested to perform a Softmax optimization over the different levels of the class hierarchy to enable knowledge transfer from seen to unseen classes. Here, we rather rely on the prototypical networks and introduce the hierarchy knowledge thanks to the definition of hierarchical prototypes. The overall idea is to regularize the latent space by putting closer classes that are in the same branch of the class hierarchy, and pushing apart classes that have common ancestors in higher levels of the class hierarchy

To properly formulate our approach, given an episode, we first compute the prototypes per class which are prototypes at the leaf-level of the class hierarchy $\mathcal{H}$ (following Eq. 1). We then compute the hierarchical prototypes by aggregating the leaf-level prototypes according to $\mathcal{H}$. The prototypes of the super-classes $c \in C_e^l$ (the hierarchical prototypes) at level l ($1 < l < L$ with $l = 1$ the root node and $L = \text{height}(\mathcal{H})$) are denoted as $\mathcal{P}_l = \{p_l^c\}_{c \in C_e^l}$ and computed as the mean of support samples of the super-class sub-tree S_l^c similarly to Eq. 1:

$$p_l^c = \frac{1}{|S_l^c|} \sum_{(x_i, y_i) \in S_l^c} f_\Phi(x_i) \tag{4}$$

Note that when $l = L$, the prototypes at level l are the prototypes at the lowest level of $\mathcal{H}$ (leaf-level prototypes).

The hierarchical prototypical network outputs a distribution over classes for each query sample $x_q \in Q$ at different levels of $\mathcal{H}$, based on a Softmax over the distances to the prototypes of each level l in $\mathcal{H}$. We then formulate the probability of predicting the query features $f_\Phi(x_q)$ and the prototype p_l^c of its super-class c at level l in $\mathcal{H}$ as formulated in Eq. 3 as:

$$p_\Phi(y_q^l = c|x_q) = \frac{\exp(-d(f_\Phi(x_q), p_l^c))}{\sum_{c' \in C_e^l} \exp(-d(f_\Phi(x_q), p_l^{c'}))}, \tag{5}$$

where y_q^l is the ancestor of y_q at level l, C_e^l represents the super-classes at level l at the current episode.

We therefore optimize a new loss function given as

$$\mathcal{L}_{\mathcal{H}-\text{proto}} = \sum_{l=2}^{L} \lambda_l \mathcal{L}_l \tag{6}$$

where $\lambda_l = \frac{\gamma^{l-1}}{\sum_{l'=2}^{L} \gamma^{l'-1}}$, γ is a hyper-parameter that controls the importance of each level in the hierarchy and $\sum_{l=2}^{L} \lambda_l = 1$. $\mathcal{L}_l$ represents the prototypical network loss at level l of the class hierarchy $\mathcal{H}$.

As such, we can tune the importance of each level of the hierarchy into the learning process: by choosing low values of γ, we put more importance into organizing the higher levels of the hierarchy; a value close to one gives the same importance for all the levels; a high value tends to behave like the *flat* cross entropy loss formulation.

4 Few-Shot Learning for Remote Sensing Scene Classification

We evaluate the performance of our hierarchical prototypical approach in a few-shot scene classification task. We first present the remote sensing scene dataset we consider in our study, since its labels are hierarchically organized Then, we describe the parameters and hyper-parameters setting. Finally, in order to assess the interest of introducing semantic knowledge into the few-shot scene classification task, we compare the classification results of the proposed approach to some baseline methods for the 5-way 5-shot and 5-way 1-shot tasks.

4.1 Dataset Description

The NWPU-RESISC45 [4] dataset is a widely used benchmark for remote sensing image scene classification. It consists of 31 500 images of 256 × 256 pixels; the spatial resolution varies from approximately 30 to 0.2 m per pixel. It covers 45 scene categories, each with 700 RGB images, which can be organized hierarchically. Following [12] in which the authors propose a hierarchical organization of the scene classes of the PatternNet [25] remote sensing scene dataset, we construct a tree-like arrangement of these scene classes which reflects their semantic relationships. We note that the leaf level of the constructed class hierarchy corresponds to the original scene classes of the dataset. A sub-tree of the 3−level label tree is shown in Fig. 3.

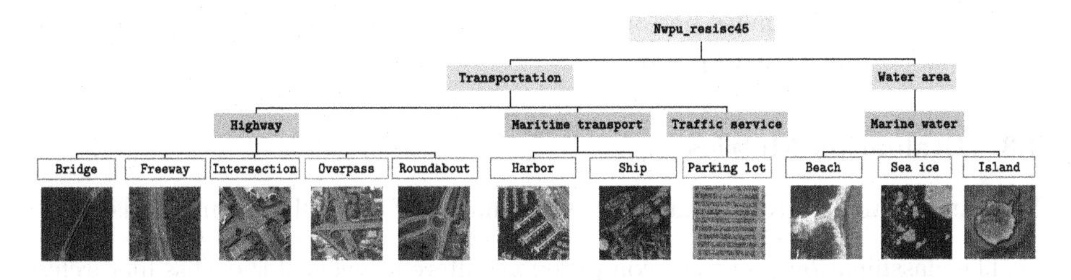

Fig. 3. Sub-tree of the proposed label tree for the NWPU-RESISC45 remote sensing dataset. The leaves correspond to the classes, the distance between two given classes is the height of the subtree at the Lowest Common Ancestor (LCA) node, and can take one of the following values: 0, 1, 2, and 3. The meta-train, meta-validation, and meta-test categories are leaves with red, green, and blue boxes respectively. (Color figure online)

For a fair comparison, we adopt the same split as done in [22]. We split the dataset into three disjoint subsets: meta-training D_{base}, meta-validation D_{val}, and meta-test D_{novel} containing 25, 8, and 12 categories, respectively. We note that the meta-validation set is used for hyper-parameter selection in the meta-training step. The meta-training set is further divided into three subsets: training, validation, and test sets. In our experiments, we follow [22] and resize all the images to 80 × 80 pixels to fit our designed feature extractor.

4.2 Implementation Details

Following recent FSRSSC studies [10, 22–24], we utilize ResNet-12 as a backbone for feature extraction. We also adopt the pre-training strategy as suggested in [22] to better initialize the meta-learner feature extractor.

We train our meta-learner for 1000 epochs with an early stopping of 50 epochs. The best model parameters were obtained within the first 300 epochs. In standard deep learning, an epoch implies that the entire train set passes through the deep neural network once. However, in meta-learning, an epoch is a set of episodes randomly sampled from the base set D_{base}, which we set to 1000 episodes per epoch. We optimize the model based on the average loss of 4 episodes, i.e. the batch size is set to 4 episodes. We use SGD optimizer to update the network parameters with a momentum set to 0.9 and a weight decay set to 0.0005. The learning rate is fixed to 0.001. After each training epoch, we test our model on a validation set D_{val} by randomly sampling 1000 episodes, the network weights with the lowest validation loss are retained as the best results. For the hyper-parameter γ, we assigned different values ($\gamma = 1$, $\gamma < 1$ and$\gamma > 1$) in order to observe its impact on the framework performances.

For the meta-testing stage, we conduct a 5-way 1-shot and 5-way 5-shot classification following the widely used meta-learning protocol. We evaluate the best model on 2000 randomly sampled episodes from the test set D_{novel}. Following the FSL evaluation protocol [17], for 5-way K-shot episode, we randomly sample 5 classes from the unseen classes C_{novel}, K images per class to form the support set S, and 15 images per class to form the query set Q, making a total of $5 \times (K + 15)$ images per episode.

4.3 Evaluation Metrics

We use two metrics to evaluate the performance of the different methods:

- The classification accuracy, computed at different levels of the class hierarchy;
- The hierarchical precision [16] which is defined as the total number of common ancestors between the predicted class and the true class divided by the total number of ancestors of the predicted classes:

$$hp = \frac{\sum_i |\hat{Y}_i \cap Y_i|}{|\sum_i \hat{Y}_i|} \tag{7}$$

where $\hat{Y}_i = \{\hat{y}_i \cup Ancestor(\hat{y}_i, \mathcal{H})\}$ is the set consisting of the most specific predicted class for test example i and all its ancestor classes in $\mathcal{H}$ except the root node and $Y_i = \{y_i \cup Ancestor(y_i, \mathcal{H})\}$ is the set consisting of the most specific true class for test example i and all its ancestor classes in $\mathcal{H}$ except the root node.

For all evaluation metrics, we report the average of the test episodes with a 95% confidence interval.

4.4 Experimental Results

In both 5-way K-shot configurations, K = 1 or 5, we compare our method to the original *flat* prototypical network [17] and to the approach proposed in [22] that uses the cosine metric as a similarity function, which we denote by *ProtoNet* and *c-ProtoNet* respectively. We re-implement both methods with their related parameter setting according to [22] and use ResNet-12 as a backbone for a fair comparison. We also compare our prototypes (namely *h-ProtoNet*) with the results yielded by the soft-label method [1], which allows taking into account the class hierarchy within the learning process. Results are provided in Table 1 for $K = 5$ and Table 2 for $K = 1$.

Table 1. 5-shot classification results computed on the test set of the NWPU-RESISC45 dataset at different levels of the class hierarchy: overall acc represents the classification accuracy at the leaves (level 4) and thus the NWPU-RESISC45 classes; L3-acc and L2-acc give the accuracy at level 3 and level 2, respectively; hp is the hierarchical precision. All accuracy results are averaged over 2000 test episodes and are reported with a 95% confidence interval.

Method	hyp-param	Overall acc	L3-acc	L2-acc	hp
ProtoNet [17]	/	83.76 ± 0.13	84.80 ± 0.04	85.62 ± 0.09	84.72 ± 0.08
c-ProtoNet [22]	10	80.21 ± 0.59	82.11 ± 1.80	84.81 ± 4.08	82.38 ± 2.16
Soft-labels [1]	4	84.22 ± 0.25	85.35 ± 0.23	86.19 ± 0.23	85.25 ± 0.23
h-ProtoNet (ours)	0.5	84.90 ± 0.25	86.01 ± 0.22	86.72 ± 0.23	85.88 ± 0.22
h-ProtoNet (ours)	1	$\mathbf{85.11 \pm 0.23}$	$\mathbf{86.10 \pm 0.22}$	$\mathbf{86.81 \pm 0.22}$	$\mathbf{86.01 \pm 0.21}$
h-ProtoNet (ours)	2	84.95 ± 0.23	85.93 ± 0.22	86.65 ± 0.20	85.85 ± 0.22

For both 1-shot and 5-shot cases, our proposed *h-ProtoNet* achieves the highest accuracy and outperforms both flat prototypes and the soft-labels hierarchical loss. We obtain the best performance with $\gamma = 1$, that is to say when all the (hierarchical) prototypes have the same weights. When we put more weights on the prototypes that correspond to the higher level of the hierarchy (corresponding to nodes close to the root, $\gamma < 1$) or to those that correspond to the leaves ($\gamma > 1$), we obtain degraded performances, that are still better than the other methods. Note that this value of $\gamma = 1$ would have been selected if we perform a cross-validation on the validation set. We argue that the improvement observed in the case of the hierarchical prototypes is due to an efficient regularization of the latent space, with a loss that encourages leaves within the same branch of the level hierarchy to be closer. As such, the performances at level 2 and 3 are improved, but also the overall accuracy.

Table 2. 1-shot classification results computed on the test set of the NWPU-RESISC45 dataset at different levels of the class hierarchy: overall acc represents the classification accuracy at the leaves (level 4) and thus the NWPU-RESISC45 classes; L3-acc and L2-acc give the accuracy at level 3 and level 2, respectively; hp is the hierarchical precision. All accuracy results are averaged over 2000 test episodes and are reported with a 95% confidence interval.

Method	hyp-param	Overall acc	L3-acc	L2-acc	hp
ProtoNet [17]	/	65.67 ± 0.46	67.39 ± 0.45	69.49 ± 0.45	67.52 ± 0.44
c-ProtoNet [22]	10	65.64 ± 0.45	67.52 ± 0.45	69.62 ± 0.45	67.59 ± 0.44
Soft-labels [1]	3	65.65 ± 0.45	67.24 ± 0.45	69.56 ± 0.45	65.65 ± 0.45
h-ProtoNet (ours)	0.5	$67.23 + 0.45$	$\mathbf{69.02 \pm 0.45}$	$\mathbf{71.41 \pm 0.45}$	$\mathbf{69.22 \pm 0.43}$
h-ProtoNet (ours)	1	$\mathbf{67.25 \pm 0.45}$	68.94 ± 0.45	71.23 ± 0.45	69.14 ± 0.43
h-ProtoNet (ours)	2	66.86 ± 0.45	68.74 ± 0.45	70.92 ± 0.45	68.84 ± 0.44

5 Conclusion and Future Works

Few-shot learning has captured the attention of the remote sensing community thanks to the great success it has achieved in other fields. In many cases, when dealing with the problem of scene classification, the organization of the classes is defined in a hierarchical manner, with classes being semantically closer than some others. In this work, we present a novel prototypical network which defines hierarchical prototypes that match the nodes of the label hierarchy[1]. We evaluate our method on a benchmarked [4] remote sensing scene dataset in a few-shot learning context and we show that hierarchical prototypes ensure a regularization of the latent space, providing higher performance than *flat* prototypes but also than a competitive hierarchical loss introduced in another context.

In future work, we plan to investigate the use of the hierarchical prototypes on other tasks such as semantic segmentation, where we consider adding spatial information among regions to output meaningful hierarchical prototypes. We also intend to use graph prototypical networks instead of prototypical networks, which better take into account the class relationships. We further consider relying on other metric spaces than the Euclidean one, *e.g.* hyperbolic spaces that are known to better encode the distances when the data are hierarchically-organized. Thus, a follow-up of this work could be to build hyperbolic prototypes to enforce the hierarchical information into the learning process.

Acknowledgement. This work was supported by the ANR Multiscale project under the reference ANR-18-CE23-0022.

[1] We recently became aware of a paper that proposes a similar approach to classify audio data in the FSL context [7]. The difference lies rather in the experimental part in which we use a deeper network and a pre-training step.

References

1. Bertinetto, L., Müller, R., Tertikas, K., Samangooei, S., Lord, N.A.: Making better mistakes: leveraging class hierarchies with deep networks. In: CVPR, pp. 12503–12512. Computer Vision Foundation/IEEE (2020)
2. Chen, Z., et al.: Multi-level semantic feature augmentation for one-shot learning. IEEE Trans. Image Process. **28**(9), 4594–4605 (2019)
3. Cheng, G., et al.: SPNet: siamese-prototype network for few-shot remote sensing image scene classification. IEEE Trans. Geosci. Remote. Sens. **60**, 1–11 (2022)
4. Cheng, G., Han, J., Lu, X.: Remote sensing image scene classification: benchmark and state of the art. Proc. IEEE **105**(10), 1865–1883 (2017)
5. Cheng, G., Yang, C., Yao, X., Guo, L., Han, J.: When deep learning meets metric learning: remote sensing image scene classification via learning discriminative CNNs. IEEE Trans. Geosci. Remote Sens. **56**(5), 2811–2821 (2018)
6. Esam, O., Yakoub, B., Naif, A., Haikel, A., Farid, M.: Using convolutional features and a sparse autoencoder for land-use scene classification. Int. J. Remote Sens. **37**(10), 2149–2167 (2016)
7. Garcia, H.F., Aguilar, A., Manilow, E., Pardo, B.: Leveraging hierarchical structures for few-shot musical instrument recognition. In: ISMIR, pp. 220–228 (2021)
8. Li, A., Luo, T., Lu, Z., Xiang, T., Wang, L.: Large-scale few-shot learning: knowledge transfer with class hierarchy. In: CVPR, pp. 7212–7220. Computer Vision Foundation/IEEE (2019)
9. Li, L., Han, J., Yao, X., Cheng, G., Guo, L.: DLA-MatchNet for few-shot remote sensing image scene classification. IEEE Trans. Geosci. Remote. Sens. **59**(9), 7844–7853 (2021)
10. Li, X., Li, H., Yu, R., Wang, F.: Few-shot scene classification with attention mechanism in remote sensing. J. Phys. Conf. Ser. **1961**, 012015 (2021)
11. Liu, L., Zhou, T., Long, G., Jiang, J., Zhang, C.: Many-class few-shot learning on multi-granularity class hierarchy. CoRR abs/2006.15479 (2020)
12. Liu, Y., Liu, Y., Chen, C., Ding, L.: Remote-sensing image retrieval with tree-triplet-classification networks. Neurocomputing **405**, 48–61 (2020)
13. Miller, G.A.: WordNet: a lexical database for English. Commun. ACM **38**(11), 39–41 (1995)
14. Nogueira, K., Penatti, O.A.B., dos Santos, J.A.: Towards better exploiting convolutional neural networks for remote sensing scene classification. Pattern Recognit. **61**, 539–556 (2017)
15. Shi, X., Salewski, L., Schiegg, M., Welling, M.: Relational generalized few-shot learning. In: BMVC. BMVA Press (2020)
16. Silla, C.N., Jr., Freitas, A.A.: A survey of hierarchical classification across different application domains. Data Min. Knowl. Discov. **22**(1–2), 31–72 (2011)
17. Snell, J., Swersky, K., Zemel, R.S.: Prototypical networks for few-shot learning. In: NIPS, pp. 4077–4087 (2017)
18. Sun, X., et al.: Research progress on few-shot learning for remote sensing image interpretation. IEEE J. Sel. Top. Appl. Earth Obs. Remote Sens. **14**, 2387–2402 (2021)
19. Sung, F., et al.: Learning to compare: relation network for few-shot learning. In: CVPR, pp. 1199–1208. Computer Vision Foundation/IEEE Computer Society (2018)
20. Vinyals, O., Blundell, C., Lillicrap, T., Kavukcuoglu, K., Wierstra, D.: Matching networks for one shot learning. In: NIPS, pp. 3630–3638 (2016)

21. Yang, F., Wang, R., Chen, X.: SEGA: semantic guided attention on visual prototype for few-shot learning. CoRR abs/2111.04316 (2021)
22. Zhang, P., Bai, Y., Wang, D., Bai, B., Li, Y.: Few-shot classification of aerial scene images via meta-learning. Remote Sens. **13**(1), 108 (2021)
23. Zhang, P., Fan, G., Wu, C., Wang, D., Li, Y.: Task-adaptive embedding learning with dynamic kernel fusion for few-shot remote sensing scene classification. Remote Sens. **13**(21), 4200 (2021)
24. Zhang, P., Li, Y., Wang, D., Wang, J.: RS-SSKD: self-supervision equipped with knowledge distillation for few-shot remote sensing scene classification. Sensors **21**(5), 1566 (2021)
25. Zhou, W., Newsam, S.D., Li, C., Shao, Z.: PatternNet: a benchmark dataset for performance evaluation of remote sensing image retrieval. CoRR abs/1706.03424 (2017)

TS-QUAD: A Smaller Elastic Ensemble for Time Series Classification with No Reduction in Accuracy

Jason Lines(✉) and George Oastler

University of East Anglia, Norwich Research Park, Norwich, UK
{j.lines,g.oastler}@uea.ac.uk

Abstract. The Elastic Ensemble (EE) is a time series classification (TSC) ensemble that includes eleven nearest neighbour (NN) classifiers that use variations of eight elastic distance measures. While EE offers an accurate solution for TSC in the time domain, its relatively slow run-time is a weakness. This has led to new algorithms, such as Proximity Forest and TS-CHIEF, that have iterated on the design of EE by taking the same elastic measures and incorporating them into tree-based ensembles. These enhancements were implemented successfully and led to faster and more accurate time domain classifiers and, as such, development on the original EE algorithm subsided.

However, in this work we make the simple hypothesis that the original design of EE contains distance measures that capture the same discriminatory features, and as such, the ensemble includes redundant classifiers. If this were true, EE could perform to the same level in terms of accuracy with significantly less computation. If proven true this would have interesting implications to the design of algorithms such as Proximity Forest and TS-CHIEF that are based on the original EE implementation. To investigate this, we form a simple categorisation of the distance measures within EE and form four groups. We take one measure from each group, building an ensemble of four 1-NN classifiers that we call TS-QUAD: the Time Series QUARtet of distance-based classifiers. We demonstrate that this ensemble is able to match EE in terms of accuracy over 10 resamples of 85 datasets while containing fewer than 50% of the original EE constituents, implying that other elastic distance-based TSC ensembles could benefit from the design philosophy of TS-QUAD.

Keywords: Time series · Classification · Elastic distance measures

1 Introduction

The Elastic Ensemble (EE) [12] is a time series classification (TSC) ensemble that combines eleven nearest neighbour (NN) classifiers built with eight distinct elastic distance measures. The motivation for creating EE was that, at the time, the commonly used gold-standard for TSC was a 1-NN classifier coupled with

M. El Yacoubi et al. (Eds.): ICPRAI 2022, LNCS 13364, pp. 221–232, 2022.
https://doi.org/10.1007/978-3-031-09282-4_19

Dynamic Time Warping (DTW) and a warping window parameter set through cross-validation. This led to variants of DTW being proposed in the literature, such as derivative [11] and weighted DTW [10], as well as other competing elastic distance measures such as Time Warp Edit (TWE) distance [15] and the Move-Split-Merge (MSM) distance [25]. While various approaches were proposed and evaluated in the literature, none significantly outperformed DTW 1-NN in terms of accuracy.

In [12], it was hypothesised that, even though these measures did not perform differently in terms of accuracy when combined with 1-NN classifiers, the measures themselves may detect similarity in different ways. It was proposed that combining classifiers built with each of these measures would detect a wider range of discriminatory features than using a single measure alone. EE was created to test this hypothesis by coupling the elastic measures each with a 1-NN classifier and combining predictions through a weighted voting scheme that was informed by training accuracy estimates. The results of experiments over the UCR datasets supported this hypothesis as EE outperformed all of its constituent classifiers, including DTW 1-NN, and all other TSC approaches that were published in the literature at the time.

Since EE was first proposed the field of TSC has grown rapidly and a range of diverse and effective algorithms have been introduced into the literature. Such algorithms include the Collective of Transformation-based Ensembles (COTE) [2], HIVE-COTE: the Hierarchical Vote Ensemble Collective of Transformation-based Ensembles [13], ROCKET [6], Proximity Forest (PF) [14], InceptionTime [7], and TS-CHIEF [24]. These algorithms are notable because each has now been shown to significantly outperform EE over the UCR datasets in terms of accuracy, but an interesting observation is that EE has been critical to the development of many successive state-of-the-art approaches. While ROCKET and InceptionTime are based on convolutional kernels and deep learning approaches respectively, PF, COTE and TS-CHIEF each incorporate the eight elastic distance measures that were first combined in EE and also use the same parameter options as proposed by EE, while the first version of HIVE-COTE contained EE itself as a constituent module to operate in the time domain.

It is clear that EE has influenced numerous algorithms, but development and refinement of the ensemble has all but ceased due to the relatively slow run-time of the nearest neighbour classifiers within EE. Efforts have been made to demonstrate that training and testing decisions can be significantly faster for EE through restricted neighbourhoods and randomised parameter searchers [19] but, in general, there was little need until now to revisit EE since subsequent algorithms such as PF are faster and more accurate than EE.

We do revisit the design of EE in this work however due to a simple observation that the original EE algorithm in [12] was designed to significantly outperform the gold standard at the time of DTW-1NN. While run-time was noted in this work, it was not a priority in the design of EE and it was not considered whether all distance measures were required in the final EE since its introduction was a legitimate step-forward in the state of the art for TSC. Thus, we hypothesise that there may be underlying redundancy between some of the distance measures that were selected for EE and it is worth investigating. We believe that it is likely that we can build a subset of EE that will perform to the same level of accuracy as the whole ensemble while requiring far less computation. This finding would be of note because, while EE may not be widely used in TSC anymore, leading algorithms such as PF and TS-CHIEF are based on the original design of EE and may also include redundant distance measures. We choose to investigate this hypothesis with EE as it is a deterministic algorithm, unlike PF and TS-CHIEF that each include random selection, so it is clearer to demonstrate that the differences in performance are based on constituent selection alone rather than random chance.

We start by grouping the distance measures into four high-level and intuitive groupings and nominate a single measure from each group to include in a new subset of EE. We call this *TS-QUAD: the Time Series QUARtet of distance-based classifiers* for the purposes of this work, and results over 10 resamples of 85 UCR TSC problems demonstrate that TS-QUAD is no less accurate than EE while containing less than half of the constituent classifiers, and half of the original distance measures, of EE. This finding indicates that further research and refinement may be possible of subsequent elastic TSC ensembles such as PF and TS-CHIEF.

2 Background and Related Work

We define a time series $T = <x_1, x_2, ..., x_m>$ as an ordered sequence of m real values. The ordering of attribute values is typically by units of time, but this is not a requirement. For example, electromagnetic spectroscopy readings are typically recorded in nanometres, not units of time, but we would consider this data a time series under our definition. Further, time series data can be univariate or multivariate depending on the number of dimensions or channels in the incoming data streams. In this work, we constrain our research efforts to the univariate case for classification of time series data.

For the supervised task of TSC, each series T_i must have an associated class label y_i. The objective of TSC is to use a set of n time series $\mathbf{T} = \{T_1, T_2, ..., T_n\}$, with associated class labels $Y = \{y_1, y_2, ..., y_n\}$, as training data to learn a function that maps from the space of all possible series to the space of all possible class labels. Then, when previously unseen series with unknown class labels are presented, predictions can be made to classify the unknown cases as one of the possible class values.

As alluded to earlier, TSC is a very active area of research and many diverse algorithms have been proposed and evaluated on a large number of TSC datasets (for example, [1] contains a large experimental comparison). We focus on EE as the starting point for this work, which performs classification in the time domain on raw series data, but it should be noted that a variety of other algorithms exist and work with discriminatory features that are discovered in other transformation-based domains and the current state of the art for TSC in terms of accuracy, HIVE-COTE V2.0 [18] (HC2) is an ensemble that is formed with classifiers built over a range of different domains. Such individual domains include shapelet-based approaches that detect discriminatory features within phase-independent subsequences [8,9,26], interval-based approaches that focus on specific intervals within series [3,17], and histogram-based algorithms that extract features through counting the occurrence of repeated patterns to make classification decisions [16,22,23]. Recently, convolutional and deep learning approaches have shown promising results for TSC, such as InceptionTime [7] and ROCKET [6], while other approaches such as HIVE-COTE [13], HC2 and TS-CHIEF [24] are hybrid approaches that combine classifiers over multiple domains, such as the time, frequency and shapelet domains.

2.1 Classification in the Time Domain

Before HC2 and the other contemporary TSC algorithms were proposed, a large amount of research effort in the field focused on developing *elastic* distance measures to couple with nearest neighbour classifiers. The approach to perform classification in the time domain by measuring distances between series was popularised by the early success of using DTW with 1-NN classifiers and a warping window set through cross-validation (such as in [20,21]). Given the success of this approach, many subsequent efforts iterated on this design by proposing alternative time-series similarity measures to couple with 1-NN classifiers. These included variations of DTW, such as derivative [11] and weighted [10] DTW, and other specialised methods such as those that extended edit-distance approach to similarity (e.g. [4]) and hybrids based approaches such as TWE [15] and MSM [25]. While these proposed measure were often compared in experiments to DTW 1-NN, conclusions were anecdotal and no measure was demonstrated to significantly outperformed DTW-1NN over a large number of datasets.

2.2 The Elastic Ensemble (EE) and Extensions

EE was created to leverage from the wide range of elastic distance measures that had been introduced in the TSC literature in order to combine the different predictions of individual measures to produce a result that was more accurate than any approach in isolation. We will briefly reintroduce EE in this section, but to avoid retreading existing ground, we direct the interested reader to [12] for a more in-depth discussion and full implementation details of EE.

In total, EE contains eleven 1-NN classifiers that are coupled with versions of eight elastic distance measures. The first three 1-NN classifiers use measures that do not contain parameters to be set (Euclidean 1-NN, full window DTW 1-NN, full window derivative DTW 1-NN) and the remaining classifiers each use one of eight distance measures that require parameters to be set in training. The constituent classifiers in EE are summarised in Fig. 1.

The elastic 1-NN classifiers in EE are combined through a weighted vote, where weights are established in training while parameters are optimised. Each

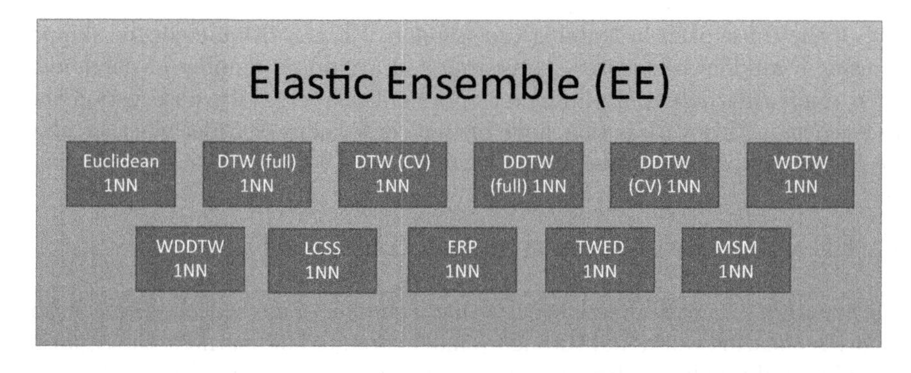

Fig. 1. A graphical representation of EE and the constituent classifiers that it contains. Eight of the eleven classifiers require distance measure parameters to be set in training, while the remaining three approaches (Euclidean, DTW full, DDTW full) do not require parameters to be set.

constituent is given 100 possible parameter options (which was originally motivated by DTW using windows in the range of 1%–100%) and leave-one-out cross-validation is used to determine which parameter setting performs best in training for each constituent classifier. The subsequent EE uses the best parameter options found in training for each constituent and also its corresponding training estimate to weight test predictions in a proportional vote. For example, if WDTW-1NN within the ensemble had a training accuracy of 87% for a given dataset, in testing, WDTW-1NN would be given a weight of 0.87 for its vote. By applying this weighting scheme to all constituent classifiers within EE, rather than using a simple majority vote, test classification over the UCR datasets [5] was significantly improved.

A clear downside of EE is that 1-NN classifiers are lazy classifiers, requiring an $O(N)$ pass of the data for each classification decision. This is further slowed by the elastic measures each having $O(m^2)$ run-time complexities for series of length m, and when combined with the training experiments that are required to find measure parameters and constituent voting weights, EE becomes a time-consuming algorithm to use. This has motivated work such as [14] where Proximity Forest (PF) was proposed as an improvement to EE. PF addressed these run-time issues by taking the eight distance measures from EE and making two key changes. First, 1-NN classifiers are not used, and they are replaced with tree-based classifiers that form an ensemble for test classification. Second, the same parameter ranges were considered for the elastic measures, but random selection is used when assessing potential splits within internal trees of PF. As a result, PF is much faster than EE in practice while still utilising the same elastic measures and parameter options. TS-CHIEF [24] is a further continuation of this research, using a similar structure and the same measures and parameter options as EE and PF in combination with trees that are built with features from other transformation domains. Finally, it is worth noting that the underlying training scheme within EE has also been investigated, with [19] showing that over

90% of the time taken in training the standard EE algorithm could be skipped by using a random parameter grid-search and a reduced number of neighbours when comparing potential parameter options. However, a key observation that we leverage in this work is that none of these extensions consider whether *all* of the elastic distance measures within EE, PF and TS-CHIEF are required.

3 EE with Fewer Constituents: TS-QUAD

Our hypothesis for this investigation is that a number of internal classifiers within EE are replicating work, and through removing redundant learners, the resulting ensemble could make predictions with significantly less computation but no loss in accuracy. If this holds, it will have important implications for PF and TS-CHIEF; at its simplest, it would suggest that these classifiers could be built to the same level more quickly, as fewer parameter and measure combinations would need to be evaluated to produce an equivalent classifier. Importantly, however, there is also the possibility that this could lead to more accurate classifiers. The algorithm to build PF defaults to include 100 constituent tree classifiers; if the 100 internal learners are using complimentary measures and parameter options that detect the same discriminatory features, diversity within the ensemble will naturally be lower. However, with redundant measures reduced, the likelihood of the 100 internal learners being more diverse would be increased and this may lead to a more accurate ensemble overall, and this would also then translate to TS-CHIEF if true. However, investigating the effect on PF and TS-CHIEF is beyond the scope of this work as we wish to make a direct comparison between the inclusion and exclusion of constituent measures and classifiers. EE is a better choice for this goal as it is a deterministic algorithm and the differences between a full and reduced ensemble would not be explained by random chance. For this reason, we also do not include the clear speedups provided in [19] as this introduces randomness into the parameter selections for internal classifiers and the relative speedups for EE and a subset of EE would also be consistent.

To investigate whether we can remove constituent classifiers from EE we start by creating a simple, intuitive grouping of the elastic measures in Table 1. Our rationale for these groupings is that we do not believe that EE requires multiple measures that are designed to operate in similar manners. We wish to create an ensemble that only contains measures that have different design objectives, so we have created a high-level grouping that is based on the intuition behind each of the measures. We have also disregarded the full-window options for DTW and derivative DTW, as well as Euclidean distance, as these are already redundant if the parameterised versions of DTW and derivative DTW can recreate Euclidean distance and the full window equivalents in cases where those parameter options would be optimal.

The first group in Table 1, *time domain warping*, includes the classic DTW algorithm and weighted DTW (WDTW). The original DTW measure is applied to raw time series, and WDTW is also applied to the raw data but uses weights to manipulate warping paths rather than a fixed cutoff. As DTW and WDTW

Table 1. The eight elastic distance measures first used together in EE placed into four high-level groupings. One measure was selected for TS-QUAD from each of the four groups and this is denoted in the table using *.

Time domain warping	Derivative warping	Edit-distance	Hybrid measures
DTW	***DDTW****	***LCSS****	***MSM****
WDTW*	WDDTW	ERP	TWE

are conceptually very similar and can result in identical distances with certain data and parameter options, they are clear candidates to group together.

Similarly, the second group in Table 1 contains derivative DTW (DDTW) and weighted derivative DDTW (WDDTW) into a *derivative warping* group. These measures are very similar to their origin measures, DTW and WDTW, and are both based on DTW with the variation that similarity is measured on the first-order derivatives of the time series, rather than directly on the raw data.

Thirdly, group three is titled *edit-distance* and includes the two distance measures from EE that are based around the idea of edit-distance. A full description of ERP and LCSS is given in [12], but briefly, these two measures are not based on DTW and instead measure the effort required to transform one series into another through operations such as additions, deletions and replacements. Edit-distance approaches are more common in other data mining applications, such as text mining, but have been successfully implemented for real-valued data by using threshold values and penalty functions.

Finally, the fourth group is named *hybrid measures* and it includes MSM and TWE. Both of these measures incorporate facets of time warping and edit-distance, and hence have been grouped together due to this high-level design similarity of incorporating characteristics from both the warping and edit-distance groups.

Our hypothesis is that including multiple measures from each of these groups in the same ensemble would introduce redundancy, rather than increasing diversity, and is therefore unnecessary computation. To test this, we select one distance measure from each group in Table 1. We do not wish to overfit the measure selections or introduce bias through looking at test results, so we use simple assumptions and practical knowledge, rather than classification accuracies, to make these decisions. From groups one and two we select WDTW and DDTW for use in our reduced ensemble. Our justification for using these two measures is slightly nuanced, but we believe it is more likely to result in diversity if one measure uses weighting and one uses a traditional warping window. We could select DTW and WDDTW, but we choose instead to select WDTW and DDTW as these two measures were the specific contributions of two TSC research papers [10,11], while WDDTW was a secondary contribution after the main WDTW measure and DTW was first used in other fields with WDTW posed as an improvement upon it. We do not expect this rationale to make a large difference overall however, and it is likely that using DTW and WDDTW would result in similar coverage to using WDTW and DDTW if our hypothesis is correct. For groups three and four, our decisions are simpler; timing experiments were carried out in [12] and demonstrated that LCSS was faster than ERP, and MSM was faster than TWE on the same data. We use this prior knowledge to select LCSS and MSM respectively for convenience as these timing results can be recreated simply without introducing bias or observing any results from real data. Since our hypothesis is that the discriminatory features captured by measures within the same group will be consistent regardless of run-time it is therefore sensible to prioritise faster measures.

Our final ensemble contains four elastic distance measures: WDTW, DDTW, LCSS and MSM. Each is combined with a 1-NN classifier and form part of a smaller elastic ensemble. For the purposes of this work, we call this new ensemble TS-QUAD (**T**ime-**S**eries **QUA**rtet of **D**istance-based classifiers). We do not expect TS-QUAD to compete with the state of the art, but in this work it will help to either support or refute our hypothesis that EE, PF and TS-CHIEF contain redundant distance measures that could be removed without reducing accuracy.

4 Experimental Procedure

We compare TS-QUAD to EE over 10 resamples of the UCR TSC problems [5] using the same 85-dataset version of the repository that has been widely used in recent work [1,13,14,24]. As discussed previously, the primary motivation for this research is not to outperform state-of-the-art algorithms such as HIVE-COTE with TS-QUAD, but rather the motivation is to demonstrate that four elastic measures can perform as well together as the full set of eight that are used by EE. To this end we compare TS-QUAD directly to EE in our experiments. The datasets are resampled using the same random seeds as the first 10 resamples in [1] to ensure that results are reproducible and comparable (with the first 'resample' being the default train/test split of the data), and we also use the same implementations of the distance measures and 1-NN classifiers that were originally used for EE in [12] to ensure that there are no differences caused by inconsistent implementations. The source code for the distance measures and classifiers is freely available in the open source Java toolkit `tsml` and can be found here[1], while the code to create consistent resamples of the dataset can also be found within the same toolkit here[2].

[1] https://github.com/uea-machine-learning/tsml/tree/master/src/main/java/tsml/classifiers/legacy/elastic_ensemble.

[2] https://github.com/uea-machine-learning/tsml/blob/master/src/main/java/utilities/InstanceTools.java.

5 Results

The results of EE and TS-QUAD over 10 resamples of the 85 UCR datasets are summarised in Table 2 and the full results are given in Table 3. It can be seen from the summarised results that there is very little to choose from between TS-QUAD and EE in terms of both average accuracy and average rank. EE has a slightly superior rank over the 85 problems, with 1.494 versus 1.506, while TS-QUAD in fact has a higher average accuracy than EE with 81.16% and 80.89% over these experiments.

Table 2. The average accuracies and ranks of EE and TS-QUAD over the 85 UCR datasets. The accuracies are averaged over 10 resamples, and the average rank is calculated by first ranking each classifier on their respective average accuracy for a given dataset, and then averaging the ranks across all 85 datasets. Overall, EE won on 42 datasets, TS-QUAD on 41, and they tied on two.

	EE	TS-QUAD
Average accuracy	80.89%	**81.16%**
Average rank	**1.494**	1.506

There is no significant difference in accuracy between EE and TS-QUAD, confirmed by both a paired t-test and a Wilcoxon signed-rank test. This result is a very positive indication that our original hypothesis holds true and that we do not need to use all eight distance measures that were originally combined in [12] to produce a competitive ensemble of elastic-based 1-NN classifiers. While the results of TS-QUAD do not challenge the state of the art, and were never expected to, they do suggest that further investigation is required to verify whether this finding is true when based to other time series ensembles that built upon the design principles established by the introduction of EE, most notably PF and TS-CHIEF. We also note that it may be possible to further improve upon TS-QUAD by optimising the constituent measures that are included and it would likely be possible to post-process all combinations of the EE constituents to produce a more accurate subset. However, it would not be constructive to optimise the ensemble in this way as it would likely lead to overfitting on the UCR datasets specifically. We believe TS-QUAD is a fair subset of EE, as it is based on an intuitive and high-level grouping of measures, but it is not intended to be solution to TSC problems itself. Its main purpose is to motivate further research effort in the area of elastic measure selection and we believe these results achieve this goal.

Table 3. Average accuracies over the 85 UCR TSC problems for EE and TS-QUAD. The accuracies reported are averaged over 10 resamples of each dataset (please note that some of the dataset names have been shortened for presentation, but each dataset is identical to those used in other work such as [1].

Dataset	EE	TS-QUAD	Dataset	EE	TS-QUAD
Adiac	**67.16**	66.45	MedicalImages	76	**76.38**
ArrowHead	86.06	**86.17**	MiddlePhalanxAge	59.55	**64.55**
Beef	56	**58.67**	MiddlePhalanxCorrect	78.11	**78.63**
BeetleFly	77.5	**78**	MiddlePhalanxTW	51.56	**54.68**
BirdChicken	**86.5**	83	MoteStrain	87.26	**87.83**
CBF	98.59	**99.39**	NonInvasiveFT	**84.94**	83.4
Car	80.83	**82.83**	NonInvasiveFT2	**91.39**	90.35
ChlorineConcentration	66.43	**68.93**	OSULeaf	**81.9**	80.95
CinCECGTorso	94.62	**95.78**	OliveOil	87	**87.67**
Coffee	**98.21**	97.86	PhalangesCorrect	77.82	**78.64**
Computers	72.32	**73.64**	Phoneme	**30.16**	28.41
CricketX	**81.08**	79.54	Plane	**100**	99.81
CricketY	**78.9**	77.26	ProximalPhalanxAgeGroup	79.71	**82.93**
CricketZ	**80.31**	79.38	ProximalPhalanxCorrect	82.99	**83.81**
DiatomSizeRed.	94.87	**95.75**	ProximalPhalanxTW	75.95	**77.56**
DistalPhalanxAge	74.68	**75.25**	RefrigerationDevices	65.33	**67.95**
DistalPhalanxCorrect	**76.23**	75.87	ScreenType	55.73	**56.24**
DistalPhalanxTW	65.25	**66.83**	ShapeletSim	82.72	**91.22**
ECG200	**89.2**	88.6	ShapesAll	88.5	**87.97**
ECG5000	93.68	**93.8**	SmallKitchenAppliances	69.55	**70.24**
ECGFiveDays	85.39	**88.58**	SonyAIBORobotSurface1	78.49	**79.63**
Earthquakes	73.17	**73.53**	SonyAIBORobotSurface2	88.61	**88.91**
ElectricDevices	**81.43**	81.41	StarlightCurves	93.92	**94.62**
FaceAll	96.6	**97.07**	Strawberry	95.57	**95.59**
FaceFour	86.48	**90.91**	SwedishLeaf	**91.98**	91.46
FacesUCR	94.83	**96.68**	Symbols	**95.58**	94.32
FiftyWords	**82.31**	81.85	SyntheticControl	**99.4**	99.07
Fish	**91.49**	90.97	ToeSegmentation1	**77.68**	77.5
FordA	73.74	**74.9**	ToeSegmentation2	**90**	89.92
FordB	**74.95**	74.94	Trace	**99.5**	**99.5**
GunPoint	**96.87**	96.8	TwoLeadECG	**95.49**	94.14
Ham	73.52	**74.1**	TwoPatterns	**100**	99.99
HandOutlines	**88.62**	88.22	UWaveGestureLibraryAll	**96.94**	96.71
Haptics	**44.19**	43.93	UWaveGestureLibraryX	**80.63**	79.04
Herring	57.03	**58.13**	UWaveGestureLibraryY	**72.95**	71.21
InlineSkate	**47.44**	46.64	UWaveGestureLibraryZ	**72.49**	70.97
InsectWingbeatSound	**57.66**	57.48	Wafer	99.71	**99.73**
ItalyPowerDemand	**95.27**	95.07	Wine	**85.74**	**85.74**
LargeKitchenAppliances	**81.68**	80.69	WordSynonyms	**77.63**	77.26
Lightning2	82.95	**83.11**	Worms	**63.38**	62.47
Lightning7	**75.07**	71.78	WormsTwoClass	**72.08**	70.91
Mallat	**95.95**	95.45	Yoga	88.47	**88.5**
Meat	**97.83**	97.33			

6 Conclusions, Future Work and Extensions

In this work we have investigated whether the Elastic Ensemble (EE) [12] contains distance measures that capture overlapping discriminatory features. We hypothesised that a number of measures within EE were redundant, and that we could therefore form a subset of constituents from EE that would perform no worse under experimental conditions in terms of accuracy but with significantly less computation. We formed this subset by first grouping each of the distance measures from EE together into simple and intuitive categories. We proposed four categories and used one elastic measure from each group, in combination with a 1-NN classifier, to form TS-QUAD. TS-QUAD contains four internal 1-NN classifiers, rather than the eleven (built with eight distance measures) that are contained within EE. We demonstrated that, over 10 resamples of 85 datasets, there is no significant difference in terms of accuracy when comparing EE to TS-QUAD. This work has demonstrated that it is indeed possible to perform as well as the full EE while only using half of the original distance measures that were contained by the full ensemble. This finding suggests that future work should be conducted to investigate whether similar improvements could be made to algorithms that are informed by the original design of EE, such as PF and TS-CHIEF, and this may lead to faster and more accurate elastic-based TSC ensembles.

References

1. Bagnall, A., Lines, J., Bostrom, A., Large, J., Keogh, E.: The great time series classification bake off: a review and experimental evaluation of recent algorithmic advances. Data Min. Knowl. Discov. **31**(3), 606–660 (2016). https://doi.org/10.1007/s10618-016-0483-9
2. Bagnall, A., Lines, J., Hills, J., Bostrom, A.: Time-series classification with COTE: the collective of transformation-based ensembles. IEEE Trans. Knowl. Data Eng. **27**, 2522–2535 (2015)
3. Baydogan, M., Runger, G., Tuv, E.: A bag-of-features framework to classify time series. IEEE Trans. Pattern Anal. Mach. Intell. **25**(11), 2796–2802 (2013)
4. Chen, L., Ng, R.: On the marriage of Lp-norms and edit distance. In: Proceedings of 30th International Conference on Very Large Databases (VLDB) (2004)
5. Dau, H., et al.: The UCR time series archive. IEEE/CAA J. Automatica Sinica **6**(6), 1293–1305 (2019)
6. Dempster, A., Petitjean, F., Webb, G.: ROCKET: exceptionally fast and accurate time series classification using random convolutional kernels. Data Min. Knowl. Discov. **34**, 1454–1495 (2020)
7. Fawaz, H., et al.: InceptionTime: finding AlexNet for time series classification. Data Min. Knowl. Discov. **34**(6), 1936–1962 (2020)
8. Grabocka, J., Schilling, N., Wistuba, M., Schmidt-Thieme, L.: Learning time-series shapelets. In: Proceedings of 20th ACM SIGKDD International Conference on Knowledge Discovery and Data Mining (2014)
9. Hills, J., Lines, J., Baranauskas, E., Mapp, J., Bagnall, A.: Classification of time series by shapelet transformation. Data Min. Knowl. Discov. **28**(4), 851–881 (2013). https://doi.org/10.1007/s10618-013-0322-1

10. Jeong, Y., Jeong, M., Omitaomu, O.: Weighted dynamic time warping for time series classification. Pattern Recognit. **44**, 2231–2240 (2011)
11. Keogh, E., Pazzani, M.: Derivative dynamic time warping. In: Proceedings of 1st SIAM International Conference on Data Mining (2001)
12. Lines, J., Bagnall, A.: Time series classification with ensembles of elastic distance measures. Data Min. Knowl. Discov. **29**(3), 565–592 (2014). https://doi.org/10.1007/s10618-014-0361-2
13. Lines, J., Taylor, S., Bagnall, A.: Time series classification with HIVE-COTE: the hierarchical vote collective of transformation-based ensembles. ACM Trans. Knowl. Discov. Data **12**(5), 1–36 (2018)
14. Lucas, B., et al.: Proximity forest: an effective and scalable distance-based classifier for time series. Data Min. Knowl. Discov. **33**(3), 607–635 (2019)
15. Marteau, P.: Time warp edit distance with stiffness adjustment for time series matching. IEEE Trans. Pattern Anal. Mach. Intell. **31**(2), 306–318 (2009)
16. Middlehurst, M., Large, J., Cawley, G., Bagnall, A.: The temporal dictionary ensemble (TDE) classifier for time series classification. In: Hutter, F., Kersting, K., Lijffijt, J., Valera, I. (eds.) ECML PKDD 2020. LNCS (LNAI), vol. 12457, pp. 660–676. Springer, Cham (2021). https://doi.org/10.1007/978-3-030-67658-2_38
17. Middlehurst, M., Large, J., Bagnall, A.: The canonical interval forest (CIF) classifier for time series classification. In: 2020 IEEE International Conference on Big Data (Big Data), pp. 188–195. IEEE (2020)
18. Middlehurst, M., et al.: HIVE-COTE 2.0: a new meta ensemble for time series classification. Mach. Learn. Online First, 1–33 (2021). http://link.springer.com/article/10.1007/s10994-021-06057-9
19. Oastler, G., Lines, J.: A significantly faster elastic-ensemble for time-series classification. In: Yin, H., Camacho, D., Tino, P., Tallón-Ballesteros, A.J., Menezes, R., Allmendinger, R. (eds.) IDEAL 2019. LNCS, vol. 11871, pp. 446–453. Springer, Cham (2019). https://doi.org/10.1007/978-3-030-33607-3_48
20. Rakthanmanon, T., et al.: Addressing big data time series: mining trillions of time series subsequences under dynamic time warping. ACM Trans. Knowl. Discov. Data **7**(3), 1–31 (2013)
21. Rath, T., Manamatha, R.: Word image matching using dynamic time warping. In: Proceedings of Computer Vision and Pattern Recognition (2003)
22. Schäfer, P.: The BOSS is concerned with time series classification in the presence of noise. Data Min. Knowl. Discov. **29**(6), 1505–1530 (2014). https://doi.org/10.1007/s10618-014-0377-7
23. Schäfer, P., Leser, U.: Fast and accurate time series classification with WEASEL. In: Proceedings of the ACM on Conference on Information and Knowledge Management, pp. 637–646 (2017)
24. Shifaz, A., Pelletier, C., Petitjean, F., Webb, G.I.: TS-CHIEF: a scalable and accurate forest algorithm for time series classification. Data Min. Knowl. Discov. **34**(3), 742–775 (2020). https://doi.org/10.1007/s10618-020-00679-8
25. Stefan, A., Athitsos, V., Das, G.: The move-split-merge metric for time series. IEEE Trans. Knowl. Data Eng. **25**(6), 1425–1438 (2013)
26. Ye, L., Keogh, E.: Time series shapelets: a novel technique that allows accurate, interpretable and fast classification. Data Min. Knowl. Discov. **22**(1–2), 149–182 (2011)

Machine Learning

Shop Signboards Detection Using the ShoS Dataset

Mrouj Almuhajri[1,2(✉)] and Ching Y. Suen[1]

[1] Centre for Pattern Recognition and Machine Intelligence, Concordia University, Montreal, QC H3G 2W1, Canada
mr_almuh@encs.concordia.ca, suen@cse.concordia.ca

[2] Department of Computer Science, Saudi Electronic University, Riyadh, Saudi Arabia
m.almuhajri@seu.edu.sa

Abstract. This work was driven by the possibility of enabling beneficial applications for humans and municipal agencies utilizing deep learning techniques to detect shop signboards. Data is the foundation of successful AI-based applications. Despite the abundance of data, providing datasets for such applications is a challenge as they have to be refined and characterized accurately for better performance. This paper describes the process of collecting the ShoS dataset from Google Street Views for the detection of the signboards of shops on streets. A total of 10k storefront signboards were captured and fully annotated within 7500 images. The ShoS datasets were tested by running different baseline methodology using one-stage detectors YOLO and SSD. Out of the tested methods and variances, the YOLOv3 yields the highest performance reaching 94.23% (mAP@0.5).

Keywords: Shop signboard detection · Dataset · Object detection · YOLO · SSD · Deep learning

1 Introduction

Despite the massiveness of street view images provided by Google, collecting storefront images and annotating them is a hard and time consuming task that is prone to human errors due to the intensive work it requires. Literature shows that detecting and classifying storefronts from Google view images is often negatively impacted by the lack of annotations or having inaccurate ones [9,10,20]. This work was driven by the possibility of enabling beneficial applications for municipal agencies, humans, and other applications related to transportation.

Municipal government agencies issue policies and regulations to govern the design of storefronts and their signboards. Although human inspectors are usually utilized to ensure adherence to such policies and guidelines, AI-based systems can identify, classify, and check shops' signboard regulations with improvement in speed and accuracy. For instance, the city of Westmount in Quebec issued regulations governing the design of storefronts and their signboards including language, size, lettering, and graphic elements [3].

M. El Yacoubi et al. (Eds.): ICPRAI 2022, LNCS 13364, pp. 235–245, 2022.
https://doi.org/10.1007/978-3-031-09282-4_20

Detecting the shop signboards is the first step for further potential applications including store classification, which may facilitate exploring neighborhoods and identifying locations of interest for different types of users, such as tourists and vision-impaired people leveraging smart phones.

The main contributions of this work are: 1) provide the ShoS dataset for the public for several research purposes including but not limited to shop signboards detection; 2) report outcomes of different baseline methodology and applications on the ShoS dataset including YOLO and SSD.

2 Related Work

2.1 Street View Imagery Object Detection

In [20] study, the authors aimed to detect the whole storefronts given street panoramic views using MultiBox model [5] which uses a single CNN based on GoogLeNet [17] with a 7×7 grid. A coarse sliding window mechanism was applied followed by non-maximum suppression to make fewer predictions of bounding boxes. This work found difficulty annotating that huge number of the dataset, so they used less amount of data in testing. For evaluation, they compared their work with selective search, multi-context heat MCH map, and human performance. Results revealed that MultiBox surpasses the first two methods as MultiBox gets a recall of 91% compared to 62% for selective search. Moreover, MCH could not detect the boundary of storefronts precisely. This was due to the fact that storefronts are more exposed to noise and they can abut each other.

Similarly, another recent study [10] proposed a system composed of several models for detecting the whole storefront from street views and classify it in further models. The detector was based on YOLOv3 [13] as they removed the layers responsible for detecting small objects. The authors evaluated their work using their limited dataset and compared it to SSD[8] and Faster RCNN[15]. Their methodology got mAP@0.50 = 79.37% which outperforms the others with 74.3% and 78.9% respectively.

For that, some research results have been published in a similar area which is License Plate Detection (LPD). A lot of attention has been devoted to LPD with the enhancement of real-time object detection models. In [6] work, the first two models of YOLO [11] and [12] were used in a multi-stage manner to detect vehicles first using Fast-YOLO with IoU set to 0.125, and then the detected vehicle is cropped and fed into YOLOv2 network with an extremely low threshold to make sure they got all possibilities within the vehicle patch. Thus, the box with a higher confidence score is considered. This way, they were able to get high precession and recall nearly to 99%. In addition, in [1] work, authors introduced a YOLO-inspired solution for LPD system as they trained and tested several models with different hyper parameter values in order to save computational processing time and power. A recall ratio of 98.38% is achieved outperforming two commercial products (OpenALPR and Plate Recognizer) significantly.

Another work [14] focused on providing a small and fast model for LPD so that it could work on embedded systems. The proposed system is based on

Mobilenet-SSD (MSSD) to detect license plates. The authors further optimized the system by introducing feature fusion methods on the MSSD model in order to extract context information and hence better detection. The results revealed that their proposed system is 2.11% higher than the MSSD in terms of precision, and it is also faster than MSSD by 70 ms.

Despite that the enhancement done on LPD field is dramatically significant, things could be different with shop signboards as they take various shapes and forms compared to licence plates. This visual variability may make it challenging for machines to detect them. Also, all the previous mentioned works used the whole storefront in their systems and faced some crucial issues in detection because of 1) the limitation of existing datasets, 2) the boundaries of storefronts are not clear enough to be learned. This work intends to overcome these challenges by building a large-scale dataset with full annotation where the focus is on the signboards only and then train some one-stage object detection models on the collected dataset to examine its performance.

2.2 Storefront Dataset

Street View Text (SVT) dataset [18] is one of the earliest public datasets that focused on the signage of retail stores. It contains images of street views that include storefronts from Google Map. These images had been harvested using Amazon's Mechanical Turk service[1]. The dataset has 350 images in which each image has one single store signboard. The total number of words in these images is 725. A set of 100 images with a total of 211 words was designated as the training set. The Annotation for each image has been done by Alex Sorokin's Annotation Toolkit[2] which generates an xml format. For each image, business name and address are recorded in addition to image resolution, lexicon, and bounding boxes of words in the signage. The lexicon words have been collected from the top 20 business results that came out of searching all nearby business stores.

Another Dataset [9] was collected also using Google Street View with Google collaboration. Unfortunately, the dataset is not provided for the public even though the authors were contacted! The dataset contains 1.3 million street images with geo-information. They were collected from different urban areas in many cities across Europe, Australia, and the Americas. The annotation was done through some operators who generate bounding boxes around business-related information including signboards however, the text was extracted using OCR software. In this study, the authors aimed to classify street view storefronts using their own set of 208 unique labels/classes.

Moreover, a Chinese shop signs dataset (ShopSign) [21] has been published for the public. It contains images of real street views for shop signboards. The images were collected by 40 students for more than two years using 50 different types of cameras. The ShopSign dataset has 25,770 Chinese shop sign

[1] http://mturk.com.

[2] http://vision.cs.uiuc.edu/annotation/.

images with geo-locations which include a total of 4,072 unique Chinese characters/classes. The annotation was done manually in a text-line-based manner with the help of 12 members using quadrilaterals. The dataset is large scaled, and it is considered sparse and unbalanced. Moreover, the ShopSign dataset has big environmental and material diversity. Unfortunately, this dataset is based on Chinese characters with only limited samples of English scripts.

3 The ShoS Dataset

3.1 Data Collection

The **Shop Signboard Dataset ShoS** has been collected using Google Street View (GSV). This version of the dataset was collected from 51 cities in

Fig. 1. Samples from the ShoS Dataset illustrated with the bounding box annotations

Table 1. Statistical descriptives of the number of signboard (region_count) per image

Descriptives	Region_count
N	10000
Missing	0
Mean	1.63
Median	1.00
Standard deviation	0.844
Variance	0.712

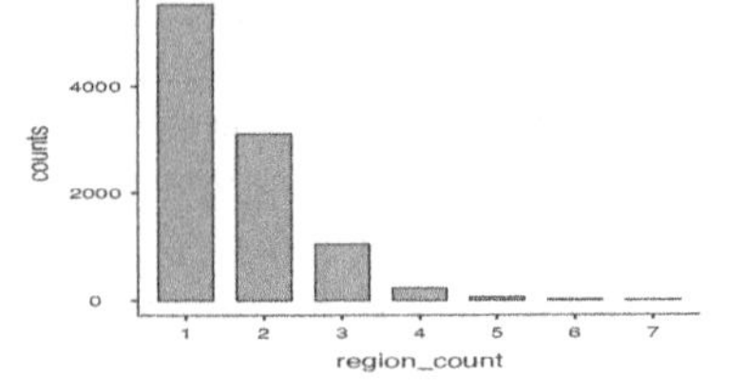

Fig. 2. Bar blot of the number of signboard (region_count) per image

Canada and the USA including Toronto, Vancouver, Ottawa, Calgary, Edmonton, Chicago, Los Angeles, San Francisco, New York City, Seattle, Miami, and Boston. Using GSV, screenshot images of storefronts were taken after some adjustments to ensure clarity of the image. The recorded scene includes one or more shop signboards with a minimum of one store per image and a maximum of 7 stores per image (Fig. 2). The average number of stores per image is 1.6 and more statistical descriptives are provided in Table 1. View angles were selected in a way that guarantees signboard visibility. The samples were collected by the researchers at first and by hired freelancers later through Upwork[3] freelance platform. Multiple revision cycles were completed to improve the quality of the collected data; this is further detailed below. The completed process of collecting and annotating the dataset took around one year.

The ShoS dataset contains 10k signboards within 7500 images of multiple resolutions, but mainly in 3360×2100 and 1280×1024 pixels. It is available for public for multiple research purposes. Figure 1 show some samples from the dataset.

3.2 Data Annotation

The ShoS Dataset was annotated using VGG Image Annotator (VIA) [4] which was developed by Visual Geometry Group at the University of Oxford. VIA is a manual annotation tool that is characterized by its simplicity and lightweight. It does not need any installation, and it works online with an interface or offline as an HTML file. VIA satisfied the requirements of this research as it enables adding more attributes to image files and bounding boxes where many tools do not. It also can generate annotation files as JSON and CSV files however, additional modifications to the CSV file were needed to meet the research requirements. The final CSV file was then used to generate Pascal VOC XML and text files for each image through Python scripts.

For each image file, the following attributes were recorded: image name, image width, image height, and the number of bounding boxes in the image. Similarly, for each bounding box in each image, these attributes were annotated: top left coordinates (xmin, ymin), bottom right coordinates (xmax, ymax), width, height. Also, each bounding box was marked if it is occluded or not where shop signboards can be occluded by trees, tree branches, traffic signs, big vehicles, spotlights, shadow, and some other shop signs that are positioned for pedestrians. The signboard is considered occluded if at least 20% of the text on the sign is covered. About 9% of the ShoS signboards are occluded. Figure 3 shows some samples from the CSV annotation file for the ShoS dataset.

Revising and cleaning the collected data was a time consuming task requiring multiple steps since the majority of the data was collected by freelancers. First, the hired freelancers were provided with a guideline to follow during data collection, such as avoiding some board types like painted glass, light, and board-less signs. An initial review was performed to accept or reject the collected images

[3] https://www.upwork.com/.

filename	image width	image height	region count	region id	xmin	ymin	width	height	xmax	ymax	occluded
img403.png	1280	823	2	0	469	242	211	114	680	356	no
img403.png	1280	823	2	1	776	249	176	127	952	376	no
img404.png	1280	823	1	0	660	229	450	69	1110	298	no
img405.png	3360	2100	2	0	831	580	966	251	1797	831	no
img405.png	3360	2100	2	1	1918	620	1175	206	3093	826	no
img406.png	1280	823	1	0	810	229	84	90	894	319	no

Fig. 3. Some samples from the CSV annotation file for the ShoS dataset

based on the given criteria. Once accepted, the freelancers annotated the images based upon more detailed instructions. Finally, the annotation file was processed using a Python script to avoid null values and mismatched attributes.

3.3 Challenges and Limitation

During data collection, multiple challenges were faced that limited the overall diversity of real world store signboards. The main challenges have been classified into three categories detailed below:

A) Google Street View Challenges. Some GSV factors impact the clarity of shop signboards. GSV collects street views by taking panoramic view images and stitching them together [2]. Stitching images can create irregular shapes with repetitive or incomplete parts. Moreover, environmental factors may affect the clarity of GSV images, such as rain which leads to foggy lens and thus foggy images. In addition, GSV images can be obstructed by traffic on the street such as buses and large vehicles. All of these factors can obstruct shop signboards or impact the quality of their screenshots.

B) Signboard Material Challenges. Different materials can be used to build shop signboards including mirror, glass, wood, or even bare wall. The study in [21] identified some of these material types as 'hard' for the detection and recognition process. Therefore, the number of signboards that are made of these material types were minimized from the ShoS dataset as much as possible.

C) Signboard Position Challenges. Some shops place their signboards in abnormal positions. For example, shop signage can be perpendicular to the storefront in order to attract pedestrians. Also, it is possible to find shop signboards on top of buildings without an actual storefront. Capturing these types of signboards could confuse the learning process as they do not reflect the normal view of a storefront with a signboard. Thus, such images were eliminated from the ShoS dataset.

4 Experiments

For signboard detection, one-stage object detectors YOLOv3 [13] and SSD [8] were utilized. The models make several predictions in a single pass using convolutional neural networks. Several backbones, pre-trained base networks, were used based on the object detector where the chosen YOLO model uses Darknet53 pre-trained on the ImageNet dataset[16] and SSD model uses MobileNetv2 FPNLite pre-trained on COCO dataset [7].

The ShoS dataset was preprocessed in order to train the YOLO and SSD models. All images were converted from png into jpg format and resized to 960×720 as this image size helped balance image quality and image processing time. Bigger image sizes could not be handled due to the huge amount of memory they required during training while smaller image sizes reduced the model performance. Then, two input resolutions were chosen for training: 640×640 and 320×320 plus two color schemes: RGB and grayscale. Thus, we would be able to see how the resolution and color factors could affect the models' accuracy.

The data was split into train and test sets with a ratio of 80/20 respectively. This process had to take into account the fact that some images had a single store while other images included multiple stores and hence had a proportionally equal amount from each group in the train and test sets. Furthermore, a second run was done with about 10% of the ShoS dataset random signboards were blurred and provided as true negative samples, and the results were significantly higher in term of mean average precision.

The number of classes c was set to one which is "Signboard". The number of batches was set as 64 and 16 for the smaller and bigger input resolutions respectively, and the learning rate was 0.001. Some random augmentations were used including brightness, height shift, rescale, rotation, and zoom with respect to the overall structure of the image is not destroyed in order to make the models robust to different variations as suggested in [19].

The training was stopped after 5k iterations for YOLO and after 8k iterations for SSD as the results were plateauing. The output of the inference stage was a bounding box for each signboard coupled with its confidence score. Finally, the redundant overlapping bounding boxes with low confidence scores were eliminated using Non-maximum Suppression.

5 Results and Discussion

The experiments were performed for both models YOLO and SSD on Google Colab Pro[4] which assigned a GPU machine with an option of "high-RAM" usage. Detection was considered correct if the value of intersection over union IoU was 0.5 or higher as recommended in previous studies of licence plate detection [6]. The models were tested for several variances of average precision over the four variations mentioned before for the input resolutions and color schemes. Based on the results shown in Table 2, YOLOv3 with the higher input resolution of 640×640 and in RGB color scheme works the best reaching a mean average precision of 94.23% whereas SSD reached a mAP of 90.4% at IoU $= 0.5$ with a confidence score set to 0.25. Therefore, the spatial distribution of labels directly impacts the detection of small objects (signboards) at a lower resolution, as

[4] https://colab.research.google.com.

Fig. 4. Results from YOLO3 640 showing high accuracy of detecting signboards even when they are occluded. Green bounding boxes indicate the ground truth and pink denotes all predications. (Color figure online)

Table 2. Results of one-stage detectors over mean Average Precision of 0.5 and 0.75 and the recall at IoU = 0.5

Detector	Input resolution	Image color	mAP@0.5(%)	mAP@0.75(%)	Recall%
YOLO3	320 × 320	RGB	92.0	66.09	91
	640 × 640	RGB	**94.23**	**76.76**	**94**
	320 × 320	Grayscale	91.2	64.09	89
	640 × 640	Grayscale	91.88	69.0	91
SSD-Moblilenet2	320 × 320	RGB	88.8	74.08	54
	640 × 640	RGB	90.4	76.84	53
	320 × 320	Grayscale	85.5	70.0	49
	640 × 640	Grayscale	84.6	68.8	47

they are harder to detect. Figure 4 displays some sample results obtained by YOLOv3-640 and SSD-Mobilenet2-fpnlite-640 models showing the superiority of YOLOv3. The YOLO model was robust enough to predict even partially occluded signboards. It is also noticed that both detectors could detect most of the signboards even the ones that are missed by annotators intentionally because of the limitations mentioned before. This allows a more accurate future stage for shops classification based on their signboards. Figures 5 and 6 illustrate both methodology performance. It is noticed that the average loss for all YOLO variants reached to a value less than 1 (0.07 in its ultimate case). On the other hand, the loss is computed differently in SSD as there several losses where one of them is based on cross-entropy loss and the other is Smooth L1 loss. At the end both losses are combined together to compute the final loss which also reached a small value (0.02 in its ultimate case).

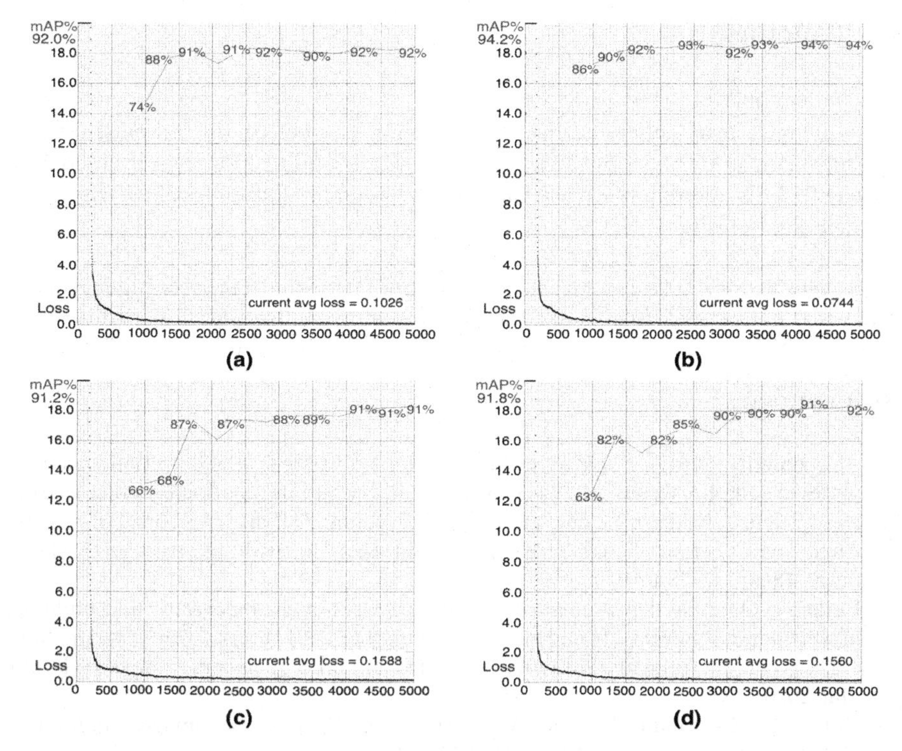

Fig. 5. Average loss (blue) and mean average precision mAP (red) for YOLO experiments. (a) RGB-320; (b) Grayscale-320; (c) RGB-640; (d) Grayscale-640. (Color figure online)

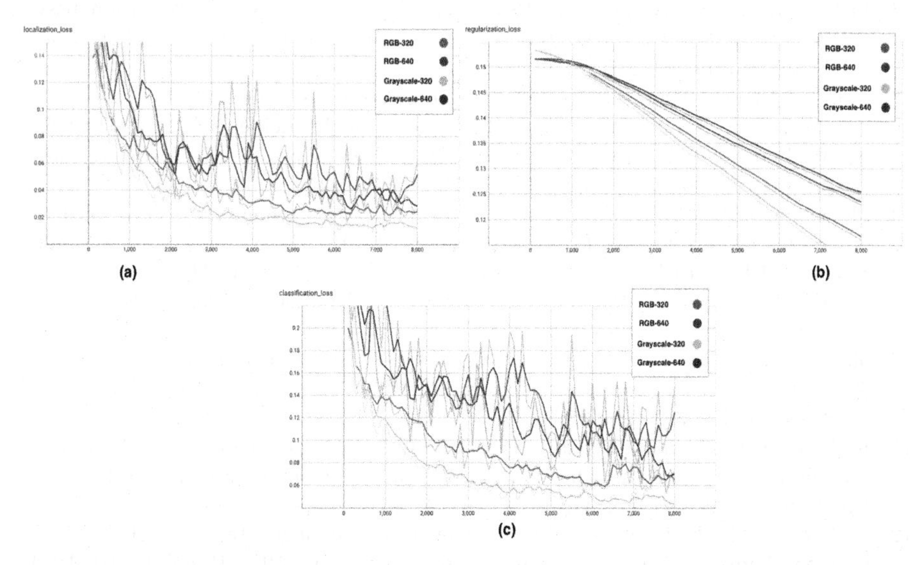

Fig. 6. (a) Localization, (b) regularization, and (c) classification loss charts for SSD experiments with a smooth factor set to 0.6

6 Conclusion

This paper contributes by providing the ShoS dataset with complete annotations for shop signboards detection. Several experiments were conducted on the ShoS datasets using one-stage object detection methods, and results are presented and discussed. This allows a more accurate future stage for shops classification based on their signboards.

Data Availability. The dataset will be made public for research purposes upon request from CENPARMI research manager Nicola Nobile at nicola@cenparmi.concordia.ca

References

1. Al-qudah, R., Suen, C.Y.: Enhancing yolo deep networks for the detection of license plates in complex scenes. In: Proceedings of the Second International Conference on Data Science, E-Learning and Information Systems, Dubai, UAE, pp. 1–6 (2019)
2. Anguelov, D., et al.: Google street view: capturing the world at street level. Computer **43**(6), 32–38 (2010)
3. Building, planning department of the city of Westmount: renovating and building in westmount - storefronts and signage, September 2001. https://www.westmount.org/wp-content/uploads/2014/07/7-Storefronts_and_Signage.pdf. Accessed 30 Mar 2020
4. Dutta, A., Zisserman, A.: The {VIA} annotation software for images, audio and video, **5**. arXiv preprint arXiv:1904.10699 (2019)
5. Erhan, D., Szegedy, C., Toshev, A., Anguelov, D.: Scalable object detection using deep neural networks. In: Proceedings of the IEEE Conference on Computer Vision and Pattern Recognition, Columbus, Ohio, USA, pp. 2147–2154 (2014)
6. Laroca, R., et al.: A robust real-time automatic license plate recognition based on the yolo detector. In: 2018 International Joint Conference on Neural Networks (IJCNN), Rio, Brazil, pp. 1–10 (2018)
7. Lin, T.Y., et al.: Microsoft COCO: common objects in context (2015)
8. Liu, W., et al.: SSD: single shot multibox detector. In: Leibe, B., Matas, J., Sebe, N., Welling, M. (eds.) ECCV 2016. LNCS, vol. 9905, pp. 21–37. Springer, Cham (2016). https://doi.org/10.1007/978-3-319-46448-0_2
9. Movshovitz-Attias, Y., et al.: Ontological supervision for fine grained classification of street view storefronts. In: Proceedings of the IEEE Conference on Computer Vision and Pattern Recognition, Boston, MA, USA, pp. 1693–1702 (2015)
10. Noorian, S.S., Qiu, S., Psyllidis, A., Bozzon, A., Houben, G.J.: Detecting, classifying, and mapping retail storefronts using street-level imagery. In: Proceedings of the 2020 International Conference on Multimedia Retrieval, ICMR 2020, pp. 495–501. Association for Computing Machinery, Dublin, Ireland (2020). https://doi.org/10.1145/3372278.3390706
11. Redmon, J., Divvala, S., Girshick, R., Farhadi, A.: You only look once: unified, real-time object detection. In: The IEEE Conference on Computer Vision and Pattern Recognition (CVPR), Las Vegas, NV, USA, June 2016
12. Redmon, J., Farhadi, A.: Yolo9000: better, faster, stronger. In: The IEEE Conference on Computer Vision and Pattern Recognition (CVPR), Honolulu, HI, USA, July 2017

13. Redmon, J., Farhadi, A.: YOLOv3: an incremental improvement. arXiv preprint arXiv:1804.02767 (2018)
14. Ren, J., Li, H.: Implementation of vehicle and license plate detection on embedded platform. In: 2020 12th International Conference on Measuring Technology and Mechatronics Automation (ICMTMA), Phuket, Thailand, pp. 75–79 (2020)
15. Ren, S., He, K., Girshick, R., Sun, J.: Faster R-CNN: towards real-time object detection with region proposal networks. In: Cortes, C., Lawrence, N.D., Lee, D.D., Sugiyama, M., Garnett, R. (eds.) Advances in Neural Information Processing Systems 28, pp. 91–99. Curran Associates, Inc. (2015). http://papers.nips.cc/paper/5638-faster-r-cnn-towards-real-time-object-detection-with-region-proposal-networks.pdf
16. Russakovsky, O., et al.: ImageNet large scale visual recognition challenge. Int. J. Comput. Vis. **115**(3), 211–252 (2015). https://doi.org/10.1007/s11263-015-0816-y
17. Szegedy, C., et al.: Going deeper with convolutions. In: Proceedings of the IEEE Conference on Computer Vision and Pattern Recognition, Boston, MA, USA, pp. 1–9 (2015)
18. Wang, K., Belongie, S.: Word spotting in the wild. In: Daniilidis, K., Maragos, P., Paragios, N. (eds.) ECCV 2010. LNCS, vol. 6311, pp. 591–604. Springer, Heidelberg (2010). https://doi.org/10.1007/978-3-642-15549-9_43
19. Xie, X., Xu, X., Ma, L., Shi, G., Chen, P.: On the study of predictors in single shot multibox detector. In: Proceedings of the International Conference on Video and Image Processing. ICVIP 2017, pp. 186–191. ACM, New York (2017). https://doi.org/10.1145/3177404.3177412. http://doi.acm.org.lib-ezproxy.concordia.ca/10.1145/3177404.3177412
20. Yu, Q., et al.: Large scale business discovery from street level imagery. arXiv preprint arXiv:1512.05430 (2015)
21. Zhang, C., et al.: Shopsign: a diverse scene text dataset of Chinese shop signs in street views. arXiv preprint arXiv abs/1903.10412 (2019)

One-Shot Decoupled Face Reenactment with Vision Transformer

Chen Hu and Xianghua Xie(✉)

Department of Computer Science, Swansea University, Swansea, UK
X.Xie@Swansea.ac.uk

Abstract. Recent face reenactment paradigm involves estimating an optical flow to warp the source image or its feature maps such that pixel values can be sampled to generate the reenacted image. We propose a one-shot framework in which the reenactment of the overall face and individual landmarks are decoupled. We show that a shallow Vision Transformer can effectively estimate optical flow without much parameters and training data. When reenacting different identities, our method remedies previous conditional generator based method's inability to preserve identities in reenacted images. To address the identity preserving problem in face reenactment, we model landmark coordinate transformation as a style transfer problem, yielding further improvement on preserving the source image's identity in the reenacted image. Our method achieves the lower head pose error on the CelebV dataset while obtaining competitive results in identity preserving and expression accuracy.

Keywords: Face reenactment · Vision transformer · Optical flow · Facial landmark

1 Introduction

Face reenactment is an image generation task. In the one-shot setting, given a pair of human face images, called the source and the driving, respectively, the face in the generated image should not only have the same identity as the source image, but also share the same pose and expression in the driving image. Practical applications of face reenactment include video conferencing and film production. In video conferencing, the speaker's face can be reenacted to match the face motion of a translator [20]. For film production, substitute actors can dub an iconic character with mouth movements and expressions properly mapped to the original character's face.

Early studies [4,12,19,20,22] on face reenactment primarily focused on fitting faces from images to 3D models, then morphing 3D faces and rendering the reenacted results. These methods require a large quantity of video frames as inputs and are limited to reenacting specific identities. More recent studies [7,17,18,24,26,27,29] propose one-shot or few-shot face reenactment and utilise optical flow to map pixels from the source image to the reenacted image, image

M. El Yacoubi et al. (Eds.): ICPRAI 2022, LNCS 13364, pp. 246–257, 2022.
https://doi.org/10.1007/978-3-031-09282-4_21

warping then becomes an essential operation for these methods. Image warping on convolutional neural networks (CNN) was first proposed in [10], where the model can estimate an optical flow map that warps skewed digits back to the regular view, improving the classification accuracy. For face reenactment, image warping means estimating an optical flow that determines how pixel values should be sampled from the source image or its feature maps such that the desired reenacted image can be generated.

Since obtaining images for different people with the exact same poses and expressions is infeasible in practice, a now widely adopted self-supervised learning paradigm was proposed in [24]. Given a source image sampled from a video sequence, a corresponding driving image of the same person is randomly chosen from the same video, this makes supervised learning possible as the driving image is the expected reenactment result. The self-supervised strategy subsequently leads to the identity preserving problem described in [7]. The model is only supervised from optical flow estimation for the same person. When applied to reenacting faces with different identities, defected images may be generated, making the person in the reenacted image looks more similar to the one in the driving image. Inspired by 3DMM [3], authors of [7] approached this issue by proposing the landmark transformer, which breaks down 3D facial landmark coordinates into a base 3D face, and principal components that controls the person-specific shape and expression of the face. By estimating corresponding principal component coefficients, landmark transformer modifies landmark coordinates of the driving image to be more fitting to the identity of the source image. However, the performance of [7] is limited by the expressiveness of derived principal components. The work of [27] estimates 3DMM parameters for source and driving images, the authors explicitly exclude the identity information of driving images by constructing reenacted 3D faces using only the identity parameters of source images. This method achieves the state-of-the-art performance in identity preserving, yet currently there is no 3DMM annotaion for face reenactment datasets, and the optical flow estimation module in [27] requires heavy computational resource, because it is a graph convolutional neural network [16] that runs on the source and the reenact mesh each with 53,215 vertices.

In a latest work [26], the authors also utilised landmark transformer to transform landmark coordinates of the driving image. They estimated an global optical flow for the source image based on landmark heatmaps [1] derived from transformed coordinates, while facial landmarks such as the nose and the mouth are separately reenacted. Inspired by this strategy, we also decoupled the reenactment of the entire face and facial landmarks. NeuralHead [28] is another reenactment method that relies on facial landmark coordinates. Compared to [7,17,18,24,26,27], NeuralHead obtained competitive results on head pose and expression accuracy, however, the performance on identity preserving is significantly lower. Authors of [7] believe that this is an indirect evidence of the lack of identity-preserving capacity in methods based on adaptive instance normalization [9], we argue that this is the immediate effect of feeding a conditional GAN with inappropriate conditions. The image generator of NeuralHead directly takes face sketches generated by landmark coordinates of driving images as input. When reenacting different identities, no information on the identity of the source image is encoded into NeuralHead's input. This suggests that when a reenactment method, e.g. NeuralHead, is conditioned on unmodified landmark coordinates of the driving image, such method can achieve great performance in reenacting poses and expressions without considering the identity of the source image. In contrast, a method that does not require any landmark coordinates, such as X2face, can easily outperform the conditioned method on identity preserving though poses and expressions are less accurate.

Considering the implication of performance and limitations of [28], our method directly estimate the global optical flow from the source and driving image without any prior. Additionally, we use Vision Transformer [6] for optical flow estimation. Vision Transformer is an extension of the attention-based neural network [21] to computer vision tasks. Unlike CNNs that are characterised by weight sharing and locality, Vision Transformer has less inductive bias [13], attention weights are dynamically computed depending on the input and features are aggregated from all elements in the input sequence instead of an neighbouring area. Although experiments show that Vision Transformer would require much more parameters and tens of millions training examples to reach the same level of performance as CNN [6], we show that a shallow Vision Transformer is also a good optical flow estimator for face reenactment.

As for individual landmark components, we use face sketches generated by landmark coordinates of the driving face for reenactment. Our approach to the identity preserving problem is aligning the mean and variance of the driving face's landmark coordinates with those of the source face. Experiments show that this approach effectively improve the performance of our models on identity preserving.

2 Methods

Figure 1 shows the overall framework of our proposed one-shot face reenactment method. The source and driving image are first fed into the facial feature extractor, extracted features for the source and driving image are concatenated and sent to a multi-layer perceptron (MLP) and transpose convolutional layers to estimate an optical flow map, which later warps the feature map of the source image in the face reenactment module. The landmark reenactment module is responsible for individually reenacting the left eye, the right eye, the nose and the mouth of the source image. As shown in Fig. 1, only cropped parts in the source image and the face sketch are sent to this module. The face reenactment module takes the source image, the estimated optical flow map and reenacted landmark parts as input and generates the reenacted face image.

2.1 Facial Feature Extractor and Optical Flow Estimation

Facial feature extractor is responsible for extracting and aggregate image features for optical flow estimation. The extractor is comprised of a Vision Transformer

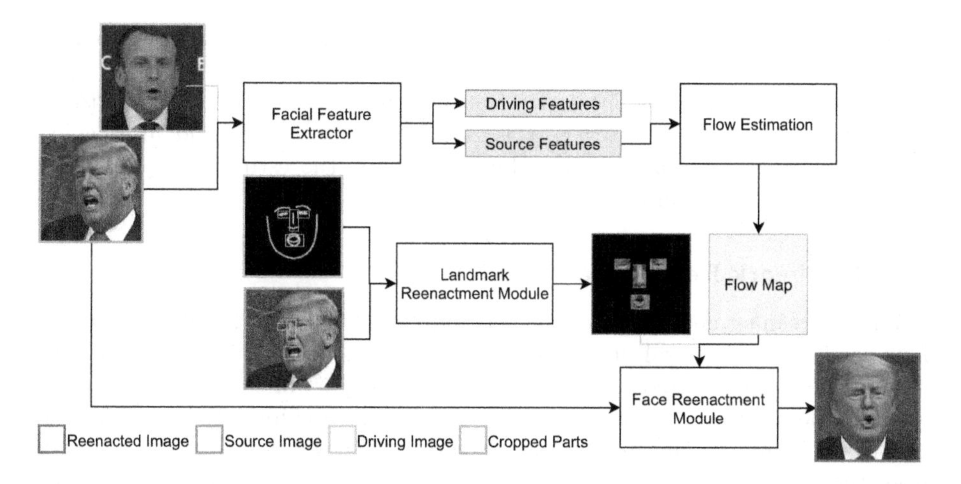

Fig. 1. The overall architecture of proposed method.

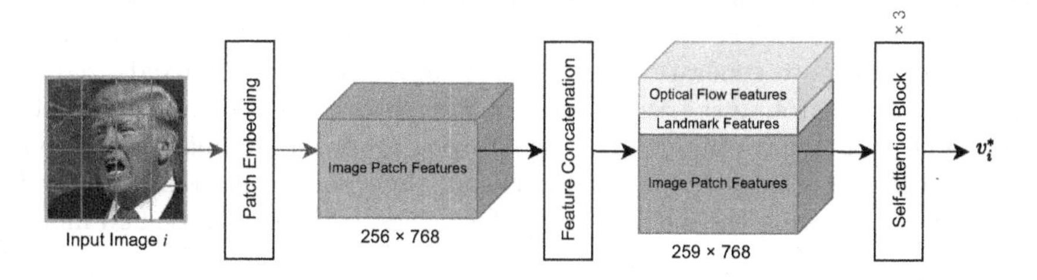

Fig. 2. Architecture of facial feature extraction module

with three layers. The architecture of this module is shown in Fig. 2. An input image i with size 224×224 is divided into 256 patches with size 14×14. Each image patch is embedded into a 768-dimensional vector, resulting in a 256×768 tensor v_i for an input image. In addition, a tensor $t \in \mathbb{R}^{3\times768}$ with learnable initial values are concatenated to v_i, the first two rows of t store features for the optical flow estimation, and the third row of t contains features for landmark coordinate regression, which acts as an auxiliary task that helps the model perceive human faces. After an input image being embedded into $v_i \in \mathbb{R}^{259\times768}$, it further goes through three self-attention layers. The self-attention process is given as follows.

$$Q = v_i W_q,\ K = v_i W_k,\ V = v_i W_v \tag{1}$$

$$\alpha = softmax(QK^T/\sqrt{d_k}),\ v_i^* = \alpha V \tag{2}$$

where $W_q \in \mathbb{R}^{768\times d_q}$, $W_k \in \mathbb{R}^{768\times d_k}$ and $W_v \in \mathbb{R}^{768\times d_v}$ are learn-able parameters, $d_q = d_k = d_v = 768$, $\alpha \in \mathbb{R}^{259\times259}$ is the attention score given the input tensor v_i, and $v_i^* \in \mathbb{R}^{259\times768}$ is the output of the self-attention operation, it further goes through an MLP layer to yield the final result of a transformer block.

Optical flow features for the source and the driving image are denoted by $u_s, u_d \in \mathbb{R}^{2\times768}$ respectively. u_s and u_d are first compressed to $\mathbb{R}^{2\times128}$ then reshaped to $\mathbb{R}^{1\times256}$, next, these two features are concatenated and sent to an MLP, resulting in $f \in \mathbb{R}^{1\times6272}$, f is reshaped to $\mathbb{R}^{7\times7\times128}$ and after going through a series of transpose convolutional layers, the estimated optical flow $f^* \in \mathbb{R}^{2\times224\times224}$ is obtained.

2.2 Landmark Reenactment Module

Landmark reenactment modules reenacts individual facial landmarks, it contains four convolutional neural networks that share the same architecture, however, each of them is dedicated to reenacting a different part of the face, namely the left eye, the right eye, the nose and the mouth. The architecture of each neural network is similar to an autoencoder. Figure 3(a) shows the crop of the mouth from the source image, along with its counterpart from the face sketch of the driving image are first sent to three convolution layers, with the size of feature maps reduced by half through max pooling, then feature maps of the RGB mouth crop and that of the face sketch are element-wise added and sent to transpose convolution layers to generate the reenacted parts. All crops are fixed-sized and they are cropped around the centre point of corresponding landmark coordinates. The sketch of a face is obtained by first drawing 68 facial landmark points on a 224×224 image with pure black background, then points are connected by B-spline curves, drawing the outlines of the face, eyes, eye brows, nose and mouth.

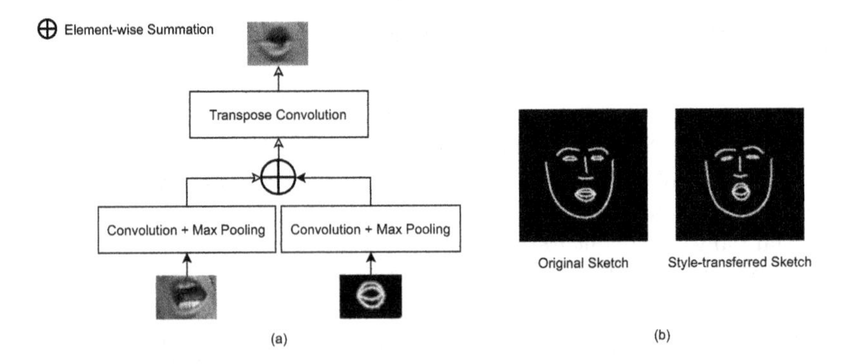

Fig. 3. (a) The architecture of landmark reenactment module. (b) An example of landmark style transfer.

When all parts are reenacted, they are directly placed on another blank 224×224 image I_p, and their centre point all align with the centre point of corresponding parts in the driving sketch.

Landmark Style Transfer. Although our landmark reenactment module relies on the face sketch generated by driving landmark coordinates, no modification on landmark coordinates is needed during training as source images and driving images share the same identity. When we reenact faces with different identities, this leads to the identity preserving problems described in Sect. 1 due to the identity mismatch between the source image and the driving sketch. To remedy this, we modify driving landmark coordinates by treating it as a style transfer problem. Inspired by [9], to adapt the driving person's landmark coordinates to the landmark style of the source person, we align the mean and variance of the driving coordinates $lmk_{driving}$ with those of the source coordinates lmk_{source},

$$lmk_{reenact} = \frac{lmk_{driving} - \mu_{driving}}{\sigma_{driving}} \times \sigma_{source} + \mu_{source} \tag{3}$$

$\mu_{source}, \sigma_{source}, \mu_{driving}, \sigma_{driving}$ can be obtained by computing the mean and variance of each person's landmark coordinates in the dataset, no learning is involved in this process. We also shift $lmk_{reenact}$ such that its centre point is at the same location as $lmk_{driving}$. Figure 3(b) shows an example the driving face sketch generated by the original landmark coordinates and the one generated by style-transferred coordinates.

2.3 Face Reenactment Module

The face reenactment module is a U-Net-like convolutional neural network with only one skip-connection in the middle, Fig. 4 shows its overall architecture. The source image is first sent to three convolutional layers with the size of its feature map r being reduced to 58×58, then the estimated optical flow map f^* (Sect. 2.1) with size 224×224 is resized to match the size of r and warps r, yielding the warped feature map r^*. The image I_p with reenacted landmark parts from the landmark reenactment module (Sect. 2.2) is also resized to 58×58 and concatenated to r^*. The concatenated feature map $r^*_{cat.}$ continues to go through intermediate convolutional layers with no change in feature map size, then r^* is concatenated to $r^*_{cat.}$ through the skip connection, the resulting feature map is further upsampled through bilinear interpolation and processed by convolution layers to generate the final reenacted image. The use of bilinear upsampling is aiming for alleviating the checkerboard artifact in images generated by convolutional neural networks [14].

2.4 Loss Function

All modules of our method are jointly trained in the adversarial and self-supervised fashion. Adversarial [15] loss is essential for image generation tasks, and since driving images are groundtruths for training face reenactment models, L1 loss on pixel values and the perceptual loss [11] are adopted. We also use the GAN feature matching loss [23], as it can stabilize and speed up the training of image generation tasks when groundtruth images are available. Lastly, we also consider the L1 loss for landmark coordinate regression for the auxiliary task

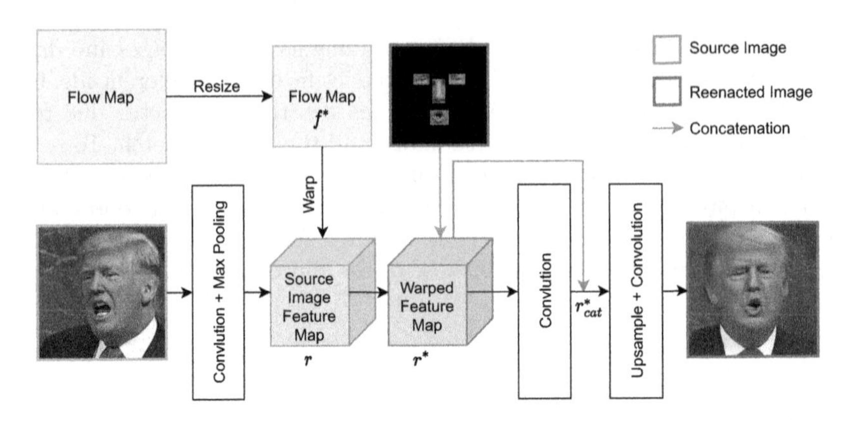

Fig. 4. The overall architecture of face reenactment transformer

described in Sect. 2.1. A linear combination of above losses is suffice to train our proposed method, the loss function J is given by,

$$J = \sum_{k=0}^{5} \lambda_i J_i \tag{4}$$

where J_0 is the L1 loss of regressed landmark coordinates, J_1 is the GAN feature matching loss, J_2 is the adversarial loss, we let $\lambda_0 = \lambda_1 = \lambda_2 = 1$; J_3 is an L1 loss for pixel values of reenacted landmark parts in Sect. 2.2, and $\lambda_3 = 5$; J_4 is the perceptual loss of reenacted images, $\lambda_4 = 10$; J_5 is the L1 loss for pixel values of the entire reenacted image, $\lambda_5 = 20$. We find that putting more weight on the L1 loss of pixel values prevents the model from generating unexpected artifacts, and the emphasis on perceptual loss helps obtaining faces and shoulders with more realistic shapes.

3 Experiments

We evaluated our methods on the CelebV [25] dataset following protocols in [7]. CelebV is a dataset with video frames for five celebrities, each of them has around 40k images. The evaluation focuses reenactment with different identities, namely the person in the source image is different from the one in the driving image.

3.1 Model Variants

We tested two model variants: the baseline model, denoted by **ViT**, has three Vision Transformer layers for facial feature extraction, and the **ResNet-34** model with all Vision Transformer layers in the baseline model replaced by a ResNet-34 [8] backbone for feature extraction. In [6], a modified ResNet-50 (25M parameters) outperforms the base 12-layer Vision Transformer (86M parameters) on ImageNet top-1 accuracy by 10% with a pre-training dataset of 10M images. Given that there are three Vision Transformer layers (19M parameters) in our baseline model, we hence choose ResNet-34 (21M parameters) for comparison, which is shallower than ResNet-50. Additionally, we applied landmark style transfer described in Sect. 2.2 to both models and evaluated their performance accordingly. Models with landmark style transfer are denoted by ViT+LSt and ResNet-34+LSt.

3.2 Metrics

Cosine similarity (CSIM) measures the quality of identity preserving by comparing the distance between face embedding vectors of source images and reenacted images, where embedding vectors are estimated by the pre-trained face recognition model ArcFace [5]; the root mean square error of the head pose angles (PRMSE), and the ratio of identical facial action unit values (AUCON) compares driving images and reenacted images, PRMSE tells how accurately the head pose is reenacted, and AUCON represents how close the reenacted expression is to that of the driving image. Both head pose angles and action unit values are estimated by OpenFace [2].

Table 1. Evaluation results of reenactment with different identities on CelebV following protocols in [7]. Values in bold stands for the best results, underlined values are the second best ones. The upward arrow indicates the larger the value, the better the performance, the downward arrow means a smaller value is better.

Model	CSIM↑	PRMSE↓	AUCON↑	Source of optical flow
Mesh Guided GCN [27]	**0.635**	3.41	0.709	3D faces
MarioNETte [7]	0.520	3.41	<u>0.710</u>	Raw coordinates
MarioNETte+LT [7]	0.568	3.70	0.684	Transformed coordinates
NeuralHead-FF [28]	0.108	3.30	**0.722**	No optical flow
X2face [24]	0.450	3.62	0.679	Raw images
ResNet-34	0.570	**2.57**	0.695	Raw images
ResNet-34+LSt	0.616	3.78	0.650	Raw images
ViT	0.568	<u>2.77</u>	0.692	Raw images
ViT+LSt	<u>0.620</u>	3.87	0.646	Raw images

3.3 Analysis

Table 1 shows the metrics of our methods compared to other methods evaluated under the same protocol, including types of input that the optical flow estimation is based on. Figure 5 shows the qualitative results of our model variants as well as typical failure cases. Among our proposed methods, the model with ResNet-34 as the backbone of optical flow estimator shows the best performance, achieving lower head pose error than previous work. The use of landmark style transfer significantly boosts the identity preserving capability of our methods while decreasing the head pose and expression accuracy. Distorted input and large head pose are two challenging cases for our method, a distorted driving image results in a face which is more similar to the distorted shape, and a large head pose induces misaligned facial landmarks in the reenacted image. Detailed analysis is presented in following sections.

Fig. 5. Qualitative results of proposed models. The last two rows are typical failure cases, our method is sensitive to distortion in images and struggles with very large poses.

Comparison of Methods. Unlike other methods that involve image warping, optical flows estimated by X2face are directly applied to images instead of feature maps, no module is responsible for refining the warped results, hence X2face generally performs poorly in recent literature. NeuralHead-FF was implemented by authors of [7] without meta-learning in the original paper [28]. As described in Sect. 1, NeuralHead-FF generates faces from face sketches of driving images, it does not estimate any optical flow. Mesh Guided GCN benefits from 3D models in which the driving identity is completely discarded. We believe the 3DMM parameter estimator and mesh down-sampling are the main sources of error for [27], as there is no 3DMM annotation for face reenactment datasets and loss-less down-sampling is not feasible for general surfaces [16]. MarioNETte estimates optical flows from feature maps of face sketches generated by original landmark coordinates of source and driving images, these optical flows are exerted on feature maps instead of raw images. Face sketches in MarioNETte+LT are generated from landmark coordinates transformed by the landmark transformer. Without modification on landmark coordinates, our ResNet-34 and ViT achieve lower PRMSE than previous methods. The use of landmark style transfer boosts CSIM for both ResNet-34 and ViT, though ViT benefits more from it. Compared to the landmark transformer in [7], our landmark style transfer better promotes the quality of identity preserving but suffers more on the accuracy of pose and expression, this is because our method is more closely related to how images in the dataset are captured, and each person's preferred poses and expression intensity, landmark coordinates transformed by our method are more similar to how the person behaves in the recorded video.

Performance of Vision Transformer. ResNet-34 performs slightly better than ViT, nonetheless, the shallow Vision Transformer in our proposed method obtains satisfactory results, which is on par with pure CNN methods such as [7]. Since the estimated optical flow operates on feature maps extracted by CNN, ResNet, which is also a CNN, can perceive optical flows that are more compatible with these feature maps. Current architectures of Vision Transformer make them natural feature extractors, even so, due to the need for image warping in face reenactment, CNN is still the dominant and more direct way of image synthesis, reenactment methods that adopt Vision Transformer for image generation need further study.

Effects of Landmark Reenactment Module. Regarding the use of landmark style transfer, we notice the same pattern that presents in MarioNETte and MarioNETte+LT: the improvement on the quality of identity preserving comes at the cost of less accurate head poses and expressions. This is because both our method and [7] leverage face sketches generated by landmark coordinates for reenactment. When those coordinates are modified, reenacted images are subsequently altered. We notice the alteration brought by landmark style transfer favors faces in frontal view, but performs poorer when faces have large poses. For instance, in the first row of Fig. 5, with the landmark coordinates of the driving image being transferred to the style of the source image, the eyes and mouth in the reenacted image are properly opened, yet in the second row of Fig. 5, the style-transferred coordinates make the mouth region less truthful to the expression in the driving image. As mentioned above, we believe the effectiveness of landmark style transfer is closely related to how training images are captured and the preferred expression intensity of each person. In terms of the strategy of placing reenacted landmarks at the same location as in the driving image, the difference in CSIM and PRMSE before and after the use of landmark style transfer indicates that this is a strong prior for lowering head pose error, but it is leaking the driving identity to the reenacted image.

4 Conclusions

In this paper, we propose a one-shot face reenactment framework in which the overall face and individual landmarks are reenacted separately. Vision Transformer is used to estimate the optical flow that warps the entire source image while landmarks are individually reenacted by corresponding sketches through CNN. We further propose landmark style transfer to alleviate the identity mismatching problem. Compared to other methods, we achieved more accurate head poses and the proposed landmark style transfer better preserves identities that other methods that also rely on facial landmark coordinates. One possible future work is to investigate the use of Vision Transformer for the image synthesis stage in face reenactment.

References

1. Amos, B., Ludwiczuk, B., Satyanarayanan, M.: OpenFace: a general-purpose face recognition library with mobile applications. Technical report, CMU-CS-16-118, CMU School of Computer Science (2016)
2. Baltrusaitis, T., Zadeh, A., Lim, Y.C., Morency, L.P.: OpenFace 2.0: facial behavior analysis toolkit. In: 13th IEEE International Conference on Automatic Face Gesture Recognition (2018)
3. Blanz, V., Vetter, T.: A morphable model for the synthesis of 3D faces. In: SIGGRAPH (1999)
4. Cheng, Y.T., et al.: 3D-model-based face replacement in video. In: SIGGRAPH (2009)
5. Deng, J., Guo, J., Xue, N., Zafeiriou, S.: ArcFace: additive angular margin loss for deep face recognition. In: CVPR (2019)
6. Dosovitskiy, A., et al.: An image is worth 16x16 words: transformers for image recognition at scale. arXiv: 2010.11929 (2020)
7. Ha, S., Kersner, M., Kim, B., Seo, S., Kim, D.: MarioNETte: few-shot face reenactment preserving identity of unseen targets. In: AAAI (2020)
8. He, K., Zhang, X., Ren, S., Sun, J.: Deep residual learning for image recognition. arXiv: 1512.03385 (2015)
9. Huang, X., Belongie, S.: Arbitrary style transfer in real-time with adaptive instance normalization. In: ICCV (2017)

10. Jaderberg, M., Simonyan, K., Zisserman, A., Kavukcuoglu, K.: Spatial transformer networks. In: NIPS (2015)
11. Johnson, J., Alahi, A., Fei-Fei, L.: Perceptual losses for real-time style transfer and super-resolution. In: Leibe, B., Matas, J., Sebe, N., Welling, M. (eds.) ECCV 2016. LNCS, vol. 9906, pp. 694–711. Springer, Cham (2016). https://doi.org/10.1007/978-3-319-46475-6_43
12. Kim, H., et al.: Deep video portraits. ACM Trans. Graph. **37**, 1–14 (2018)
13. Liu, Y., et al.: A survey of visual transformers. arXiv: 2111.06091 (2021)
14. Odena, A., Dumoulin, V., Olah, C.: Deconvolution and checkerboard artifacts. Distill **1**, e3 (2016)
15. Radford, A., Metz, L., Chintala, S.: Unsupervised representation learning with deep convolutional generative adversarial networks. arXiv: 1511.06434 (2016)
16. Ranjan, A., Bolkart, T., Sanyal, S., Black, M.J.: Generating 3D faces using convolutional mesh autoencoders. In: Ferrari, V., Hebert, M., Sminchisescu, C., Weiss, Y. (eds.) ECCV 2018. LNCS, vol. 11207, pp. 725–741. Springer, Cham (2018). https://doi.org/10.1007/978-3-030-01219-9_43
17. Siarohin, A., Lathuilière, S., Tulyakov, S., Ricci, E., Sebe, N.: First order motion model for image animation. In: Advances in Neural Information Processing Systems (2019)
18. Siarohin, A., Lathuilière, S., Tulyakov, S., Ricci, E., Sebe, N.: Animating arbitrary objects via deep motion transfer. In: CVPR (2019)
19. Suwajanakorn, S., Seitz, S.M., Kemelmacher-Shlizerman, I.: What makes tom hanks look like tom hanks. In: ICCV (2015)
20. Thies, J., Zollhöfer, M., Stamminger, M., Theobalt, C., Nießner, M.: Face2Face: real-time face capture and reenactment of RGB videos. In: CVPR (2016)
21. Vaswani, A., et al.: Attention is all you need. In: NIPS (2017)
22. Vlasic, D., Brand, M., Pfister, H., Popović, J.: Face transfer with multilinear models. ACM Trans. Graph. (2005)
23. Wang, T.C., Liu, M.Y., Zhu, J.Y., Tao, A., Kautz, J., Catanzaro, B.: High-resolution image synthesis and semantic manipulation with conditional GANs. In: CVPR (2018)
24. Wiles, O., Koepke, A.S., Zisserman, A.: X2Face: a network for controlling face generation using images, audio, and pose codes. In: Ferrari, V., Hebert, M., Sminchisescu, C., Weiss, Y. (eds.) ECCV 2018. LNCS, vol. 11217, pp. 690–706. Springer, Cham (2018). https://doi.org/10.1007/978-3-030-01261-8_41
25. Wu, W., Zhang, Y., Li, C., Qian, C., Loy, C.C.: ReenactGAN: learning to reenact faces via boundary transfer. In: Ferrari, V., Hebert, M., Sminchisescu, C., Weiss, Y. (eds.) ECCV 2018. LNCS, vol. 11205, pp. 622–638. Springer, Cham (2018). https://doi.org/10.1007/978-3-030-01246-5_37
26. Yao, G., et al.: One-shot face reenactment using appearance adaptive normalization. arXiv: 2102.03984 (2021)
27. Yao, G., Yuan, Y., Shao, T., Zhou, K.: Mesh guided one-shot face reenactment using graph convolutional networks. In: 28th ACM International Conference on Multimedia (2020)
28. Zakharov, E., Shysheya, A., Burkov, E., Lempitsky, V.: Few-shot adversarial learning of realistic neural talking head models. In: ICCV (2019)
29. Zeng, X., Pan, Y., Wang, M., Zhang, J., Liu, Y.: Realistic face reenactment via self-supervised disentangling of identity and pose. In: AAAI (2020)

ADG-Pose: Automated Dataset Generation for Real-World Human Pose Estimation

Ghazal Alinezhad Noghre, Armin Danesh Pazho, Justin Sanchez, Nathan Hewitt, Christopher Neff(✉), and Hamed Tabkhi

University of North Carolina, Charlotte, NC 28223, USA
{galinezh,adaneshp,jsanch19,nhewitt,cneff1,htabkhiv}@uncc.edu

Abstract. Recent advancements in computer vision have seen a rise in the prominence of applications using neural networks to understand human poses. However, while accuracy has been steadily increasing on State-of-the-Art datasets, these datasets often do not address the challenges seen in real-world applications. These challenges are dealing with people distant from the camera, people in crowds, and heavily occluded people. As a result, many real-world applications have trained on data that does not reflect the data present in deployment, leading to significant underperformance. This article presents ADG-Pose, a method for automatically generating datasets for real-world human pose estimation. ADG-Pose utilizes top-down pose estimation for extracting human keypoints from unlabeled data. These datasets can be customized to determine person distances, crowdedness, and occlusion distributions. Models trained with our method are able to perform in the presence of these challenges where those trained on other datasets fail. Using ADG-Pose, end-to-end accuracy for real-world skeleton-based action recognition sees a 20% increase on scenes with moderate distance and occlusion levels, and a 4× increase on distant scenes where other models failed to perform better than random.

Keywords: Human pose etimation · Real-world · Data generation

1 Introduction

Human Pose Estimation has seen vast improvements in recent years. This accuracy increase has led to their adoption in real-world applications that benefit from understanding human poses. Smart surveillance, public safety, medical assistance [3,11,14]; are examples of real-world applications that rely on pose information. Unfortunately, despite the current State-of-the-Art (SotA) achieving upwards of 80–90% accuracy on popular datasets, that accuracy often fails to transfer to real-world scenarios. The number of high-quality datasets with human pose annotations is alarmingly small, as creating them is expensive and

G. Alinezhad Noghre and A. Danesh Pazho — Authors have equal contribution.

M. El Yacoubi et al. (Eds.): ICPRAI 2022, LNCS 13364, pp. 258–270, 2022.
https://doi.org/10.1007/978-3-031-09282-4_22

time-consuming. Real-world applications are often trained on one of these few datasets, regardless of whether the dataset represents the type of scenes present in deployment.

The disconnect of the training data and inference data (i.e. data seen during deployment) often leads to high-accuracy models, when tested on datasets, underperforming in real-world applications. This disconnect is exceptionally strong in applications that need to detect persons in crowded scenes, heavily occluded persons, or persons very distant from the camera, particularly if the application uses bottom-up pose estimation. A few datasets have been introduced to address some of these issues [12,16,27], but they all only address a single issue at a time. Further, they use different skeletal structures, making it difficult to utilize them to train a single network. As such, there is a need for datasets that fill the gaps that are left by the current offering.

This article proposes ADG-Pose, a method for generating datasets designed specifically for real-world applications. ADG-Pose allows for the customization of the data distribution along three axes: distance from the camera, crowdedness, and occlusion. ADG-Pose uses high-accuracy models trained on existing datasets to annotate ultra-high resolution images. From there, high-resolution images are created that fit within the distribution parameters set by the user, resulting in a machine annotated dataset customized towards the target real-world application. To validate our method, we create Panda-Pose, a custom dataset suited towards parking lot surveillance. We take a model previously trained on COCO [13] and train it on Panda-Pose. We provide comparisons between the two models on both COCO and Panda-Pose, including F1-score to account for false negatives. We also provide qualitative results that show what validation accuracy fails to; models trained on Panda-Pose detect people completely missed by those trained on COCO. Often, these are not even annotated, whether because they are too distant from the camera, in too large a crowd, or too occluded, and do not contribute to validation accuracy.

As a final test of real-world viability, we compare how models trained on Panda-Pose and those trained on COCO affect end-to-end accuracy when used as a backbone for real-world skeleton-based action recognition on the UCF-ARG dataset [6]. When using Panda-Pose for training, we see an increase of **20%** and **30%** on the ground and rooftop scenarios respectfully. For the rooftop scenario, the COCO-trained models resulted in an accuracy equivalent to random guessing.

In summary, this paper encompasses the following contributions:

1. We identify and formulate the data gaps and limitations of existing publicly available datasets for real-world human pose estimation.
2. We propose ADG-Pose, a novel method for the automated creation of new datasets that address real-world human pose estimation, customizing for distance from camera, crowdedness, and occlusion.[1]

[1] Code available at https://github.com/TeCSAR-UNCC/ADG-Pose.

3. We present Panda-Pose, an extension over the existing Panda dataset, to demonstrate the benefits of ADG-Pose to address real-world pose estimation in smart video surveillance applications.
4. We further demonstrate the benefits of ADG-Pose and Panda-Pose in context of real-world skeleton-based action recognition.

2 Related Work

Keypoint-based human pose estimation can largely be separated into two main categories: top-down methods that work off person crops and bottom-up methods that work off entire scenes. Top-down methods are generally used for single person pose estimation and are assumed to have person crops provided to them [9,17,21]. Top-down methods can be adapted for multi-person pose estimation by attaching them to an assisting detection network that generates person crops [4, 8]. In contrast to top-down methods, bottom-up methods look at the entire scene image and detect all keypoints for all persons at once, using further processing to group them to each individual [2,5,10,19,25]. Bottom-up methods are often less computationally complex than top-down methods, as top-down methods have to process data for each individual separately, scaling linearly with the number of persons. In contrast, bottom-up approaches have static computation regardless of the number of persons in a scene. This has led to some works focusing on lightweight inference and real-time performance [15,18].

MPII [1] contains 25k images with 40k persons. Images are taken from YouTube videos and have annotations for 16 keypoint skeletons. COCO [13] contains over 200k images and 250k person instances. COCO has 17 keypoint pose annotations for over 150k persons and is widely used to train and validate SotA models. AI Challenger [24] consists of 300k images containing persons labeled with 14 keypoint skeletons. CrowdPose [12] attempts to address the lack of crowded scenes in the previous three datasets. Where MPII, AI Challenger, and COCO have distributions that greatly favor scenes with a low number of persons, CrowdPose creates its dataset by sampling from the other three in a way that guarantees a uniform distribution in the crowdedness of the scenes. CrowdPose contains 20k images with 80k persons annotated with AI Challenger style keypoint skeletons. [27] introduces a new benchmark, OCHuman, that focuses on heavily occluded scenes. Maintaining an average IoU of 0.67, OCHuman has 4731 images and 8110 persons annotated with COCO-style keypoint skeletons. Tiny People Pose [16] consists of 200 images and 585 person instances labeled with modified MPII style keypoint skeletons. The images are focused on persons far from the camera that take consist of very few pixels. The motivation is to address the lack of distant persons in common human pose datasets. Similar focus on distant detection has been seen in object detection [7,22].

3 Real-World Pose Estimation Challenges

There are many challenges when using human pose estimation in real-world applications. Take smart surveillance as an example. The types of locations surveillance cameras are placed are widely varied, even for a single system. In a shopping mall cameras will be installed in stores, hallways, food courts, and parking lots. In a store the camera will be closer to people, there will be fewer people in the scene, and occlusions from the merchandise will be common. In hallways and food courts there will be lots of people at medium to long distances to cameras and crowded scenes and occlusions will be prevalent. In parking lots people will often be very far from the camera and often partially occluded by vehicles. Overall, we have identified three main challenges of real-world human pose estimation:

1. **Wide Variety of Distances:** from an algorithmic perspective, this translates to the number of pixels a person takes up in an image. This can also be looked at as the scale of a person compared to the total image resolution.
2. **Occlusions:** where a person is partially obscured by a part of the environment or another person.
3. **Crowded Scenes:** many real-world applications will require pose estimation in highly crowded locations. In addition to occlusion, a large number of people can make accurately detecting the poses very challenging.

The major limitation in creating a model that can address all these issues is the data used for training. The most popular datasets (MPII [1], AI Challenger [24], COCO [13]) mostly consist of unoccluded people who are relatively close to the camera in non-crowded scenes. While specialized datasets have been introduced to address some of these concerns (CrowdPose [12], OCHuman [27], Tiny People Pose [16]), they each only address a single issue at a time, and their diverse annotation style and validation methods make it challenging to utilize them all for training a single model. Currently, no single dataset can adequately address the three main challenges of real-world human pose estimation.

Fig. 1. Ground truth keypoint annotations (green) from COCO dataset. (Color figure online)

Figure 1 displays keypoint annotations from the most prolific keypoint dataset, COCO. Note how distant persons or those in crowded scenes are not annotated. In the upper left image, all the persons riding elephants are unlabeled. On the bottom right image, the vast majority of the crowd is unlabeled. In the remaining images, persons distant from the camera are unlabeled, despite being clearly visible. To be fair, hand annotating all these unlabeled people would be both difficult and time-consuming, so their absence is understandable. COCO's annotation files include a number of all null keypoint annotations to go along with people who might be in the image but are not annotated. During validation, if extra skeletons that don't have annotations are detected, the number of null key points will be subtracted. COCO automatically disregards all but the 20 skeletons with the highest confidence. This is to make sure the networks are not unjustly penalized for estimating skeletons for unlabeled people. Additionally, accuracy on standard datasets is largely reported based on the "Precision" metric, while the "Recall" metric (which includes false negatives) is often ignored. So even if false negatives still occur, they are automatically disregarded by standard validation metrics (i.e. COCO validation).

These limitations can disproportionately affect bottom-up approaches, often preferred for real-world applications due to their much lower computational complexities and much better real-time execution capabilities. In contrast to top-down approaches, bottom-up methods aim to detect persons on their own. The lack of labels can hurt them in both **training**, where they do not learn to detect distance people, and **validation**, where they will not be penalized for the large majority of their false negatives (hallucinating persons that are not actually there).

4 ADG-Pose

We propose ADG-Pose, a method of Automated Dataset Generation for real-world human pose estimation. ADG-Pose aims to address all three mentioned challenges in the previous section. ADG-Pose enables users to determine the person scale, crowdedness, and occlusion density distributions of the generated datasets, allowing for training environments that better match the distributions of the target application.

Figure 2 shows the three main stages of ADG-Pose. First, a high accuracy top-down human pose estimation model is used to label ultra-high resolution images. By utilizing ultra-high resolution images and a top-down approach, we can mitigate potential issues with annotating distant people as the absolute resolution of the person crops will still be large enough to ensure high accuracy. Second, we take the fully annotated ultra-high resolution images and generate semi-random crops from them. These crops are semi-random because we introduce user-defined parameters to ensure the final dataset will match the desired statistics. First, the user can determine the resolution range to take crops at. To better detect distant persons, larger resolution crops can be used and downscaled to the desired input resolution, thus mimicking larger distances. Second, the user

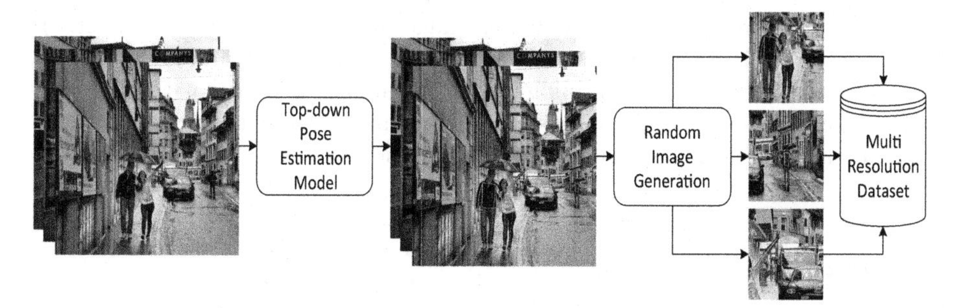

Fig. 2. Custom dataset generation. Beginning with ultra high resolution images, a pretrained top-down pose estimation model is used to generate high accuracy keypoint annotations. Semi-random cropping is used to generate numerous high resolution images inline with user specified statistic, forming the new dataset.

can determine the maximum, minimum, and mean number of persons in a crop. This allows for customization of how crowded a scene is. Third, the user can specify the desired average IoU between people in the crop, tweaking the overall level of occlusion in the dataset. After these crops are made and the statistics verified, the resulting images and annotations are synthesized into a new multi-resolution dataset. Additional user-defined parameters include the total size of the dataset, "train/val/test splits", image aspect ratio, and skeleton/validation style, which must be compatible with the top-down model used for annotation.

Panda-Pose: As a use-case, we choose a real-world application of smart security in an outdoor parking lot environment. For skeleton and validation style, we choose COCO [13] as it is currently the most prominent in the field. We use HRNet-w32 [21] for our top-down annotation model and choose PANDA [23] as our base dataset. PANDA is a gigapixel-level human-centric dataset with an extremely wide field of view ($\sim$1 km^2). It contains bounding box annotations for persons, with some scenes containing up to 4k persons. There are 555 frames across four outdoor scenes, which would normally be far too few for training. However, high density and extreme resolution (25k $\times$ 14k) result in significant information per scene and more than adequate generated images. Additionally, the wide variance in poses, scales, and occlusions allows us to create a range of challenging datasets for different user specifications. We call the resulting dataset Panda-Pose.

For the first specification, parking lots will likely include people quite distant from the camera, resulting in a very small scale. As such, Panda-Pose targets a person scale distribution on the smaller side. Since detecting small-scale persons is more complicated than a large-scale person, we heavily weigh the lower end of the scale spectrum, as can be seen in Fig. 3. The wide field of view of most parking lot security cameras will allow for a fair amount of people in the scene, though there is usually enough space that occlusions, while present, will be less than that of more crowded indoor scenes. As such, we target a relatively high number of people per image ($\sim$9) and a moderate amount of occlusions ($\sim$0.33).

We also set a maximum of 30 people per image (for fair comparisons in Sect. 5). Our aspect ratio is 4:3, the maximum resolution is 3840×2880, and the minimum is 480×360. There are 83k training, and 21k validation images with 775k and 202k annotated skeletons, respectively. 4% of images are without annotations. Training and validation splits have matching distributions.

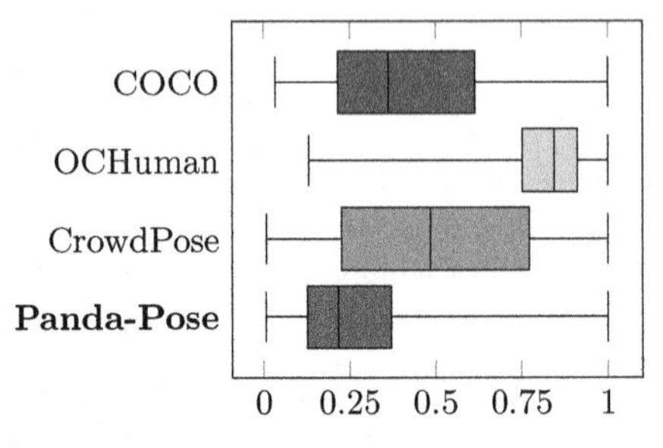

Fig. 3. Person scale distributions across datasets.

Table 1. Person density and occlusion (IoU) across datasets.

Dataset	Persons per image	Average IoU
MPII	1.6	0.11
AI Challanger	2.33	0.12
COCO	1.25	0.11
OCHuman	1.72	0.67
CrowdPose	4	0.27
Tiny People Pose	2.93	–
Panda-Pose	**9.33**	**0.33**

Figure 3 and Table 1 present the statistics of Panda-Pose compared to existing popular datasets. Note: stats for Tiny People Pose could not be gathered because the dataset is not publicly available. Overall, the scale distribution in Panda-Pose leans noticeably smaller than other datasets. The closest is COCO, whose scale is about 1.7X larger at every quartile and whose minimum is 5X larger. Additionally, COCO's persons per image and average IoU are significantly lower than Panda-Pose (7.5X and 3X, respectively), putting it well outside our desired statistic. Looking at average IoU, CrowdPose [12] comes close enough to seem a suitable replacement. However, CrowdPose has $\frac{1}{2}$ the number of persons per image, and their scale distribution is even worse than COCO's for our application. OCHuman [27] has twice the average IoU, making it far more occluded than Panda-Pose. This could be argued to be a benefit, as detecting with occlusions is significantly more challenging. However, people in OCHuman are generally very close to the camera, taking up nearly the whole image with an average scale of 0.844. All this shows that while other datasets can address part of the challenges for our chosen application, only Panda-Pose addresses them all, matching the desired statics for training and validation.

5 Results and Evaluation

To validate the efficacy of ADG-Pose, we train a bottom-up pose estimator on Panda-Pose (Sect. 4) and use it to compare Panda-Pose with the baseline COCO [13] dataset. For the bottom-up pose estimator, we use EfficientHRNet [15] for its lightweight and real-time execution capabilities, making it more suitable for real-world applications. In addition, its scalability allows us to test with different network complexities. In this article, we use EfficientHRNet's H_0 and H_1 models. EfficientHRNet by default limits the number of detections to 30, fitting with the COCO dataset. To more fairly compare, we take the same approach when training and validating with our dataset. Training on Panda-Pose starts with pretrained models and is fine-tuned for 150 epochs with a learning rate of $1e-5$ for H_0 and $1e-6$ for the larger H_1.

Table 2. Precision, recall, and F1-score on COCO val.

Method	Backbone	Input size	AP	AR	F1
Trained on COCO					
OpenPose [2]	–	–	61.0	–	–
Hourglass [17]	Hourglass	512	56.6	–	–
PersonLab [19]	ResNet-152	1401	66.5	–	–
PifPaf [10]	ResNet-152	–	67.4	–	–
HigherHRNet [5]	HRNet-W32	512	67.1	–	–
HigherHRNet [5]	HRNet-W48	640	69.8	–	–
LOGO-CAP [25]	HRNet-W32	512	69.6	–	–
LOGO-CAP [25]	HRNet-W48	640	72.2	–	–
EfficientHRNet-H_0 [15]	EfficientNet-B0	512	64.8	69.6	67.1
EfficientHRNet-H_1 [15]	EfficientNet-B1	544	66.3	70.7	68.4
trained on Panda-Pose					
EfficientHRNet-H_0 [15]	EfficientNet-B0	512	50.6	59.2	54.6
EfficientHRNet-H_1 [15]	EfficientNet-B1	512	48.9	56.8	52.6

Evaluation on COCO: To show how H_0 trained on Panda-Pose compares with SotA models trained on COCO, we conduct validation on the COCO dataset. Table 2 contains accuracy when validated on COCO val (including precision, recall, and F1-score) while Fig. 4 shows qualitative examples from validation. Looking at the reported validation accuracy, the Panda-Pose trained H_0 performs significantly worse than all other models. However, when looking at actual examples from the validation set, we see a completely different story. As discussed in Sect. 3 ground truth annotations are missing from distant people or in crowded scenes. This leads to lots of missed detections from COCO trained models, as seen in the center row. Multiple persons in the crowded scene on the left and distant people in the middle and right image are not detected. The Panda-Pose model is able to detect all persons in the first two images and only misses the single most distant person in the last image. However, since these people are not annotated on the COCO dataset, the COCO model does not get penalized for missing them and the Panda-Pose model does not benefit from being able to detect them, at least as far as COCO validation is concerned. However, real-world applications like our test case would weigh being able to detect distant persons much higher. Additionally, while the Panda-Pose model is not perfect, it also attempts to detect highly occluded persons. Looking at the leftmost image, the network greatly misinterprets that person's pose by trying to predict key points for the highly occluded person behind the man serving the ball. Meanwhile, the COCO model does not even detect that person. Another thing to note is how the H_1 Panda-Pose model with an input resolution of 768 actually performed worse than H_0 on COCO val. This is caused by lower resolution COCO images' upscaling to fit the higher input resolution, leading to additional noise. This is in line with the conclusions made in [5].

Table 3. Precision, recall, and F1-score of EfficientHRNet models on Panda-Pose.

Method	Backbone	Input size	AP	AR	F1
trained on COCO					
EfficientHRNet-H_0	EfficientNet-B0	512	20.2	24.0	21.9
EfficientHRNet-H_1	EfficientNet-B1	544	21.1	25.1	23.4
trained on Panda-Pose					
EfficientHRNet-H_0	EfficientNet-B0	512	31.4	38.7	34.7
EfficientHRNet-H_1	EfficientNet-B1	512	34.6	44.0	38.7
EfficientHRNet-H_0	EfficientNet-B0	768	36.5	44.0	39.9
EfficientHRNet-H_1	EfficientNet-B1	768	41.3	49.9	45.2

Evaluation on Panda-Pose: As explored in Sect. 3, the COCO dataset does not accurately represent our target real-world application. Since Panda-Pose was created to closely match our target application we look at how the performance of models trained on COCO compare with those trained on Panda-Pose. This dataset is significantly more challenging than COCO, with **7.5**× the number of persons per image, **3**× the occlusions, and a significant shift in distribution towards smaller scale persons. As seen in Table 3, EfficientHRNet-H_0 trained on COCO barely reaches past **20%** AP and has an F1-score of **21.9%**. Moving to the H_1 model increases AP to **21.1%** and F1 to **23.4%**. In contrast H_0 trained on Panda-Pose reaches an AP of **31.4%** and F1 of **34.7%**, and increase of **1.5**× and **1.6**× respectively. Increasing the resolution of H_0 to 768 increases AP to **36.5%** and F1 to **39.9%**, which is a **15%** increase with no other changes to the model. Notably, increases to 768 resolution have a negative effect on COCO accuracy [5], but since Panda-Pose is much higher resolution, performance is improved. This effect is even more prominent than simply increasing the model size without changing the resolution. However, changing the model size to H_1 and the resolution to 768, we see an AP of **41.3%** and F1 of **45.2%**, double what was achievable with the COCO model.

While these results are important, the COCO trained models are at an obvious disadvantage having not trained on Panda-Pose. In addition to the clear challenges of scale, crowdedness, and occlusions, COCO models must combat general domain shift that Panda-Pose models do not. As such, we must use a third dataset unseen by both COCO and Panda-Pose models.

Fig. 4. Top: COCO ground truth keypoints (green). Middle: H_0 predictions when trained on COCO. Bottom: H_0 predictions when trained on Panda-Pose. In all cases, red boxes denote unannotated or undetected persons. (Color figure online)

Case Study - Action Recognition: Continuing with the use case of parking lot surveillance, we assess the end-to-end performance of real-world action recognition on the UCF-ARG dataset [6]. UCF-ARG consists of 10 actions by 12 actors on three different high resolution (1920×1080) cameras. We focus on the "Ground" and "Rooftop" cameras, as the aerial camera does not fit our use case. We utilize a spatial-temporal graph convolutional network which uses a graph-based formulation to construct dynamic skeletons [26], and add attentive feedback to predict actions, as in [20]. The skeletal poses come from H_0.

The COCO trained model achieves **60%** accuracy on Ground and **10%** accuracy on Rooftop, the latter of which is random guessing. As seen in Fig. 5, the COCO trained model is completely unable to detect the highly distant persons in Rooftop. The model trained on Panda-Pose is able to achieve much better results of **81%** on Ground and **40%** on Rooftop. Not only is it able to detect more persons in Ground, leading to a **1.35**$\times$ increase in end-to-end accuracy, but it can effectively detect people in Rooftop where the COCO model failed. The significantly smaller person scale distribution of Panda-Pose gives models

Fig. 5. Sample images from UCF-ARG Ground (left) and Rooftop (right) with COCO (blue) and Panda-Pose (pink) predictions. (Color figure online)

the ability to accurately detect people much farther from the camera than other datasets, which is an ability completely overlooked in COCO's validation. However, the quality of the poses does slightly suffer from lack of information of very distant persons, as can be seen in Fig. 5. These results emphasize the efficacy of Panda-Pose and ADG-Pose for real-world applications.

6 Conclusion

In this article we presented ADG-Pose for generating datasets for real-world human pose estimation. Current SotA datasets do not always address the challenges faced by real-world applications, which often leads to unexpected under performance. By using ultra-high resolution images and high accuracy neural networks, ADG-Pose allows users to customize datasets towards their chosen application by determining the data distribution along the axes of crowdedness, occlusion, and distance from the camera. We have shown through quantitative and qualitative analysis how validation on current SotA datasets can fail to properly address the challenges of real-world applications, and we have provided real-world skeleton based action recognition as a use case to show how our method produces models better suited for real-world applications.

Acknowledgements. This research is supported by the National Science Foundation (NSF) under Award No. 1831795 and NSF Graduate Research Fellowship Award No. 1848727.

References

1. Andriluka, M., Pishchulin, L., Gehler, P., Schiele, B.: 2D human pose estimation: new benchmark and state of the art analysis. In: IEEE Conference on Computer Vision and Pattern Recognition (CVPR), June 2014 (2014)
2. Cao, Z., Hidalgo, G., Simon, T., Wei, S., Sheikh, Y.: Openpose: realtime multi-person 2D pose estimation using part affinity fields. arXiv preprint arXiv:1812.08008 (2018)
3. Chen, K., et al.: Patient-specific pose estimation in clinical environments. IEEE J. Transl. Eng. Health Med. **6**, 1–11 (2018). https://doi.org/10.1109/JTEHM.2018.2875464

4. Chen, Y., Wang, Z., Peng, Y., Zhang, Z., Yu, G., Sun, J.: Cascaded pyramid network for multi-person pose estimation. arXiv preprint arXiv:1711.07319 (2017)
5. Cheng, B., Xiao, B., Wang, J., Shi, H., Huang, T.S., Zhang, L.: Higherhrnet: scale-aware representation learning for bottom-up human pose estimation (2019)
6. For Research in Computer Vision, U.C.: UCF-ARG dataset. https://www.crcv.ucf.edu/data/UCF-ARG.php
7. Etten, A.V.: You only look twice: rapid multi-scale object detection in satellite imagery (2018)
8. Fang, H., Xie, S., Tai, Y., Lu, C.: RMPE: regional multi-person pose estimation. In: 2017 IEEE International Conference on Computer Vision (ICCV), pp. 2353–2362 (2017)
9. Johnson, S., Everingham, M.: Learning effective human pose estimation from inaccurate annotation. In: CVPR 2011, pp. 1465–1472 (2011)
10. Kreiss, S., Bertoni, L., Alahi, A.: Pifpaf: composite fields for human pose estimation. arXiv preprint arXiv:1903.06593 (2019)
11. Kumar, D., T, P., Murugesh, A., Kafle, V.P.: Visual action recognition using deep learning in video surveillance systems. In: 2020 ITU Kaleidoscope: Industry-Driven Digital Transformation (ITU K), pp. 1–8 (2020). https://doi.org/10.23919/ITUK50268.2020.9303222
12. Li, J., Wang, C., Zhu, H., Mao, Y., Fang, H.S., Lu, C.: Crowdpose: efficient crowded scenes pose estimation and a new benchmark. In: Proceedings of the IEEE/CVF Conference on Computer Vision and Pattern Recognition (CVPR), June 2019 (2019)
13. Lin, T.Y., et al.: Microsoft coco: common objects in context (2014)
14. Neff, C., Mendieta, M., Mohan, S., Baharani, M., Rogers, S., Tabkhi, H.: Revamp2t: real-time edge video analytics for multicamera privacy-aware pedestrian tracking. IEEE Internet Things J. **7**(4), 2591–2602 (2020). https://doi.org/10.1109/JIOT.2019.2954804
15. Neff, C., Sheth, A., Furgurson, S., Middleton, J., Tabkhi, H.: EfficientHRNet. J. Real-Time Image Process. **18**(4), 1037–1049 (2021). https://doi.org/10.1007/s11554-021-01132-9
16. Neumann, L., Vedaldi, A.: Tiny people pose. In: Jawahar, C.V., Li, H., Mori, G., Schindler, K. (eds.) ACCV 2018. LNCS, vol. 11363, pp. 558–574. Springer, Cham (2019). https://doi.org/10.1007/978-3-030-20893-6_35
17. Newell, A., Yang, K., Deng, J.: Stacked hourglass networks for human pose estimation. arXiv preprint arXiv:1603.06937 (2016)
18. Osokin, D.: Real-time 2D multi-person pose estimation on CPU: lightweight openpose. arXiv preprint arXiv:1811.12004 (2018)
19. Papandreou, G., Zhu, T., Chen, L., Gidaris, S., Tompson, J., Murphy, K.: Personlab: person pose estimation and instance segmentation with a bottom-up, part-based, geometric embedding model. arXiv preprint arXiv:1803.08225 (2018)
20. Sanchez, J., Neff, C., Tabkhi, H.: Real-world graph convolution networks (RW-GCNS) for action recognition in smart video surveillance. In: Symposium on Edge Computing (SEC), pp. 121–134. ACM/IEEE (2021). https://doi.org/10.1145/3453142.3491293
21. Sun, K., Xiao, B., Liu, D., Wang, J.: Deep high-resolution representation learning for human pose estimation. arXiv preprint arXiv:1902.09212 (2019)
22. Van Etten, A.: Satellite imagery multiscale rapid detection with windowed networks. In: 2019 IEEE Winter Conference on Applications of Computer Vision (WACV), Jan 2019 (2019). https://doi.org/10.1109/wacv.2019.00083

23. Wang, X., et al.: Panda: a gigapixel-level human-centric video dataset. In: 2020 IEEE International Conference on Computer Vision and Pattern Recognition (CVPR). IEEE (2020)
24. Wu, J., et al.: Large-scale datasets for going deeper in image understanding. In: 2019 IEEE International Conference on Multimedia and Expo (ICME), Jul 2019 (2019). https://doi.org/10.1109/icme.2019.00256
25. Xue, N., Wu, T., Zhang, Z., Xia, G.S.: Learning local-global contextual adaptation for fully end-to-end bottom-up human pose estimation (2021)
26. Yan, S., Xiong, Y., Lin, D.: Spatial temporal graph convolutional networks for skeleton-based action recognition. In: Thirty-Second AAAI Conference on Artificial Intelligence (2018)
27. Zhang, S.H., et al.: Pose2seg: detection free human instance segmentation. In: Proceedings of the IEEE/CVF Conference on Computer Vision and Pattern Recognition (CVPR), June 2019 (2019)

Deep Reinforcement Learning for Autonomous Navigation in Robotic Wheelchairs

Sotirios Chatzidimitriadis(✉) and Konstantinos Sirlantzis

Intelligent Interactions Research Group, School of Engineering, University of Kent, Canterbury CT2 7NT, UK
{sc866,K.Sirlantzis}@kent.ac.uk

Abstract. We propose a novel efficient method for autonomous navigation of nonholonomic mobile robots within complex indoor environments, with application to Electric Powered Wheelchairs (EPW). It is designed and developed using the Deep Reinforcement Learning (RL) framework. Specifically, an end-to-end navigation model is devised utilizing an "off-policy" RL algorithm, which fully exploits information from a realistic setup to perform map-less, collision-free navigation. The model takes as input noisy sensor readings and produces moving commands for the mobile robot, thus, mapping a flow of environmental observations to a *continuous space* of driving actions, to reach a desired target. The effectiveness and efficiency of the proposed approach is tested through experiments in simulation, in both seen and unseen environments, and is compared to human performance, as well as state-of-the-art motion planners. The results show that our trained planner is not only able to navigate the nonholonomic mobile robot (EPW) through the challenging scenarios with significantly high success rates, but also, it outperforms the baseline methods in a range of performance aspects.

Keywords: Autonomous navigation · Powered wheelchair · Robotic wheelchair · Assistive technologies · Reinforcement learning

1 Introduction

People with motor, sensory, or even cognitive impairments, rely on the daily use of wheelchairs to satisfy their mobility needs. Many of those people, especially the ones with severe conditions, need Electric Powered Wheelchairs (EPW) to compensate for their disability. It is not uncommon, that EPW users, due to poor motor control, inconvenient control interfaces, fatigue, or other reasons, face difficulties with coping with daily maneuvering tasks. In those cases, an

This work is supported by the Assistive Devices for empowering dis-Abled People through robotic Technologies (ADAPT) project. ADAPT is selected for funding by the INTERREG VA France (Channel) England Programme which is co-financed by the European Regional Development Fund (ERDF).

M. El Yacoubi et al. (Eds.): ICPRAI 2022, LNCS 13364, pp. 271–282, 2022.
https://doi.org/10.1007/978-3-031-09282-4_23

autonomous navigation system would be greatly beneficial in alleviating part of their daily burden and enhance their independence.

A robotic, or smart, wheelchair integrates a standard EPW with an onboard computer and sensors, in order to allow the incorporation of technologies originally developed for mobile robots. The current state-of-the-art in the field of EPW navigation includes systems capable of performing obstacle avoidance, simultaneous localization and mapping (SLAM), path planning and motion control. The majority of the autonomous navigation solutions [4,8,13] rely on constructing a map of an environment, and utilizing a global planner, along with a localization method and a local planner to reach a desired goal in the map.

We focus our work in a different direction by adopting a learning approach to the problem of navigation in EPWs, and by taking advantage of the recent advances in the Reinforcement Learning (RL) field. We believe that such an approach can tackle several drawbacks of the traditional methods: a) the need of a map, b) high computational costs, c) extensive hyperparameter tuning and d) expensive sensors. Our aim is to develop a smart wheelchair system, capable of autonomously navigating complex indoor environments, in a collision-free manner and without the need of perfect knowledge of the area in which the robot will move. We choose to use a sensor setup that is low-cost, low-bandwidth and that can be easily installed on a real EPW. The main contributions of this paper are:

- Propose a RL-based motion planner for robotic wheelchairs, which can outperform the traditionally used navigation methods in various aspects.
- Utilize a realistic and low-cost sensor setup for tackling complex navigation tasks on nonholonomic mobile robots in the continuous action space.
- Design of a reward function with emphasis on safety and proposal of an additional safety layer that promotes collision-free navigation.

In the following section related work is presented with a focus on learning based methods. Section 3 describes the problem formulation and the methodology that was followed. The experimental setup, along with the training process and the method's evaluation, are shown in Sect. 4. In Sect. 5 we state our conclusions and suggest possible topics for future research.

2 Related Work

In terms of EPW navigation, the state-of-the-art relies on traditional path planning methods, often applied with some variations. Aiming for indoor navigation, the method introduced in [15] integrated points of interest into a floor plan, in which an adjacency matrix was added to enable the use of the $A^{\star}$ algorithm for path planning. Gao et al. [3] focused on synthesizing 3-D landmark maps for localization of a smart wheelchair, with the mapping process, however, requiring a high fidelity sensor suite, including two LiDAR modules and a digital video camera. Morales et al. [10] augmented the standard geometric map built via SLAM to a comfort map and used a modification of the $A^{\star}$ algorithm for path planning. In [8] the ROS navigation stack was integrated with the EPW to perform mapping, localization and planning. Similarly, the authors in [13] used SLAM, along with the global planner provided by ROS, combined with an adaptive controller to account for the changing system dynamics. Finally, Grewal et al. [4] utilized computer vision to identify possible destinations for the user to choose, before applying Dijkstra's algorithm along with the Dynamic Window Approach to navigate towards the chosen target. However, the destination scanning process takes a long time to complete, and requires high computational power (e.g. laptop or PC) integrated to the wheelchair.

Moving to the machine learning framework for mobile robot navigation, many works have utilized Supervised learning (SL) with deep neural networks, that has proven to be a powerful tool to classify and process data [1]. Learning from demonstrations and inverse reinforcement learning (IRL) are other major paradigms which utilize deep learning [7,11], however, these methods heavily rely on high-quality demonstration data, which can be hard and very time-consuming to collect. There are works where SL is combined with RL, as in [16], which trains a global planner by mimicking an expert, and a local planner that is trained with deep Q-learning. The switching strategy between the planners, though, is simplistic, the global planner can only navigate towards a specific number of goals, and both planners work with discrete actions. In a pure RL framework, many works rely solely on vision to perform navigation, either through RGB or depth camera sensors [9,17]. The issues, though, commonly present in those approaches, are the high computational demands in both training and testing time, their poor transferability to the real world, due to the discrepancies between it and the simulation environment, while they also operate in the discrete action space. Lastly, Tai et al. [14] is one of the few works that learns a continuous control policy for a Kobuki based turtlebot, relying only on sparse 10-dimensional laser ranges, the robot's velocity and the relative target position.

Our method, is based on a pure RL framework, and addresses the problem of navigation in the continuous action space, which for us is a necessary requirement in order to be able to produce smooth trajectories for the EPW user, while enabling fine maneuvers often needed in indoor environments. Moreover, we propose a system with a sensor setup that can be easily transferred from simulation to the real world and that is relatively low-cost. Therefore, we choose to use ultrasonic sensors, with appropriately modeled measurement uncertainty, instead of RGB cameras or LiDARs, and which are also more suitable for covering a bulkier robot frame such as that of an EPW. Additionally, Inertial Measurement Unit (IMU) measurements are included as part of the state space, which is not found in other works. We found that providing self orientation is especially important for a non-symmetrically shaped platform (as opposed for example to the turtlebot platform used in [14]), and also the pitch measurement allows the agent to take into account inclinations, which is of critical importance for wheelchairs. Finally, we utilize a small and efficient neural network architecture contrary to complex architectures used in similar works, or the very demanding path planning algorithms that are usually implemented for EPW navigation.

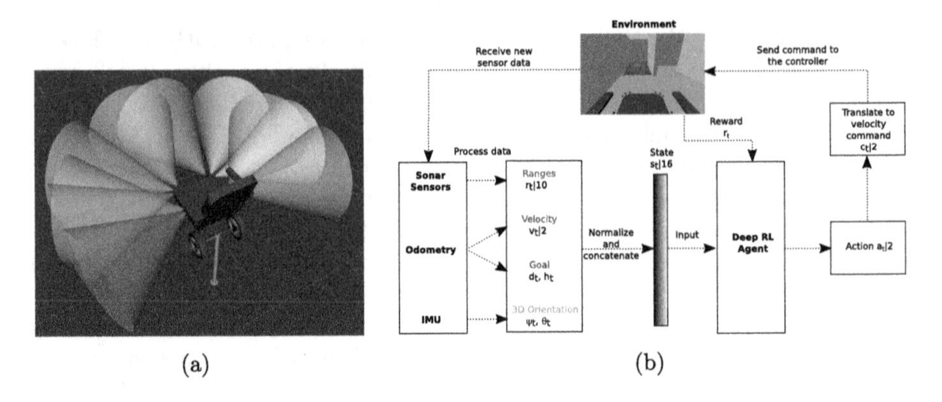

Fig. 1. (a) The virtual wheelchair model (b) The flowchart of the system

3 Methodology

3.1 MDP Formulation

This work focuses on an end-to-end learning framework for performing mapless autonomous navigation in complex environments. We model our problem as an episodic *Markov Decision Process* (MDP), with finite time horizon T. A MDP is a tuple $(\mathcal{S}, \mathcal{A}, \mathcal{T}, \mathcal{R})$, where $\mathcal{S}$ is a set of continuous states, $\mathcal{A}$ a set of continuous actions, $\mathcal{T}$ an unknown transition function and $\mathcal{R}$ the reward function. We denote the discrete timestep within an episode with $t \in \{0, 1, .., T-1\}$. The state transition dynamics $\mathcal{T}(s_{t+1}|s_t, a_t)$ map a state-action pair at time t onto a distribution of states at time $t+1$, with $s_t \in \mathcal{S}$ and $a_t \in \mathcal{A}$. The agent, at each timestep, chooses its actions according to a policy $a_t = \pi(s_t)$, then applies them to the environment, observes a new state s_{t+1} and receives a reward $r(s_t, a_t, s_{t+1}) \in \mathcal{R}$. Given this setting, the goal is to find an optimal policy $\pi^\star$ that achieves the maximum expected return $G_t = \sum_{t=0}^{T} \gamma^t r(s_t, a_t, s_{t+1})$ from all states, where $\gamma \in [0, 1)$ is a scalar discount factor.

State Space. Since our aim is to transfer our system into the real world and for a real purpose, the arrangement of sensors that was chosen was such to closely resemble the real EPW of our robotic experiments. The sensors that were used in our virtual model, as shown in Fig. 1a, consist of 10 ultrasonic sensors (with Gaussian distributed noise $\mathcal{N}(0, 0.01)$) surrounding the EPW, a pair of wheel encoders that provide odometry information, as well as an IMU. The sonar sensors are positioned in a way to fully cover the front view, as well as the sides of the EPW, with minimal overlapping between them. Each of the sonar sensors has a 50° field of view and can measure up to 3 m far. By utilizing the sensors described above, we form the state space which consists of: 10 sonar

Table 1. Reward function terms

(distance) $\mathbf{r_d}$ =	(sensor) $\mathbf{r_s}$ =	(goal) $\mathbf{r_g}$ =
-0.25 if $\lvert d_t \rvert < d_{min}$	-0.5 if $s_{any} < 1.5 s_{min}$	1.0 if current goal achieved
$-1.5/log(-d_t)$ if $d_t < 0$	-0.25 if $s_{any} < 2.5 s_{min}$	5.0 if final goal achieved
0 otherwise	0 otherwise	0 otherwise

range measurements, the linear and angular velocity of the robot provided by the odometry, the distance and heading to the current goal calculated from the current position of the robot, along with the current goal's position, and finally the pitch and the yaw of the robot converted from the quaternions provided by the IMU. The yaw gives the agent a sense of its own direction, while the pitch is important to identify inclinations, as for example when climbing up a ramp. In total, the above measurements form a state space of 16 continuous variables, which are normalized in $[0, 1]$ before being fed to the actor-critic networks.

Actions. We introduce two available actions to the agent, which correspond to the commands that need to be sent to the differential drive controller to move the virtual wheelchair. Those are the linear and angular velocities, in the range of $[-1, 1]$ for easier convergence of the neural network, which are then remapped to the actual desired velocities that will be sent to the controller and drive the EPW. The differential drive kinematics, in terms of robot velocities, can be expressed as follows:

$$v = \frac{v_R + v_L}{2} \qquad \omega = \frac{v_R - v_L}{d}, \tag{1}$$

where v is the platform body's linear velocity, ω is its angular velocity, $v_{R,L}$ are the drive wheel velocities (right and left respectively) and d is the axial distance between the two drive wheels.

Rewards. To ingrain our agent with the desired behavior, we define the reinforcement learning signal received from the environment, which is our reward function at timestep t, as follows:

$$r(s_t, a_t, s_{t+1}) = l_d \cdot r_d(s_t, s_{t+1}) + l_s \cdot r_s(s_{t+1}) + l_g \cdot r_g(s_{t+1}), \tag{2}$$

where l_d, l_s and l_g are scaling factors. The analytical expression of each term is presented in Table 1.

r_d is the reward related to the distance difference from the current goal, between two consecutive timesteps ($d_t = \|p_{t+1}^{x,y} - g_i^{x,y}\| - \|p_t^{x,y} - g_i^{x,y}\|$, $p_t^{x,y}$ being the robot's position at timestep t and $g_i^{x,y}$ being the current goal's position). The first branch of this reward penalizes the agent for not moving (when the distance difference is below a specified threshold, denoted as d_{min}), which is observed in situations such as when the robot gets stuck at a wall corner, or when trying to get up a ramp but does not accelerate enough. The second branch of the positional reward, returns a reward proportional to the logarithm of the distance difference. The reasoning behind this is that the odometry can return values differing by several orders of magnitude, which we want to squash down to sensible scalar values that are not far apart, by utilizing the logarithmic function.

r_s is an auxiliary sensor reward to penalize dangerous proximity to obstacles, by defining two danger zones, and penalizing when any of the range sensors (indicated as s_{any}) returns a reading smaller than a multiple of the minimum safety range (s_{min}), at which we consider that we have crashed. This reward is designed to provide the robot with safety awareness, and thus act as an extra safety feature for the particular application, given the increased risks of driving an EPW. Lastly, r_g indicates the reward for reaching the current goal within a specified radius of 0.5 m. For crashing we penalize the agent by setting the total reward as $r(s_t, a_t) = r_{crash} = -100$.

Terminal States. The episode is reset when the robot crashes, when it manages to reach the endgoal, as well as when it remains in the same position for several consecutive steps (stuck or not moving), so as not to fill the replay buffer (used with off-policy RL methods) with useless experience and slow down training. It also resets when the maximum number of allowed steps is exceeded, which discourages the robot from retaining a low linear speed when not necessary, since it has to complete the track before the episode resets.

3.2 Solving the MDP

For solving the above MDP we choose to use the Soft Actor Critic Algorithm (SAC) [5]. SAC is an off-policy algorithm that is used with continuous action spaces and trains a policy that maximizes a trade-off between expected return and entropy, in order to increase the randomness of the policy and boost exploration. The reasoning behind this choice is three-fold. First, the use of the continuous action space, which is a motivation for this work to allow smoother control of the mobile robot enabling complex maneuvers. Second, the proven success of the particular algorithm for solving similar MDPs in an efficient way, being a sample efficient and stable algorithm. Third, the fact that SAC requires relatively little hyper-parameter tuning compared to other RL algorithms. The objective function that is optimized in SAC for the policy network is shown below:

$$J(\pi) = \sum_{t=0}^{T} \mathbb{E}_{\boldsymbol{s_t}, \boldsymbol{a_t} \sim p_\pi} [r(s_t, a_t) + \alpha \mathcal{H}(\pi(\cdot|s_t))], \tag{3}$$

where $\mathcal{H}$ is the entropy of the policy and α is a parameter which controls the trade-off between the reward and the entropy.

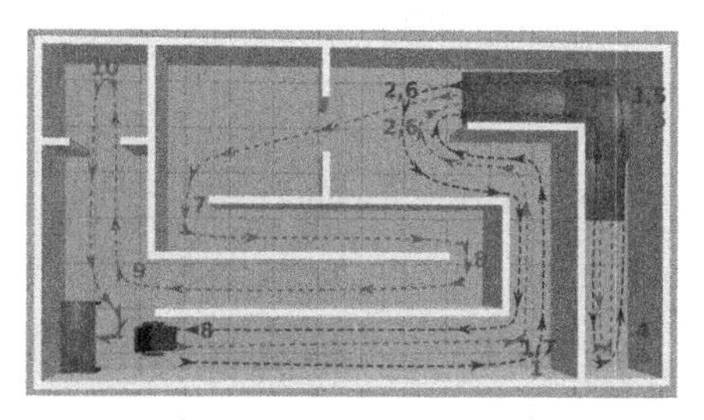

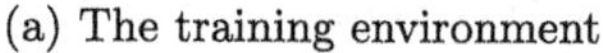

(a) The training environment

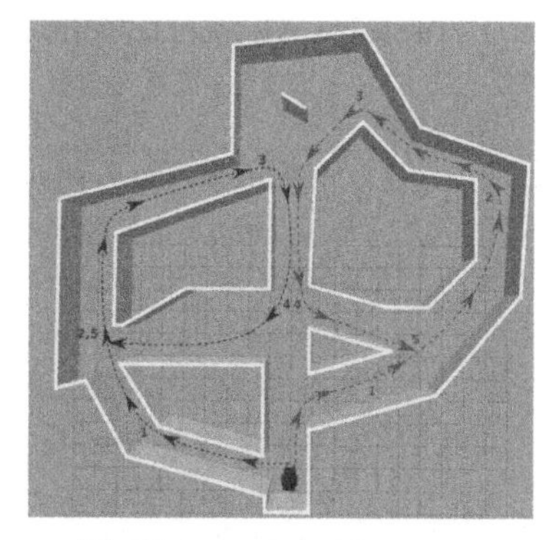

(b) The unseen environment

Fig. 2. The virtual scenarios implemented in Gazebo. The green and red lines indicate the desired paths for the 1st and the 2nd scenario respectively, whereas the numbers show the approximate locations of the subgoals along those paths. (Color figure online)

4 Experiments and Results

4.1 Training

Setup. For training the autonomous agent, we follow the real-world trial scenarios defined in the ADAPT project to test wheelchair user skills according to the Wheelchair Skills Test (WST) [6] protocol. The WST describes a range of driving skills needed for assessing the capacity and performance of an EPW user, including a series of challenging tasks as shown in Table 2. The track is split into two scenarios, which in turn include a number of subgoals the agent needs to accomplish, in order to fully navigate the paths as marked in Fig. 2a. At each training episode a scenario is selected randomly, as well as a random subgoal within that scenario. The initial pose of the robot is also randomised, within some bounds, along the track. The reasoning behind this is that we want to integrate diverse experience for the replay buffer, so that our agent learns faster, while minimizing the risk of the model getting stuck at a local minima, by converging early on to a weak policy unable to explore further and improve its strategy. Our system setup is implemented using ROS, acting as its backbone to allow communication between the components, while Gazebo is used as our simulation environment to conduct the agent training and evaluation.

Training Details. The SAC algorithm's hyperparameter were tuned through trial and error, resulting in the parameters shown in Fig. 3b. The actor critic neural network architecture utilized standard Multilayer Perceptrons (MLP). During training, the performance of the agent was periodically evaluated in a separate test environment, over the span of 5 episodes, in order to identify and save the best one. The maximum linear speed of the robot was set to 1.5 m/s, while the angular velocity was bound in $[-1, 1]$ rad/s.

Table 2. Wheelchair Skills Test tasks integrated in scenario 2 (Fig. 2a)

Subgoal	Task
1	Perform 90° turn in narrow corridor (1.5 m width)
2	Position for ascending inclined ramp (1.4 m width)
3	Ascent of 5% incline
4	Descent 10% incline and turn in place in narrow corridor
5	Ascent of 10% incline
6	Descent of 5% incline
7	Pass through 90 cm door and perform 90° turn in very narrow space
8	Perform U-turn in very narrow corridor (1 m width)
9	Exit corridor performing a wide turn
10	Enter lift area through 90 cm door and turn in place to exit lift
11	Position under desk/table (for working, eating etc.)

4.2 Evaluation

Trained Agent. For evaluating the proposed method, we first repeated the training process five times, using different random seeds, resulting in five policies representing the best agent of each run. Performing several runs was done to gather quantitative results, and test our method's sensitivity to the stochasticity involved in the training process. Figure 3a presents the results, in terms of average reward over the training course. We observe that given enough training time the models converge to similar achieved reward, which shows that the method is robust to randomness between different runs. This robustness is enhanced by enabling the agent to start off at various points of the course, as well as the deterministic nature of the environment. Additionally, all models resulted in high entropy policies (in the context of RL entropy measures the randomness in actions), which is indicative of their ability to generalize and adapt to situations not experienced before.

(a) Average reward during training

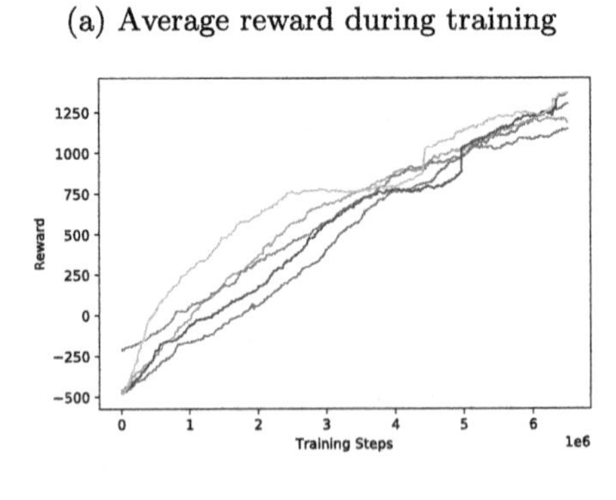

(b) SAC hyperparameters

Parameter	Value
Optimizer	Adam
Learning rate	3e-4
Discount(γ)	0.99
Replay buffer size	10e6
Num. of hidden layers (all nets.)	2
Num. of hidden units per layer	256
Num. of samples per minibatch	256
Nonlinearity	ReLU
Training steps	6.5e6

Fig. 3. RL Agent training information

The performance of the trained agents was initially tested on the scenarios they were trained on, for a span of 100 episodes on each scenario. An important innovation we employ during testing time is the addition of an extra *safety mechanism*, to aid collision-free navigation. The mechanism activates when any of the range sensor measurements is below the minimum safety threshold (s_{min}) and the chosen action would move the robot towards the direction of the obstacle. Instead of resetting the episode as in during training, we simply issue a zero command to the controller to prevent the crash, and also allow the agent to continue its task if it manages pick an action from the stochastic policy that would move it away from the obstacle. In Table 3 we present the average success rate of fully navigating each scenario, along with the number of collisions, as well as the completion time of our best performing agent, both with and without the extra safety layer. We observe that the RL agent scores a high success rate (88%) for the first scenario, while the success drops for the second scenario (74%) due to the very demanding maneuvers that are required for completion. Enabling the safety mechanism drastically improves the success rates of the agent, while reducing the collisions to zero, only for a very slight trade-off in completion times.

We then tested the models in a different, unseen scenario (Fig. 2b), in order to evaluate how well our method has generalized in terms of driving behaviour and goal tracking. Compared to Fig. 2a, this one is less linear, more open spaced and requires slightly less complex maneuvers to navigate. Again, we design two separate paths along the track, each with its respective subgoals, while the results are presented in Table 3. We observe that the agent has not overfitted to the specific scenarios it was trained on, rather, it can navigate an unseen environment with high success rates, comparable to those of the training environment. The number and the positions of the defined subgoals are set arbitrarily, but placing them relatively close to each other and before steep changes in the map topology, helps the agent progress the track more smoothly, given the absence of a global knowledge of the map. Again, by applying the extra safety layer we observe a significant increase of the agent's success.

Baseline Comparison. The deep-RL trained motion planner was compared with human performance, as well as with two widely used motion planners. For a fair comparison, we provided both the humans and the path planners with the same subgoals and velocity limits as the RL agent. For the human trials we setup a *hardware-in-the-loop* (HIL) simulation, incorporating a real joystick controller connected via a USB-to-TTL Serial interface to a Linux machine running the simulation. Eight healthy human participants were given some time to familiarize themselves with the setup and were then asked to navigate the scenarios as fast and accurately as possible. The trials were not stopped in case of a crash, as was done with the RL agent.

For implementing traditional path planning we utilized the navigation stack provided by ROS. We initially created a 2-D occupancy grid map, using laser-based SLAM, and for localizing the robot in the map we used the Adaptive

Table 3. Performance statistics on the two environments. For the path planners only success/failure and completion times are marked.

Experiment		Training env. (Fig. 2a)			Unseen env. (Fig. 2b)		
Scenario	Method	Success	Collisions	Time	Success	Collisions	Time
Sc.1 (Green line)	RL	88%	0.12	53.5 s	86%	0.14	45.2 s
	RL(safe)	98%	0	54.7 s	94%	0	46.6 s
	HUM	87.5%	1.6	77.8 s	100%	0.4	47.2 s
	TEB	✓	N/A	75.8 s	✓	N/A	58.7 s
	DWA	✗	N/A	143.1 s	✓	N/A	103.4 s
Sc.2 (Red line)	RL	74%	0.26	79.4 s	87%	0.13	47.8 s
	RL(safe)	89%	0	82.8 s	97%	0	49.3 s
	HUM	75%	5.9	118.7 s	100%	2.4	62.3 s
	TEB	✗	N/A	–	✓	N/A	65.2 s
	DWA	✗	N/A	210.9 s	✓	N/A	94.6 s

Monte Carlo Localization approach. For producing a global plan we utilized the A* algorithm, whereas for generating velocity commands for collision-free path following we experimented both with the Dynamic Window Approach (DWA) [2] and the Time Elastic Bands (TEB) approach [12]. The relevant results are presented in Table 3. We observe that some of the human participants were not able to complete the scenarios of the training environment, which was due to getting stuck in tight spots and not being able to reverse. Overall, it was quite challenging to avoid crashing, at least not without moving extremely slowly. We also notice that the path planners were unable to fully complete the scenarios of the training environment. Even though the global planner managed to create a valid path to the goals, the local planners were unable to produce the necessary moving commands to guide the robot through specific spots, and thus the navigation was aborted. With DWA the robot speed was quite slow, while the planner was particularly problematic with rotating on the spot. On the other hand, TEB's overall performance was better than DWA, producing smoother trajectories and driving the robot faster. However, it was still unable to navigate the robot through tight spots and narrow pathways, despite our best efforts to tune it properly. These results occurred even after extensive tuning of various parameters of the planners, such as the inflation radius of obstacles in the costmap, the footprint of the robot, path and goal related cost factors etc. In the unseen environment, which is simpler in terms of the required maneuvers, both the humans and the planners were successful in navigating the given scenarios.

Discussion. Including human participants in this study was mainly aimed at putting into perspective the challenging task of controlling a bulky mobile platform. Naturally, the perceived task for a user would be quite different in the real world compared to the simulation, but still, the participants who focused on completing the trials as fast as possible had a significant number of collisions, whereas those who focused on accuracy had large completion times. This indicates the challenge of combining speed and accuracy for non-expert users when fine maneuvering is required and without the help of an assistive system. The traditional path planners both failed in completing the most challenging scenario, while they were successful in the easier tasks. However, they both required extensive tuning and proved to be slower in achieving the tasks, while being significantly more computationally intensive compared to the RL approach. When measured on the same hardware, the average frequency at which drive commands were sent resulted 7 Hz with TEB, 13 Hz with DWA 115 Hz with RL. This is an important factor to consider when deploying the solution in a real world robot with an onboard computer.

5 Conclusions

In this paper, we proposed a RL-based method for autonomously navigating complex indoor environments, only relying on low-cost onboard sensors of a differential drive robot. We focused our application on EPWs and provided a robust reward function, with a strong emphasis on collision-free navigation and wheelchair user safety. Results show that the learned policy can effectively complete challenging tasks and also adapt to new ones, with our aim lying in providing an option for effortless and safe navigation in the daily routine of EPW users. On top of the policy's output we apply a simple but effective control mechanism to further promote safety. Our method is able to handle cases the baseline methods are unable to, while being less computationally intensive. Future work will focus on validating the method's performance in the real world as a priority, and on extending the method for capturing dynamic environments. Finally, we are also interested in taking into account the human-comfort factor by including it as part of our reward function (e.g. punishing trajectories with abrupt accelerations).

References

1. Chen, C., Seff, A., Kornhauser, A., Xiao, J.: DeepDriving: learning affordance for direct perception in autonomous driving. In: Proceedings of the IEEE International Conference on Computer Vision 2015 Inter(Figure 1), pp. 2722–2730 (2015). https://doi.org/10.1109/ICCV.2015.312
2. Dieter, F., Wolfram, B., Sebastian, T.: The Dynamic Window Approach to Collision Avoidance, pp. 137–146 (1997). https://www.ri.cmu.edu/pub_files/pub1/fox_dieter_1997_1/fox_dieter_1997_1.pdf
3. Gao, C., Sands, M., Spletzer, J.: Towards autonomous wheelchair systems in urban environments. In: Howard, A., Iagnemma, K., Kelly, A. (eds.) Field and Service Robotics. Springer Tracts in Advanced Robotics, vol. 62, pp. 13–23. Springer, Heidelberg (2009). https://doi.org/10.1007/978-3-642-13408-1_2
4. Grewal, H.S., Thotappala Jayaprakash, N., Matthews, A., Shrivastav, C., George, K.: PCL-based autonomous wheelchair navigation in unmapped indoor environments. In: 2018 9th IEEE Annual Ubiquitous Computing, Electronics and Mobile Communication Conference, UEMCON 2018, pp. 291–296 (2018). https://doi.org/10.1109/UEMCON.2018.8796660

5. Haarnoja, T., Zhou, A., Abbeel, P., Levine, S.: Soft actor-critic: off-policy maximum entropy deep reinforcement learning with a stochastic actor. In: 35th International Conference on Machine Learning, ICML 2018, vol. 5, pp. 2976–2989 (2018)
6. Kirby, R.L., Swuste, J., Dupuis, D.J., MacLeod, D.A., Monroe, R.: The Wheelchair Skills Test: a pilot study of a new outcome measure. Arch. Phys. Med. Rehabil. **83**(1), 10–18 (2002). https://doi.org/10.1053/apmr.2002.26823
7. Kretzschmar, H., Spies, M., Sprunk, C., Burgard, W.: Socially compliant mobile robot navigation via inverse reinforcement learning. Int. J. Robot. Res. **35**, 1289–1307 (2016). https://doi.org/10.1177/0278364915619772
8. Li, R., Wei, L., Gu, D., Hu, H., McDonald-Maier, K.D.: Multi-layered map based navigation and interaction for an intelligent wheelchair. In: 2013 IEEE International Conference on Robotics and Biomimetics, ROBIO 2013, pp. 115–120, December 2013. https://doi.org/10.1109/ROBIO.2013.6739445
9. Mirowski, P., et al.: Learning to navigate in complex environments. In: 5th International Conference on Learning Representations, ICLR 2017 - Conference Track Proceedings (2019)
10. Morales, Y., Kallakuri, N., Shinozawa, K., Miyashita, T., Hagita, N.: Human-comfortable navigation for an autonomous robotic wheelchair. In: IEEE International Conference on Intelligent Robots and Systems, pp. 2737–2743 (2013). https://doi.org/10.1109/IROS.2013.6696743
11. Pfeiffer, M., Schaeuble, M., Nieto, J., Siegwart, R., Cadena, C.: From perception to decision: a data-driven approach to end-to-end motion planning for autonomous ground robots. In: Proceedings - IEEE International Conference on Robotics and Automation, pp. 1527–1533 (2017). https://doi.org/10.1109/ICRA.2017.7989182
12. Rösmann, C., Feiten, W., Wösch, T., Hoffmann, F., Bertram, T.: Efficient trajectory optimization using a sparse model. In: 2013 European Conference on Mobile Robots, pp. 138–143 (2013). https://doi.org/10.1109/ECMR.2013.6698833
13. Sinyukov, D., Desmond, R., Dickerman, M., Fleming, J., Schaufeld, J., Padir, T.: Multi-modal control framework for a semi-autonomous wheelchair using modular sensor designs. Intel. Serv. Robot. **7**(3), 145–155 (2014). https://doi.org/10.1007/s11370-014-0149-7
14. Tai, L., Paolo, G., Liu, M.: Virtual-to-real deep reinforcement learning: continuous control of mobile robots for mapless navigation. In: IEEE International Conference on Intelligent Robots and Systems, September 2017. https://doi.org/10.1109/IROS.2017.8202134
15. Yayan, U., Akar, B., Inan, F., Yazici, A.: Development of indoor navigation software for intelligent wheelchair. In: INISTA 2014 - IEEE International Symposium on Innovations in Intelligent Systems and Applications, Proceedings, pp. 325–329 (2014). https://doi.org/10.1109/INISTA.2014.6873639
16. Zhou, X., Gao, Y., Guan, L.: Towards goal-directed navigation through combining learning based global and local planners. Sensors (Switzerland) **19**(1) (2019). https://doi.org/10.3390/s19010176
17. Zhu, Y., et al.: Target-driven visual navigation in indoor scenes using deep reinforcement learning. In: Proceedings - IEEE International Conference on Robotics and Automation, pp. 3357–3364 (2017). https://doi.org/10.1109/ICRA.2017.7989381

Understanding Individual Neurons of ResNet Through Improved Compositional Formulas

Rafael Harth(✉)

Department of Information Security, University of Stuttgart, Stuttgart, Germany
Rafael.Harth@gmail.com

Abstract. Compositions of concepts from human-annotated datasets, e.g., "chair OR table", have been shown to approximate latent representations of image classifiers better than single concepts. In this work, we introduce the Close Algorithm, which improves performance according to the IoU metric by utilizing the non-logical connectors CLOSE-TO, WITH, and EXPAND. We consider the shortcomings of current approaches, discuss possible causes, and review a small user study we have run to collect evidence on this point. We also introduce a metric that discourages the reliance on scene-level annotations. (The code to replicate the technical results (along with additional sample images) can be accessed at https://github.com/rafaelharth/indres).

Keywords: Machine learning · Image classification · Interpretability

1 Introduction

Neural networks achieve state-of-the-art performance on many tasks but are infamously hard to understand. Existing explainability methods typically focus on local approximations [16,20], textual explanation modules [5,13,15], saliency maps [2,11,22], or pointing to examples [6,21] or influential training data [19]. In contrast, scant attention has been paid to individual neurons, and almost no work has focused on understanding and predicting neuron activations in detail.

In the context of image processing, human-annotated concepts from a densely labeled dataset provide a possible starting point for this problem [23]. Thresholding neuron activations allows computing their similarity with such concepts using metrics for the overlap between two sets, such as Intersection over Union (IoU). This method reveals that, e.g., the eleventh neuron in the final hidden layer of ResNet-18 trained on places365 is most similar to the concept "highway".

This approach can be improved by connecting several concepts into formulas [17], e.g., "(highway OR field-cultivated) AND NOT sky". In this work, we build on this approach by introducing the non-logical connectors CLOSE-TO, WITH, and EXPAND (Sect. 3). We discuss problems with IoU as a metric and suggest an alternative (Sect. 4). We show that incorporating the three new connectors improves accuracy according to either metric, observe that it is still poor, and

M. El Yacoubi et al. (Eds.): ICPRAI 2022, LNCS 13364, pp. 283–294, 2022.
https://doi.org/10.1007/978-3-031-09282-4_24

suggest possible reasons (Sect. 5). To provide evidence on this point, we review a small study in which two trained annotators were asked to take the role of the algorithm in predicting neuron activations for four different neurons (Sect. 6).

2 Related Work

In [12], Gonzalez-Garcia et al. aim to answer whether "CNNs learn semantic parts in their internal representation" using the PASCAL-Part dataset [7] as the source of ground truth. They match bounding boxes with individual neurons or combinations of neurons from AlexNet, finding that "34 out of the 105 semantic part classes emerge", which they call a "modest number".

Using Broden, a richer dataset with 1197 annotated concepts, Zhou et al. [23] find more promising results with their approach called "Network Dissection". They show that human-understandable concepts naturally emerge in hidden layers of neural networks but are lost under basis transformations of the latent representation, making them artifacts of the specific training procedure rather than an inevitable side-effect of discriminatory power. However, these results rely on an inclusive notion of emergence: the similarity between annotated concepts and neuron activations, while easily clearing the threshold for statistical significance, is usually mild.[1] Mu and Andreas [17] improve this level of similarity by matching neurons to combinations of several human-annotated concepts. This is the most direct predecessor of our work.

Fong and Vedaldi [10] introduce a method that learns a vector $\mathbf{w}_C \in \mathbb{R}^K$ for each concept C, where K is the number of neurons in a specific layer. Thus, each concept is assigned a linear combination of neurons, which improves predictive quality substantially compared to the 1:1 mapping introduced in [23].[2] Using one-hot vectors recovers single neuron mappings as a special case.

In an attempt to unify different approaches for interpreting image classifiers, [18] provides a rich set of visualizations showing how a network's latent representation evolves across layers, including visualizations that combine the representations of all neurons into a single image. [9] and [3] study individual neurons in language processing tasks. [8] provides a toolkit for analyzing individual neurons in practice.

3 Algorithmic Compositional Explanations

3.1 Setup

Following [17], we examine the 512 individual neurons (or "filters") from the last hidden layer of ResNet-18 [14] trained on places365 [24]. To predict neuron activations algorithmically, we use the Broden dataset introduced in [23].

[1] While mean IoU scores are not reported in the paper, [17] finds a mean of 0.059 for ResNet in what (as far as we can tell) is an identical setting.

[2] Even though this similarity is also measured by IoU, a quantitative comparison to our results is not possible because [10] does not examine neurons from ResNet.

In Broden, images are annotated with 1197 different classes that each belong to one of the six categories 'color', 'object', 'part', 'material', 'scene', and 'texture', where the last two categories annotate on a per-image basis, the remaining ones on the pixel level (112×112). Annotations are non-overlapping within each category but can overlap between categories, e.g., the same pixel can be annotated as 'car' (object), 'car dealership' (scene), and 'gray' (color). Broden combines several datasets, but only images from Ade20k [25] have been used in this work.

Neurons from the last hidden layer of ResNet output a 7×7 grid of numbers for each input image. This induces a division of each image into 49 cells, and we write $\mathbf{C}$ to denote the set of all cells from images in Ade20k so that each neuron n can be viewed as a function $n : \mathbf{C} \to \mathbb{R}$.

In this setting, each choice of a threshold $t_n \in \mathbb{R}$ induces a binary function $f_n : \mathbf{C} \to \{1, 0\}$, where $f_n(c) = 1$ iff $n(c) > t_n$. We call f_n the *neuron mask* for n and the value $\frac{1}{|\mathbf{C}|} \sum_{c \in \mathbf{C}} f_n(c) \in [0, 1]$ the *coverage* of f_n. Following [23] and [17], we choose thresholds t_n such that each neuron mask has coverage 0.5%.

To make human-annotated concepts comparable with neuron masks, they have been downsampled from their 112×112 resolution to 7×7 using block-based downsampling with a threshold of 100 (i.e., for each pixel-based class, each image is divided into 49 16×16 blocks corresponding to the cells in $\mathbf{C}$, and the class is considered to activate on that block if it activates on at least 100 of the 256 pixels). Image-level classes are converted to 49 or 0 activated cells, respectively. Previous approaches [4,17,23] instead rescale neuron activations to the 112×112 resolution using bilinear upsampling, but this makes the approach computationally infeasible given the connectors introduced in the upcoming Section. Given that the 7×7 neuron activations constitute the ground truth for this task, it is also unclear whether upsampling is desirable.

3.2 Connecting Annotated Concepts

In [17], human-annotated concepts are combined using the logical connectors AND, OR, and AND NOT, but many non-logical connectors are also possible.

Motivated by the observation that some neurons seem to care about two concepts appearing concurrently, we have introduced the binary connectors CLOSE TO and WITH, which restrict a given neuron mask f_n to cells where a second mask f_m activates within a two-cell radius (CLOSE TO) or anywhere in the same image (WITH). Furthermore, we found that some neurons that care about a specific concept also activate on cells adjacent to the concept. To capture this behavior, we have introduced the unitary connector EXPAND that widens the area of a single concept.

Formally, writing $\vee, \wedge, \neg$ to denote logical connectors, f_n, f_m for neuron masks, $C, D, E, F \in \mathbf{C}$ for cells, $\mathrm{im}(C)$ for the set of the 49 cells in the image corresponding to C, and $N(C)$ for the set of (at most 21) cells in the 5×5 square with corners removed around C, the three connectors can be defined as follows:

- $(f_n \text{ WITH } f_m)(C) := f_n(C) \wedge \bigvee_{D \in \mathrm{im}(C)} f_m(D)$.

- $(f_n \text{ CLOSE TO } f_m)(C) := f_n(C) \wedge \bigvee_{D \in N(C)} f_m(D)$. Furthermore, we define $(f_n \text{ CLOSE } f_m) := ((f_n \text{ CLOSE TO } f_m) \text{ OR } (f_m \text{ CLOSE TO } f_n))$. Note that $(f_n \text{ CLOSE } f_m)$ is treated as a formula of length 2.
- $\text{EXPAND}(f_n)(C) := f_n(C) \vee \bigvee_{(D,E,F) \in \text{adjacent}^3(C)} f_m(D) \wedge f_m(E) \wedge f_m(F)$, where $\text{adjacent}^3(C)$ is the set of all triples of three different cells adjacent to C (diagonal adjacency is permitted). EXPAND is applied to singular concepts only and does not increase formula length. We abbreviate it by the postfix -X, e.g., we write chair-X rather than EXPAND(chair).

One thing to keep in mind is the difference between the accuracy of an approximation (as measured by, e.g., IoU) and how much it helps a human understand the concept. For example, we will show in Sect. 5 that increasing the length of formulas increases IoU for either algorithm, but a formula of length 10 may still be less useful than one of length 3. We believe that the non-logical connectors introduced above (including the abbreviation "A CLOSE B") are intuitively simple and thus helpful for genuine understanding.

Throughout the paper, we refer to the algorithm using the new connectors as the "Close Algorithm" and the algorithm relying exclusively on AND, AND NOT, and OR as the "standard algorithm". We refer to masks produced by formulas from either algorithm as "label masks".

4 Locality and the ImRoU Metric

As mentioned in Sect. 3.1, Broden contains both pixel- and scene-level annotations. Scene-level annotations are made on a per-image basis, meaning that each image is either annotated fully or not at all. When optimizing for IoU with formula length 3, the standard algorithm finds a set of formulas in which over half of all primitive labels are scene-level.

At first glance, one may suspect that this reflects behaviors exhibited by the corresponding neuron masks. However, Fig. 1 shows that even neuron masks whose formula contains three scene-level annotations predominantly activate on small parts of their images (red graph), if they activate at all. This makes the algorithm's reliance on scene-level annotations intuitively undesirable. Furthermore, comparing them to neuron masks whose formulas contain zero scene-level annotations (blue graph) shows only marginal differences.

One way to discourage scene-level annotations is to add a penalty term that disproportionately affects false positives in images where neurons activate strongly. Given two masks $f_n, f_m : \mathbf{C} \to \{0,1\}$ (think of one neuron-, and one label mask), let N and M be the sets of cells on which they activate, i.e., $N = \{c \in \mathbf{C} : f_n(c) = 1\}$. One can compute a "random intersection" for each image I, which is equal to the expected size of the intersection $N \cap M$ if all cells of M were chosen uniformly at random out of I (see Fig. 2 for an example). Based on this, we introduce the metric ImRoU_r (**I**ntersection **m**inus **R**andom Intersection **o**ver **U**nion), which is computed by subtracting r times the random intersection (summed over all images) before dividing by the union. Formally,

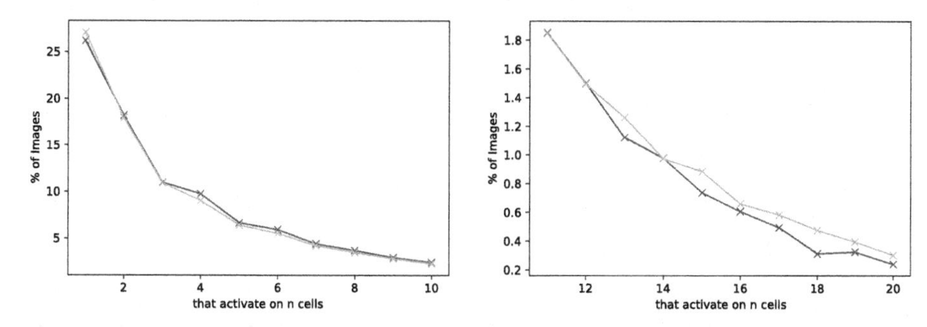

Fig. 1. Relative frequencies of images where neurons activate on exactly n cells, for different values of n, averaged across all neurons with zero (blue) and three (red) scene-level annotations in the formula of length three found by the standard algorithm. Most images (94.5% and 94.7% for the blue and red group, respectively) have no activations at all; the percentages shown are of only the set of images with nonzero activations. This was done to make the graphs readable. (Color figure online)

$$\text{ImRoU}_r^{\text{not-normalized}}(N, M) = \frac{\sum_{I \in \mathbf{I}} |N \cap M \cap I| - r \cdot \frac{1}{|I|} \cdot |M \cap I| \cdot |N \cap I|}{|N \cup M|}. \quad (1)$$

where $\mathbf{I}$ is the set of all images. Normalized ImRoU_r is obtained by dividing the above expression by the maximally achievable score for a given neuron mask.[3] We write ImRoU_r to refer to normalized ImRoU_r throughout the paper.

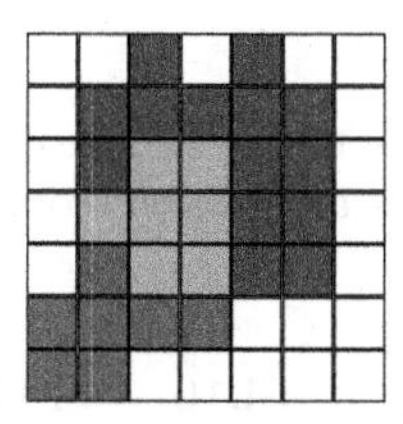

Fig. 2. An example illustrating the concept of random intersection. A neuron mask (red) and label mask (blue) intersect at 7 cells (purple). As the neuron mask covers 14 cells, choosing 21 cells in this grid at random would lead to an expected intersection of 6 cells, which means that the label mask achieves an intersection of 7 against a random intersection of 6. With $r = 0.75$, this leads to a value of 2.5 (as supposed to 6) in the respective summand in the nominator of (1). (Color figure online)

Choosing a value for r is non-trivial. With $r = 1$, every scene-level annotation achieves a score of 0 regardless of neuron behavior as the real intersection is always equal to the random intersection, which is intuitively undesirable. Thus,

[3] If the neuron mask is N, this can be computed as $(|N| - (r/|I|) \sum_{I \in \mathbf{I}} |N \cap I|^2)/|N|$.

we have used $r = .75$ for all results reported on in this paper. Figure 3 compares masks found by the Close Algorithm optimizing for $\text{ImRoU}_{.75}$ with masks found by the standard algorithm optimizing for IoU.

5 Results

5.1 Scene-Level Annotations

When the standard algorithm is optimized for IoU, it finds $(52, 146, 196, 118)$ formulas using $(0, 1, 2, 3)$ scene-level annotations, whereas the Close Algorithm finds $(120, 197, 136, 59)$. When $\text{ImRoU}_{.75}$ is optimized for instead, the numbers change to $(331, 153, 23, 5)$ and $(398, 100, 14, 0)$, respectively. While it will come as no surprise that $\text{ImRoU}_{.75}$ discourages scene-level annotations, it is also worth noting that the standard algorithm uses them more than the Close Algorithm. As shown in the upcoming Section, the Close Algorithm improves upon the accuracy of the standard algorithm according to either metric. Thus, these results may indicate that improving approximation quality will disincentivize scene-level annotations naturally.

5.2 Scores

Table 1 provides a quantitative comparison between the Close- and standard algorithm.[4] While the Close Algorithm does better, its absolute accuracy remains poor. E.g., if the neuron and label masks have the same coverage, an IoU score of 0.1 means that more than 80% of the positive predictions made by the label masks are inaccurate.

Table 1. IoU and $\text{ImRoU}_{.75}$ scores of the standard vs. Close Algorithm for formula lengths 3 and 10. Each cell shows mean/median scores in % for the respective setting.

	IoU		$\text{ImRoU}_{.75}$	
	FL3	**FL10**	**FL3**	**FL10**
Standard	8.4/7.5	9.9/9.2	6.1/5.2	7.2/6.5
Close	9.3/8.4	11.3/10.4	7.3/6.4	8.9/7.9

We can identify at least two different hypotheses to explain this:[5]

[4] Results for individual neurons differ from those in [17] because we use downsampling to make annotations comparable (see Sect. 3.1), but the difference is mild and does not systematically skew in either direction. At formula length 10, the standard algorithm achieves a mean IoU of 0.099 (rounded to 3 decimal places) in both cases.

[5] In [17], Mu and Andreas find diminishing returns of predictive performance from raising the formula length beyond 10, which is evidence against the third hypothesis that neurons frequently combine more than ten human concepts.

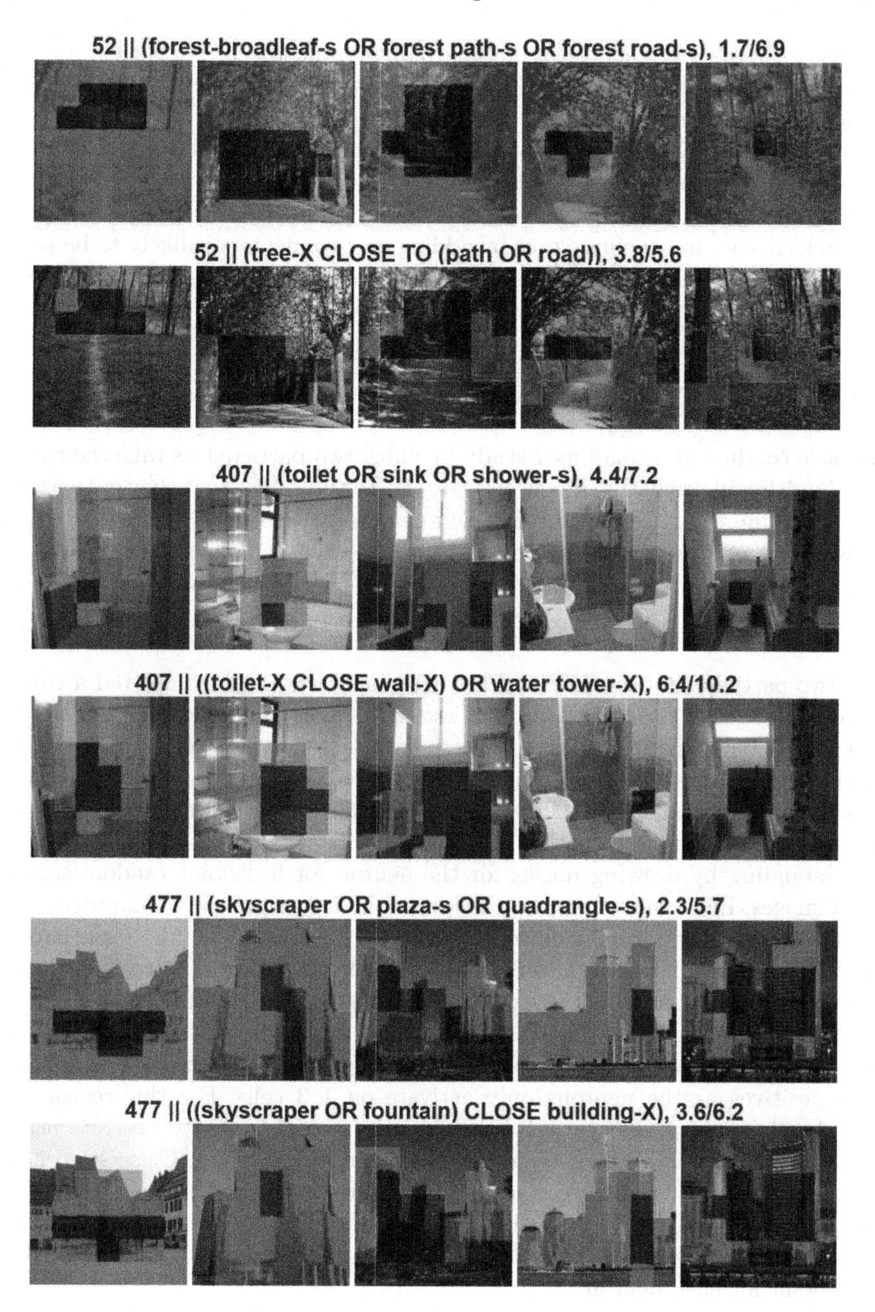

Fig. 3. Examples of masks found by the standard algorithm optimizing for IoU (first row) vs. masks found by the Close Algorithm optimizing for ImRoU$_{.75}$ (second row), at formula length 3. Here, the neuron masks are shown in red and the masks found by the algorithm in blue; intersected areas are purple. Scene-level concepts have the postfix -s. The numbers at the end of each line denote ImRoU$_{.75}$ and IoU scores in %. The three neurons shown here have been selected to be illustrative rather than at random. (Color figure online)

Hypothesis (1): neurons combine human concepts in ways that are not represented by AND, OR, AND NOT, CLOSE-TO, WITH, and EXPAND, but could be represented by different connectors.

Hypothesis (2): neurons activate on concepts that are not annotated in the Broden dataset, such as the edges of objects.

Differentiating between these hypotheses is important to guide future research as, e.g., improving scores by adding new connectors is likely to be possible insofar as problems are due to (1) rather than (2). However, the hypotheses are not mutually exclusive.

6 User Study

We have conducted a small user study in which two participants take the role of the algorithm in predicting image activations. To the extent that they outperform the algorithm, their descriptions for their neurons are evidence on the distinction between hypotheses (1) and (2) mentioned in Sect. 5.

6.1 Study Design

The two participants were selected among people who have completed a course in computer science or statistics and did well on a pilot study with a similar task. Each participant was given access to a large set of images and ground-truth neuron masks through a simple web-based application. The application allows hand-drawing masks and displays the $\text{ImRoU}_{.75}$ score averaged across those masks. After training for 40 min, participants were asked to test their understanding by drawing masks for the neuron for a disjoint random sample of 60 images. Each participant had access to the algorithmically computed label masks (but not the formula) for one of the two neurons. After the task, participants were asked to provide a brief description of their neuron (up to 2 sentences) and to describe interesting patterns they noticed (up to 10 sentences).

As mentioned in Sect. 4, neurons typically do not activate at all on over 95% of images. Furthermore, over 55% of the remaining images are still approximately false positives as the neurons only activate on 1–3 cells. For this reason, we considered it acceptable to only include images with nonzero activations, as otherwise, the task becomes tedious for the participants. The Close Algorithm was retrained on this altered data set, achieving mean and median $\text{ImRoU}_{.75}$ scores of .158 and .152, respectively (up from .089 and .079). Image subsets shown to annotators have been sampled uniformly and subsequently pruned to be disjoint for each neuron.

6.2 Results

Participants outperformed the algorithm on all four neurons. Table 2 shows the quantitative results; Table 3 contrasts the short description given by the human with the formulas found by the Close Algorithm. The participants completed neurons 353 and 329 first, respectively. Access to label masks had a slight negative correlation with relative performance (mean performance relative to the algorithm on neurons with/without access was 1.261 and 1.277, respectively).

Table 2. ImRoU$_{.75}$ scores achieved by human annotators ("Human Score") vs. the Close Algorithm ("CA Score") on the test set (60 images, uniformly sampled), where "Ratio" denotes $\frac{\text{Human Score}}{\text{CA Score}}$

Neuron	Human score	CA score	Ratio	Access
69	0.240	0.170	1.412	No
154	0.213	0.187	1.142	Yes
329	0.072	0.063	1.142	No
353	0.220	0.159	1.379	Yes

6.3 Discussion

The descriptions given by the participants include evidence for both hypotheses – in fact, this is already true for just neuron 69. "[T]he front left pocket of a pool table" could be algorithmically annotated using a new LEFT-OF connector, whereas "rectangles on the face of things" would require a new ground-truth annotation of shapes rather than objects. Other descriptions in the latter category include "potted plants in the forefront of images" (this would require differentiating between foreground and background), "the area where you can sit and reach a table", and "where you would sit on a bed". Conversely, "vertically hung clothes" could in principle be found algorithmically, though this would be difficult.

To get a qualitative sense of this task, consider the following response to the "describe interesting patterns" question for neuron 353:

> At first I thought the filter was just selecting tables and chairs (and that seems to be what the label mask is filtering on), but there was definitely a tendency to only pick the areas that were within reach of a surface, so a chair alone may not necessarily be highlighted, but a chair with an end table would definitely be, but just the area above the chair, and the surface within reach. For something like a couch or a bed, it would only highlight the side by the table. As the images were more complex, the area highlighted tended to be smaller, so a table with 12 chairs that filled the image would have a smaller proportion highlighted than a small table with a single chair. It also tended to select the side closest to the camera, I think, though I just realized that was what it was doing after the case, and it may not really be the case, but there was a bias to a specific side.

Insofar as these observations reflect true behaviors of the neuron, the response may shed further light on why the task remains challenging to do algorithmically. Determining that a neuron cares about a particular object may fail to

Table 3. Descriptions given by human annotators vs. formulas found by the Close Algorithm (trained on the subset of only images with nonzero activations)

N#	Human description	Close algorithm formula
69	Dark windows/doors/corridors/pits; windows or rectangles on the face of things (e.g. bulletin boards/lattices); the top/middle of the first cabinet on the right, the front left pocket of a pool table	(((door-X OR pool table OR house) AND NOT kitchen-s) OR drawer OR elevator door OR elevator OR telephone booth OR hovel OR arcade machine)
154	Snowy mountains, greenhouses (especially ceilings)	((((((mountain OR ice) CLOSE TO sky-X) OR greenhouse OR tent OR iceberg OR canopy) AND NOT greenhouse-indoor-s) OR truck) AND NOT wall-X)
329	Bedsheets, curtains, shelves, people's center of mass/chest area, rough stone structures including sculptures, pool tables, potted plants in the forefront of images	(bed-X OR rock OR person OR apparel OR sofa-X OR shirt-X OR armchair OR cliff OR viaduct-X OR aqueduct-X)
353	The area where you can sit and reach a table, and the area above that table, including chairs, couches, toilets, and where you would sit on a bed. Also, vertically hung clothes and occasionally organizers with books/clothes	(table-X OR cradle-X OR chair-X OR shirt-X OR apparel-X OR pillow-X OR jacket-X OR cushion-X OR back-X OR back pillow-X)

translate into a good score if the solution misses out on subtleties of this kind. The CLOSE-TO connector can plausibly help with this, but it often remains a crude approximation, e.g., it cannot determine whether a table is within reach of a chair since the spatial distance in the scene is not strictly proportional to the cell-based distance in the image. In fact, the Close Algorithm did not choose any non-logical connectors for neuron 353 other than EXPAND, proving that the CLOSE-TO connector is not helpful for predicting this particular neuron.

One may argue that the existing metrics are unfairly harsh as they fail to take proximity into account: if the label mask predicts an incorrect cell, it makes no difference whether the predicted cell is adjacent to a cluster of correct cells or in an entirely different image. Unfortunately, a metric that cares about distance is computationally expensive, making this problem difficult to address.

Due to the small sample size, these results do not permit a more quantitative analysis. However, future experiments including more participants may make this possible.

Finally, these results show that (a) it is possible for humans to outperform the algorithm on this task, and (b), there is a substantial similarity between human descriptions and algorithmic formulas.[6] This is worth pointing out as there is precedent of interpretability tools failing comparable "sanity checks" [1].

[6] For all four neurons, there has been an overlap between the set of objects picked by the algorithm and the human description. E.g., doors, mountains, beds, tables.

References

1. Adebayo, J., Gilmer, J., Muelly, M., Goodfellow, I., Hardt, M., Kim, B.: Sanity checks for saliency maps. In: Bengio, S., Wallach, H., Larochelle, H., Grauman, K., Cesa-Bianchi, N., Garnett, R. (eds.) Advances in Neural Information Processing Systems, vol. 31. Curran Associates, Inc. (2018). https://proceedings.neurips.cc/paper/2018/file/294a8ed24b1ad22ec2e7efea049b8737-Paper.pdf
2. Bach, S., Binder, A., Montavon, G., Klauschen, F., Müller, K.R., Samek, W.: On pixel-wise explanations for non-linear classifier decisions by layer-wise relevance propagation. PLOS ONE **10**(7), 1–46 (2015). https://doi.org/10.1371/journal.pone.0130140
3. Bau, A., Belinkov, Y., Sajjad, H., Durrani, N., Dalvi, F., Glass, J.: Identifying and controlling important neurons in neural machine translation. In: International Conference on Learning Representations (2019). https://openreview.net/forum?id=H1z-PsR5KX
4. Bau, D., Zhu, J.Y., Strobelt, H., Lapedriza, A., Zhou, B., Torralba, A.: Understanding the role of individual units in a deep neural network. In: Proceedings of the National Academy of Sciences (2020). https://doi.org/10.1073/pnas.1907375117. https://www.pnas.org/content/early/2020/08/31/1907375117
5. Camburu, O.M., Rocktäschel, T., Lukasiewicz, T., Blunsom, P.: e-SNLI: natural language inference with natural language explanations. In: Bengio, S., Wallach, H., Larochelle, H., Grauman, K., Cesa-Bianchi, N., Garnett, R. (eds.) Advances in Neural Information Processing Systems, vol. 31. Curran Associates, Inc. (2018). https://proceedings.neurips.cc/paper/2018/file/4c7a167bb329bd92580a99ce422d6fa6-Paper.pdf
6. Chen, C., Li, O., Tao, C., Barnett, A.J., Su, J., Rudin, C.: This Looks like That: Deep Learning for Interpretable Image Recognition. Curran Associates Inc., Red Hook (2019)
7. Chen, X., Mottaghi, R., Liu, X., Fidler, S., Urtasun, R., Yuille, A.: Detect what you can: detecting and representing objects using holistic models and body parts. In: Proceedings of the 2014 IEEE Conference on Computer Vision and Pattern Recognition, CVPR 2014, pp. 1979–1986. IEEE Computer Society, USA (2014). https://doi.org/10.1109/CVPR.2014.254
8. Dalvi, F., et al.: NeuroX: a toolkit for analyzing individual neurons in neural networks. In: Proceedings of the AAAI Conference on Artificial Intelligence, vol. 33, pp. 9851–9852, July 2019. https://doi.org/10.1609/aaai.v33i01.33019851
9. Durrani, N., Sajjad, H., Dalvi, F., Belinkov, Y.: Analyzing individual neurons in pre-trained language models. In: Proceedings of the 2020 Conference on Empirical Methods in Natural Language Processing (EMNLP), pp. 4865–4880. Association for Computational Linguistics, Online, November 2020. https://doi.org/10.18653/v1/2020.emnlp-main.395. https://aclanthology.org/2020.emnlp-main.395
10. Fong, R., Vedaldi, A.: Net2Vec: quantifying and explaining how concepts are encoded by filters in deep neural networks. In: Proceedings of the IEEE Conference on Computer Vision and Pattern Recognition (CVPR), June 2018
11. Fong, R.C., Vedaldi, A.: Interpretable explanations of black boxes by meaningful perturbation. In: 2017 IEEE International Conference on Computer Vision (ICCV), pp. 3449–3457 (2017). https://doi.org/10.1109/ICCV.2017.371
12. Gonzalez-Garcia, A., Modolo, D., Ferrari, V.: Do semantic parts emerge in convolutional neural networks? Int. J. Comput. Vision **126**, 476–494 (2017)

13. Hase, P., Zhang, S., Xie, H., Bansal, M.: Leakage-adjusted simulatability: can models generate non-trivial explanations of their behavior in natural language? In: Findings of the Association for Computational Linguistics: EMNLP 2020, pp. 4351–4367. Association for Computational Linguistics, Online, November 2020. https://doi.org/10.18653/v1/2020.findings-emnlp.390. https://aclanthology.org/2020.findings-emnlp.390
14. He, K., Zhang, X., Ren, S., Sun, J.: Deep residual learning for image recognition. In: 2016 IEEE Conference on Computer Vision and Pattern Recognition (CVPR), pp. 770–778 (2016). https://doi.org/10.1109/CVPR.2016.90
15. Kim, J., Rohrbach, A., Darrell, T., Canny, J., Akata, Z.: Textual explanations for self-driving vehicles. In: Ferrari, V., Hebert, M., Sminchisescu, C., Weiss, Y. (eds.) ECCV 2018. LNCS, vol. 11206, pp. 577–593. Springer, Cham (2018). https://doi.org/10.1007/978-3-030-01216-8_35
16. Lundberg, S.M., Lee, S.I.: A unified approach to interpreting model predictions. In: Guyon, I., et al. (eds.) Advances in Neural Information Processing Systems, vol. 30. Curran Associates, Inc. (2017). https://proceedings.neurips.cc/paper/2017/file/8a20a8621978632d76c43dfd28b67767-Paper.pdf
17. Mu, J., Andreas, J.: Compositional explanations of neurons. In: Larochelle, H., Ranzato, M., Hadsell, R., Balcan, M.F., Lin, H. (eds.) Advances in Neural Information Processing Systems, vol. 33, pp. 17153–17163. Curran Associates, Inc. (2020). https://proceedings.neurips.cc/paper/2020/file/c74956ffb38ba48ed6ce977af6727275-Paper.pdf
18. Olah, C., et al.: The building blocks of interpretability. Distill **3** (2018). https://doi.org/10.23915/distill.00010
19. Pruthi, G., Liu, F., Kale, S., Sundararajan, M.: Estimating training data influence by tracing gradient descent. In: Larochelle, H., Ranzato, M., Hadsell, R., Balcan, M.F., Lin, H. (eds.) Advances in Neural Information Processing Systems, vol. 33, pp. 19920–19930. Curran Associates, Inc. (2020). https://proceedings.neurips.cc/paper/2020/file/e6385d39ec9394f2f3a354d9d2b88eec-Paper.pdf
20. Ribeiro, M., Singh, S., Guestrin, C.: "Why should I trust you?": explaining the predictions of any classifier. In: Proceedings of the 2016 Conference of the North American Chapter of the Association for Computational Linguistics: Demonstrations, pp. 97–101. Association for Computational Linguistics, San Diego, June 2016. https://doi.org/10.18653/v1/N16-3020. https://aclanthology.org/N16-3020
21. Ribeiro, M.T., Singh, S., Guestrin, C.: Anchors: high-precision model-agnostic explanations. In: Proceedings of the AAAI Conference on Artificial Intelligence, vol. 32, no. 1, April 2018. https://ojs.aaai.org/index.php/AAAI/article/view/11491
22. Selvaraju, R.R., Cogswell, M., Das, A., Vedantam, R., Parikh, D., Batra, D.: Grad-CAM: visual explanations from deep networks via gradient-based localization. In: 2017 IEEE International Conference on Computer Vision (ICCV), pp. 618–626 (2017). https://doi.org/10.1109/ICCV.2017.74
23. Zhou, B., Bau, D., Oliva, A., Torralba, A.: Interpreting deep visual representations via network dissection. IEEE Trans. Pattern Anal. Mach. Intell. **41**(9), 2131–2145 (2019). https://doi.org/10.1109/TPAMI.2018.2858759
24. Zhou, B., Lapedriza, A., Khosla, A., Oliva, A., Torralba, A.: Places: a 10 million image database for scene recognition. IEEE Trans. Pattern Anal. Mach. Intell. **40**, 1452–1464 (2017)
25. Zhou, B., et al.: Semantic understanding of scenes through the ADE20K dataset. Int. J. Comput. Vision **127**(3), 302–321 (2018). https://doi.org/10.1007/s11263-018-1140-0

Visual Transformer-Based Models: A Survey

Xiaonan Huang[1], Ning Bi[1,2], and Jun Tan[1,2](✉)

[1] School of Mathematics and Computational Science, Sun Yat-Sen University, Guangzhou 510275, People's Republic of China
huangxn27@mail2.sysu.edu.cn, {mcsbn,mcstj}@mail.sysu.edu.cn
[2] Guangdong Province Key Laboratory of Computational Science, Sun Yat-Sen University, Guangzhou 510275, People's Republic of China

Abstract. After Transformer was first proposed by Vaswani et al. [1] in 2017, Transformer model has revolutionized and become the dominant methods in the field of natural language processing (NLP) which has achieved significant achievement. Transformer was first applied to Computer Vision fields in 2020, which called Vision Transformer (ViT) proposed by Dosovitskiy et al. ViT achieved state-of-the-art on image classification tasks at that time. In the past two years, the proliferation of Transformer in CV proves the effectiveness and breakthrough in various tasks including image classification, object detection, segmentation and low-level image tasks. In this paper, we focus on a review of Transformer-based models improved by ViT and Transformer backbones which is suitable for all kinds of image-level tasks, analyzing their improvement mechanisms, strengths and weaknesses. Furthermore, we briefly introduce the effective improvement of self-attention mechanism. In the end of this paper, some prospects have been put forward for future development on basis of the above Transformer-based models.

Keywords: Visual transformer · Self-attention · Deep learning

1 Introduction

Transformer is a Seq2Seq model proposed by Vaswani et al. [1] in 2017, which was first applied to machine translation tasks and achieved significant improvement. Subsequently, researchers applied Transformer to various tasks of natural language processing (NLP) for modeling and experimentation [2–6]. Devlin et al. [2] proposed a pre-training of deep bidirectional language representation model called BERT, which achieved an absolutely substantial improvement in 11 tasks in the NLP field surpassing the LSTM-based seq2seq methods. Then BERT flourishes the application of Transformer on various NLP tasks. The GPT-3 model proposed by Brown et al. [3] is a super large-scale autoregressive language model with 175 billion parameters and 45 TB of data for training, which is more than 10 times larger than all previous non-sparse model parameters. The model has demonstrated excellent modeling capabilities and made breakthroughs in many downstream tasks including translation, question-answering, and several tasks requiring on-the-fly reasoning or domain adaption.

M. El Yacoubi et al. (Eds.): ICPRAI 2022, LNCS 13364, pp. 295–305, 2022.
https://doi.org/10.1007/978-3-031-09282-4_25

In addition, many variants (RoBERTa [4], ALBERT [5], XLNet [6], etc.) based on the above results have also promoted the rooting and development of Transformer in NLP field. Nowadays, Transformer has become the most effective and preferred method on multiple NLP tasks. The general idea is to pre-train on a large corpus and then fine-tune parameters according to specific target data to achieve strong performance.

The prominent performance of Transformer on NLP tasks has attracted many researchers to try to apply it to computer vision tasks. On the one hand, many Transformer enhanced CNN models have been proposed. On the other hand, it is available to use a pure Transformer architecture on CV tasks. The first model of employing Transformer structure migration to the field of CV is ViT [7], which is the first time a pure Transformer model is proposed to an image classification task, demonstrating the versatility of Transformer without convolutions. Based on thoughts and room for improvement of Transformer, many Transformer-based models on CV tasks have been proposed, while some general Transformer backbones for dense prediction have been proposed as well. Thus, Transformer-based models are not just for image-level tasks such as image classification. They also bring breakthroughs in pix-level tasks such as object detection and segmentation tasks, low-level image processing, video understanding, and so on.

This paper will focus on an overview of the Transformer-based model for image-level tasks and general Transformer-based backbone. The rest of the paper is organized as follows: Sect. 2 introduces the original Transformer mechanism. Section 3 discusses the pioneering work of the first Transformer-based model for image classification—ViT. Section 4 is the central part of the paper, which introduces various Transformer-based ViT variants and general backbones. In Sect. 5, we summarize the models mentioned above and make a comparison among them.

2 Transformer

Transformer [1] is a multi-layered architecture with an encoder-decoder structure that discards recurrence and convolution entirely by using attention mechanisms and point-wise feed-forward networks. The overall architecture, Attention mechanism, and other vital components are described in the following sub-sections.

2.1 Transformer Architecture

As shown in Fig. 1(a), the encoder is composed of 6 identical layers stacked, containing two sub-layers of each layer. The first sub-layer is a multi-head self-attention mechanism, and the second is a position-wise fully connected feed-forward Neural network (FFNN), which is connected by residual connectors and a layer-normalization (LN) layer.

The decoder is also made up of 6 identical layers. In addition to the same two sub-layers as the encoder, the decoder inserts another multi-head attention that interacts with encoders and decoders. In this attention, key-value pairs K and V come from the output of encoders, and Q comes from decoders. The masking mechanism is added to ensure output for a specific position comes from the known output of the previous.

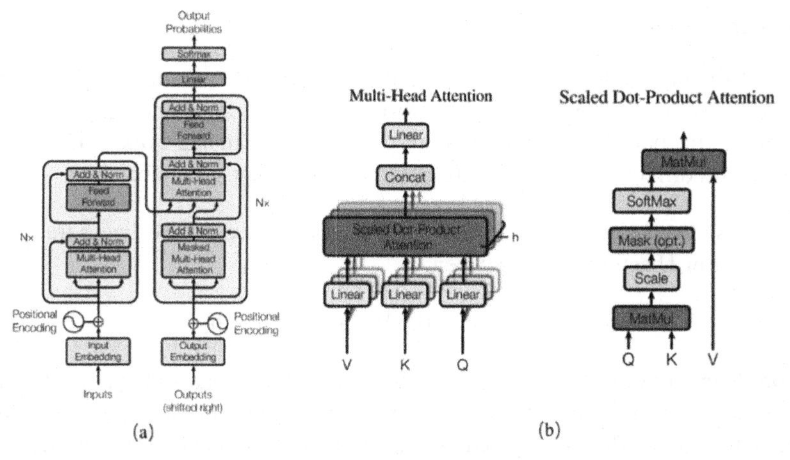

Fig. 1. (a) Transformer architecture. (b) (left) Scale dot-product attention. (Right) Multi-head attention consists of several attention layers running in parallel [1].

2.2 Attention

The idea of attention was proposed in the 1990s, whose principle is to assign weights to the segmented targets. Mnih et al. [9] embedded the attention mechanism into the RNN model for image classification tasks in 2014; Bahdanau et al. [10] applied this mechanism to machine translation tasks for the first time, the first time attempt on NLP tasks. On this basis, many computing methods of attention mechanism have been proposed, such as additive attention (AA) [11], MLP attention [12], and bilinear attention. In this Transformer block, Scaled Dot-Product Attention and Multi-head Attention are employed.

Scaled Dot-Product Attention. Compute the dot products of querys with all keys and apply a softmax function to obtain the weight on the values after dividing by $\sqrt{d_k}$:

$$\mathrm{Attention(Q, K, V)} = \mathrm{softmax}\left(\frac{\mathrm{QK^T}}{\sqrt{\mathrm{d_k}}}\right)\mathrm{V} \tag{1}$$

Multi-head Attention. Q, K, and V are linearly transformed and input into the zoom dot product attention. Each time it is a single-head attention process, and the parameters between the heads are not shared. Concatenate the attention output of h heads, and perform a linear transformation to get the result of multi-head attention. 'Multi-head attention allows the model to jointly attend to information from different representation subspaces at different positions.'

$$\mathrm{MultiHead(Q, K, V)} = \mathrm{Concat(head_1, \ldots, head_h)W^O}$$
$$\mathrm{head_i} = \mathrm{Attention(QW_i^Q, KW_i^K, VW_i^V)}$$

Where parallel heads $h = 8$, W_i represents the parameter matrix of projection.

2.3 Other Components

Positional Encoding. In order to capture the sequence information of the sequence without recursion and convolution, Transformer adds positional encoding to the input embedding at the bottom of the encoder and decoder stack. In this work, sine and cosine functions with different frequencies are used for absolute position encoding.

Position-wise Feed-Forward Networks. FFN is composed of two linear transformations with a ReLU activation in between:

$$\mathrm{FFN}(x) = \max(0, xW_1 + b_1)W_2 + b_2$$

Residual Connections. Borrowing from the ResNet [13], each sublayer of the Transformer encoder and decoder inserts a skip connection which adds the input to a nonlinear change in the input, effectively avoiding the problem of'gradient disappearance'.

3 ViT (Vision Transformer)

The vision Transformer model (ViT) proposed by Dosovitskiy et al. [7] in 2020 gets rid of the reliance of visual tasks on CNNs, and proves a pure Transformer architecture can also achieve outstanding performance on image classification tasks. In order to input a 1D sequence of token embeddings, 2D images of size H $\times$ W $\times$ C are split into patches and flattened into a 1D sequence as the input matrix of size N $\times$ (P^2C), where $N = HW/P^2$ is the number of patches. A learnable embedding like BERT's class token is added in front of the above sequence for image classification. The joint embeddings sever as input to the encoder. ViT utilizes only the standard transformer's encoder, whose output precedes an MLP head. In ViT, the image is divided into fixed-length 14 $\times$ 14 or 16 $\times$ 16 blocks (Fig. 2).

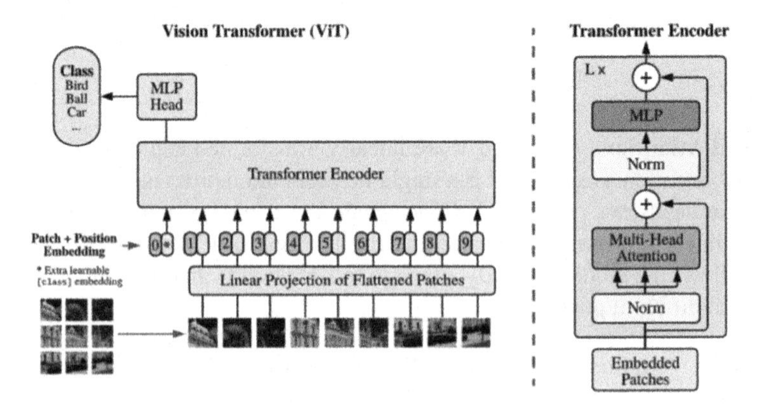

Fig. 2. ViT architecture and transformer encoder [7].

When pre-trained on large-scale image annotation datasets, ViT advanced on image classification tasks and achieved state-of-the-art. Significantly, the best performance of ViT reaches the accuracy of 88.55% on ImageNet, 90.72% on ImageNet-ReaL, 94.55% on CIFAR-100, and 77.63% on the VTAB suite of 19 tasks.

Though ViT, as a pioneering work of the Transformer-based architecture on CV, has opened up a new idea for improvement on image classification tasks, the limitation of ViT are pretty obvious: (1) This method is only ideal when pre-trained on large-scale datasets (such as JFT-300M [14]), otherwise the experimental accuracy is significantly lower than CNNs model. (2) Simple image segmentation and tokenization cannot model local structures such as edges and lines, resulting in low efficiency of training; (3) Computational complexity on ViT has a quadratic relationship with the size of images. The above disadvantages make the model quite limited, but this also lay the groundwork for subsequent improvements to ViT.

4 Transformer-Based Models

In this section, methods classified according to its applicable tasks. We divide them into two categories: ViT variants which can only be employed on image-level tasks (image classification), and general backbone which can be applied to both image-level and pixel-level tasks (including image classification, target detection and segmentation tasks) (Fig. 3).

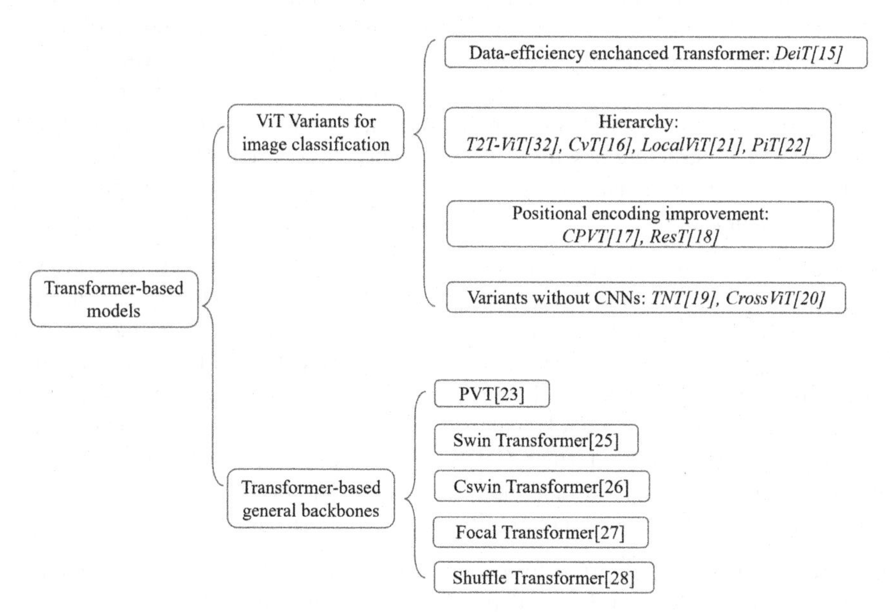

Fig. 3. Taxonomy of transformer-based models

4.1 ViT Variants for Image Classification

In the past two years, researchers have applied convolutional mechanisms or components into Transformer architecture, or simply optimized the internal structure of Transformer, which has greatly improved ViT. The following shows some research ideas of optimization: improve the utilization efficiency of training set through data enhancement, such as DeiT [15]; construct hierarchy architecture to enhance the richness of feature extraction, such as T2T-VIT [32], CvT [16], LocalViT [21]; improve positional encodings, such as CPVT [17] and ResT [18]; adjust Transformer structure, such as TNT [19], CrossViT [20].

Data-Efficiency Enhanced Transformer
DeiT. Without convolution operation, DeiT [15] introduced a token-based distillation method into ViT to improve training efficiency, so as to achieve a top-1 accuracy of 83.1% only using ImageNet data for training. In addition, a teacher-student strategy specific for Transformer is proposed in which the distillation token is inserted to enable students to learn from the teacher network through attention. The distillation strategy of DeiT is to add a distillation token at the end of the sequence of decoder blocks. Similar to the class token, it interacts with other patches through the self-attention layer to reproduce the teacher network prediction label. This token also learns through backpropagation.

Hierarchy
T2T-ViT. Based on ViT, T2T-VIT [32] proposes a token-to-token (T2T) Transformer architecture. A T2T block is inserted between Transformer layers to implement tokenization, which aggregates adjacent tokens into a single token recursively, with the length of tokens decreasing as the number of layers increases. This design achieves hierarchy for enhancing feature richness. On this basis, an efficient vision Transformer with a deep and narrow structure based on CNN thoughts is proposed. The disadvantage of VIT-T2T is that the concatenation of multiple tokens greatly increases the computational and storage complexity.

CvT. Wu et al. [16] proposed an architecture of convolutional vision Transformer (CvT) this year, integrating convolution into the two sublayers of Transformer architecture which achieves 87.7% top-1 accuracy in ImageNet. Convolution is introduced to ViT through two primary modifications: a convolutional Transformer block leveraging a convolutional projection replacing the linear projection and a hierarchy of Transformers containing a new convolutional token embedding. The design of CvT combines advantages of both CNNs and Transformer: CNNs enhances the local receptive field, achieves weight sharing and spatial subsampling; Transformer applications facilitate dynamic attention, global context fusion and excellent generalization capabilities.

LocalViT. Compared with Transformer, which aims at global feature extraction, LocalViT [21] introduces a 3×3 depthwise convolution in feed-forward networks and augments the locality mechanism for information exchange locally for Transformer.

PiT. Pooling-based Vision Transformer (PiT [22]) applies the pooling idea of CNNs to Transformer. Its method is to reshape 2D tokens into spatial tensors with spatial structure, pool the result through a deep-wise convolution, and reshape it into 2D tokens. PiT implements hierarchy like CvT and T2T-ViT.

Positional Encoding Improvement
CPVT, ResT. CPVT [17] proposed conditional positional encoding (CPE) based on convolution, which is an implicit encoding method that changes according to the size of input images. It replaces the pre-defined positional encoding used in ViT and enables Transformer to process input images of any size without interpolation preprocessing, thus enhancing the flexibility of the task. A new variable length position encoding is designed in ResT [18], which is constructed as spatial attention and can also process input images of arbitrary size without interpolation and fine-tuning.

Transformer Internal Architecture Adjustment Without CNNs Thought
TNT. The innovation point of TNT [19] (Transformer in Transformer) is to perform Transformer operations on each interior token based on ViT. An external Transformer module and an internal Transformer module are used to extract both image-level and pixel-level information.

CrossViT. In order to fully extract features of tokens, CrossViT [20] designed a dual-branch Transformer and a token fusion module based on interactive attention. The branch encoders of two Transformers are independent of each other. Images are divided into tokens of different sizes and input into the encoder branches of two Transformers respectively. The output results are fused with block information through a token fusion module based on interactive attention, so as to achieve the purpose of obtaining more image features. It is worth noting that interactive attention block is designed to combine the class token from one branch as query with a sequence of tokens in the other branch, which is linear in terms of computation and memory.

4.2 Transformer-Based General Backbone

The ViT variants in Sect. 4.1 optimize ViT with the goal of advancing image classification tasks, and creatively proposes multiple models with less computational complexity and richer feature extraction that do not require large data pre-training. In this section, generic backbones that can be applied to both image-level and pixel-level tasks are introduced, with improvements to both the Transformer architecture and attention mechanism.

PVT [23], as a convolution-free backbone, introduces a sinking pyramid structure and combines it with Transformer decoders, opening the door for Transformer backbone and decoder to combine for high-resolution downstream tasks. Swin Transformer [25] put forward the idea of shifted windows for the first time, using window attention to realize connection between Windows and realize the linear computational complexity with respect to image size. In the past six months, based on the window idea proposed by Swin Transformer, many general backbones for image classification, object detection and segmentation tasks have been proposed, such as Cswin Transformer [26], Focal Transformer [27], Shuffle Transformer [28], Twins Transformer [29] and so on. These methods are all described below.

PVT. PVT [23] draws on the pyramid idea of CNNs to construct a hierarchical pure Transformer architecture with a shrinking feature pyramid, forming multi-scale feature maps for dense prediction tasks. Initially, images are divided into 4 * 4 fine-grained image patches. With the network deepening, the number of tokens and calculation decreases. The resolution of feature map also decreases with the deepening of network and the number of channels increases.

In this method, Spatial reduced attention (SRA) is used to replace the multi-head attention layer (MHA). The proposed global sub-sampling attention is calculated with the same size of Q, the width and height of K and V are reduced to 1/R so that the model is lightweight to reduce the consumption of computation and memory. PVTv2 [24] further improves the above architecture: convolution is introduced to extract local continuous features; Positional encoding is extracted locally by embedding overlapping blocks with zero padding. Pooling layers and linear complexity are also designed. The improved PVT performs even better than Swin Transformer on specific tasks.

Swin Transformer. A Swin Transformer [25] block consists of a window multi-head attention (WMSA) or shifting window multi-head attention (SW-MSA) with two layers of MLPs. Swin Transformer realizes window amplification by down-sampling of image, forming hierarchical pyramid structure, scaling down the original attention to window scale, ensuring good local perception. By shifting windows to carry on interaction between windows. As the network deepens, perception field increases, so that local perception and global perception are closely combined.

Swin Transformer fundamentally solves the drawbacks of ViT complexity, realizes the linearization of computational complexity, and achieves state-of-the-art on multiple tasks. The proposal of attention in windows has inspired other researchers to further improve window attention, as shown in Cswin Transformer and Focal Transformer as follows.

Cswin Transformer. Drawing lessons from Swin Transformer [25], Cswin Transformer [26] introduces a Cross-Shaped Window self-attention mechanism for computing self-attention in the horizontal and vertical stripes in parallel that form a cross-shaped window, with each stripe obtained by splitting the input feature into stripes of equal width. Locally-enhanced positional encoding (LePE) is proposed as well, which naturally supports arbitrary image resolutions, and is effectively friendly for downstream tasks.

Focal Transformer. Focal self-attention [27] called FSA is proposed to conduct differentiated granularity processing near and far from target tokens: small-size window is applied near Query patch to achieve fine granularity, while large-size window is applied far away to achieve coarse granularity. The information of multiple tokens is carried out sub-windows pooling and aggregation, which makes receptive field guaranteed and computation reduced.

Shuffle Transformer [28]. By combining ShuffleNet [33] idea of replacement with Transformer, Huang proposed spatial replacement to build long-distance cross-window relations, and the neighbor window connection module was used to enhance the connectivity between neighbor Windows. Then, we integrate spatial permutation with neighbor window connections to construct Shuffle Transformer Block to build rich cross-window connections.

5 Discussions and Conclusions

The basic structure of Transformer, the first Transformer method ViT applied to CV and a series of variants are introduced in this paper. For image classification tasks, data enhancement can reduce the pre-training process and improve the training efficiency. A series of seep hierarchical structures similar to CNNs are designed to effectively enhance feature richness. The improvement of positional coding can better apply the position information of pictures to Transformer-based models. The application of t attention operations within blocks can reduce computational complexity.

For all image-level tasks including image classification, object detection and segmentation, general backbones design based on Transformer applies Transformer to a variety of image tasks. The window-wised idea is put forward, and self-attention is calculated inside the divided window, so that the computational complexity is linearly correlated with the image size. Many self-attention methods have also been proposed to reduce complexity and achieve global and local information interaction.

Acknowledgments. This work was supported by Guangdong Province Key Laboratory of Computational Science at the Sun Yat-sen University (2020B1212060032), the National Natural Science Foundation of China (Grant no. 11971491, 11471012).

References

1. Vaswani, A., et al.: Attention is all you need. In: Advances in Neural Information Processing Systems, pp. 5998–6008 (2017)
2. Devlin, J., Chang, M.W., Lee, K., Toutanova, K.: BERT: pre-training of deep bidirectional transformers for language understanding (2018). arXiv preprint arXiv:1810.04805
3. Brown, T.B., et al.: Language models are few-shot learners (2020). arXiv preprint arXiv:2005.14165
4. Liu, Y., et al.: Roberta: a robustly optimized BERT pretraining approach (2019). arXiv preprint arXiv:1907.11692
5. Lan, Z., Chen, M., Goodman, S., Gimpel, K., Sharma, P., Soricut, R.: Albert: a lite bert for self-supervised learning of language representations (2019). arXiv preprint arXiv:1909.11942
6. Yang, Z., Dai, Z., Yang, Y., Carbonell, J., Salakhutdinov, R.R., Le, Q.V.: XLNet: generalized autoregressive pretraining for language understanding. In: Advances in Neural Information Processing Systems, vol. 32 (2019)
7. Dosovitskiy, A., et al.: An image is worth 16x16 words: transformers for image recognition at scale (2020). arXiv preprint arXiv:2010.11929
8. Posner, M.I.: Attention: the mechanisms of consciousness. Proc. Natl. Acad. Sci. **91**(16), 7398–7403 (1994)
9. Mnih, V., Heess, N., Graves, A.: Recurrent models of visual attention. In: Advances in Neural Information Processing Systems, pp. 2204–2212 (2014)

10. Bahdanau, D., Cho, K., Bengio, Y.: Neural machine translation by jointly learning to align and translate (2014). arXiv preprint arXiv:1409.0473
11. Zheng, G., Mukherjee, S., Dong, X.L., Li, F.: OpenTag: open attribute value extraction from product profiles. In: Proceedings of the 24th ACM SIGKDD International Conference on Knowledge Discovery & Data Mining, pp. 1049–1058, July 2018
12. Yang, Z., Yang, D., Dyer, C., He, X., Smola, A., Hovy, E.: Hierarchical attention networks for document classification. In: Proceedings of the 2016 Conference of the North American Chapter of the Association for Computational Linguistics: Human Language Technologies, pp. 1480–1489, June 2016
13. He, K., Zhang, X., Ren, S., Sun, J.: Deep residual learning for image recognition. In: Proceedings of the IEEE Conference on Computer Vision and Pattern Recognition, pp. 770–778 (2016)
14. Sun, C., Shrivastava, A., Singh, S., Gupta, A.: Revisiting unreasonable effectiveness of data in deep learning era. In: Proceedings of the IEEE International Conference on Computer Vision, pp. 843–852 (2017)
15. Touvron, H., Cord, M., Douze, M., Massa, F., Sablayrolles, A., Jégou, H.: Training data-efficient image transformers & distillation through attention. In: International Conference on Machine Learning, pp. 10347–10357. PMLR, July 2021
16. Wu, H., et al.: CvT: Introducing convolutions to vision transformers (2021). arXiv preprint arXiv:2103.15808
17. Chu, X., Zhang, B., Tian, Z., Wei, X., Xia, H.: Do we really need explicit position encodings for vision transformers?. arXiv e-prints, arXiv-2102 (2021)
18. Zhang, Q., Yang, Y.:. ResT: an efficient transformer for visual recognition (2021). arXiv preprint arXiv:2105.13677
19. Han, K., Xiao, A., Wu, E., Guo, J., Xu, C., Wang, Y.: Transformer in transformer (2021). arXiv preprint arXiv:2103.00112
20. Chen, C.F., Fan, Q., Panda, R.: CrossViT: cross-attention multi-scale vision transformer for image classification (2021). arXiv preprint arXiv:2103.14899
21. Li, Y., Zhang, K., Cao, J., Timofte, R., Van Gool, L.: LocalViT: bringing locality to vision transformers (2021). arXiv preprint arXiv:2104.05707
22. Heo, B., Yun, S., Han, D., Chun, S., Choe, J., Oh, S.J.: Rethinking spatial dimensions of vision transformers (2021). arXiv preprint arXiv:2103.16302
23. Wang, W., et al.: Pyramid vision transformer: a versatile backbone for dense prediction without convolutions. arXiv e-prints, arXiv-2102 (2021)
24. Wang, W., et al.: PVTv2: improved baselines with pyramid vision transformer (2021). arXiv preprint arXiv:2106.13797
25. Liu, Z., et al.: Swin transformer: hierarchical vision transformer using shifted windows (2021). arXiv preprint arXiv:2103.14030
26. Dong, X., et al.: CSWin transformer: a general vision transformer backbone with cross-shaped windows (2021). arXiv preprint arXiv:2107.00652
27. Yang, J., et al.: Focal self-attention for local-global interactions in vision transformers (2021). arXiv preprint arXiv:2107.00641
28. Huang, Z., Ben, Y., Luo, G., Cheng, P., Yu, G., Fu, B.: Shuffle transformer: rethinking spatial shuffle for vision transformer (2021). arXiv preprint arXiv:2106.03650
29. Chu, X., et al.: Twins: revisiting the design of spatial attention in vision transformers. In: Thirty-Fifth Conference on Neural Information Processing Systems, May 2021
30. Lin, T.Y., Goyal, P., Girshick, R., He, K., Dollár, P.: Focal loss for dense object detection. In: Proceedings of the IEEE International Conference on Computer Vision, pp. 2980–2988 (2017)
31. He, K., Gkioxari, G., Dollár, P., Girshick, R.: Mask R-CNN. In: Proceedings of the IEEE International Conference on Computer Vision, pp. 2961–2969 (2017)

32. Yuan, L., et al.: Tokens-to-token ViT: training vision transformers from scratch on ImageNet (2021). arXiv preprint arXiv:2101.11986
33. Zhang, X., Zhou, X., Lin, M., Sun, J.: ShuffleNet: an extremely efficient convolutional neural network for mobile devices. In: Proceedings of the IEEE Conference on Computer Vision and Pattern Recognition, pp. 6848–6856 (2018)

Stochastic Pairing for Contrastive Anomaly Detection on Time Series

Guillaume Chambaret[1,3(✉)], Laure Berti-Equille[2], Frédéric Bouchara[3], Emmanuel Bruno[3], Vincent Martin[1], and Fabien Chaillan[1]

[1] Naval Group, 199 av. P. G. de Gennes, Ollioules, France
[2] ESPACE-DEV, IRD, Montpellier, France
[3] LIS UMR 7020 CNRS/AMU/UTLN, Université de Toulon, Toulon, France
guillaume.chambaret@lis-lab.fr

Abstract. Anomaly detection for predictive maintenance is a significant concern for industry. Unanticipated failures cause high costs for experts involved in maintenance policy. Traditional reconstruction-based anomaly detection methods perform well on multivariate time series but they do not consider the diversity of samples in the training dataset. An abrupt change of operating conditions, which is labeled as anomaly by experts, is often not detected due to the lack of sample diversity. Besides, obtaining large volumes of labeled training data is cumbersome and sometimes impossible in practice, whereas large amounts of unlabelled data are available and could be used by unsupervised learning techniques. In this paper, we apply the principles of contrastive learning and augmentation in a self supervised way to improve feature representation of multivariate time series. We model a large variety of operating conditions with an innovative distance based stochastic method to prepare an anomaly detection downstream task. Our approach is tested on NASA SMAP/MSL public dataset and shows good performance close to the state-of-the-art anomaly detection methods.

Keywords: Time series regression · Augmentation · Contrastive learning · Anomaly detection

1 Introduction

Industry devices such as ships, spacecrafts, engines are typically monitored from sensor-based multivariate time series, for which anomaly detection is critical for service quality management of the organization owning the devices. However, due to complex temporal dependence and multiplicity of examples, it is often though to model diversity of operational modes. For aerospace complex systems, monitoring is frequently designed on several telemetry channels (Fig. 1) in order to capture various behaviours. Due to the limited number of samples, domain experts determine labels on few portions of time series which appear to be abnormal. The drawback of this approach is generally the lack of data and the lack of labels characterizing operational modes and/or failure occurrences. In particular

M. El Yacoubi et al. (Eds.): ICPRAI 2022, LNCS 13364, pp. 306–317, 2022.
https://doi.org/10.1007/978-3-031-09282-4_26

automated methods have to deal with too few samples relative to the diversity of pre-existing normal operating conditions. The emergence of machine learning techniques allowed the design of data-driven systems where labels entered by human experts are mainly used to validate models trained on normal samples to detect deviations. These labels are useful to anticipate failure but they do not necessarily provide information about operational modes of the system. Frequent contributions propose to split multivariate time series into windows of fixed length in order to reconstruct them with autoencoding techniques. The gap of reconstruction is then interpreted as an anomaly score where peeks correspond to potential anomalies. Our experiments are conducted on NASA Soil Moisture Active Passive (SMAP) and Mars Science Laboratory (MSL) datasets, proposed by [6], containing respectively 55 and 27 channels (Fig. 1). Full data from each channel is split into two sets (train/test). Test series contain labeled anomaly segments used to compute performance metrics. In this paper, we propose the following contributions: (1) an innovative augmentation based method to design tensor pairs for contrastive learning on time series, (2) an application of self supervised contrastive learning to multivariate time series anomaly detection, and (3) an exploration of associated settings impact on anomaly detection performance.

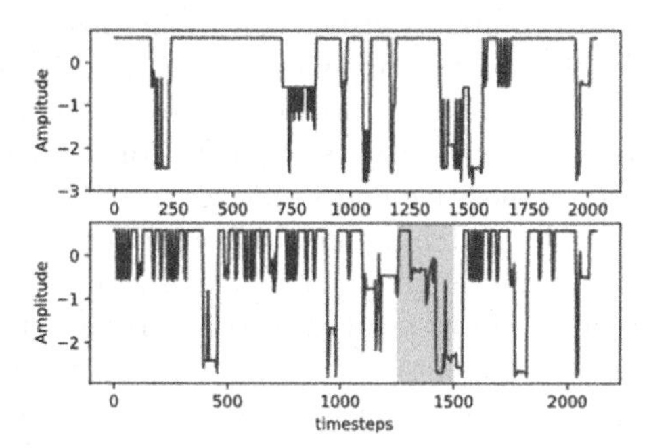

Fig. 1. Example of normalized feature measured for a single spacecraft channel with normal operating conditions (top) versus testing (bottom with an highlighted anomaly).

2 Related Works

2.1 Reconstruction Based Time Series Anomaly Detection

Anomaly detection is the task of detecting unseen events in data. Therefore, different unsupervised methods [2] have been proposed including reconstruction-based methods. These ones aim to compare the distance between a real input (time window) and its prediction after regression on relative features. Increasingly frequent use of autoencoders made these methods more popular in the last few years. We can mention Deep Autoencoding Gaussian Mixture Model (DAGMM) [5] which models the density distribution of series by connecting an encoder to a gaussian mixture model. Variational autoencoders, which learn a prior distribution of data, are gradually replacing traditional recurrent autoencoders. In that way, Su et al. [1] proposed a stochastic recurrent neural network to learn robust multivariate time series representations with stochastic variable connections and a normalizing flow inference. The hierarchical variational autoencoder of Li et al. [4] achieves a blend of temporal dependencies and intermetric dependencies. The latter one corresponds to non linear relationships between features for a given period and modelled by embeddings. Generative models are also employed for unsupervised anomaly detection. For example, [24] proposed Tad-GAN, a generative adversarial network with cycle consistency loss. This one measures time series reconstruction and is associated to a critic which measures the quality of mapping in latent space.

2.2 Self Supervised Contrastive Learning

Contrastive learning is a recent technique popularized by computer vision community to learn an embedding space in which similar samples are close to each other while dissimilar ones are far apart. One common way to proceed is by using siamese networks [14] consisting of two encoders sharing weights and trained with a contrastive loss. In computer vision, contrastive loss [12] repulses different images (negative pairs) while attracting views of the same image (positive pairs). Recently, Chen et al. [11] proposed a projection network trick that maps representations to the space where the loss is applied. Contrastive learning assumes the possibility of designing positive and negative pairs. For image classification, this task is often realized by matching images from different classes to build negative pairs. In the meantime, augmented images by common techniques (e.g., rotating, flipping, burring) are associated to their original images to form positive pairs. When labels are missing or unavailable, positive/negative pairs could be obtained with other techniques in order to learn representations in a self-supervised approach [11]. Self-supervision task could be realized by augmenting the samples to still obtain positive pairs while negative pairs are designed by another techniques. For example, semantic information about the datasets have been successfully used for patient biosignals. In that way, negative pairs are built by mixing samples from different individuals [15]. We can also mention the use of unrelated examples for audio signals which do not share same contexts [16].

2.3 Time Series Augmentation

Augmenting time series dataset is frequently used to reduce generalization error in classification tasks. Whereas in image dataset, the meaning is kept by rotating, flipping or transforming the images, augmenting time series requires some minimal assumptions. For aperiodic signals, like spacecraft multivariate time series, traditional signal processing methods can be employed. For example, jittering (adding noise), scaling, magnitude or time warping [10,17] can be used without loss of meaning. Recently, specific augmentation techniques to mix existing samples (pattern mixing) rather than applying "naïve" operators have been proposed to create new training examples by computing DTW [19] or shape-DTW [20] distances between real samples. Forestier et al. [9] proposed a method to create new samples based on random multivariate time series selection with DTW comparisons. More recently, Iwana et al. [3] introduced a guided DTW-warping to select samples with more diversity. Finally, we can cite generative models as recurrent conditional GAN [18]. The last one generates new samples conserving class property of different tensors.

3 Our Approach

In this paper, we propose to learn multivariate time series representations for unsupervised anomaly detection. First, as it is commonly done in unsupervised anomaly detection, we split training time series data into windows of fixed length (unchanged for every considered series). Then, we design pairs of windows by random draws on the set formed by the whole windows. In order to get so-called negative pairs, we use a distance-based approach to select dissimilar samples. The so-called positive pairs are then built with augmentation techniques. Once these operations achieved, a siamese network, composed of two encoders, is trained to learn a joint representation for pairs of windows. The network is completed by the trick proposed by Chen et al. [11]. In other words, a simple projection network maps the embeddings to the final L2-normalized low dimensional representation where the contrastive loss is applied. Finally, for detection process, an anomaly score is inferred from embedding vectors computed for testing windows. The best threshold is determined by the searching method proposed by [1] where an anomaly segment is correctly detected if at least one threshold crossing occurs.

3.1 Preprocessing and Stochastic Pairing

For each multivariate time series (training data), we first apply a z-score scaling. This is then applied to corresponding test series. At first sight, we have no expert knowledge to determine which portion belongs to which operating mode. Note that different conditions can appear multiple times across multiple time segments. Therefore, considering multiple time windows can naively capture operating patterns. The samples are simply obtained by splitting the complete series into fixed-size windows. This task produces a dataset D where we can assume variable operating conditions depending on the position of the window along the global time series. We proceed then to pairing (Fig. 2). We split equally and randomly D into 2 datasets D_1, D_2 such that $D_1 \sqcup D_2 = D$. The first one is used for reality modelling. The second one is used to make random batch of windows. Given a window W extracted from D_1, we first apply an augmentation operator to obtain another window W', (W, W') forms a positive pair. To get a negative pair, we extract a batch $B = (W_1, ..W_p)$ from D_2 and we choose then the most dissimilar windows of B related to W. Similarity is determined by computing Shape-DTW distance d between W and the observed windows of B.

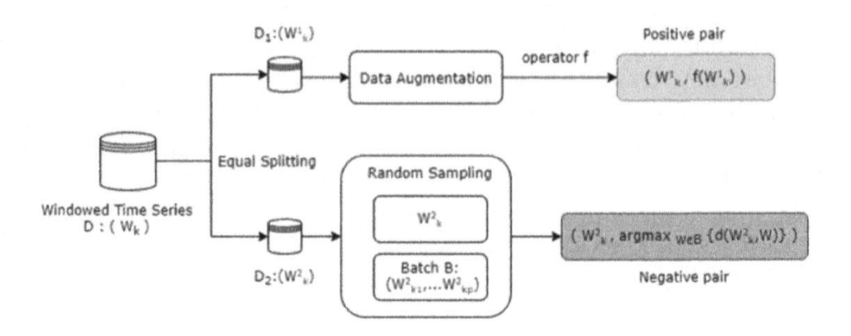

Fig. 2. Pairing process on multivariate time series.

3.2 Shape-Dynamic Time Warping

Shape-DTW is a variation of classic Dynamic Time Warping (DTW) [19] proposed by Zhao et al. [20]. It improves distance measure for time series with shape descriptors rather than traditional alignments. Consider two multivariate time series $r = (r_1,\ldots,r_i,\ldots,r_I)$ and $s = (s_1,\ldots,s_i,\ldots,s_J)$ with sequence lengths I and J, respectively. DTW seeks for that minimizes Euclidean distance between aligned series. To proceed, DTW tests different warping in order to get the best alignment which minimizes global cost under constraints with dynamic programming. Solving DTW implies to compute a given cumulative sum matrix D using Eq. 1:

$$D(i,j) = C\left(r_i, s_j\right) + \min_{(i',j') \in \{(i,j-1),(i-1,j),(i-1,j-1)\}} D\left(i', j'\right) \tag{1}$$

where $D(i,j)$ refers to cumulative sum of i-th and j-th elements, and $\mathrm{C}(r_i, s_j)$ is defined as the local distance between r_i and s_j. For next steps, as is often the case, Euclidean distance will be used as cost function for DTW computations with constant warping window equal to sample length. Finally, global distance for $r = (r_1,\ldots,r_i,\ldots,r_I)$, and $s = (s_1,\ldots,s_i,\ldots,s_J)$ is defined as $D(I,J)$. To compute shape-DTW, element-wise matching is replaced by shape descriptors matching. For a series r, a descriptor d at position i is defined as an extracted sub-series of r with length $l : d_{r_i} = \left(r_{i-\lceil \frac{1}{2}l \rceil},\ldots,r_i,\ldots,r_{i+\lfloor \frac{1}{2}l \rfloor}\right)^{\top}$. To complete descriptors located at the beginning of r (respectively at the end), zero-padding is applied to the left of the sub-series (respectively to the right). Then, series (r,s) are replaced by series of descriptors $((d_{r_0},\ldots,d_{r_I}),(d_{s_0},\ldots,d_{s_J}))$ in the previous DTW computation (Eq. 1). This method which tends to align descriptors instead of points is commonly used to cope with misalignment of time series. This is the case in particular when specific peeks might induce a high DTW distance measurement (Fig. 3). Due to processing local time series (windows) and improper alignments, we choose this distance rather than the classic DTW.

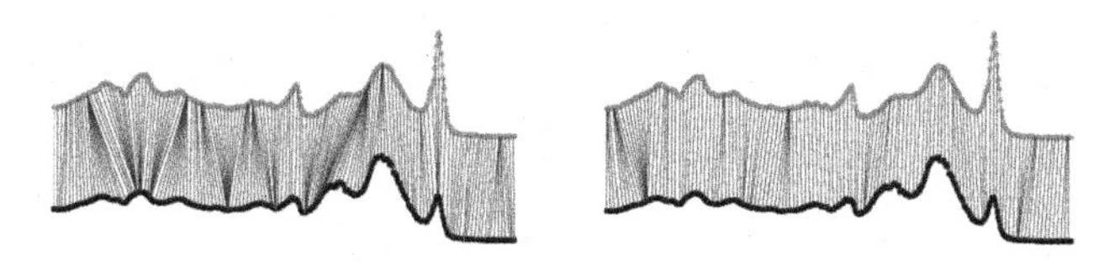

Fig. 3. DTW and Shape-DTW (right) alignments where cost increase due to curve pinchs is mitigated by the use of descriptors [20].

3.3 Augmentation Methods

To augment windows of the first partitioned dataset D_1 and then form positive pairs (Fig. 2), we use the following operators:

- **Identity**: the positive pair is obtained by duplication of the given window;
- **Noising**: random Gaussian noise is added to each feature with mean $\mu = 0$ and standard deviation $\sigma = 0.05$;
- **Magnitude Scaling**: each feature is summed to a scalar derived from a Gaussian distribution with mean $\mu = 1$ and standard deviation $\sigma = 0.1$;
- **Time Warping**: Time Warping based on a random smooth warping curve generated with cubic spline with 4 knots at random magnitudes with $\mu = 1$ and $\sigma = 0.2$;
- **Dual Averaging**: averaging the window with another one based on shape DTW computation on a batch from the first partition (as it is done for negative pairs).

Note that, above parameters of different methods have been obtained with tuning in a range magnitude proposed proposed by Um et al. [17]. In order to enrich previous datasets by various methods, a weighted combination of previous methods is tested with random weights such that the sum of weights equals 1. We call it mixed augmentation.

3.4 Learning Architecture

In this section, we detail in Fig. 4 the architecture we propose to encode features. The siamese network consists of two encoding pipelines (one by window extracted from a given pair). Encoding networks are the same for each ones and share their weights. As it is suggested by [11], the outputs of pipelines are linked to a simple projection network where the contrastive loss is applied. Projection network consists in a single layer perceptron of size 32 which will be unchanged for follow-up applications.

As processing time series implies naturally recurrent aspects, we propose to use double stacked long-short term memory layers [22] (LSTM) with downstream fully connected (FC) layers as a first way to encode pairs. The second proposed encoder is a VGG-like network [23] which consists of 2 stacked monodimensional convolutional layers. Parameters for each encoder are given below:

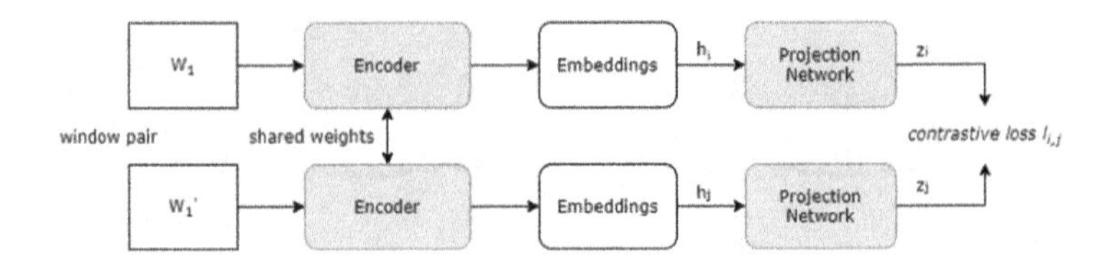

Fig. 4. Siamese architecture with projection networks.

- **Recurrent Encoder**: LTSM [128]- LSTM [64]-FC [64]. *Tanh* activation. Dropout [0.1] after recurrent layers. Embedding (output) dimension: 64.
- **Convolutional Encoder**: 2 * [Conv1D [filters: 64, kernel size: 3 strides: 1]- MaxPooling1D]- 2 * [Conv1D [filters: 32, kernel size: 3 strides: 1]- MaxPooling1D]- FC[1024]- FC[128]. ReLu activation. Dropout [0.3] after FC layers. Embedding (output) dimension: 128.

Selected loss for training is the Normalized Temperature-scaled Cross Entropy (NT-Xent) [11] defined in Eq. 2:

$$\mathrm{l}_{i,j} = -\log \frac{\exp\left(sim\left(\mathbf{z}_i, \mathbf{z}_j\right)/\tau\right)}{\sum_{k=1}^{2N} 1_{[k \neq i]} \exp\left(sim\left(\mathbf{z}_i, \mathbf{z}_k\right)/\tau\right)} \tag{2}$$

where sim represents the cosine similarity between input vectors. τ is the temperature parameter (equals to 1 for this contribution) and N is the batch size.

3.5 Anomaly Score

After training the siamese network, we aim to determine an anomaly score (AS) related to testing windows and based on embedding representation. The key idea is to consider the separating property of contrastive learning which tends to take away abnormal windows from an averaging pattern (operating mode for industrial time series). In order to achieve this, we compute the Frobenius distance between embeddings of a given testing window W_{test} and the mean representations of training windows in the latent space. So, considering the encoded vector $E(W_{test})$, the anomaly score is defined as follows (Eq. 3):

$$AS\left(W_{test}\right) = \left\| E\left(W_{test}\right) - \overline{\left\{E\left(W_{training}\right)\right\}} \right\|_2 \tag{3}$$

For convenience, mean representation of training windows is computed once before anomaly score processing. To limit noise and extreme peeks, exponential weighted moving average smoothing is applied to the computed score (Eq. 3).

3.6 Detection Method

Anomalies are often stretched on time-segments which are longer than the length of sliding windows. We propose to use the point-adjust detection already employed by [1,4]. This approach allocates a label to every observed window. If it contains at least one point of anomaly segment, label will be 1, 0 otherwise. The goal is now to find the best threshold for the given metrics (Eq. 4):

$$Precision = \frac{TP}{TP + FP}, \; Recall = \frac{TP}{TP + FN} \quad F_1 = 2\frac{Precision \cdot Recall}{Precision + Recall} \tag{4}$$

A high precision means that the model will limit the number of false positive windows. For sensitive systems with low risk-tolerance, precision will be the first criterion of the detector. High recall is associated to a low number of undetected true anomalies. Depending on the situation, a prioritization decision has to be formulated to privilege a metric. F1 score is a popular trade-off between previous metrics to evaluate the quality of detection. It can be used without industrial assumptions and it is often proposed as single metric to compare detection methods. To evaluate our approach, we use a fixed threshold. If anomaly score is higher than this one on a single point, the window containing the point will be detected as anomaly window. In other words, its predicted label will be 1. On the contrary, windows below the threshold will have a predicted label equals to 0. To find the optimal threshold, we use the F_1 score as a criterion. We adjust the value of the threshold by a grid search procedure to select the threshold corresponding to the best F_1 value.

4 Experiments on Public Datasets

Experiments are conducted on MSL and SMAP public datasets [6]. Testing series are labelled with anomaly segments. For every experiment run, we suppose a fixed length for each window of 32. The mixed augmentation (combination of each augmentation method) is applied for positive pairing with best weights determined by random search: (0.36, 0.28, 0.11, 0.04, 0.21). Batch size for negative pairing will be initially fixed to 15 and explored in next section. For training process, Adam optimizer [7] is used to train the model. Each model is trained for 250 epochs with a learning rate $5 \times 10e{-4}$. To control the loss variation, train/validation partition of ratio 80/20 is applied. To reduce the overall training time, an early stopping is applied when the validation loss did not decrease for more than 15 epochs. Experiments are conducted with tensorflow [8] (v 2.4.1) and CUDA-GPU acceleration on Nvidia Quadro RTX 5000 device. We give results compared to other unsupervised methods proposed in literature in Table 1. LSTM encoding achieves better performance than VGG-encoder for both datasets. As we can observe, autoencoding techniques [1] remain the most adapted models but they have to process the complete dataset rather than trying to model data with a given fraction as we made with augmented pairs. These methods perform the best possible reconstruction regardless of the existence of anomalies in the input window. Our method achieves comparable performance and can be adapted to limited samples augmented to obtain as many pairs as needed for training. Although our approach is limited to anomalies based on

Table 1. SMAP/MSL results for the proposed encoders compared to state-of-the-art.

Method	SMAP			MSL		
	P	R	F1	P	R	F1
TadGAN [24]	0.523	0.835	0.643	0.490	0.694	0.574
MRONet [21]	0.487	0.833	0.615	0.521	0.806	0.632
Hundman et al. [6]	0.855	0.835	0.844	0.926	0.694	0.793
OmniAnomaly [1]	0.758	0.974	0.852	0.914	0.888	0.900
VGG-contrastive	0.708	0.852	0.763	0.845	0.903	0.869
LSTM-contrastive	0.751	0.923	**0.827**	0.860	0.891	**0.874**

existing contrast between windows, it could allow exhaustive normality modelling by augmentation techniques. However, our architecture works with different encoding methods, so it will be suited for contextual anomalies that are often produced in altered operating conditions. In next section we observe the influence of parameters of pairing process on performance. For conciseness, results will be given for SMAP dataset with LSTM encoder in network.

5 Effects of Parameter Settings

5.1 Augmentation Techniques

In this section, we aim to study the influence of augmentation techniques on performance metrics. Every augmentation method is tested as a single augmentation applied to every window from the first partition (positive pair design). As we can see in Table 2, augmentations methods sharply differ in terms of performance. First, it appears, that a combination of methods performs well than separated ones.

Table 2. Separate evaluation of augmentation techniques used for positive pairing. "Mixed" refers to a weighted combination of augmentations (0.36, 0.28, 0.11, 0.04, 0.21).

Method	P	R	F1
Identity	**0.801**	0.765	0.782
Noising	0.788	0.826	0.807
Magnitude scaling	0.641	0.722	0.679
Time warping	0.414	0.603	0.491
Dual averaging	0.700	**0.942**	0.803
Mixed	0.751	0.923	**0.827**

Obviously, the positive pairs need diversity in order to model similarity between windows sharing contextual information. As we previously mentioned, mixed augmentation has been obtained by random search on weight combinations (with 30 iterations). The best weights do not strictly correspond to the linear combination of metrics. Besides, we can notice that our architecture can consider pairing without augmentation in order to get the best precision. This result can be explained by the increasing number of false positives induced by an excessive augmentation which tends to add noise. For the next sections, augmentation method will be the mixed one.

5.2 Batch Parameters

In this section, we study the influence of batch parameters. First we observe its size in terms of negative pairing with mixed augmentation. At a first glance, selecting a high number of windows in a batch will improve the contrast between windows for negative pairs. The bias induced by stochastic sampling will consequently be reduced. However, large batch sizes will eliminate pairs with a moderate similarity which might be useful to model soft contrast. Thus, a decrease of recall is expected due to a high sensitive contrast required. As can be seen on Fig. 5a, optimal batch size is around 15 windows. For high batch sizes, contrast modelling relies on redundant pairs. It causes a significant decrease of performance in terms of recall and F_1-score. But moderate increase of size tends to slightly improve the precision. This can be useful for monitoring system with scarce anomalies. Another way to limit the bias due to the batching process is to post-process the negative pairs by observing the shape-DTW distances between paired windows. For a fixed batch size of 15, we observe how varying elimination ratio of the lowest shape-DTW pairs impact metrics. Note that in order to work with a constant number of negative pairs, deleted pairs are replaced by duplicating those with the highest shape-DTW. In other words, ratio corresponds to percentage of deleted windows from the batch. As it is shown on Fig. 5b, post-process batch by mitigating similar pairs may slightly improve detection. The method is clearly limited to small ratios but implies less computations than raising the batch size as it was done just before.

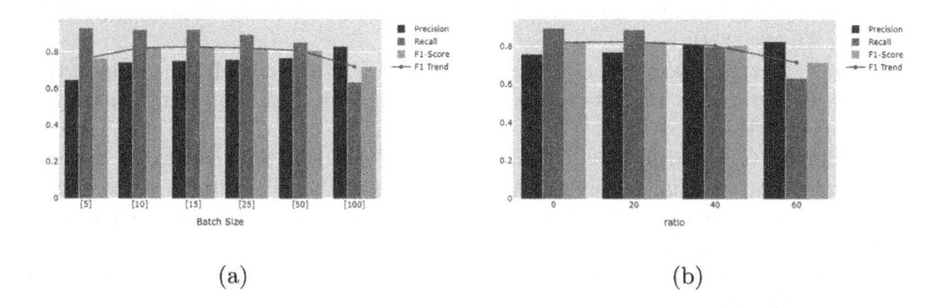

Fig. 5. Metrics variations according to batch size and ratio mitigation

6 Conclusion

We proposed an application of contrastive learning to anomaly detection with a method dealing with missing assumptions, as is the case for unsupervised anomaly detection. Our approach has been successfully tested on two public datasets and tend to demonstrate that our pairing design is intrinsically linked to the nature of data. This method and the siamese architecture are generic and can be adapted to model several phenomena with an enhancing tolerance to noise. In addition, the unsupervised representations allow us to explore other downstream tasks. For example, with provided labels, it is possible to infer the class (anomaly/normal) of windows from latent representations. It has to be optimized in terms of precision and recall according to industry requirements. Future developments will focus on local anomaly scoring by comparing sequences of consecutive windows instead of computing distance to a mean embedding vector. Another possible extension could also consist in an incremental learning to aggregate previous detected anomalies to pairing process.

Acknowledgements. This material is based on research fund by Naval Group. The views and results contained herein are those of the authors and should not be interpreted as necessarily representing the official policies of Naval Group.

References

1. Su, Y., Zhao, Y., Niu, C., Liu, R., Sun, W., Pei, D.: Robust anomaly detection for multivariate time series through stochastic recurrent neural network. In: Proceedings of the 25th ACM SIGKDD International Conference on Knowledge Discovery & Data Mining, pp. 2828–2837, July 2019
2. Blázquez-García, A., Conde, A., Mori, U., Lozano, J.A.: A review on outlier/anomaly detection in time series data. ACM Comput. Surv. (CSUR) **54**(3), 1–33 (2021)
3. Iwana, B.K., Uchida, S.: Time series data augmentation for neural networks by time warping with a discriminative teacher. In: 2020 25th International Conference on Pattern Recognition (ICPR), pp. 3558–3565. IEEE, January 2021
4. Li, Z., et al.: Multivariate time series anomaly detection and interpretation using hierarchical inter-metric and temporal embedding. In: Proceedings of the 27th ACM SIGKDD Conference on Knowledge Discovery & Data Mining, pp. 3220–3230, August 2021
5. Zong, B., et al.: Deep autoencoding gaussian mixture model for unsupervised anomaly detection. In: International Conference on Learning Representations, February 2018
6. Hundman, K., Constantinou, V., Laporte, C., Colwell, I., Soderstrom, T.: Detecting spacecraft anomalies using LSTMs and nonparametric dynamic thresholding. In: Proceedings of the 24th ACM SIGKDD International Conference on Knowledge Discovery & Data Mining, pp. 387–395, July 2018
7. Kingma, D.P., Ba, J.: Adam: a method for stochastic optimization. arXiv preprint arXiv:1412.6980 (2014)

8. Abadi, M., et al.: TensorFlow: a system for large-scale machine learning. In: 12th USENIX Symposium on Operating Systems Design and Implementation (OSDI 16), pp. 265–283 (2016)
9. Forestier, G., Petitjean, F., Dau, H.A., Webb, G.I., Keogh, E.: Generating synthetic time series to augment sparse datasets. In: 2017 IEEE International Conference on Data Mining (ICDM), pp. 865–870. IEEE, November 2017
10. Wen, Q., et al.: Time series data augmentation for deep learning: a survey. arXiv preprint arXiv:2002.12478 (2020)
11. Chen, T., Kornblith, S., Norouzi, M., Hinton, G.: A simple framework for contrastive learning of visual representations. In: International Conference on Machine Learning, pp. 1597–1607. PMLR, November 2020
12. Hadsell, R., Chopra, S., LeCun, Y.: Dimensionality reduction by learning an invariant mapping. In: 2006 IEEE Computer Society Conference on Computer Vision and Pattern Recognition (CVPR 2006), vol. 2, pp. 1735–1742. IEEE, June 2006
13. Oord, A.V.D., Li, Y., Vinyals, O.: Representation learning with contrastive predictive coding. arXiv preprint arXiv:1807.03748 (2018)
14. Melekhov, I., Kannala, J., Rahtu, E.: Siamese network features for image matching. In: 2016 23rd International Conference on Pattern Recognition (ICPR), pp. 378–383. IEEE, December 2016
15. Kiyasseh, D., Zhu, T., Clifton, D.A.: CLOCS: contrastive learning of cardiac signals across space, time, and patients. In: International Conference on Machine Learning, pp. 5606–5615. PMLR, July 2021
16. Fonseca, E., Ortego, D., McGuinness, K., O'Connor, N.E., Serra, X.: Unsupervised contrastive learning of sound event representations. In: ICASSP 2021–2021 IEEE International Conference on Acoustics, Speech and Signal Processing (ICASSP), pp. 371–375. IEEE, June 2021
17. Um, T.T., et al.: Data augmentation of wearable sensor data for Parkinson's disease monitoring using convolutional neural networks. In: Proceedings of the 19th ACM International Conference on Multimodal Interaction, pp. 216–220, November 2017
18. Esteban, C., Hyland, S.L., Rätsch, G.: Real-valued (medical) time series generation with recurrent conditional GANs. arXiv preprint arXiv:1706.02633 (2017)
19. Sakoe, H., Chiba, S.: Dynamic programming algorithm optimization for spoken word recognition. IEEE Trans. Acoust. Speech Signal Process. **26**(1), 43–49 (1978)
20. Zhao, J., Itti, L.: shapeDTW: shape dynamic time warping. Pattern Recogn. **74**, 171–184 (2018)
21. Baireddy, S., et al.: Spacecraft time-series anomaly detection using transfer learning. In: Proceedings of the IEEE/CVF Conference on Computer Vision and Pattern Recognition, pp. 1951–1960 (2021)
22. Hochreiter, S., Schmidhuber, J.: Long short-term memory. Neural Comput. **9**(8), 1735–1780 (1997)
23. Simonyan, K., Zisserman, A.: Very deep convolutional networks for large-scale image recognition. arXiv preprint arXiv:1409.1556 (2014)
24. Geiger, A., Liu, D., Alnegheimish, S., Cuesta-Infante, A., Veeramachaneni, K.: TadGAN: time series anomaly detection using generative adversarial networks. In: 2020 IEEE International Conference on Big Data (Big Data), pp. 33–43. IEEE, December 2020

Visual Radial Basis Q-Network

Julien Hautot[1(✉)], Céline Teuliere[1], and Nourddine Azzaoui[2]

[1] Université Clermont Auvergne, Clermont Auvergne INP, CNRS, Institut Pascal, 63000 Clermont-Ferrand, France
{julien.hautot,celine.teuliere}@uca.fr

[2] Laboratoire de Mathématiques Blaise Pascal, 63100 Clermont-Ferrand, France
azzaoui.nourddine@uca.fr

Abstract. While reinforcement learning (RL) from raw images has been largely investigated in the last decade, existing approaches still suffer from a number of constraints. The high input dimension is often handled using either expert knowledge to extract handcrafted features or environment encoding through convolutional networks. Both solutions require numerous parameters to be optimized. In contrast, we propose a generic method to extract sparse features from raw images with few trainable parameters. We achieved this using a Radial Basis Function Network (RBFN) directly on raw image. We evaluate the performance of the proposed approach for visual extraction in Q-learning tasks in the Vizdoom environment. Then, we compare our results with two Deep Q-Network, one trained directly on images and another one trained on feature extracted by a pretrained auto-encoder. We show that the proposed approach provides similar or, in some cases, even better performances with fewer trainable parameters while being conceptually simpler.

Keywords: Reinforcement learning · State representation · Radial basis function network · Computer vision

1 Introduction

Reinforcement learning (RL) has made significant progress in recent years, allowing the use of policy and value-based algorithms on images to perform tasks in fully observable contexts [8,23,29]. However, when the state space is more complex or partially observable, learning remains harder. Solutions are introduced by implementing additional learning modules like Long Short Term Memory (LSTM) [12] or enlarging the networks by adding convolutional layers [14].

Another strategy to facilitate the learning of an agent in a complex visual environment is to reduce the dimension of the state space [20]. This can be accomplished by extracting relevant features from the images using learning based methods such as auto-encoder [18]. The dimension of the state space has a large impact on how these solutions are implemented. Indeed, an auto-encoder needs lots of parameters to encode large states and hence its training is time and energy consuming.

M. El Yacoubi et al. (Eds.): ICPRAI 2022, LNCS 13364, pp. 318–329, 2022.
https://doi.org/10.1007/978-3-031-09282-4_27

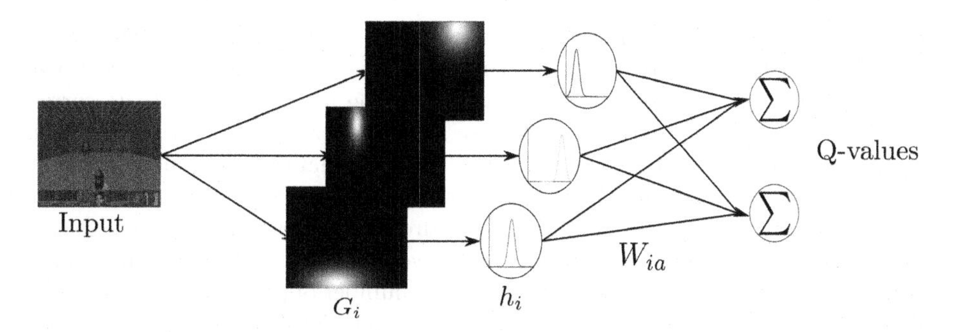

Fig. 1. Visual Radial Basis Q-Network architecture. Input raw image are filtered by spatial Gaussian filters G_i then Gaussian activation h_i are applied on all the filtered pixels and Q-values are calculated by a linear combination of h_i and W_ia the weight between activation h_i and output $Q(S, a)$

Furthermore using sparse representation in RL has been proven to be efficient [22], this can be done with Radial Basis Function Networks (RBFN) [3,11, 24,26] a well know function approximator used for classification and regression tasks [32]. Since its success in deep learning, the idea of using RBFN in RL has emerged and encountered a great interest especially in non-visual tasks applications [5,6,16]. In all these works, RBFN are however not applied directly on raw pixel, but rather on features extracted from the environment that involve pre-training steps.

Contributions. In this paper, we aim to train an agent in a partially observable environment, with only raw pixel inputs and without prior knowledge, i.e., without pre-training or additional information. We extend the RBFN to extract random sparse features from visual images. Our major contribution is the design and the analysis of a generic features extraction method based on RBFN for visual inputs. We evaluate our extracted features performance in a Q-learning setting and compare the result with state-of-the-art methods. We used Vizdoom as the virtual environment [15] where visual tasks are hard to solve with classic RL algorithms [16].

Paper Organisation. In Sect. 2, we present a brief review of related approaches, then we introduce the theoretical background in Sect. 3. In Sect. 4 we present our RBFN method and analyse the extracted features in Sect. 5. Finally Sect. 6 presents an evaluation of the method on two different visual RL tasks and compare the performances against state-of-the-art approaches.

2 Related Works

State representation learning methods are popular approaches to reduce the state dimension used in visual RL. In the survey [20], Lesort et al. distinguished several categories of approaches for state representation learning. Auto-encoders can be used to extract features by reconstructing input images [13,18,25], or by forward model learning to predict the next state given the actual state and the corresponding action [19]. Learning an inverse model to predict the action knowing states can also be used to extract features that are unaffected by uncontrollable aspect of the environment [33]. Prior knowledge can also be used to constrain the state space and extract conditional features [10]. These learning representation methods typically require to train a network upstream of an RL algorithm, which can be time-consuming due to the large number of parameters or the environment dimension. Even when the state representation is trained parallel with the agent as in [27] or when unsupervised learning is used as in [1,30], the training is still time-consuming since multiple convolutional networks are trained. Unlike the current state-of-the-art, our method does not rely on pre-training or convolutional network; instead the features are extracted using a combination of Radial Basis Function (RBF) without training nor prior knowledge.

RBFNs have been recently used as feature extractors for 3-D point cloud object recognition [7]. They achieved similar or even better performances compared to the state-of-the-art with a faster training speed. Earlier, in [9] RBF-based auto-encoder showed the efficiency of RBFN as feature extractors prior to classification tasks. One key property of RBFN activation is their sparsity; for each input, only a few neurons will be activated. This is advantageous for RL as it imposes locality of activation avoiding catastrophic interference and keeping stable value which allows bootstrapping [22]. Applying directly RBFN on high dimensional images is challenging and has not been yet much explored in the literature. Other sparse representations, such as extreme machine learning or sparse coding, have been investigated but none have been extended to visual RL as their computing cost tends grows exponentially with the input dimension. One solution in the literature is to reduce the inputs dimension with convolution [21,28].

3 Background

3.1 Reinforcement Learning

In RL we consider an agent interacting with an environment through actions a, states s and rewards r. The environment is modelled as a Markov decision process (MDP). Such processes are defined by the tuple $\langle S, A, T, R \rangle$, where S and A are the states and action spaces, $T : S \times A \rightarrow S$ is the transition probability to go from a state $s \in S$ to another state $s' \in S$ by performing an action $a \in A$. $R : S \times A \rightarrow \mathbb{R}$ is the reward function. At each time step, the agent will face a state $s \in S$ and choose an action $a \in A$ according to its policy $\pi : S \rightarrow A$. The environment will give back a reward $r = R(s, a)$ and the probability of reaching s' as the next state is given by $T(s, a, s')$. The goal of the agent is to find a policy which maximizes its expected return, which we define as the cumulative discounted reward along time-step t, i.e., $R_t = \sum_{k=0}^{\infty} \gamma^k r_{t+k+1}$, where γ is the discounted rate determining the actual value of future reward.

We chose to evaluate our state representation method in a Q-learning [31] setting. To optimize the policy, Q-learning estimates the state-action value function (Q-value) which represents the quality of taking an action, $a \in A$, in a state, $s \in S$, following a policy π. $Q^{\pi}(s, a)$ is defined by

$$Q^{\pi}(s, a) := \mathbb{E}_{\pi}[R_t | s_t = s, a_t = a]. \tag{1}$$

The optimal policy can then be estimated by approximating the optimal Q-value given by the Bellman equation such that

$$Q^{*}(s, a) = \mathbb{E}_{s'}[r + \gamma \max_{a'} Q^{*}(s', a')]. \tag{2}$$

In Deep Q-learning [23], the optimal Q-value is approximated by a neural network parametrized by θ. At each time-step Q-values are predicted by the network, then the agent chooses the best action according to an exploration strategy. The agent experiences $\langle s_t, a_t, s_{t+1}, F\rangle$ are stored into a replay memory buffer D where F is a Boolean indicating if the state is final or not. Parameters of the Q-Network θ are optimized at each iteration i to minimize the loss $L_i(\theta_i)$ for a batch of state uniformly chosen in the replay buffer D, defined by

$$L_i(\theta_i) = \begin{cases} \mathbb{E}_{(s,a,r,s') \sim U(D)}[(r - Q(s, a; \theta_i))^2] \text{ if } \text{F} \\ \mathbb{E}_{(s,a,r,s') \sim Rb}[(r + \gamma \max_{a'} Q(s', a'; \bar{\theta_i}) - Q(s, a; \theta_i))^2] \text{ otherwise.} \end{cases} \tag{3}$$

To stabilize the training a target network is used with parameters $\bar{\theta}$ which is periodically copied from the reference network with parameters θ.

3.2 Radial Basis Function Network (RBFN)

The network is composed of three layers: the inputs $\mathbf{X}$, the hidden layers ϕ compose of RBFs and the output layers $\mathbf{Y}$. A RBF is a function ϕ defined by its center μ and its width σ as

$$\phi(\mathbf{X}) = \phi(||\mathbf{X} - \mu)||, \sigma), \quad \text{where } ||.|| \text{ is a norm.} \tag{4}$$

In this paper we will consider Gaussian RBF with the Euclidean norm defined as

$$\phi_g(\mathbf{X}) = \exp\left(\frac{||\mathbf{X} - \mu||^2}{2\sigma^2}\right). \tag{5}$$

A RBFN computes a linear combination of N RBF:

$$y_i(\mathbf{X}) = \sum_{j=1}^{N} w_{ij} \cdot \phi(||\boldsymbol{X} - \mu_j||, \sigma_j), \tag{6}$$

where, w_{ij} is a learnable weight between output y_i and hidden RBF layer ϕ_j.

RBFN are fast to train due to the well-localized receptive fields that allow activation of few neurons for one input. The farther the input value is from the receptive field of the neuron, the closer output value is to zero.

4 Method

Our method focuses on the projection of high dimensional input state spaces into a lower dimensional space by combining Gaussian receptive filters and RBF Gaussian activations. Our network architecture is shown in Fig. 1. Each receptive field can be seen as the attention area of the corresponding neuron. The attention area of a neuron i, for a pixel p in a state S (of shape $w \times h$) with coordinates (p_x, p_y) is defined as follows:

$$G_{i,p_x,p_y} = \exp\left(-\left(\frac{(p_x/w - \mu_{x,i})^2}{2\sigma_{x,i}^2} + \frac{(p_y/h - \mu_{y,i})^2}{2\sigma_{y,i}^2}\right)\right), \tag{7}$$

where, $\mu_{x,i}, \mu_{y,i} \in [0,1]$ define the center of the Gaussian function along spatial dimension and $\sigma_{x,i}, \sigma_{y,i} \in [0,1]$ are the standard deviations. $\mathbf{G_i} \in \mathcal{M}_{w \times h}$ is the full matrix that defines the spatial attention of a neuron. Given the attention area, the activation of the hidden neuron i is computed using a Gaussian RBF activation function weighted by $\mathbf{G_i}$:

$$\mathbf{h}_i(\mathbf{S}) = \exp\left(-\frac{\sum((\mathbf{S} - \mu_{z,i}) \odot \mathbf{G}_i)^2}{2\sigma_{z,i}^2}\right), \tag{8}$$

where, $\mu_{z,i} \in [0,1]$ is the center and $\sigma_{z,i} \in [0,1]$ the standard deviation of the RBF intensity Gaussian activation function. Symbol $\odot$ is the Hadamard product, i.e., the element-wise product. Parameters $\mu_{z,i}$ and $\sigma_{z,i}$ have the same size as the input channel.

To test the efficiency of our extraction we use the extracted features as the state in a Q-learning algorithms where the Q-value will be approximated by a linear combination of N_g Gaussian neurons activations.

$$Q(s,a) = \sum_{i=0}^{N_g} w_{ai} \times h_i(s), \tag{9}$$

where, w_{ai} is the weight between the action a and the neuron i. On each step the input image is passed to the RBF layer and the computed features are saved in the replay buffer. Then during each training iteration a batch of random features is chosen from the replay memory buffer and the weights are updated using a gradient descent step (Adam [17]) to minimize Eq. (3).

4.1 Selection of RBF Parameters

There are 6 hyper-parameters for each Gaussian unit. Centers of Gaussian filters $\mu_{x,y}$ and centers of Gaussian activation μ_z are chosen uniformly between 0 and 1 as we need to cover all the state space. The standard deviations $\sigma_{x,y,z}$ influence the precision of the activation of a neuron, i.e., the proximity between pixel intensities weighted by attention area and intensity center of the neuron. In that way RBF layer allows activation of few neurons for a particular image.

The hyper-parameters are chosen at the beginning and never changed during training.

After empirical experiments and based on the work of [4] which used also Gaussian attention area, for all the study we choose 2001 neurons for gray and 667 neurons for rgb inputs as each neuron has 3 intensity center, one for each canal. The choice of standard deviations is as follows: $\sigma_z = 1$ and $\sigma_{x,y}$ uniformly chosen in $[0.02 - 0.2]$.

4.2 Vizdoom Scenarios

We evaluate our method on two Vizdoom scenarios to show the robustness of our network to different state dimensions and partially observable tasks. Scenarios are defined as follows:

Basic Scenario. In this task the agent is in a square room, its goal is to shoot a monster placed on a line in front of him. At each episode the monster has a different position while the agent spawns all the time in the same place. In this scenario the agent has the choice between 8 possible actions: move right, move left, shoot, turn left, turn right, move forward, move backward and do nothing. In this configuration the agent can be in a state where the monster is not visible. The agent gets a reward of 101 when the shoot hits the monster, -5 when the monster is missed and -1 for each iteration. The episode is finished when the agent shoots the monster or when it reaches the timeout of 300 steps.

Health Gathering Scenario. In this task the agent is still in a square room but the goal is different, the agent has to collect health packs to survive. It has 100 life points at the beginning of the episode, each iteration the agent looses some life points, if the agent reaches a health pack it gains some life point. The episode ends when the agent dies or when it reaches 2100 steps. Reward is designed as follows: $r_t = \text{life}_{t+1} - \text{life}_t$. Possible actions are move forward, move backward, turn left, turn right, do nothing. All the health packs spawn randomly and the agent spawns in the middle of the room.

5 Analysis of Pattern Activations

In this section we put in evidence the sparsity of our network, and analyse the activation patterns of our neurons and their differences. We then present an example of feature targeted by a RBF neuron.

We generated 1 000 states from both scenarios in gray and rgb with a random policy and a random "skip frame" between 0 and 12 in order to cover all the

Table 1. Distribution of the active neurons on 1000 states with 20 different RBF parameters initialisation. Per cent of the total number of neurons (2001).

	Basic		Health gathering	
	Gray	RGB	Gray	RGB
Active neurons (aN)	$32 \pm 1\%$	$31 \pm 1\%$	$29 \pm 6\%$	$32 \pm 5\%$

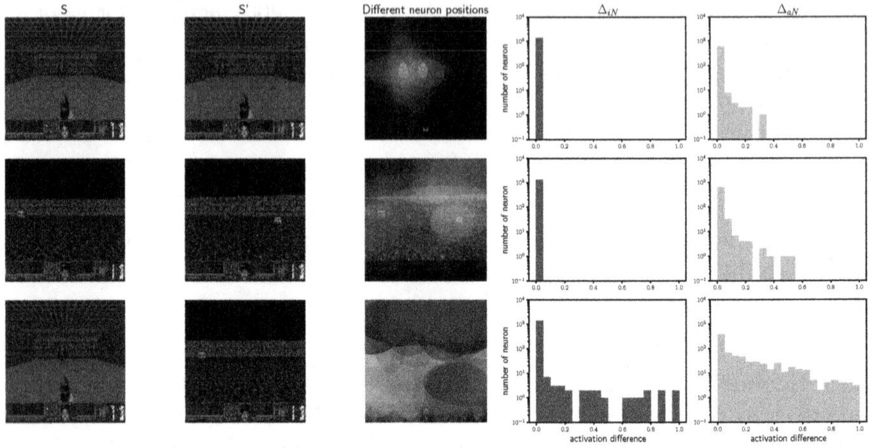

Fig. 2. Comparison of neurons activity on different states for one seed. Histograms represent $\Delta_N = |N(s) - N(s')|$ with N the neurons activation (iN, aN). Neuron positions represent the position of the different neurons with $|S - S'|$ in the background. *Top:* comparison for two close states in basic scenario. *Middle:* comparison of two close states in the health gathering scenario. *Bottom:* comparison between both scenarios

state space, i.e., each random action is repeated a certain number of time. In each scenario we can classify the neurons into two categories: inactive neurons (iN) which have an activation always inferior to 0.01 and active neurons (aN) which have an activation superior to 0.01 in some states. Table 1 gives the percentage of aN on the total number of neurons for 20 different seeds in each configuration. We can see that even with a random generation of Gaussian neurons we have stable distribution, around 30% of activated neurons, across different random seeds, state spaces and scenarios.

Figure 2 highlights the difference in activation for iN and aN between two frames. The first observation is that iN can be used to differentiate two scenarios as some iN of basic scenario become aN in health gathering scenario, those neurons describe the scenario rather than the state. The active neurons, have also more differences between two scenarios than two states, but they have a non negligible number of neurons that differ between the states. These neurons describe particular features as shown in the neuron position column. Indeed, in the basic scenario, the position of different aNs are around the monster, for health gathering there is more differences between both frames so more different neurons. However, we identified 3 main areas, two on both health packs and one on the upper side of the right wall. Between both scenarios, the different iNs and aNs are distributed over the entire image with more differences on the top for the iN as the ceiling is characteristic of the scenario.

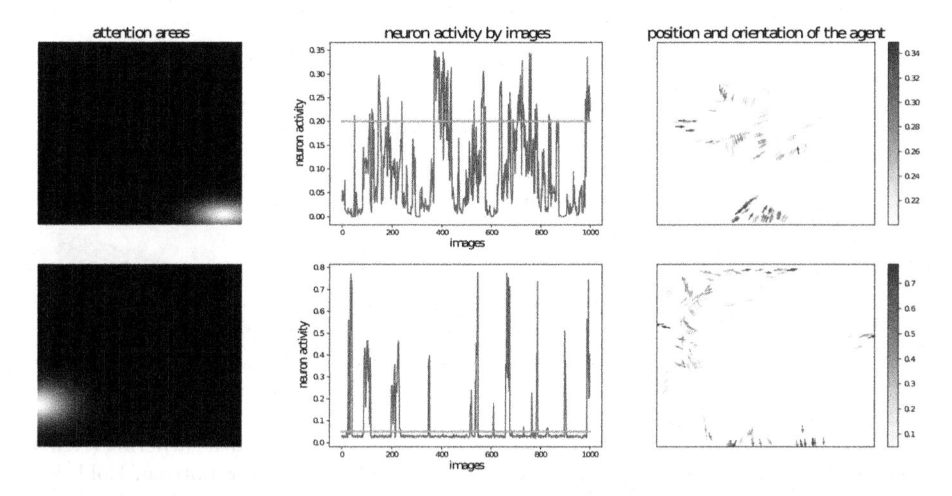

Fig. 3. Study of the activity of two neurons, in both scenarios. Health gathering scenario on top and basic scenario at the bottom. The arrow on the last column represents the agent's position when the neuron activity is below the threshold (orange line), the color represents the amplitude of the activation. (Color figure online)

In Fig. 3 we study two different neuron activations, one for each scenario, on 5000 images, and we print the position and orientation of the agent (black arrow) when the neuron is activated or inactivated under a certain threshold. In the basic scenario the neuron fires only when the agent has a wall at its left. Whereas, in the health gathering the neuron is activated when the agent is not facing a wall but rather when the floor is in the neuron attention area. Each aN gives a direct or indirect information about the environment, the monster can be identified by a neuron that gets activated on the wall; indeed, when this neuron will face the monster it will be deactivated indicating that there is something in front of the agent but it is not necessarily the monster. This is why a combination of different activations is needed to get a complete information.

All the neurons formed a pattern activation specific for each scenario, and inside this pattern there is small variation helping to differentiate states in the scenario. We show in the next section that this combination can provide enough information about the environment for Q-learning to predict relevant Q-values.

6 Reinforcement Learning Application

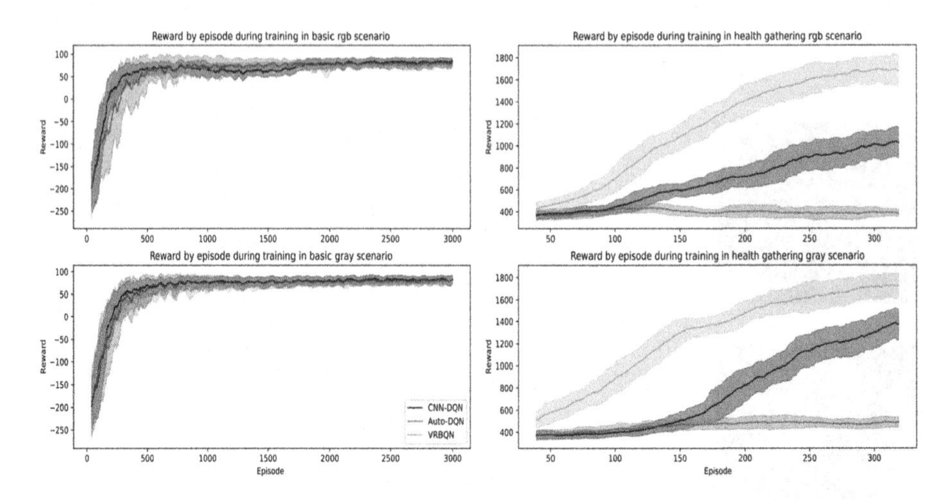

Fig. 4. Comparison of 3 different approaches on basic (left) and health gathering (right) task on 20 different seeds. Rgb inputs for the top and gray for the bottom. Bold line represents the mean and transparent area the standard deviation. The plotted rewards for health gathering scenario is the number of alive step

In the following section we compare our algorithm on two different Vizdoom tasks, basic and health gathering scenarios, with a CNN-DQN, a convolutional network trained directly on pixels, and an autoencoder-DQN where the RL algorithm is applied on features extracted from a pre-trained CNN auto-encoder. Both CNN are similar to the one used in [23] with one more convolutional layer as the inputs image are bigger, 120×160. Both scenarios have different characteristics, basic scenario has a sparse reward while health gathering reward is dense. Training is done with gray and RGB input state to check the robustness of tested networks to different input spaces. The dimension of the used images is 120×160. We stack two consecutive frames to form a state providing information about movement and we used a "skip frame" of 6 to train faster.

Agents are trained during 100k training steps. The RL part of CNN-DQN and autoencoder-DQN used target networks updated every 1000 iterations. An epsilon-greedy policy is used during training with epsilon starting to decay after 1000 training steps: it goes from 1 to 0.1 in 10 000 training step. A learning rate of 0.00025 and a batch size of 64 are used.

Our method, V-RBQN, does not require a target network as the features are sparse and the approximation of the Q-value is stable and can efficiently bootstrap. In addition, we did not use any exploration strategy and we used a learning rate of 0.01 and a batch size of 256.

For the basic scenario, the left curves in Fig. 4 show that all the methods converge to the maximum reward. Both methods that trained the agent on

Table 2. Reward on 1000 episode of basic and health gathering scenario for 3 different algorithms. Score is calculated with mean ± standard deviation on 20 different seeds. V-RBQN (only aN) represents the reward when testing without inactive neurons.

Scenario	Basic		Health gathering	
	Gray	rgb	Gray	rgb
basicDQN	**86 ± 6**	**86 ± 6**	1519 ± 751	1092 ± 716
Autoencoder-DQN	86 ± 7	85 ± 7	601 ± 357	438 ± 384
V-RBQN	85 ± 8	85 ± 9	**1809 ± 543**	**1778 ± 573**
V-RBQN (only aN)	85 ± 8	84 ± 9	1799 ± 571	1690 ± 635

extracted features have a larger variance during training than when training directly on images with convolution. This high variance is due to the imprecision of the features which can be too close for 2 different states that require 2 different actions to maximize the Q-value. For example when the monster is not perfectly in front of the weapon, the agent can be in a situation where the features are similar and so the Q-value for shoot, turn left and right are very close, the agent will oscillate between those three actions until it shoots the monster. In the health gathering scenario, which is more difficult to solve with Q-learning [16], the autoencoder method does not find an optimal solution and V-RBQN performs better that the CNN-DQN. Both state-of-the-art methods converge to a behavior where the agent can get stuck in walls, whereas our method alleviates this problem by having special local and sparse neurons activations. Test results in Table 2 demonstrate the robustness of our method to different state spaces. Indeed, for the same number of training steps, our method gets similar results with different inputs size, i.e., corresponding to gray and rgb images, whereas CNN-DQN and autoencoder-DQN have a bigger variance and a smaller reward for rgb input when comparing with gray input for a given time-step.

Finally, we realized another test to highlight the sparsity of our network. We tested the learned weights only on the aNs for each scenario without the contribution of the iNs. Results in Table 2 show that the iNs are not required to solve a task. This allows faster forward passes as the quantity of neurons is divided by a factor of three when dealing with a specific scenario.

7 Conclusion

In this paper we have extended the Radial Basis Function Network to handle feature extraction in images. We put into light the sparsity and locality properties of our network by analyzing the extracted features. We then show the usefulness of these extracted features by using them as inputs of partially observable visual RL tasks. Despite its simplicity our Visual Radial Basis Q-Network (V-RBQN) gives promising results on two scenarios, i.e., the basic and the health gathering tasks, even with different input channel sizes. Thanks to the sparsity of the extracted features and their locality, the proposed approach outperforms the evaluated baseline while having less trainable parameters, without any exploration strategy nor target network. In addition, the inactive neurons can be omitted without hindering the efficiency which allows to reduce the size of the network by a factor of three. One of the research direction will be to find generic RBF parameters, by training them on different types of images to be optimal regardless the input images. Future work will also consider the extension of this approach to continuous action spaces and other RL algorithms.

References

1. Anand, A., et al.: Unsupervised state representation learning in Atari. CoRR abs/1906.08226 (2019). arXiv: 1906.08226
2. Asadi, K., Parikh, N., Parr, R.E., Konidaris, G.D., Littman, M.L.: Deep radial-basis value functions for continuous control. In: Proceedings of the Thirty-Fifth AAAI Conference on Artificial Intelligence (2021)
3. Broomhead, D.S., Lowe, D.: Radial basis functions. Multi-variable functional interpolation and adaptive networks. Technical report, Royal Signals and Radar Establishment Malvern (United Kingdom) (1988)
4. Buessler, J.L., et al.: Image receptive fields for artificial neural networks. Neurocomputing **144**, 258–270 (2014). https://doi.org/10.1016/j.neucom.2014.04.045
5. Capel, N., Zhang, N.: Extended radial basis function controller for reinforcement learning. CoRR abs/2009.05866 (2020). arXiv: 2009.05866
6. Cetina, V.U.: Multilayer perceptrons with radial basis functions as value functions in reinforcement learning. In: ESANN (2008)
7. Chen, W., et al.: Deep RBFNet: point cloud feature learning using radial basis functions. CoRR abs/1812.04302 (2018). arXiv: 1812.04302
8. Christodoulou, P.: Soft actor-critic for discrete action settings. CoRR abs/1910.07207 (2019). arXiv: 1910.07207
9. Daoud, M., et al.: RBFA: radial basis function autoencoders. In: 2019 IEEE Congress on Evolutionary Computation (CEC), pp. 2966–2973 (2019). https://doi.org/10.1109/CEC.2019.8790041
10. Finn, C., et al.: Deep spatial autoencoders for visuomotor learning. In: 2016 IEEE International Conference on Robotics and Automation (ICRA), pp. 512–519 (2016). https://doi.org/10.1109/ICRA.2016.7487173
11. Hartman, E.J., et al.: Layered neural networks with gaussian hidden units as universal approximations. Neural Comput. **2**(2), 210–215 (1990). https://doi.org/10.1162/neco.1990.2.2.210
12. Hochreiter, S., Schmidhuber, J.: Long short-term memory. Neural Comput. **9**(8), 1735–1780 (1997). https://doi.org/10.1162/neco.1997.9.8.1735
13. van Hoof, H., et al.: Stable reinforcement learning with autoencoders for tactile and visual data. In: 2016 IEEE/RSJ International Conference on Intelligent Robots and Systems (IROS), pp. 3928–3934 (2016). https://doi.org/10.1109/IROS.2016.7759578
14. Justesen, N., et al.: Deep learning for video game playing. IEEE Trans. Games **12**(1), 1–20 (2020). https://doi.org/10.1109/TG.2019.2896986
15. Kempka, M., et al.: ViZDoom: a doom-based AI research platform for visual reinforcement learning. In: 2016 IEEE Conference on Computational Intelligence and Games (CIG), pp. 1–8 (2016). https://doi.org/10.1109/CIG.2016.7860433

16. Khan, A., et al.: Playing first-person shooter games with machine learning techniques and methods using the VizDoom game-AI research platform. Entertainment Comput. **34**, 100357 (2020). https://doi.org/10.1016/j.entcom.2020.100357
17. Kingma, D.P., Ba, J.: Adam: a method for stochastic optimization. In: Bengio, Y., LeCun, Y. (eds.) 3rd International Conference on Learning Representations, ICLR 2015, San Diego, CA, USA, 7–9 May 2015, Conference Track Proceedings (2015)
18. Lange, S., et al.: Batch reinforcement learning. In: Reinforcement Learning, vol. 12, pp. 45–73. Springer, Heidelberg (2012). https://doi.org/10.1007/978-3-642-27645-3_2
19. Leibfried, F., et al.: Model-based stabilisation of deep reinforcement learning. CoRR abs/1809.01906 (2018). arXiv: 1809.01906
20. Lesort, T., et al.: State representation learning for control: an overview. Neural Netw. **108**, 379–392 (2018). https://doi.org/10.1016/j.neunet.2018.07.006
21. Liu, H., Li, F., Xu, X., Sun, F.: Active object recognition using hierarchical local-receptive-field-based extreme learning machine. Memetic Comput. **10**(2), 233–241 (2017). https://doi.org/10.1007/s12293-017-0229-2
22. Liu, V., et al.: The utility of sparse representations for control in reinforcement learning. Proc. AAAI Conf. Artif. Intell. **33**, 4384–4391 (2019). https://doi.org/10.1609/aaai.v33i01.33014384
23. Mnih, V., et al.: Human-level control through deep reinforcement learning. Nature **518**(7540), 529–533 (2015). https://doi.org/10.1038/nature14236
24. Moody, J., Darken, C.: Learning with localized receptive fields. Yale University, Department of Computer Science (1988)
25. Nair, A., et al.: Visual reinforcement learning with imagined goals. CoRR abs/1807.04742 (2018). arXiv: 1807.04742
26. Park, J., Sandberg, I.W.: Approximation and radial-basis-function networks. Neural Comput. **5**(2), 305–316 (1993). https://doi.org/10.1162/neco.1993.5.2.305
27. Pathak, D., et al.: Curiosity-driven exploration by self-supervised prediction. In: 2017 IEEE Conference on Computer Vision and Pattern Recognition Workshops (CVPRW), pp. 488–489. IEEE (2017). https://doi.org/10.1109/CVPRW.2017.70
28. Rodrigues, I.R., et al.: Convolutional extreme learning machines: a systematic review. Informatics **8**(2), 33 (2021). https://doi.org/10.3390/informatics8020033
29. Schulman, J., et al.: Proximal policy optimization algorithms. CoRR abs/1707.06347 (2017). arXiv: 1707.06347
30. Srinivas, A., et al.: CURL: contrastive unsupervised representations for reinforcement learning. CoRR abs/2004.04136 (2020). arXiv: 2004.04136
31. Sutton, R.S., Barto, A.G.: Reinforcement Learning: An Introduction, 2nd edn. Adaptive Computation and Machine Learning Series. The MIT Press (2018)
32. Wu, Y., et al.: Using radial basis function networks for function approximation and classification. ISRN Appl. Math. **2012**, 1–34 (2012). https://doi.org/10.5402/2012/324194
33. Zhong, Y., et al.: Disentangling controllable object through video prediction improves visual reinforcement learning. In: 2020 IEEE International Conference on Acoustics, Speech and Signal Processing (ICASSP), pp. 3672–3676 (2020). https://doi.org/10.1109/ICASSP40776.2020.9053819

GANs Based Conditional Aerial Images Generation for Imbalanced Learning

Itzel Belderbos[1], Tim de Jong[2], and Mirela Popa[1(✉)]

[1] Department of Data Science and Knowledge Engineering, Faculty of Science and Engineering, Maastricht University, 6200 MD Maastricht, The Netherlands
mirela.popa@maastrichtuniversity.nl

[2] Statistics Netherlands, 6401 CZ Heerlen, The Netherlands
tja.dejong@cbs.nl

Abstract. In this paper, we examine whether we can use Generative Adversarial Networks as an oversampling technique for a largely imbalanced remote sensing dataset containing solar panels, endeavoring a better generalization ability on another geographical location. To this cause, we first analyze the image data by using several clustering methods on latent feature information extracted by a fine-tuned VGG16 network. After that, we use the cluster assignments as auxiliary input for training the GANs. In our experiments we have used three types of GANs: (1) conditional vanilla GANs, (2) conditional Wasserstein GANs, and (3) conditional Self-Attention GANs. The synthetic data generated by each of these GANs is evaluated by both the Fréchet Inception Distance and a comparison of a VGG11-based classification model with and without adding the generated positive images to the original source set. We show that all models are able to generate realistic outputs as well as improving the target performance. Furthermore, using the clusters as a GAN input showed to give a more diversified feature representation, improving stability of learning and lowering the risk of mode collapse.

Keywords: Generative adversarial networks · Imbalanced learning · Deep learning

1 Introduction

In recent years, remote sensing data has become increasingly accessible and therefore prominent as a source of fine-grained information about the globe. Recent improvements in supervised classification of remote sensing images have also made this type of data more interesting for a wide range of application fields—official statistics in particular. In this paper, we focus on the improvement of CNNs trained for classification of roof-top solar panel installations in aerial images. A well-know problem in remote sensing is the generalization ability of deep learning models across various geographical areas. One of the frequently occurring underlying causes is the class imbalance problem: the binary

M. El Yacoubi et al. (Eds.): ICPRAI 2022, LNCS 13364, pp. 330–342, 2022.
https://doi.org/10.1007/978-3-031-09282-4_28

classification model is biased towards the over-represented class when the class distribution is imbalanced [3]. The bias towards the majority class is even more severe in the case of high-dimensional data, such as images. Additionally, an imbalance is notably prevalent in the field of solar panel recognition, as the number of rooftops without solar panels largely outnumbers the number of rooftops with a solar panel, making it more expensive to obtain positive samples for an aerial image dataset. Acquiring more labeled data for the training set in order to improve this balance is expensive and time-consuming, which leads to the need for semi-supervised or unsupervised learning techniques. There are various techniques which aim to address this issue, such as oversampling, undersampling and ensemble learning. Oversampling techniques, and in particular Synthetic Minority Oversampling Technique (SMOTE), are most widely used. SMOTE identifies the k nearest neighbors for every minority sample based on the Euclidean distance. Nonetheless, for high-dimensional data such as RGB images, too many dimensions lead to every sample to appear equidistant. As these techniques are more focused on this local neighborhood information, these techniques may not be suitable for synthetic image generation [8]. Recently, Generative Adversarial Networks (GANs) have gained attention as an oversampling and data augmentation technique for high-dimensional data, as research has demonstrated that synthetic GAN images are effective as additional minority samples in order to improve the resulting classification performance. The vanilla GAN [5] consists of two neural networks with contradicting objectives: a generator and a discriminator. GANs are able to model and imitate the real data distribution in an antagonistic manner. Douzas et al. [4] successfully compared the performance of GANs with other oversampling techniques for binary class data on 71 datasets and found that GANs outperform the other methods. However, generating the under-represented class with exclusively these minority samples might be difficult, as there might not be sufficient minority data to train a GAN. A conditional GAN, which is able to condition the image generation on a specific class, would be more suitable for this oversampling task as it makes use of all data—positives and negatives. In this way, the GAN can learn from a larger feature space to generate samples for the minority class [10]. Moreover, Deep Convolutional GANs (DGGANs) [12] are an extension of the vanilla GAN, where the fully connected blocks are replaced by convolutional blocks. Another improvement in the GAN architecture is the Wasserstein GAN (WGAN) [2], which uses another loss function instead of the binary cross-entropy loss. With the addition of gradient penalty (WGAN-GP) to stabilize learning, it diminishes the vanishing gradient problem the original GAN has [6]. Various researchers have tried to investigate combinations of different models to tackle the imbalance problem. Shamsolmoali et al. [13] have integrated Capsule Neural Networks and GANs to generate the minority class. A more end-to-end framework is proposed by Mullick et al. [11], which came up with a framework consisting of a discriminator, generator and classifier to address class imbalance. The generator learns to generate the minority class which are misclassified, whereas the classifier learns to classify samples as minority or majority class. However, the above mentioned works are highly focused on solving the class imbalance in empirical datasets, such as MNIST and ImageNet, while we make use of a real-world remote sensing dataset, which is created by Statistics Netherlands for analysis of sustainability indicators in The Netherlands. To our knowledge, oversampling the minority class in an imbalanced case with GANs has not been performed before in the field of solar panel classification. Although GANs have been used to address the lack of annotated remote sensing data (e.g. MARTA GAN [7], SiftingGAN [9]), these remote sensing GAN frameworks are not aimed at solar panel image generation and classification. Also, they are not designed to generate data of the specific under-represented class in case of class imbalance, but rather add more labeled data from every class when the dataset is small. Therefore, we propose a performance comparison of several new GAN frameworks to oversample the under-represented class in aerial solar panel datasets, such that a better classification performance on another geographical location is attained. Instead of directly making use of the positive class as input for the conditional GAN, we subdivide the classes based on their encoded feature information. This division is retrieved by clustering on feature embeddings extracted by a fine-tuned VGG16 network, and these clusters are corroborated by visualizing their samples in a lower dimension. Accordingly, we are able to further ensure heterogeneity of image generation, provide a better feature representation and decrease the risk that the generator only generates one single mode. To our knowledge, tackling the class imbalance with GANs conditioned on this type of auxiliary information has not been performed before in the field of remote sensing and/or solar panel data. Also, we avoid constructing architectures which are overly complex, such that relative computational efficiency is assured, making the proposed models realistically applicable in real-world challenges.

2 Methods

2.1 Datasets

The *source* dataset covers aerial images around Heerlen area (The Netherlands) and has a resolution of 200×200 pixels. It contains 23 847 labeled images, with 4672 positives (20%) and 19 175 negatives (80%). The *target* set covers aerial images from the South of province Limburg (The Netherlands), consisting of 39 506 labeled images, with 36 693 negatives (93%) and 2813 positives (7%). For this imbalanced ratio, a VGG11-based classification model fine-tuned on the source set gives an accuracy, precision and recall of 87.19%, 94.81% respectively 57.10% on the Zuid-Limburg target set. Even though 42.90% of the positives are misclassified as negative, the target accuracy is still high due to only consisting of 7% positives. The model does not have difficulty with classifying the negatives, derived from the high precision value, appearing to be highly biased towards the negative class, while at the same time being overly prudent with classifying samples as positive. Hence, for the comparison between classification performances, we will focus on improving the recall on the Zuid-Limburg target set as our performance metric. For computational efficiency purposes, a sample of 10 000 images is taken from the source dataset to cluster the images and train the GANs. This new set contains all the 4672 positives (47%) and 5328 (53%) negatives. Since we will not generate negatives with the GAN, this omission of negatives is not significant. In contrary, when training the classifier to evaluate the GANs performance, we use the complete source dataset of 23 847 labeled images.

Preprocessing: The research procedure consists of three parts: (1) a preprocessing step where the data is clustered based on its class and features, followed by (2) the generation of synthetic images by means of different types of GANs, and (3) an evaluation of the classification performance after adding the generated data. This is summarized in Fig. 1. First, a VGG16 network, fine-tuned on the Heerlen source samples, is used as a feature extractor. The output of the last flatten layer is used, providing latent vectors of 12800 dimensions. These embeddings are the input for clustering methods, which divide the samples into multiple groups. This information is used as the conditional input for the GAN, which generates the fakes images.

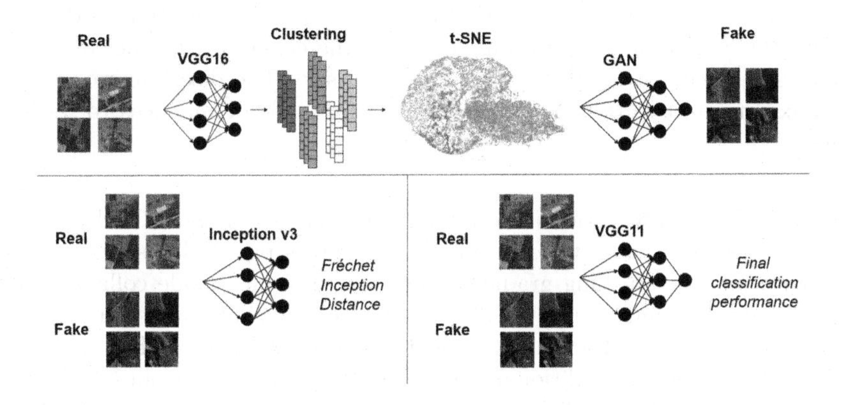

Fig. 1. Experimental design of research procedure

Clustering: The clustering methods are performed on the feature embeddings generated with the fine-tuned VGG16 network. These resulting clusters are provided as auxiliary information for the GANs. The clusterings are computed with KMeans and hierarchical clustering, with Euclidean distance and cosine similarity as distance measures. For the evaluation, The Silhouette score and Calinski-Harabasz (CH) score are used, as these metrics do not require access to the ground truth labels. The Silhouette score is bounded between -1 and $+1$, and a score of -1 implies poor clustering, while a score of $+1$ is optimal. The CH score is not bounded and is desired to be as high as possible.

2.2 Generative Adversarial Networks

Generative Adversarial Network (GAN) is a deep learning based technique that consists of two antagonistic neural networks which have opposite objectives. Eventually, the goal of the GAN is to generate images which are indistinguishable from the real images, as the fake distribution gradually simulates the real distribution. In the original GAN, the discriminator is a classifier which determines whether a given image originated from the real or generative distribution, by evaluating the conditional probability of the class (real/fake) Y, given the features X. In contrary, the generator aims to produce samples which are close to the real data by modeling its feature distribution, evaluating the probability of the features/data X. It effectuates this imitation by learning a mapping between a latent input vector and the space of the data. Since the discriminator makes a distinction between two classes, the binary cross-entropy (BCE) cost function is used to determine the GAN loss. An improvement of the vanilla GAN is the Deep Convolutional GAN [12], which performs downsampling with the convolutional stride and upsampling with transposed convolutions, rather than using fully connected layers. Another advancement is the addition of an auxiliary class condition to the input of the GAN, which adds an extra condition to the input of both the generator and discriminator. For the generator, the noise vector is concatenated with a one-hot vector of the class Y. The discriminator receives this auxiliary information by an addition of the one-hot matrices to its input images.

Wasserstein GAN: One of the main disadvantages of the BCE loss is that it approaches zero when the discriminator outputs probabilities close to 0 or 1, which leads to vanishing gradients. This could induce mode collapse, which implies that the generator is stuck at generating one type of sample (mode) which has shown to trick the discriminator, as it has stopped learning. This problem is even more severe in unconditional GANs, since the generator is not compelled to generate multiple classes. To combat this inconvenience, Wasserstein GANs are introduced by Arjovsky, Chintala and Bottou [1,2]. The WGAN considers a loss function based on the Earth Mover's Distance (EMD), also called Wasserstein-1 distance, which computes the minimum effort required to transform the real distribution to the generative distribution. The main benefit of the EMD compared to BCE loss is that its output values are unbounded, which diminishes its susceptibility to vanishing gradient problems. In this setting, the discriminator is known as a 'critic', as it evaluates a distance rather than probabilities of classes. However, the Wasserstein GAN has the stability requirement that the critic's gradient norm is at most 1 for every possible input, which is controlled by 1-Lipschitz continuity. There are multiple ways to enforce 1-L continuity on the Wasserstein GAN. The first way is weight clipping [2]: imposing the critic's weights to be between bounds, meaning that the weight values which are lower or higher than these bounds are 'clipped' to these bounds. However, the main risk of this method is that it inhibits the learning of the critic. Another method is adding a gradient penalty, a form of regularization of the critic's gradient introduced by Gulrajani et al. [6]. Using these considerations, a new Wasserstein loss function can be derived, by incorporating gradient penalty and a penalty weight λ:

$$\min_{g}\max_{c}\mathbb{E}(c(x)) - \mathbb{E}(c(g(z))) + \lambda\mathbb{E}(\|\nabla c(\hat{x})\|_2 - 1)^2 \tag{1}$$

Self-attention GAN: Although Deep Convolutional GANs are good in generating images with geometric structures, DCGANs sometimes fail to generate the complete object accurately. This is due to the convolutional filters in the DCGAN, having receptive fields which might not be sufficiently large to discover non-local structures in the image. Therefore, the concept of self-attention applied to GANs is introduced by Zhang et al. [14], which improves the evaluation of which part of the feature map should receive more attention. This is particularly interesting in the field of solar panel recognition, as the solar panels cover a small fraction of the image. The concept of self-attention uses three representation matrices: query (Q), key (K) and value (V) matrices. Conceptually, the query matrix entails the representation of every position related to itself; the key matrix contains the representation of every position with respect to other positions; the value gives a weight for the attention at every position. The importance of two specific positions relative to each other is computed by the dot product of the query (Q) and key (K) matrices, which is called dot product attention. This dot product is converted to a probability distribution by means of a softmax. The computation and all the other details of Self-Attention GAN are described in [14].

3 Evaluation

Since we are generating images, we can subjectively observe how realistic the samples are. For the evaluation of GANs, two characteristics of the images are important: fidelity and diversity. The fidelity is defined as the quality (e.g. blurriness or realism) of the generated images. The diversity refers to the variety/heterogeneity of the images. However, we will also quantitatively evaluate the images by means of the Fréchet Inception Distance and classification performance increase. *The Fréchet Inception Distance (FID)* is an evaluation metric which computes a high-level feature distance between the real and fake images and is considered as a quantitative indicator of diversity and fidelity. The ImageNet pre-trained Inception-v3 network is widely used as the state-of-the-art feature extractor for FID evaluation. The output of the model is defined by the last pooling layer, which gives an encoded representation of the features in the image of 2048 dimensions. In our experiments, we used a subsample of 512 feature vectors for both real and fake images to compute the FID scores.

A second quantitative metric is assessing whether adding synthetic positives to the source dataset leads to a *classification performance increase in the target set.* For training, we split the source dataset into a train, validation and test

Table 1. Evaluation metrics clustering

Dataset	Method	Linkage	Distance	Silhouette score	Calinski-harabasz score
Source set	Kmeans		Euclidean	**0.51**	**1675.70**
	Hierarchical	Ward	Euclidean	0.43	1207.40

set in the ratio (70:20:10). It is made sure that the percentage of positives is 20% in all datasets, analogous to the original source dataset. The architecture of this model is based on VGG11, where the last 4 convolutional blocks are retrained, while freezing the first 4 convolutional blocks. After adding synthetic positives, the classifier with the same hyperparameter settings is trained on this new dataset, and its performance metrics are compared with the baseline model. For every experiment, we run the classification model three times and report the average performance.

Influencing the Generation: (a) *Subset of Clusters.* Due to the usage of the clusters, we could have more control over the generation of positives by selecting a subset of clusters we would like to generate. (b) *Truncation trick* The generation can also be influenced by adjusting the noise vector. The values within this vector are sampled from a Gaussian distribution, which implies that values closer to zero occur more frequently in the generator's input during GAN training. These values will generally also lead to higher quality images, as the generator has seen these noise values more regularly during training. The downside is that these images will be less diverse. With this trick, we can influence the generation of images by truncating the values in the noise vectors provided to the trained GAN.

4 Results and Discussion

4.1 Data Preprocessing

In Table 1, the performance metrics for both KMeans and hierarchical clustering are shown. KMeans is evaluated with the Euclidean distance and the optimum number of clusters is $k = 5$, value based on experimentation. As hierarchical clustering has several parameters to tune (e.g. number of clusters, affinity, linkage type), only the best experimental combinations are shown in the table, while we explored all combinations. We can see that KMeans has the best Silhouette and CH score of 0.51 respectively 1675.70. Therefore, as a next step we evaluated the class distribution within the KMeans clusters. Four clusters (0, 2, 3, and 4) consist of more than 99% positives, while cluster 1 contains roughly all the negatives. However, 25% of the samples within cluster 1 are positive instead of negative. Since we will use the positive clusters as conditional input for the GANs to generate new positives, this implies that the positives hidden in the negative cluster will not be included in generation. Further exploration shows that these positives in cluster 1 are the samples that are mostly misclassified by the classification model. Hence, it might be interesting to include these positives in GAN training, since adding more of these type of generated positives to the dataset might enable the classifier to improve on these samples. Therefore, a possible solution is to split the negatives from this cluster into cluster 1 (the split positives) and a newly created cluster 5 (the negatives). We will compare the GAN performances achieved by considering four scenarios: training the GAN with the 2 original classes as input, the original 5 clusters, the 6 clusters and the 5 clusters where the positives are omitted from the 'negative' cluster.

4.2 Generation and Evaluation

We will test three different types of GANs: the conditional vanilla GAN, the conditional Wasserstein GAN and the conditional Self-Attention GAN. We will also condition the GANs on two types of auxiliary inputs: the original binary class and the generated clusters. For all training, a GPU (Tesla-V100-SXM2) of 32 GB and CUDA version 11.1 is used. For all models, the images are resized from $200 \times 200 \times 3$ to $96 \times 96 \times 3$, as experimentation showed that resizing the images to this resolution provided more realistic outputs as well as being more computationally efficient. We noticed that adding too many synthetic samples to the source set would mean that there are proportionally a lot more synthetic positives than real positives in the dataset, which could make the classification model focus more on the fake positives. Experimentation with several proportions of added synthetic positives showed that the percentage of positives in the source set increasing from 19.59% to 35.13% consistently gave the best results. This implies the new source set consists of 45.0% real positives and 55.0% fake positives out of all positives. Therefore, all experiments below make use of these proportions to enable an analogous and equitable comparison of results. As already mentioned, for every experiment we run the classification model three times and report the average performance.

Vanilla GAN: The optimal architecture for the vanilla conditional GAN with binary cross-entropy loss has a generator with 6 convolutional blocks and a discriminator with 4 convolutional blocks. The batch size is 256, noise dimension 64, learning rate 0.0002 and we used the Adam optimizer. It makes use of normal initialization for both the convolutional and batch normalization layers. The model was trained for 600–2000 epochs.

Comparing the Generator Input: We test four different GAN inputs: the original 2 classes (A), the 5 original clusters (B), 5 clusters with the positives in the 'negative' cluster completely omitted from the dataset (C), and 6 clusters with the positives in the 'negative' cluster separated (D). The results are shown in Table 2. The results show that the 6 clusters with the split positives gives the best FID (198.85) and recall increase (2.91%) compared to the baseline model.

Table 2. Performance comparison of vanilla GAN

Model	Input	Output	FID	Accuracy	Recall	Precision
Baseline				0.8719	0.5710	0.9481
A	2 classes	1-dim	251.6	0.8728	0.5918	0.9237
B	5 clusters (original)	1-dim	220.6	0.8731	0.5971	0.9182
C	5 clusters (positives omitted)	1-dim	292.6	0.8736	0.5972	0.9227
D	6 clusters	1-dim	**198.85**	0.8747	**0.6001**	0.9208
E	6 clusters	8-dim	**185.58**	0.8747	**0.6037**	0.9180

Figure 2 shows a random set of generated images, in which every row represents a cluster and the last row represents the negative cluster. The models which make use of the clusters as input (B and D) have a higher/worse FID value as well as higher observed fidelity and diversity than the model A, which uses the classes as input. However, completely omitting the positives from the negative cluster (model C) increases the FID, which could be due to not having sufficient data.

Comparing Discriminator Output: The results show that the 8-dimensional output (model E) provides a better FID score (185.58) than the scalar prediction of model D (198.85). Additionally, model E gives the highest increase in recall, namely 3.27%. A grid of generated images is shown in Fig. 3.

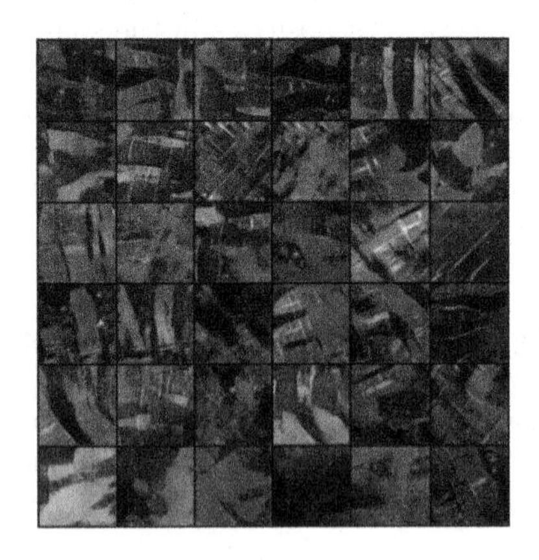

Fig. 2. Generated images Vanilla GAN (model D)

Fig. 3. Generated images Vanilla GAN (model E)

Wasserstein GAN: The second type of GAN we evaluate is the conditional Deep Convolutional WGAN. In order to ensure 1-Lipschitz continuity of the critic, we can impose gradient penalty or weight clipping. We evaluated several variations of the WGAN: WGAN without any 1-L enforcement, WGAN with gradient penalty and WGAN with gradient clipping. The optimal generator and critic architecture both consist of 5 blocks. The models are run for a varying number of epochs between 600–2000, with noise dimension 64, batch size 256 and learning rate 0.0002. We experiment with both optimizers Adam and RMSprop, as the authors of the vanilla WGAN [2] state that a momentum-based optimizer such as Adam may destabilize training, while the authors of the WGAN-GP [6] found that Adam outperforms RMSprop. Moreover, updating the critic multiple times before updating the generator is introduced for the WGAN-GP, as we want to avoid that the generator overpowers the critic due to not having a penalty.

WGAN with Gradient Penalty: In Table 3, the results for some of the WGAN models with gradient penalty are shown. Model H is the WGAN without any penalty or 1-L enforcement. It generates good images until the 250th epoch, after which the model destabilizes and fails to generate realistic results. Hence, for its FID calculation, the model at the 250th epoch is chosen, which shows a relatively high diversity and medium realistic results and the highest recall increase of 3.52%. The other models (I until L) make use of gradient penalty. The WGAN with penalty weight 10, 2 updates for the critic before updating the generator and optimizer RMSprop (model I) shows the best FID of 193.51 and highest recall increase of 2.90%. A sample of generated images from model I is shown in Fig. 4. The table also shows that increasing the critic repeats from 2 to 5 in model L worsens the performance drastically, as the critic might overpower the generator.

Table 3. Performance comparison of WGAN

Model	Penalty weight	Critic repeats	Optimizer	Clip value	FID	Accuracy	Recall	precision
Baseline						0.8719	0.5710	0.9481
H	None	1	Adam		232.6	0.8761	**0.6062**	0.9219
I	10	2	RMSprop		**193.51**	0.8741	0.6000	0.9201
J	15	1	RMSprop		200.88	0.8735	0.5995	0.9175
K	10	1	Adam		251.3	0.8710	0.5703	0.9456
L	10	5	Adam		332.1	0.8703	0.5698	0.9442
M			Adam	0.01	**181.82**	0.8864	**0.6324**	0.9269
P			RMSprop	0.02	207.04	0.8735	0.6020	0.9240
Q			Adam	0.03	210.06	0.8792	0.6144	0.9211

WGAN with Weight Clipping: For the WGAN with weight clipping, various clip values are examined. The results of some models with various parameters are shown in Table 3. Model M, P and Q show the results with clip value 0.01, 0.02 respectively 0.03. Model M showed the best FID value of 181.82. The model increases the target recall with 6.14%, while model Q with clip value 0.03 increases the metric with 4.34%.

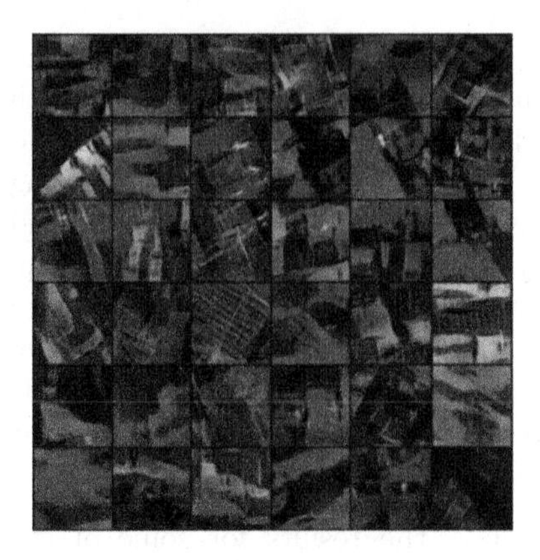

Fig. 4. Generated images WGAN with GP (model I)

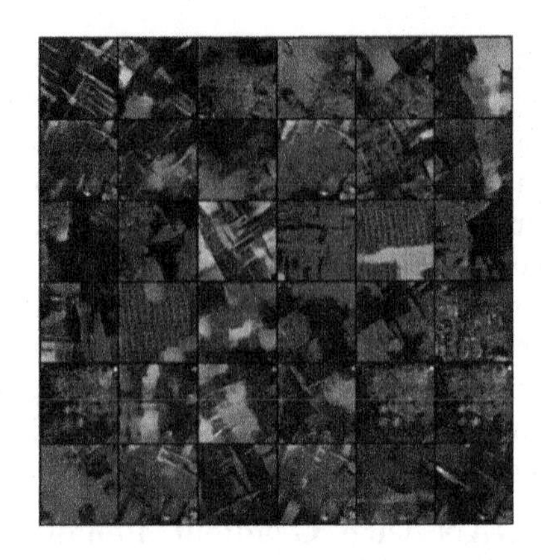

Fig. 5. Generated images SA-GAN (model R)

Table 4. SA-GAN comparison

Model	Attention blocks	Loss	FID	Accuracy	Recall	Precision
Baseline				0.8719	0.5710	0.9481
R	1	BCE	**209.68**	0.8750	**0.6022**	0.9213
S	2	BCE	240.97	0.8739	0.5964	0.9232

Self-attention GAN: The Self-Attention (SA) GAN paper states that spectral normalization in both the generator and discriminator improves the performance of the SA-GAN [14]. However, analogous to the results for the WGAN, spectral normalization destabilized the GAN. Moreover, both WGAN with weight clipping and WGAN with gradient penalty did not show stable results. However, the SA-GAN with BCE loss did show more stable results. In Table 4, the results for the two best models are shown. Both models use the BCE loss. In model R, both the generator and discriminator consist of 5 convolutional blocks, while the attention block is placed after the second block. In model S, an extra attention block is placed after the second convolutional block. Table 4 shows that the model with one attention block delivered the highest FID of 209.68. Also, the recall rate improved with 3.12%. A sample of generated images is shown in Fig. 5. The sample shows that the solar panels are visible, although it contains many images which seem more unrealistic and nonsensical than previous models.

5 Conclusion

This research was focused on finding a suitable oversampling method to address the class imbalance in an aerial image dataset, in order to improve the classification performance on a target set covering another geographical location.

Originally, the model is biased towards the majority group, being overly prudent with classifying a sample as positive, resulting in a low recall rate of 57.10% in the target set. For the generation of synthetic minority samples, we made use of three different GAN architectures: the conditional vanilla GAN, conditional Wasserstein GAN with different 1-Lipschitz continuity enforcements and the Self-Attention GAN. Instead of directly making use of the positive class as condition input for the GAN, we subdivided the class based on clusters on fine-tuned VGG16-based feature embeddings. Accordingly, we were able to further ensure heterogeneity of image generation and guarantee a feature representation based on multiple modes. While all models led to an increase in recall for the target set, the Wasserstein GAN with weight clipping provided the largest recall increase of 6.14%, while also achieving the best FID of 181.82. Nonetheless, the experiments have shown that these models are highly sensitive to hyper-parameter and architecture settings while also being computationally complex, making the process expensive. Moreover, one of the main challenges is the relative size of the solar panel in the image, as it covers a small part of the image. For future work we propose investigating whether these issues could be addressed, by further improving the GAN architecture with state-of-the-art techniques, such as injecting more random noise with Adaptive Instance Normalization, substituting the noise vector by a Noise Mapping Network, adding skip connections and/or progressively growing to speed up the training time.

References

1. Arjovsky, M., Bottou, L.: Towards principled methods for training generative adversarial networks. arXiv preprint arXiv:1701.04862 (2017)
2. Arjovsky, M., Chintala, S., Bottou, L.: Wasserstein gan. arXiv preprint arXiv:1701.07875 (2017)
3. Buda, M., Maki, A., Mazurowski, M.A.: A systematic study of the class imbalance problem in convolutional neural networks. Neural Netw. **106**, 249–259 (2018)
4. Douzas, G., Bacao, F.: Effective data generation for imbalanced learning using conditional generative adversarial networks. Expert Syst. Appl. **91**, 464–471 (2018)
5. Goodfellow, I., et al.: Generative adversarial nets. In: Advances in Neural Information Processing Systems, pp. 2672–2680 (2014)
6. Gulrajani, I., Ahmed, F., Arjovsky, M., Dumoulin, V., Courville, A.C.: Improved training of Wasserstein gans. In: Advances in Neural Information Processing Systems, pp. 5767–5777 (2017)
7. Lin, D., Fu, K., Wang, Y., Xu, G., Sun, X.: MARTA GANs: unsupervised representation learning for remote sensing image classification. IEEE Geosci. Remote Sens. Lett. **14**(11), 2092–2096 (2017)
8. Lusa, L., et al.: Evaluation of smote for high-dimensional class-imbalanced microarray data. In: 11th International Conference on Machine Learning and Applications (2012)
9. Ma, D., Tang, P., Zhao, L.: SiftingGAN: generating and sifting labeled samples to improve the remote sensing image scene classification baseline in vitro. IEEE Geosci. Remote Sens. Lett. **16**(7), 1046–1050 (2019)
10. Mariani, G., Scheidegger, F., Istrate, R., Bekas, C., Malossi, C.: BAGAN: data augmentation with balancing GAN. arXiv preprint arXiv:1803.09655 (2018)

11. Mullick, S.S., Datta, S., Das, S.: Generative adversarial minority oversampling. In: Proceedings of the IEEE/CVF International Conference on Computer Vision, pp. 1695–1704 (2019)
12. Radford, A., Metz, L., Chintala, S.: Unsupervised representation learning with deep convolutional generative adversarial networks. arXiv:1511.06434 (2015)
13. Shamsolmoali, P., Zareapoor, M., Shen, L., Sadka, A.H., Yang, J.: Imbalanced data learning by minority class augmentation using capsule adversarial networks. Neurocomputing (2020)
14. Zhang, H., Goodfellow, I., Metaxas, D., Odena, A.: Self-attention generative adversarial networks. In: International Conference on Machine Learning, pp. 7354–7363. PMLR (2019)

Augment Small Training Sets Using Matching-Graphs

Mathias Fuchs[1(✉)] and Kaspar Riesen[1,2]

[1] Institute of Computer Science, University of Bern, 3012 Bern, Switzerland
{mathias.fuchs,kaspar.riesen}@inf.unibe.ch

[2] Institute for Informations Systems, University of Applied Sciences Northwestern Switzerland, 4600 Olten, Switzerland
kaspar.riesen@fhnw.ch

Abstract. Both data access and data acquisition have become increasingly easy over the past decade, leading to rapid developments in many areas of intelligent information processing. In many cases, the underlying data is complex, making vectorial structures rather inappropriate for data representation. In these cases graphs provide a versatile alternative to purely numerical approaches. Regardless the representation formalism actually used, it is inevitable for supervised pattern recognition algorithms to have access to large sets of labeled training samples. In some cases, however, this requirement cannot be met because the set of labeled samples is inherently limited. In a recent research project a novel encoding of pairwise graph matchings is introduced. The basic idea of this encoding is to formalize the stable cores of pairs of patterns by means of graphs, termed matching-graphs. In the present paper we propose a novel scenario for the use of these matching-graphs. That is, we employ them to enlarge small training sets of graphs in order to stabilize the training of a classifier. In an experimental evaluation on four graph data sets we show that this novel augmentation technique improves the classification accuracy of an SVM classifier with statistical significance.

Keywords: Graph matching · Matching-graphs · Graph edit distance · Graph augmentation

1 Introduction and Related Work

Pattern recognition is an important field of research that attempts to solve diverse problems such as emotion recognition [21], person re-identification [14] or signature verification [10], to name just three examples. The very first step in any pattern recognition scenario is to solve the data representation challenge. In terms of data representation, graphs are a good alternative to feature vectors because they can encode more information than merely an ordered list of real

Supported by Swiss National Science Foundation (SNSF) Project Nr. 200021_188496.

M. El Yacoubi et al. (Eds.): ICPRAI 2022, LNCS 13364, pp. 343–354, 2022.
https://doi.org/10.1007/978-3-031-09282-4_29

numbers. Due to their power and flexibility, graphs can be found in various pattern recognition applications that range from gait recognition [2], over link-fault detection [13], to object recognition [15].

Most of the graph based pattern recognition methods available are based on some sort of *graph matching* [7]. Graph matching describes the task of quantifying pairwise graph proximity. *Graph edit distance* [4,20], introduced about 40 years ago, is acknowledged as one of the most flexible graph distance models available to date. The major advantage of this paradigm over other distance measures (like *graph kernels* [3] or *graph neural networks* [23]) is, that graph edit distance provides more information than merely a dissimilarity score. In particular, graph edit distance gives us the information that states which subparts of the underlying graphs actually match with each other (known as *edit path*). In a recent work [8] the authors of the present paper suggest to explicitly use the matching information of graph edit distance to encode stable parts of pairs of graphs in a novel data structure called *matching-graph.*

According to [12], Mercer's famous comment, "There is no data like more data," was made at Arden House in 1985. The authors of [1] even argue that more data is more important than better algorithms. At least we agree that labeled training data is one of the most crucial prerequisites for the development and evaluation of supervised pattern recognition methods. This applies in particular for deep learning methods [17,22] which perform better the more examples of a given phenomenon a network is exposed to. However, in real-world applications, we are often faced with the fact that the amount of training data is limited (for various reasons). The main contribution of the present paper is to propose a novel and systematic way of increasing the amount of training data for graph based pattern recognition. The basic idea is to compute matching-graphs for any pair of training graphs available. In this way, the amount of training data can be increased virtually at any size.

The proposed process of creating matching-graphs in order to enlarge training sets is similar in spirit to graph augmentation approaches [27,28]. However most of these approaches augment the graphs by altering edge information only. Moreover, these approaches often rely on a single sample of a graph. In our approach, however, we generate new graphs based on information captured in the edit path resulting from pairs of graphs. The graphs generated this way include both edge and node modifications. Our main hypothesis is that this novel method provides a natural way to create realistic and relevant graphs that are actually useful during training of pattern recognition algorithms.

The remainder of this paper is organized as follows. Section 2 makes the paper self-contained by providing basic definitions and terms used throughout this paper. Next, in Sect. 3, a detailed description of the data augmentation process is given in conjunction with the general procedure of creating matching-graphs. Eventually, in Sect. 4, we provide empirical evidence that our approach of generating training samples is able to improve the classification accuracy of an existing classification system. Finally, in Sect. 5, we conclude the paper and discuss some ideas for future work.

2 Basic Definitions

The following definition allows us to handle arbitrarily structured graphs with unconstrained labeling functions.

Let L_V and L_E be finite or infinite label sets for nodes and edges, respectively. A *graph* g is a four-tuple $g = (V, E, \mu, \nu)$, where

- V is the finite set of nodes,
- $E \subseteq V \times V$ is the set of edges,
- $\mu : V \rightarrow L_V$ is the node labeling function, and
- $\nu : E \rightarrow L_E$ is the edge labeling function.

In some algorithms it is necessary to include *empty "nodes"* and/or *empty "edges"*. We denote both empty nodes and empty edges by ε.

When graphs are used to represent different objects, a measure of distance or similarity is usually required. We employ *graph edit distance* as basic dissimilarity model. One of the main advantages of graph edit distance is its high degree of flexibility, which makes it applicable to virtually all types of graphs.

Given two graphs g and g', the basic idea of graph edit distance is to transform g into g' using some *edit operations*. A standard set of edit operations is given by *insertions*, *deletions*, and *substitutions* of both nodes and edges. We denote the substitution of two nodes $u \in V_1$ and $v \in V_2$ by $(u \rightarrow v)$, the deletion of node $u \in V_1$ by $(u \rightarrow \varepsilon)$, and the insertion of node $v \in V_2$ by $(\varepsilon \rightarrow v)$. For edge edit operations we use a similar notation.

A set $\{e_1, \ldots, e_s\}$ of s edit operations e_i that transform a source graph g completely into a target graph g' is called an *edit path* $\lambda(g, g')$ between g and g'. Let $\Upsilon(g, g')$ denote the set of all edit paths transforming g into g' while c denotes the cost function measuring the strength $c(e_i)$ of edit operation e_i. The graph edit distance can now be defined as follows.

Let $g = (V_1, E_1, \mu_1, \nu_1)$ be the source and $g' = (V_2, E_2, \mu_2, \nu_2)$ the target graph. The *graph edit distance* between g and g' is defined by

$$d_{\lambda_{\min}}(g, g') = \min_{\lambda \in \Upsilon(g, g')} \sum_{e_i \in \lambda} c(e_i). \tag{1}$$

Optimal algorithms for computing the edit distance of two graphs are typically based on combinatorial search procedures. It is known that finding an exact solution for graph edit distance is an NP-complete problem [9]. Thus, applying graph edit distance to large graphs is computationally demanding, or even intractable.

In order to reduce the computational complexity of graph edit distance computation, several approximation algorithms have been proposed in the literature [5,6]. In this paper we use the often employed approximation algorithm BP [18,24]. This specific algorithm reduces the problem of graph edit distance computation to an instance of a linear sum assignment problem for which several efficient algorithms exist. The approximated graph edit distance between g and g' computed by algorithm BP is termed $d_{\mathrm{BP}}(g, g')$ from now on.

3 Augment Training Sets by Means of Matching-Graphs

The general idea of the proposed approach is to increase the size of a given training set by means of *matching-graphs*. Matching-graphs are built by extracting information on the matching of pairs of graphs and by formalizing and encoding this information in a data structure. Matching-graphs can be interpreted as denoised core structures of the underlying graphs. The idea of matching-graphs initially emerged in [8] where they are employed for improving the overall quality of graph edit distance. The matching-graphs used in this paper are adapted for graph set augmentation and are created in a slightly different way as originally proposed.

Formally, we assume k sets of training graphs $G_{\omega_1}, \ldots, G_{\omega_k}$ stemming from k different classes $\omega_1, \ldots, \omega_k$. For all pairs of graphs stemming from the same class ω_l, the graph edit distance is computed by means of algorithm BP [18]. Hence, we obtain a (sub-optimal) edit path $\lambda(g, g') = \{e_1, \ldots, e_s\}$ for each pair of graphs $g, g' \in G_{\omega_l} \times G_{\omega_l}$. Each edit operation $e_i \in \lambda(g, g')$ can either be a substitution, a deletion or an insertion of a node including the corresponding edge edit operation.

Eventually for each edit path $\lambda(g, g')$, matching-graphs are built. In its initial definition [8], a matching-graph $m_{g \times g'}$ represents nodes as well as edges of g and g' that have been matched under the usage of some specific model. That is, a matching-graph basically represents the substituted subparts of two underlying graphs.

In our specific case, however, the matching-graphs are created according to the following procedure. We randomly select a certain percentage $p \in [0, 1]$ of all s edit operations available in $\lambda(g, g')$, where p is a user defined parameter. Hence, we obtain a partial edit path $\tau(g, g') = \{e_1, \ldots, e_t\ \} \subseteq \lambda(g, g')$ with $t = \lfloor p \cdot s \rfloor$ edit operations only. Then each edit operation $e_i \in \tau(g, g')$ is applied on both graphs g and g' according to the following rules:

- If e_i refers to a substitution it is applied on both g and g', which means that the labels of the matching nodes are swapped in the respective graphs.
- If e_i refers to a deletion, e_i is applied on g only.
- If e_i refers to an insertion, e_i is applied on g' only. This means that the node that would be inserted in g (according to e_i), is deleted in g' instead.

When all selected edit operations of $\tau(g, g')$ are applied on both graphs g and g', we obtain two novel graph representations $m_{g \times g'}$ and $m_{g' \times g}$ (one based on the source graph g and one on the target graph and g'). Both matching-graphs represent intermediate graphs between the two underlying training graphs. If p is set to 1.0, all edit operations from the complete edit path $\lambda(g, g')$ are considered during the matching-graph creation. Note, however, that according to our rules, deletions and insertions are uniquely applied on the source or the target graph, respectively. Hence, in this particular parameter setting we obtain two matching-graphs that are subgraphs from the original graphs. With parameter values $p < 1.0$, however, we obtain matching-graphs in which possibly some of the nodes are either deleted from g or g' and some other nodes are potentially altered according to their labeling (due to substitutions).

In Fig. 1 a visual example of a possible matching-graph which stems from the matching of a source graph and target graph is given. The complete edit path is given by $\lambda = \{(1 \rightarrow c), (2 \rightarrow \varepsilon), (\varepsilon \rightarrow d), (0 \rightarrow a), (3 \rightarrow b), (\varepsilon \rightarrow e)\}$. The possible matching-graph, showed in a frame in Fig. 1b, is created with $p = \frac{1}{3}$, resulting in the partial edit path $\tau(g, g') = \{(1 \rightarrow c), (2 \rightarrow \varepsilon)\}$, that consists of $t = 2$ edit operations only. For the sake of clarity, we show the matching-graph resulting from the source graph only.

In our evaluations we observe that the proposed process might lead to isolated nodes in the resulting matching-graphs. Although many graph matching algorithms can actually handle isolated nodes, we still remove them from our matching-graphs. The rationale for this heuristic is that we aim at building small and robust cores of the graphs with nodes that are actually connected to at least one other node in the obtained formalism.

The whole procedure of creating matching-graphs described above is individually repeated for each class of training graphs $G_{\omega_1}, \ldots, G_{\omega_k}$. Assuming n training graphs per class this results in $k \cdot n(n-1)$ matching-graphs in total. These matching-graphs can now directly be used to augment the corresponding training sets.

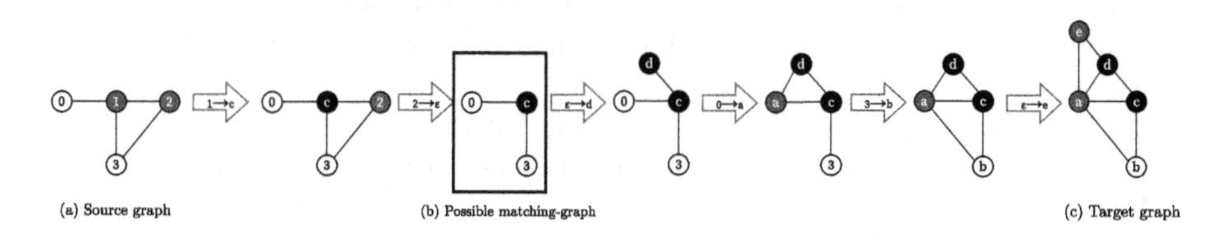

(a) Source graph
(b) Possible matching-graph
(c) Target graph

Fig. 1. An example of an edit path and the resulting matching-graph.

4 Experimental Evaluation

4.1 Experimental Setup

On the basis of the following experimental evaluation we aim to research whether or not matching-graphs can be used to augment small training sets to reliably increase the accuracy of a classification algorithm. In order to answer this question, we artificially reduce existing graph data sets to simulate limited training data. This is achieved by randomly selecting 10 training graphs per class for each data set. In order to avoid overly simple or very difficult data sets (that might be created by random chance), we repeat the random process of creating small data sets 20 times. The same accounts for training set augmentation by means of our matching-graphs which is also repeated 20 times.

As basic classification system a Support Vector Machine (SVM) that exclusively operates on a similarity kernel $\kappa(g, g') = -d_{\mathrm{BP}}(g, g')$ is used [16]. Note that any other data-driven classifier could be used in our evaluation as well. However, we feel that the SVM is particularly suitable for our evaluation because of its pure and direct use of the underlying distance information.

The primary reference system is trained on the reduced training data, denoted as $\text{SVM}_R(-d_{\text{BP}})$. Our novel approach, denoted as $\text{SVM}_{R}+(-d_{\text{BP}})$ is trained on the same training samples of the reduced sets but uses also the created matching-graphs. For the sake of completeness we also compare our novel framework with a secondary reference system, viz. an SVM that has access to the full training sets of graphs (before the artificial reduction is carried out), denoted as $\text{SVM}_F(-d_{\text{BP}})$.

4.2 Data Sets

By representing atoms as nodes and bonds as edges, graphs can actually represent chemical compounds in a lossless and straightforward manner. We evaluate our novel approach on the following four data sets that all represent molecules stemming from two classes.

- The **Mutagenicity** data set is split into two classes, containing mutagenic and non-mutagenic compounds, respectively. Mutagenicity refers to the ability of a chemical compound to cause DNA mutations.
- The **NCI1** data set [26][1] originates from anti-cancer screens and is split into molecules that have activity in inhibitioning the growth of non-small cell lung cancer and those that have no activity.
- The third data set **COX-2** originates from [25] and contains cyclooxygenase-2 (COX-2) inhibitors with or without in-vitro activities against human recombinant enzymes.
- The fourth and last data set **PTC(MR)** stems from the predictive toxicology challenge [11] and consists of compounds that are potentially carcinogenic.

The nodes of all data sets represent the atoms and are labeled with their chemical symbol. The edges of the graphs of the PTC(MR) data set are labeled with the information about the chemical bonds between the atoms. The edges of all other sets are unlabeled.

In Table 1 we show the size of the original training sets F and the size of the reduced sets R and augmented sets $R+$ (which is actually the same for each data set).

4.3 Validation of Metaparameters

In Table 2 an overview of all parameters that are optimized is presented. For algorithm BP, that approximates the graph edit distance, the cost for node and edge deletions, as well as a weighting parameter $\gamma \in [0, 1]$ that is used to trade-off the relative importance of node and edge edit costs are often optimized [18,19].

[1] https://ls11-www.cs.tu-dortmund.de/staff/morris/graphkerneldatasets.

Table 1. The total number of graphs in the full training set (F), the artificially reduced training set (R), and the augmented training set (R+).

Data set	F	R	R+
Mutagenicity	1,500	20	200
NCI1	2,465	20	200
COX-2	280	20	200
PTC(MR)	206	20	200

However, for the sake of simplicity we employ unit cost of 1.0 for deletions and insertions of both nodes and edges and optimize the weighting parameter γ only (on all data sets). For the creation of the matching-graphs – actually also dependant on the cost model – the same weighting parameter is independently optimized. In addition to this we optimize the percentage p of the edit path operations that are used for the matching-graph creation. For the SVM classificator itself, parameter C is optimized to trade off between the size of the margin and the number of misclassified training examples.

Table 2. Description and evaluated values of all parameters.

Parameter	Description	Evaluated values
γ	Parameter to scale node and edge costs during the computation of the graph edit distance and matching-graph creation. The higher the value the more important are the node edit operations.	$\{0.05, 0.10, \ldots, 0.90, 0.95\}$
p	The relative amount of edit operations used from the complete edit path λ	$\{0.25, 0.50, 0.75, 1.0\}$
C	Weighting parameter for SVM	$\{10^{-4}, 5 \cdot 10^{-4}, 10^{-3}, 5 \cdot 10^{-3}, 10^{-2}, 5 \cdot 10^{-2}, 10^{-1}, 5 \cdot 10^{-1}, 10^{0}, 10^{1}, 10^{2}\}$

4.4 Test Results and Discussion

In Fig. 2 we show the reference accuracies of $\text{SVM}_R(-d_{\text{BP}})$ as well as the accuracies of our system $\text{SVM}_{R}+(-d_{\text{BP}})$ as bar charts for all 20 random iterations on all four data sets. The iterations are ordered from the worst to the best performing reference accuracy. On the NCI1 and COX-2 data sets we observe that the SVM that relies on the matching-graphs performs better than, or at least equal as, the reference systems in all iterations. On the other two data sets Mutagenicity and PTC(MR) our system outperforms the reference system in 19 out of 20 iterations. In general we report substantial improvements over the respective baselines for almost all iterations and data sets. There is a tendency that the improvement is particularly large in iterations where the reference system performs poorly (most likely due to an unfortunate random selection of training samples which in turn might lead to overfitting). This is visible on all the data sets, but it is particularly well observable on the COX-2 and PTC(MR) data sets. For example on the COX-2 data set we outperform the reference system by about 30% points during the first two iterations (from 47.3% to 77.4% and from 51.6% to 82.8%, respectively). On PTC(MR) we see a similar pattern for the first three iterations, where our system increases the accuracy with about 20% points (from 41.4% to 62.8%, from 41.4% to 60% and from 47.1% to 70%). This underlines the usefulness of the systematic augmentation by means of matching-graphs, especially when small sets of rather poor training samples are available only.

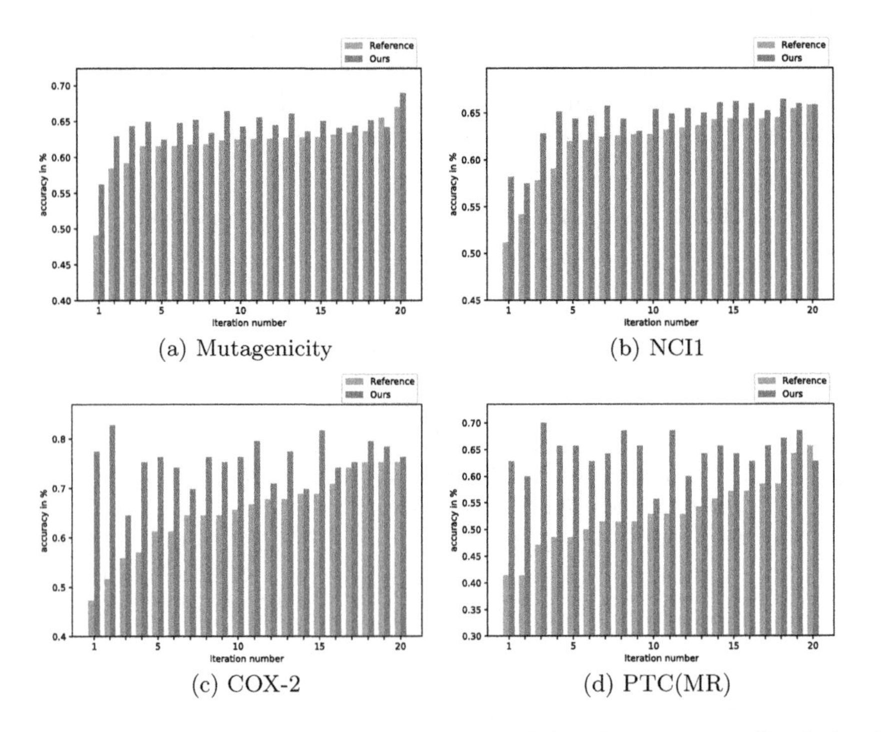

Fig. 2. Classification accuracies of all 20 iterations of the reference system (bright bars) compared to our novel system that additionally uses the matching-graphs for training (dark bars).

In Table 3 we compare the classification accuracy of our novel system with both reference systems in tabular form. To this end, we aggregated the results of the 20 iterations and show the mean classification accuracies (including the standard deviation). We observe that the mean classification accuracy of our approach is better than the first reference system on all data sets. On NCI1 our system outperforms the reference system in all iterations (as seen in Fig. 2). Eight of the 20 improvements are statistically significant[2]. Eight out of 19, 11 out of 20, and 13 out of 19 improvements are statistically significant on the other data sets, respectively.

On Mutagenicity and NCI1 the novel system does not reach the classification accuracy of the second reference system $\text{SVM}_F(-d_{\text{BP}})$ that has access to the full training data. Most of the deteriorations are statistically significant. However, we have to keep in mind that it was not our main goal to improve the full system, but to show that our approach is able to substantially improve a system that has access to a small data set only. From this point of view, it is rather surprising that our novel approach outperforms the second reference system on average on the other two data sets. We actually observe an immense improvement of about 10 percentage points on both data sets.

In Table 3 it is also visible that our system becomes more robust, as the standard deviation is smaller for each data set for $\text{SVM}_{R+}(-d_{\text{BP}})$ compared to $\text{SVM}_R(-d_{\text{BP}})$. It is also worth to note that on both Mutagenicity and PTC(MR), the average validation accuracy of our system lies closer to the average test accuracy, compared to the reference system, which might indicate a better generalization of our system (validation results are not shown due to the lack of space).

Table 3. Classification accuracies of two reference systems ($\text{SVM}_R(-d_{\text{BP}})$ and $\text{SVM}_F(-d_{\text{BP}})$) and our novel system $\text{SVM}_{R+}(-d_{\text{BP}})$. Symbols ⓧ/ⓨ indicate a statistically significant improvement and ❶x/❶y (filled x/y) indicate a statistically significant deterioration in x, y of the 20 iterations when compared with the first and second reference system, respectively (using a Z-test at significance level $\alpha = 0.05$).

	Reference systems		Ours
Data set	$\text{SVM}_R(-d_{\text{BP}})$	$\text{SVM}_F(-d_{\text{BP}})$	$\text{SVM}_{R+}(-d_{\text{BP}})$
Mutagenicity	61.8 ± 3.5	69.1	**64.3** ± 2.4 ⑬/ ⓳
NCI1	62.0 ± 3.8	68.6	**64.5** ± 2.4 ⑧/ ⓱
COX-2	65.2 ± 7.8	71.3	**75.6** ± 4.3 ⑪/ ③
PTC(MR)	53.1 ± 6.3	54.3	**64.6** ± 3.4 ⑧/ ⑤

5 Conclusion and Future Work

The present paper is concerned with the problem of training a classifier based on small sets of training samples. We focus our research on graph based pattern representation. The complete process is based on matching-graphs, which can be pre-computed by means of suboptimal graph edit distance computations on

[2] The statistical significance is computed via Z-test using a significance level of $\alpha =$ 0.05.

training graphs. The basic idea of matching-graphs is to formalize the matching between two graphs by defining a novel graph that reflects the core of each graph. This underlying core can be interpreted as a stable part of each graph.

The novelty of the present paper is that we use these matching-graphs in order to augment small training sets of graphs. That is, we systematically produce matching-graphs for each pair of training graphs and are thus able to substantially increase even very small sets of training graphs. The goal of this augmentation process is to make pattern recognition based on small labeled sets more robust and ultimately improve the downstream training of a classification algorithms.

By means of an experimental evaluation on four artificially reduced graph data sets, we empirically confirm that our novel approach is able to significantly outperform a classifier that has access to the small training data set only. Moreover, in some particular cases we can even report that our novel approach is able to outperform a system that has access to the full set of training graphs.

In future work we envision several rewarding avenues to pursue. First we feel that it could be beneficial to apply our approach in conjunction with graph neural networks, as these models are even more sensitive to the size of the training set. Furthermore, our approach can also be applied in conjunction with the full training sets in order to further improve existing classification approaches that already rely on relatively large sets of training graphs.

References

1. Banko, M., Brill, E.: Mitigating the paucity-of-data problem: exploring the effect of training corpus size on classifier performance for natural language processing. In: Proceedings of the First International Conference on Human Language Technology Research, HLT 2001, San Diego, California, USA, 18–21 March 2001. Morgan Kaufmann (2001). https://aclanthology.org/H01-1052/
2. Battistone, F., Petrosino, A.: TGLSTM: a time based graph deep learning approach to gait recognition. Pattern Recogn. Lett. **126**, 132–138 (2019). https://doi.org/10.1016/j.patrec.2018.05.004, https://www.sciencedirect.com/science/article/pii/S0167865518301703. Robustness, Security and Regulation Aspects in Current Biometric Systems
3. Borgwardt, K.M., Ghisu, M.E., Llinares-López, F., O'Bray, L., Rieck, B.: Graph Kernels: state-of-the-art and future challenges. Found. Trends Mach. Learn. **13**(5–6), 24–94 (2020). https://doi.org/10.1561/2200000076
4. Bunke, H., Allermann, G.: Inexact graph matching for structural pattern recognition. Pattern Recogn. Lett. **1**(4), 245–253 (1983). https://doi.org/10.1016/0167-8655(83)90033-8
5. Carletti, V., Gaüzère, B., Brun, L., Vento, M.: Approximate graph edit distance computation combining bipartite matching and exact neighborhood substructure distance. In: Liu, C.-L., Luo, B., Kropatsch, W.G., Cheng, J. (eds.) GbRPR 2015. LNCS, vol. 9069, pp. 188–197. Springer, Cham (2015). https://doi.org/10.1007/978-3-319-18224-7_19
6. Chen, X., Huo, H., Huan, J., Vitter, J.S.: Fast computation of graph edit distance. CoRR abs/1709.10305 (2017). http://arxiv.org/abs/1709.10305

7. Conte, D., Foggia, P., Sansone, C., Vento, M.: Thirty years of graph matching in pattern recognition. Int. J. Pattern Recogn. Artif. Intell. **18**(3), 265–298 (2004). https://doi.org/10.1142/S0218001404003228
8. Fuchs, M., Riesen, K.: Matching of matching-graphs - a novel approach for graph classification. In: 25th International Conference on Pattern Recognition, ICPR 2020, Virtual Event/Milan, Italy, 10–15 January 2021, pp. 6570–6576. IEEE (2020). https://doi.org/10.1109/ICPR48806.2021.9411926
9. Garey, M.R., Johnson, D.S.: Computers and Intractability: A Guide to the Theory of NP-Completeness. W. H. Freeman, San Francisco (1979)
10. Ghosh, S., Ghosh, S., Kumar, P., Scheme, E., Roy, P.P.: A novel spatio-temporal Siamese network for 3D signature recognition. Pattern Recogn. Lett. **144**, 13–20 (2021). https://doi.org/10.1016/j.patrec.2021.01.012, https://www.sciencedirect.com/science/article/pii/S0167865521000258
11. Helma, C., King, R.D., Kramer, S., Srinivasan, A.: The predictive toxicology challenge 2000–2001. Bioinformatics **17**(1), 107–108 (2001). https://doi.org/10.1093/bioinformatics/17.1.107
12. Jelinek, F.: Some of my best friends are linguists. Lang. Resour. Eval. **39**(1), 25–34 (2005). https://doi.org/10.1007/s10579-005-2693-4
13. Kenning, M., Deng, J., Edwards, M., Xie, X.: A directed graph convolutional neural network for edge-structured signals in link-fault detection. Pattern Recogn. Lett. **153**, 100–106 (2022). https://doi.org/10.1016/j.patrec.2021.12.003, https://www.sciencedirect.com/science/article/pii/S016786552100430X
14. Li, Z., Shao, H., Niu, L., Xue, N.: Progressive learning algorithm for efficient person re- identification. In: 25th International Conference on Pattern Recognition, ICPR 2020, Virtual Event/Milan, Italy, 10–15 January 2021, pp. 16–23. IEEE (2020). https://doi.org/10.1109/ICPR48806.2021.9413306
15. Madi, K., Paquet, E., Kheddouci, H.: New graph distance for deformable 3D objects recognition based on triangle-stars decomposition. Pattern Recogn. **90**, 297–307 (2019). https://doi.org/10.1016/j.patcog.2019.01.040, https://www.sciencedirect.com/science/article/pii/S0031320319300627
16. Neuhaus, M., Bunke, H.: Bridging the Gap between Graph Edit Distance and Kernel Machines, Series in Machine Perception and Artificial Intelligence, vol. 68. WorldScientific (2007). https://doi.org/10.1142/6523
17. Pereira, F., Norvig, P., Halevy, A.: The unreasonable effectiveness of data. IEEE Intell. Syst. **24**(02), 8–12 (2009). https://doi.org/10.1109/MIS.2009.36
18. Riesen, K., Bunke, H.: Approximate graph edit distance computation by means of bipartite graph matching. Image Vis. Comput. **27**(7), 950–959 (2009). https://doi.org/10.1016/j.imavis.2008.04.004
19. Riesen, K., Bunke, H.: Classification and clustering of vector space embedded graphs. In: Emerging Topics in Computer Vision and Its Applications, pp. 49–70. World Scientific (2012). https://doi.org/10.1142/9789814343008_0003
20. Sanfeliu, A., Fu, K.: A distance measure between attributed relational graphs for pattern recognition. IEEE Trans. Syst. Man Cybern. **13**(3), 353–362 (1983). https://doi.org/10.1109/TSMC.1983.6313167
21. Schoneveld, L., Othmani, A., Abdelkawy, H.: Leveraging recent advances in deep learning for audio-visual emotion recognition. Pattern Recogn. Lett. **146**, 1–7 (2021). https://doi.org/10.1016/j.patrec.2021.03.007, https://www.sciencedirect.com/science/article/pii/S0167865521000878
22. Shorten, C., Khoshgoftaar, T.M.: A survey on image data augmentation for deep learning. J. Big Data **6**, 60 (2019). https://doi.org/10.1186/s40537-019-0197-0

23. Singh, S., Steiner, B., Hegarty, J., Leather, H.: Using graph neural networks to model the performance of deep neural networks. CoRR abs/2108.12489 (2021). https://arxiv.org/abs/2108.12489
24. Stauffer, M., Tschachtli, T., Fischer, A., Riesen, K.: A survey on applications of bipartite graph edit distance. In: Foggia, P., Liu, C.-L., Vento, M. (eds.) GbRPR 2017. LNCS, vol. 10310, pp. 242–252. Springer, Cham (2017). https://doi.org/10.1007/978-3-319-58961-9_22
25. Sutherland, J.J., O'Brien, L.A., Weaver, D.F.: Spline-fitting with a genetic algorithm: a method for developing classification structure-activity relationships. J. Chem. Inf. Comput. Sci. **43**(6), 1906–1915 (2003). https://doi.org/10.1021/ci034143r
26. Wale, N., Watson, I.A., Karypis, G.: Comparison of descriptor spaces for chemical compound retrieval and classification. Knowl. Inf. Syst. **14**(3), 347–375 (2008). https://doi.org/10.1007/s10115-007-0103-5
27. Zhao, T., Liu, Y., Neves, L., Woodford, O.J., Jiang, M., Shah, N.: Data augmentation for graph neural networks. In: Thirty-Fifth AAAI Conference on Artificial Intelligence, AAAI 2021, Thirty-Third Conference on Innovative Applications of Artificial Intelligence, IAAI 2021, The Eleventh Symposium on Educational Advances in Artificial Intelligence, EAAI 2021, Virtual Event, 2–9 February 2021, pp. 11015–11023. AAAI Press (2021). https://ojs.aaai.org/index.php/AAAI/article/view/17315
28. Zhou, J., Shen, J., Yu, S., Chen, G., Xuan, Q.: M-evolve: structural-mapping-based data augmentation for graph classification. IEEE Trans. Netw. Sci. Eng. **8**(1), 190–200 (2021). https://doi.org/10.1109/TNSE.2020.3032950

Progressive Clustering: An Unsupervised Approach Towards Continual Knowledge Acquisition of Incremental Data

Akshaykumar Gunari(✉), Shashidhar V. Kudari, Ramesh Ashok Tabib, and Uma Mudenagudi

Center of Excellence for Visual Intelligence (CEVI), KLE Technological University, Hubli, India
akshaygunari@gmail.com, {ramesh_t,uma}@kletech.ac.in

Abstract. In this paper, we propose a categorization strategy to handle the incremental nature of data by identifying concepts of drift in the data stream. In the world of digitalization, the total amount of data created, captured, copied, and consumed is increasing rapidly, reaching a few zettabytes. Various fields of data mining and machine learning applications involve clustering as their principal component, considering the non-incremental nature of the data. However, many real-world machine learning algorithms need to adapt to this ever-growing global data sphere to continually learn new patterns. In addition, the model needs to be acquainted with the continuous change in the distribution of the input data. Towards this, we propose a clustering algorithm termed as Progressive Clustering to foresee the phenomenon of increase in data and sustain it until the pattern of the data changes considerably. We demonstrate the results of our clustering algorithm by simulating various instances of the incremental nature of the data in the form of a data stream. We demonstrate the results of our proposed methodology on benchmark MNIST and Fashion-MNIST datasets and evaluate our strategy using appropriate quantitative metrics.

Keywords: Unsupervised learning · Incremental data · Concept drift

1 Introduction

Many machine learning applications require learning algorithms to capture both spatial features and temporal behaviour in data. Existing algorithms lack ability to capture temporal dependencies in a natural, data-driven manner. Training a neural network also typically assumes that the data is non incremental in nature. However, in the real world, additional data accumulates gradually and the model requires training on the arrival of new data. To this end, Incremental Learning, a.k.a Continual Learning or Lifelong Learning, that learns from data arriving sequentially receives increasing attention. Dynamically growing data requires models preservation of previously learnt knowledge and acquire new knowledge.

M. El Yacoubi et al. (Eds.): ICPRAI 2022, LNCS 13364, pp. 355–367, 2022.
https://doi.org/10.1007/978-3-031-09282-4_30

A widely studied setting in this field is image classification tasks, namely Class Incremental Learning (CIL) [1], where the data of new classes arrive phase by phase. In CIL, the data of classes arrive phase by phase, resulting in the change of the data distribution, forcing the model to adapt to such changes in the data.

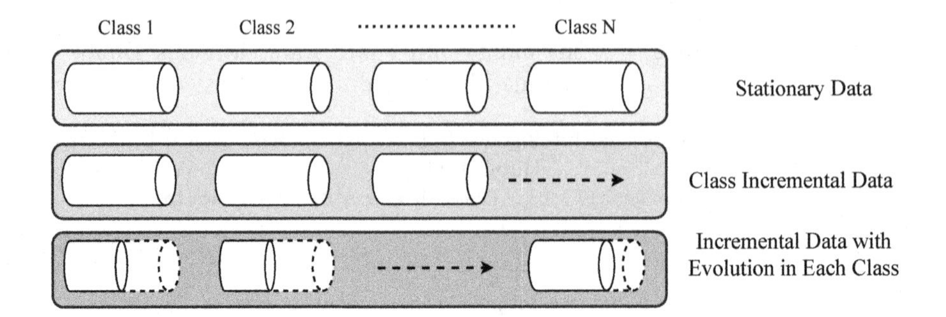

Fig. 1. Different scenarios of data advent in real time applications.

In CIL, a set of new classes needs to be learned in each phase, as depicted in Fig. 1(middle row). The following three assumptions that exist in CIL are: (i) the number of classes across different phases is fixed; (ii) classes appearing in earlier phases will not appear in later phases again; (iii) training samples are well-balanced across different classes in each phase. However, these assumptions do not hold true in many real world applications. Towards this, we design an algorithm to generate data that has different number of classes in each phase with varied sample size for each class (Fig. 1 bottom row). Towards such applications, where data accumulates dynamically, we demonstrate the learning process of dynamically growing data as shown in Fig. 2. The data arriving is stored in data chunks d to learn and acquire its knowledge to $memory(d)$. Acquisition of knowledge from currently availed data is a repetitive process adding to $memory(D)$ which represents the knowledge acquired by the model L_D over aggregate of all data D. Model learnt on previous data serves for learning a part $d^{'}$ of currently arrived data d. Concept drift has to be handled if existing over the stream of data to update the overall knowledge acquired by the model L_D. We develop our proposed strategy *Progressive Clustering* in this fashion to train incremental data.

Crowd-sourcing facilitates desired data at scale and involves task owners relying on a large batch of supposedly anonymous human resources with varying expertise contributing a diversified amount of data. In our case, we are interested in obtaining a large image corpus that is dynamically growing in nature. A pictorial representation of dynamically growing datasets where the increment is not merely in class, but also in the distribution of each class can be seen in Fig. 1 (bottom row). In such scenarios, statistical properties of the cluster assignment, which the model is trying to predict may change over time. An essential step in this problem is to formulate an efficient categorization method that detects

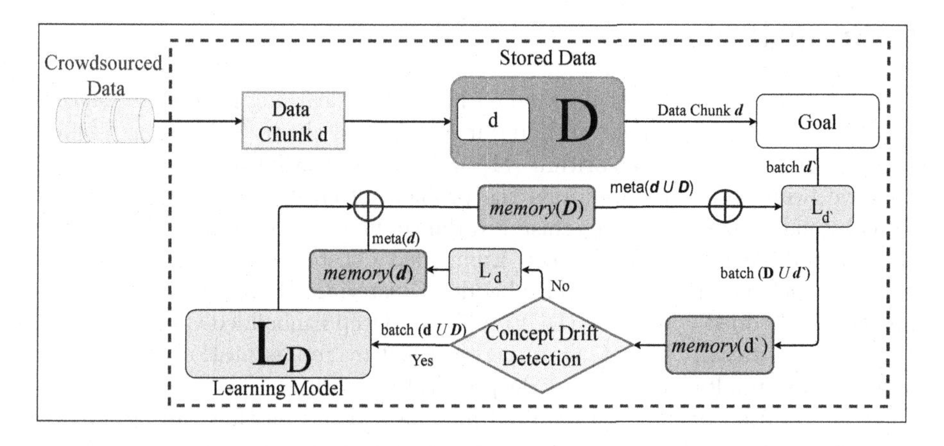

Fig. 2. Overview of incremental learning.

and updates such changes in data distribution. Towards this, we summarize our contributions as follows:

- We set up an environment that simulates the dynamically growing datasets, considering increments with respect to class and in the distribution of each class.
- We propose a novel strategy to handle the incremental nature of the data
  - that clusters the current data chunk from antecedent models knowledge.
  - that adapts to the change in the behaviour of the data over time.
  - to design deep dynamically growing models that adjust themselves with the distribution of the dataset.
- We show proposed strategy *Progressive Clustering* can be used as a plug-in in many state-of-the-art techniques reducing the number of times the whole data has to be re-clustered.
- We experiment *Progressive Clustering* on a MNIST [10] and Fashion MNIST [17] datasets showing comparable results with the state-of-the-art methodologies that are proposed towards clustering using consistent performance through various evaluation metrics.

The organization of this paper is as follows. In Sect. 2, we study various methods proposed for deep embedded clustering and incremental learning as a part of literature review. In Sect. 3, we discuss the proposed Progressive Clustering architecture that handles to categorize dynamically growing (incremental data) by detecting concept drift in the data stream. In Sect. 4, we describe the incremental data generated to carry out the experimentation and discuss the various metrics used for measuring the performance of the proposed strategy. Section 5 demonstrates the experimental results obtained by Progressive Clustering on MNIST and Fashion-MNIST dataset. In Sect. 6, we provide concluding remarks.

2 Related Works

Clustering has been extensively studied in machine learning in terms of feature selection, distance functions, grouping methods, and cluster validation. Various variants of the k-means algorithm [11] and Gaussian Mixture Models (GMM) [2] have been proposed to address the problem of clustering in higher dimensions by maximizing the inter-cluster variance when the data is projected into the lower dimensional space. Deep Embedded Clustering (DEC) [18] and its variants, such as Improved Deep Embedded Clustering (IDEC) [4], Deep Convolutional Embedded Clustering (DCEC) [5] and Deep Embedded Clustering with Data Augmentation (DEC-DA) [6] perform feature representations and cluster assignments simultaneously using deep neural networks.

The evolution of big data required incremental setting that can be directly applied to deep models with online/continual updating and adaptation. Many supervised incremental learning methods have been proposed that can be classified as *Regularization-based methods*, *Architecture-based methods*, and *Rehearsal-based methods*. Traditional work on continual learning starts from a set of randomly initialized network parameters θ, and each upcoming data with the either updates entire θ or partial θ. Regularization approaches [8,16] constrain weight update by adding a regularization term min, the loss function. Parametric isolation approaches [12,13] allocate a subset of weights for previous tasks and prune the rest to learn new data. Segmented training [3] approach freezes important weights to preserve learned knowledge and keeps the secondary weights to learn new tasks. Network expansion approaches [15,19] grow new branches or parameters to include new knowledge. Memory replay approaches [14] train the model with a small subset of previously seen data.

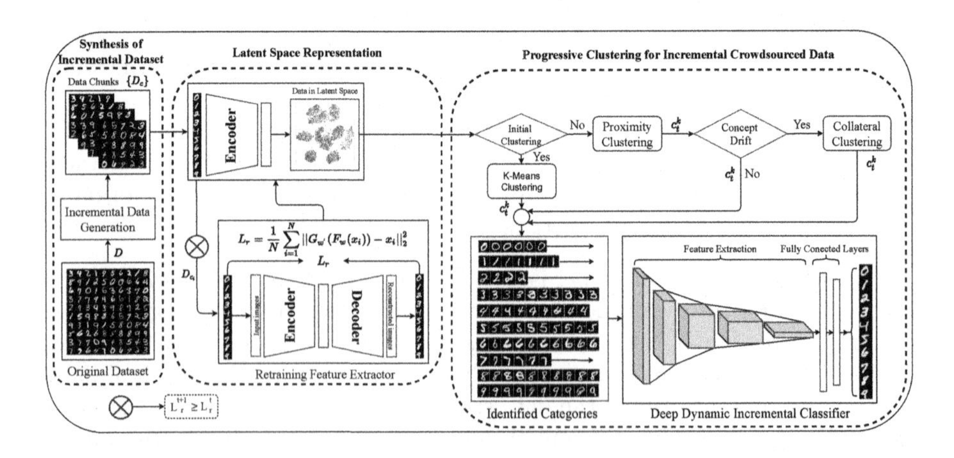

Fig. 3. Progressive clustering

In many practical applications where the data is availed incrementally, we observe the changes in the response of the model and the ground truth predictor variables over time. This results in the deterioration of the predictive performance of these models. This phenomenon called concept drift occurs when the concepts associated with the data change, as the new data arrive.

3 Progressive Clustering

We propose a clustering strategy termed as *Progressive Clustering* that handles the dynamically growing datasets as shown Fig. 3. Progressive clustering identifies the newly evolving clusters and updates the clusters as the newly availed data from current data chunks are added to previously identified clusters. The change in the data distribution is identified in to handle concept drift in the data stream. Algorithm 1 shows the incremental clustering of data using *Progressive Clustering.*

Algorithm 1: Progressive Clustering

Input : Incremental Dataset $D = \sum_{i=1}^{N_c}\{D_{c_i}\}$, where N_c = Number of Data Chunks.

Output: Clusters $C = \{c_1, c_2, c_3 \dots c_k\}$

$update(\phi_{\theta_i}, D_{c_i})$ ▷ Sect. 3.2
$C_t \leftarrow kmeans(D_{c_i}, k)$ ▷ Sect. 3.3
for $i \leftarrow 2$ **to** N_c **do**
  if $(L_{r+1}) \leqslant \eta \cdot L_r$ **then**
    $update(\phi_{\theta_i}, D_{c_i})$ ▷ Sect. 3.2
  end if
  $d_{c_i} \leftarrow getEmbeddings(D_{c_i}, \phi_{\theta_i})$
  if $ConceptDrift(d_{c_i})$ **then**
    $C_t \leftarrow kmeans(D_{c_i}, k)$ ▷ Sect. 3.5
  end if
  $C_t \leftarrow proximityClustering(C_{t-1}, d_{c_i})$ ▷ Sect. 3.4
end for
$C \leftarrow C_t$
return C

3.1 Incremental Data Generation for Progressive Clustering

To simulate the environment of dynamically arriving data, we propose an algorithm that takes any image dataset as input and outputs a set of *Data Chunks* consisting of different number of samples from each class. Algorithm 2 limitations of CIL are alleviated by allowing classes to appear in a realistic manner across multiple phases. Specifically, we characterize each phase by the appearing classes and the number of samples appearing in each class. In our setting, these quantities are sampled from probabilistic distributions. Thus, different realistic scenarios can be simulated by varying these distributions. We use this setting of incremental data advent as the input to our proposed clustering algorithm, *Progressive Clustering* in absence of target variables.

Algorithm 2: Incremental Data Generation for Progressive Clustering

Input : Dataset S as $S = \sum_{i=1}^{N} \{X_i\}$, $X_i = \sum_{j=1}^{M_i} \{x_j^i\}$ where N=Number of Classes, X_i = Class i, $n = \sum_{k=1}^{N} \{M_k\}$, M_k=Number of Images in class k, m=Number of Images in each data Chunk.

Output: Incremental Dataset $D = \sum_{i=1}^{N_c} \{D_{c_i}\}$, where N_c = Number of Data Chunks, D_{c_i} is data chunk i.

```
D = ∅                                   ▷ Initialize an empty set to store data chunks.
c = m
for i ← 1 to N_c do
    d = ∅                                ▷ For each data chunk
    t = random(1, N)                     ▷ Number of classes to choose in data chunk D_ci
    for j ← 1 to t do
        s = random(10, c)                ▷ Number of samples to choose in class j
        d_c = random_collection(X_j, s)  ▷ Choose s samples from class j
        updateDataChunk(d)               ▷ Add d_c to d
        X_i = X_i − d_c
        c = m − c
    end for
    addDataChunk(d, D)                   ▷ Add data chunk d to D
end for
return D
```

3.2 Latent Space Representation

An autoencoder is used to encode the input image into a compressed and meaningful representation, and then decode it back such that the reconstructed image is similar as possible to the original one. These self-supervised architectures aim at combining discriminative and representational properties by learning simultaneously an encoder-generator map. An autoencoder, can be formally defined as a function

$$arg\ min_{F_w, G_w}\ E[\Delta(x, G_w(F_w(x)))] \quad (1)$$

where E is the expectation over the distribution of x, and Δ is the reconstruction loss function, which measures the distance between the output of the decoder and the input. The latter is usually set to be the l_2-norm.

We design a convolutional autoencoder (CAE) ϕ_{θ_i}, with the foremost data D_{c_i} availed, to map from higher dimensional to lower dimensional space for the initial latent space representation. To circumvent the misspend of training the autoencoder on the arrival of a new batch, which is a tedious task, the autoencoder trained on the previous data is validated on the newly-arrived data with the tolerance factor of η in reconstruction loss over the Mean Squared Error (MSE) loss of the previously trained data. This tolerance factor depends upon the size and performance of the data on previous data chunk. Hence, the autoencoder is trained only if $(L_{r+1}) \leqslant \eta \cdot L_r$, where $\eta \geq 1$ and

$$L_r = \frac{1}{n}\sum_{i=1}^{n} ||G_w(F_w(x_i)) - x_i||_2^2. \tag{2}$$

3.3 Initial Clustering

The data mapped to the lower dimensional space by CAE as discussed in Sect. 3.2 is clustered by initializing cluster centres with k-means algorithm where number of cluster centres k is estimated from elbow method. We cache the following four parameters from each of the identified clusters i.e.,

$$C_k^t = \{x_k^t, \lambda_k^t, \psi_k^t, \beta_k^t\} \tag{3}$$

where,

x_k^t is the centroid of cluster c_k^t,
λ_k^t is maximum distance threshold of cluster c_k^t,
ψ_k^t is current number of records assigned to cluster c_k^t,
β_k^t is the cluster growth rate at timestamp t.

The four parameters $\{x_k^t, \lambda_k^t, \psi_k^t, \beta_k^t\}$ are used to facilitate the incremental learning of the algorithm.

3.4 Proximity Clustering

On the arrival of new data chunk, the four parameters as defined in Eq. 3 from previously identified clusters, $C^{t-1} = \{c_1^{t-1} \dots c_k^{t-1}\}$ are used for assigning the cluster labels to each of instance o_j^t of current data chunk. Hence, each instance o_j^t of the data chunk S^t, is assigned to one of the previously identified clusters, satisfying the condition, $min(dist(o_j^t, C^{t-1})) \leqslant \tau \cdot \lambda_i^{t-1}$ where, τ is the tolerance region till which a data point is accepted by the cluster c_i^t. $dist(o_j^t, c_k^{t-1})$ is the distance between the data point o_j^t and the cluster centre x_k^{t-1}, λ_i^{t-1} is the maximum distance threshold of nearest cluster c_i^{t-1}.

Lifelong learning algorithm also needs the updation to the centroids for which the new data points that are being associated to. To achieve the stability of the model, once good coverage of the data set has been reached, updating of the centroids should recede. Towards this, we consider two parameters, mean μ and standard deviation σ which are directly proportional to the change in the centroids. The centroid update change is then modulated by the moving average, ρ such that the update rules for mean and variance are given by,

$$\mu^t = \alpha\mu^{t+1} + (1-\alpha)(x_i^{t-1} - o_j) \tag{4}$$

$${\sigma^t}^2 = \beta{\sigma^{t-1}}^2 + (1-\beta)|(o_j - \mu^{t-1}) - {\sigma^{t-1}}^2| \tag{5}$$

A metric for each centroid which reflects the normalized standard deviation of that centroid's updates over time is maintained as,

$$\rho_x^t = \frac{2}{1 + e^{-\frac{\sigma^{t2}}{1+\mu^t}}} - 1 \tag{6}$$

The online computation of normalized standard deviation, ρ is as, $\rho^t = c\rho^{t-1} + (1-c)\rho t - 1$.

To guarantee unbiased treatment of all centroids, regardless of the input sample distribution, Pseudo-Entropy (PE) is incorporated which is calculated as,

$$PE = \frac{1 - \sum x_i^t \cdot log(x_i^t)}{log(D)} \tag{7}$$

where, D is the dimension of the data point. We finally update centroid x_i^t as,

$$x^t = x^{t-1} - |x^t - o_j| \cdot \rho^{t-1} \cdot \phi^{t-1} \cdot (PE) \tag{8}$$

where ϕ^t is the step size. When the direction in movement of cluster centroid is similar, the estimated centroid is moving consistently in the same direction between updates, and once it gets close to the true cluster centroid the step size is reduced for the convergence.

3.5 Detection of Concept Drift

Concept drift literature has given a probabilistic definition of concept [9]. Authors in [7] define a concept as the prior class probabilities $P(Y)$ and class conditional probabilities $P(X|Y)$. As $P(Y)$ and $P(X|Y)$ uniquely determines the joint distribution $P(X,Y)$ and vice versa, this is equivalent to defining a concept as the joint distribution $P(X,Y)$. For this reason we adopt definition for stream categorization. As the impact of concept drift reduces the predictive performance of the incremental/continual learning model, we try to detect these concept drifts as early as possible. If the number of outliers exceeds the predefined threshold, the algorithm must detect the newly evolved clusters and the change in the distribution of the data.

3.6 Collateral Clustering

To retain the previously learnt knowledge, the detected concept drift must be made sure if it is temporal or sustainable concept drift. Temporal concept drift may tend to disappear if the data stream revert to the previous concept. Hence, on the detection of concept drift, clusters are assigned for the present data with respect to the of previous data chunks that are retained.

3.7 Deep Dynamic Incremental Classification

In this paper, we consider the problem of incrementally training the deep model considering the concept drift with the stream data. After arrival of each data chunk from the stream, clusters will be redefined as new clusters may be evolved with growth in each previously identified cluster. To solve catastrophic forgetting we must find an optimal trade-off between *rigidity* (being optimized in previously learnt distribution) and *plasticity* (being open to learn new distribution). The simplest way to train a new model would be to train the entire model every time a new data chunk is availed. However, because deep neural networks can get very large, this method will become very expensive.

At the first task, the model is trained with l_1 regularization. This ensures sparsity in the network, i.e. only some neurons are connected to other neurons. This can be useful in achieving the goal of generalization of the model.

$$minimize_{w^t} \; L(w^t; w^{t-1}, x_i) + \mu \sum_{l=1}^{L} ||w^t|| \tag{9}$$

The W^t denotes the weights of the model at time t. D_t denotes training data at time t. μ is the regularization strength. L denotes the layers of the network from the first layer to the last. When the next data chunk is availed, a sparse linear classifier is fit on the last layer of the model, then the network is trained using:

$$minimize_{w^t_{L,t}} \; L(w^t_{L,t}; w^{t-1}_{1:L-1}, D_t) + \mu \sum_{l=1}^{L} ||w^t_{L,t}||_1 \tag{10}$$

4 Experimental Setup

4.1 About the Datasets

We use MNIST and Fashion-MNIST datasets to validate our Progressive Clustering. Both the datasets consists of 70,000 grayscale images of resolution (28×28) pixels belonging to 10 classes. We divide the datasets into the data chunks of 7,000 images as discussed in Algorithm 2 from each dataset which serves as the incremental data. We generated incremental dataset containing 10 data chunks for both MNIST and Fashion-MNIST dataset. Each data chunk contained different number of samples from each class.

4.2 Evaluation Metrics

For evaluating the proposed strategy Progressive Clustering and comparing with state of the art methods, we use Unsupervised Clustering Accuracy (ACC), Normalized Mutual Information (NMI), Adjusted Rand Index (ARI) each of which are discussed below.

Unsupervised Clustering Accuracy (ACC): It uses a mapping function m to find the best mapping between the cluster assignment output c of the algorithm with the ground truth y which can be defined as:

$$ACC = max_m \frac{\sum_{i=1}^{N} 1\{y_i = m(c_i)\}}{N} \tag{11}$$

For the given image x_i, let c_i be resolved cluster label and y_i be the ground truth label, m is the delta function that equals one if $x = y$ and zero otherwise. m maps each cluster label c_i to the equivalent label from the datasets. The best mapping can be found by using the Kuhn-Munkres algorithm.

Normalized Mutual Information (NMI): It measures the mutual information $I(y, c)$ between the cluster assignments c and the ground truth labels y and is normalized by the average of entropy of both ground labels $H(y)$ and the cluster assignments $H(c)$, and can be defined as:

$$NMI = \frac{I(y, c)}{\frac{1}{2}[H(y) + H(c)]} \tag{12}$$

Adjusted Rand Index (ARI): It computes a similarity measure between two clusterings by considering all pairs of samples and counting pairs that are assigned in the same or different clusters in the predicted and true clusterings. It is defined as:

$$ARI = \frac{Index - ExpectedIndex}{MaxIndex - ExpectedIndex} \tag{13}$$

5 Results and Discussions

5.1 Evaluation Methodology

For the proposed strategy to categorize incremental data, we evaluate the performance of our model on each of the discrete modules. For evaluating Progressive Clustering, we use three standard unsupervised performance metrics i.e., ACC [Sect. 4.2], NMI [Sect. 4.2] and ARI [Sect. 4.2]. The labels assigned at the time of Progressive Clustering are used for training Deep Dynamic Incremental Classifier as the target variables. To evaluate the classifier, we use supervised accuracy (Accuracy). However, the overall performance of the proposed strategy can be given by the ACC (Eq. 11), which is calculated between the result of Deep Dynamic Incremental Classifier versus the original labels of the images.

5.2 Qualtitative Study

In this section, we discuss the effectiveness of our framework on MNIST and Fashion-MNIST datasets. We can find that our strategy Progressive Clustering attains comparable results with the state-of-the-art methodologies that are

Table 1. Results showing different quantitative metrics (average over 10 data chunks) depicting the performance of various clustering strategies on MNIST and Fashion MNIST datasets. It can be observed that the Progressive Clustering strategy can be used as a plug-in in many state-of-the-art techniques reducing the number of times the whole data has to be re-clustered.

Methodology	Number of times reclustered	Dataset							
		MNIST				Fashion-MNIST			
		ACC	NMI	ARI	Accuracy	ACC	NMI	ARI	Accuracy
K-Means	10	0.5385	0.4680	0.3229	0.9524	0.4737	0.5116	0.3473	0.9498
SEC	10	0.8037	0.7547	0.6542	0.9587	0.5124	0.5008	0.4245	0.9587
SAE+k-means	10	0.7817	0.7146	0.8658	0.9564	0.5370	0.5563	0.5474	0.9429
CAE+k-means	10	0.8490	0.7927	0.8798	0.9584	0.5833	0.6084	0.4449	0.9587
DEC	10	0.8408	0.8128	0.7831	0.9655	0.518	0.546	0.5139	0.9327
IDEC	10	0.8421	0.8381	0.5406	0.9587	0.529	0.557	0.4098	0.9547
DEC-DA	10	0.9861	0.9622	0.9447	0.9651	0.586	0.636	0.5484	0.9645
DCEC	10	0.8897	0.8849	0.5319	0.9691	0.584	0.638	0.5156	0.9459
Progressive k-means	**8**	0.5221	0.4631	0.2965	0.9324	0.4583	0.4587	0.3327	0.9149
Progressive SEC	**8**	0.7424	0.7021	0.6954	0.9234	0.4464	0.3984	0.3547	0.9258
Progressive SAE+k-means	**8**	0.7124	0.6857	0.7894	0.9132	0.4865	0.5132	0.5474	0.9174
Progressive CAE+k-means	**6**	0.8126	0.6972	0.8123	0.9129	0.5514	0.5127	0.4415	0.9107
Progressive DEC	**6**	0.7792	0.7462	0.7536	0.9097	0.4997	0.5165	0.4741	0.9057
Progressive IDEC	**6**	0.8056	0.7862	0.5125	0.9234	0.5174	0.5475	0.3687	0.9157
Progressive DEC-DA	**6**	0.9157	0.9165	0.9014	0.9324	0.5547	0.6234	0.5654	0.9268
Progressive DCEC	**6**	0.8265	0.7896	0.5123	0.9557	0.5844	0.5672	0.5074	0.9215

proposed for clustering. Table 1 shows that the proposed methodology achieves good results without re-clustering every data chunk on its arrival. It can be observed that algorithms defined in Sect. 3 can be plugged in to modify the state-of-the-art clustering methods to train the data in incremental fashion. The dataset is divided into the data chunks of 7000 images each, with varied number of images from each class in each data chunk. The CAE and SAE is pretrained end-to-end for 400 epochs, with the batch size of 256 using Adam optimizer with default parameters. The convergence threshold is set to 0.1%. Families of DEC are trained for 50,000 iterations.

6 Conclusion

In this paper, we proposed a categorization strategy to handle the incremental nature of the data by identifying concept drift in the data stream. Our method automatically discovers newly occurring object categories in unlabelled data and is used to train a classifier that can be used for various downstream tasks such as content based image retrieval systems, image data segregation etc. We proposed an algorithm to alleviate the problem of concept drift by designing progressive clustering algorithm capable of handling continually arriving data. We demonstrate our results on standard MNIST and Fashion-MNIST datasets to show our methodology shows comparable performance to state-of-the-art clustering algorithms which will have to be trained from scratch on the arrival of each data chunk. Deploying incremental learning algorithms for critical applications warrants circumspection and is still a work in progress and we believe our work is a step in this direction.

Acknowledgement. This project is partly carried out under Department of Science and Technology (DST) through ICPS programme - Indian Heritage in Digital Space for the project "CrowdSourcing" (DST/ ICPS/ IHDS/ 2018 (General)) and "Digital Poompuhar" (DST/ ICPS/ Digital Poompuhar/ 2017 (General)).

References

1. Castro, F.M., Marín-Jiménez, M.J., Mata, N.G., Schmid, C., Karteek, A.: End-to-end incremental learning. arXiv abs/1807.09536 (2018)
2. Chen, J., Zhang, L., Liang, Y.: Exploiting gaussian mixture model clustering for full-duplex transceiver design. IEEE Trans. Commun. **67**(8), 5802–5816 (2019). https://doi.org/10.1109/TCOMM.2019.2915225
3. Du, X., Charan, G., Liu, F., Cao, Y.: Single-net continual learning with progressive segmented training. In: 2019 18th IEEE International Conference on Machine Learning and Applications (ICMLA), pp. 1629–1636 (2019). https://doi.org/10.1109/ICMLA.2019.00267
4. Guo, X., Gao, L., Liu, X., Yin, J.: Improved deep embedded clustering with local structure preservation, August 2017. https://doi.org/10.24963/ijcai.2017/243
5. Guo, X., Liu, X., Zhu, E., Yin, J.: Deep clustering with convolutional autoencoders. In: Liu, D., Xie, S., Li, Y., Zhao, D., El-Alfy, E.S. (eds.) Neural Information Processing, ICONIP 2017. LNCS, vol. 10635, pp. 373–382. Springer, Cham (2017). https://doi.org/10.1007/978-3-319-70096-0_39
6. Guo, X., Zhu, E., Liu, X., Yin, J.: Deep embedded clustering with data augmentation. In: Zhu, J., Takeuchi, I. (eds.) Proceedings of The 10th Asian Conference on Machine Learning. Proceedings of Machine Learning Research, vol. 95, pp. 550–565. PMLR, 14–16 November 2018. http://proceedings.mlr.press/v95/guo18b.html
7. Hoens, T., Polikar, R., Chawla, N.: Learning from streaming data with concept drift and imbalance: an overview. Prog. Artif. Intell. **1**(1), 89–101 (2012). https://doi.org/10.1007/s13748-011-0008-0, Copyright: Copyright 2021 Elsevier B.V., All rights reserved
8. Kirkpatrick, J., et al.: Overcoming catastrophic forgetting in neural networks. Proc. Natl. Acad. Sci. **114**(13), 3521–3526 (2017). https://doi.org/10.1073/pnas.1611835114, https://www.pnas.org/content/114/13/3521
9. Kuncheva, L.I.: Classifier ensembles for changing environments. In: Roli, F., Kittler, J., Windeatt, T. (eds.) MCS 2004. LNCS, vol. 3077, pp. 1–15. Springer, Heidelberg (2004). https://doi.org/10.1007/978-3-540-25966-4_1
10. LeCun, Y., Cortes, C.: MNIST handwritten digit database (2010). http://yann.lecun.com/exdb/mnist/
11. Li, Y., Wu, H.: A clustering method based on k-means algorithm. Physics Procedia **25**, 1104–1109 (2012). https://doi.org/10.1016/j.phpro.2012.03.206
12. Mallya, A., Davis, D., Lazebnik, S.: Piggyback: adapting a single network to multiple tasks by learning to mask weights (2018)
13. Mallya, A., Lazebnik, S.: PackNet: adding multiple tasks to a single network by iterative pruning, pp. 7765–7773, June 2018. https://doi.org/10.1109/CVPR.2018.00810

14. Rebuffi, S.A., Kolesnikov, A., Sperl, G., Lampert, C.H.: ICARL: incremental classifier and representation learning. In: 2017 IEEE Conference on Computer Vision and Pattern Recognition (CVPR), pp. 5533–5542 (2017). https://doi.org/10.1109/CVPR.2017.587
15. Rusu, A.A., et al.: Progressive neural networks (2016)
16. Tabib, R.A., et al.: Deep features for categorization of heritage images towards 3D reconstruction. Procedia Comput. Sci. **171**, 483–490 (2020). https://doi.org/10.1016/j.procs.2020.04.051, https://www.sciencedirect.com/science/article/pii/S1877050920310176, Third International Conference on Computing and Network Communications (CoCoNet 2019)
17. Xiao, H., Rasul, K., Vollgraf, R.: Fashion-MNIST: a novel image dataset for benchmarking machine learning algorithms (2017)
18. Xie, J., Girshick, R., Farhadi, A.: Unsupervised deep embedding for clustering analysis (2016)
19. Yoon, J., Yang, E., Lee, J., Hwang, S.J.: Lifelong learning with dynamically expandable networks (2018)

Malware Detection Using Pseudo Semi-Supervised Learning

Upinder Kaur(✉), Xin Ma, Richard M. Voyles, and Byung-Cheol Min

Purdue University, West Lafayette, IN 47907, USA
{kauru,maxin,rvoyles,minb}@purdue.edu

Abstract. Malware, due to its ever-evolving nature, remains a serious threat. Sophisticated attacks using ransomware and viruses have crippled organizations globally. Traditional heuristic and signature-based methods have failed to keep up and are easily evaded by such programs. Machine learning-based methods can alleviate this concern by detecting inherent and persistent structures in the malware unrecognized by heuristic methods. Supervised learning methods have been used previously, but they need vast labeled datasets. Semi-supervised learning can address these issues by leveraging insights gained from unlabeled data. In this paper, we present a novel semi-supervised learning framework that can identify malware based on sparsely labeled datasets. This framework leverages the global and local features learned by the combination of k-NN and CNN to generate pseudo labels for efficient training using both labeled and unlabeled samples. The combined loss of the models regularizes the neural network. The performance of this framework is compared against popular semi-supervised approaches such as LapSVM, TSVM, and label propagation on the Embers dataset. The proposed framework achieved a detection accuracy of 72% with just 10% of the labeled training samples. Hence, these results demonstrate the viability of semi-supervised methods in large-scale malware detection systems.

Keywords: Malware detection · Semi-supervised learning · Pseudo labeling · Code analysis

1 Introduction

Malware detection is one of the emerging areas for the application of Artificial Intelligence (AI). Malware is an ever-evolving threat that continues to plague the digital world; from data theft to ransomware, it can have deleterious effects resulting in damages worth millions. Current anti-virus software utilizes multiple methods to detect malicious software, the most common being signature/template matching with internal libraries of pre-identified malware. While this approach is successful for the vast majority of malware attacks of low

The authors acknowledge the support of the USDA from Grants 2018-67007-28439 and 2019-67021-28990 in the fulfillment of this work.

M. El Yacoubi et al. (Eds.): ICPRAI 2022, LNCS 13364, pp. 368–379, 2022.
https://doi.org/10.1007/978-3-031-09282-4_31

sophistication, there is a growing minority of adversarial malware agents that display a high degree of sophistication in both their attack vectors and their ability to disguise themselves. Furthermore, this approach requires enormous libraries that are expensive to both maintain and cross-check. With nearly a million new viruses being detected every day, there is a need for more adaptive and self-evolving methodologies, as recognized by security experts [1].

Machine learning can be an effective tool in identifying malware. Stochastic and learning models can evolve with the malware without the need for explicit re-programming. Learning-based malware detection systems are of two main types - dynamic and static. In dynamic analytical systems, runtime behavior such as API calls, execution behavior, and instructions are analyzed to classify programs as malware [3,17]. This approach captures behavioral patterns and while it may seem more intuitive to develop, it demands an isolated environment for the identification of behavior. Customized virtual machine testbeds needed for such analysis are not only expensive but accrue significant computational costs. Also, intelligent malware might have the ability to recognize such testbeds and could potentially avoid discovery [15].

On the other hand, static analysis for malware detection concentrates on analyzing the executable binary to search for patterns that can foretell maliciousness. The emphasis is on inferring the potential of malicious behavior from raw byte structures of the executable. This approach does not require any special test environments and is computationally less expensive. Further, it acts as a security system that can prevent the execution of malicious software. Static analysis using byte n-grams and strings were the early attempts to detect malware, but not only are they computationally expensive and promote overfitting, but they also showed low-performance [14].

Nevertheless, static analysis based on supervised approaches using neural networks on portable executables (PE) has shown better performance [12,13,19,25]. Deep learning on metadata features, contextual byte features, and 2D histograms from the PE files resulted in a detection rate of 95% [19]. LSTMs have also been used to learn from domain knowledge extracted using n-gram methods [12]. This work was further extended using convolutional neural networks (CNN) with temporal max-pooling in the MalConv model [13] which resulted in state-of-the-art performance. Moreover, visualization techniques that convert binary executable into images for identifying malware have also been attempted [10,23,24]. Such systems employed CNN and deep neural networks to identify textural patterns in malware images. In a recent work, static analysis using a clustering approach with deep neural networks showed promising results in a supervised learning setting [16]. Similar endeavours have been attempted in optimizing the performance and reducing the computational overloads by using ant-colony clustering with a CNN [7]. Although these methods achieved high detection rates, they still rely on large labeled datasets for a supervised approach to malware detection.

The need for extensive labeled datasets, that covers all major classes of malware, for supervised models is often unmet. Labeling instances entail a time-consuming process of analyzing binaries which are further complicated by the scale of malware distribution. Published works in this area have mostly used private datasets which have made cross-evaluation of models difficult [12,14,18,25]. The use of private datasets can be attributed to the fact that while malware can be downloaded easily, good software is often proprietary with limitations set on its public distribution. Moreover, with new malware being introduced every day, such a dataset would need constant updates and labeling. Hence, a semi-supervised approach with few labelled instances can be of great use in this area. Moreover, semi-supervised frameworks can overcome the disproportionate distribution of malware to benign instances in the datasets, thereby delivering better detection rates.

In this work, we propose a novel semi-supervised framework that assigns pseudo-labels using both clustering and feature-based models. The clustering approach maps global features while local features are identified using CNN. This framework is tested on an extensive and publicly available malware dataset. The performance is compared to that of some of the popular models in semi-supervised learning. This framework is the first step in building an extensive semi-supervised system for the task of malware detection from static analysis.

2 Related Work

2.1 Semi-Supervised Learning

Semi-supervised learning (SSL) is a learning methodology that is primarily used when there is limited availability of labelled data [11]. SSL relies on learning inherent structures in the data from the unlabeled samples to make predictions to make up for the lack of labeled samples. The use of SSL is particularly important in fields where the data is subject to frequent change, such as image classification, text classification [9], and emotion recognition [27]. SSL models have been successful in achieving performance comparable to pure supervised learning methods with using just a fraction of the labeled samples [22]. In malware detection, few examples of semi-supervised learning have been reported in published works. Initial approaches used opcode-frequency features with SVM classifier for semi-supervised malware detection [4,18]. Santos et al. [18] achieved an accuracy of 83% with 50% labelled data using an SVM model on a dataset of 100 PE files. Biased-SVM (bSVM) have also been used in SSL for malware detection with a reported detection rate of 87.65% with 82.8% of labelled samples [4]. However, the need is to investigate newer approaches of SSL for malware detection which can improve performance even with a lower fraction of labeled samples.

2.2 Pseudo-Labeling

In pseudo-labeling, the classifier is trained on the labeled dataset and predictions are derived for all the unlabeled data. These predictions are also called pseudo-labels and only the ones predicted with a certain threshold are added to the labelled dataset to retrain the classifier [8]. Initially, pseudo labeling was just limited to a fine-tuning stage [8]; however, pseudo-labeling has also been used to derive hard labels for unlabeled samples [20]. They introduced a loss term to encourage intra-class compactness and inter-class separation. Further, graph-based label propagation has also been used for generating pseudo-labels. We propose to combine two methods to generate pseudo labels for a binary classification task. To the best of our knowledge no work exists which uses both clustering and an CNN model-based approach to detect malware in large datasets.

3 Proposed Framework

Malware dataset distribution can be extensive, as instances can have varied and diverse characteristics, especially those designed for a full operating system environment. At the high level, the malware classified into ransomware, trojans, worms, etc. At the low level, even singular statements and functions can cause an executable to exhibit malicious behavior. Further, malware designers often create malicious binaries using functions and structure similar to that of good programs which helps them evade signature-based anti-virus software. Therefore, the need for a framework for this application is to be able to capture both local as well as global invariance. Hence, we propose the use of a k-NN clustering algorithm along with a CNN to generate pseudo labels.

CNN excels in finding local features, but mapping those local features to the global distribution is a challenge for them. On the other hand, k-NN clustering identifies the global distribution of the instances in the dataset, thereby building a global map based on the distance between them. This global connectivity when leveraged against the local feature detection capability of a CNN, creates a model that possess the ability to comprehend both spatial and local associativity. To the best of our knowledge, no such framework has been proposed.

3.1 Model

The model for generating the pseudo labels is an ensemble of the k-NN clustering and the CNN. Given a dataset D, with $D_L = \{x_{L_1}, ...x_{L_n}\}$ labeled instances and $D_u = \{x_{u_1}, ...x_{u_m}\}$ unlabeled instances, we build a cluster k on the labeled dataset. Subsequently, the labeled instances are used to train the CNN model, as shown in Fig. 1. For this model, we chose k empirically by testing the performance for a range of 1 to 300. The CNN model consists of two 1-dimensional convolutional layers with activation function rectified linear units (ReLU). The convolutional layers are then connected to a max pooling layer with batch normalization. Following this, we flatten the inputs and pass them to the fully connected network of four dense layers with dropout and ReLU activation function. Finally, the activation layer decides the output based on the sigmoid activation function. Adam was used as the optimizer for the CNN and loss was calculated as binary cross entropy.

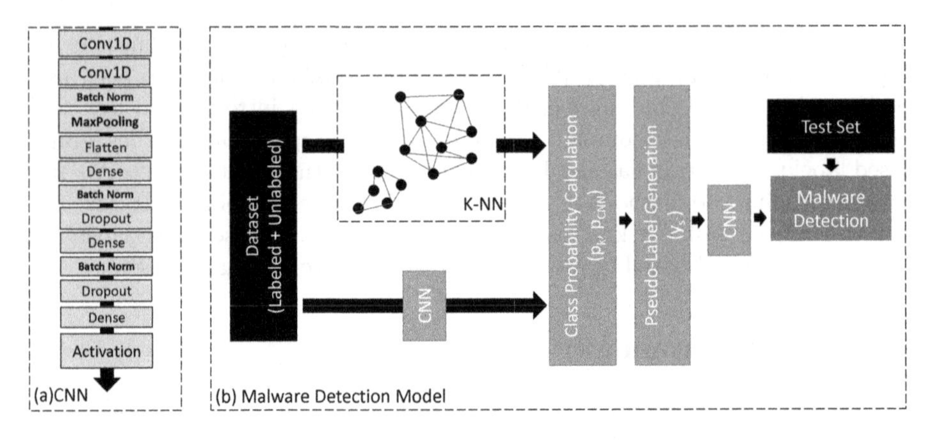

Fig. 1. (a) The representative CNN structure with a 1-dimensional convolutional layer, batch normalization layer, max pooling layer, flatten layer, dense fully-connected layers with dropout, and activation layer. (b) The full flowchart of the framework.

After initial training on the labeled samples, the probabilities are calculated for the unlabeled samples from both the k-NN (p_k) and CNN (p_{CNN}) as per Algorithm 1. The class for each unlabeled instance is then decided based on a weighted average of these probabilities. The weighted average is calculated as:

$$p_{u_i} = p_k(x_{u_i}) * \lambda_k + p_{CNN}(x_{u_i}) * \lambda_{CNN} \tag{1}$$

where the influence of the k-NN and CNN models in deciding the label are controlled using λ_k and λ_{CNN}, respectively. Notably, $\lambda_k + \lambda_{CNN} = 1$. A threshold t is used to finally assign class 0 (good software) and class 1 (malware),

$$y_{s'} = \begin{cases} 1, if\, p_{u_i} > t \\ 0, \text{otherwise.} \end{cases} \tag{2}$$

The generated pseudo labels $y_{s'}$ are then stacked with the true labels from the labelled instances y_L. These are then used to retrain the classifier for final training and then tested on the test set.

The combined loss includes the binary cross entropy loss of the CNN model as well as the l1-norm of the predictions by k-NN and CNN. Mathematically, this is formulated as,

$$\mathcal{L}_{total}(x_{ui}) = \mathcal{L}_{l_1} + \mathcal{L}_{BCE} \tag{3}$$

where the $\mathcal{L}_{l_1}$ for a batch size of k is defined as,

$$\mathcal{L}_{l_1} = \frac{1}{k} \sum_{i=1}^{n} \|p_k(x_{u_i}) - p_{CNN}(x_{u_i})\| \tag{4}$$

Algorithm 1. Pseudo-Label Generation

```
Input: Labeled Samples D_L, Unlabeled Samples D_U
Output: Pseudo Labels y_s'
for all input labeled samples, D_L do
   mapKNN( D_L, D_U,k)
      calculate p_k(x_{u_i})
   trainCNN(D_L, D_U, epochs T, batch-size B)
   for epoch ∈ [1,....,T] do
      fit CNN model
      return p_CNN(x_{u_i})
   end for
end for
for all input unlabeled samples, D_U do
   Calculate Class Probability p_{u_i}
   if p_{u_i} > t then
      y_s' = 1
   else
      y_s' = 0
   end if
end for
return y_s'
```

and $\mathcal{L}_{BCE}$ which represents the binary cross entropy loss of the CNN model is defined as,

$$\mathcal{L}_{BCE} = -\frac{1}{k}\sum_{i=1}^{k}\left[y_t \times \log\left(f_\theta\left(x_{u_i}\right)\right) + (1-y_t) \times \log\left(1-f_\theta\left(x_{u_i}\right)\right)\right] \quad (5)$$

where y_t is the target label vector for the batch, with f_θ being the CNN model with the input of x_{u_i} samples.

The hyper-parameters in this model are the number of neighbors for k-NN, the filters, epochs, mini-batch size, and the learning rate for the CNN model. For the pseudo-labelling step, the weights for each model and the threshold are also hyper-parameters. The mean square error and accuracy were also monitored during the training of the model.

3.2 Regularization

Regularizing models is essential especially when dealing with a lower number of input instances. Overfitting on the smaller subset of input instances will impact the overall performance of the model. Hence, we use batch normalization in the CNN model. Dropout layers were also incorporated among the fully connected layers to prevent overfitting [21]. The batch size, the number of neighbours, number of epochs, the learning rate, and the optimizer was empirically tuned to optimize the performance and reduce overfitting.

4 Experiments

4.1 Dataset

Embers [2] PE malware dataset was used for the validation of the proposed framework. This dataset contains 800,000 training samples, of which 200,000 are unlabeled, and 200,000 test samples. The PE header files are processed to extract header, import, strings, histograms, byte histograms, section and general information which is stored as features. This distribution of unlabelled, labeled and test features made this dataset an ideal candidate for this framework. Moreover, since this dataset is publicly available, the results on this dataset can be used in future publications for comparison by the community.

4.2 Comparison Methods

Due to the paucity of similar investigation on publicly available malware datasets, we select some of the popular semi-supervised methods for comparison in this study. Transductive SVM (TSVM) [5], Laplacian-SVM (lapSVM) [26], and label propagation with k-NN kernel [6] for the comparing of performance of the proposed framework. TSVM assumes that the decision boundary lies in the lower density regions of the feature space, whereas LapSVM makes a manifold assumption for the distribution. Both these approaches have been extensively used in semi-supervised learning for their ability to learn from fewer labeled samples. Label propagation is an iterative method that generates pseudo labels by iterative training and testing on a set of labeled and unlabeled data. The k-NN kernel was used in the implementation as it allows a direct comparison with teh proposed framework. Further, hyper-parameter tuning using grid search was completed to select some of the hyperparameters such as number of neighbors, lambda, and gamma. The radial basis function (RBF) kernel was used for the two SVM models.

4.3 Training and Evaluation

Training and validation were completed using instances from the training set and the testing instances were selected from the test set. The number of labelled samples selected were: 1,000, 10,000, 30,000, and 60,000. The unlabeled samples were kept equivalent to the number of labeled samples. The test samples were kept at 20% of the final training set (with pseudo labels). The evaluation metrics selected were accuracy of detection and the error rates. Three-fold cross validation was used in the experiments and the error rates were calculated as the average of the mean square error (MSE) for each fold. All experiments were conducted on a cluster with 32 2.3 GHz Intel Xeon E5-2686 v4 (Broadwell) processors, 224 GB DDR4 memory, and 2 NVIDIA Tesla V100 GPUs with 5120 CUDA cores and 640 tensor cores.

5 Results and Discussion

The performance of the models, with varying number of labelled images, was compared to evaluate the effectiveness of the proposed framework. The error rates for all the methods under examination are reported in Table 1. The accuracy of LapSVM and TSVM did increase linearly with addition of more labeled samples, however the training slowed exponentially. This can be attributed to the extensive distribution of the dataset. Due to the spread of the feature space, both LapSVM and TSVM did not find suitable decision hyperplanes, but LapSVM did perform better than TSVM. Notably, training had to be abandoned at 100,000 instances for these two models as the size of the data resulted in kernel crashes even after feature reduction.

Table 1. Error rates for the semi-supervised frameworks on the Ember dataset with the varying number of labeled samples.

Models	Labeled samples			
	1,000	10,000	30,000	60,000
LapSVM	0.52	0.48	0.32	0.29
TSVM	0.55	0.42	0.36	0.32
Label propagation	0.59	0.38	0.42	0.50
Proposed framework	0.52	0.42	0.39	0.27

The accuracy of the models is plotted in Fig. 2. The increase in accuracy with the increase in the labeled data was consistent till the 30,000 labelled instance level. After, this label propagation reported a decline in accuracy. This can be attributed to the propagation of errors in the iterative process of label propagation. In the proposed framework, this was corrected by deciding the label from the weighted average of two models. The proposed framework outperformed all the other methods, with an accuracy of 72% with just 60,000 labeled instances from the entire 600,000 training set labeled samples. The training loss for the 60,000 samples iteration is shown in Fig. 3. We notice a sharp decline with few peaks as new classes of malware are encountered by the model as it learns the training set.

In terms of scalability, our proposed method proved to be the best choice. For LapSVM and TSVM, training could not be completed beyond 60,000 labeled samples, as frequent kernel crashes limited the training. In case of labeled propagation, the training took considerably more time than the proposed method.

This experiment also sheds light on the complexity of the dataset, in terms of semi-supervised learning. Most semi-supervised learning methods assume make either clustering or a manifold assumption. However, this vast and complex dataset represent a large distribution which made it difficult for baseline models to identify decision boundaries. Nevertheless, our proposed framework leveraged

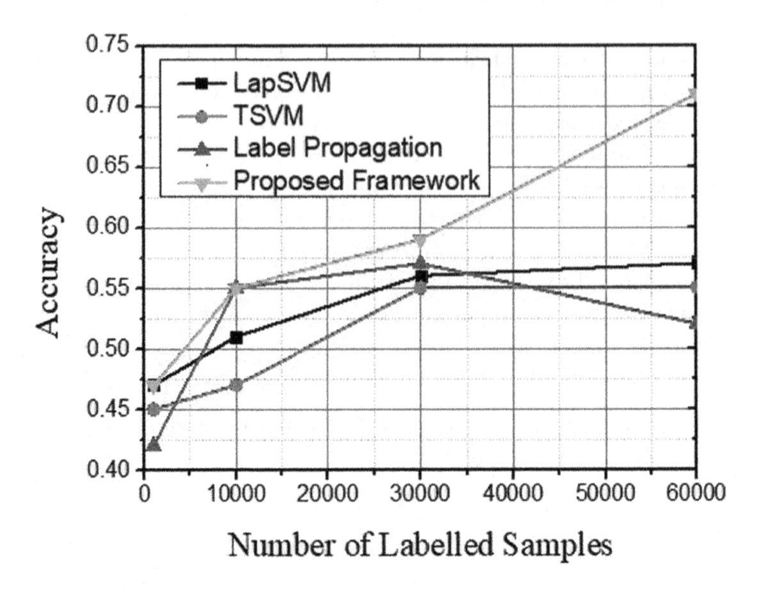

Fig. 2. The plot of accuracy with respect to the number of labeled samples for LapSVM, TSVM, label propagation, and the proposed framework.

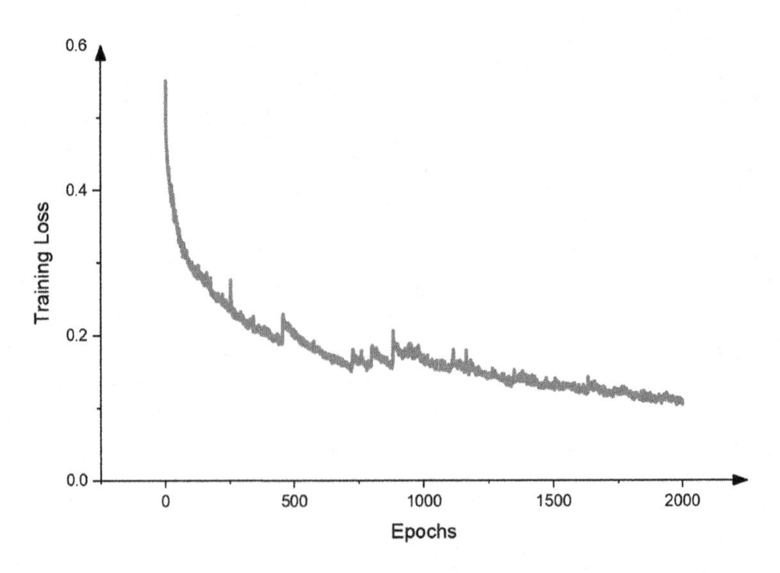

Fig. 3. The training loss plot for the CNN model while training with 60,000 labeled samples.

the local and global correlation in features to achieve effective performance. The reason behind the success of our framework is the ensemble of two intrinsically different methods, each compensating for the other to provide accurate classification.

6 Conclusion

In this paper, we address the ever-evolving challenge of detecting malware by proposing a pseudo-labelling-based semi-supervised learning framework. This framework leverages both local and global correlation among instances in the feature space to decide pseudo labels for the classes. While traditional and supervised method need extensive, updated, and labeled libraries and datasets to detect malware, this framework achieved an overall accuracy of 72% with just 10% of the labeled samples from the entire data set of 600,000 training samples. Moreover, this framework can be scaled, and can be deployed easily with existing methods. In the future, we plan to extend this method for online semi-supervised malware detection to cover zero-day attacks and anomalies.

References

1. Almeshekah, M.H., Spafford, E.H.: Planning and integrating deception into computer security defenses. In: Proceedings of the 2014 New Security Paradigms Workshop, pp. 127–138 (2014)
2. Anderson, H.S., Roth, P.: EMBER: an open dataset for training static PE malware machine learning models. CoRR abs/1804.04637 (2018). http://arxiv.org/abs/1804.04637
3. Athiwaratkun, B., Stokes, J.W.: Malware classification with LSTM and GRU language models and a character-level CNN. In: 2017 IEEE International Conference on Acoustics, Speech and Signal Processing (ICASSP), pp. 2482–2486 (2017)
4. Bisio, F., Gastaldo, P., Zunino, R., Decherchi, S.: Semi-supervised machine learning approach for unknown malicious software detection. In: 2014 IEEE International Symposium on Innovations in Intelligent Systems and Applications (INISTA) Proceedings, pp. 52–59. IEEE (2014)
5. Bruzzone, L., Chi, M., Marconcini, M.: A novel transductive svm for semisupervised classification of remote-sensing images. IEEE Trans. Geosci. Remote Sens. **44**(11), 3363–3373 (2006)
6. Fujiwara, Y., Irie, G.: Efficient label propagation. In: International Conference on Machine Learning, pp. 784–792 (2014)
7. Huang, H., Deng, H., Sheng, Y., Ye, X.: Accelerating convolutional neural network-based malware traffic detection through ant-colony clustering. J. Intell. Fuzzy Syst. **37**(1), 409–423 (2019)
8. Lee, D.H.: Pseudo-label: the simple and efficient semi-supervised learning method for deep neural networks. In: Workshop on Challenges in Representation Learning, ICML, vol. 3 (2013)
9. Miyato, T., Dai, A.M., Goodfellow, I.: Adversarial training methods for semi-supervised text classification. arXiv preprint arXiv:1605.07725 (2016)

10. Nataraj, L., Karthikeyan, S., Jacob, G., Manjunath, B.S.: Malware images: visualization and automatic classification. In: Proceedings of the 8th International Symposium on Visualization for Cyber Security, VizSec 2011. Association for Computing Machinery, New York (2011). https://doi.org/10.1145/2016904.2016908
11. Oliver, A., Odena, A., Raffel, C., Cubuk, E.D., Goodfellow, I.J.: Realistic evaluation of deep semi-supervised learning algorithms. Curran Associates Inc. (2018)
12. Raff, E., Barker, J., Sylvester, J., Brandon, R., Catanzaro, B., Nicholas, C.: Malware detection by eating a whole exe. In: AAAI Workshop on Artificial Intelligence for Cyber Security (2018)
13. Raff, E., Sylvester, J., Nicholas, C.: Learning the PE header, malware detection with minimal domain knowledge. In: Proceedings of the 10th ACM Workshop on Artificial Intelligence and Security, pp. 121–132, AISec 2017. Association for Computing Machinery, New York (2017). https://doi.org/10.1145/3128572.3140442
14. Raff, E., et al.: An investigation of byte n-gram features for malware classification. J. Comput. Virol. Hacking Tech. **14**(1), 1–20 (2016). https://doi.org/10.1007/s11416-016-0283-1
15. Raffetseder, T., Kruegel, C., Kirda, E.: Detecting system emulators. In: Garay, J.A., Lenstra, A.K., Mambo, M., Peralta, R. (eds.) ISC 2007. LNCS, vol. 4779, pp. 1–18. Springer, Heidelberg (2007). https://doi.org/10.1007/978-3-540-75496-1_1
16. Rezaei, T., Manavi, F., Hamzeh, A.: A PE header-based method for malware detection using clustering and deep embedding techniques. J. Inf. Secur. Appl. **60**, 102876 (2021)
17. Rieck, K., Trinius, P., Willems, C., Holz, T.: Automatic analysis of malware behavior using machine learning. J. Comput. Secur. **19**(4), 639–668 (2011). http://dblp.uni-trier.de/db/journals/jcs/jcs19.html#RieckTWH11
18. Santos, I., Sanz, B., Laorden, C., Brezo, F., Bringas, P.G.: Opcode-sequence-based semi-supervised unknown malware detection. In: Herrero, Á., Corchado, E. (eds.) CISIS 2011. LNCS, vol. 6694, pp. 50–57. Springer, Heidelberg (2011). https://doi.org/10.1007/978-3-642-21323-6_7
19. Saxe, J., Berlin, K.: Deep neural network based malware detection using two dimensional binary program features. In: 2015 10th International Conference on Malicious and Unwanted Software (MALWARE), pp. 11–20 (2015)
20. Shi, W., Gong, Y., Ding, C., Ma, Z., Tao, X., Zheng, N.: Transductive semi-supervised deep learning using min-max features. In: Ferrari, V., Hebert, M., Sminchisescu, C., Weiss, Y. (eds.) ECCV 2018. LNCS, vol. 11209, pp. 311–327. Springer, Cham (2018). https://doi.org/10.1007/978-3-030-01228-1_19
21. Srivastava, N., Hinton, G., Krizhevsky, A., Sutskever, I., Salakhutdinov, R.: Dropout: a simple way to prevent neural networks from overfitting. J. Mach. Learn. Res. **15**(1), 1929–1958, 102876 (2014)
22. Tarvainen, A., Valpola, H.: Mean teachers are better role models: weight-averaged consistency targets improve semi-supervised deep learning results. In: Advances in Neural Information Processing Systems, pp. 1195–1204 (2017)
23. Venkatraman, S., Alazab, M.: Use of data visualisation for zero-day malware detection. Secur. Commun. Netw. **2018** (2018)
24. Venkatraman, S., Alazab, M., Vinayakumar, R.: A hybrid deep learning image-based analysis for effective malware detection. J. Inf. Secur. Appl. **47**, 377–389 (2019)
25. Vinayakumar, R., Alazab, M., Soman, K.P., Poornachandran, P., Venkatraman, S.: Robust intelligent malware detection using deep learning. IEEE Access **7**, 46717–46738 (2019)

26. Zhang, X., Zhu, P., Tian, J., Zhang, J.: An effective semi-supervised model for intrusion detection using feature selection based LapSVM. In: 2017 International Conference on Computer, Information and Telecommunication Systems (CITS), pp. 283–286. IEEE (2017)
27. Zhang, Z., Ringeval, F., Dong, B., Coutinho, E., Marchi, E., Schüller, B.: Enhanced semi-supervised learning for multimodal emotion recognition. In: 2016 IEEE International Conference on Acoustics, Speech and Signal Processing (ICASSP), pp. 5185–5189. IEEE (2016)

Information Extraction

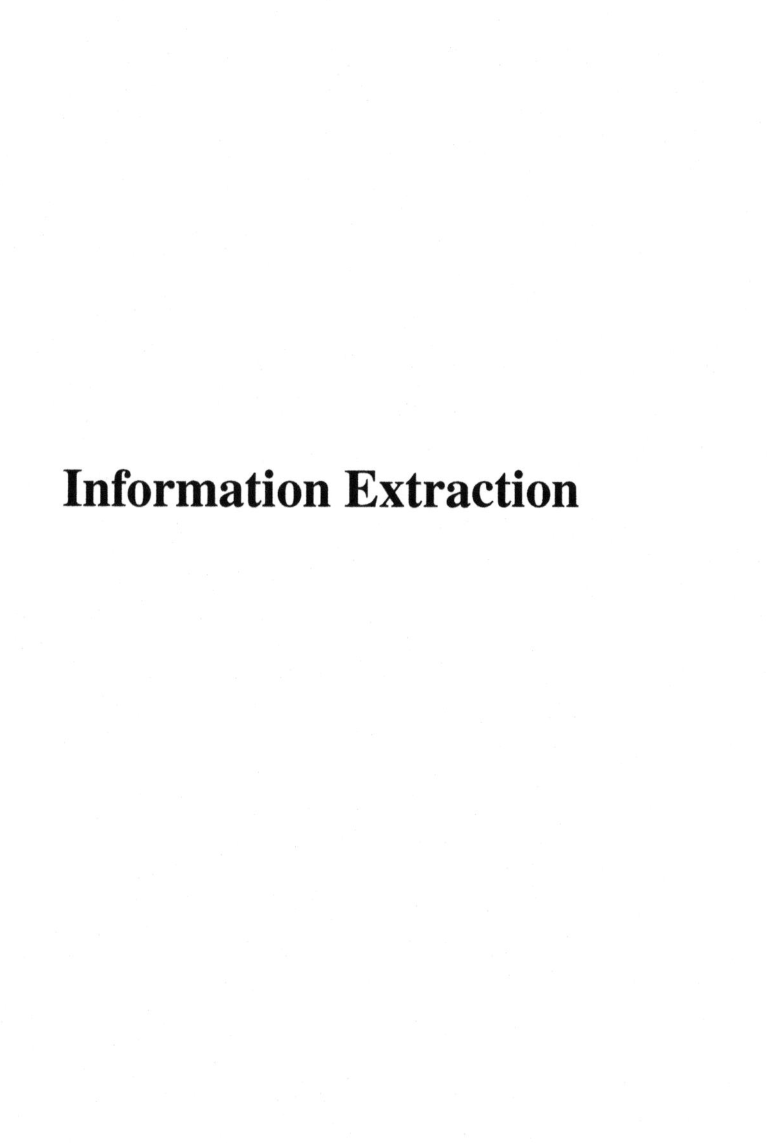

Temporal Disaggregation of the Cumulative Grass Growth

Thomas Guyet[1(✉)], Laurent Spillemaecker[2], Simon Malinowski[3], and Anne-Isabelle Graux[4]

[1] Inria Centre de Lyon, Villeurbanne, France
thomas.guyet@inria.fr
[2] ENSAI, Université Rennes 1, Rennes, France
[3] Inria/IRISA, Université Rennes 1, Rennes, France
[4] PEGASE, INRAE, Institut Agro, 35590 Saint Gilles, France
anne-isabelle.graux@inrae.fr

Abstract. Information on the grass growth over a year is essential for some models simulating the use of this resource to feed animals on pasture or at barn with hay or grass silage. Unfortunately, this information is rarely available. The challenge is to reconstruct grass growth from two sources of information: usual daily climate data (rainfall, radiation, etc.) and cumulative growth over the year. We have to be able to capture the effect of seasonal climatic events which are known to distort the growth curve within the year. In this paper, we formulate this challenge as a problem of disaggregating the cumulative growth into a time series. To address this problem, our method applies time series forecasting using climate information and grass growth from previous time steps. Several alternatives of the method are proposed and compared experimentally using a database generated from a grassland process-based model. The results show that our method can accurately reconstruct the time series, independently of the use of the cumulative growth information.

Keywords: Time series · Auto-regressive models · Forecasting · Agronomy

1 Introduction

In 2019, grasslands covered 12.7 million hectares in France, i.e. about 44% of the useful agricultural surface and 20% of the national land. Therefore, grasslands play an important role, especially by providing ecosystem services such as forage production, climate change mitigation through soil carbon storage, biodiversity maintenance, etc.

The forage production service provided by grasslands is intimately linked to the way the grass grows and therefore to the specific conditions of the year in question. The grass growth depends on various factors: the water and nutrient resources of the soil, the climate (primarily the radiation useful for photosynthesis, the temperature that regulates the functioning of the plants and the rainfall),

M. El Yacoubi et al. (Eds.): ICPRAI 2022, LNCS 13364, pp. 383–394, 2022.
https://doi.org/10.1007/978-3-031-09282-4_32

the management applied by the farmer (mowing, grazing, fertilization) and the grassland vegetation. This growth therefore also depends on the growth that took place on the previous days and that contributed to the establishment of this leaf area.

Information about the grass growth during the year is essential to some simulation models of cattle herds that simulate the use of this resource to feed animals on pasture or at barn (with hay or grass silage). But information on grass growth is rarely available. The challenge is therefore to design a service that estimates this growth over the year, for example by 10-day periods.

Grasslands are used by farmers to feed their animals. They can be grazed and/or cut to produce preserved fodder such as hay or grass silage. The total amount of grazed grass as well as the cut grass during the year corresponds to what is called the "annual valuation" of the grassland (expressed in tons of dry matter per hectare and per year). Information on the annual valuation of French grasslands is often available. In this work, we have assumed that annual valuation allows us to estimate the *cumulative annual growth* of the grass (i.e., the total grass growth over a year), and therefore we assume that the cumulative annual growth is available. We will discuss the assumption that this information is available in the results.

Our problem is then to disaggregate the cumulative annual grass growth to reconstruct the dynamics of the growth over the year using time series describing the climate of the year.

We propose to approach this problem as a task of forecasting time series. Our problem is not to forecast future values of grass growth. Indeed, time series forecasting methods are used to estimate values of a time series, especially as a function of exogenous variables, such as climate. The main contribution of the present work is therefore to adapt these methods to our problem.

In the remaining of the article, we first present the data used in this study in Sect. 2. Section 3 presents the formalization of the problem as well as the various methods proposed. These methods are then evaluated in Sect. 4. Before concluding, Sect. 5 positions our approach among those of the state of the art.

2 Data

For learning and evaluating a model for predicting a time series of grass growth, a database was available from simulations by the STICS model [3][1], which is a process-based and deterministic crop model.

The simulations were carried out at the scale of France at a high spatial resolution corresponding to pedoclimatic units (PCU), resulting from the crossing of the climatic information (*SAFRAN* grid point) and soil information (soil mapping units), and for which the surface of grassland is significant. The outputs of the simulations correspond to 30-year time series (1984–2013) at daily time step.

[1] STICS Model: https://www6.paca.inra.fr/stics/.

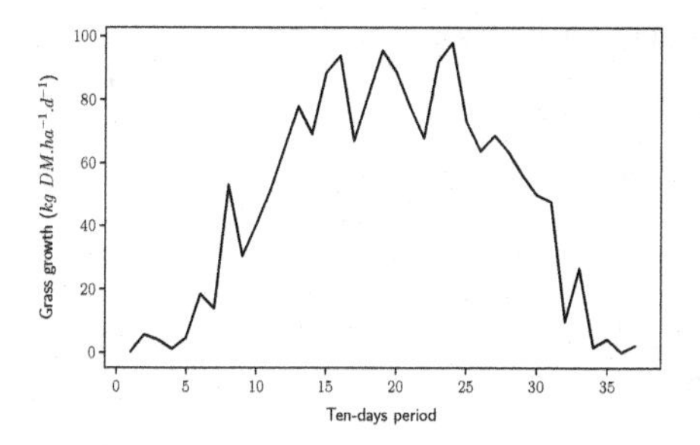

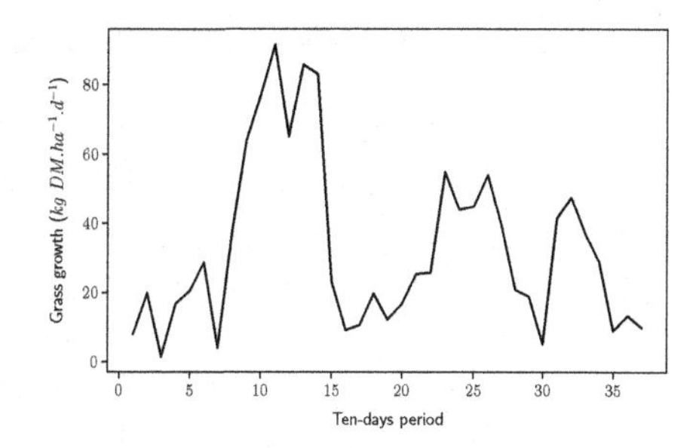

Fig. 1. Examples of annual grass growth curve for two different PCUs with different climatic conditions. In the case on the right, there is a sharp decrease in growth in summer, probably due to lack of rainfall.

Each PCU is associated with a 30-year climate (1984–2013), one to two main soils, one to two main grassland types, and for each grassland type, 1 to 18 farming modes. Within the same PCU, there can be up to 72 grassland simulations. In practice there is an average of ten simulations per PCU.

Figure 1 illustrates two examples of grass growth simulations extracted from this database. The two curves have different shapes due to seasonal climatic conditions more or less favorable to the grass growth.

In the context of this work, we limited ourselves to data from the Brittany region. We selected only the useful variables, namely the daily growth of the grasslands and the daily climatic data. The cumulative growth was obtained by summing the daily growth over a year. We excluded the years of grassland installation because they have a particular grass growth pattern.

The daily growth and climate data were aggregated to the 10-day period (as a sum or an average, see Table 1), i.e. over a period of ten consecutive days. Each annual series thus contains 37 values. Agronomists estimated that during 10 days, the growth varies little. Thus, this period length is sufficient for expecting accurate disaggregation.

The dataset consists of 477 439 series [6]. Each series contains 10 variables summarized in Table 1: the pair $(id, annee)$ identifies a series of 37 periods of 10 days, the variable measuring growth (to be reconstructed) and the exogenous variables that describe the climate (temperature, rainfall and radiation). The de Martonne index (im) is an index of aridity that integrates temperature and rainfall information [9]. To conduct our experiments, only the last five years (2009 to 2013) were used to reduce computation time.

3 Methodology

In this section, we first formalize the problem of disaggregating a time series as a machine learning problem. Then, Sect. 3.2 presents variants of the proposal using alternative representations of a time series (differentiated or cumulative series). Finally, Sect. 3.3 discusses the choices of initial values for the reconstructed series.

Table 1. Description of the different variables in the dataset.

Variable	Aggregation	Definition (unit)
id	–	Identifier of the simulated PCU
year	–	Simulation year
period	–	Identifier of the period of ten consecutive days
T_{min}	Min	Minimum temperature (°C)
T_{max}	Max	Maximum temperature (°C)
T_{avg}	Avg	Average temperature (°C)
Rain	Sum	Total rainfall (mm)
RG	Sum	Global Radiation (J.cm^{-2})
im	–	Martonne index defined by: $I = 37 \times \frac{Rain}{T_{avg}+10}$ (mm.°C^{-1})
growth	avg	Average daily grass growth over the 10-day period (kg DM.ha^{-1}.d^{-1}, *DM* meaning Dry Matter)

3.1 Formalization and General Approach

In our disaggregation problem, an example is a couple $\langle C, \boldsymbol{Y}\rangle$ where $C \in \mathbb{R}$ is the value of the cumulative growth and $\boldsymbol{Y} = \boldsymbol{y}_1, \ldots, \boldsymbol{y}_n$ is a multivariate time series of size n where $\boldsymbol{y}_t \in \mathbb{R}^k$ for all $t \in [1, n]$. $\boldsymbol{Y}$ represents the climate data of the year considered.

The objective of the disaggregation is to construct a time series $\widehat{X} = \hat{x}_1, \ldots, \hat{x}_n$ in such a way that we have $\sum_{t=1}^{n} \hat{x}_t = C$ and that $\widehat{X}$ is as close as possible to the original time series X. So we aim to minimize the mean square error (MSE) between X and $\widehat{X}$.

The approach proposed in this work consists in using a time series forecasting technique to reconstruct $\widehat{X}$ step by step. The aim is to estimate $\hat{x}_t$ according to the previous values of $\widehat{X}$, but also to the values of the exogenous time series.

If we consider an autoregressive model of order p ($AR(p)$), $\hat{x}_t$ is obtained by the following equation:

$$\hat{x}_t = b + \sum_{i=1}^{p} \varphi_i \hat{x}_{t-i} + \sum_{j=0}^{p} \boldsymbol{\psi}_j \cdot \boldsymbol{y}_{t-j} = f_{(\varphi, \boldsymbol{\psi})}\left(\hat{x}_{t-1,\ldots,t-p}, \boldsymbol{y}_{t,\ldots,t-p}\right) \quad (1)$$

where $\varphi_i \in \mathbb{R}$, $b \in \mathbb{R}$ and $\boldsymbol{\psi}_j \in \mathbb{R}^k$ are the model parameters. The order of the model, p, designates the number of past values that are taken into account for the prediction.

Note that Eq. 1 only considers time series values strictly before t to predict $\hat{x}_t$, but since the exogenous values are known, the exogenous data of $\boldsymbol{Y}$ at date t is used in the prediction.

More generally, we wish to estimate $\hat{x}_t$ as a function of $\hat{x}_{t-1}, \ldots, \hat{x}_{t-p}$, and we note f_θ this estimation function where θ represents the parameters of this function. In the experiments, we compared three classes of functions: linear regression, support vector regression (SVR) and random forests (RF).

Our disaggregation problem turns out to be a machine learning problem. We have to estimate the parameters θ of a forecasting model f_θ from a training dataset. A time series $\widehat{X}$ is then reconstructed by recursively applying this forecasting model. Nevertheless, it is necessary to add assumptions about the initial values of the time series to apply the forecasting model the first time (see Sect. 3.3).

3.2 Pre and Post Processings

Three pre-processings of the time series have been proposed: no-preprocessing (raw time series), "differentiated" time series and "cumulative" time series. In the two latter cases, we transform X without modifying the exogenous time series ($\boldsymbol{Y}$).

The time series differentiation subtracts the growth for the $(d-1)$-th 10-day period from the growth of the d-th 10-day period. The learning problem is then to be able to reconstruct accurately the derivative of the growth, rather than the growth itself. The reconstruction of the growth time series is done step by step. The value of the differentiated time series must first be predicted and then integrated (cumulated with the previous values) to reconstruct the growth time series. The interest of this approach is to leave the choice of the initialization of the growth free during the integration step. Thus, the reconstruction of the growth ensures to have a cumulative values equals to C (see post-processings).

The time series cumulation sums all the values of the previous periods of 10 days. This is the inverse path of time series differentiation. Our forecasting problem thus becomes to reconstruct accurately this partial cumulative growth. During the reconstruction phase, the learned forecasting model reconstructs the cumulative time series which is then derived to obtain the growth time series. The interest of the cumulation is to potentially ease the learning problem since the predicted function is monotonic.

In addition, three post-processings have been proposed: no post-processing, rescaling and translation. The objective of a post-processing is to enforce the cumulative of the reconstructed time series to equal exactly the known cumulative value C. Rescaling consists in applying the scale factor $\frac{C}{\sum_{i=1}^{n} \hat{x}_i}$ to all values of the time series obtained by the prediction model. Translation consists in adding the value $C - \sum_{i=1}^{n} \hat{x}_i$ to all values of the time series obtained by the prediction model.

3.3 Order of Models and Initialization

The next step is the choice of the parameter p, i.e., the number of past values to be taken into account to predict the next one. Then, the first p values of the growth must be provided to initiate the disaggregation. This parameter must be chosen so that it is large enough to give an accurate prediction and, at the same time, it is as small as possible to not require the use of too much *a priori* initial values. Domain experts decided to set $p = 3$, which corresponds approximately to a month (30 days), and to initiate the reconstruction from the January, a period during which the growth is small and does not changes too much.

Table 2. Initializations of the first 3 values for the preprocessing of a series $X = \langle x_1, \ldots, x_n \rangle$.

Initialization	Type of preprocessing		
	Raw	Differentiated	cumulative
Concrete	x_1, x_2, x_3	$x_1, x_2 - x_1, x_3 - x_2$	$x_1, x_1 + x_2, x_1 + x_2 + x_3$
Average	$9, 9, 9$	$0, 0, 0$	$9, 18, 27$

Two different initializations of the growth are possible using either the raw time series, or an *a priori* value. In this second case, we choose to set a value that corresponds to the average of the concrete growth over each of the first three periods of 10 days and for all the available series (9 kg DM.ha^{-1}.d^{-1}). Note that the first type of initialization requires information that is not always available in practice, so we would like to compare the second type of initialization with this optimal case.

For the cumulative and differentiated time series, the initialization values are deduced from the previous assumptions. The choices for the initializations are summarized in Table 2.

4 Experiments and Results

The methods were implemented in Python. Three regression models were investigated: linear regression (*lm*), Support Vector Regression (SVR) [1] (Gaussian kernel, configured with $C = 100$) and random forests (RF) [2] (limited to 100 trees). We choose the hyper-parameters to make a trade-off between accuracy and efficiency. It has been evaluated on small subsets of the data. Other hyper-parameters of the methods are the default ones. Due to the large amount of data, the training of the random forests and the SVRs, required to sample the dataset using only the last 5 years of data (total amount of 76 918 series).

Combining the different types of regression and preprocessing yields 9 different growth prediction models:

- three preprocessings: raw, differentiated (*diff*), and cumulative (*cumul*);
- three regression models: *lm*, SVR and *RF*;

These models are then combined with several possibilities for disaggregation:

- two initializations: concrete or average initialization (at 9 kg DM.ha^{-1}.d^{-1}) of the first three values;
- use of two post-processings to match the sum of values of the disaggregate time series with the cumulative annual growth C: scale factor (*scale*) or translation (*trans*).

Each of these models was learned on the training set and then evaluated on the test set data. The training set represents 70% of the sampled set (30% for the test set). Since we wish to have a model that generalizes well for different

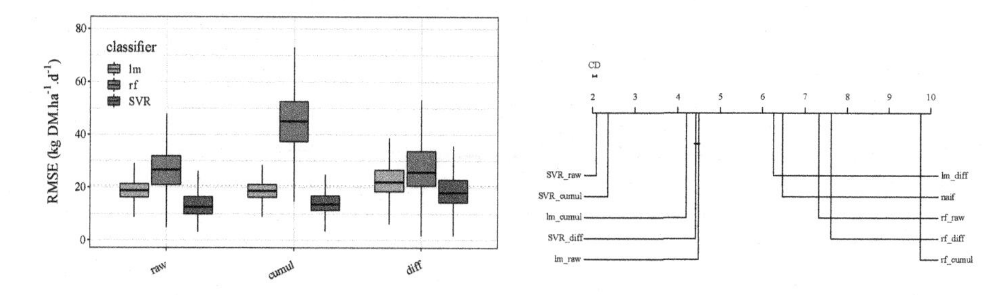

Fig. 2. Comparison of RMSE between different classifiers and preprocessings. On the left: error distributions; on the right: critical difference diagram. The dashed line indicates the RMSE of the naive model.

exogenous data, we choose to split the dataset according to climate: the climate time series of the test set are different from all the climate time series in the learning set. We used *SAFRAN* grid points to split the dataset: the time series of 328 grid points are used for learning, and the time series of the remaining 141 grid points are used for testing.

The accuracy of the time series disaggregation is evaluated by the root mean square error (RMSE). The smaller the better.

As a baseline, we propose a naive model which generates always the average time series. This time series has been computed as the average of 10-day growth values for each time series on the training dataset. The average RMSE of this naive model is 20.6 kg DM.ha^{-1}.d^{-1}. Then, we expect to lower this error with our proposal.

In the rest of this section, we start by giving the results of the comparisons of our nine models with an average initialization. In a second step, we analyze the error committed by the model due to the choice of the initialization, then we analyze the accuracy improvement obtained by using the information of the cumulative growth C. Finally, Sect. 4.4 illustrates qualitatively the results of the disaggregation.

4.1 Comparison of the Prediction Models

In this section, we compare our nine forecasting models (three pre-processed data and three types of regressor) and the naive model. In these experiments, time series were initialized with the average initial values and no post-processing adjustment were applied.

Figure 2 on the left represents the RMSE distributions. For the RF, SVR and *lm* classifiers (all pre-treatments combined), the average RMSE are respectively 35.3 kg DM.ha^{-1}.d^{-1}, 16.8 kg DM.ha^{-1}.d^{-1} and 20.7 kg DM.ha^{-1}.d^{-1} for the raw time series. The better results are achieved with SVR. The random forest model shows surprisingly poor performance compared to the other approaches. It may comes from a model overfitting due to the default hyper-parameters of the RF which iw not necessarily suitable for regression tasks. Compared to the average model, only SVR performs better on average.

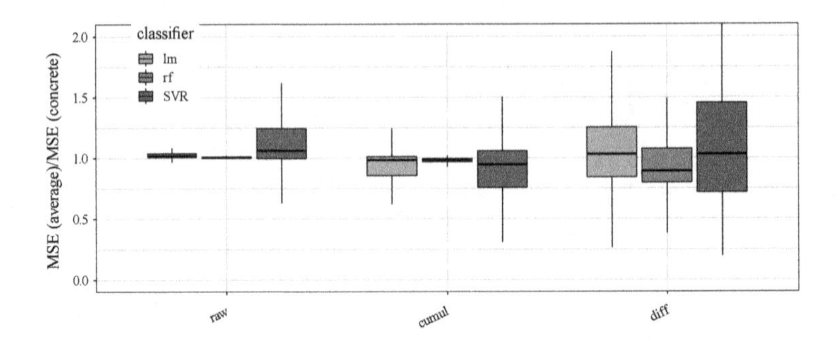

Fig. 3. Ratio of RMSE with an average initialisation to RMSE with concrete initialisation. A value greater than 1 indicates that using an average growth value for the first three 10-day periods to initialize the time series is worse than using concrete growth values, and vice versa.

The cumulative time series have rather reduced RMSE for the linear (*lm*) and SVR models, on the contrary the RF performance worsens in this case.

Figure 2 on the right illustrates the same results in a synthetic way by a critical difference diagram. The diagram confirms that the approaches with SVR are significantly better. The solutions based on cumulation are also rather interesting (except when combined with RF). Most of the models based on linear regression and SVR models are significantly better than the naive model. This comparison is based on peer-to-peer differences for each series to be disaggregated (Nemenyi test with $\alpha = 5\%$).

4.2 Effect of Approximating the First Values

This section investigates the errors related to the initialisation of the first grass growth values. It addresses the following question: has the approximation by an a priori average grass growth value an impact on the accuracy of the model prediction? Figure 3 visualizes the ratios of RMSE with average initialisation and MSE with concrete initialisation.

We observe that on average the ratios are very close to 1. This means that the use of the average initialization does not introduce significant error. Nevertheless, we note a strong presence of outliers, in particular when using the cumulative or the differentiated time series. These outliers are also observed when using the SVR on the raw time series.

Finally, we can also see that in some cases, the use of the average initialisation improves the model predictions (ratio < 1).

4.3 Improvements by Post-processings

This section investigates the accuracy improvement by applying a post-processing. Indeed, the post-processing makes benefit from an additional information: the cumulative growth C. Then we expect to lower the RMSE.

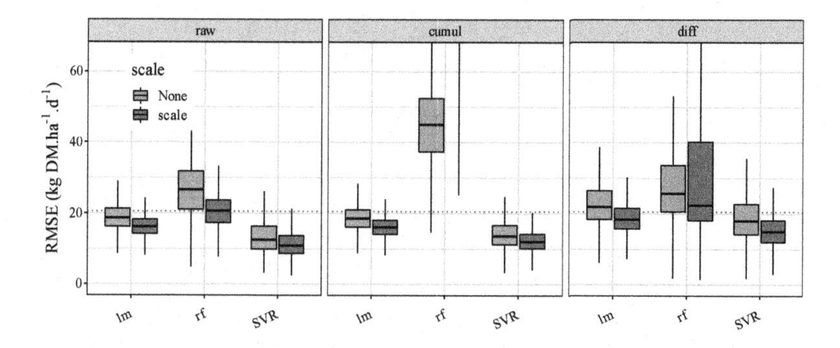

Fig. 4. Comparison of RMSE with and without the use of a scaling factor in post-processing (use of the cumulative growth C). The box of RF with scaling factor applied on the cumulative time series can not be show on the graph to keep it readable. The dashed line indicates the RMSE of the naive model.

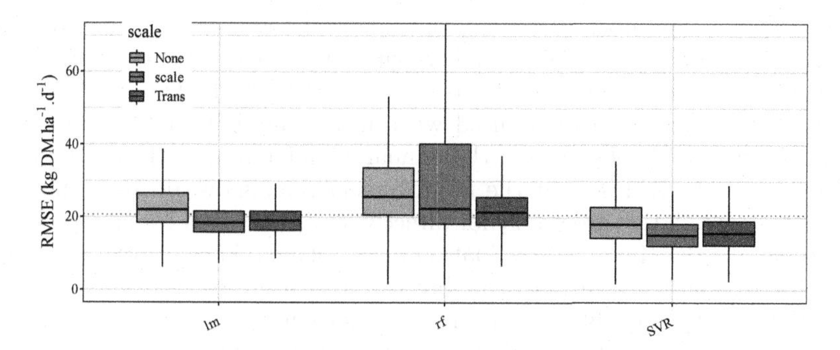

Fig. 5. Comparison of the RMSE according to the post-processing applied to the differentiated series: without post-processing, scaling or translation of the curve (using the cumulative growth C). The dashed line indicates the RMSE of the naive model.

We start by looking at the errors while applying the scale factor. We can see from the graph in Fig. 4 that this post-processing improves the RMSE in most settings. At the median, for the SVR applied without preprocessing, the improvement is ≈84%. The results of RF with cumulative time series continues to contrast with the others.

Finally, we complement the analysis with the comparisons of the three alternatives of post-processing: translation, scaling factor or without post-processing. This comparison is meaningful only in the case of the differentiated time series.

The results are given in Fig. 5. Compared to the previous graph, this figure adds the case of the translation. We observe that the performances of scaling are similar to that of translation. But, translation can induce negative growth values. Such values are not acceptable from a biological point of view. Therefore, although attractive from a methodological point of view, the solution with a translation post-processing turns out to be not usable in practice. Furthermore, the practical use of scaling tends to show an interest in improving disaggregation by using knowledge of the annual aggregate.

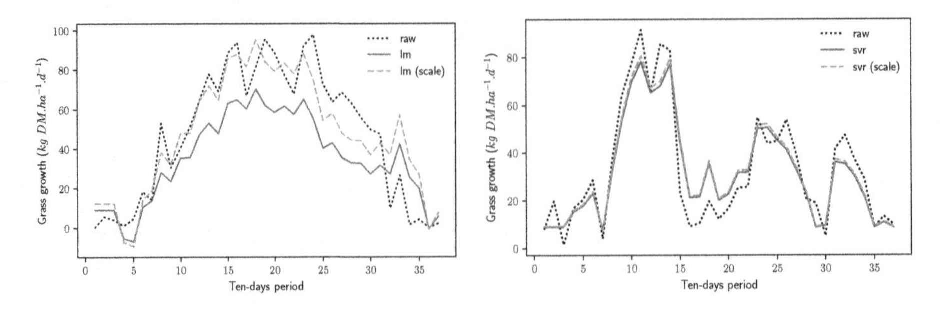

Fig. 6. Examples of disaggregation of cumulative growth with *lm* (on the left) and SVR (on the right, RMSE: 6.9 kg DM.ha^{-1}.d^{-1}). The example on the left illustrates the effect of post-processing (RMSE before: 17.5 kg DM.ha^{-1}.d^{-1}, after: 11.1 kg DM.ha^{-1}.d^{-1}).

From these experiments, we can conclude that the best disaggregation solution is the one based on a SVR classifier, without preprocessing the growth series (SVR_raw). The average error of this model is 12.4 ± 4.3 kg DM.ha^{-1}.d^{-1}. This disaggregation solution can be used with an average initialization of the first three 10-day periods. The use of the annual cumulative growth (C) is interesting to reduce the RMSE, but the improvement remains weak. Remember that this annual cumulative growth is not directly accessible: in the long run, it could be estimated from the annual valuation of grasslands, known from agricultural statistics or interviews with farmers, but the error resulting from this estimation could mitigate the benefit of using this information.

It should be noted that if SVR requires a long computation time (several hours in learning and about ten seconds in inference), learning a linear model takes only a few seconds.

4.4 Qualitative Evaluation of Reconstructions

Figure 6 illustrates the disaggregation results obtained for the two time series of Fig. 1.[2] In both cases, the treatments were carried out without pre-processing and with an average initialization (one can note that the first three values are constant). The figure shows that the linear model (*lm*) underestimates growth in summer. The scaling factor corrects this defect, but induces additional errors in winter. On the right curves, we see that the original time series is very well reconstructed despite some important changes. In this case, the linear model does not fit well to these changes.

5 Related Work

The term *disaggregation* sometimes corresponds to a signal processing task that aims to separate signals from different sources that are mixed in the same signal,

[2] Disaggregation can be tested on-line: https://disaggregation.herokuapp.com.

for example in a power consumption signal [5]. This type of problem does not correspond to ours.

For time series, *temporal disaggregation* refers to methods to reconstruct a high frequency time series consistent with a lower frequency time series (the sum or average of the values of the high frequency series). It is a kind of oversampling. It is used in econometrics to refine annual, monthly or quarterly estimates of indicators at finer time scales. The seminal work in this field is the Chow and Lin algorithm [4] of which many variants have been proposed. Nevertheless, in this approach of the problem, it is necessary to have regular data about the grass growth. However, we have only one cumulative value per example in our case. The application of this type of problem is therefore likely to be inefficient.

The disaggregation problem can also be seen as a special case of a more general problem: that of estimating individual values from aggregated data. This problem is also frequently encountered in economic applications where statistical data (for example, voting statistics) are known only for groups of people, but not individually. Mathematically, it is a matter of reconstructing a joint distribution from marginal distributions. For our application, the marginal would be the aggregate and we aim to reconstruct the distribution for the different 10-day periods. This type of problem can be solved for example by *Iterative Proportional Fitting* (IPF) algorithms or ecological inference [8].[3] For the latter approach, Quinn [10] proposes a variant that takes into account temporal dependencies between values by making the assumption on dynamics. Nevertheless, the hypotheses on these dynamics can be difficult to propose, so we preferred an approach focused only on the data.

Finally, the field of machine learning has also been interested in this type of problem, notably by proposing alternatives to IPF based on Sinkhorn normal forms [7]. This formulation brings the IPF problem closer to the optimal transport problem. Nevertheless, it does not take into account the specificity of time series data.

6 Conclusion

We presented the temporal disaggregation of the annual cumulative grass growth. We addressed this problem by using a time series forecasting, using available exogenous climate data. Through our experiments, we identified a method based on the learning of a SVR model with an average RMSE lower than 12.4 ± 4.3 kg DM.ha^{-1}.d^{-1}. The experiments showed that the initialization can be done using the average values of the first three 10-day periods without worsen the results. It is worth noting that the good performances of the approach is also due to available climatic variables that are known to be strongly related to the grass growth.

Finally, the experiments showed that the annual cumulative growth improves the accuracy of the model. Nevertheless, this improvement is small and the availability of reliable information on this annual cumulative growth is not guaranteed

[3] The term *ecological inference* does not particularly refer to ecological data.

in the future. If the initial problem was to disaggregate this quantity, the results are in fact very good without using it directly. Thereafter, it does not seem necessary to pursue its use.

Then, the first perspective is to better investigate the hyper-parameters of the models. More specifically, the RF overfitting may be corrected with better choices of the hyper-parameters. In addition, regularisation (Lasso or Ridge) may be evaluated. The second perspective of this work is the investigation of time series intrinsic regression [11] as a new possible solution for our problem. The third perspective of this work is to explore other variants. In particular, the initial choice of the period length may be changed. Reducing this period, for example to the week, will likely help the auto-regressive algorithms to be more accurate, and thus improve the disaggregation. Finally, the selected prediction model will feed a dairy farming simulation model called FARM-AQAL developed in the framework of the European project GENTORE.

References

1. Awad, M., Khanna, R.: Support vector regression. In: Awad, M., Khanna, R. (eds.) Efficient Learning Machines: Theories, Concepts, and Applications for Engineers and System Designers, pp. 67–80. Apress, Berkeley, CA (2015). https://doi.org/10.1007/978-1-4302-5990-9_4
2. Breiman, L.: Random forests. Machine Learning **45**(1), 5–32 (2001)
3. Brisson, N., et al.: An overview of the crop model STICS. Eur. J. Agron. **18**(3–4), 309–332 (2003)
4. Chow, G.C., Lin, A.: Best linear unbiased interpolation, distribution, and extrapolation of time series by related series. Rev. Econ. Stat. **53**(4), 372–375 (1971). https://doi.org/10.2307/1928739
5. Figueiredo, M., de Almeida, A., Ribeiro, B.: Home electrical signal disaggregation for non-intrusive load monitoring (NILM) systems. Neurocomputing **96**, 66–73 (2012)
6. Graux, A.I.: Growth and annual valorisation of breton grasslands simulated by STICS, and associated climate. Portail Data INRAE (2021). https://doi.org/10.15454/FD9FHU
7. Idel, M.: A review of matrix scaling and sinkhorn's normal form for matrices and positive maps. arXiv preprint arXiv:1609.06349 (2016)
8. King, G., Fox, J.: A solution to the ecological inference problem: reconstructing individual behavior from aggregate data. Can. J. Sociol. **24**(1), 150 (1999)
9. de Martonne, E.: Aréisme et indice d'aridité. Comptes rendus de L'Academie des Sciences **182**, 1395–1398 (1926)
10. Quinn, K.M.: Ecological inference in the presence of temporal dependence. In: Ecological Inference: New Methodological Strategies, pp. 207–233. Cambridge University Press (2004)
11. Tan, C.W., Bergmeir, C., Petitjean, F., Webb, G.I.: Time series extrinsic regression. Data Min. Knowl. Disc. **35**(3), 1032–1060 (2021). https://doi.org/10.1007/s10618-021-00745-9

Extraction of Entities in Health Domain Documents Using Recurrent Neural Networks

Erick Barrios González[1], Mireya Tovar Vidal[1(✉)], Guillermo De Ita Luna[1], and José A. Reyes-Ortiz[2]

[1] Faculty of Computer Science, Benemerita Universidad Autonoma de Puebla, 14 sur y Av, C.U., San Claudio, Puebla, Mexico
erick.barrios@alumno.buap.mx, mireya.tovar@correo.buap.mx

[2] Universidad Autonoma Metropolitana, Av. San Pablo Xalpa 180, Azcapotzalco, 02200 Mexico City, Mexico
jaro@azc.uam.mx

Abstract. This paper reviews the subtask "A" of *eHealth-KD challenge 2021*, using a strategy oriented to the use of recurrent neural networks. In subtask "A" the entities are identified by document and their types (Concepts, actions, predicates, and references). This paper mainly compares various word embedding models, annotation styles in BIO, BILOU, and an own annotation style to distinguish entities composed of more than one word from entities of a single word. Is also proposed a solution based on POS tagging to improve the results of systems that use recurrent neural networks by changing the pre-processing. An evaluation process was performed with the following well-known metrics: precision, recall, and F_1.

Keywords: Entity extraction · Bidirectional long short-term memory · Natural language processing

1 Introduction

Natural language processing (NLP) methods are increasingly being used to extract knowledge from unstructured health texts. The organization of medical information can be helpful in clinical analyses, reduce the number of medical errors, or help make more appropriate decisions in some instances. Currently, it is easier to have medical information in electronic format and even to have that information structured. However, information in traditional media (such as publications, academic manuscripts, clinical reports) is of little use in selecting the most appropriate information in each case, whether in the clinical or research setting. Therefore, it exists the necessity for creating new ways of extracting knowledge from health texts and for the information to be comprehensive and reliable for any study or analysis to be carried out with that information.

M. El Yacoubi et al. (Eds.): ICPRAI 2022, LNCS 13364, pp. 395–406, 2022.
https://doi.org/10.1007/978-3-031-09282-4_33

Therefore, subtask "A" of *eHealth-KD challenge 2021* proposes identifying entities of a document and their respective types [13]. These entities are all relevant terms (of a single word or multiple words) representing semantically essential elements in a sentence. There are four types of entities:

- Concept: Identify a term, concept, relevant idea in the domain of knowledge of sentence.
- Action: Identify a process or modification of other entities. It can be indicated by a verb or verbal construction or by nouns.
- Predicate: Identifies a function or filter from a set of elements, which has a semantic label in the text, and is applied to an entity with some additional arguments.
- Reference: Identifies a textual element that refers to an entity (of the same sentence or a different one).

In Fig. 1 there are examples of how entities would be classified into concepts, actions, predicates, and references. For example, "asma" (asthma), "enfermedad" (disease), "vías respiratorias" (respiratory tract) are concepts, the word "afecta" (affects) is an action, the word "esta" (this) is a reference, and "mayores" (older) is a predicate.

Fig. 1. Entity recognition example [13].

This paper explores two strategies, a solution based in a own annotation style to distinguish entities composed of more than one word from entities of a single word, and a solution based on POS tagging to improve performance in learning models based on recurrent neural networks to identify entities in a corpus of the health domain.

The document is structured as follows: Sect. 2 presents the works related to this research. Section 3 shows the proposed solution for the identification of entities. Section 4 shows the results obtained. Finally, Sect. 5 contains the conclusion.

2 Related Work

The following describes work related to the identification of entities mainly using recurrent neuronal networks:

In [8] an entity identification model for any domain in general is presented. This model combines a bidirectional LSTM network and conditional random fields (BiLSTM-CRF) adding "Multi-Task Learning" (MTL) and a framework "called Mixture of Entity Experts" (MoEE). This work uses information "from CoNLL-2003 English NER (Named entity recognition)", the entities found are classified into 4 types: people, locations, organizations and miscellaneous. Experiments were made with different word embeddings; the model used FastText (freeze settings) model and obtained a 69.53% with the measure F_1.

In *eHealth-KD challenge 2019* in [5] a BILOU annotation scheme is used. The architecture inputs are represented by vectors, POS tag embedding and word embedding respectively, two types of rules have been applied to the result of deep learning: The first set of rules is aimed at correcting frequent errors expanding or reducing the scope of a detected keyword phrase, or modifying its type.

Also in *eHealth-KD challenge 2019* in [1] a system is proposed with a strategy that uses BiLSTM with a CRF (Conditional random fields) layer for the identification of entities. In addition, domain-specific word embeds are used. For each token that the sentence was divided into, the input for that token consists of a list of three feature vectors: Character encodings, POS tagging vectors, and word indexes.

In [2] an architecture based on a BiLSTM with a CRF classifier was proposed. The corresponding classes are encoded in BIO annotation style.

During *eHealth-KD challenge* in 2020, [12] uses the BMEWO-V tag system and BiLSTM layers as contextual encoders. The label "None" is included in the latter for cases where there is no entity present.

Also in *eHealth-KD challenge 2020* in [4] the proposed system uses the BILUOV tagger that uses a character encoding layer to transform the representation of the characters of each token into a single vector that captures the morphological dependencies of the token. The character encoding layer consists of an embedded layer, followed by a BiLSTM layer. Four independent instances are trained with this architecture, each one corresponding to a type of entity.

Finally, in *eHealth-KD challenge* in 2021, in the system proposed in [11] it obtains fourth place with a solution based on BiLSTM aimed at embedding words and characters; it also makes use of information POS of spacy and the BILUOV tagger.

3 Proposed Solution

The proposed solution for the detection of entities, of subtask "A" of *eHealth-KD challenge*, is divided into two stages described below.

3.1 Information Pre-processing

This section shows the basic structure for pre-processing, the description of the corpus, the description of the word embedding models, and the description of the tagging patterns used.

Pre-processing Structure: For the pre-processing of the information, the following steps have been considered:

1. Cleaning the text: In this step the corpus provided is divided into several sentences and irrelevant signs are eliminated.
2. Tagging: The sentences from the previous step are tokenized and their POS tagging is added to each word.
3. Annotation style: In this step, a vector is created for each annotation style, as well as vectors of the additional information attached.
4. Information vectors: The vectors of words and characters are converted into vectors of numbers, a dictionary of terms is created, where each term has its equivalent in number.
5. Word Embedding Model: This model receives all the words, tags, and expressions before they are vectorized to convert the information into an array of vectors.

Tagging: Grammar tagging (part-of-speech tagging) complements the information in the text; for this, it is essential to consider that grammatical tagging is usually different for Spanish and English and depends on the tool used to tag. That is why two spacy libraries will be used, one for English (in_core_web_lg of 714 mb) and another for Spanish (is_core_news_lg of 542 mb), but they have the same tagging format.

In order to improve the performance of the systems, it is proposed to attach additional information using POS tagging.

From the training corpus provided, content is made of the appearance of each POS tag as an entity. For example, there are 342 nouns as entities within all the sentences in the training body (nouns appear most often as entities within the text).

For each entity that consists of more than one word, its occurrences are counted according to the POS tagging pattern. For example, in the entity "asilos de ancianos" (nursing homes), the pattern would be "NOUN ADP NOUN." An example of how the frequency of these patterns is captured is shown in Table 1.

Table 1. Frequency of appearance of entities (made up of more than one word) based on POS tagging.

POS tagging pattern	Frequency
NOUN ADJ	33
PROPN PROPN	9
NOUN ADP NOUN	8
NOUN ADP PROPN	6
PROPN PROPN PROPN	3

Finally, with the POS tagging and the patterns found, it is intended to build a proposal for a system where words are classified according to the frequency of their appearance.

Annotation and Proposal Styles: For the annotation styles, the following styles have been considered: BIO (Beginning, Inside, Outside), BILOU (Beginning, Inside, Last, Outside, Unique) [7] and an own style annotation aimed at differentiating entities that consist of more than one word from those that do not. To implement the annotation style, we consider the classification of the entities (concepts, actions, predicates, and references) and add the label "None" for the words in the text that do not belong to any group of entities mentioned above.

Table 2. Example of own annotation style.

Token	Tag
Algunos	Predicate
asilos	P_Concept
de	P_Concept
ancianos	P_Concept
cuentan	O_
con	O_
unidades	Concept
de	O_
cuidados	Action

The own annotation style proposed is shown in Table 2, which we will call the annotation style "P", the labels that begin with the prefix "P_" refer to the entities that are made up of more than one word, "O_" for words that are not entities and no prefix for words that are single word entities. As mentioned, this annotation style is aimed at differentiating entities that are made up of more than one word that are not, and gives a simpler approach than the BIO and BILOU annotation style provide.

Information Vectors: The information on the frequency of the POS tagging was manually classified into 6 ranges: very high frequency (0.75–1), high frequency (0.5–0.75), medium frequency (0.35–0.5), low frequency (0.1–0.35), very low frequency (0–0.1) and no frequency (0). The classification is obtained from the probability of occurrence of the patterns found. It is calculated within a range of 0 to 1, the frequency of appearance of a tag is divided into the frequency of appearance of that tag recognized as an entity. For example, if 678 nouns appear and only 534 times those nouns are entities, the words that are tagged as a noun have a probability of appearing of $(534/678) = 0.78$ and a probability of 0 if not never appears as an entity. For entities made up of more than one word, sequences that fulfill previously established patterns were searched and subsequently classified as previously shown using the BIO (prefixes B_, I_, O_) or BILOU (prefixes B_, I_, L_, O_, U_) annotation style. In Table 3, we can see how the sequence of words would look, with the annotation style added.

Table 3. Example of tag sequence created with annotation style BIO and BILOU.

Word	POS	BIO	BILOU
algunos	DET	B_LOW_FRECUENCY	U_LOW_FRECUENCY
asilos	NOUN	B_LOW_FRECUENCY	B_LOW_FRECUENCY
de	ADP	I_LOW_FRECUENCY	I_LOW_FRECUENCY
ancianos	NOUN	I_LOW_FRECUENCY	L_LOW_FRECUENCY
cuentan	VERB	B_MEDIUM_FRECUENCY	U_MEDIUM_FRECUENCY
con	ADP	B_VERYLOW_FRECUENCY	U_VERYLOW_FRECUENCY

3.2 Identification of Entities

For the identification of entities, it is proposed to use two systems, one BiLSTM with CNN and the other BiLSTM with CRF.

In Fig. 2, we can see how the pre-processing output files are the input for the entity identification system; each system will return a vector of numbers as a result, which must be converted using the term dictionaries to get the final file in BRAT format. For the training and prediction of the network, we have three different vectors; these are considered the "X" axis: Vector of words, vector POS and vector probabilities POS. In contrast, the vector with the annotation styles that contains the entity classification for training is the "Y" axis.

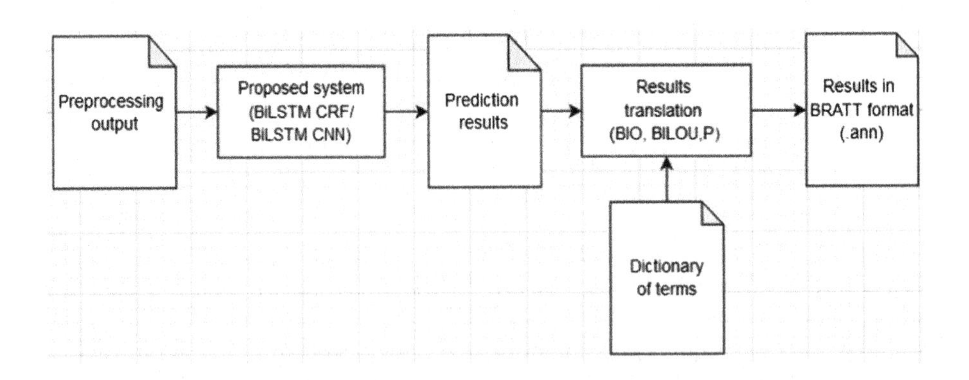

Fig. 2. Steps to identify entities.

Table 4. Format example *BRAT standoff.*

T1 Concept 3 10; 11 19 sistema vascular
T2 Predicate 26 29 red
T3 Concept 33 38; 39 49 vasos sanguíneos
T4 Concept 54 60 cuerpo

4 Results

4.1 Description of the Corpus

The corpus provided by *eHealth Challenge 2021* will be used. These corpora are classified mainly in 2 ways:

The corpus provided by *eHealth Challenge 2021* will be used for the preprocessing part. These corpora are classified mainly in 2 ways:

- Training (For system training): Made up of 100 sentences and approximately 822 distinct words in spanish (vocabulary).
- Testing (For system test): Made up of 100 sentences, 50 in english and 50 in spanish, with approximately a vocabulary with approximately 531 distinct words in spanish and approximately 607 distinct words in english.

Each corpus comprises two files, one ".ann" that contains the answers, and another ".txt" that contains the text to be treated. The file ".txt" is organized by sentences, for example, "El sistema vascular es la red de vasos sanguíneos del cuerpo." As shown in Table 4, the entities and relationships are correctly classified in BRAT standoff format.

4.2 Pre-processing Results

This section shows the results obtained from the pre-processing stage:

The training corpus (training) provided has 728 entities (464 concept type, 73 predicate type, 18 reference type, and 173 action type); all entities are in Spanish. For the evaluation corpus (testing), we have a total of 934 entities, of which 451 are in Spanish (323 concept type, 37 predicate type, 6 reference type, and 85 action type) and 483 are in English (364 concept type, 63 predicate type, two reference type, and 54 action type).

4.3 Results: Word Embedding

Several embedding patterns as well as various text have been compiled in order to create a corpus and various word embedding patterns. A Wikipedia library for Python was used to create this corpus, allowing searching and saving the information in texts. In Table 5, different features are shown, such as the number of words used for their training, dimensions, the language, and the tool used for creating the model.

Table 5. Word embedding models.

Tool	Algorithm	Words	Dimension	Language	Source
Wor2vec.	*Skip-gram*	20 million	490	Spanish	Created
Wor2vec.	*Cbow*	20 million	490	Spanish	Created
FastText.	*Skip-gram*	20 million	490	Spanish	Created
FastText.	*Skip-gram*	40 million	360	Spanish/English	Created
FastText.	*Skip-gram*	40 million	700	Spanish/English	Created
FastText.	*Cbow*	600 billion	300	English	*FastText* [10]
FastText.	*Skip-gram*	600 billion	300	English	*FastText* [10]
FastText.	*Skip-gram*	16 billion	300	English	*FastText* [10]
GloVe.	–	42 billion	300	English	*stanford.edu* [6]

We can see in Table 5 that half of the models described were created from the compiled corpus that is made up of 40 million words with texts in English and Spanish, with an approximate 50% per language, approximately a vocabulary of 900,000 different words, and a total size of 360 MB. The other half of the embedding models were obtained from their respective official sources [10] and [6].

Table 6. Example of tag sequence created with annotation style BIO and BILOU.

Word	POS	BIO	BILOU
algunos	DET	B_LOW_FRECUENCY	U_LOW_FRECUENCY
asilos	NOUN	B_LOW_FRECUENCY	B_LOW_FRECUENCY
de	ADP	I_LOW_FRECUENCY	I_LOW_FRECUENCY
ancianos	NOUN	I_LOW_FRECUENCY	L_LOW_FRECUENCY
cuentan	VERB	B_MEDIUM_FRECUENCY	U_MEDIUM_FRECUENCY
con	ADP	B_VERYLOW_FRECUENCY	U_VERYLOW_FRECUENCY

4.4 System Results for Entity Identification

This section shows the results of the systems proposed to identify entities. First, the systems obtained are presented, and finally, the results obtained evaluating the systems.

System BiLSTM-CRF: The architecture of this system is mainly composed of a layer BiLSTM and a layer CRF that benefits the classification of entities, the architecture of this system is specifically composed of: 1 Embedding layer, 3 BiLSTM layers with 490 units, 1 LSTM layer with 980 units, one dense layer with nine units and 1 CRF layer with nine units.

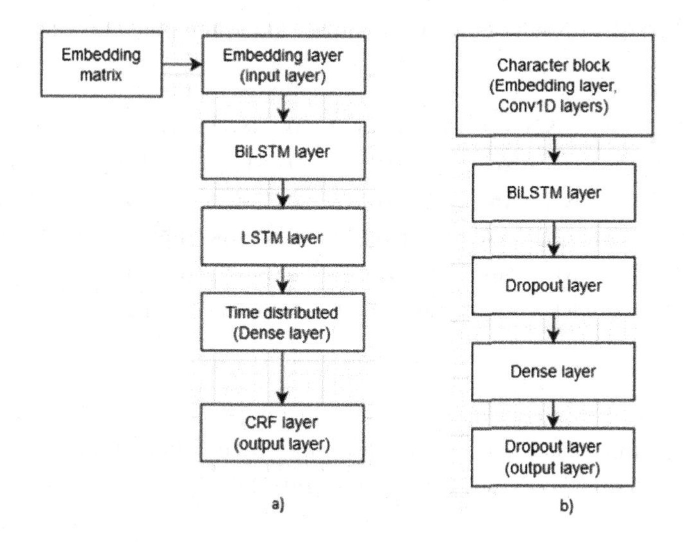

Fig. 3. a) Architecture BiLSTM-CRF, b) Architecture BiLSTM-CNN.

In Fig. 3, we can see the order of the layers used in that system. Finally, the network was trained with 21 epochs and a batch size of 110.

System BiLSTM-CNN: The architecture of this system is mainly composed of BiLSTM layers and CNN layers oriented to character embedding [9]. The character block is in charge of analyzing the words at the character level later to perform the classification, employing a BiLSTM network [3]. The architecture of this system is specifically composed of: 1 block of characters CNN, 1 BiLSTM layer with 128 units, one dropout layer with 128 units with a dropout rate of 0.5, 1 dense layer with 128 units, and one dropout layer with nine units with a dropout rate of 0.5.

In Fig. 3 we can see the order of the layers used in that system. Finally, the network trained with 21 epochs and a batch size of 110.

4.5 Evaluation of the Proposed Systems

The evaluation was performed with the evaluation corpus provided by [13]. For this, the precision, recall, and F_1 metrics proposed by [13] were used.

The results were obtained from the average of 20 executions of each model. The best results were obtained with FastText embedding models. The model that worked best was the self-created one with 20 million words and 490 dimensions (FastText).

In Table 7 A comparison of the annotation styles in the different entity identification systems is shown. It can be seen that the "P" annotation style got the best results at F_1 on both systems. In Table 7 is shown that "P" annotation style is better than BIO and BILOU annotation styles for this case.

Table 7. System results for entity identification, comparing annotation styles.

System	Recall	Precision	F_1
BiLSTM-CNN - Annotation P	**0.66852**	**0.48535**	**0.56169**
BiLSTM-CNN - Annotation BIO	0.68438	0.47151	0.55817
BiLSTM-CNN - Annotation BILOU	0.67668	0.46965	0.55407
BiLSTM-CRF - Annotation P	**0.67858**	**0.52135**	**0.58949**
BiLSTM-CRF - Annotation BIO	0.68005	0.49503	0.57263
BiLSTM-CRF - Annotation BILOU	0.69358	0.47524	0.56396

In Table 8. A comparison of the systems with the "P" annotation style is shown, including the POS tagging proposal with different annotation styles. POS tagging proposal does not give an improvement.

Table 8. Results of systems for identification of entities, comparing the POS tagging proposal.

System	Recall	Precision	F_1
BiLSTM-CNN - Annotation P (base)	**0.66852**	**0.48535**	**0.56169**
BiLSTM-CNN (P) - POS Annotation P	0.64834	0.48068	0.55165
BiLSTM-CNN (P) - POS Annotation BIO	0.63449	0.48971	0.55201
BiLSTM-CNN (P) - POS Annotation BILOU	0.65229	0.48264	0.55407
BiLSTM-CRF - Annotation P (base)	**0.67858**	**0.52135**	**0.58949**
BiLSTM-CRF (P) - POS Annotation P	0.67502	0.51250	0.58211
BiLSTM-CRF (P) - POS Annotation BIO	0.63101	0.51020	0.56201
BiLSTM-CRF (P) - POS Annotation BILOU	0.63633	0.51950	0.57103

4.6 Results of the Systems Proposed in *eHealth-KD Challenge 2021*

Table 9 shows a comparison of the results of subtask "A" with the participants of the *eHealth-KD challenge 2021*. It is important to note that these results of our proposal were after the *eHealth-KD challenge 2021*. Finally, Table 9 shows the neural network architecture on which the system of each participant is based.

Table 9. Comparison of results from subtask "A" (results obtained after the *eHealth-KD challenge 2021.*)

Team	Precision	Recall	F_1	Architecture
PUCRJ-PUCPR-UFMG	0.71491	0.69733	0.70601	BERT
Vicomtech	0.69987	0.74706	0.68413	BERT
IXA	0.61372	0.69840	0.65333	BERT
UH-MMM	0.54604	0.68503	0.60769	BiLSTM
Proposed system	**0.52135**	**0.67858**	**0.58949**	**BiLSTM**
uhKD4	0.51751	0.53743	0.52728	BiLSTM
Yunnan-Deep	0.52036	0.27166	0.33406	BiLSTM

5 Conclusion

The exposed BiLSTM architectures were implemented in this work. The novelties proposed in this work were the proposed solution directed to POS tagging and the "P" annotation style. Despite implementing the proposal directed to POS tagging with different annotation styles, in Table 8 can be seen that the implemented proposal decreases the score F_1 of the systems. However, the proposed "P" annotation style slightly improves compared to the other annotation styles reviewed in this article.

Finally, the best result obtained with a system based on a BiLSTM network is *0.60769* in F_1, and the best-proposed system has a result of *0.5894*, as shown in Table 9, for which it can be considered as an acceptable result for a BiLSTM network. However, it is expected to explore other forms of pre-processing that can help to improve the F_1 of the systems.

References

1. Alvarado, J.M., Caballero, E.Q., Pérez, A.R., Linares, R.C.: UH-MAJA-KD at eHealth-KD challenge 2019. Deep learning models for knowledge discovery in Spanish eHealth documents. In: Cumbreras, M., et al. (eds.) Proceedings of the Iberian Languages Evaluation Forum co-located with 35th Conference of the Spanish Society for Natural Language Processing, IberLEF@SEPLN 2019, CEUR Workshop Proceedings, Bilbao, Spain, 24 September 2019, vol. 2421, pp. 85–94. CEUR-WS.org (2019). http://ceur-ws.org/Vol-2421/eHealth-KD_paper_9.pdf
2. Bravo, À., Accuosto, P., Saggion, H.: LaSTUS-TALN at IberLEF 2019 eHealth-KD challenge. Deep learning approaches to information extraction in biomedical texts. In: Cumbreras, M.Á.G., et al. (eds.) Proceedings of the Iberian Languages Evaluation Forum co-located with 35th Conference of the Spanish Society for Natural Language Processing, IberLEF@SEPLN 2019. CEUR Workshop Proceedings, Bilbao, Spain, 24 September 2019, vol. 2421, pp. 51–59. CEUR-WS.org (2019). http://ceur-ws.org/Vol-2421/eHealth-KD_paper_5.pdf
3. Chiu, J.P.C., Nichols, E.: Named entity recognition with bidirectional LSTM-CNNs. CoRR abs/1511.08308 (2015). http://arxiv.org/abs/1511.08308

4. Consuegra-Ayala, J.P., Palomar, M.: UH-MatCom at eHealth-KD challenge 2020. In: Cumbreras, M.Á.G., et al. (eds.) Proceedings of the Iberian Languages Evaluation Forum (IberLEF 2020) co-located with 36th Conference of the Spanish Society for Natural Language Processing (SEPLN 2020), Málaga, Spain, 23 September 2020. CEUR Workshop Proceedings, vol. 2664, pp. 112–124. CEUR-WS.org (2020). http://ceur-ws.org/Vol-2664/eHealth-KD_paper4.pdf
5. Fabregat, H., Fernandez, A.D., Martínez-Romo, J., Araujo, L.: NLP_UNED at eHealth-KD challenge 2019: deep learning for named entity recognition and attentive relation extraction. In: Cumbreras, M.Á.G., et al. (eds.) Proceedings of the Iberian Languages Evaluation Forum co-located with 35th Conference of the Spanish Society for Natural Language Processing, IberLEF@SEPLN 2019, Bilbao, Spain, September 24th, 2019. CEUR Workshop Proceedings, vol. 2421, pp. 67–77. CEUR-WS.org (2019). http://ceur-ws.org/Vol-2421/eHealth-KD_paper_7.pdf
6. Pennington, J., Socher, R., Manning, C.D.: GloVe: global vectors for word representation (2015). https://nlp.stanford.edu/projects/glove/
7. Linet, C.Z.J.: Reconocimiento de entidades nombradas para el idioma español utilizando Conditional Random Fields con características no supervisadas. Universidad Católica San Pablo - Perú, Tesis de maestría (March 2017)
8. Liu, Z., Winata, G.I., Fung, P.: Zero-resource cross-domain named entity recognition. CoRR abs/2002.05923 (2020). https://arxiv.org/abs/2002.05923
9. Ma, E.: Besides word embedding, why you need to know character embedding? (2018). https://towardsdatascience.com/besides-word-embedding-why-you-need-to-know-character-embedding-6096a34a3b10
10. Mikolov, T., Grave, E., Bojanowski, P., Puhrsch, C., Joulin, A.: Advances in pre-training distributed word representations. In: Proceedings of the International Conference on Language Resources and Evaluation, LREC 2018 (2018)
11. Monteagudo-García, L., Marrero-Santos, A., Fernández-Arias, M.S., Cañizares-Díaz, H.: UH-MMM at eHealth-KD challenge 2021. In: Proceedings of the Iberian Languages Evaluation Forum, IberLEF 2021 (2021)
12. Pérez, A.R., Caballero, E.Q., Alvarado, J.M., Linares, R.C., Consuegra-Ayala, J.P.: UH-MAJA-KD at eHealth-KD challenge 2020. In: Cumbreras, M.Á.G., et al. (eds.) Proceedings of the Iberian Languages Evaluation Forum (IberLEF 2020) co-located with 36th Conference of the Spanish Society for Natural Language Processing (SEPLN 2020), Málaga, Spain, 23 September 2020. CEUR Workshop Proceedings, vol. 2664, pp. 125–135. CEUR-WS.org (2020). http://ceur-ws.org/Vol-2664/eHealth-KD_paper5.pdf
13. Piad-Morfis, A., Estevez-Velarde, S., Gutiérrez, Y., Almeida-Cruz, Y., Montoyo, A., Muñoz, R.: Overview of the eHealth knowledge discovery challenge at IberLEF 2021. Proces. del Leng. Natural **67**, 233–242 (2021). http://journal.sepln.org/sepln/ojs/ojs/index.php/pln/article/view/6392

An Overview of Methods and Tools for Extraction of Knowledge for COVID-19 from Knowledge Graphs

Mariya Evtimova-Gardair(✉) and Nedra Mellouli(✉)

IUT Montreuil, Laboratoire d'Intelligence Artificielle et Sémantique des Données, University Paris 8, Paris, France
{m.evtimovagardair,n.mellouli}@iut.univ-paris8.fr
https://www.iut.univ-paris8.fr/

Abstract. The sanitary crisis provoked from the virus COVID-19 push researchers and practitioners to explore and find solutions to stamp the pandemic problem. Therefore many productions of various scientific papers and knowledge graphs are publicly accessible in internet. In this article is defined an overall description of the search engines available for COVID-19 information. A brief review of the knowledge graphs available for COVID-19 information is performed. This paper is an overview of the main relevant knowledge graph-based methods contributing in COVID-19 knowledge extraction and understanding. Furthermore, it is proposed a state-of-the-art of knowledge reasoning methods on COVID-19.

Keywords: Knowledge graph · COVID-19 · Extraction of information · Reasoning · Information searching · Artificial intelligence · Web search · Information retrieval

1 Introduction

Despite the enormous available information on the internet for COVID-19 for the experts, it is still a challenging task to find an answer to complicated questions that require linking multiple sources of information. A reasonable solution for this problem can be found when using knowledge graph technologies. Knowledge graphs have the structure to use complex types of entities and attributes with their links and constraints. More widely, knowledge graphs have an inherent notion of structure, which allows us to declare complex types of entities and attributes, their linkage and constraints. It can also be defined as methods for named-entity extraction. The content of the article is constructed from four main sections. In the first section is presented a review of the COVID-19 searching systems and COVID-19 knowledge graphs. Then in the second section is described the possible challenges when constructing COVID-19 knowledge graph. In the last part the classification of the usage of the reasoning algorithms for COVID-19 information is presented [1].

University Paris 8.

M. El Yacoubi et al. (Eds.): ICPRAI 2022, LNCS 13364, pp. 407–418, 2022.
https://doi.org/10.1007/978-3-031-09282-4_34

2 COVID-19 Knowledge Graphs and Search Engines

2.1 Search Engines in Internet for COVID-19 Information

There are available in internet the following search engines for COVID-19 disease literature: Sketch Engine COVID-19, Sinequa COVID-19 Intelligent Search, Microsoft's CORD19 Search, and Amazon's CORD19 Search. They include different searched technologies like knowledge graphs and semantics or simple keyword text search. But these tools return the searched results without using the possibility to visualize the relations that could be used for knowledge discovery [2]. Furthermore, some searching systems like COVID-19 papers browser, CoronaSearch and CovidScholar calculate embeddings when perform querying with phrases or concepts and retrieve documents using the nearest-neighbor algorithm to generate their results. But other systems constrain the query vocabulary to entities in already available knowledge graph. For example, the COVID-19 Navigator[1] contain data from CORD-19, Medline, PubMed Open Access, ClinicalTrials.gov, patents from the US Patent Office and UMLS(Unified Medical Language System) that have a possibility to make a request to entities using UMLS terminology. Also the interface of the SPIKE-CORD [3] supports boolean queries using UMLS concepts and semantic types. From the other side, the system for searching of information SPIKE-CORD use as a pattern regular expressions in order to control the returned results when searching [4]. In [4] is presented a list of 39 data mining systems and their characteristics. The information was collected from the public representation of the CORD-19 web page and from COVID-19 papers and preprints represented in the CORD-19 corpus and from the social media. All data mining systems that are presented in the list from the article [4] provide easy search and investigation functionality. But some of the systems support more specific function as text understanding tasks (Ex. summarization, question answering or claim verification). It is important to mention that many of the proposed systems use transparent techniques or include reproducible source code. Furthermore, search systems like: Covidex, fatcat, DOC Search, COVID-19 Intelligent Insight, Covid AI-powered Search, COVID-19 Navigator and CovidScholar gather data from different sources, so that to supplement the proposed information for COVID-19 and to increase the quality of the searched systems [4]. List of the sources that are used in the searched system include: CORD-19, LitCovid, ClinicalTrials.gov, Lens, Dimensions, documents from the WHO or CDC websites and more. Other systems also leverage external knowledge bases for entity linking, such as Vapur [5], which links to ChemProt, COVID-19 Navigator and EVIDENCEMINER [6], which link to UMLS, or AWS CORD-19 Search that implement external knowledge from the Comprehend Medical knowledge base. DOC Search[2] and COVID-SEE [7] are systems that incorporate extracted PICO[3](the abbreviation come from Patient Problem Intervention Comparison or Control and Outcome) elements and relationships about visualization and

[1] https://acd-try-it-out.mybluemix.net/preview.
[2] https://docsearch.algolia.com/.
[3] https://canberra.libguides.com/c.php?g=599346&p=4149722.

search that are more important for the visualization of the results to the clinical trial papers [8].

2.2 Introduction of Leading Knowledge Graphs for COVID-19 and Data Sets

When the COVID-19 pandemic started, the amount of web data for COVID-19 is increased dramatically as a response of the pandemic. That lead to the construction of many knowledge graphs, so as to provide reasonable information. DBpedia is a cross-language project that is created to extract structured content from the information created in the Wikipedia project. DBpedia contains a lot of information and also contains various informations information about COVID-19. DBpedia data is organized in categories and geographical regions. Wikidata is a multilingual open, linked and structured knowledge graph that supports 280 languages and is accessible for editing by both humans and machines. Wikidata contains information in different domains and supports more than 280 language versions of Wikipedia with a common source of structured data [8]. The data model for COVID-19 information in wikidata is organized in three main categories SARS-CoV-2, COVID-19 and COVID-19 pandemic [9]. Then these categories are interlinked with subcategories as Human, Disease, Chemical compound, Clinical trial, Vaccine candidate, Treatment, Big city, Type of medical test, COVID-19 dashboard, Sovereign state, Scholarly article, Disease outbreak, COVID-19 tracing application, Protein, Gene, Taxon, Biological process, Symptom, Medical specialty. Other sources that propose knowledge graphs for COVID-19 are the following [10]:

1. LG-COVID-19 HOTP[4]- transform scientific literature
2. COVID graph[5]- combining literature, case statistics and genomic and molecular data
3. Knowledge graph of COVID-19 Literature[6]- drug trials, unstructured literature, drug and genome sequence data
4. Blender Lab COVID-KG[7]- COVID graph that is focused on drug repurposing

Knowledge graphs that propose more general information about COVID-19:

1. SPOKE[8] contain information about treatment, disease, genes, proteins and their structural data, drugs, and drug side effects, pathways, proteins, genes, anatomic terms, phenotypes and microbiome
2. KnetMiner[9] contain information about genes, proteins, diseases, phenotypes, genome and sequences

[4] https://lg-covid-19-hotp.cs.duke.edu/.
[5] https://covidgraph.org/.
[6] https://ds-covid19.res.ibm.com/.
[7] http://blender.cs.illinois.edu/covid19/.
[8] https://spoke.ucsf.edu/.
[9] https://knetminer.com/.

A description of COVID-19 information is presented in Comparative Toxigenomics Database[10]. Commonly used when building up a knowledge graph about COVID-19 information, is the dataset CORD-19 that is with open access[11]. The data set CORD-19 integrate scientific paper, about COVID-19, that increase in a daily basis. Furthermore, the name of the searching instrument using PubMed COVID-19 publications is LitCovid [11], containing over 52 000 papers that are increasing constantly. Another available tools are WHO's COVID-19 set or the Centers for Disease Control and Prevention abbreviated as (CDC) that maintain own COVID-19 research articles database[12]. Moreover, the database Medline contain more general data, that include references and abstracts, in life sciences and biomedical data that are also accessible from pubMed[13]. It is also important to mention that in internet is available the pubMed knowledge graph datasets[14]. Furthermore, an article about Pubmed construction of knowledge graphs is published [12].

3 Definition of Constraints When Building COVID-19 Knowledge Graph

3.1 COVID-19 Data Constraints

The constraints in COVID-19 data can be observed when integrating different data sources such as defined from the interoperability, granularity, quality control, data accessibility or scalability. Defining the information about COVID-19 represent challenges [13]:

- The COVID-19 data is increasing constantly during the pandemic so that the information accessible in the knowledge graph need to be set constantly up to date so that the data representation model to remain flexible and scalable.
- Embedded knowledge about COVID-19 increase and the data relationships that are defined from the virus information and the past diseases.
- The pandemic of COVID-19 impacts all the human domains and activities and also affects the presentation of the data related with COVID-19.
- Providing accessible data from human communities concerning COVID-19 can be accessible to humans and machines. More often the pandemic data also include a lot of use cases.

The constraint limitation can be separated into 4 categories:

[10] http://ctdbase.org/.
[11] https://www.semanticscholar.org/cord19.
[12] https://www.cdc.gov/library/researchguides/2019novelcoronavirus/researcharticles.html.
[13] https://pubmed.ncbi.nlm.nih.gov/.
[14] http://er.tacc.utexas.edu/datasets/ped.

Table 1. Table with knowledge graphs for COVID-19.

Knowledge graph for COVID-19	Specific information	General categories included	Items	Languages
WikiData	When the concept is not a particular Wikipedia page it is not presented in DBpedia. For example "vaccine candidate" is only represented in WikiData	SARS-CoV-2, COVID-19, COVID-19 pandemic	<17000	50 languages (English, French, German, Spanish, Chinese, Arabic, Japanese, Russian)
DBpedia	DBpedia cover the information of Covid 19 that is available in WikiData	SARS-CoV-2, COVID-19, COVID-19 pandemic	8727	50 languages (English, French, German, Spanish, Chinese, Arabic, Japanese, Russian)
LG-COVID-19 HOTP	Literature graph composed of not only articles (graph nodes) that are relevant to the study of coronavirus, but also in and out citation links (directed graph edges) to base navigation and search among the articles	COVID-19 literature	485097	English
COVID graph	CovidGraph was developed from nonprofit collaboration of researchers, software developers, data scientists, and medical professionals. In April 2021, CovidGraph became part of HealthECCO	Publications, case statistics, genes and functions, molecular data, and more	128053-papers, 1700-clinical trials	English
Knowledge graph of COVID-19 Literature	IBM is providing free access to its COVID-19 Knowledge Graph, which is part of its Corpus Processing Service	Literature, DrugBank, GenBank, Trials	180547	English
Blender Lab COVID-KG	Knowledge extraction from scientific papers about corona virus (CORD-19 dataset), Link prediction for new hypothesis generation and ranking, Question answering for scientists to search related hypotheses and knowledge graphs, and provide evidence from source text and images	Gene, Disease, Chemical, Organism	50752 - Gene nodes, 10781 - Disease nodes, 5738 - Chemical nodes, 535 - Organism nodes	English

3.2 Respect the Quality of the Data When Constructing Knowledge Graph

The quality challenge impact the knowledge graph data because of the reliability of the data and also the quality of the searched results return from the knowledge graph. The sources that are used for the construction of the knowledge graph need to be reliable and trustful so that the knowledge graph information to respects the quality. Another aspect is also the quality of the algorithms used in different artificial intelligence modules in the knowledge graph. It is necessary to ensure that the quality of the algorithms are good enough with precision and recall so that it could be used for the semantic searching of information The searching is a primary service provided from the knowledge graphs. Furthermore, AI(artificial intelligence) has been developed as an important direction especially in the medical domain. Also, the quality defined to the knowledge graphs will increase the usage of the knowledge graphs from the stakeholders that can have an impact to their future development. The extraction of relations can also impact the quality as the human interaction cannot be completely supported.

3.3 Scale Constraints in Knowledge Graph Construction

Scale provide a challenge when the data increase until reaching the Big Data conformity. And that concern each different categories such as geographic domain, organization, social domain. Another constrain to the scale is defined from the presence of the privacy from the private companies when introducing the COVID-19 knowledge graph applications.

3.4 Constraints Defined from Interface Presentation Tools and Visualizations

An application using KG(knowledge graph) that have more adapted interface to the users is more popular than applications that are not having user friendly interface. That makes a reflection that the user interface is more important than the implementation of significant algorithms as a back-end. Furthermore, another constraint could also be defined from the rating of the COVID-19 KG application defined from the consumers when using the corresponding application. That problem is not presented in the big organizations that provide their online services such as Wikipedia, DBpedia, google and also e-commerce companies that implement the KGs as a technology that increase the quality of the returned information to the user when the data from the experience from the system increase. Applications like this use the information gathered for each user, so that to provide more appropriate information or search results when creating an optimization. Sometimes users are not having a direct access to the KG, that is the case with google and also amazon KG. But their gathered data is applied when the user is using the application for searching of information corresponding to a particular case. The COVID-19 applications must support advanced users, as experts. The pandemic applications for COVID-19 also require support of complex requests that the particular domain experts can require. But even so, the experts also need the facility to form their request in a natural way using natural language and user friendly presentation of the returned results that are easy for exploration. Most often the visualization tool and the construction of the KG are a subject of a separate research that can reflect to non conformity. From the beginning of the pandemic COVID-19 it can be observed in internet that a lot of instruments have been published. An example for a visualization tool for COVID-19 information is the COVID Linked Data Visualizer[15] that is having also sparql point[16]. This tool is described in [6] and is constructed from the collaboration of research organizations. Another example is the portal of a private organization[17] that is defined from the private organization for commercial use. It could be observed that some of the visualization tools are provided only for general usage such as the visualization provided from the CDC organization [18] with a more simple representation. A brief review of the tools available in internet for visualization for the COVID-19 information, can show their variety and their target to different users. Some of tools are provided from research institutes and universities and provide more options and instruments and is for expert user. And another are more suitable for general users that visualize the data without including options for observation.

3.5 Social Constraints

A social challenge present the innovative technologies in front of the conservative users. From the one side the statistical information using AI can be observed from domain experts but from the other side the general user can look over it as a privacy interruption and that the technologies can reduce the implacability of the employees. The acceptance of the AI technologies concern the level of education of the society. The impact of that phenomena can be observed in the less developed countries and communities that don't have easily access to the technological advances. Then it is important to mention that applications that serve to the human society with knowledge graphs have been made technological revolution. Ii is important to mention, that the social aspect need to be observed when implementing advanced technologies.

4 Introduction to COVID-19 Reasoning from KGs

4.1 Definition of Knowledge Reasoning Applied for Extraction of COVID-19 from KGs [14]

In general, knowledge reasoning is the process from information extraction that uses well known knowledge to infer new knowledge. Early reasoning studies were

[15] http://covid19.i3s.unice.fr:8080/.
[16] http://covidontheweb.inria.fr/sparql.
[17] https://pandemic.internationalsos.com/2019-ncov/covid-19-data-visualisation.
[18] https://www.cdc.gov/coronavirus/2019-ncov/cases-updates/cdc-in-action.html.

carried out among scholars in the fields of logic and knowledge engineering. They always focused on how to draw correct conclusions from the known propositions and predicates. Unlike scholars from the Logic field who used propositions or first-order predicates to represent concepts in the objective world, the scholars from the knowledge engineering field use semantic networks to represent richer concepts and knowledge for describing the relationships between entities and attributes. Nevertheless, early KGs totally relied on expert knowledge. The entities, attributes, and relationships in the KG were entirely handcrafted by the experts in the fields. With the explosive growth of Internet data scale, traditional methods based on artificially and built knowledge bases, cannot adapt to the need when mining a large amount of knowledge. For this reason, data-driven machine reasoning methods have gradually become the main stream of knowledge reasoning research. With the development of KGs, reasoning over KGs has also increased the general concern. Referring to the definition of reasoning, we can give the definition of reasoning over KGs as:

Definition for Knowledge Reasoning Over KGs: KG is presented as KG $K = \langle E1, R, E2 \rangle$ and the relation path P, where E1, E2 define the set of entities, R describe the set of relations, then the edges from R make a link between two nodes to create a triple $(x, y, z) \epsilon E2$, generating a triplet that is not presented in the knowledge graph $G = \{(x, y, z) \mid x \epsilon E1, y \epsilon R, z \epsilon E2, (x, y, z) \backslash\epsilon G\}$ [15,16].

It is used machine learning methods to infer potential relations between entity pairs and identify erroneous knowledge based on existing data automatically with the purpose of complementing knowledge graphs. The object of knowledge reasoning is not only the attributes and relations between entities, but also the attribute values of entities and the conceptual hierarchy of ontology. For example, if an entity's COVID-19 type attribute is known, the entity's virus gene, virus taxon, virus protein and other attributes can be obtained through reasoning. The KGs can represent, generally semantic network and a semantically structured knowledge base, that can formally describe concepts and their relations that are applied in reality. Therefore, reasoning over KG have no limitation to traditional reasoning methods based on logic and rules and it can be diverse. At the same time, the KG consists of instances, which makes the reasoning methods more precise.

4.2 General Model for COVID-19 Knowledge Reasoning from KGs

It is presented a general model for COVID-19 reasoning (see Fig. 1). The KG reasoning can be defined with the following tasks:

1. Missing entity prediction- when one entity N1 and a given relation Re can predict the missing entity named N2.
2. Predicting the missing link- when one entity N1 and another entity N2 are defined to predict the missing relation Re.
3. Fact prediction- from a certain triple to predict if the fact F is true or false.

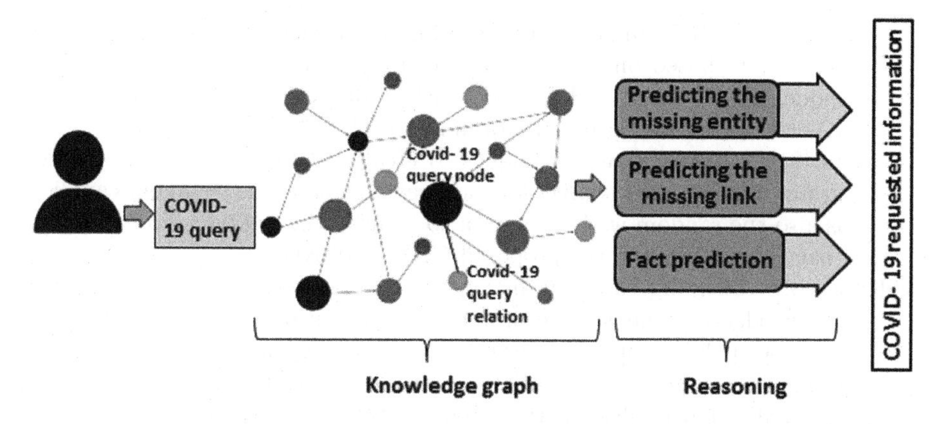

Fig. 1. General model for reasoning from knowledge graph COVID-19 information

4.3 Classification of Knowledge Reasoning Oriented for COVID-19 Entity Extraction [14]

The classification of the reasoning methods is defined concerning their severe application for COVID-19 information reasoning. The analysis conclude the usage of certain reasoning types of algorithms than another in the applications that include COVID-19 reasoning.

1. Knowledge reasoning based on logic rules
   - Knowledge reasoning based on rules
     In report [17] is proposed new, integrative, and neural network-bases discovery about COVID-19 literature. The triples were identified using filtering rules and an accuracy classifier created with BERT. In another report [18] the structure of biomedical KGs differs from graph structure rather than benchmarking data sets, which also impact the choice of algorithm for reasoning. In the report the problem is formulated as link prediction where compounds and diseases are defined as correspondence to entities in the KG. It is proposed a new method named PoLo, that implements policy-guided walks based on reinforcement learning with logical reasoning and Hetionet algorithm to integrate biomedical information. The rules are implemented using a new reward function.
   - Case based knowledge reasoning
     The literature source [19] that represents COVID-19 with case based reasoning about automatic epidemiological case report analysis and inference. A Tuple-based Multi-Task Neural Network is proposed that recognizes epidemiological entities and relations from case reports that are a part of KG so that to propose a reasonable COVID-19 infection information. The preliminary results gave promising results.
   - Knowledge reasoning based on ontology
     Article [20] integrate KG with COVID-19 information into ontology and allow researchers to apply reasoning so that to derive new knowledge

using rules. It is implemented path finding framework that calculate the path score based on the similarity distance using pre-trained word2vec model that is based on PubMed and PubMed Central (PMC) texts.

- Knowledge reasoning based on random walk algorithm
  In [21] is used various techniques to create a COVID-19 KG that integrates different data sources for the disease. Among the techniques applied is also the random walk algorithm to identify the relationship in the KG that is later build in the proposed COVID-19 KG.

2. Knowledge reasoning based on distributed representation
   - Knowledge reasoning based on tensor factorization
     In paper [22] is proposed a new tensor matrix framework for KG embedding. It uses tensor factorization tools to learn about relations and entities from KGs and implement these representations to create drug repurposing for COVID-19 that achieves 100 I% improvement concerning the other algorithms for drug repurposing tasks.
   - Knowledge reasoning on semantic matching model
     In [23] is used for COVID-19 reasoning semantic matching model. In [23] is presented KnetMiner that is an interactive online platform for gene discovery and knowledge mining that is available for COVID-19 KG.
   - Knowledge reasoning based on multi-source information In the literature is presented entity reasoning based on multiple-source information for the creation of COVID-19 KG from CORD-19 corpus, DBpedia, Wikidata and Bioportal vocabularies [18]. In [21] KGs provide a way of integrating heterogeneous data from different sources and combining different data modalities. Knowledge graph for COVID-19 produce knowledge graph for COVID-19 integrating molecular and chemical information, enabling users to conduct complex queries over relevant biological entities as well as machine learning analyses to generate graph embeddings for making predictions. That framework create a 'hub' that gather different sources of data that support COVID-19.
3. Knowledge reasoning based on neural network
   The algorithm presented in [19] paper use also neural network, so that the study can be classified also in this section when the reasoning is based on neural network.
   - Knowledge reasoning based on convolutional neural networks
     In article [24] is described reasoning with convolution neural network to detect COVID-19 pneumonia from chest XR images. In paper [25] is presented a detection of COVID-19 patients with hybrid reasoning model that use two classifiers a fuzzy interference engine and deep neural network(convolutional neural network). The research described in [26] is for extraction of information for COVID-19 drug from KGs when applying the prediction model based on Graph Convolutional Network with Attention. With the proposed model can be predicted drugs about COVID-19 disease.

5 Conclusions

With beginning of the COVID-19 pandemic the researchers have started to think about solutions that can support the people in the crisis. Consequently, in the literature are described many applications specialized for COVID-19 searching systems. Most of the systems proposed are for information extraction and expands data sources for KG construction. A brief analysis of the systems that use KGs is presented that can serve later for the development of new COVID-19 KG searching system. That rich content of COVID-19 knowledge bases provide new opportunities and challenges for the development of the knowledge reasoning technology. With the popularity of knowledge representation learning, neural networks and other technologies, a series of new reasoning methods were created and applied for the COVID-19. Many articles are recently available about the COVID-19 KG reasoning for extraction of information. The literature overview about the reasoning technologies used in the COVID-19 applications is classified and provide to observe a tendency in COVID-19 reasoning methods. That show the application of new algorithms for reasoning that are often hybrid because they consist of multiple different technologies.

References

1. Colavizza, G.: Meta-research on COVID-19: an overview of the early trends. arXiv preprint arXiv:2106.02961 (2021)
2. Wise, C., et al.: COVID-19 knowledge graph: accelerating information retrieval and discovery for scientific literature. arXiv preprint arXiv:2007.12731 (2020)
3. Papaioannou, J.-M., Mayrdorfer, M., Arnold, S., Gers, F.A., Budde, K., Löser, A.: Aspect-based passage retrieval with contextualized discourse vectors. In: Hiemstra, D., Moens, M.-F., Mothe, J., Perego, R., Potthast, M., Sebastiani, F. (eds.) ECIR 2021. LNCS, vol. 12657, pp. 537–542. Springer, Cham (2021). https://doi.org/10.1007/978-3-030-72240-1_61
4. Wang, L.L., Lo, K.: Text mining approaches for dealing with the rapidly expanding literature on COVID-19. Brief. Bioinf. **22**(2), 781–799 (2020)
5. Köksal, A., et al.: Vapur: a search engine to find related protein-compound pairs in COVID-19 literature. arXiv preprint arXiv:2009.02526 (2020)
6. Chen, X., Jia, S., Xiang, Y.: A review: knowledge reasoning over knowledge graph. Exp. Syst. Appl. **141**, 112948 (2020)
7. Verspoor, K., et al.: Brief description of COVID-SEE: the scientific evidence explorer for COVID-19 related research. In: Hiemstra, D., Moens, M.-F., Mothe, J., Perego, R., Potthast, M., Sebastiani, F. (eds.) ECIR 2021. LNCS, vol. 12657, pp. 559–564. Springer, Cham (2021). https://doi.org/10.1007/978-3-030-72240-1_65
8. Michel, F., et al.: Covid-on-the-web: knowledge graph and services to advance COVID-19 research. In: Pan, J.Z., et al. (eds.) ISWC 2020. LNCS, vol. 12507, pp. 294–310. Springer, Cham (2020). https://doi.org/10.1007/978-3-030-62466-8_19
9. Turki, H., et al.: Representing COVID-19 information in collaborative knowledge graphs: the case of Wikidata. Semantic Web Preprint, pp. 1–32 (2021)
10. Chen, Q., Allot, A., Zhiyong, L.: LitCovid: an open database of COVID-19 literature. Nucleic Acids Res. **49**(D1), D1534–D1540 (2021)
11. Xu, J., et al.: Building a PubMed knowledge graph. Sci. Data **7**(1), 1–15 (2020)

12. Kejriwal, M.: Knowledge graphs and COVID-19: opportunities, challenges, and implementation. Harv. Data Sci. Rev. (2020)
13. Menin, A., et al.: Covid-on-the-Web: exploring the COVID-19 scientific literature through visualization of linked data from entity and argument mining. Quant. Sci. Stud. **2**(4), 1301–1323 (2021)
14. Al-Moslmi, T., Gallofre Ocana, M., L. Opdahl, A., Veres, C.: Named entity extraction for knowledge graphs: a literature overview. IEEE Access **8**, 32862–32881 (2020)
15. Baclawski, K., et al.: Ontology summit 2020 communiqué: knowledge graphs. Appl. Ontol. **16**, 229–247 (2020)
16. Zhang, R., et al.: Drug repurposing for COVID-19 via knowledge graph completion. J. Biomed. Inf. **115**, 103696 (2021)
17. Wang, X., et al.: Automatic textual evidence mining in COVID-19 literature. arXiv preprint arXiv:2004.12563 (2020)
18. Liu, Y., Hildebrandt, M., Joblin, M., Ringsquandl, M., Raissouni, R., Tresp, V.: Neural multi-hop reasoning with logical rules on biomedical knowledge graphs. In: Verborgh, R., et al. (eds.) ESWC 2021. LNCS, vol. 12731, pp. 375–391. Springer, Cham (2021). https://doi.org/10.1007/978-3-030-77385-4_22
19. Wang, J., et al.: Accelerating epidemiological investigation analysis by using NLP and knowledge reasoning: a case study on COVID-19. In: AMIA Annual Symposium Proceedings, vol. 2020. American Medical Informatics Association (2020)
20. Zhang, P., et al.: Toward a coronavirus knowledge graph. Genes **12**(7), 998 (2021)
21. Reese, J.T., et al.: KG-COVID-19: a framework to produce customized knowledge graphs for COVID-19 response. Patterns **2**(1), 100155 (2021)
22. Kanatsoulis, C.I., Nicholas D.S.: TeX-Graph: coupled tensor-matrix knowledge-graph embedding for COVID-19 drug repurposing. In: Proceedings of the 2021 SIAM International Conference on Data Mining (SDM). Society for Industrial and Applied Mathematics (2021)
23. Hearnshaw, J., Brandizi, M., Singh, A., Rawlings, C., Hassani-Pak, K.: Organizing knowledge to enable faster data interpretation in COVID-19 research. F1000Research **10**, 703 (2021)
24. Zeiser, F.A., Costa, C.A., Ramos, G.O., Bohn, H., Santos, I., Righi, R.R.: Evaluation of convolutional neural networks for COVID-19 classification on chest X-rays. In: Britto, A., Valdivia Delgado, K. (eds.) BRACIS 2021. LNCS (LNAI), vol. 13074, pp. 121–132. Springer, Cham (2021). https://doi.org/10.1007/978-3-030-91699-2_9
25. Shaban, W.M., Rabie, A.H., Saleh, A.I., Abo-Elsoud, M.A.: Detecting COVID-19 patients based on fuzzy inference engine and deep neural network. Appl. Soft Comput. **99**, 106906 (2021)
26. Che, M., Yao, K., Che, C., Cao, Z., Kong, F.: Knowledge-graph-based drug repositioning against COVID-19 by graph convolutional network with attention mechanism. Fut. Internet **13**(1), 13 (2021)

Explaining Image Classifications with Near Misses, Near Hits and Prototypes

Supporting Domain Experts in Understanding Decision Boundaries

Marvin Herchenbach[1,2(✉)], Dennis Müller[1,2], Stephan Scheele[1,3], and Ute Schmid[1,3]

[1] Sensory Perception and Analytics | Comprehensible AI, Fraunhofer Institute for Integrated Circuits IIS, Erlangen, Germany
{stephan.scheele,ute.schmid}@iis.fraunhofer.de

[2] Friedrich-Alexander-Universität Erlangen-Nürnberg, Erlangen, Germany
{marvin.herchenbach,dennis.mueller}@fau.de

[3] Otto-Friedrich-Universität Bamberg, Bamberg, Germany

Abstract. We propose a method for explaining the results of black box image classifiers to domain experts and end users, combining two example-based explanatory approaches: Firstly, *prototypes* as representative data points for classes, and secondly, contrastive example comparisons in the form of *near misses* and *near hits*. A prototype *globally* explains the relevant characteristics for a entire class, whereas near hit and near miss explain the *local* decision boundary of a specific prediction. To combine both types of explanations within one framework is novel and we propose that presenting both types of explanations is especially helpful for domain experts in visual domains. To improve the faithfulness of the explanations, we investigated an unbiased, generic embedding and a model-related (model-specific) embedding for handling the images. The proposed approaches are evaluated regarding parameter selection and suitability on two different data sets – the well-known MNIST and a real-world industrial quality control data set. Finally, it is shown how global and local example-based explanation can be combined and realized within a demonstrator.

Keywords: Explainable AI · Example-based explanation · Prototypes · Near misses · Near hits

1 Introduction

Machine learning (ML) based image classification algorithms, such as deep neural networks, are increasingly employed in settings where transparency and comprehensibility of decisions are crucial such as medical diagnostics or industrial quality control. Research on *explainable artificial intelligence* (XAI) is addressing

M. El Yacoubi et al. (Eds.): ICPRAI 2022, LNCS 13364, pp. 419–430, 2022.
https://doi.org/10.1007/978-3-031-09282-4_35

these requirements [1] by providing techniques to support the decision making of ML black-box models and thereby allow users to develop justified trust [14]. Many XAI methods identify the most relevant information in the input for the classifier decision. While this information is helpful for model developers, e.g., to detect overfitting [13], it might be not expressive enough to explain model decisions for domain experts such as medical experts or quality engineers [14].

Cognitive science research provides theories as well as empirical evidence that explanations by examples are highly effective for humans to grasp complex concepts [7,11,12]. Therefore, we consider in this paper two kinds of examples, with the specific goal of explaining *image classifier* AI models to end users and domain experts without expertise in machine learning:

1. *Prototypes*, representing *typical* representative instances of some image class as a *global* explanation of the model, and
2. *Near hits and misses* of some given input, representing examples from the training data similar to the input image and from the same (or opposite, respectively) class, as *local* explanations.

In combination, prototypes, near hits and near misses allow users to get a better understanding of information considered relevant as well as of the decision boundaries of a given classification algorithm.

Numerous algorithms for computing prototypes of a given data set exist. In this paper, we primarily use [8], a widely used state-of-the-art approach based on *Maximum Mean Discrepancy* (see Subsect. 3.1 for details). ProtoDash [4] builds on the former, but at time of writing, no adequate implementation with sufficient adaptability for our experiments could be found. We additionally use *Partitioning around Medoids* [15] as a baseline approach for comparison; an improved version of a simple k-Medoids clustering algorithm [6], where we interpret the associated medoids of each cluster as prototypes.

Near hits and misses (*NHM*s) as relating to classified data are much less well covered by the existing literature, especially as an explanatory tool. One notable exception is [11], where NHMs are computed specifically for Prolog clauses to explain classifications in the context of *Inductive Logic Programming.* Conceptually however, finding close matches of a given input according to some metric is a ubiquitous tool in many distinct areas, such as in feature selection [17] or – more closely related to our purposes – in *content-based image retrieval* [5].

For providing more faithful explanations, we differentiate between two vector embeddings for handling images: a *model-specific* relying on the CNN-based classification model to be explained, and a *model-agnostic* allowing obtain another embedding unbiased by our data sets and unrelated to our classification model.

In the following, we describe the algorithms used for example-based explanations with focus on their evaluation for two data sets – the classic MNIST and a real-world data set of casting manufacturing image data for industrial quality control [2]. We start in Sect. 2 with describing the setup for our experiments, i.e. the data sets and classifier models used, and a brief overview of the final user-centric architecture. Sections 3 and 4 deal with prototypes and near hits and misses, respectively, the algorithms used, their parameters and our evaluations thereof. Lastly, in Sect. 5 we present our demonstrator implementation.

2 Methodology

2.1 Data Sets

We primarily use [2] for our experiments; a data set consisting of 1100 grayscale images of cast metal components of size 512×512 labelled with one of two classes, "ok" (419 entries) and "defective" (681 entries), see Fig. 1. The entries of the latter class show various kinds of defects, e.g., blow holes, abrasions, scratches etc. (see Fig. 1a). Notably, the data set is highly homogeneous in that the objects in the images are very similar to each other (except for the defects, which are usually subtle), but differ with respect to features that are irrelevant for purposes of classification, e.g., lighting conditions and angle (see Fig. 1b). The data set occasionally contains multiple images from different angles of the same object, which makes it especially interesting for the purpose of evaluating near hits and misses.

(a) defective. (b) ok.

Fig. 1. Some examples from the casting data set [2].

For comparison, we additionally use the MNIST data set of handwritten digits [9]. Since the casting data set is restricted to two classes, we correspondingly restrict MNIST to two classes – namely "1" and "7" (each consisting of 7877 and 7293 entries, respectively), which are uniformly white digits on black background, but differ significantly in their shapes within their respective classes.

2.2 Models and Embeddings

For each of our two data sets, we trained a small standard convolutional neural network (CNN) with three convolutional and two fully connected layers on the respective classification tasks, with resulting accuracies of 96.82% and 99.72% respectively.

These models actually serve two purposes: Firstly, they naturally serve as toy classifier models to be explained by our overall approach. Secondly, we can use feature extraction on the models to obtain embeddings for our images, which should be sensitive to those aspects of an image that relate to its inferred class. We consequently expect these embeddings to map images with similar *class-relevant* features near each other, leading to more informative near hits and misses. However, it should be noted that by using embeddings depending on the classifier model, our approach is *model-specific*. That is, it is required that the model to be explained is a neural network (or otherwise induces a suitable vector embedding). We therefore additionally use a generic state-of-the-art image classification model (VGG16 [16]) to obtain a second embedding unbiased by our data sets and unrelated to our classifier model, allowing us to remain *model-agnostic*. We refer to the embedding obtained via feature extraction on our classifier models as $\mathtt{E}_C$, and the one using VGG16 as $\mathtt{E}_{\mathtt{VGG}}$. We will occasionally use the raw image vectors for comparison, which we denote as the (trivial) embedding $\mathtt{E}_0$.

2.3 Architecture Overview

Figure 2 shows our approach as envisioned in practice. A user selects an image, for instance, of an industrial manufacturing component, which is classified by a CNN (or other black-box model). The inferred label is used to obtain a set of prototypes with the same label from the training data set. Both the label and the input image – under some vector embedding – are used to select a number of comparable near hits and misses from the training set. All three combined are provided to the user, allowing to better comprehend both the returned classification by comparing it to prototypical samples and the most similar (ground-truth labelled) elements from the training data (near hits), as well as the decision boundary in a contrastive manner via the near misses.

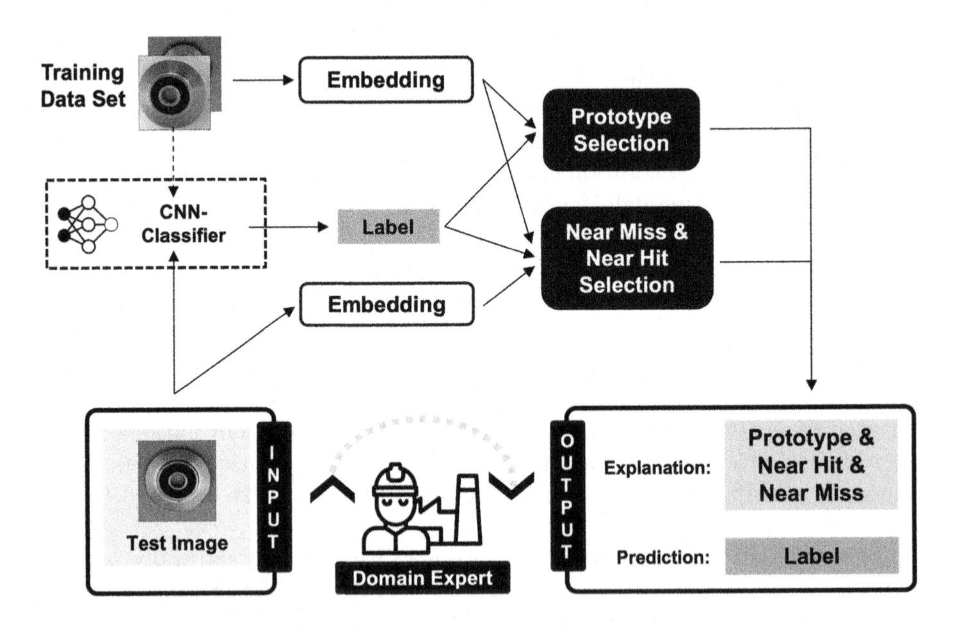

Fig. 2. Overview of the implemented architecture.

3 Prototype Selection

3.1 Prototype Selection Using Maximum Mean Discrepancy

Kim et al. [8] propose an approach for prototype selection based on *Maximum Mean Discrepancy* (MMD), a similarity measure on distributions, rather than individual data points: Given (finite approximations for) distributions X, Y, then the expression

$$\begin{aligned}\texttt{MMD}^2(X,Y) := & \frac{1}{|X|^2}\sum_{x_1,x_2\in X} k(x_1,x_2) + \frac{1}{|Y|^2}\sum_{y_1,y_2\in Y} k(y_1,y_2) \\ & - \frac{2}{|X|\cdot|Y|}\sum_{x\in X, y\in Y} k(x,y)\end{aligned}$$

approaches 0, as X and Y become more similar with respect to a Hilbert space of testing functions with reproducing kernel k. For our purposes, we use the radial basis kernel function $k(x, y) := e^{-\gamma||x-y||}$ for a real-valued scaling parameter γ. We can use this for selecting prototypes as follows:

Given a set of embedded data points X with $|X| = n$ and a kernel function $k : X \times X \to \mathbb{R}$, our objective is to find a subset $S \subseteq X$ with $|S| = m$ such that $\texttt{MMD}^2(X, \varnothing) - \texttt{MMD}^2(X, S)$ is maximized, which can be simplified to the following cost function:

$$J(S) := \frac{2}{nm}\sum_{x\in X, s\in S} k(x,s) - \frac{1}{m^2}\sum_{s_1,s_2\in S} k(s_1,s_2)$$

The remaining aspects of the selection algorithm are straight-forward (see Algorithm 1).

Algorithm 1. Prototype selection algorithm, adapted from [8].

Input: m, X
  $S = \varnothing$
  while $|S| < m$ **do**
    foreach: $x \in X \setminus S, j_x = J(S \cup \{x\}) - J(S)$ **do**
      $S = S \cup \{\text{argmax } \{j_x | x \in X\}\}$
  end while
Return: S

Surprisingly, [8] suggests using raw image data as input for the algorithm. While this works well for some data sets, e.g., MNIST, we agree with [10] that feature embeddings should yield better results in general. Nevertheless, we compare both variants.

3.2 Parameter Selection

Algorithm 1 depends on two parameters: The number m of desired prototypes and the scaling factor γ of the kernel function. To determine the optimal value for the latter, [10] suggests training a 1-Nearest-Neighbour (1-NN) algorithm on the selected prototypes to classify an test set. Additionally, we used a k-fold cross-validation averaged for robustness. Notably, the best value for γ seems to depend on both the underlying data set and the embedding used (see Fig. 3).

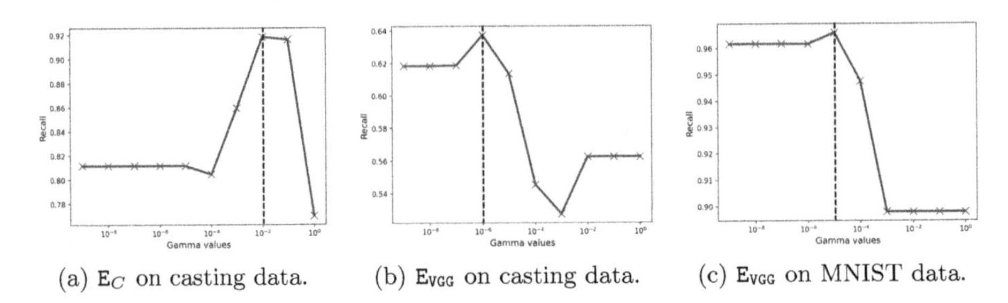

(a) $\mathtt{E}_C$ on casting data. (b) $\mathtt{E}_{\mathtt{VGG}}$ on casting data. (c) $\mathtt{E}_{\mathtt{VGG}}$ on MNIST data.

Fig. 3. γ-Values plotted against recall on two data sets and two embeddings while using 1-NN.

Regarding m, the natural but expensive approach would be a survey on end-users. Instead, we opt for an analytical approach by considering two methods:

1. We perform an *Elbow method* based on a k-Means algorithm, plotting the *distortion* (i.e. the sum of square distances from each point to its assigned cluster center) wrt. the number of clusters/prototypes (see Fig. 4a).
2. We use the fact that $\mathtt{MMD}^2(X, S)$ gives us a measure of how "representative" the elements of S are with respect to our full data set X. We therefore consider a *Scree plot* (see Fig. 4b) of the $\mathtt{MMD}^2$-value against m.

We applied both methods on all three embeddings E_0, E_C and $E_{\mathtt{VGG}}$, and on both data sets, and observe at which values the respective curves flatten. In all cases, this happens noticeably at a value of about $m = 3$, which strongly suggests that more than three prototypes do not convey significantly more information. However, note that the optimal number should vary depending on the specific data set under consideration.

3.3 Evaluation

Similarly to our strategy for selecting parameters, we evaluate the resulting prototypes using a 1-NN approach with respect to the training data set. We additionally use an off-the-shelf *Partitioning around Medoids* [15] k-Medoids clustering algorithm as a baseline approach. The results are shown in Table 1.

Overall, the MMD-based approach performs mostly better than k-Medoids, although the difference is surprisingly small. As expected, the embedding $\mathtt{E}_C$

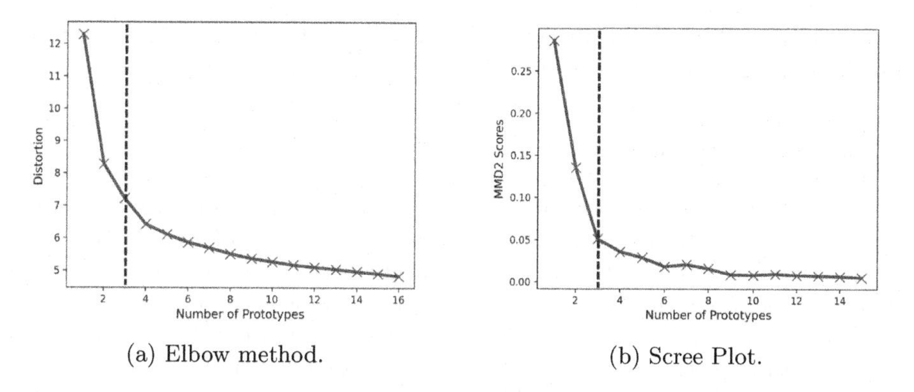

(a) Elbow method.

(b) Scree Plot.

Fig. 4. Representative plots using an Elbow method (a) and a Scree plot (b).

Table 1. Results of 1-NN algorithm trained selected prototypes, evaluated with respect of the embedding based on accuracy (best performance in bold).

	Casting			MNIST		
	E_0	E_C	E_{VGG}	E_0	E_C	E_{VGG}
MMD	0,6682	**0,9273**	**0,6591**	**0,9649**	**0,9995**	**0,9750**
k-Medoids	**0,6864**	0,9136	0,6136	0,9598	**0,9995**	0,9653

obtained via feature extraction on the classifier model itself shows consistently better results than the alternative embeddings. Surprisingly, the unbiased embedding (E_{VGG}) is also superior to the raw data (E_0) on the casting data set, while not on MNIST - probably due to the simple structure and uniform background.

Figure 5 shows the resulting prototypes of our primary data set. Notably, the defective prototypes using E_C cover exactly the three primary kinds of defects occurring in the data set - a blowhole in the first, abrasions in the second, and a scratch in the third, whereas the E_{VGG} based prototypes are noticeably less diverse

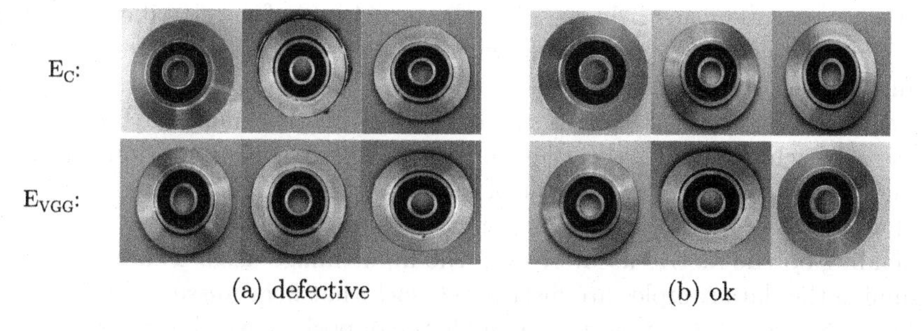

(a) defective

(b) ok

Fig. 5. Selected prototypes of the casting data set.

in that respect. Like the corresponding data samples themselves, the prototypes for the "ok" class are largely very similar, regardless of the embedding used.

4 Near Miss and Hit Selection

Regarding NHMs, our algorithm is conceptually straight-forward (see Algorithm 2). Given a data sample e, we choose as a subset X of our *training* data either those samples with the same inferred label as e (near hits) or those with a different label (near misses). Then we compare each element of X to e by some given metric $m : \mathbb{R}^n \times \mathbb{R}^n \to \mathbb{R}$: (i) The euclidean metric $\sqrt{\sum_i (x_i - y_i)^2}$, (ii) the manhattan metric $\sum_i |x_i - y_i|$ and (iii) the cosine metric $1 - x \cdot y / \|x\| \cdot \|y\|$, again using all three of our embeddings.

Algorithm 2. Near Miss/Hit Algorithm.

Input: e data sample, X data set, m metric
  $L = \varnothing$
  foreach: $x \in X \setminus \{e\}$ **do**
    $L = L \cup \{\langle x, m(x, e)\rangle\}$
  sort L by second component
Return: L

4.1 Evaluation

Evaluating the accuracy of NHMs *analytically* is considerably difficult in that no *objective* measure of similarity – especially with respect to those features that are relevant for classification – exists, which could serve as a baseline comparison. While this applies equally to prototypes, this problem becomes a lot more prominent here, where comparisons between individual pairs of data samples need to be considered. Ideally, we would evaluate the possible vector embeddings and metrics in a large-scale user study. In lieu of that, we opted for manually inspecting random samples of NHMs on both data sets with varying parameters.

One clear and unsurprising result is the superiority of the classifier embedding E_C. This is particularly noticeable with *near misses* on the MNIST data set. Figure 6 shows some near misses for the class "7" for both embeddings. Notably, the near misses obtained using E_C all have something resembling a corner at the upper end, which could indicate a number 7, whereas using $\mathsf{E}_{\mathsf{VGG}}$ quickly yields plain lines, much more reminiscent of a 1.

Furthermore, the near misses using E_C seem to differ much more rarely depending on the metric used, or even the input image used. This makes sense, assuming the data samples are distributed such that near misses reduce to those data samples which most closely resemble the opposite class. For example, Fig. 7 shows the first five near hits for an image of class "1", which are notably similar for all three metrics and for several input images.

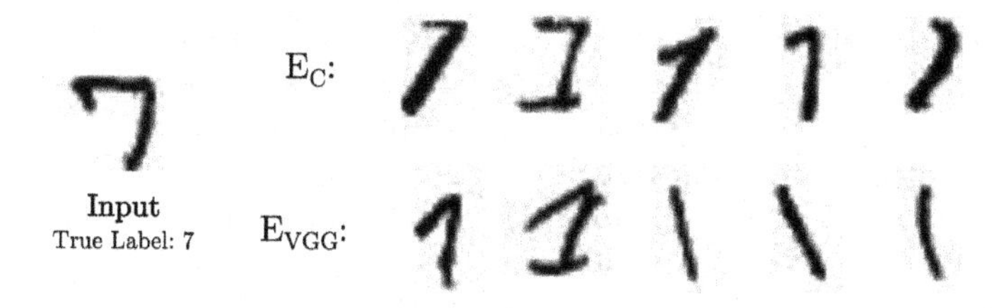

Fig. 6. Near misses for an input of class "7".

Fig. 7. Regularly occurring near hits for the class "1".

The advantage of E_C over E_{VGG} is much less noticeable on the casting data set (see Fig. 8), however. We conjecture that the homogeneity of the data set allows for either embedding to primarily focus on the relevant differences, i.e. exactly the defects, since even generic embeddings should largely be able to abstract from rotation, angle and similar unimportant variations.

With respect to the metric used, different choices yield different, but very similar results (equal in only ≈30% of cases). In fact, we could not notice a clear advantage of either over the others, regardless of the choice of embedding, with possibly a slight advantage of euclidean and manhattan distances over cosine.

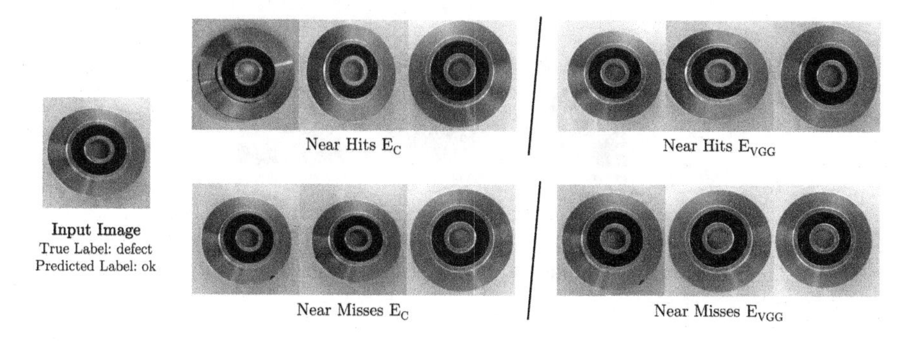

Fig. 8. E_C-based NHMs exhibits more striking features regarding the example input image, to indicate faster this misclassified image of class "defective"

5 Demonstrator

We implemented a web-based interactive demonstrator (see Fig. 9). A user can choose a model-specific (E_C) or model-agnostic (E_{VGG}) embedding, one of our two example data sets, a metric (cosine, euclidean, manhattan), the number of near hits and misses to show, and an input image from the test sets. The system then displays the input image itself, its classification according to the CNN, the corresponding probability, prototypes for the classes and near hits and misses with their corresponding distances according to the metric chosen. The demonstrator, and all code relating to our evaluations is available online[1].

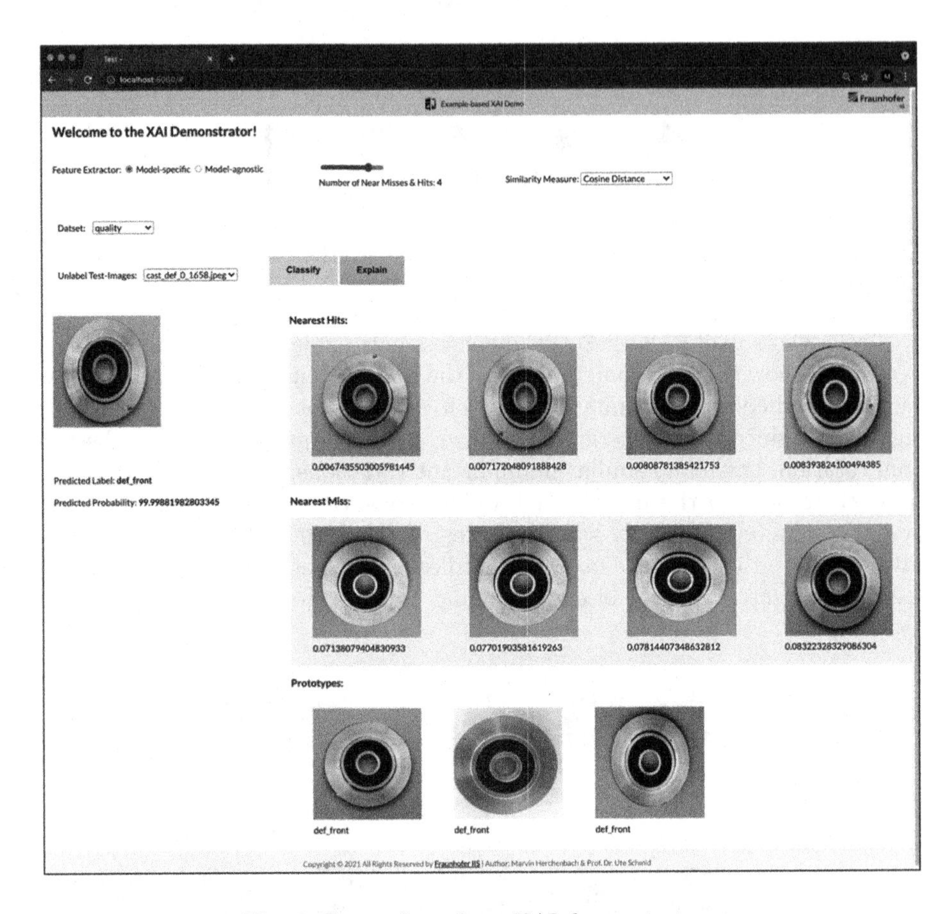

Fig. 9. Screenshot of our XAI demonstrator.

6 Conclusion and Future Work

We presented an example-based XAI approach for image classification models providing prototypes as global explanation, as well as near misses and hits to explain the local decision boundary of a prediction. Our experiments showed that model-specific embeddings are more informative with respect to decision boundaries than model-agnostic ones. In a next step, more advanced prototype

[1] https://gitlab.cc-asp.fraunhofer.de/sees/vis-ml2022-mh.

selection algorithms can be evaluated, e.g., re-implementing the ProtoDash algorithm from [4].

Although there already exists some empirical evidence showing that humans can profit from these types of example-based explanations [7,11], we plan to conduct user studies to evaluate the helpfulness of our demonstrator for the visual quality control task. Performance accuracies for predictions of class decisions of the CNN models will be compared for (a) visual highlighting, (b) prototype explanations, (c) near hit and miss explanations, and both prototype and near hit/miss explanations. Another useful enhancement could be highlighting the dissimilarities or similarities between the test image and the near miss or hit by using saliency maps – e.g. similarity based saliency maps stemming from CBIR [3] – to enable much more precise and faster indication of the decision boundaries to the domain expert. Finally, the user interface of the demonstrator can be improved with respect to intuitive interaction, ease of information acquistion, and positive user experience.

References

1. Adadi, A., Berrada, M.: Peeking inside the black-box: a survey on explainable artificial intelligence (XAI). IEEE Access **6**, 52138–52160 (2018). https://doi.org/10.1109/ACCESS.2018.2870052
2. Dabhi, R.: Casting product image data for quality inspection (2020). https://www.kaggle.com/ravirajsinh45/real-life-industrial-dataset-of-casting-product
3. Dong, B., Collins, R., Hoogs, A.: Explainability for content-based image retrieval. In: IEEE Conference on Computer Vision and Pattern Recognition (CVPR) Workshops, pp. 95–98 (2019)
4. Gurumoorthy, K.S., Dhurandhar, A., Cecchi, G., Aggarwal, C.: Efficient data representation by selecting prototypes with importance weights. In: Proceedings IEEE International Conference on Data Mining (ICDM), pp. 260–269 (2019). https://doi.org/10.1109/ICDM.2019.00036
5. Hameed, I.M., Abdulhussain, S.H., Mahmmod, B.M.: Content-based image retrieval: a review of recent trends. Cogent Eng. **8**(1) (2021). https://doi.org/10.1080/23311916.2021.1927469
6. Kaufmann, L., Rousseeuw, P.: Clustering by means of medoids. In: Data Analysis Based on the L1-Norm and Related Methods, pp. 405–416 (1987)
7. Kenny, E.M., Ford, C., Quin, M., Keane, M.T.: Explaining black-box classifiers using post-hoc explanations-by-example: the effect of explanations and error-rates in XAI user studies. Artif. Intell. **294**, 103459 (2021)
8. Kim, B., Khanna, R., Koyejo, O.: Examples are not enough, learn to criticize! criticism for interpretability. In: Proceedings of the 30th International Conference on Neural Information Processing Systems, NIPS 2016, pp. 2288–2296. Curran Associates Inc., Red Hook, NY, USA (2016). https://doi.org/10.5555/3157096.3157352. ISBN 9781510838819
9. LeCun, Y., Cortes, C., Burges, C.J.: The MNIST database of handwritten digits (1998). http://yann.lecun.com/exdb/mnist/
10. Molnar, C.: Interpretable Machine Learning. A Guide for Making Black Box Models Explainable, p. 247 (2019). https://christophm.github.io/interpretable-ml-book

11. Rabold, J., Siebers, M., Schmid, U.: Generating contrastive explanations for inductive logic programming based on a near miss approach. Mach. Learn., 1–22 (2021, online first). https://doi.org/10.1007/s10994-021-06048-w
12. Renkl, A.: Toward an instructionally oriented theory of example-based learning. Cogn. Sci. **38**(1), 1–37 (2014). https://doi.org/10.1111/cogs.12086
13. Samek, W., Montavon, G., Vedaldi, A., Hansen, L.K., Müller, K.-R. (eds.): Explainable AI: Interpreting, Explaining and Visualizing Deep Learning. LNCS (LNAI), vol. 11700. Springer, Cham (2019). https://doi.org/10.1007/978-3-030-28954-6
14. Schmid, U.: Interactive learning with mutual explanations in relational domains. In: Muggleton, S., Chater, N. (eds.) Human-Like Machine Intelligence, pp. 338–354. Oxford University Press (2021)
15. Schubert, E., Rousseeuw, P.J.: Faster k-medoids clustering: improving the PAM, CLARA, and CLARANS algorithms. In: Amato, G., Gennaro, C., Oria, V., Radovanović, M. (eds.) SISAP 2019. LNCS, vol. 11807, pp. 171–187. Springer, Cham (2019). https://doi.org/10.1007/978-3-030-32047-8_16
16. Simonyan, K., Zisserman, A.: Very deep convolutional networks for large-scale image recognition. In: 3rd International Conference on Learning Representations, ICLR 2015 - Conference Track Proceedings, pp. 1–14 (2015)
17. Urbanowicz, R.J., Meeker, M., La Cava, W., Olson, R.S., Moore, J.H.: Relief-based feature selection: introduction and review. J. Biomed. Inf. **85**, 189–203 (2018). https://doi.org/10.1016/j.jbi.2018.07.014

Adaptive Threshold for Anomaly Detection in ATM Radar Data Streams

Achraf Krim Rahaoui[1(✉)], Théobald de Riberolles[1], and Jiefu Song[1,2]

[1] Activus Group, 2 Chemin du Pigeonnier, 31100 Toulouse, France
{achraf.krimrahaoui,theobald.deriberolles,jiefu.song}@activus-group.fr
[2] IRIT - Université Toulouse I Capitole, 2 Rue du Doyen Gabriel Marty, 31042 Toulouse Cedex 09, France

Abstract. Intrusion Detection Systems (IDS) are capital instruments for protecting ATM networks against intrusion, and subsequently ensuring the integrity of air traffic. An anomaly detection approach in such systems enables the detection of multiple types of attacks with the aid of a threshold as a criterion for differentiating between normal activity and unusual events in the network. IDS with fixed threshold fail to detect the presence of patterns in the data, thus hampering proper detection ability, and requiring regular human intervention. Detection ability of IDS can be improved by establishing an automated system that recognises pattern shifts in evolving data streams and adjusts the threshold accordingly. Our work focuses on designing an algorithm to recognize the occurrence of new patterns and adjust the threshold consequently for enhanced anomaly detection, whilst offering flexibility for different frameworks and scalability to cope with large data streams. In this article, we present an adaptive threshold approach based on extreme value theory, which aims to automatically detect concept drifts in radar data streams. We evaluate our method in a practical scenario of anomaly detection on time series data collected by air traffic radars across France and show that we can achieve a threefold performance improvement over a standard approach using a fixed threshold.

Keywords: Anomaly detection · Concept drift · Time series

1 Introduction

Surveillance radars for air traffic monitor the behaviour of an aircraft during the course of a flight. Such communications between surveillance radars and aircraft are recorded and transferred over a private network linking the various air traffic management (ATM) entities. Nevertheless, the effort to connect multiple ATM systems, which were previously operating in a closed environment, is resulting in the disruption of previous security features, thereby exposing the entire system to attacks. In order to ensure security in the ATM network, intrusion detection systems (IDS) that can provide a hybrid of misuse and anomaly detection are deployed. Since attacks are not yet widespread in ATM networks, malicious

M. El Yacoubi et al. (Eds.): ICPRAI 2022, LNCS 13364, pp. 431–442, 2022.
https://doi.org/10.1007/978-3-031-09282-4_36

actions are barely defined, thus an IDS based on misuse detection is unable to detect unknown attacks. As air traffic increases, it is necessary to ensure the reliability and relevance of the detections of all types of attacks. Existing approaches based on a fixed threshold trigger numerous false alarms, resulting in the failure to meet the criterion of relevance of an IDS. Hence, the importance of introducing an alternative approach that breaks away from the classical approach in order to respond to the qualities of an IDS.

We aim to provide a solution centred on concept drift recognition, with improved anomaly detection over a fixed threshold due to the dynamic adjustment of the threshold following the occurrence of drifts. The proposed solution intended to be flexible and scalable, with the potential to be used in different frameworks and to process high volumes of data. In this article, we present an adaptive threshold approach based on extreme value theory (EVT), which aims to automatically detect concept drifts in radar data streams. We evaluate our method in a practical scenario of anomaly detection on time series data collected by air traffic radars across France and show that we can achieve a threefold performance improvement over a standard approach using a fixed threshold. We also present a protocol for processing radar data to perform anomaly detection, as it constitutes a preliminary step in order to asses our method.

We structure this article as follows. Section 2 presents the state of the art and related work. In Sect. 3 we present the VPOT approach and provide a breakdown of our methodology. In Sect. 4 we provide the experimental framework and discuss the outcomes. Finally, in Sect. 5 we review our progress and consider the directions for future work.

2 Related Work

The existing approaches for anomaly detection through machine learning include outlier detection (Lazarevic et al. [1]), classification (Bhuyan et al. [2]) and semi-supervised learning techniques (de Riberolles et al. [3]). In all of the approaches discussed, anomalies are detected via a fixed threshold. The capacity of a fixed threshold is compromised by the presence of fluctuating data, which will often require human intervention to correct the threshold. Considering that under this approach the threshold is computed on the observed data set, calculating the threshold on a relatively small data set will result in a poor extrapolation of the threshold in data streams. It will thus be required to calculate it on fairly large data sets in order to capture the overall behaviour. However, the processing time of this threshold will be significantly long, especially when the data set processed is large, thereby affecting its scalability. An effective approach to ensure that manual intervention is not required to make adjustments, and to reduce computing time through automation, is to employ an adaptive threshold, which is a mechanism that has the ability to recognise the presence of new behaviour patterns in the observed data in order to calculate a threshold on that basis. In order to develop an adaptive threshold, numerous strategies have been presented in the scientific literature. Machine learning related methods are addressed for detecting concept drift and computing the threshold. Esposito et al. [4] present a method that relies on Cohen's Kappa coefficient as a metric to ascertain the threshold. This method is suitable for classification algorithms as it does not constrain the training of the model being used. However, the drawing of random samples in the process of calculating the threshold risks breaking the time series continuity, resulting in a poor representation of the behaviour of the data. Probabilistic approaches rely on the results of probability theory, Ali et al.[5] study the automation of the threshold used for anomaly detection systems in an effort to improve the detection capability of zero-day attacks in the traffic of a computer network. To address this aim, a recognition algorithm based on Markov chains is used to predict abnormal scores, leading to an a priori threshold that fits these predictions. An extension of the work of Ferragut et al. [6], who reformulate the notion of anomaly based on a probabilistic approach, is proposed by Bridges et al. [7]. In their studies, the distribution of incoming data is assumed to be known and a guideline is suggested to build a threshold –either fixed or automated– in a generic form that would depend on the data flow and the number of alarms allowed.

An interesting insight is brought by combining the using of sliding windows and probabilistic tools. T. Wang et al. [8] present a martingale-based method to learn the regularity of the observed data in a sliding window of variable size and to identify the shifts in the data stream. The threshold is computed according to a global factor that ascertains the confidence level of the detection. On the other hand, H. Wang [9] defines a threshold for incoming observations by conducting a wavelet analysis and the resulting confidence interval obtained by using the Central Limit Theorem over a sequence of data on a sliding window of fixed size. On their part, Clark et al. [10] present a method for detecting concept drifts through a sliding window based approach that relies on a statistical test, with the threshold being adjusted accordingly. Finally, Siffer et al. [11] suggest the use of a threshold derived from the results of the extreme value theory. The threshold is defined from the quantiles of a generalized Pareto distribution, in dependence on the sensitivity chosen to differentiate between normal and abnormal data.

We have discussed several approaches to establish a threshold that can adapt to the nature of the data. In their majority, these approaches rely on statistical tests or sliding windows, assuming that the theoretical distribution of the data is known. Nevertheless, in a practical framework, the nature of data is constantly changing. Hence, making an a priori assumption on the nature of the data or the abnormal scores constrains the computation of the threshold to a single case of the model. After a thorough review of the methods discussed, we will consider the potential of linking a probabilistic approach with a sliding window system to provide a solution with a level of flexibility that facilitates the inclusion of an adaptive threshold in the operational environment of an IDS. Existing approaches focus on either detecting concept drift or on computing the threshold, and are often restricted to specific frameworks. We propose a generic approach involving concept drift detection and robust threshold calculation. With this insight, we design an automated method that employs sliding windows of variable size, along the introduction of a non-parametric test to detect concept drifts in fluctuating data. To achieve better efficiency, the threshold is obtained by using an extreme value theory approach. On completion, we perform a benchmarking analysis of the approaches VATU [10] and DSPOT [11] with our approach when applied to surveillance radar data from ATM networks.

3 Method

In this section we present our approach VPOT that combines the VATU [10] and DSPOT [11] concepts for developing an adaptive threshold capable of identifying concept drifts. We also establish a guideline for obtaining an anomaly score from radar data, on which our method will be evaluated.

3.1 VPOT Approach

VATU approach addresses the detection of concept drift zones in Gaussian distributions via the z-test. To perform the test, two sliding windows are dedicated for the comparison of the last monitored and new incoming scores. However, the z-test is bounded by its inability to perform on non-Gaussian distributions. To ensure compatibility with scores from different distributions, we have introduced the Kolmogorov-Smirnov test in VPOT, which is applied on the scores in the two sliding windows. In contrast to VATU, where the threshold is calculated by a linear combination of the mean and standard deviation of the scores, a more advanced threshold calculation is possible with DSPOT. This approach based on the EVT, and more accurately on the Peaks Over Threshold (POT) method, allows to compute a threshold without prior knowledge of the distribution of the scores. A crucial aspect is that EVT results, and the subsequent application of the POT method, require the scores to be independent and identically distributed (iid), which is not met in a realistic scenario such as presented in this study. On the case of the scores we generate, they are dependent on each other if the distance between them is less than or equal to the size of the window used for computing the scores. Nevertheless, this dependence weakens as two scores become more distant from each other. By analysing the autocorrelation of the scores (Fig. 1), we observe a decreasing degree of correlation as the lag increases. This outcome, which is consistent with the scoring method, suggests that the dependency between two scores is short-term. Under the condition of short-term dependency, the same results of the EVT can be applied as for the iid variables [12,13].

Moreover, in broad strokes, the POT method is based on the Pickands-Balkema-De Haan theorem [14,15] and is applied for ascertaining the probability of an anomalous event. The method, however, is considered for situations where the scores do not vary considerably, and to ensure this condition, a change of variables $X' = X - M_d$, where M_d is the moving average over the last d scores, is introduced. Finally, the maximum likelihood method is used to ascertain the

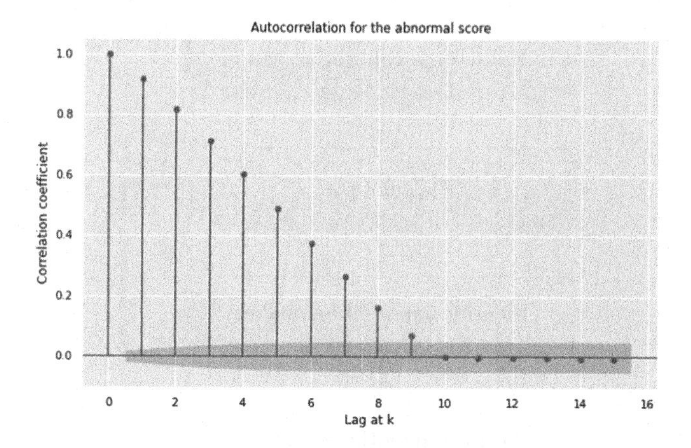

Fig. 1. Autocorrelation of the scores in relation to the lag k

extreme quantile to be used as a threshold for identifying abnormal activity. In DSPOT, the extreme quantile is computed with every new observation. In contrast, in VPOT, every time a drift is detected, the extreme quantile is computed over the scores in a third window that includes both the observed and the incoming scores, thus improving the computational efficiency.

Following a similar procedure as in VATU, we regularly update the scores stored in the third window. The purpose of this update is to prevent a stationary threshold in the case where concept drifts are not present or not properly detected. In the following diagram (Fig. 2), we present the steps of the VPOT algorithm.

3.2 Methodology

In order to evaluate the performance of the discussed methods, we produce scores that capture the degree of abnormality in a sequence of data. In the following paragraphs we will briefly describe the process leading to the setting of our adaptive threshold.

Initially, we collect the features of interest from raw data stored in network packet records. We then proceed to the preparation of the data to be transferred to the autoencoder model for its training. For a brief overview, following on [3], we consider an autoencoder consisting of GRU (Gated Recurrent Units) cells. After concluding the training of the model, we artificially introduce anomalies that represent spoofing attacks in the test samples. The last step in the process consists in comparing the reconstruction provided by the autoencoder with the input data by using a metric –abnormal score– derived from the cosine similarity. Once the scores are computed, we then set up the threshold –fixed or adaptive– to identify anomalies in the testing data sets. On these scores, adaptive threshold algorithms employ sliding windows to identify concept drifts that occur, and set the threshold in accordance with the incoming data. Our protocol is described in Fig. 3.

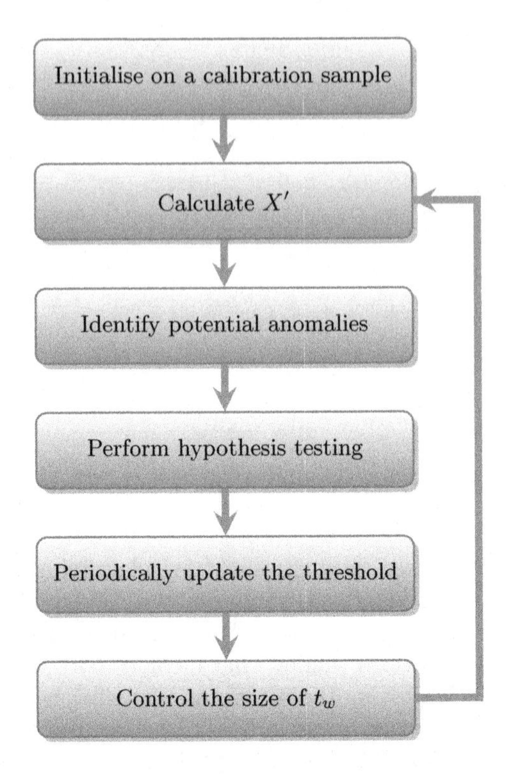

Fig. 2. Algorithm VPOT proceeding

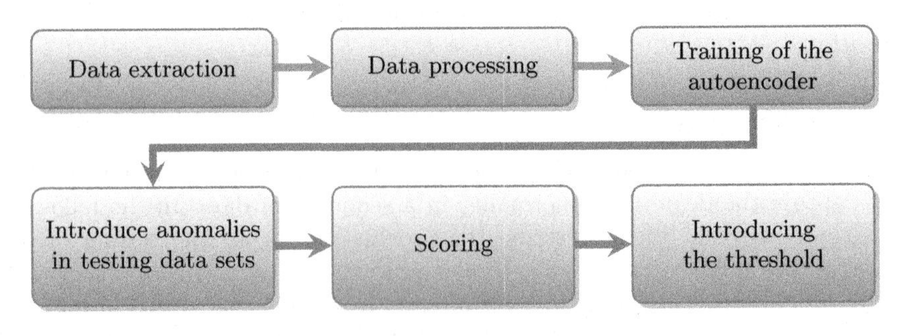

Fig. 3. Stages of anomaly detection using an autoencoder

4 Experimental Assessment

In this section, we will provide our experimental protocol, followed by an overview of the experimental data sets and their corresponding abnormal scores. Finally, we will evaluate and discuss the results of the three methods VATU, DSPOT and VPOT, including their performance with respect to a fixed threshold.

4.1 Experimental Protocol

The purpose of our experiments is twofold. First, to evaluate the ability of our algorithm to identify the areas where concept drift occurs. Our second aim is to assess the effectiveness of the threshold to be adjusted in such a way to detect a maximum of anomalies –criterion of reliability– and to raise the fewest false alarms –criterion of relevance–. For these experiments we formulate the following assumptions. We set ourselves in a realistic framework, in which the data is complex, with the occurrence of different patterns that result in concept drifts in data and subsequently in anomalous scores. The data set used for training the autoencoder consists of real world data from normal air traffic activity. On the other hand, the data sets used for testing include anomalies corresponding to spoofing attacks where information have been altered. In order to measure the scalability of our solution, we chose test samples with size of 3 million records that represent 5% of all records over a 24-h time span.

We perform our experiments in a virtual machine under the following environment: 12 CPUs x Intel Xeon(R) Silver 4216 CPU @ 2.10 GHz, 62.8 GB of RAM, 214.7 GB of disk memory, a 256-bit LLVM 11.0.0 GPU, running on a 64-bit Ubuntu 20.04.2 LTS system. The runtime of the algorithms varies with the sample size. However, we can differentiate the algorithms based on their rapidity. In the following table, we have illustrated the average runtime of the reviewed methods on the larger samples (Table 1).

Table 1. Table of performances

Algorithm	Sample size	Average runtime
VATU	3×10^6	14 s
DSPOT	1×10^6	4 h 36 min 47 s
VPOT	3×10^6	1 min 35 s
Fixed threshold	3×10^6	38 min 54 s

In view of the considerably high execution time for the DSPOT algorithm for large sample sizes, we have opted to rely on the results generated by a one-time execution of the algorithm. Given this constraint, we also choose to benchmark the other algorithms under the same conditions to provide a more fair comparison.

4.2 Data Set

The data at our disposal corresponds to the captured messages sent by surveillance radars for civil aviation air traffic. Raw network capture files (.pcap) contain 4 h of records, with the average size of each file being 700 Mb, which varies depending on the traffic at the time of recording. To facilitate the analysis and processing of such data, we transform the raw capture files into .csv files.

With real world data being used, anomalies are artificially introduced into the data set. Hence, it is not convenient to fix permissible false alarm rates for the framework. Our data sets are built from a collection of information retrieved from different aircraft. This information enables us to identify an aircraft – aircraft address (ACAddr)– and track its position –in polar coordinates (RHO, THETHA)– and route –flight level (FL), calculated ground speed (CGS) and calculated heading (CHdg)–, to identify the radar station transmitting the messages to the network –system identification code (SIC)–, and the timestamp (TS). In view of this background, and the importance of considering the reporting time of the transmitted messages, the data collection under study consists of a multivariate time series. For this paper, we will use a training data set consisting of 12 million records registered over a 24-h period. As data collected since the start of the Covid-19 pandemic constitute an unprecedented scenario, it becomes a serious challenge to characterise a pattern of normal air traffic activity. Our finality being to develop a generic support tool for the air traffic controller, by using data from normal activity, we can assess the benefits of our approach with a real world data set. Therefore, we will be focusing on data collected prior to the pandemic. More precisely, the data set used for training the autoencoder consists of 12 million records, that were retrieved on 24/09/2019. For testing, we use two distinct data sets, each one consisting of 3 million records retrieved on 25/09/2019 and 26/09/2019, over a 4-h time frame corresponding to the peak of air traffic throughout the day in order to gather the more relevant information.

4.3 Benchmarking

Before evaluating the performance of the proposed algorithms, we tuned the parameters of each method to define the optimal setting. The window size is adjusted to allow enough data to compute the threshold. A narrow margin of error is assigned to the test that identifies concept drift. The likelihood of an anomaly occurring is typically low, therefore we opt for large quantiles that enable the recognition of anomalies. We employed the following metrics as benchmarks: precision, recall, accuracy and F1 score. We therefore suggest the following settings for each algorithm (Table 2):

Table 2. Table of optimal settings

Algorithm	Window size	Significance level of the test	Probability (quantile)
VATU	$T = 300$	alpha = 0.05	–
DSPOT	$d = 150$	–	$q = 0.01$ ($z_{0.99}$)
VPOT	$T = 2000$	alpha = 0.05	$q = 0.01$ ($z_{0.99}$)

Taking these settings as a reference, we conducted a benchmark of the performances achieved by the VATU, DSPOT and VPOT algorithms on sub-samples of different sizes, along with the ones achieved by using a fixed threshold. To define the fixed threshold, we selected the threshold s^* that presented the lowest false positive rate (FPR) amongst the thresholds that exhibited a true positive rate (TPR) superior to a certain value δ that is arbitrarily adopted in consideration of the capacity of the autoencoder: $s^* = \underset{s}{\operatorname{argmin}}\{FPR(s); TPR(s) \geq \delta, s \in \mathcal{S}\}$, with $\mathcal{S}$ being the set of the fixed thresholds s used to calculate the ROC curve.

4.4 Observation

After running the algorithms on the scores achieved on subsamples of sizes ranging from 50,000 to 3 million records from the test data sets, we provide the following remarks.

The first remark is that an adaptive threshold provides a better overall performance (Fig. 4 and 6) than the fixed threshold. However, it shows less sensitivity compared to a fixed threshold (Fig. 5 and 7). On the smaller samples, VATU, DSPOT and VPOT have similar performance and sensitivity for the first test data set (Fig. 4 and 5), whereas we perceive a gap in performance and sensitivity between VPOT and DSPOT for the second data set (Fig. 6 and 7). On medium and large samples for both test data sets, both VATU and VPOT maintain the same level of efficiency, with a slightly decreasing sensitivity in spite of a slight decline in the efficiency of VPOT for the second test data set on medium samples. An efficiency decay is noticeable for DSPOT on both data sets. As a result, it appears that overall VPOT shows slightly better results, while VATU and DSPOT exhibit similar performances, all three performing significantly better than a fixed threshold.

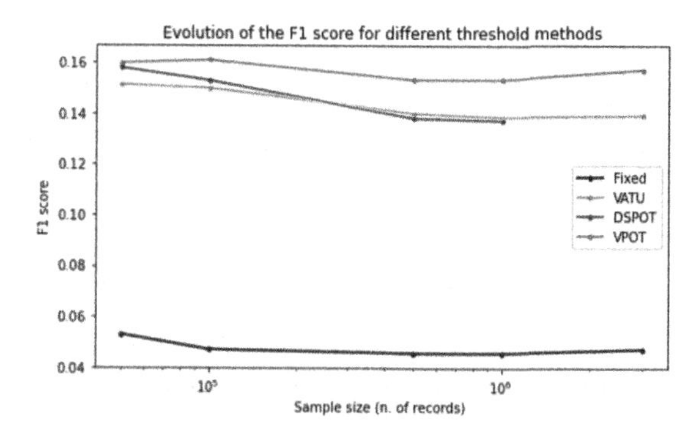

Fig. 4. F1 score for test data set collected on 25/09/2019

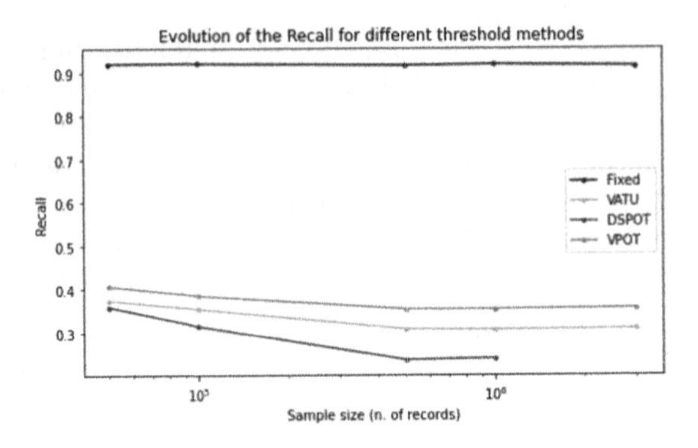

Fig. 5. Recall for test data set collected on 25/09/2019

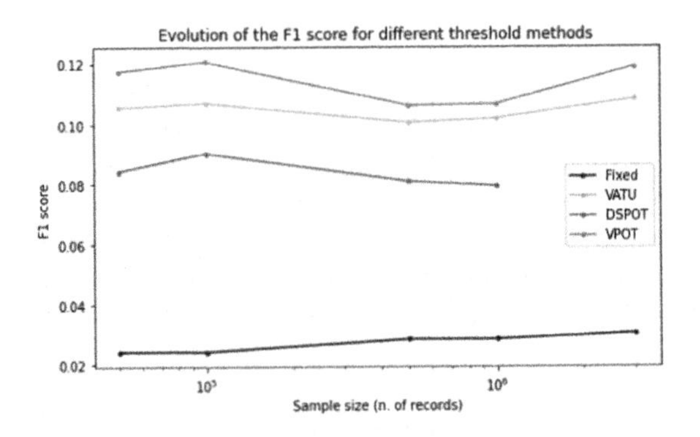

Fig. 6. F1 score for test data set collected on 26/09/2019

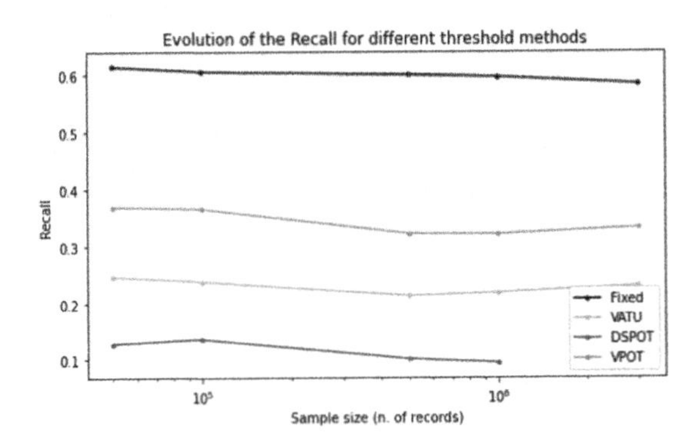

Fig. 7. Recall for test data set collected on 26/09/2019

4.5 Discussion

Firstly, we shall stress that while the fixed threshold ensures a better detection of the introduced anomalies, it triggers frequent false alarms that cause a decrease in precision and a consequent poor performance. Regarding accuracy, the use of an adaptive threshold produces fewer false alarms, yielding improved precision as compared to the fixed threshold. Both methods VATU and VPOT use the scores within a sliding window (t_w) of reasonably small size to calculate the threshold. This means that the calculated thresholds depend to a lesser extent on the previous scores, ensuring a better fit to the observed patterns, which in turn provides consistency to the methods. In contrast, DSPOT's method of calculating the threshold considers the excesses of all previous observations. As a consequence, a substantial impact is caused by the excesses of data showing a different behavioural pattern and therefore the calculated threshold is increasingly less dependent on the actual data. This allows us to understand the decrease in performance experienced as the sample size increases. We can attribute the enhanced efficiency of the VPOT method to the fact that the EVT provides a threshold that is more adapted to the observed data compared to using a linear combination of the mean and the standard deviation, particularly by using only the excesses within the sliding window. On the second data set, the decay in efficiency experienced by all threshold methods suggests that effectiveness of such methods is higher for data sets corresponding to the following day of the data set used for training the autoencoder.

5 Conclusion and Future Work

In this paper, we have discussed the interest of a developing an adaptive threshold approach for detecting anomalies in ATM networks. To overcome the limitations of an IDS based on a fixed threshold, we have defined an algorithm –VPOT– based on an adaptive threshold approach that provides improved performance, while being consistent, accurate and fast on high volume data streams.

From an overall standpoint, this approach brings us closer to the requirements –reliability and relevance– for an IDS in a wider international ATM network. However to achieve operability in a real life application, certain aspects can be further addressed. In particular, transition areas between data from two separate aircraft are interpreted as anomalies by the autoencoder model, yielding a higher scores that trigger numerous false alarms, thus reducing the performance of the threshold. We therefore contemplate a more extensive handling of concept drift [16] in order to identify transition zones more accurately, and introducing machine learning-based approaches for concept drift detection [17].

In addition, the capacity of the autoencoder is an underlying factor in our protocol, therefore to enhance its efficiency, we intend to conduct continual learning of the model, which will enable us to yield more accurate scores.

References

1. Lazarevic, A., Ertöz, L., Kumar, V., Ozgur, A., Srivastava, J.: A comparative study of anomaly detection schemes in network intrusion detection. In: SDM 2003, May 2003, vol. 3 (2003). https://doi.org/10.1137/1.9781611972733.3
2. Bhuyan, M.H., Bhattacharyya, D.K., Kalita, J.K.: Network anomaly detection: methods, systems and tools. IEEE Commun. Surv. Tut. **16**(1), 303–336 (2014). https://doi.org/10.1109/SURV.2013.052213.00046

3. de Riberolles, T., Song, J., Zou, Y., Silvestre, G., Larrieu, N.: Characterizing radar network traffic: a first step towards spoofing attack detection. In: 2020 IEEE Aerospace Conference, pp. 1–8 (2020). https://doi.org/10.1109/AERO47225.2020.9172292
4. Esposito, C., Landrum, G.A., Schneider, N., Stiefl, N., Riniker, S.: GHOST: adjusting the decision threshold to handle imbalanced data in machine learning. J. Chem. Inf. Model. **61**(6), 2623–2640 (2021). https://doi.org/10.1021/acs.jcim.1c00160
5. Ali, M.Q., Al-Shaer, E., Khan, H., Khayam, S.A.: Automated anomaly detector adaptation using adaptive threshold tuning. ACM Trans. Inf. Syst. Secur. **15**(4), 1–30 (2013). https://doi.org/10.1145/2445566.2445569
6. Ferragut, E., Laska, J., Bridges, R.: A new, principled approach to anomaly detection. In: 2012 11th International Conference on Machine Learning and Applications, December 2012, vol. 2, pp. 210–215 (2012). https://doi.org/10.1109/ICMLA.2012.151
7. Bridges, R., Jamieson, J., Reed, J.: Setting the threshold for high throughput detectors: a mathematical approach for ensembles of dynamic, heterogeneous, probabilistic anomaly detectors. In: 2017 IEEE International Conference on Big Data (Big Data), December 2017, pp. 1071–1078 (2017). https://doi.org/10.1109/BigData.2017.8258031
8. Wang, T., Lu, G.-L., Liu, J., Yan, P.: Adaptive change detection for long-term machinery monitoring using incremental sliding-window. Chin. J. Mech. Eng. **30**(6), 1338–1346 (2017). https://doi.org/10.1007/s10033-017-0191-4
9. Wang, H.: Anomaly detection of network traffic based on prediction and self-adaptive threshold. Int. J. Fut. Gener. Commun. Netw. **8**(6), 205–214 (2015). https://doi.org/10.14257/ijfgcn.2015.8.6.20
10. Clark, J., Liu, Z., Japkowicz, N.: Adaptive threshold for outlier detection on data streams. In: 2018 IEEE 5th International Conference on Data Science and Advanced Analytics (DSAA), pp. 41–49 (2018). https://doi.org/10.1109/DSAA.2018.00014
11. Siffer, A., Fouque, P.A., Termier, A., Largouët, C.: Anomaly detection in streams with extreme value theory. In: KDD 2017, August 2017, pp. 1067–1075 (2017). https://doi.org/10.1145/3097983.3098144
12. Leadbetter, M., Lindgren, G., Rootzén, H.: Extremes and Related Properties of Random Sequences and Processes. SSS, Springer, New York (1983). https://doi.org/10.1007/978-1-4612-5449-2
13. Poon, S.-H., Rockinger, M., Tawn, J.: Modelling extreme-value dependence in international stock markets. Stat. Sin. **13**(4), 929–953 (2003). https://doi.org/10.2139/ssrn.302961. Institute of Statistical Science, Academia Sinica
14. Balkema, A.A., de Haan, L.: Residual life time at great age. Ann. Probab. **2**(5), 792–804 (1974). https://doi.org/10.1214/aop/1176996548
15. Pickands III, J.: Statistical inference using extreme order statistics. Ann. Stat. **3**(1), 119–131 (1975). https://doi.org/10.1214/aos/1176343003
16. Hoens, T.R., Polikar, R., Chawla, N.V.: Learning from streaming data with concept drift and imbalance: an overview. Prog. Artif. Intell. **1**(1), 89–101 (2012). https://doi.org/10.1007/s13748-011-0008-0
17. Harries, M., Horn, K.: Detecting concept drift in financial time series prediction using symbolic machine learning (July 1996)

Covid-19 Vaccine Sentiment Analysis During Second Wave in India by Transfer Learning Using XLNet

Anmol Bansal, Seba Susan(✉), Arjun Choudhry, and Anubhav Sharma

Department of Information Technology, Delhi Technological University, New Delhi, India
seba_406@yahoo.in

Abstract. The Covid-19 pandemic has created a world-wide crisis from the perspectives of health and economy. Vaccination is one of the prime means by which herd immunity could be developed. Social media platforms such as Twitter has played a major role in building public opinion as the vaccination drive got underway in several countries. In this paper, we present a tweet-based sentiment analysis of the two popularly administered vaccines in India Covishield and Covaxin during the second wave of the pandemic in India, from March 2021 to September 2021, which was attributed to the Delta mutant of the coronavirus. We use unlabeled Covid-19 vaccine-related tweets downloaded from a large-scale dataset from March 2021 to September 2021, and employ transfer learning for classifying the unlabeled tweets. The contributions of this paper are: - sentiment analysis of unlabeled vaccine-related tweets by training a transformer model on pre-trained XLNet (transformer) features derived from a labeled non-Covid Twitter dataset, a time-line of public sentiments for the two vaccines administered in India, and word clouds of high-frequency adjective unigrams after sentiment analysis, as evidence.

Keywords: Sentiment analysis · Covid-19 · Vaccine · Twitter · Unlabeled tweets · Covishield · Covaxin · XLNet · Transformer

1 Introduction

Covid-19 has spread world-wide for almost two years now, and has claimed more than 4.7 million lives. To counter the virus and develop herd immunity, vaccination drives are underway in all countries. Since their introduction, vaccines have received mixed reviews, which vary along with time as more awareness is spread among the masses [1]. Twitter is a social media platform used by 320 million people worldwide, and it has played a significant role in building public opinion about the Covid-19 vaccines [2]. Vaccine hesitancy and vaccine controversies need to be timely identified by the governments in order to take sufficient remedial actions, as asserted in several works [1, 3]. In India, the vaccination drive started in January 2021 after the first wave of the pandemic had abated. Covishield and Covaxin are the two popularly administered vaccines in India. An analysis of the tweets posted since March 2021 when the second

M. El Yacoubi et al. (Eds.): ICPRAI 2022, LNCS 13364, pp. 443–454, 2022.
https://doi.org/10.1007/978-3-031-09282-4_37

wave started in India due to the Delta mutant of the coronavirus, till the abatement of the second wave in September 2021, would reveal the public sentiments for the two vaccines over time as the second wave progressed, and this is the task undertaken in this paper.

We particularly analyze unlabeled tweets since, as of now, it is difficult to get sentiment annotations for the Covid-19 related tweets since the pandemic situation is new and evolving. Some researchers have manually annotated tweets spread over a limited time span to train machine learning models [4–6]. However, training machine learning models with insufficient data may lead to overfitting or underfitting, rendering these models unfit to classify unseen test data. A list of Artificial Intelligence (AI) tools used for text mining from Covid-19 related social media posts is given in [7]. There are two main approaches for tackling unlabeled tweets. The first approach is to perform unsupervised sentiment analysis using sentiment lexicons that yield sentiment scores for each tweet, such as SentiWordNet, VADER, TextBlob or AFINN [8–11]. Sometimes, sentiment scores are used to identify phrase patterns that are associated with different sentiments [12, 13]. A majority of the researchers have adopted this approach for the sentiment analysis of Covid-19 tweets, examples being: - Yousefinaghani *et al.* (2021), Hu *et al.* (2021), Liu and Liu (2021), and Na *et al.* (2019) [2, 14–16] who used VADER, Marcec and Likic (2021) [17] who used AFINN, Sattar and Arifuzzaman (2021) [18] who used TextBlob and VADER. In [19], VADER, TextBlob and SentiWordNet were used to label news headlines into positive and negative sentiments. These annotations were then used to train a transformer model RoBERTa for sentiment classification. However, this method places a dependency on the efficacy of the three unsupervised techniques used for sentiment labeling. The second approach for handling unlabeled tweets is to train a model using a labeled dataset and apply it to classify the unlabeled tweets, a concept known as transfer learning [5, 20], which is the approach adopted in this paper. Recently, transfer learning was used successfully for sentiment classification of unlabeled social media posts related to the human papillomavirus [21]. One example of transfer learning related to Covid-19 text mining is the Covid-TWITTER-BERT model [22] which is a transformer-based model pre-trained on Covid-19 tweets, that can be fine-tuned for various text-based classification tasks. There are two main concerns while using a pre-trained model: - the selection of the labeled dataset and the choice of the classifier. In this paper, we use XLNet introduced by Yang *et al.* in 2019 [23], which is a recently introduced pre-trained transformer model, for supervised learning of the labeled *US Airlines* Twitter dataset which is a benchmark for tweet-based sentiment analysis. The trained model is then used to classify the unlabeled tweets related to the Covid-19 vaccines as positive, negative or neutral. The rest of this paper is organized as follows. Section 2 presents the methodology of the proposed sentiment analysis, Sect. 3 discusses the dataset, experimental setup and the results, and Sect. 4 summarizes the conclusions of the paper.

2 Methodology

This work is motivated by the need for testing the public sentiments related to the two vaccines popularly administered in India - Covishield and Covaxin, as the majority of the Indian population has already taken at least one dose of the two vaccines till date. Covishield is the Oxford Astrazeneca vaccine, while Covaxin is an Indian vaccine now approved by WHO. We obtained tweets in the duration of the second Covid-19 wave in India from March 2021 to September 2021, that are devoid of any sentiment annotations, from a large-scale Covid-19 Vaccine tweet dataset available online. The details of the dataset are discussed in Sect. 3. The tweets in the duration of the second wave in India are unannotated, which is an obstacle for supervised learning. In order to classify the unlabeled tweets into positive, negative and neutral sentiments, we perform transfer learning by pre-training a transformer model on XLNet features derived from the *US Airlines* tweet dataset [24] which is one of the benchmark datasets for tweet-based sentiment analysis. XLNet is an auto-regressive pretrained transformer model with multi-head self attention that has achieved high accuracies for text classification tasks [25, 26] as compared to the LSTM-based models with a single attention layer between the encoder and decoder [27]. XLNet is an extension of the transformer-XL model [28] introduced in 2019, that has outperformed the simple transformer for different classification and text generation tasks [29, 30]. XLNet introduced a modified language model training objective which learns distributions for all permutation of sequence tokens. The overall process flow for the proposed method is shown in Fig. 1.

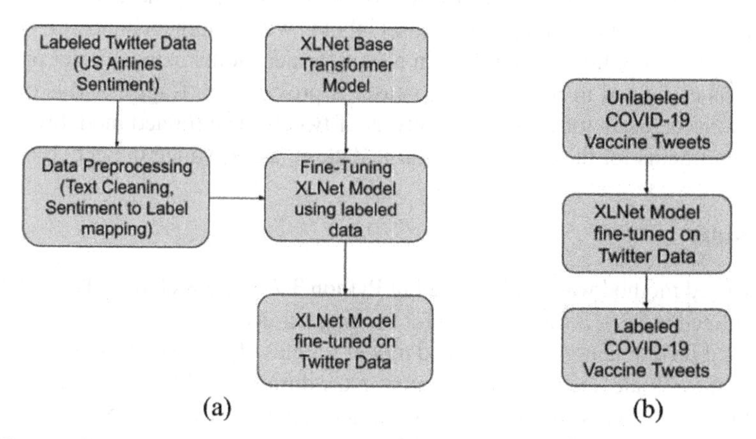

Fig. 1. Process flow: (a) Pre-training the XLNet model using *US Airlines* tweets (b) Classification of Covid-19 vaccine-related tweets using the pre-trained XLNet model.

The pre-training process is depicted in Fig. 1 (a) where the XLNet model is pre-trained on the *US Airlines* tweets that are sentiment annotated. A three-fold cross-validation is used for training the XLNet model on the *US Airline* tweets. In the second phase of our experiments, shown in Fig. 1 (b), the pre-trained XLNet model is used to classify the unlabeled Covid-19 vaccine-related tweets pertaining to the two vaccines – Covishield and Covaxin, that were popularly administered in India. The tweets so labeled are analyzed using time-line graphs to determine if the overall attitude towards vaccines has undergone a change, and if there is a boost in the general positivity of the social media users towards Covid-19 vaccines, during the course of the pandemic. We present the word clouds of high frequency adjective unigrams as evidence.

3 Experimentation and Results

3.1 Dataset Preparation

The Covid-19 vaccine dataset[1] contains tweets collected using tweepy in Python by Gabriel Preda. It contains tweets for seven different vaccines and has been updated till October 1st 2021 with a total of 197870 tweets. We separated out the tweets pertaining to either Covishield (also known as Astrazeneca) or Covaxin. We have not considered the tweets having a mention of both the vaccines, for the sake of simplicity. The total number of Covaxin tweets segregated by this procedure were 59,000 in number while Covishield tweets were 16,000 in number. The tweets were cleaned of URLs and links to websites, and all sentences were converted to lower case. Due to the absence of labels in Covid-19 vaccine dataset, a separate dataset labeled with sentiment annotations - the *US Airline* tweets dataset, was used to train a transformer model using XLNet pre-trained features, as explained in Sect. 2. This dataset is provided on Kaggle and is one of the most popular datasets for sentiment analysis of tweets. The trained model was used to predict sentiments for the unlabeled vaccine dataset, as explained in Sect. 2.

3.2 Results

The proposed method was implemented in Python 3.7 on a 2.8 GHz CPU. The methodology outlined in Sect. 2 was followed for training a transformer model using the labeled dataset, and further applying the trained model for classifying the unlabeled tweets pertaining to Covishield and Covaxin vaccines in the duration of March 2021 to September 2021. Table 1 presents the results of sentiment analysis for the *US Airlines* dataset using 80:20 train:test split with three-fold cross-validation, and a learning rate of 0.001, trained for 100 epochs. As observed, the XLNet model outperformed the unsupervised techniques of VADER and TextBlob, and supervised learning by Bi-LSTM and BERT models for sentiment analysis of the *US Airlines* tweets dataset, in terms of both accuracy and F1-score.

[1] https://www.kaggle.com/gpreda/all-covid19-vaccines-tweets.

Table 1. Sentiment analysis of US Airline tweets dataset using different classification frameworks.

Method	Accuracy (%)	F1-score
VADER	45.3	0.536
TextBlob	44.4	0.446
Bi-LSTM	81.1	0.801
BERT	84.2	0.843
XLNet	85.8	0.856

It was noted that the removal of stopwords and punctuations lowered the accuracy of our XLNet model. As observed from the confusion matrix plotted in Fig. 2 for the *US Airlines* tweets dataset, the XLNet model was able to correctly classify 85% of the positive tweets and 92% of the negative tweets. The model had some difficulty in distinguishing between the negative and neutral sentiments, but the precision and recall for both positive and negative tweets were high.

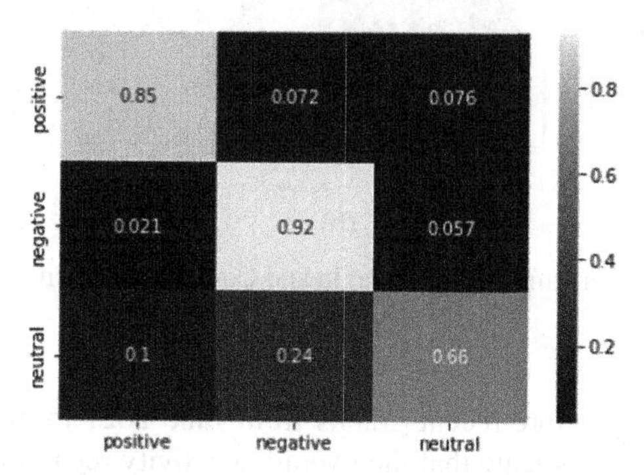

Fig. 2. Confusion matrix of the XLNet model trained on the *US Airlines* tweets dataset.

The transfer-learned XLNet model is now used for classifying the Covid-19 vaccine-related tweets into three classes: positive, negative and neutral. Figure 3 summarizes the sentiment classification results for the two vaccines in the form of bar charts. The neutral class is not shown since neutral tweets are mostly informational tweets and have no direct bearing on the understanding of the public sentiment. Our model classifies 11.14% of the Covaxin tweets as negative and 6.21% as positive; the rest are neutral tweets. Covishield tweets also follow a similar trend with 17.79% negative and 9.2% positive tweets. The positivity about Covishield only slightly exceeds that of Covaxin. The negative sentiment exceeds the positive sentiments for both vaccines due to apprehensions regarding the vaccination process during the course of the second wave of the pandemic in India. We next analyze time-line graphs to understand the changing public opinion in the duration of March 2021 to September 2021. Figure 4 shows the time-line graphs from March 2021 to May 2021 when the peak of the second wave was observed in India.

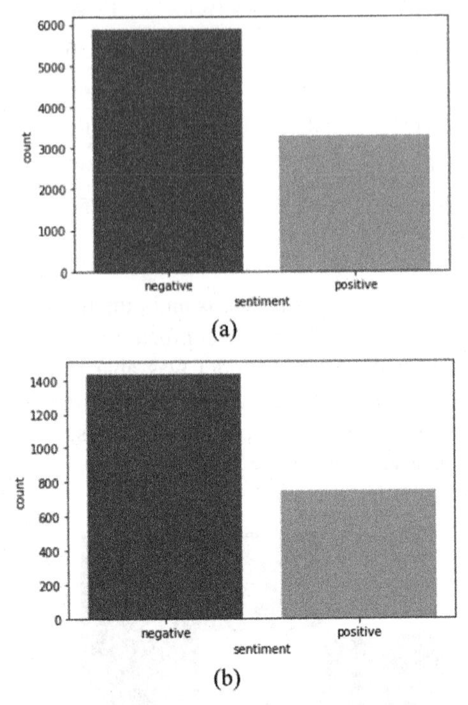

Fig. 3. Results of sentiment analysis of Covaxin and Covishield vaccine tweets by the proposed method.

Figure 5 shows the more recent graphs from June 2021 to September 2021. The graphs in Figs. 4 and 5 indicate that the overall negativity regarding both the vaccines (indicated by the blue line in both the graphs) reduces over time, with peaks observed in March, April and June. The positivity rate showed a spike in July 2021 possibly because of the reduction in the number of Covid-19 cases after the second wave in May 2021 subsided. However, the positivity is still low for both the vaccines, as observed from the graphs in Fig. 4.

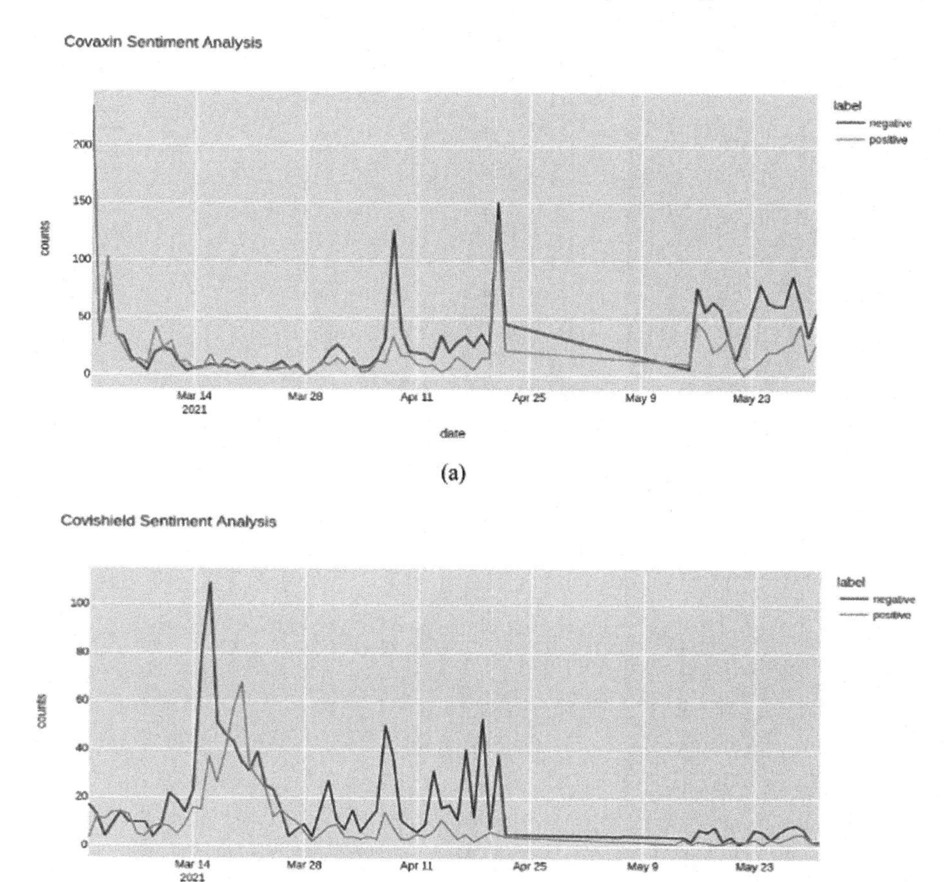

(b)

Fig. 4. Time-line graphs of public sentiments for (a) Covaxin and (b) Covishield vaccines from March 2021 to May 2021.

The term frequency in Natural Language Processing refers to the number of times a unigram occurs in a document. The set of highest frequency terms or unigrams indicates the class of the document [31]. We plot the word clouds of highest frequency adjective unigrams in Fig. 6 for the positive sentiments of Covaxin from the duration of March-May 2021, and also from June-September 2021. Likewise, we also plot the word clouds for the Covishield vaccine in Fig. 7.

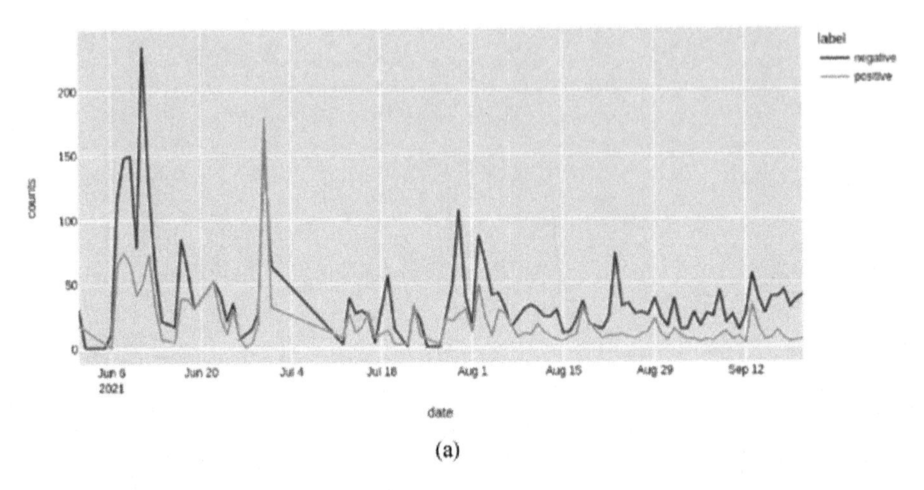

(a)

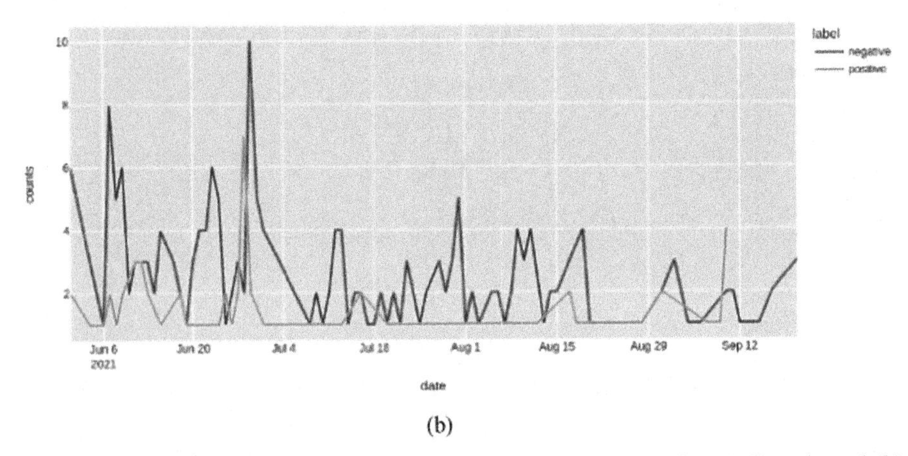

(b)

Fig. 5. (From top to bottom) Time-line graphs of public sentiments for (a) Covaxin and (b) Covishield vaccines from June 2021 to September 2021.

In the initial phase, from March 2021 to May 2021, Covishield garnered a lot of positive comments as observed from the large number of adjectives in Fig. 7 (a) as compared to Covaxin in Fig. 6 (a). It is noteworthy that the frequency of positive words used for Covaxin has increased as compared to Covishield in the more recent times (June to September 2021) as observed from the higher frequency of the adjectives "*good*", "*great*" and "*effective*" in Fig. 6 (b). Another notable fact is the mention of 2nd dose found in both word clouds pertaining to the June to September 2021 time span, which indicates the increased positivity in public sentiments towards vaccinations over time. Further analysis shows that people have expressed their appreciation towards Covaxin with words such as "*indian*" and "*indigenous*" to showcase the fact that Covaxin was

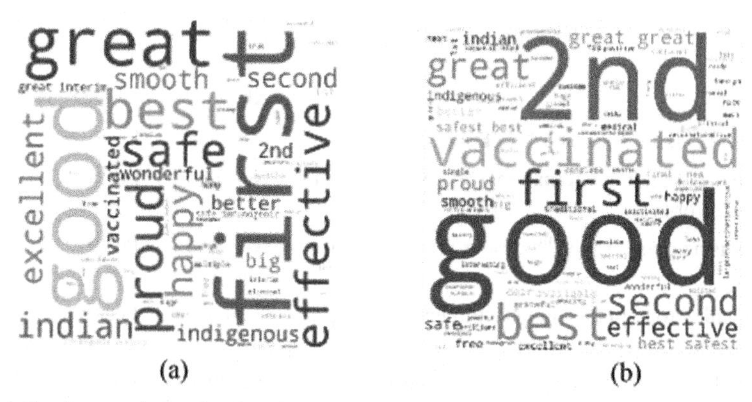

Fig. 6. Adjective word clouds of positive sentiments for Covaxin from (a) March 2021 to May 2021 (b) June 2021 to September 2021.

Fig. 7. Adjective word clouds of positive sentiments for Covishield from (a) March 2021 to May 2021 (b) June 2021 to September 2021.

made in India. We show some negative tweets in Table 2, that showcase the advantage that XLNet has over the unsupervised techniques of VADER and TextBlob. The last tweet containing mixed reviews is labeled as negative by XLNet since it was unable to detect the smiley emoticon that was correctly recognized by VADER and TextBlob.

Table 2. Instances of negative sentiment analysis.

Tweets	XLNet	VADER/TextBlob
But I will not take it because it's not safe	Negative	Positive
#Covaxin is not finding international takers even when supplied free of cost	Negative	Positive
#Covaxin is no good as the 2nd dose is reportedly not available	Negative	Positive
I am beginning to regret having #AstraZeneca vaccine. It's full of controversy	Negative	Positive
Arm hurts but head feels like it's been stomped… other than that I'm happy	Negative	Positive
Youngest cousin with his first vaccine shot:) #Covaxin Hyderabad, slots not easy	Negative	Positive

4 Conclusion

In this paper, supervised sentiment analysis of unlabeled tweets related to the two vaccines popularly administered in India: Covaxin and Covishield, was made possible by transfer learning using the latest transformer model XLNet, that is trained on a labeled non-Covid Twitter dataset. The transfer-learned model outperformed the unsupervised techniques of VADER and TextBlob that are currently used by most researchers for vaccine sentiment analysis, especially for the classification of the negative tweets. Analyzing the Covid-19 vaccine tweets dataset revealed that the negative tweets were more in case of both vaccines as compared to the positive tweets. The positive sentiments were found to have increased in the duration of June 2021 to September 2021 as the second wave gradually abated in India, as compared to the initial phase of March 2021 to May 2021 when the second wave attributed to the Delta variant peaked in India. The positive adjectives for the Indian-made domestic vaccine - Covaxin have increased as evident from the higher frequencies of the words – "*great*", "*best*", "*efficient*" and "*good*". Analyzing the tweets in two temporal phases for both the vaccines was beneficial as we were able to observe the public sentiments towards the two vaccines, and the vaccination process in general, as the second wave of the pandemic peaked and abated in India.

References

1. Rosenbaum, L.: Escaping catch-22—overcoming Covid vaccine hesitancy. N. Engl. J. Med. **384**(14), 1367–1371 (2021)
2. Yousefinaghani, S., Dara, R., Mubareka, S., Papadopoulos, A., Sharif, S.: An analysis of Covid-19 vaccine sentiments and opinions on Twitter. Int. J. Infect. Dis. **108**, 256–262 (2021)

3. Krishnan, G.S., Sowmya Kamath, S., Sugumaran, V.: Predicting vaccine hesitancy and vaccine sentiment using topic modeling and evolutionary optimization. In: Métais, E., Meziane, F., Horacek, H., Kapetanios, E. (eds.) Natural Language Processing and Information Systems, NLDB 2021. LNCS, vol. 12801, pp. 255–263. Springer, Cham (2021). https://doi.org/10.1007/978-3-030-80599-9_23
4. Bl, M., Midha, S., Ramana Murthy Oruganti, V.: Sentiment analysis in Indian sub-continent during Covid-19 second wave using twitter data. In: 2021 IEEE 9th Region 10 Humanitarian Technology Conference (R10-HTC), pp. 1–6. IEEE (2021)
5. Liu, S., Li, J., Liu, J.: Leveraging transfer learning to analyze opinions, attitudes, and behavioral intentions toward Covid-19 vaccines: social media content and temporal analysis. J. Med. Internet Res. **23**(8), e30251 (2021)
6. To, Q.G., et al.: Applying machine learning to identify anti-vaccination tweets during the Covid-19 pandemic. Int. J. Environ. Res. Public Health **18**(8), 4069 (2021)
7. Nguyen, T.T., Nguyen, Q.V.H., Nguyen, D.T., Hsu, E.B., Yang, S., Eklund, P.: Artificial intelligence in the battle against coronavirus (Covid-19): a survey and future research directions. arXiv preprint arXiv:2008.07343 (2020)
8. Vashishtha, S., Susan, S.: Fuzzy interpretation of word polarity scores for unsupervised sentiment analysis. In: 2020 11th International Conference on Computing, Communication and Networking Technologies (ICCCNT), pp. 1–6. IEEE (2020)
9. Hutto, C., Gilbert, E.: VADER: a parsimonious rule-based model for sentiment analysis of social media text. In: Proceedings of the International AAAI Conference on Web and Social Media, vol. 8(1) (2014)
10. Loria, S., Keen, P., Honnibal, M., Yankovsky, R., Karesh, D., Dempsey, E.: Textblob: simplified text processing. In: Secondary TextBlob: Simplified Text Processing, vol. 3 (2014)
11. Koto, F., Adriani, M.: A comparative study on twitter sentiment analysis: Which features are good? In: Biemann, C., Handschuh, S., Freitas, A., Meziane, F., Métais, E. (eds.) NLDB 2015. LNCS, vol. 9103, pp. 453–457. Springer, Cham (2015). https://doi.org/10.1007/978-3-319-19581-0_46
12. Ghosh, M., Gupta, K., Susan, S.: Aspect-based unsupervised negative sentiment analysis. In: Hemanth, J., Bestak, R., Chen, J.I.Z. (eds.) Intelligent Data Communication Technologies and Internet of Things, pp. 335–344. Springer, Singapore (2021). https://doi.org/10.1007/978-981-15-9509-7_29
13. Vashishtha, S., Susan, S.: Highlighting keyphrases using senti-scoring and fuzzy entropy for unsupervised sentiment analysis. Expert Syst. Appl. **169**, 114323 (2021)
14. Hu, T., et al.: Revealing public opinion towards Covid-19 vaccines using Twitter data in the United States: a spatiotemporal perspective. medRxiv (2021)
15. Na, T., Cheng, W., Li, D., Lu, W., Li, H.: Insight from NLP analysis: Covid-19 vaccines sentiments on social media. arXiv preprint arXiv:2106.04081 (2021)
16. Liu, S., Liu, J.: Public attitudes toward Covid-19 vaccines on English-language Twitter: a sentiment analysis. Vaccine **39**(39), 5499–5505 (2021)
17. Marcec, R., Likic, R.: Using Twitter for sentiment analysis towards AstraZeneca/Oxford, Pfizer/BioNTech and Moderna Covid-19 vaccines. Postgrad. Med. J., 1–7 (2021)
18. Sattar, N.S., Arifuzzaman, S.: Covid-19 vaccination awareness and aftermath: public sentiment analysis on twitter data and vaccinated population prediction in the usa. Appl. Sci. **11**(13), 6128 (2021)
19. Ghasiya, P., Okamura, K.: Investigating covid-19 news across four nations: a topic modeling and sentiment analysis approach. IEEE Access **9**, 36645–36656 (2021)
20. Nigam, K., McCallum, A.K., Thrun, S., Mitchell, T.: Text classification from labeled and unlabeled documents using EM. Mach. Learn. **39**(2), 103–134 (2000)

21. Zhang, L., Fan, H., Peng, C., Rao, G., Cong, Q.: Sentiment analysis methods for hpv vaccines related tweets based on transfer learning. In: Healthcare, vol. 8(3), p. 307. Multidisciplinary Digital Publishing Institute (2020)
22. Müller, M., Salathé, M., Kummervold, P.E.: Covid-twitter-bert: a natural language processing model to analyse covid-19 content on twitter. arXiv preprint arXiv:2005.07503 (2020)
23. Yang, Z., Dai, Z., Yang, Y., Carbonell, J., Salakhutdinov, R., Le, Q.V.: XLNet: generalized autoregressive pretraining for language understanding. In: Proceedings of the 33rd International Conference on Neural Information Processing Systems, pp. 5753–5763 (2019)
24. Rane, A., Kumar, A.: Sentiment classification system of twitter data for US airline service analysis. In: 2018 IEEE 42nd Annual Computer Software and Applications Conference (COMPSAC), vol. 1, pp. 769–773. IEEE (2018)
25. Sweidan, A.H., El-Bendary, N., Al-Feel, H.: Sentence-level aspect-based sentiment analysis for classifying adverse drug reactions (ADRs) using hybrid ontology-XLNet transfer learning. IEEE Access **9**, 90828–90846 (2021)
26. He, X., Li, V.O.: Show me how to revise: ımproving lexically constrained sentence generation with XLNet. In: Proceedings of the AAAI Conference on Artificial Intelligence, vol. 35(14), pp. 12989–12997 (2021)
27. Goel, R., Vashisht, S., Dhanda, A., Susan, S.: An empathetic conversational agent with attentional mechanism. In: 2021 International Conference on Computer Communication and Informatics (ICCCI), pp. 1–4. IEEE (2021)
28. Dai, Z., Yang, Z., Yang, Y., Carbonell, J.G., Le, Q., Salakhutdinov, R.: Transformer-XL: attentive language models beyond a fixed-length context. In: Proceedings of the 57th Annual Meeting of the Association for Computational Linguistics, pp. 2978–2988 (2019)
29. Koo, J., Lee, J.H., Pyo, J., Jo, Y., Lee, K.: Exploiting multi-modal features from pre-trained networks for Alzheimer's dementia recognition. arXiv preprint arXiv:2009.04070 (2020)
30. Goel, R., Susan, S., Vashisht, S., Dhanda, A.: Emotion-aware transformer encoder for empathetic dialogue generation. In: 2021 9th International Conference on Affective Computing and Intelligent Interaction Workshops and Demos (ACIIW), pp. 1–6. IEEE Computer Society (2021)
31. Susan, S., Keshari, J.: Finding significant keywords for document databases by two-phase Maximum Entropy Partitioning. Pattern Recogn. Lett. **125**, 195–205 (2019)

Improving Drift Detection by Monitoring Shapley Loss Values

Bastien Zimmermann(✉) and Matthieu Boussard(✉)

Research and Development, Craft.AI, Paris, France
{bastien.zimmermann,matthieu.boussard}@craft.ai

Abstract. Along the deployment of Machine Learning models rises an inherent need for monitoring, where model performances should be tracked as well as potential drifts. In a live environment, with evolving data, the risk is for the model to become ill-adapted for the given situation. The failure to detect drift while leading to a performance deterioration could also cause side effects due to model over-trust. Informing the user of any anomaly upon detection is the key to enabling any action. We propose Shap-ADWIN, a novel approach improving the performance of state-of-the-art drift detectors such as ADWIN by leveraging the information brought by Shapley Loss Values.

While common practice is to monitor the evolution of the loss of models at most for every predicted instance, the proposed solution monitors each individual instance and features the Shapley Loss value. Whenever the loss is attributed more toward a given feature the information becomes more contrasted, which enables a better detection. Indeed the signal-to-noise ratio is higher on that feature and allows the detector to leverage that information. The opposite case being equal Shapley values that are just the Loss under-scaled for every feature. Moreover, noise over the output would be equally distributed along with each Shapley Loss value of every feature providing lower information to noise ratio and allows a more reliable detection. We provide: a restricted proof, experiments and source code. Results were obtained using synthetically generated data presenting diverse types of drift, showing the performance of Shap-ADWIN over ADWIN.

Keywords: Shapley values · Drift-detection · ADWIN

1 Introduction

With the general development of Artificial Intelligence (AI) and Machine Learning (ML) algorithms, the risk for AI applications to encounter edge cases in which the systems perform or react in an unplanned or unexpected way rises. Consequently, it becomes essential to monitor the deployed models, that is to say, control the performances and impacts of the system in its environment. One major problem is unstable data dependencies, [13] as some inputs signals are unstable as they qualitatively and/or quantitatively change behavior over time.

All these evolutions can induce a performance degradation, the model being ill-suited to new environments or events. ML solutions facing drifts have to

M. El Yacoubi et al. (Eds.): ICPRAI 2022, LNCS 13364, pp. 455–466, 2022.
https://doi.org/10.1007/978-3-031-09282-4_38

change, re-adapt themselves as the solution they offer is no longer relevant. Drift monitoring presents three main challenges: identifying important changes over the data distribution, identifying the inadequacy of the ML model with respect to its context, and identifying key points to leverage in order to get the model back on track. Our study is focused on the first challenge: Determining when the underlying data distribution suddenly changes into a different one and hinders the model's behavior. While any unforeseen or unexpected change in the data is relevant in most cases, the point of interest is the model behavior. Although common approaches monitor the input data and the model loss separately, [10] presents the decomposition of the loss among the model's input features in order to improve problems identification and debugging.

In this article, we introduce Shap-ADWIN (Sect. 3), a novel algorithm to better detect this phenomenon. It combines interventional Shapley values and the Adaptive Windowing drift detector [1] in order to produce a more reliable and efficient detection. After computing the Shapley values, a detector is fed each feature Shap-Loss values. There is one Drift detector per feature, each dealing with the loss attribution for every value taken by this feature. Experimental results point that the newly introduced algorithm detects the drift more often and earlier compared to the alternative without Shapley values. Drifts can have many different characteristics, they may occur in the feature distributions, in the label distribution or it can even be the underlying concept learned that is changing. Furthermore, each one of these drifts may occur differently, with diverse patterns. A drift might be very sudden, abrupt or it may appear gradually. Accordingly to this diversity, our experimental setting is based around the generation of synthetic datasets presenting various drifts cases. Across the majority of the studied scenarios, Shap-ADWIN is shown to perform better compared to ADWIN w.r.t the metrics exposed. The code used for the experiments is available in a Github repository and can be found as supplementary material. https://github.com/craft-ai/shap-adwin

After first exploring related work on Drift Detection and Shapley values, we introduce our novel drift detector Shap-ADWIN. Along with the intuition behind the functioning of our approach a restricted mathematical proof is provided. Further on, experimental results are presented demonstrating the improvement brought by Shap-ADWIN over ADWIN and the impact on the detection of: the Shapley values background set, noise on the target label, and the variation of the detector hyper-parameter.

2 Related Work

2.1 Drift Detection

Calling *concept* the learned target, a *concept drift* is any change of the underlying data distribution. Drift velocity, severity, and patterns vary, designated as abrupt when the distribution transition is sudden or gradual when it changes progressively, it is incremental when the probability that observed instances belong to the new concept increases over time while the probability of the ones belonging to the previous concept decreases.

Over the different characteristics, drifts can be grouped into different types. [14] identifies the three types of drifts:

- A *Covariate Drift*: The input distribution changes over time.
- A *Prior probability shift*: The output distribution changes over time
- A *Concept shift* The relation between input and output changes over time.

In order to determine when those drifts occur, and doing so the fastest way possible, different drift detection methods exist. Obtaining this information is the keystone to any adaptation mechanism. Four types of drift detection methodologies exist [6]. These methods are based on either: Sequential analysis, Control Charts, Monitoring of two distribution or Contextual.

The evaluation of drift detectors can be made through many domain-dependant points of view. Not all drift detectors respond to the same requirements, thus evaluation metrics may differ. When dealing with well-identified drift, for instance when using synthetic datasets, the detector's performance can be measured through earliest detection, detection frequency, and mean duration until detection. These metrics allow clear and comparable results.

A classical robust detector is the ADaptive WINdowing drift (ADWIN) detector [1]. Through the monitoring of differences between distributions and the sliding window, it aims to the optimal window to handle best the concept drift. While old samples should be discarded as they aren't representative anymore, they might still be representative of an important learning aspect. Adjusting the window is one example of handling the stability-plasticity dilemma. The algorithm automatically adjusts the size of the window to keep a sufficient enough number of samples to detect a significant enough change in means.

ADWIN has a unique parameter [7]: the confidence level δ making it robust as there is no possibility of ill-tweaking other parameters. This real value between 0 and 1 impacts directly the cut threshold ϵ_{cut} this is the detection threshold. Moreover, as exposed by [14] ADWIN reaches some of the best results on benchmark data representative of many different drifts.

2.2 Shapley Values

In 1951 Lloyd Shapley introduced the Shapley Value as a solution to distribute the total value of a coalition to each player's contributions. It is a *"fair"* manner of sharing the payout of a game. The Shapley values $\phi_i(v)$ for a game v are the unique allocations that satisfy the following properties: With N the set of all players, S a given coalition of players, v the game-defining value function, ϕ_i Shapley value for player i.

1. **Efficiency:** The allocations add up to the difference in value between the grand coalition and the empty coalition.

$$\sum_{i \in N} \phi_i(v) = v(N) - v(\{\varnothing\}) \tag{1}$$

2. **Monotonicity:** If a player i increases a game v value more than they would for game v' for all possible remaining sets of players, then i's attribution for v should be greater than or equal to his attribution in v'.
3. **Symmetry:** Two players i, j that make equal marginal contribution to all coalitions receive the same allocation.
4. **Dummy:** A player i making 0 marginal contribution receives 0 allocation.
5. **Linearity:** For two games v and v' and their respective allocations $\phi_i(v)$ and $\phi_i(v')$, then the cooperative game defined as their sum $v = v'$ has allocations defined as the sum of each game's allocations.

$$\phi_i(v + v') = \phi_i(v) + \phi_i(v') \; ; \; \phi_i(av) = a\phi_i(v) \tag{2}$$

Thanks to those desirable properties, the Shapley values have been widely used in different contexts, notably in Artificial Intelligence. They can provide an estimation of the contribution of an algorithm to a portfolio, data valuation for a machine learning model, model agnostic approach to explain the output of machine learning models, [11], global feature contribution with additive importance measures [4], feature selection or even explaining non-linear model output transformations (such as the model's loss) [10].

This unique allocation, the Shapley value for the feature i of the game v takes the following form:

$$\phi_i(v) = \sum_{S \in N \setminus \{i\}} \frac{|S|!(|N| - |S| - 1)!}{|N!|}(v(S \cup i) - v(S)). \tag{3}$$

It is the average marginal contribution of that player for all possible permutations of remaining players:

2.3 Shapley Values for Machine Learning

Oppositely to the game-theory case it is not possible to assign credit for a ML model through Shapley values directly as most models require inputs with values for every feature, rather than a subset of features. To obtain local feature attribution it is required to define a set function $v(S)$ that is a *lift* of the original model $f(x) : \mathbb{R}^m \rightarrow \mathbb{R}^1, m \in \mathbb{N}$ [3,12]. In this context we assume the model to be a game where each feature is a player, the value of the game is the model output and the rules are defined by the representation learned by the model. While the choice of the lift is influential, the Shapley values computed throughout this study will use the *interventional conditional expectation*:

$$v(S) = \mathbb{E}_D[f(x)|do(X_S)]. \tag{4}$$

J. Pearl *do* operator for causal inference breaks the dependence between features [8]. It requires a background Distribution D (cf Sect. 4.1) that the foreground, sample to explain x^f will be compared to. For a single background instance x^b:

$$\mathbb{E}_D[f(x^f)|do(x_S)] = f(h^S), h_i^S = \begin{cases} x_i^f & \text{if } i \in S \\ x_i^b & \text{otherwise} \end{cases} \tag{5}$$

$$\phi_i(f, x^e, D) = \frac{1}{|D|} \sum_{x^b \in D} \phi_i(f, x^e, x^b). \tag{6}$$

This interventional approach is described to better reflect the model behavior [2], yet it can lead to computing Shapley values on points that are away from the true data manifold [5]. TreeSHAP detailed in [10] allows to compute quickly and exactly the interventional Shapley values for tree based algorithms.

2.4 Shapley Loss Values

Loss attribution through Shapley values provides different insights in comparison to the model output alternative. The interventional approach using a background distribution allows us to explain non linear transformations of the model output such as the loss. These local feature attributions that explain the per-sample loss can be used to identify the impact of a covariate shift with feature attributions [3] or signal problems that would have been hidden [10].

It defines as important the features whose absence degrades the model performances through this notion of predictive power of feature subsets (difference between the mean prediction and the one over features in our subset).

Given a loss function l, an instance x and its label y the reduction in risk over the mean prediction is defined as follow [4]:

$$v_{f,x,y}(S) = l(f_\varnothing(x_\varnothing), y) - l(f_S(x_S), y). \tag{7}$$

3 Shap-ADWIN: Drift Detection on Shapley Values

In order to improve the performance of a drift detector, we leverage the Shapley values loss attributions. By assigning a single detector to every single feature it monitors the feature Shapley loss values for each instance.

In this context, the signals seen by the detectors are continuous, even for classification problems the observation is focused on the log-loss resulting from the model output likelihood. Aside from the continuous constraint our method is detector agnostic. While we don't rely on any specific aspect, ADWIN is convenient as it simplifies the parameter-tuning task by relying on a single hyperparameter (δ) and performs well in many scenario. The ADWIN detector algorithm can be found in the appendix or in [1].

In the following algorithm Ad_i indicates the ADWIN detector receiving the Shapley values of the feature i, '*raises a Detection*' is used to indicate the detector returning a positive output signaling a Drift. $\phi_i(x)$ designates the Shapley Loss value of Feature i of the instance X. The computation of those values can be obtained with the TreeShap algorithm for a LGBM model using the logloss.

The complexity at each instance is

$$\mathcal{O}(\underbrace{(|D| \times (\#Nodes) \times (\#trees))}_{\text{TreeShap, D: Background set}} + \underbrace{log(W)}_{\text{ADWIN}} \times (\#feat)). \tag{8}$$

```
Result: Shap-ADWIN
for each feature i do
| Initialize Ad_i an ADWIN detector on feature i
end
for each instance x do
    compute φ(x) Shapley Loss Values of instance x for each feature i do
        Update Ad_i ADWIN detector with φ_i(x)
        if Ad_i raises a Detection then
        | output Detection
        end
    end
end
```

Algorithm 1: The Shap-ADWIN algorithm

3.1 Intuition

Due to the nature of Shapley loss values and the Symmetry axiom (cf 2.2), one could argue that the impact of noise on the loss should be the same across all features. As the detector leverages the information and ignores the noise, the bigger the ratio of information to noise the better the detector performs. The noisier the signal the more difficult it gets for scale-independent detectors to identify the occurrence of potential drifts.

Suppose now that the noise impact is uniform across all features, i.e. the loss increases uniformly with noise regardless of which feature it is from. Any discrepancy in information on a feature would be differently dispatched through Shapley values, whereas, the noise effect would be equally shared across every feature. The worst case being when the feature having equal contributions then the attributions would be a de-scaled version of the overall loss, any scale independent detector would then perform equally well.

3.2 Mathematical Foundations

Let's suppose that our model cannot learn from the noise ϵ and that our loss function f takes the following form: With F the set of features

$$f(x+\epsilon) = g(x) + h(\epsilon) \text{ , Where: } h(\epsilon) = \sum_{i \in F} \epsilon_i$$

Thanks to the Linearity property of Shapley values (Eq. 2), the Shapley value for the loss on feature i is:

$$\phi_{i,f}(x+\epsilon) = \phi_{i,g}(x) + \phi_{i,h}(\epsilon) = \phi_{i,g}(x) + \epsilon_i$$

We then define the following information to noise ratios for respectively Shapley values ϕ and the loss f:

$$R_{\phi_i} = \frac{\phi_{i,g}}{\epsilon_i}; R_f = \frac{g(x)}{\epsilon} \text{ , Where: } \epsilon = \sum_{i \in F} \epsilon_i; \epsilon_i, \epsilon \in \mathbb{R}^*$$

Theorem 1. *Let* $i \in F$, $\epsilon_i = \frac{\epsilon}{n}$ *with* $\epsilon \in \mathbb{R}^*$ *and* $n = |F|$

$$\exists k \text{ such as } R_{\phi_k} \geq R_f$$

Proof. Thanks to the efficiency property (Eq. 1) we can write:

$$\frac{g(x)}{\epsilon} = \frac{\sum \phi_{i,g}}{\epsilon}$$

$$\exists k, R_{\phi_k} \geq R_f \iff \exists k, \frac{\phi_{k,g}}{\epsilon_k} \geq \frac{\sum_{i \in F} \phi_{i,g}}{\epsilon}$$

Depending on the sign of ϵ we can chose either $max(\phi)$ or $min(\phi)$ as index k.

Whenever this inequality is verified, a drift detector will perform better on a feature Shapley-Loss attributions. (Cf 3.1)

With a more general definition of the noise (removing the $\forall i \in F$, $\epsilon_i = \frac{\epsilon}{n}$ constraint), it is possible to show that: the ratio between the discrepancies among Shapley values and the discrepancies among noise values being bigger than the ratio of a given feature k Shapley value and its noise is sufficient to have: $R_{\phi_k} \geq R_f$. Having bigger discrepancies among Shapley values than discrepancies among noise values is sufficient to ensure a better ratio on one feature Shapley value.

4 Experimental Results

Most experiments are based on a synthetically generated circle dataset. This dataset is defined using a fixed number of features where for each point each feature value is randomly sampled. The labels are generated by a hyper-sphere, if the point is inside the label is True otherwise False, this is our circle concept. Note that this simple concept is convenient as it cannot be perfectly learned by tree based models due to its curved nature.

The data is generated in two steps. First is the feature generation; with a default number of three, for each feature, the values are sampled from a uniform distribution over $[0, 1)$. The second is setting the decision boundary; each instance is checked to be inside or outside of the decision boundary (hyper-sphere) and the label is respectively set to "True" and "False".

That generative process is then modified to incorporate a drift pattern in it.

1. **Abrupt Concept Drift:** At index i change the hyper-sphere decision boundary to other parameters (center coordinates and radius).
2. **Gradual Concept Drift:** From index i to index $i + Width$ move the hyper-sphere decision boundary center by $\delta_t = \frac{center_B - center_A}{Width}$ at each step.
3. **Covariate Drift:** For a given feature and a given zone (range of indexes) limit the feature values to be sampled from a uniform distribution over [a,b), where $a >= 0$ and $b <= 1$

By default, any part of the generated data that is not modified by any drift pattern is assigned a hyper-sphere of $center = (0.4, 0.4, 0.4), radius = 0.25$ in 3 dimensions as a default decision boundary. For each Drift case the change can be applied along a single axis or using all available dimensions.

The other datasets used are classical methods taken from the drift literature:

1. **Sine1** (Abrupt concept drift): Two attributes x and y uniformly distributed in $[0, 1]$. The class is define according to $y = sin(x)$ positive if under the curve; negative otherwise. At a drift point, the class labels are reversed.
2. **Sine2**: Identical to Sine1 with $y = 0.5 + 0.3 * sin(3\pi x)$.
3. **Stagger** (with abrupt concept drift): This dataset contains three nominal attributes, namely *size*, *color*, and *shape*. The positive decision shifts from $[color = red$ and $size = small]$ to $[color = green$ or $shape = circular]$.

Without loss of generality, the model used is LGBMClassifier [9] with default parameters to use Tree-SHAP and minimize computational costs by having efficient computation of exact Shapley values.

Each detector performance is evaluated using: False and True positive rates (FP, TP) of detection, Min, Mean, Median, Max, and standard deviation (STD). The aforementioned metrics are the respective statistical function computed on several drift detection simulation e.g. the mean detection over 50 iteration of ADWIN on the Sine1 dataset. The unit is the number of instances and the origin is the drift starting point.

Overall results are presented in Fig. 1. The methods are ranked based on TP then Median, Mean, and STD. For each row-pair the best performing method is in bold. $+, -, =$ indicate the relative performance with respect to the other method, the colors green and red indicate respectively a better and a worse relative performance. The unit is in number of instances.

The Shap-ADWIN drift detector outperforms ADWIN in all but one Drift scenario (cf. Fig. 1). Drifts impacting a single feature increase the performance discrepancies between Shap-ADWIN and ADWIN compared to drift on all features. When the drift is localized on a single variable all indicators present bigger discrepancies, except minimum detection in the gradual concept drift case. The worst-case makes Shap-ADWIN slightly less stable with a higher standard deviation and higher mean detection, however, the median detection is equal i.e. in half of the cases both approaches detect the problem before the same median point (Fig. 2). This occurs for an Abrupt Covariate Drift on all features, all other scenarios present Shap-ADWIN as the better alternative.

4.1 Background Dataset

Interventional Shapley Values require a background dataset for their computation. This set of points is estimated to represent the prior over our data. Common practice is to sample at random a sufficient amount of points and it provides sound results. To investigate the impact of different background sets on Drift detection, 4 heuristics were developed where each background is filled

Drift	Method	FP	TP	Min	Mean	STD	Max	Median
Gradual Concept - A	**SHAP**	0.01	1.0	459	1686	236	2187	1675
	ADWIN	-0.01	-0.24	-64	+976	+300	+2208	+992
Gradual Concept - B	**SHAP**	0.0	1.0	779	1501	201	1931	1451
	ADWIN	=	=	+576	+326	+58	+608	+368
Abrupt Concept - A	**SHAP**	0.0	1.0	75	307	77	459	331
	ADWIN	+0.01	-0.06	+192	+1312	+821	+2752	+1120
Abrupt Concept - B	**SHAP**	0.0	1.0	107	323	76	523	331
	ADWIN	=	=	-32	+152	+193	+1728	+64
Abrupt Covariate - A	**SHAP**	0.0	1.0	119	289	147	1399	279
	ADWIN	=	-0.01	=	+131	+178.00	+1248	+96
Abrupt Covariate - B	SHAP	0.0	1.0	23	73	28	183	55
	ADWIN	=	=	=	-8	-11.00	-96	=
Stagger - single Drift	**SHAP**	0.0	1.0	103	159	16	167	167
	ADWIN	=	=	+64	+8	-16.00	=	=
Sine 1 - single Drift	**SHAP**	0.0	1.0	71	71	0	71	71
	ADWIN	=	=	+32	+32	=	+32	+32
Sine 2 - single Drift	**SHAP**	0.0	1.0	39	47	21	103	39
	ADWIN	=	=	+32	+24	-21.00	-32	+32

Fig. 1. Shap-ADWIN and ADWIN drift detector relative performances facing Drift. (A: single feature drift, B: all features drift)

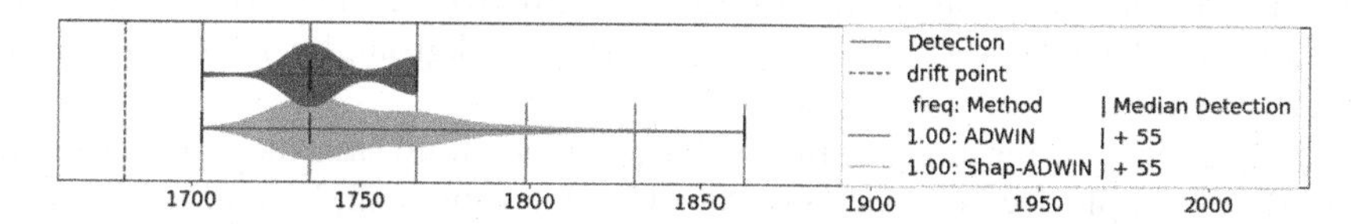

Fig. 2. Detection Distribution per detector over 50 iterations Covariate Abrupt Drift on all features (Most competitive case) (violins present the probability density smoothed by a kernel density estimator)

picking from a pool of consecutive instances in the training set: **Small background:** 2 points at random, **Best background:** 10% lowest loss points, **Worse background:** 10% highest loss points, **Random background:** 10% points at random.

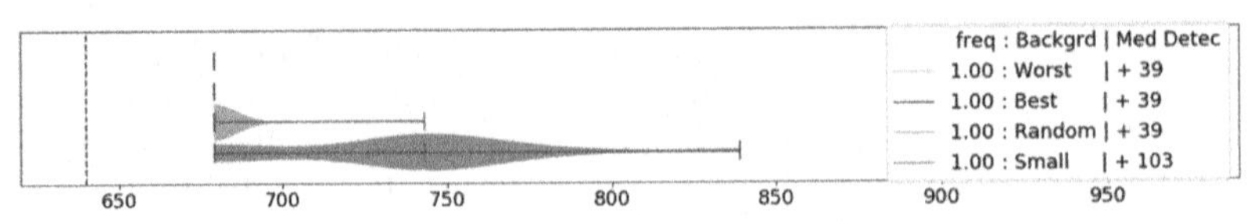

(a) Background impact on detection distribution - Sine2 dataset - ShapAdwin

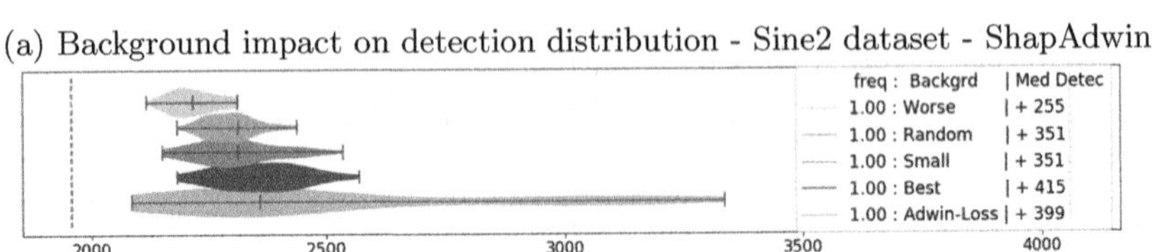

(b) Background impact on detection distribution - Circle abrupt concept Drift

Fig. 3. Background heuristics impact on detection

Results Fig. 3a was generated using a Sine2 dataset comporting a single abrupt concept drift. The background choice is the only varying factor, in this case it has a very small impact. Picking values under-representative of our data such as outliers can lead to worse performances the small backgrounds do not contain sufficient information and the resulting average detection takes longer.

Best and Worse background filling methods results are sensibly different compared to the random alternative. Changing the information in the background dataset that represents our prior does have an impact on the distribution of the resulting Shapley values. Coincidentally, the Best background performs relatively better than its alternatives Fig. 3b.

Finding efficient methods to fill the background could save many resources as TreeSHAP complexity is linear in terms of background samples and it is used at every sample. For a stable stream that drifts rarely a small efficient background would be highly beneficial.

4.2 Influence of Noise on Drift Detection

To investigate the impact of noise, we flipped at random 5% of labels in the dataset. Figure 4 Compare the performances on the same dataset with and without noise for both detectors. For Shap-ADWIN the noise has no impact on the detection rate and a small increase in detection latency is seen. ADWIN fails to detect reliably in a noisy context and the detection latency increases significantly. Our method is particularly fitted to overcome this kind of noise.

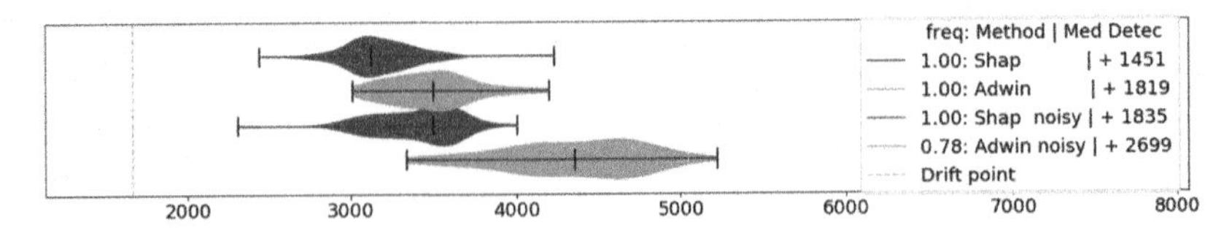

Fig. 4. Noise impact on detec distrib; Gradual concept drift on all feat. ($\delta = 0.01$)

4.3 Influence of Sensitivity of the Detector

We investigate the influence of the δ hyper-parameter for the drift detector ADWIN. The confidence level indicates the sensitivity selected for the detector, the higher the more confident the detector is.

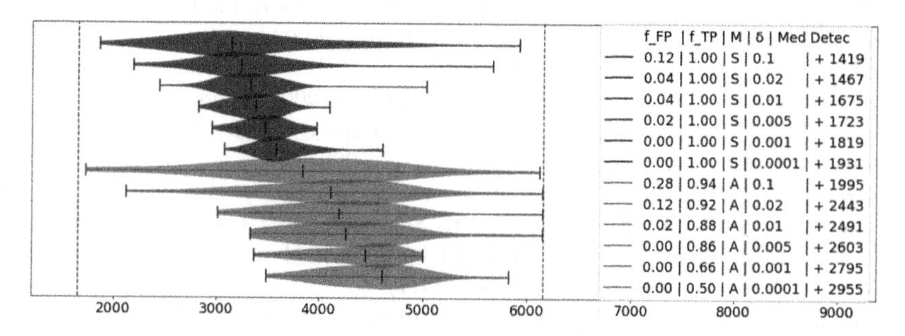

Fig. 5. Impact of ADWIN δ on Detection Distribution (**S**: Shap-ADWIN, **A**: ADWIN, **f_FP**: freq False Positive, **f_TP**: freq True Positive)

Figure 5 is generated comparing ADWIN and Shap-ADWIN detection policies for several values of δ, re-generating the dataset (gradual concept drift - CIRCLE on all 3 features and a transition period of 2000 instances) several times. The top section presents the false detection i.e. occurring before the drift appearance. The bottom one contains true detection.

Within the range of δ tested, Shap-ADWIN is better than any ADWIN as it has and earlier, more reliable and more consistent detection. High δ values cause some false detection, however, there is no clear difference between Shap-ADWIN and ADWIN here, the choice of δ has more impact than the method chosen. Here, Shap-ADWIN is better than ADWIN regardless of any δ choice.

5 Conclusion

Combining the strength of drift detectors with Shapley values provides a more reliable and more stable drift detection. The new approach proposed monitors the loss on each feature for a ML model with an ADWIN drift detector fed with Shapley Loss values. We showed that this result holds regardless of global noise or the detector's tuning. Shap-ADWIN is a better alternative to ADWIN. Finally, the choice of the background dataset is non-trivial and some filling heuristics can provide several advantages for both detection performance and complexity. Improving drift detection brings substantial benefits to any deployed ML-based systems, which is why it is essential to keep improving those methods.

In future work, we'll include this new detector in a re-training setting and experiment with its performances on real-world datasets getting closer to a real-life deployment setting.

References

1. Bifet, A., Gavaldà, R.: Learning from time-changing data with adaptive windowing, vol. 7, April 2007. https://doi.org/10.1137/1.9781611972771.42
2. Chen, H., Janizek, J.D., Lundberg, S., Lee, S.I.: True to the model or true to the data? arXiv:2006.16234 [cs, stat], June 2020
3. Chen, H., Lundberg, S.M., Lee, S.: Explaining a series of models by propagating local feature attributions. CoRR abs/2105.00108 (2021)
4. Covert, I., Lundberg, S., Lee, S.: Understanding global feature contributions through additive importance measures. CoRR abs/2004.00668 (2020)
5. Frye, C., Rowat, C., Feige, I.: Asymmetric shapley values: incorporating causal knowledge into model-agnostic explainability (2020)
6. Gama, J., Žliobaitė, I., Bifet, A., Pechenizkiy, M., Bouchachia, A.: A survey on concept drift adaptation. ACM Comput. Surv. **46**(4), 44:1–44:37 (2014)
7. Gomes, H.M., et al.: Adaptive random forests for evolving data stream classification. Mach. Learn. **106**(9), 1469–1495 (2017)
8. Janzing, D., Minorics, L., Blöbaum, P.: Feature relevance quantification in explainable AI: a causality problem. arXiv abs/1910.13413 (2020)
9. Ke, G., et al.: LightGBM: a highly efficient gradient boosting decision tree. In: Guyon, I., et al. (eds.) Advances in Neural Information Processing Systems, vol. 30 (2017)
10. Lundberg, S.M., et al.: From local explanations to global understanding with explainable AI for trees. Nat. Mach. Intell. **2**, 56–67 (2020)
11. Lundberg, S.M., Lee, S.I.: A unified approach to interpreting model predictions. In: Advances in Neural Information Processing Systems 30 (2017)
12. Merrill, J., Ward, G., Kamkar, S., Budzik, J., Merrill, D.C.: Generalized integrated gradients: a practical method for explaining diverse ensembles. arXiv abs/1909.01869 (2019)
13. Sculley, D., et al.: Hidden technical debt in machine learning systems. In: Annual Conference on Neural Information Processing System (2015)
14. Souza, V.M.A., dos Reis, D.M., Maletzke, A.G., Batista, G.E.A.P.A.: Challenges in benchmarking stream learning algorithms with real-world data. Data Min. Knowl. Discov. **34**(6), 1805–1858 (2020)

Interpolation Kernel Machine and Indefinite Kernel Methods for Graph Classification

Jiaqi Zhang[1], Cheng-Lin Liu[2,3], and Xiaoyi Jiang[1(✉)]

[1] Faculty of Mathematics and Computer Science, University of Münster, Einsteinstrasse 62, 48149 Münster, Germany
xjiang@uni-muenster.de

[2] National Laboratory of Pattern Recognition, Institute of Automation of Chinese Academy of Sciences, Beijing 100190, People's Republic of China

[3] School of Artificial Intelligence, University of Chinese Academy of Sciences, Beijing 10049, People's Republic of China

Abstract. Graph kernels have been studied for a long time and applied among others for graph classification. In this paper we bring two novel aspects into the graph processing community. Currently, the backbone for kernel-based classification is solely the support vector machine. We introduce the interpolation kernel machine for this purpose. In addition, for both support vector machine and interpolation kernel machine, many kernels used in practice do not satisfy the formal requirements (e.g. positive definiteness). We thus introduce extensions of the standard version to indefinite kernel methods. We argue and experimentally demonstrate why these two aspects should be considered for graph classification. One of our conclusions will be that the interpolation kernel machine is a good alternative of support vector machine. Consequently, we will propose an extended experimental protocol. With this work we contribute to increasing the methodological plurality in the graph processing community.

1 Introduction

Kernel-based methods in machine learning have sound mathematical foundation and provide powerful tools in numerous fields. In addition to classification and regression [7,22], they also have successfully contributed to other tasks such as clustering [34], dimensionality reduction (e.g. PCA [15]), consensus learning [25], computer vision [17], and recently to studying deep neural networks [10].

Graph kernels provide a way to compute similarities between graphs [13,16, 27]. As such they can be used for graph classification, in particular with Support Vector Machine (SVM) but not only. Graph kernels have been studied for a long time. In this work we address two aspects that are unexplored in the literature so far: interpolation kernel machine (IKM) and indefinite kernel methods.

First, we will look at a particular class of kernel-based classification methods, the so-called IKM, which has undeservedly hardly received attention in the literature. The recent work [3] brought it more attention in the research community

M. El Yacoubi et al. (Eds.): ICPRAI 2022, LNCS 13364, pp. 467–479, 2022.
https://doi.org/10.1007/978-3-031-09282-4_39

and serves as the base of our work. Despite the diversity in the design of graph kernels, their use for classification is rather monotonous, namely by using support vector machines (SVM). This is also reflected in the recent survey papers for graph kernels: "The criteria used for prediction are SVM for classification" [13]; "We performed classification experiments using the C-SVM implementation LIBSVM" [16]; "In the case of graph kernels, to perform graph classification, we employed a Support Vector Machine (SVM) classifier and in particular, the LIBSVM implementation" [27]. This is not a surprise due to the dominance of SVM in machine learning in general. However, SVM is not the only choice one can have. In this work we will demonstrate the power of IKM for graph classification.

Second, kernel methods typically require some properties of the kernel function to be satisfied. For instance, the SVM is formulated for positive semidefinite kernels. Similarly, IKMs require positive definite kernels. In practice, however, many kernels are not of these two types. Therefore, the standard version of the kernel method (SVM or IKM) cannot be applied. Instead, we need to apply indefinite kernel methods to cope with such cases.

This paper does not present new methods for graph classification. Instead, it can be understood as a position paper. We bring the two aspects sketched above into the graph processing community. We argue and experimentally demonstrate why they should be considered. One of our conclusions will be that IKM is a good alternative of SVM. Consequently, we will propose an extended experimental protocol that is beyond the currently dominating practice.

The remainder of the paper is organized as follows. We present the fundamentals of graph kernels in Sect. 2. The IKM is introduced in Sect. 3. Then, we discuss the indefinite kernel methods for both SVM and IKM in Sect. 4. The experimental results are presented in Sect. 5, which motivates an extended experimental protocol in Sect. 6. Finally, Sect. 7 concludes the paper.

2 Graph Kernels

A kernel function $k(x, y)$ over the space of graphs $\mathcal{G}$ is defined by $k\colon \mathcal{G} \times \mathcal{G} \to \mathbb{R}$ with a related transformation $\phi : \mathcal{G} \to \mathcal{H}_k$ into a Hilbert space $\mathcal{H}_k$ so that $k(x, y) = \langle \phi(x), \phi(y) \rangle$, i.e. the kernel function corresponds to the scalar product in $\mathcal{H}_k$. If for any $n \in \mathbb{N}$ and all sets of n graphs, $g_1, g_2, ..., g_n \in \mathcal{G}$, a kernel $k(x, y)$ gives rise to a positive semidefinite kernel (Gram) matrix $K \in \mathbb{R}^{n \times n}$ with elements $K(i, j) = k(g_i, g_j)$, then it is called a *positive semidefinite* (PSD) kernel. Making the requirement stronger to ask for positive definite kernel matrix, then the kernel is *positive definite* (PD). Note that the terminology in the literature is not consistent. Some researchers define positive definite kernels as those with positive semidefinite kernel matrix [6]. The terminology used in our work is due to its clarity and helps to avoid potential confusion.

Dozens of graph kernels have been developed [13,16,27], which focus on specific structural properties of graphs. The key design ideas behind these graph kernels differ, e.g. based on Weisfeiler-Lehman test of graph isomorphism [31], paths [4], and graph decomposition [21]. Meanwhile, public graph kernel libraries are also available [12,32].

3 Interpolation Kernel Machines

Kernels are an efficient way to compute the similarity of two samples in a high dimensional space. In this section we introduce a technique to fully interpolate the training data using kernel functions, known as kernel machines [3,11]. Note that this term has been often used in research papers (e.g. [9,37]), where variants of support vector machines are effectively meant. For the sake of clarity we will use the term "interpolation kernel machine" throughout the paper.

Let $X = \{x_1, x_2, \ldots, x_n\} \subset \Omega^n$ be a set of n training samples with their corresponding targets $Y = \{y_1, y_2, \ldots, y_n\} \subset \mathcal{T}^n$ in the target space. The sets are sorted so that the corresponding training sample and target have the same index. A function $f : \Omega \to \mathcal{T}$ interpolates this data iif:

$$f(x_i) = y_i, \quad \forall i \in 1, \ldots, n \tag{1}$$

Representer Theorem. Let $k : \Omega \times \Omega \to \mathbb{R}$ be a PSD kernel for some domain Ω, X and Y a set of training samples and targets as defined above, and $g : [0, \infty) \to \mathbb{R}$ a strictly monotonically increasing function for regulation. We define E as an error function that calculates the loss L of f on the whole sample set with:

$$E(X,Y) = E((x_1, y_1), ..., (x_n, y_n)) = \frac{1}{n} \sum_{i=1}^{n} L(f(x_i), y_i) + g(\|f\|) \tag{2}$$

Then, the function $f^* = \text{argmin}_f\{E(X,Y)\}$ that minimizes the error E has the form:

$$f^*(z) = \sum_{i=1}^{n} \alpha_i k(z, x_i) \quad \text{with } \alpha_i \in \mathbb{R} \tag{3}$$

The proof can be found in many textbooks, e.g. [30]. While this statement of the representer theorem gives sufficient conditions on the regularizer, an interesting theoretical extension was given in [1]. The authors showed that an interpolation problem (2) admits solutions representable in the form (3) *if and only if* the regularizer is a nondecreasing function of the Hilbert space norm, thus providing a complete characterization of regularizers that give rise to representer theorems. The recent work [29] studies the same problem in a more general context where the regularizer does not have to be norm-based.

The family of representer theorems like the above is among the fundamental results of learning theory. They allow us to express the optimal solution of certain risk minimization problems in the form (2) as linear combination of expansions in terms of the training samples. Since the various variants of SVM optimization problems can be casted into (2) [30], the representer theorem builds the theoretical foundation for the powerful SVMs. They operate in the finite dimensional space of the training samples mapped into feature space. This is particularly attractive since for many popular PSD kernels, the Hilbert space is known to be infinite dimensional [30].

We now can use f^* from Eq. (3) to interpolate our training data. Note that the only learnable parameters are $\alpha = (\alpha_1, \ldots, \alpha_n)$, a real-valued vector with the same length as the number of training samples. Learning α is equivalent to solving the system of linear equations:

$$K(\alpha_1^*, ..., \alpha_n^*)^T = (y_1, ..., y_n)^T \tag{4}$$

where $K \in \mathbb{R}^{n \times n}$ is the kernel matrix. In case of PD kernel k the kernel matrix K is invertible. Therefore, we can find the optimal α^* to construct f^* by:

$$(\alpha_1^*, ..., \alpha_n^*)^T = K^{-1}(y_1, ..., y_n)^T \tag{5}$$

After learning, the interpolation kernel machine then uses the interpolating function from Eq. (3) to make prediction for test samples. Note that solving the optimal parameters α^* in (5) in a naive manner requires computation of order $\mathcal{O}(n^3)$ and is thus not feasible for large-scale applications. A highly efficient solver EigenPro has been developed [20] to enable significant speedup for training on GPUs. Another recent work [35] applies an explainable AI technique for sample condensation of interpolation kernel machines.

In this work we focus on classification problems. In this case $f(z)$ is encoded as a one-hot vector $f(z) = (f_1(z), \ldots f_c(z))$ with $c \in \mathbb{N}$ being the number of output classes. This requires c times repeating the learning process above, one for each component of the one-hot vector. This computation can be formulated as follows. Let $A_l = (\alpha_{l1}^*, ..., \alpha_{ln}^*)$ be the parameters to be learned and $Y_l = (y_{l1}, ..., y_{ln})$ target values for each component $l = 1, ..., c$. The learning of interpolation kernel machine becomes:

$$K\underbrace{\left(A_1^T, ..., A_c^T\right)}_{A} = \underbrace{\left(Y_1^T, ..., Y_c^T\right)}_{Y} \tag{6}$$

with the unique solution:

$$A = K^{-1} \cdot Y \tag{7}$$

which is the extended version of Eq. (5) for c classes and results in zero error on training data. When predicting a test sample z, the output vector $f(z)$ is not a probability vector in general. The class which gets the highest output value is considered as the predicted class. If needed, e.g. for the purpose of classifier combination, the output vector (z) can also be converted into a probability vector by applying the softmax function. We will explore this option in Sect. 4.2.

4 Indefinite Kernel Methods

We first discuss the need of indefinite kernel methods. Then, the different possibilities of indefinite kernel methods will be presented. Due to our focus on IKM in this paper we will start with indefinite IKMs and continue with indefinite SVMs.

4.1 Need of Indefinite Kernel Methods

Kernel-based methods typically require some properties of the kernel function to be satisfied. The SVM is formulated for PSD kernels. Similarly, interpolation kernel machines require PD kernels to guarantee the invertibility of kernel matrix K. If such requirements are satisfied, these kernel methods can be safely used.

The situation is more complex if these formal requirements are violated. In case of non-PSD kernels the SVM formulation is no longer guaranteed to be convex, thus resulting in a non-convex optimization problem. For interpolation kernel machines only PD kernels can guarantee the invertibility of the kernel matrix K. It is however important to point out that a violation of the formal requirement merely means no guarantee of the applicability of SVM or interpolation kernel machine in general, i.e. for all possible training datasets. Particular training datasets, however, may exist that lead to PSD and PD kernel matrix so such the kernel methods can still be applied in such specific cases.

Let $\mathcal{P}(\mathcal{G})$ denote the power set of $\mathcal{G}$, i.e. all subsets of $\mathcal{G}$, each representing a dataset of graphs. When working with some kernel method, we consider a set of datasets $\mathcal{P}^*(\mathcal{G}) \subseteq \mathcal{P}(\mathcal{G})$ that contains all datasets in $\mathcal{P}(\mathcal{G})$ violating the formal requirement of the particular kernel method. These are those datasets that cannot be handled by the standard version of the kernel method (SVM or interpolation kernel machine). $\mathcal{P}^*$ cannot be neglected. Thus, there is a need of developing indefinite kernel methods to cope with such datasets.

Many real-world applications favor the direct use of similarity measures as kernel, most of which are neither PD or PSD. There are several reasons of still using such kernels [28]. For instance, they produce good performance, but it is difficult to prove the formal requirement. In structural pattern recognition, many of the graph kernels [13,16,27] are PSD at best. The need of indefinite kernel methods is thus a real issue.

4.2 Indefinite Interpolation Kernel Machines

There was, to our knowledge, no previous work on infinite interpolation kernel machines yet. Recently, we developed five such methods [39]. A comparative study showed superior performance of two methods called **LSQ** and **CE** over the others. They will be briefly described in the following and used in our experiments.

LSQ Method. We aim at finding a subset of training data $X^* \subset X$ of maximum size such that the kernel matrix K^* corresponding to X^* is invertible. This can be easily achieved by determining the rank m of the original kernel matrix K and reducing K to m independent rows, say by Gaussian elimination. These rows after the elimination process directly specify the related m training samples from X that build the reduced training set X^*. Note that we assume a reasonably high rank m in order not to lose too many training samples. Our experimental results show that this requirement is well satisfied.

A straightforward solution here is to use the reduced X^* for training only, i.e. applying Eq. (6) and (7) using K^*. An interesting alternative turns out to be still using the complete training set X for training in order to keep as much information as possible. After training, only X^* is kept to build the learned interpolation kernel machine. In this case we need to learn the parameters $A_l = (\alpha^*_{l1}, ..., \alpha^*_{lm})$, $l = 1, ..., c$, based on the target values $Y_l = (y_{l1}, ..., y_{ln})$. The learning task formulated in Eq. (6) now evolves to:

$$K_{nm}A = Y \tag{8}$$

where $K_{nm}(i,j) = k(x_i, x_j)$, $i = 1, ..., n$, $j = 1, ..., m$. Because of $n > m$ this is an overdetermined system of linear equations. Thus, it is no longer possible to obtain zero training error. The typical solution is the least-square method that means in our case minimizing:

$$E_{\text{lq}} = ||K_{nm}A - Y||^2 \tag{9}$$

We minimize E_q by using the BFGS optimization algorithm.

CE Method. For classification, however, the least-square formulation may not be suitable. Instead, it is general practice to use the cross entropy as loss function. Let $[]_l$ be the l-th row of a matrix. Then, $[K_{nm}A]_l$, see Eq. (8), corresponds to the output vector of the interpolation kernel machine for training sample x_l and $[Y]_l$ the related target vector. The cross entropy loss is defined by:

$$E_{ce} = -\sum_{i=1}^{n}\sum_{l=1}^{c} \{[Y]_i\}_l \cdot \log\{\Gamma([K_{nm}A]_i)\}_l \tag{10}$$

where Γ is the softmax operator that converts a vector to a probability vector and the notation $\{\}_l$ means the l-th element of a vector. This formulation, however, is no longer analytically solvable. We minimize E_{ce} by BFGS optimization algorithm using the least-square solution above as initialization.

4.3 Indefinite Support Vector Machines

Indefinite SVM has been intensively studied before. This is essentially a non-convex optimization problem. The proposed techniques can be divided into four categories: kernel approximation, kernel transformation, non-convex optimization, and Kreĭn space solutions. Methods of the first two categories obtain a PD kernel from an indefinite one so that a convex solver can be applied afterwards.

Kernel Approximation: One can derive a PD kernel that is an approximation of a given indefinite kernel (e.g. [33]). The conformal transformation and conformal linear combination proposed in [23] look for a PSD matrix that is the closest to an indefinite matrix (by means of some auxiliary PSD matrix).

Kernel Transformation: The indefinite kernel matrix is modified to become PSD. Let K be a real symmetric $n \times n$ indefinite matrix. Its spectral decomposition leads to $K = U_n \Lambda_n U_n^T = \sum_{i=1}^{n} \lambda_i u_i u_i^T$, where Λ_n is a diagonal matrix of the eigenvalues λ_i of K and U_n is an orthogonal matrix whose columns u_i

correspond to the normalized eigenvectors of K. Simple kernel transformation methods [18,23] include clip (setting negative eigenvalues to zero), shift (eliminating negative eigenvalues by adding a positive constant), flip (fliping the sign of negative eigenvalues), and square (eigenvalues are squared, which is equivalent to using KK^T instead of K).

Non-convex Optimization: These optimization techniques can be used to directly deal with indefinite matrices without kernel matrix modification (see [18,36] for detailed discussion). A SMO-type optimization is applied in [5] which is the basis of the popular LIBSVM solver. The recent work [36,38] directly focuses on the non-convex primal form of IKSVM (instead of the dual form) and solves a related problem of difference of convex programming.

Kreĭn Space Solutions: There exist rather few methods of this category. The works [18] considers IKSVM in Kreĭn spaces, where the positiveness axiom is no longer required in contrast to Hilbert spaces.

Some other methods do not fit the above categorization well. For instance, the authors of [19] view the indefinite kernel as a noisy instance of a true kernel and then learn an explicit solution for the optimal kernel with a tractable convex optimization problem.

Despite this development of indefinite SVM it has been hardly used for graph classification yet. The work [14] is a typical example, which follows the research line of [2]. Many natural similarity functions are not PSD kernels. Instead of squeezing these functions into PSD versions, a theory of learning with well defined "good" similarity functions is proposed. Here it is the place where indefinite SVM should come into play to work with such non-PSD similarity functions. However, only the standard SVM was used in [14]. This is simply a practical way of doing things, as remarked in [16]: "kernel methods, such as SVMs, have been found to work well empirically also with indefinite kernels (Johansson and Dubhashi 2015), without enjoying the guarantees that apply to positive definite kernels". Doing it this way, however, the geometric interpretation of SVM (i.e. optimal hyperplane classifier by margin maximization) gets lost. Only for the subclass of non conditionally positive definite kernels there exists an alternate geometric interpretation [6] (minimization of distances between convex hulls in pseudo-Euclidean spaces).

5 Experimental Results

We have considered 18 graph datasets from various domains (see Table 1 for an overview). Six PSD graph kernels were selected for the experiments: shortest-path kernel [4], neighborhood hash kernel [8], Weisfeiler-Lehman graph kernel [31], tree-based graph decomposition kernel [21], propagation kernel [24], and pyramid match kernel [26]. The main selection criterion are the diverse design paradigms of these kernels. We used the implementations from the graph kernel library GraKeL written in Python [32]. For each pair of dataset and graph kernel, we conducted a ten-fold cross validation and report the average performance.

Table 1. Description of graph datasets.

Domain	Dataset	# graphs	# classes	avg. # nodes	avg. # edges
Chemistry	BZR	405	2	35.8	38.4
	BZR_MD	306	2	21.3	225.1
	COX2	467	2	41.2	43.5
	COX2_MD	303	2	26.3	335.1
	DHFR	467	2	42.4	44.5
	DHFR_MD	393	2	23.9	283.0
	ER_MD	446	2	21.3	234.9
	MUTAG	188	2	17.9	19.8
Biology	AIDS	2000	2	15.7	16.2
	PROTEINS	1113	2	39.1	72.8
	PROTEINS_full	1113	2	39.1	72.8
	PTC_FM	349	2	14.1	14.5
	PTC_FR	351	2	14.6	15.0
	PTC_MM	336	2	14.0	14.3
	PTC_MR	344	2	14.3	14.7
Computer vision	Cuneiform	267	30	21.3	44.8
	MSRC_9	221	8	40.6	97.9
	MSRC_21	563	20	77.5	198.3

IKM. For IKM the PSD graph kernels mostly result in non-invertible kernel matrix so that we need to resort to indefinite IKM methods. Table 2 presents the average classification accuracy of the two indefinite IKM methods. Note that these results are partly taken from [39], which is the methodological backbone for our current work with five indefinite IKM methods and contains experiments on graph datasets and additional UCI non-graph datasets. Here we further increase the number of graph datasets and graph kernels. It can be observed that **CE** tends to perform better than **LSQ**. This is not a surprise since the cross entropy loss is generally a better choice for classification than the least-square error. These results show that the indefinite IKM methods can successfully handle the indefinite cases.

The good performance of IKMs is comprehensible and even expectable. The representer theorem allows us to express the optimal solution of widely used risk minimization problems in the form (2) as linear combination of expansions in terms of the training samples. An interpolation kernel machine basically takes this form of optimal solution, Eq. (3), and directly optimizes its parameters α_i by a suitable loss function and training. In some sense the IKM thus may be understood as an ultimate way of learning based on the representer theorem.

IKM vs. SVM. For a comparative study with SVM one could use its standard version since all used graph kernels are PSD. In our study we do apply indefi-

Table 2. Performance (%) of indefinite interpolation kernel machines **LSQ** and **CE** on graph datasets. Comparison with indefinite SVMs.

Dataset	Method											
	Shortest path [4]				Neighborhood hash [8]				Weisfeiler-Lehman [31]			
	LSQ	**CE**	SVM-SMO	SVM-DC	**LSQ**	**CE**	SVM-SMO	SVM-DC	**LSQ**	**CE**	SVM-SMO	SVM-DC
BZR	79.9	85.4	80.1	83.4	75.4	76.9	77.9	78.1	78.9	80.4	78.6	78.1
BZR_MD	66.0	66.7	40.9	63.4	62.6	62.1	59.5	63.0	50.3	55.1	43.5	48.3
COX2	78.4	76.9	78.2	78.2	80.1	81.0	78.0	79.5	76.3	79.4	78.2	78.4
COX2_MD	59.8	61.1	46.2	59.5	50.3	52.6	47.9	52.2	47.7	50.6	36.3	43.0
DHFR	72.0	67.6	60.4	66.2	72.4	74.1	74.4	74.8	73.6	75.5	75.2	76.3
DHFR_MD	66.2	65.9	67.9	67.4	58.8	57.8	63.6	60.1	64.1	63.1	63.6	63.6
ER_MD	59.5	60.5	59.2	55.7	65.0	66.1	63.8	65.9	66.3	66.5	64.9	64.9
MUTAG	78.7	80.3	80.3	81.9	87.8	85.1	85.6	86.1	83.5	79.8	78.3	81.4
AIDS	98.3	98.3	99.2	99.3	99.2	99.1	99.3	99.3	95.8	94.0	97.8	98.1
PROTEINS	70.5	70.6	72.0	72.8	65.9	68.8	69.7	68.4	63.9	62.2	69.6	69.8
PROTEINS_full	70.5	70.6	71.9	72.8	66.5	69.1	69.8	68.3	63.7	62.2	69.6	69.8
PTC_FM	59.9	57.0	63.6	59.0	59.6	60.7	61.6	59.6	63.6	63.0	64.2	61.3
PTC_FR	65.5	65.3	67.9	64.4	65.0	65.6	67.3	65.5	65.5	67.0	67.9	67.5
PTC_MM	64.6	61.6	64.0	63.4	63.7	64.6	64.9	64.9	67.0	67.9	66.4	69.1
PTC_MR	53.5	57.3	55.6	60.2	64.5	64.3	62.3	64.8	61.3	60.8	62.3	62.2
Cuneiform	53.9	79.7	64.4	80.8	80.5	80.8	80.5	80.5	80.5	80.5	80.5	80.5
MSRC_9	90.5	90.0	87.8	90.0	92.8	92.8	93.7	92.8	90.5	90.5	85.1	90.1
MSRC_21	75.3	75.2	70.9	76.2	81.7	80.3	80.5	81.0	70.7	70.7	64.0	70.4
Average	70.2	71.7	68.4	71.9	71.8	72.3	72.2	72.5	70.2	70.5	69.2	70.7

Dataset	Method											
	Graph decomposition [21]				Propagation [24]				Pyramid match [26]			
	LSQ	**CE**	SVM-SMO	SVM-DC	**LSQ**	**CE**	SVM-SMO	SVM-DC	**LSQ**	**CE**	SVM-SMO	SVM-DC
BZR	74.5	74.5	78.6	78.6	75.9	75.7	78.6	79.1	75.7	80.9	81.6	82.9
BZR_MD	62.8	60.5	32.1	32.4	49.7	49.7	48.7	49.7	60.8	60.8	60.7	63.1
COX2	79.2	79.2	78.2	78.2	76.0	79.0	78.2	78.2	77.8	78.2	78.2	76.9
COX2_MD	60.2	60.8	34.4	35.7	50.9	50.6	50.6	50.2	57.8	57.8	57.5	59.4
DHFR	70.8	70.8	61.0	61.0	69.0	74.3	73.6	75.7	67.3	70.0	63.4	68.9
DHFR_MD	65.7	66.4	67.9	67.9	58.0	60.8	63.4	60.5	54.0	54.0	67.9	62.9
ER_MD	54.1	58.0	59.2	59.2	63.2	65.4	65.8	64.3	57.6	57.6	69.9	68.3
MUTAG	77.2	77.2	67.6	74.5	78.7	77.6	70.2	76.1	86.1	83.4	84.5	85.6
AIDS	85.5	85.9	82.9	84.1	91.0	89.9	93.7	95.8	99.5	99.6	99.7	99.7
PROTEINS	52.4	51.0	55.1	57.9	63.8	64.4	70.1	70.5	66.0	70.9	69.5	71.0
PROTEINS_full	63.5	63.3	63.4	57.9	63.0	62.9	69.1	70.0	67.3	69.6	70.6	70.4
PTC_FM	63.9	63.3	64.5	63.3	57.0	59.8	62.2	59.3	59.6	57.3	59.9	60.8
PTC_FR	66.7	67.5	68.4	68.1	65.5	65.5	67.0	64.4	59.0	61.0	67.0	61.5
PTC_MM	67.2	66.9	67.0	67.5	65.8	63.7	64.6	67.3	61.7	62.9	64.6	65.8
PTC_MR	55.8	55.8	58.8	56.4	57.3	62.0	57.1	60.2	55.0	53.6	58.5	55.6
Cuneiform	19.9	75.6	45.9	65.4	80.5	80.5	80.5	80.5	81.3	81.3	80.1	82.0
MSRC_9	79.6	79.6	78.7	83.7	93.7	88.7	91.7	91.4	92.8	92.8	89.1	89.1
MSRC_21	76.4	76.4	60.7	74.8	72.3	71.6	70.7	76.4	72.0	72.0	75.7	79.3
Average	65.3	68.5	62.5	64.8	68.4	69.0	69.8	70.5	69.5	70.2	72.1	72.4

Table 3. Detailed comparison of IKM methods with SVMs.

Method	**LSQ**	**CE**
SVM-SMO	46.3	47.2
SVM-DC	38.9	42.6

nite SVMs. In these test cases a convex optimization problem has to be solved. The extended non-convex solvers should come to similar result. Concretely, we selected the SMO-type optimization [5], SVM-SMO, from the popular LIBSVM solver and the recent approach based on difference of convex functions programming [36,38], SVM-DC. SVM-DC has a regularization parameter γ. For a fair comparison we have done a grid search to fix its optimal value.

The performance measures with these indefinite SVMs are also presented in Table 2. Generally, SVM-DC tends to perform better than SVM-SMO. The performance of the variant **CE** is comparable with that of SVM-DC. This similarity in performance can be further detailed by looking at the percentage of test cases where one method performs better than the other one. The total number of test cases is 108 (18 datasets, 6 graph kernels). Table 3 reveals that in 42.6% (47.2%) of test cases, **CE** is in favor compared to SVM-DC (SVM-SMO). Also the slightly weaker variant **LSQ** can outperform SVM-DC (SVM-SMO) in 38.9% (46.3%) of the test cases.

6 Extended Experimental Protocol

The results above justify a systematic consideration of IKM parallel to the popular SVM for experimentation in graph classification. We thus propose an extended experimental protocol to obtain the maximal possible graph classification performance in a particular application using some graph kernel $k(x, y)$. It consists of different courses of action dependent of the type of graph kernel:

- If $k(x, y)$ is PD, then apply the standard SVM and the standard IKM.
- If $k(x, y)$ is PSD, then apply the standard SVM and some indefinite IKM.
- Otherwise, apply some indefinite SVM and some indefinite IKM.

In each case the applied methods can be compared to select the best one. The first case will rarely happen due to lacking strict PD kernels. In other cases it is also possible to further include additional options, e.g. indefinite SVM in the second case of PSD kernels as done in our work.

7 Conclusion

In this paper have introduced two important aspects, interpolation kernel machine and indefinite kernel methods, which have not received attention in the graph processing community so far. From the results and discussions above we can make the following conclusions:

- The IKM is a good alternative of the popular SVM that is currently omnipresent in kernel-based graph classification.
- Infinite SVMs should be taken into account for non-PSD kernels, see the discussion in Sect. 4.3.

The first statement was experimentally demonstrated in this work. The second statement is a fundamental one. In practice one should always consider the indefinite SVMs in general because of their formal correctness. Consequently, we have proposed an extended experimental protocol. With this work we contribute to increasing the methodological plurality in the graph processing community.

Acknowledgments. Jiaqi Zhang is supported by the China Scholarship Council (CSC). This research has received funding from the European Union's Horizon 2020 research and innovation programme under the Marie Sklodowska-Curie grant agreement No. 778602 Ultracept.

References

1. Argyriou, A., Micchelli, C.A., Pontil, M.: When is there a representer theorem? Vector versus matrix regularizers. J. Mach. Learn. Res. **10**, 2507–2529 (2009)
2. Balcan, M., Blum, A., Srebro, N.: A theory of learning with similarity functions. Mach. Learn. **72**(1–2), 89–112 (2008)
3. Belkin, M., Ma, S., Mandal, S.: To understand deep learning we need to understand kernel learning. In: Proceedings of 35th ICML, pp. 540–548 (2018)
4. Borgwardt, K.M., Kriegel, H.: Shortest-path kernels on graphs. In: Proceedings of 5th ICDM, pp. 74–81 (2005)
5. Chen, P., Fan, R., Lin, C.: A study on SMO-type decomposition methods for support vector machines. IEEE Trans. Neural Netw. **17**(4), 893–908 (2006)
6. Haasdonk, B.: Feature space interpretation of SVMS with indefinite kernels. IEEE Trans. PAMI **27**(4), 482–492 (2005)
7. Herbrich, R.: Learning Kernel Classifiers: Theory and Algorithms. The MIT Press, Cambridge (2002)
8. Hido, S., Kashima, H.: A linear-time graph kernel. In: Proceedings of 9th ICDM, pp. 179–188 (2009)
9. Houthuys, L., Suykens, J.A.K.: Tensor-based restricted kernel machines for multi-view classification. Inf. Fusion **68**, 54–66 (2021)
10. Huang, W., Du, W., Xu, R.Y.D.: On the neural tangent kernel of deep networks with orthogonal initialization. In: Proceedings of 30th IJCAI, pp. 2577–2583 (2021)
11. Hui, L., Ma, S., Belkin, M.: Kernel machines beat deep neural networks on mask-based single-channel speech enhancement. In: Proceedings of 20th INTERSPEECH, pp. 2748–2752 (2019)
12. Jia, L., Gaüzère, B., Honeine, P.: graphkit-learn: A Python library for graph kernels based on linear patterns. Pattern Recognit. Lett. **143**, 113–121 (2021)
13. Jia, L., Gaüzère, B., Honeine, P.: Graph kernels based on linear patterns: theoretical and experimental comparisons. Expert Syst. Appl. **189**, 116095 (2022)
14. Johansson, F.D., Dubhashi, D.P.: Learning with similarity functions on graphs using matchings of geometric embeddings. In: Proceedings of 21th ACM SIGKDD International Conference on Knowledge Discovery and Data Mining, pp. 467–476 (2015)
15. Kim, C., Klabjan, D.: A simple and fast algorithm for L_1-norm kernel PCA. IEEE Trans. PAMI **42**(8), 1842–1855 (2020)
16. Kriege, N.M., Johansson, F.D., Morris, C.: A survey on graph kernels. Appl. Netw. Sci. **5**(1), 6 (2020)

17. Lampert, C.H.: Kernel methods in computer vision. Found. Trends Comput. Graph. Vis. **4**(3), 193–285 (2009)
18. Loosli, G., Canu, S., Ong, C.S.: Learning SVM in Kreĭn spaces. IEEE Trans. PAMI **38**(6), 1204–1216 (2016)
19. Luss, R., d'Aspremont, A.: Support vector machine classification with indefinite kernels. Math. Program. Comput. **1**(2–3), 97–118 (2009)
20. Ma, S., Belkin, M.: Kernel machines that adapt to GPUs for effective large batch training. In: Proceedings of 3rd Conference on Machine Learning and Systems (2019)
21. Martino, G.D.S., Navarin, N., Sperduti, A.: A tree-based kernel for graphs. In: Proceedings of 12th SIAM International Conference on Data Mining, pp. 975–986 (2012)
22. Motai, Y.: Kernel association for classification and prediction: a survey. IEEE Trans. Neural Netw. Learn. Syst. **26**(2), 208–223 (2015)
23. Muñoz, A., de Diego, I.M.: From indefinite to positive semi-definite matrices. In: Proceedings of IAPR International Workshop on Structural, Syntactic, and Statistical Pattern Recognition (SSPR), pp. 764–772 (2006)
24. Neumann, M., Garnett, R., Bauckhage, C., Kersting, K.: Propagation kernels: efficient graph kernels from propagated information. Mach. Learn. **102**(2), 209–245 (2016)
25. Nienkötter, A., Jiang, X.: Kernel-based generalized median computation for consensus learning (2021). Submitted for publication
26. Nikolentzos, G., Meladianos, P., Vazirgiannis, M.: Matching node embeddings for graph similarity. In: Proceedings of 31st AAAI, pp. 2429–2435 (2017)
27. Nikolentzos, G., Siglidis, G., Vazirgiannis, M.: Graph kernels: a survey. J. Artif. Intell. Res. **72**, 943–1027 (2021)
28. Ong, C.S., Mary, X., Canu, S., Smola, A.J.: Learning with non-positive kernels. In: Proceedings of 21st ICML (2004)
29. Schlegel, K.: When is there a representer theorem? Adv. Comput. Math. **47**(4), 54 (2021)
30. Shalev-Shwartz, S., Ben-David, S.: Understanding Machine Learning: From Theory to Algorithms. Cambridge University Press, Cambridge (2014)
31. Shervashidze, N., Schweitzer, P., van Leeuwen, E.J., Mehlhorn, K., Borgwardt, K.M.: Weisfeiler-Lehman graph kernels. J. Mach. Learn. Res. **12**, 2539–2561 (2011)
32. Siglidis, G., et al.: GraKeL: a graph kernel library in python. J. Mach. Learn. Res. **21**, 54:1–54:5 (2020)
33. Suard, F., Rakotomamonjy, A., Bensrhair, A.: Kernel on bag of paths for measuring similarity of shapes. In: Proceedings of European Symposium on Artificial Neural Networks, pp. 355–360 (2007)
34. Wang, R., Lu, J., Lu, Y., Nie, F., Li, X.: Discrete multiple kernel k-means. In: Proceedings of 30th IJCAI, pp. 3111–3117 (2021)
35. Winter, D., Bian, A., Jiang, X.: Layer-wise relevance propagation based sample condensation for kernel machines. In: Proceedings of 19th International Conference on Computer Analysis of Images and Patterns (CAIP), Part I, vol. 13052, pp. 487–496 (2021)
36. Xu, H., Xue, H., Chen, X., Wang, Y.: Solving indefinite kernel support vector machine with difference of convex functions programming. In: Proceedings of 31st AAAI, pp. 2782–2788 (2017)
37. Xue, H., Chen, S.: Discriminality-driven regularization framework for indefinite kernel machine. Neurocomputing **133**, 209–221 (2014)

38. Xue, H., Xu, H., Chen, X., Wang, Y.: A primal perspective for indefinite kernel SVM problem. Front. Comput. Sci. **14**(2), 349–363 (2020)
39. Zhang, J., Liu, C.L., Jiang, X.: Indefinite interpolation kernel machines (2022). Submitted for publication

DRN: Detection and Removal of Noisy Instances with Self Organizing Map

Rashida Hasan(✉) and Chee-Hung Henry Chu

University of Louisiana at Lafayette, Lafayette, LA, USA
{rashida.hasan1,henry.chu}@louisiana.edu

Abstract. Identification of noisy instances provides an effective solution to improve the predictive performance of machine learning algorithms. The presence of noise in a data set poses two major negative consequences: (i) a decrease in the classification accuracy (ii) an increase in the complexity of the induced model. Therefore, the removal of noisy instances can improve the performance of the induced models. However, noise identification can be especially challenging when learning complex functions which often contain outliers. To detect such noise, we present a novel approach: DRN for detecting instances with noise. In our approach, we ensemble a self-organizing map (SOM) with a classifier. DRN can effectively distinguish between outlier and noisy instances. We evaluate the performance of our proposed algorithm using five different classifiers (viz. J48, Naive Bayes, Support Vector Machine, k-Nearest Neighbor, Random Forest) and 10 benchmark data sets from the UCI machine learning repository. Experimental results show that DRN removes noisy instances effectively and achieves better accuracy than the existing state-of-the-art algorithm on various datasets.

Keywords: Noisy instances · Outlier · Noise detection · Self-organizing map · Classification

1 Introduction

The quality of data is important in constructing any machine learning model with good prediction accuracy. The presence of noise in a data set is one of the key factors for poor data quality [1]. Real world data sets are generally dirty with noise, which is usually referred to as errors, irregularities, and randomness in a data set. In the data collection process, issues such as measurement errors, incomplete, corrupted, wrong or distorted examples may be introduced [2]. These noisy data sets may affect the intrinsic characteristics of a model, since these corruptions could introduce new properties in the problem domain.

Data gathered from real world problems are therefore never perfect and often suffer from corruptions that hinder the performance of the model in terms of (i) prediction accuracy, (ii) model building time, and (iii) the size and interpretability of the model [3]. Hence it raises an important research question of how to

M. El Yacoubi et al. (Eds.): ICPRAI 2022, LNCS 13364, pp. 480–491, 2022.
https://doi.org/10.1007/978-3-031-09282-4_40

identify and eliminate the noise from a data set. The problem of noise detection generally falls into two categories, viz. (i) class noise and (ii) attribute noise. Class noise occurs when an instance is incorrectly labeled. In contrast, attribute noise refers to corruptions in the value of one or more attributes. Of the two noise categories, attribute noise can be more harmful than class noise due to the fact that some attributes are highly correlated with the class label. The complexity of detecting attribute noise is relatively higher than that of detecting class noise [3]. In addition, limited attention has been given to attribute noise. This work focuses on detecting instances with attribute noise with an aim to improve the prediction accuracy of the machine learning model.

The majority of the noise detection algorithms eliminate instances that are either misclassified by a base learner or majority of the learners [4–6]. Considering only this criterion may be too aggressive. Some work focuses on clustering based noise detection [7]. The pitfall of these works is the reliance on the sizes of the clusters for noisy instance identification. Many studies use the term noise in a broader sense of outliers [4,8]. An outlier is a data point that deviates significantly from other observations in the training set. Outliers are noisy instances but also include exceptions e.g. in the application of fraud detection, intrusion detection etc. Therefore, such an assumption may result in deleting meaningful instances.

In this work, we present a novel noise identification algorithm, referred to as DRN. The proposed method investigates (i) how an artificial neural network can be used for outlier detection; (ii) how to distinguish noise from an outlier; and (iii) what is the deciding factor for the elimination of noisy instances? We consider noise to be distinct from an outlier in that we deem a noisy sample as due to observation errors, such as during the sampling process to form the training set. The main idea is to train the Self-Organizing Map (SOM) network to obtain an approximation to the underlying density generating the data, then exploit this information to label as outlier. SOM is relatively fast and computationally inexpensive even when the dimension of the data is large [10].

Other works based on outlier detection either depend on the cluster size or consider outliers as noise [4,7,8]. In our proposed method, we distinguish noise from an outlier by utilizing the information of misclassified examples. Hence, DRN does not solely depend on either outlier information or misclassified examples only. In addition, our method is robust and fast for large data sets as well. We perform several experiments with different characteristics of data to validate our assumption. To measure the effectiveness of our method, we use 5 different classifiers—J48, Naive Bayes (NB), Support Vector Machine (SVM), k-Nearest Neighbor (k-NN), Random Forest (RF)—to show that our approach DRN can effectively and efficiently identify noisy instances from a data set.

2 Related Work

A few works were conducted on the impacts of attribute noise [3,11]. Zhu et al. [3] investigated the impact of noise at different attributes and classification accuracy. Different noise identification techniques and noise handling schemes were discussed in [11]. Wei et al. [7] presented instance noise detection based on K-means clustering algorithm with a noise factor. The noise factor metric measured the degree of an instance being noisy. K-means clustering was used to divide the data into small and large clusters. An instance belonging to a larger cluster has a lower noise factor. They attempt to distinguish outliers from noise with the help of class labels of instances. Nevertheless, the noise factor entirely depends on the cluster size. It is possible that outliers may belong to large clusters as well as small clusters [12]. Hua [13] proposed a different clustering based approach where they calculate different noise factors for different data types. They determine an instance noise label by combining different noise factors and class noise factors.

Most existing methods for instance noise detection take misclassified examples into account [5,7]. The advantages of such an approach is simple but aggressive in eliminating instances. This is because if the model is simple and not robust enough, it could output misclassified examples as well. Iqbal et al. [14] improves the classification accuracy with a combination of misclassified examples and a Laplace estimator. Many algorithms utilize the class label for noise detection. The PANDA [8] algorithm does not require the class label but it has a high computational cost because it computes the mean and standard deviation for each pair of attributes in the data set.

While there is substantial work on class noise detection, very limited research focuses on attribute noise detection due to the high complexity of the problem.

3 DRN: Our Proposed Framework

We propose an instance noise identification method that uses the self-organizing map (SOM) network in conjunction with a classifier. Unlike other outlier based methods, our method does not consider outliers as noise. In addition, it does not depend on the cluster size. The computational cost is low compared to other methods. The goal of our work is to find those noisy instances that hinder prediction accuracy. Our approach relies on a neural network called Self-Organizing Map (SOM) which uses unsupervised learning. Such type of learning gets only input data and based on that they generate outputs. When the training phase ends, it generates clusters of data. We take advantage of this inherent characteristics of SOM to find outliers. However, outliers often contain interesting and useful information about the underlying system. To address this, we utilize the instances that are misclassified by a classifier. Misclassified instances are those instances for which the predicted class is different from the actual class.

We choose 5 classifiers (J48, NB, SVM, k-NN, RF) to identify misclassified examples. The reasons for choosing these classifiers are two-fold. Firstly, J48, k-NN and RF are nonlinear classifiers which have better prediction accuracy in linearly non-separable problems. Secondly, Naive Bayes is a linear model for classification that has been found effective in many problem domains. We also choose a classifier SVM which can solve both linear and nonlinear problems. Our assumption is that there could be two reasons for a learner to output misclassified examples: (i) the model is too simple; (ii) if there is noise in the data set as noise misleads the learning process. We eliminate the first reason by employing five robust learners. Therefore, the only reason left out for misclassified examples is the presence of noise in the training data. We validate our assumption in the experiment section.

3.1 Noise and Outliers in Learning

Consider a classification problem. Let $f : X \to L$ be the unknown classifier that assigns a label $l \in L$ to a given vector $x \in X$. The objective of learning is to find, such as through adjusting parameters of a model, from among a set of hypotheses H a function $g \in H$ that approximates f. The challenge is that we do not know f except for a training set T formed by sampling X. After finding g, such as by training on T, we would like $g(x)$ as close as possible to $f(x)$ for all $x \in X$. The degree to which g can achieve $g(x) \approx f(x)$ for those x that are not in T is referred to as the generalization ability of g.

In the context of this work, an outlier is a data point that deviates significantly from other observations in T. It can result from situations such as when the distribution of X has a heavy tail. Outliers might lead to overfitting in learning, which can reduce the generalization ability of g. Noise in general can be considered outliers. But we consider noise to be distinct from an outlier in that we deem a noisy sample as due to observation errors, such as during the sampling process to form the training set T.

3.2 Self-organizing Map and Outlier

The self-organizing map (SOM) is an unsupervised learning method that reduces the feature space dimension to a lower dimensional space; it can be considered as a clustering method when subsets of observations are assigned to an SOM node based on their similarities to each other [9]. The rationale for choosing SOM in outlier detection is based on the following properties: (i) it provides cluster centers that together have a topological structure. Therefore, a cluster center and its neighbors are more similar than clusters farther away in the SOM; (ii) the process does not need to have the cluster size specified in advance.

3.3 DRN

The proposed framework for DRN is presented in Algorithm 1. Given a data set $X = N \times p$ with a class label L where N is the number of instances and p is the number of attributes and L represents the class. First, we normalize the data using min-max scaling. After that we train the SOM network with the data matrix X. We then check for outlier neurons based on the MID matrix. We train J48, NB, SVM, k-NN, RF classifiers to get the list of misclassified examples. If there are instances common in both outlier list and misclassified example list, we identify those instances as noisy instances.

Algorithm 1: DRN

Input : Data matrix X , class label L
Output: List of Noisy instances
Normalize the data to mean and unit variance
Compute the MID matrix using SOM
if $MID[i, j] >= 0.5$ **then**
  return outliers;
end
Feed the training dataset to the classifier
if *Predicted class NOT EQUAL Actual class* **then**
  return misclassified examples;
end
Compare outliers and misclassified examples
if *there is a match* **then**
  return noisy instances;
end

4 Experiments

The objective of our experiments is three-fold: (i) impact of noise in classification accuracy, (ii) how can noise removal improve prediction accuracy, (iii) can DRN outperform the state-of-the-art algorithm?

4.1 Experimental Methodology

We carried out our experiments on ten data sets taken from the UCI machine learning repository [15]. These data sets include credit card, iris, spect, glass, wdbc, wine, dermatology, ecoli, segmentation, and yeast. One of the main attractions of our algorithm is that it can handle different types of data sets. The data set characteristics are summarized in Table 1.

Table 1. Dataset characteristics

Dataset	Instances	Attributes	Class	Missing values	Dataset characteristics	Attribute characteristics	Balanced?
Credit card	690	15	2	Yes	Multivariate	Categorical, Integer, Real	No
Iris	150	4	3	No	Multivariate	Real	Yes
Spect	267	22	2	No	Multivariate	Categorical	No
Glass	214	10	7	No	Multivariate	Real	No
Wdbc	569	32	2	No	Multivariate	Real	No
Wine	178	13	3	No	Multivariate	Integer, Real	No
Dermatology	366	33	6	Yes	Multivariate	Categorical, Integer	No
Ecoli	336	8	8	No	Multivariate	Real	No
Segmentation	2310	19	7	No	Multivariate	Real	Yes
Yeast	1484	8	10	No	Multivariate	Real	No

We evaluate our approach DRN in terms of classification performance. In our experiments, we use the most popular evaluation metric, viz. prediction accuracy, to validate our results. Prediction accuracy is the ratio of number of correct predictions to the total number of samples.

We split our data sets into training and test sets. The split percentage for training is 70% and for testing 30%. Training and testing are performed 6 times. In each iteration, we randomly select our training and test sets. The final accuracy is the mean value from the six runs.

The data sets we use in our experiments are from the UCI repository. They have been testified to be appropriate by many algorithms in the literature [2]. Hence, there could be two possible scenarios: (i) these data sets may be pure without noise (ii) there could be noise in the data sets. With this in mind, we perform our experiments in two different settings. In Setting 1, we assume these data sets are noisy, so that we do not inject any artificial noise. In Setting 2, we assume these data sets are clean. Therefore, we corrupt the data with Gaussian noise. The parameter settings for Gaussian noise are as follows: mean = 0, variance = 0.5.

In our SOM implementation, we initialize it with random weights. The SOM dimension is set at 10×10, the input length is set to the number of attributes. The radius of the neighborhood, sigma, is set to 1.0. The learning rate at which the SOM learns is set to 0.3. We use the same classifiers for both noise detection and evaluation.

Our implementation of the DRN[1] algorithm uses Python 3.5. All the experiments are run on MacOS Big Sur with a 3.1 GHz CPU and 8 GB memory.

4.2 Results

We evaluated our performance results in four different scenarios : (i) DRN performance with original UCI datasets (ii) DRN performance with artificial noisy datasets (iii) DRN vs outlier (iv) DRN vs k-means based noise detection algorithm.

DRN Performance Analysis with UCI Benchmark Datasets. We compare our DRN algorithm with the accuracy of the original data set collected from the UCI repository. The blue line in Fig. 1 indicates the prediction accuracy when the datasets from UCI are used to train with a classifier; i.e., without eliminating noisy instances and without injecting artificial noise. The prediction accuracy after applying DRN is shown in orange color. The higher the prediction accuracy the better the result. In this experimental setup, first we evaluate the performance of each classifier. To examine how DRN performs, we feed each dataset into our model. The purpose of this experiment is to show the effectiveness of DRN in removing noisy instances. Figure 1 shows the prediction accuracy between original data with classifier and DRN. From Fig. 1, we can see that our algorithm DRN outperforms on 8 out of 10 datasets for J48. With the Naive Bayes (NB) classifier, our algorithm have better accuracy on 8 datasets. There

[1] https://github.com/chobi21/DRN-Noise-Identification.

are three tie results with SVM and k-NN classifier but still DRN achieves better performance on 6 datasets. Our algorithms wins 6 out of 10 datasets compared with RF classifier.

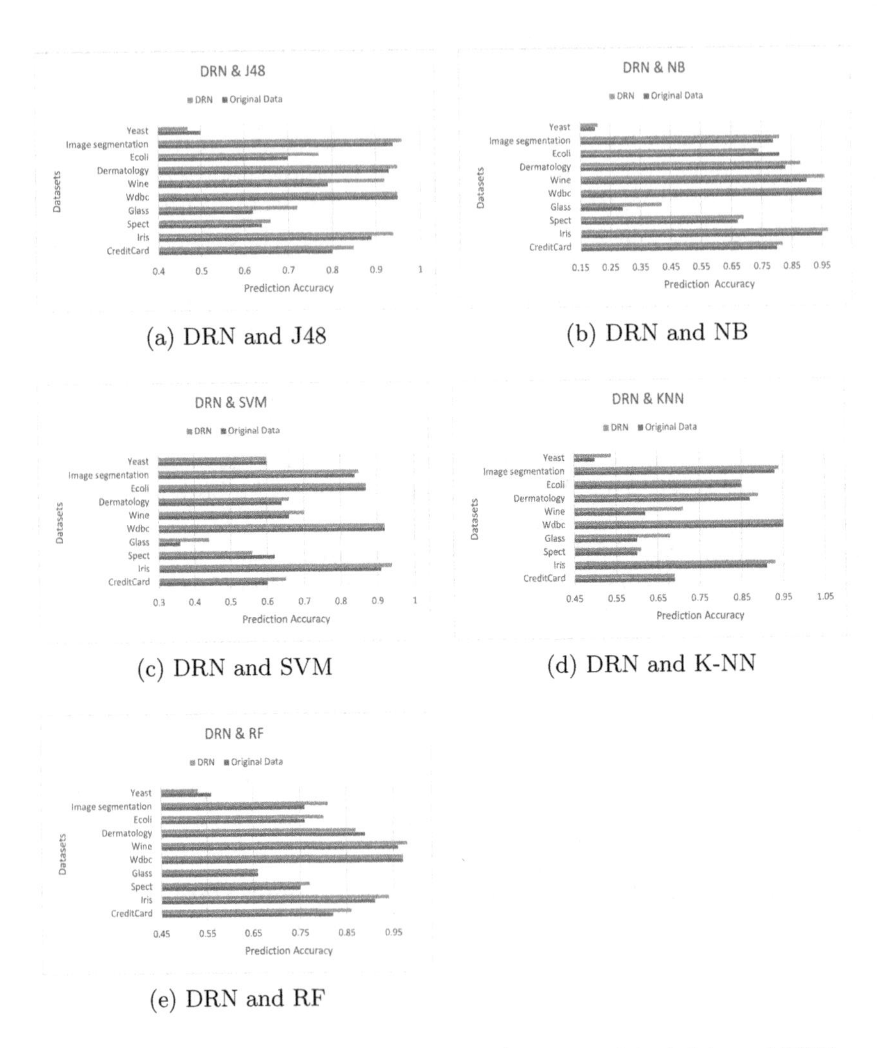

(a) DRN and J48

(b) DRN and NB

(c) DRN and SVM

(d) DRN and K-NN

(e) DRN and RF

Fig. 1. Comparison of prediction accuracy between original data and DRN.

DRN Performance Analysis with Artificial Noisy Datasets. We inject artificial Gaussian noise to the original data set. We train this corrupted data set with the five classifiers and test on prediction accuracy. From Fig. 2, on 4 classifiers out of 5 classifiers DRN achieves better performance for most of the datasets. The exception is only for Naive Bayes classifier where DRN wins fewer times compared to other classifiers. Nonetheless, DRN wins 5 times out of 10. From Fig. 2, we can see that DRN achieves better result on 8 out of 10 datasets when compared with the J48 classifier. With SVM, k-NN, and RF classifier DRN outperforms on 7 out of 10 datasets on prediction accuracy.

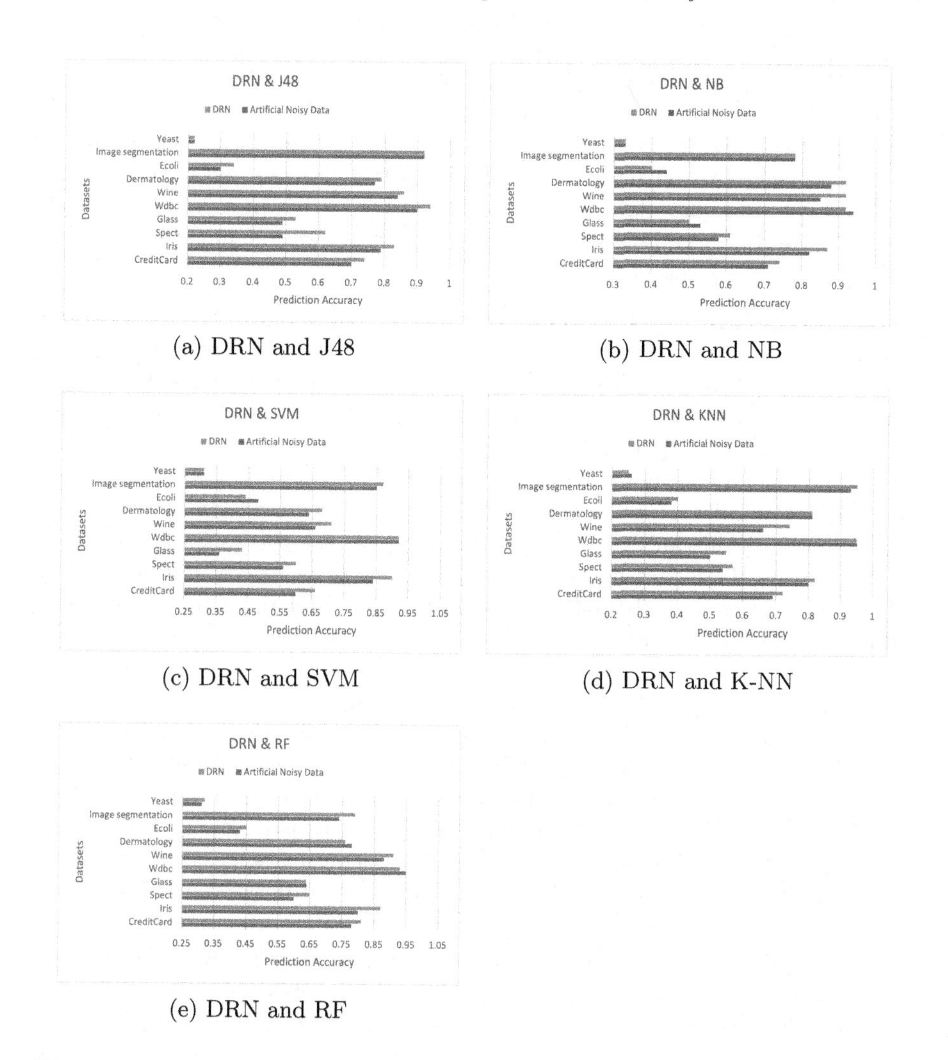

(a) DRN and J48

(b) DRN and NB

(c) DRN and SVM

(d) DRN and K-NN

(e) DRN and RF

Fig. 2. Comparison of prediction accuracy between artificial noisy data and DRN.

It is worth noting that in case of noise injection, the accuracy drops significantly. Therefore, it is evident that with the presence of noise, the model cannot learn from this data properly. The advantage of our algorithm is that even in such scenarios it improves the prediction accuracy for most of the data sets. The results from Fig. 2 demonstrates that DRN achieves higher accuracy in most of the noisy datasets. This is clear evidence that DRN is capable of removing noisy instances; hence improving the prediction performance (Table 2).

DRN vs Outlier. We also compare DRN with outliers. We examined if we only choose outliers, how it would affect the prediction performance. We obtain outliers from SOM clustering. We then remove those outliers from the original data set and train the classifiers with the remaining data set. Table 3 summarizes the results. With J48, our algorithm accuracy is better in every scenario except for wine. The performance for the wine data set is the same in J48 and slightly drops in Naive Bayes. In conjunction with Naive Bayes, DRN wins 7 times among 10. In case of k-NN and RF, DRN performs better in every dataset except iris data in k-NN and glass data in RF. The accuracy for iris in k-NN and glass in RF is a tie. With SVM, DRN wins 8 times. Therefore, we conclude that choosing outliers only hinder the performance.

DRN vs k-means Based Noise Detection Algorithm. We also present an experimental evaluation comparing our algorithm with the existing k-means based noise detection algorithm [7]. In order to have a comprehensive comparison of the existing noise detection algorithm with our algorithm, we use the same UCI datasets in the experiments.

The k-means based noise detection algorithm calculates noise factor to measure the potentiality of an instance being noisy. Based on these noise factors, they remove $p\%$ instances as noisy instances. We set $p\%$ as 20% because in reality, a given dataset is not likely to have more than 20% of its instances as noise. We use the same 10 datasets obtained from UCI repository to evaluate the performance of our algorithm with the k-means based method (Fig. 3). In iris, wdbc, and yeast dataset DRN outperforms k-means based method for each classifier. DRN wins 4 out of 5 classifiers in credit card, spect, glass, wine, dermatology, and ecoli dataset. To better understand the comparison of our algorithm with k-means based method, we average the results of five classifiers for each dataset. From Table 4, on 9 out of 10 datasets, DRN achieves better results than k-means based method. One of the important characteristics of our algorithm is that it can handle different types of datasets. For an instance, the iris dataset is a balanced dataset and ecoli is a highly imbalanced dataset. DRN performs better than k-means based method in both of these datasets.

As we stated in our experimental methodology, UCI datasets may be pure without noise. Therefore, we add Gaussian noise to these datasets. Our aim is to verify if DRN can outperform k-means based method in such settings also

Table 2. Average accuracy for original data, noisy data and DRN

Classifier	Original data	DRN	Injected noisy data	DRN
J48	0.77	0.82	0.64	0.68
NB	0.71	0.75	0.68	0.70
SVM	0.70	0.72	0.62	0.65
K-NN	0.75	0.78	0.65	0.68
RF	0.80	0.82	0.69	0.72

Table 3. Outlier accuracy vs DRN.

Datasets	J48		Naive Bayes		SVM		K-NN		RF	
	Outlier accuracy	DRN	Outlier accuracy	DRN	Outlier accuracy	DRN	Outlier accuracy	DRN	Outlier accuracy	DRN
Creditcard	0.76	0.85	0.77	0.82	0.61	0.65	0.65	0.69	0.81	0.82
Iris	0.90	0.94	0.92	0.97	0.93	0.94	0.93	0.93	0.92	0.94
Spect	0.62	0.67	0.64	0.69	0.54	0.56	0.57	0.61	0.63	0.77
Glass	0.58	0.72	0.37	0.43	0.38	0.44	0.63	0.68	0.66	0.66
Wdbc	0.90	0.95	0.94	0.95	0.86	0.92	0.92	0.95	0.93	0.97
Wine	0.92	0.92	0.97	0.96	0.70	0.70	0.68	0.71	0.93	0.98
Dermatology	0.88	0.95	0.82	0.88	0.71	0.66	0.73	0.89	0.79	0.87
Ecoli	0.75	0.78	0.79	0.75	0.86	0.87	0.81	0.89	0.74	0.80
Segmentation	0.93	0.97	0.77	0.81	0.79	0.85	0.90	0.95	0.70	0.81
Yeast	0.48	0.50	0.23	0.22	0.58	0.60	0.50	0.54	0.51	0.53

Table 4. Average accuracy obtained from 5 classifiers: DRN vs k-means based method.

Datasets	Original UCI datasets		Artificial noisy datasets	
	k-means based method	DRN	k-means based method	DRN
Creditcard	0.74	0.77	0.69	0.73
Iris	0.89	0.94	0.78	0.89
Spect	0.59	0.65	0.53	0.61
Glass	0.53	0.58	0.44	0.53
Wdbc	0.91	0.94	0.72	0.79
Wine	**0.85**	**0.85**	0.81	0.82
Dermatology	0.82	0.85	0.77	0.79
Ecoli	0.77	0.80	0.34	0.41
Image segmentation	0.85	0.87	0.84	0.86
Yeast	0.41	0.47	0.24	0.29

(Fig. 4). In the case of iris, glass, wdbc, and ecoli DRN achieves higher accuracy than k-means based method for each classifier. DRN wins 4 out of 5 classifiers in credit card, spect, wine, dermatology, and yeast dataset. Table 4 shows that DRN achieves a better result than k-means based method in all of the datasets.

From our experiment results, we make the following observations: (i) Noisy instance identification and removal indeed improve prediction performance; (ii) DRN achieves better accuracy in different data types; (iii) DRN performs better in both original data and injected noisy data; and (iv) DRN distinguishes between outlier and noise (v) DRN achieves better performance than the existing algorithm in both original and artificial UCI datasets.

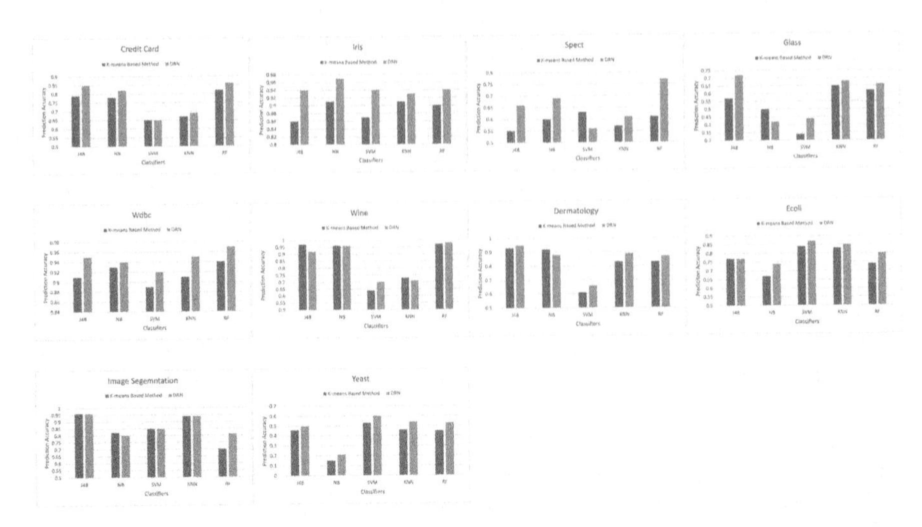

Fig. 3. Comparison of prediction accuracy between DRN and k-means based method with original UCI datasets.

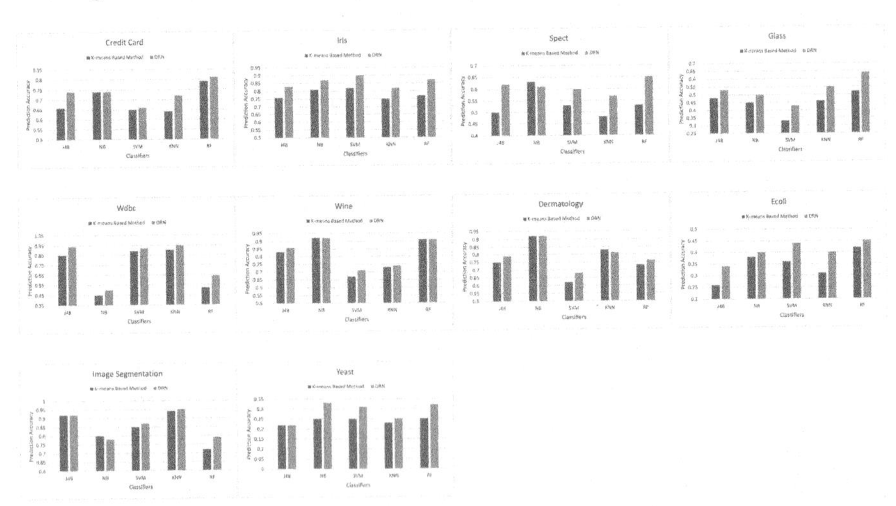

Fig. 4. Comparison of prediction accuracy between DRN and k-means based method with artificial noisy datasets.

5 Conclusions

In this work, we presented a new DRN method for detecting and eliminating noisy instances from a dataset to improve the prediction performance. Compared with the state-of-the-art algorithm k-means based noise detection, the DRN algorithm demonstrates better performance on various datasets. Our approach detects the outliers as well as separates outliers from noise. We employed a self-organizing map for outlier detection and utilized the misclassified examples for noise identification. Experimental results demonstrated that our approach DRN performs well in different datasets and improves the prediction performance in terms of accuracy. Our ongoing work is on extending our work to identify noise in an online manner both for class noise and attribute noise.

Acknowledgments. The authors thank the anonymous reviewers whose suggestions helped to clarify and improve our paper. This work was supported in part by the National Science Foundation under grant number OIA-1946231 and the Louisiana Board of Regents for the Louisiana Materials Design Alliance (LAMDA).

References

1. Han, J., Kamber, M., Pei, J.: Data Preprocessing. Data Mining, 3rd edn. The Morgan Kaufman Series in Data Management System (2012)
2. Libralon, G., Carvalho, A., Lorena, A.: Prepossessing for noise detection in gene expression classification data. J. Braz. Comput. Soc. **15**(1), 3–11 (2009)
3. Zhu, X., Wu, X.: Class noise vs attribute noise: a quantitative study. Artif. Intell. Rev. **22**(3), 177–210 (2004)
4. Gamberger, D., Lavrac, N., Groselj, C.: Experiments with noise filtering in a medical domain. In: International Conference of Machine Learning, pp. 143–151 (1999)
5. Farid, D., Zhang, L., Rahman, C., Hossain, M., Strachan, R.: Hybrid decision tree and Naive Bayes classifier for multitask classification task. Expert Syst. Appl. **41**(4), 1937–1946 (2014)
6. Sluban, B., Gamberger, D., Lavrac, N.: Ensembe-based noise detection: noise ranking and visual performance evaluation. Data Min. Knowl. Discov. **28**(2), 265–303 (2014)
7. Tang, W., Khosgoftaar, T.: Noise identification with the k-means algorithm. In: 16th IEEE International Conference on Tools with Artificial Intelligence, pp. 373–378 (2004)
8. Hulse, J., Khosgoftaar, T., Huang, H.: The pairwise attribute noise detection algorithm. Knowl. Inf. Syst. **11**(2), 171–190 (2007)
9. Kohonen, T.: The self-organizing map. Proc. IEEE **78**(9), 1464–1480 (1990). https://doi.org/10.1109/5.58325
10. Munoz, A., Muruzabal, J.: Self-organizing maps for outlier detection. Neurocomputing **18**(1–3), 33–60 (1998)
11. Gupta, S., Gupta, A.: Dealing with noise problems in machine learning data-sets: a systematic review. Procedia Comput. Sci. **161**, 466–474 (2019)
12. He, Z., Xu, X., Deng, S.: Discovering cluster-based local outliers. Pattern Recognit. Lett. **24**(9–10), 1641–1650 (2003)
13. Yin, H., Dong, H., Li, Y.: A cluster based noise detection algorithm. In: 2009 First International Workshop on Database Technology and Applications, pp. 386–389 (2009)
14. Sarker, I., Kabir, M., Colman, A., Han, J.: An improved Naive Bayes classifier-based noise detection technique for classifying user phone call behavior. In: Australian Conference on Data Mining, pp. 72–85 (2017)
15. UCI Machine Learning Repository. https://archive.ics.uci.edu/. Accessed 1 Jan 2022

Informativeness in Twitter Textual Contents for Farmer-centric Plant Health Monitoring

Shufan Jiang[1,2(✉)], Rafael Angarita[1], Stéphane Cormier[2], Julien Orensanz[3], and Francis Rousseaux[2]

[1] Institut Supérieur d'Electronique de Paris, LISITE, Paris, France
{shufan.jiang,rafael.angarita}@isep.fr
[2] Université de Reims Champagne Ardenne, CReSTIC, Reims, France
{stephane.cormier,francis.rousseaux}@univ-reims.fr
[3] Cap2020, Gradignan, France

Abstract. Data mining in social media has been widely applied in different domains for monitoring and measuring social phenomena, such as opinion analysis towards popular events, sentiment analysis of a population, detecting early side effects of drugs, and earthquake detection. Social media attracts people to share information in open environments. Facing the newly forming technical lock-ins and the loss of local knowledge in agriculture in the era of digital transformation, the urge to re-establish a farmer-centric precision agriculture is urgent. The question is whether social media like Twitter can help farmers to share their observations towards the constitution of agricultural knowledge and monitoring tools. In this work, we develop several scenarios to collect tweets, then we applied different natural language processing techniques to measure their informativeness as a source for phytosanitary monitoring.

Keywords: Crowdsensing · Social media · Smart agriculture · NLP

1 Introduction

Facing the challenge of growing population and changing alimentary habits, precision agriculture emerges to increase food production sustainability. Indeed, food production sustainability is part of the "zero hunger" goal of the 2030 Agenda for Sustainable Development of the United Nations [8]. Phytosanitary issues, including (a), abiotic stresses such as weeds, insect pests, animals, or pathogenic agents injurious to plants or plant products, and (b), biotic stresses such as floods, drought, extremes in temperature, can cause loss in food production. An important subject in precision agriculture is to improve the risk prevention tasks and measuring natural hazards within global and local aspects through real-time monitoring. We can classify mainstream real-time monitoring technologies of natural hazards into two categories [10]: (i), indirect monitoring

M. El Yacoubi et al. (Eds.): ICPRAI 2022, LNCS 13364, pp. 492–503, 2022.
https://doi.org/10.1007/978-3-031-09282-4_41

by analysing environment parameters produced by sensor networks and Internet of Things (IoT) devices to infer the probability of phytosanitary risks [23]; and (ii), direct monitoring by processing images [25]. Current precision agriculture technologies favour large-scale monoculture practices that are unsustainable and economically risky for farmers [12]. Moreover, according to the Food and Agriculture Organization of the United Nations, farms of less than 2 hectares accounted for 84% of all farms worldwide in 2019, and most of these small farms are family farms [22].

We suggest that current observation data from precision agriculture cannot represent all forms of farms, especially small farms. Recently, how to encourage the participation of farmers to share their knowledge and observations is drawing the attention of researchers [16,17]. However, local observations of farmers are not taken sufficiently into account, which results in the loss of legitimacy and the vanishing of local traditional knowledge. As [14] points out, local farmer knowledge relies on social processes for knowledge exchange, but the reducing number of farmers and the individualism weaken the local ties of blood and neighbourliness for knowledge acquisition. The diversification of professions in agricultural domain also destabilizes traditional structures of professional sociability [30].

The role of social media like Twitter in farmer-to-farmer and in farmer-to-rural-profession knowledge exchange is increasing, and it suggests that the use of Twitter among rural professionals and farmers is well evolved with open participation, collaboration (retweeting) and fuller engagement (asking questions, providing answers/replies) dominating one-way messaging (new/original tweets) [24]. Following the *social sensing* paradigm [32], individuals -whether they are farmers or not- have more and more connectivity to information while on the move, at the field-level. Each individual can become a broadcaster of information. In this sense, real-time hazard information is published in social networks such as Twitter. Indeed, Twitter enables farmers to exchange experience among them, to subscribe to topics of interest using hashtags and to share real-time information about natural hazards. Compared to paid applications, information on Twitter, presented in form of text, image, sound, video or a mixture of the above, is more accessible to the public but less formalized or structured. More and more farmers get involved in online Twitter communities by adding hashtags su as #AgriChatUK (http://www.agrichatuk.org) or #FrAgTw (https://franceagritwittos.com), to their posts on Twitter [7]. Thus, we can consider Twitter as an open tool for farmer-to-farmer knowledge exchange. This paper tackles the following question: which phytosanitary information can be automatically extracted from textual contents on Twitter, and what is the quality of this information?

The rest of this paper is organized as follows: Sect. 2 introduces our use cases and the dataset we built; Sect. 3 presents the concordances between the popularity evolution of tweets and historical records of hazards; Sect. 4 explores tweet topics using unsupervised methods and the pretraining of language models; Sect. 5 resumes lessons learned and presents future work directions.

2 Use Cases and Data Collection

We focus on detecting anomalies concerning crop health events. Possible anomalies include the time of the event -e.g., too early in the year-, the place of the event or the path taken by the pest, and the intensity of the attacks. In collaboration with experts in the agricultural domain from Cap2020 (https://www.cap2020.online/) and Arvalis (https://www.english.arvalisinstitutduvegetal.fr/index.jspz), we collected tweets concerning the following issues as observation cases:

- **User case 1: corn borer**. The corn borer (*"pyrale du maïs"* in French) is a moth native to Europe. It bores holes into the corn plant which reduces photosynthesis and decreases the amount of water and nutrients the plant can transport to the ear. Corn borers also eat the corn ear, reducing crop yield and fully damages the ear. These moths also lay their eggs on leaves of maize plant. Their larvae weaken the plant and eventually causes loss in the yield. The challenges of this use case are the following:
  - distinguish the larvae of corn borers from the larvae of other moths;
  - track their propagation timeline.
- **User case 2: yield of cereals**. The harvesting of straw cereals represents an important part of the French agricultural surface. Unexpected extreme climate events such as continuous heavy rains could result in loss in the yield. Farmers tend to express their concerns for the crops when they estimate unavoidable damages. Such concerns of yield help to predict the prices of the products. The challenges of this use case are the following:
  - index the impacted species and zones;
  - track the occurrence timeline;
  - contextualize the signals on Twitter with other data sources.
- **User case 3: barley yellow-dwarf virus (BYDV)**. The BYDV (*jaunisse nanisante de l'orge "JNO"* in French) causes the barley yellow dwarf plant disease, and is the most widely distributed viral disease of cereals. The BYDV affects the most important species of crops, reducing their yield. The BYDV can be transmitted by aphids [2]. The challenges of this use case are the following:
  - track the various symptoms depending on the species and varieties;
  - track the activities of the pest carrier of the virus in sensible season.
- **User case 4: corvids and other emerging issues**. Corvids ("corvidé OR corbeau freux OR choucas de tour OR corneille" in French) are species of birds that include crows and ravens. Corvidea can damage crops; for example, crows can pull the sprouts of cron plants and eat their kernels. The challenge of this use case are the following:
  - distinguish tweets about the attacks of corvids, while the damaged crops can be unknown or unmentioned in the text;
  - remove noises in the data, such as mentions of the famous Aesop's Fable *The Fox and the Crow*.

To study these use cases, we conceived the following methodology:

1. For each use case, we collect tweets with an initial set of keywords and a prior knowledge of the contexts of events such as cause, results, date, and region.
2. For use case 1 and 2, we plot the historical distribution of the collected tweets to verify whether the topic popularity corresponds to prior knowledge or documented data.
3. For use case 3 and 4, as there are many irrelevant tweets in the collection, we process the collected tweets with unsupervised algorithms: Latent Dirichlet Allocation [6] and K-Means [28] to extract concepts. We examine the concepts manually with domain experts to refine the scope of the topic and eventually remove tweets outside agricultural topics.
4. For the cases with a voluminous collection of tweets such as "corn borer", "BYDV" and "corvids", to tackle the challenge of distinguish observations from other agricultural topics like policies or advertisements of pesticide, we extract a subset of tweets (between 500 and 3000 distinct text values) to label: whether the text is about general information or a contextualized observation. From the labelled tweets, we build a classifier for event detection.

We use the Twitter API to collect tweets. When using the API, the matching of keyword is applied to not only the text field of a tweet, but also the username of the author or the text content of the referenced tweet. Moreover, accented and special characters are normalized to standard latin characters, which can change meanings in foreign languages or return unexpected results. For example, "maïs", which is *corn* in French, will also match "mais" which means "but" in English. Thus, we isolated accented keywords as special cases: for each accented word, we pulled all the normalized-word-filtered tweets from the Twitter API, and then we filtered them again with the accented word in our database. We saved original tweets as well as re-tweets. We have collected in total 16345 tweets about"corn borer", 3302 tweets about "BYDV", 50902 tweets about straw cereals and 38903 tweets about "corvids".

3 Histogram by Mention of Keywords

Use Case: Corn Borer. First, we want to confirm that tweets do talk about corn borers. We used "pyral" as keyword to retrieve tweets from Twitter API, then we kept the tweets that contain "maïs" to construct the dataset. We plot the number of tweets by month and by year in Fig. 1, and compare it with records of average corn borer number by trap from Arvalis (see Fig. 2). In both figures, we can observe peaks of corn borer between May and August. There is an exception in Fig. 1 since there are minor peaks in February, which correspond to the Paris International Agricultural Show (https://en.salon-agriculture.com/) when there people discussed about technologies to fight corn borers. Such exception shows that tweets collected by keywords is not precise enough.

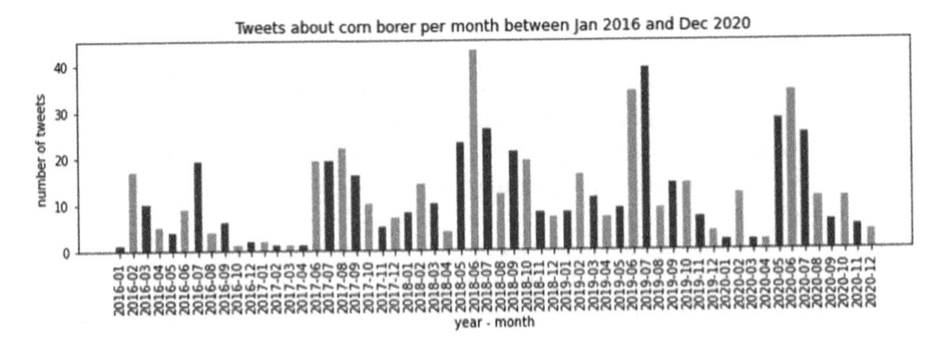

Fig. 1. Number of tweets containing "pyrale" and "maïs" by month between 2016 and 2020

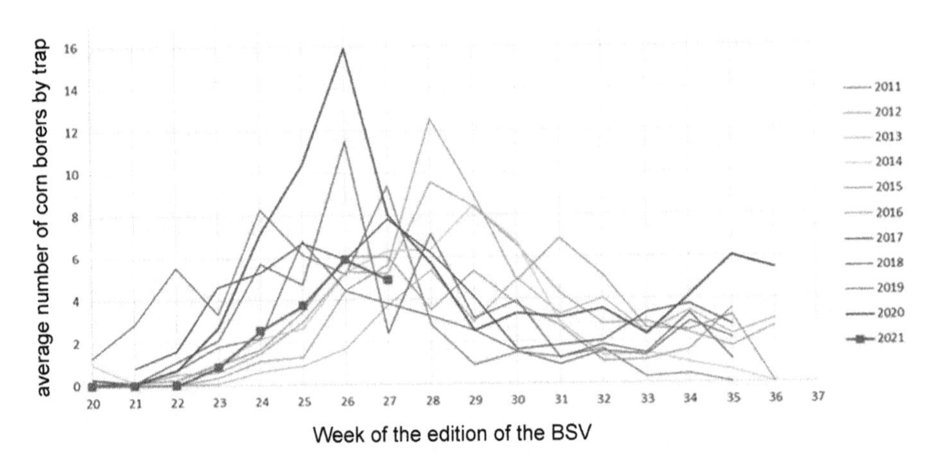

Fig. 2. Recorded averaged corn borer number by trap from [1]

Use Case: Yield of Cereals. We repeated the same data collection process for the yield of wheat. In this case, we used all the cereals in the French Crop Usage Thesaurus [27] to collect tweets (*céreales à pailles* in French). As these words are quite frequent, we add conditions to retrieve tweets containing "récolte", "moisson" or "rendement" (harvest or yield in English) and to remove tweets containing "recette" or "farine" (recipe or flour in English) to construct the final dataset of 54326 tweets between 2015 and 2020. Considering more and more people are engaged in broadcasting information about cereal production, we normalize the counts by using percentage of tweets mentioning cereal yields per month against the total mentions of each year and against the accumulated mentions of each month in 6 years (see Fig. 3). Both curves show peaks between June and September each year, which correspond to the harvest season. We can also see that the peak in 2016 is higher than the other years. This abnormal popularity corresponds to the extreme yield loss in France in 2016 due to heavy rainfalls [5]. This case shows that people tend to post more tweets when bad things happen than when everything goes well, which confirms the interest of using Twitter as a source of crop health monitoring. We also plot tweets counts since this catastrophic yield containing the keywords "récolte" and "2016" in Fig. 4. We found that this event is recalled in 2020, when people had a negative prediction for yield. We suggest that the reference of yield loss in 2016 reflects a collective memory on social media.

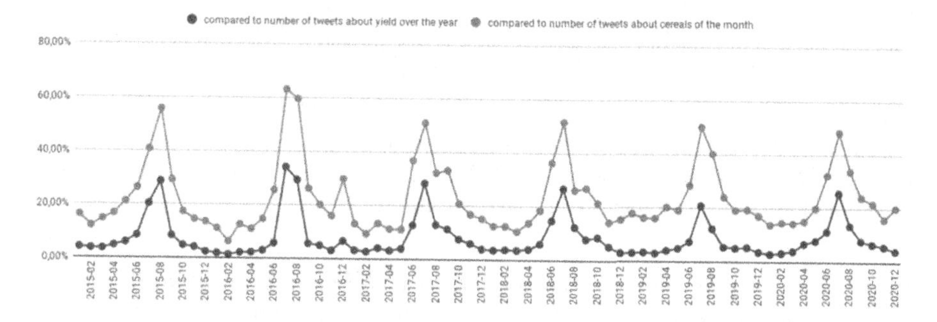

Fig. 3. Percentage of tweets concerning cereal yield between 2015 and 2020

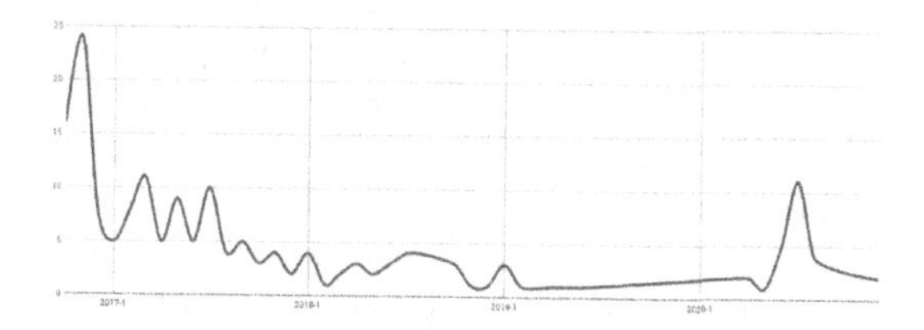

Fig. 4. Counts of tweets mentioning yield and 2016

4 Processing Tweets for Natural Hazard Detection

4.1 Topic Detection Based on Bag of Word Models

As we saw in the previous section, we have collected tweets about the natural hazard of the various use cases. The goal now is to explore in detail these tweets. We can see this task as an unspecified topic detection task [3]. Survey on topic detection [13] discussed different categories of unsupervised learning classification algorithms, including clustering techniques such as K-Means or DBSCAN, matrix factorization techniques like singular value decomposition (SVD), and probabilistic models like Latent Dirichlet Allocation (LDA) [6]. These algorithms have been created to automatically divide a collection of data into groups of similarity for browsing, in a hierarchical or partitional manner [29]. Most of the measures of similarity, such as Euclidean distance or cosine distance, can be only applied on data points in a vectorial space [15]. A simple way to project a collection of documents into vectors is to create a document-term matrix, which describes the term frequency (also called bag-of-words (BoW)) that occur in a collection of documents. In a BoW model, a document is a bag of words. Short for term frequency-inverse document frequency, TF * IDF is a formal measure of how important a term is to a document in a collection [26].

TF * IDF is defined as follows. Given a collection of N documents, define f_{ij} as the frequency of term (a word)t_i in document d_j. Then, define the term frequency TF_{ij} of term t_i in document $d_j$to be f_{ij} normalized by dividing it by the frequency f_{kj} of the maximum frequency of any term in this document: $TF_{ij} = \frac{f_{ij}}{max_k f_{kj}}$ The IDF of a term describes how much information the term provides. Suppose term t_i appears in n_i documents. Then $IDF_i = log_2(N/n_i)$. The TF * IDF score for term t_i in document d_j is defined to be $TF_{ij} \times IDF_i$. The terms with highest TF * IDF scores are often the most relevant terms to represent the topic of the document. TF matrix and TF * IDF matrix are widely used for describing the features of the document [4].

Use Case: Barley Yellow Dwarf Virus (BYDV). We searched in French for "jaunisse nanisante de l'orge" or "mosaïque jaune" and its acronym "JNO". However, there are ten times as many original tweets containing "JNO" than tweets containing "jaunisse nanisante de l'orge". The reason behind this is that "JNO" is also the acronym for other things, such as "Johny's Net Online". To collect Tweets, we used all the synonyms of "jaunisse nanisante de l'orge" presented in [31]. This list also includes the keyword "BYDV", which brings also tweets in English. Therefore, we need to look into the topics in the these tweets. Topics can be identified by finding the feature words that characterize tweets about the topic. At this stage, we do not know what are the topics among the tweets nor how many topics there are, so we cannot use keywords to filter undesired tweets. In this sense, we isolate the irrelevant tweets with the help of a clustering method as follows:

1. Removal of stop words.
2. Calculation of the TF * IDF vector for each tweet. To get a reasonable vocabulary size, we ignore terms that have a document frequency higher than 0.7 or lower than 0.01.
3. Feeding TF * IDF vectors to K-Means [29], for K between 2 and 20, find the best cluster number K using elbow method [19].
4. Calculation of the TD * IDF matrix for each cluster, examination of the 20 terms with the highest TD * IDF scores, and removal of undesired clusters.
5. Repeat step 2–4 till all the clusters talk about BYDV. An example of the final state of this cleaning process is shown in Table 1.

We executed the same step using LDA topic modelling with the document-term matrix. Both exercises succeed to distinguish tweets in English and tweets about "Johny's Net Online" from tweets about the BYDV. We find that tweets in English are classified to an isolated topic or cluster. We can observe "brassicole" and "hirondella" in a topic or a cluster, these are barley species that resist the BYDV. We can also see "puceron" (aphids in English) in both experiences.

Table 1. Top TF * IDF scored words in clusters in final state of K-Means based cleaning.

Cluster	Top TF * IDF scored words
0	année, blés, céréales, date, date semis, faire, faut, fin, jno orge, orge, précoce, pucerons, rt, variétale
1	dégâts, jno blé, orge, pucerons, rt, symptômes, virus
2	hiver, orge, orge hiver, pucerons, rt
3	année, automne, céréales, jno céréales, orge, pucerons, rt, traitement, virus, virus jno
4	année, brassicole, brassicole tolérante, brassicole tolérante jno, ceuxquifontlesessais, comportement, d'hiver, d'hiver rangs, hirondella, jno reconnue, jno reconnue brassicole, lorge, moisson, nouvelle, orge, orge brassicole, orge brassicole tolérante, orge d'hiver, orges, pucerons
5	automne, blés, hiver, jno orges, orges, orges hiver, parcelles, printemps, pucerons, rt
6	essais, faire, orge, orges, pucerons, rt, tolérantes, tolérantes jno, variétés orge, variétés tolérantes, variétés tolérantes jno
7	blé, combinaison, issue, issue combinaison, jaunisse nanisante lorge, jaunisse nanisante orge, jno jaunisse, jno jaunisse nanisante, jno maladie, jno maladie lorge, l'automne, lorge issue, l'orge issue combinaison, l'orge jno, l'orge jno maladie, maladie, maladie l'orge, maladie l'orge issue, nanisante l'orge, nanisante l'orge jno

4.2 Text Classification Based on Pre-trained Language Models

After filtering and cleaning the collected tweets, we can be almost certain that they talk about phytosanitary issues. For plant health monitoring, there is still the need for more precision. A limit of the BoW model is that it does not represent the meaning of a word. A better feature representation technique for text classification is a word embedding technique such as Word2Vec [11], where words from the vocabulary are mapped to N dimension vectors. Such vectors can be pre-trained on a large corpus and re-used for text classification tasks. The comparison between these vectors can be used to measure the similarity between words. Although word embedding may capture syntax and semantics of a word, it cannot keep the full meaning of a sentence [20]. Recent advancements in Bidirectional Encoder Representations from Transformers (BERT) [9] have showed important improvements in NLP, the multi-head attention mechanism seems to be promising for contextual representation. Next, we conduct supervised text classification based on a French BERT model CamemBERT [21], to verify whether CamemBERT can capture enough features of plant health observations.

Use Case: Corvids and Other Emerging Issues in General. In the scenario of plant health monitoring, the incompleteness of farmers' observations on

Twitter, partially resulting from the constraint on the text length, made the observation information unusable. Prior research on understanding farm yield variation [16] proposes to value them by bringing together observations from farmers and precise characterization of environmental conditions. To interconnect observation information on Twitter and other data sources, our first step is to extract tweets about observations. We define an observation as: a description of the presence of a pest or pathogens in a field in real-time. These tweets may be missing essential information, such as location, impacted crop, the developing status of the pest, damage prediction made by farmers, or suggestions of the treatment. The pest might be uncommon, as in the case of corvids, so this kind of damages are getting attention only since 2018. Thus, we can no longer filter tweets using known keywords. This observation detection is a binary classification task.

Given a small set of n labelled tweets $T = \{s_{t_1}, s_{t_2}, \dots, s_{t_n}\}$ and a language model LM. Each $s_{t_i}, s_{t_i} \in T$, is annotated with a label $o_i, o_i \in [0,1]$ indicating whether it is of an observation. s_t can be seen as a sequence of words $s = (w_1 w_2 \dots w_l)$, $s \in S, T \subset S$, $B \subset S$, where l is the length of the sequence, w is a word in natural language. To capture the features of s, we project S to a vectorial representation X using a LM. $LM(S) \rightarrow X$ can be seen as a tokenizer $f(s)$ plus an encoder $g(s')$. The tokenizer contains the token-level semantics: $f(s) \rightarrow s'$ maps sequences of words $s = (w_1 w_2 \dots w_l)$ to a sequence of token $s' = (w'_1 w'_2 \dots w'_{l'})$, where w' is the index of the token in its built-in dictionary, l' is the length of this sequence of tokens. The encoder $g(s') \rightarrow x, x \in X$ transforms s' to a continuous vectorial representation x [9]. Finally, we trained a softmax classifier with X and labels of T.

We invited experts to label 1455 core borer, BYDV and corvid tweets. Then we used the pre-trained CamemBERT base model [21] to encode tweets and train the classifier. We set the max sequence length to 128 and batch size to 16. We use Adam [18] for optimization with an initial learning rate of 2e-5. For evaluation, we plotted the precision -recall-threshold curve to find the best threshold to maximize the f1 score. To compare CamemBERT representations with BoW models, Table 2 shows the results of 5-fold cross validation of sigmoid classifier based on TDIDF vectors, and Table 3 shows the results of 5-fold cross validation of sigmoid classifier based on CamemBERT vectors. The latter is quite satisfactory. Finally, we use our classifier to predict tweets concerning natural hazards that never appeared in the training set such as wireworms ("taupin" in French, which is also a French family name). It distinguishes when "taupin" refers to a French family name or to wireworms. For an observation such as *"Pris en flagrant délit ...M. Taupin, vous êtes en état d'arrestation #maïs #masseeds"*, even though "M.Taupin" looks like is about a person, the classifier correctly classifies it to be an observation. This means that the polysemy of "taupin" is properly handled in the contextualized embedding of the tweets, and that the classifier focus on the sense of the text beyond considering only hazard names.

Table 2. Classification based on TF * IDF, with 5-fold cross-validation.

Dataset	Accuracy	Precision	Recall	f1
1	0.767123	0.539823	0.802632	0.645503
2	0.782759	0.566667	0.871795	0.686869
3	0.813793	0.620253	0.680556	0.649007
4	0.844291	0.702381	0.756410	0.728395
5	0.724138	0.536232	0.831461	0.651982

Table 3. Classification based on CamemBERT, with 5-fold cross-validation.

Dataset	Accuracy	Precision	Recall	f1
1	0.883562	0.759036	0.828947	0.792453
2	0.914384	0.857143	0.835443	0.846154
3	0.893836	0.775000	0.837838	0.805195
4	0.924399	0.913043	0.807692	0.857143
5	0.886598	0.843373	0.786517	0.813953

5 Conclusion

In this paper, we demonstrated the potential of extracting agricultural information from Twitter by using NLP techniques. The BoW model-based data clustering proves the possibility of semi-automatically browsing topics on Twitter with explainability. The language model-based supervised tweet classification experience demonstrates that, for a given concrete NLP task, language models have the potential to capture their contextual information, which can reduce manual labelling work for specific information extraction. In our scenario of plant health monitoring, the extracted tweets containing observations of farmers allow us to monitor natural hazards at the field-level. Thus, we open the possibility of conducting farmer-centric research, such as analysing and addressing the diversity of concerns and decision-making processes of different farmers. Furthermore, we can generalize our approach for the monitoring of other events on Twitter.

Ackownledgement. Thanks to Doriane HAMERNIG, Emmanuelle GOURDAIN, Olivier DEUDON, Jean-Baptiste THIBORD, Christophe GIGOT, François PIRAUX and Stéphane JEZEQUEL for their wise comments, their suggestions on the application scenarios and their contribution to Tweet annotation.

References

1. ARVALIS: Figure 2 : Evolution du nombre moyen de pyrale par piège selon l'année. https://www.arvalis-infos.fr/_plugins/WMS_BO_Gallery/page/getElementStream.jspz?id=72073&prop=image

2. ARVALIS: Jaunisse Nanisante de l'Orge (JNO) - Maladie virale sur Blé tendre, blé dur, triticale (2013). http://www.fiches.arvalis-infos.fr/fiche_accident/fiches_accidents.php?mode=fa&type_cul=1&type_acc=7&id_acc=53
3. Asgari-Chenaghlu, M., et al.: Topic detection and tracking techniques on Twitter: a systematic review. Complexity **2021**, 1–15 (2021)
4. Bafna, P., Pramod, D., Vaidya, A.: Document clustering: TF-IDF approach. In: 2016 International Conference on Electrical. Electronics, and Optimization Techniques (ICEEOT), Chennai, India, pp. 61–66. IEEE, March 2016
5. Ben-Ari, T., et al.: Causes and implications of the unforeseen 2016 extreme yield loss in the breadbasket of France. Nat. Commun. **9**(1), 1627, December 2018
6. Blei, D.M., Ng, A.Y., Jordan, M.I.: Latent Dirichlet allocation. J. Mach. Learn. Res. **3**, 993–1022 (2003)
7. Defour, T.: EIP-AGRI Brochure Agricultural Knowledge and Innovation Systems, February 2018. https://ec.europa.eu/eip/agriculture/en/publications/eip-agri-brochure-agricultural-knowledge-and
8. Desa, U., et al.: Transforming our world: the 2030 agenda for sustainable development (2016)
9. Devlin, J., Chang, M.W., Lee, K., Toutanova, K.: BERT: pre-training of deep bidirectional transformers for language understanding (2019)
10. Gao, D., et al.: A framework for agricultural pest and disease monitoring based on Internet-of-Things and unmanned aerial vehicles. Sensors **20**, 1487 (2020)
11. Goldberg, Y., Levy, O.: word2vec explained: deriving Mikolov et al'.s negative-sampling word-embedding method. arXiv preprint arXiv:1402.3722 (2014)
12. Heldreth, C., Akrong, D., Holbrook, J., Su, N.M.: What does AI mean for smallholder farmers?: a proposal for farmer-centered AI research. Interactions **28**(4), 56–60 (2021)
13. Ibrahim, R., Elbagoury, A., Kamel, M.S., Karray, F.: Tools and approaches for topic detection from Twitter streams: survey. Knowl. Inf. Syst. **54**(3), 511–539 (2017). https://doi.org/10.1007/s10115-017-1081-x
14. Ingram, J.: Farmer-scientist knowledge exchange. In: Thompson, P.B., Kaplan, D.M. (eds.) Encyclopedia of Food and Agricultural Ethics, pp. 722–729. Springer, Dordrecht (2014). https://doi.org/10.1007/978-94-007-0929-4_68
15. Irani, J., Pise, N., Phatak, M.: Clustering techniques and the similarity measures used in clustering: a survey. Int. J. Comput. Appl. **134**(7), 9–14 (2016). Foundation of Computer Science
16. Jiménez, D., et al.: From observation to information: data-driven understanding of on farm yield variation. PLoS ONE **11**(3), e0150015 (2016)
17. Kenny, U., Regan, A.: Co-designing a smartphone app for and with farmers: empathising with end-users' values and needs. J. Rural Stud. **82**, 148–160 (2021)
18. Kingma, D.P., Ba, J.: Adam: a method for stochastic optimization (2017)
19. Kodinariya, T., Makwana, P.: Review on determining of cluster in k-means clustering. Int. J. Adv. Res. Comput. Sci. Manag. Stud. **1**, 90–95 (2013)
20. Kowsari, K., et al.: Text classification algorithms: a survey. Information **10**(4), 150 (2019). arXiv: 1904.08067
21. Louis, M., et al.: Camembert: a tasty French language model. arXiv:abs/1911.03894 (2020)
22. Lowder, S., Sánchez, M., Bertini, R., et al.: Farms, family farms, farmland distribution and farm labour: what do we know today? FAO Agricultural Development Economics Working Paper (2019)

23. Olatinwo, R., Hoogenboom, G.: Weather-based pest forecasting for efficient crop protection. In: Abrol, D.P. (ed.) Integrated Pest Management, pp. 59–78. Academic Press, San Diego (2014) Chapter 4
24. Phillips, T., Klerkx, L., McEntee, M., et al.: An investigation of social media's roles in knowledge exchange by farmers. In: 13th European International Farming Systems Association (IFSA) Symposium, Farming systems: facing uncertainties and enhancing opportunities, 1–5 July 2018, Chania, Crete, Greece, pp. 1–20. International Farming Systems Association (IFSA) Europe (2018)
25. Qing, Z., et al.: A pest sexual attraction monitoring system based on IoT and image processing. J. Phys. Conf. Ser. **2005**(1), 012050 (2021)
26. Rajaraman, A., Ullman, J.D.: Data Mining, pp. 1–17. Cambridge University Press, Cambridge (2011). https://doi.org/10.1017/CBO9781139058452.002
27. Roussey, C.: French Crop Usage (2021). https://doi.org/10.15454/QHFTMX
28. Singh, V.K., Tiwari, N., Garg, S.: Document clustering using k-means, heuristic k-means and fuzzy C-means. In: 2011 International Conference on Computational Intelligence and Communication Networks, Gwalior, India, pp. 297–301. IEEE, October 2011
29. Steinbach, M., Karypis, G., Kumar, V.: A Comparison of Document Clustering Techniques, May 2000. http://conservancy.umn.edu/handle/11299/215421. Accessed 13 Dec 2021
30. Thareau, B., Daniel, K.: Le numérique accompagne les mutations économiques et sociales de l'agriculture. Sciences Eaux & Territoires Numéro **29**(3), 44 (2019)
31. Turenne, N., Andro, M.: Maladies des cultures (2017). https://doi.org/10.5281/zenodo.268301
32. Wang, D., Abdelzaher, T., Kaplan, L.: Social Sensing: Building Reliable Systems on Unreliable Data. Morgan Kaufmann (2015)

A Deep Learning Approach to Detect Ventilatory Over-Assistance

Emmanouil Sylligardos[1,2(✉)], Markos Sigalas[1], Stella Soundoulounaki[3], Katerina Vaporidi[3], and Panos Trahanias[1,2]

[1] Institute of Computer Science, Foundation for Research and Technology - Hellas (FORTH), Heraklion, Greece
{sylligardo,msigalas,trahania}@ics.forth.gr

[2] Department of Computer Science, University of Crete, Heraklion, Greece

[3] School of Medicine, Department of Intensive Care, University of Crete, Heraklion, Greece
medp2011911@med.uoc.gr, vaporidi@uoc.gr

Abstract. We propose a novel, end-to-end, decision support system, to facilitate ICU clinicians to identify ventilatory over-assistance and titrate the level of respiratory support. Our method consists of a wavelet-based algorithm to automatically segment distinct breaths in mechanical ventilator respiratory recordings, and a 1D CNN schema for the classification of new respirations. A dataset of 40 respiratory recordings, taken from 38 ICU patients, was used for quantitative performance assessment, where our approach achieved impressive results in detecting ventilatory over-assistance in a total of 76,595 distinct breath patterns. The proposed system is non-invasive, requires no changes in clinical practice and is readily applicable to contemporary mechanical ventilators. Accordingly, it facilitates efficient ventilator exploitation and reduces the risk of mechanical ventilation complications.

Keywords: Deep neural networks · Time series analysis · Mechanical ventilation · Respiration classification

1 Introduction

Mechanical Ventilation (MV) is a life-saving intervention for patients with respiratory failure. It is employed to support gas exchange and breathing in patients with respiratory failure of any cause. However, MV can cause rapid deterioration of diaphragm's endurance and strength, as a result of its inactivity. Studies [3] indicate that approximately 80% of mechanically ventilated Intensive Care Unit (ICU) patients exhibit various degrees of diaphragmatic weakness after the use of MV. This vicious cycle, where mechanical ventilation causes diaphragmatic weakness, which, in turn, necessitates prolongation of ventilatory support, can adversely affect critically ill patients and, consequently, increase health care costs, length of ICU stay and in-hospital mortality [6].

M. El Yacoubi et al. (Eds.): ICPRAI 2022, LNCS 13364, pp. 504–515, 2022.
https://doi.org/10.1007/978-3-031-09282-4_42

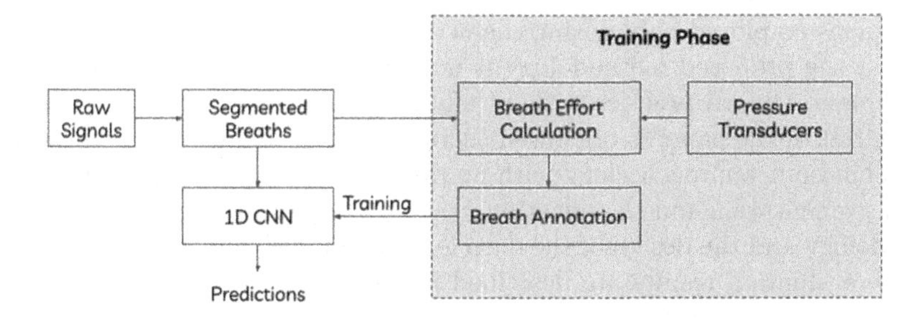

Fig. 1. The flowchart of the proposed methodology.

To prevent the development of diaphragmatic weakness, the level of ventilatory assistance should not be too high, covering entirely the patient's ventilatory demands, because, in such cases, the diaphragmatic contractions will be minimised. Yet, it is also important to always provide adequate ventilatory assistance to the patient with established diaphragmatic weakness and increased load, to prevent the development of dyspnea and distress. Therefore it is essential, when setting the level of ventilatory assistance, to meet a patient's needs both to prevent atrophy from over-assistance and to avoid distress caused by under-assistance [20].

Albeit under-assistance can often be recognized by the clinician due to patient's signs of distress (agitation, high respiratory rate, hypertension, diaphoresis), over-assistance has no overt symptoms and thus it's recognition and titration of the level of support is of paramount importance. The only method currently available at the bedside to help titrate the level of assistance is the direct measurement of diaphragmatic pressure which is relatively invasive, time consuming, and requires expertise and frequent evaluation, so it is not widely used [21]. As a result clinicians titrate the level of assistance mainly by trial and error, observing the patients for signs of under-assistance, which is obviously impractical and labour-intensive. Therefore, the design and development of a non-invasive method against ventilator over-assistance, e.g. supporting clinician's decision by serving as respiratory "smart alarm", is crucial and will be significantly beneficial for both patients and ICU personnel.

In this work, we propose a two-step, end-to-end methodology, as illustrated in Fig. 1, that non-invasively predicts the patient's diaphragmatic effort per breath, tackles the problem of ventilatory over-assistance and can readily be exploited to support clinicians' decisions. Initially, a wavelet-based technique is adopted in order to segment patients' respiratory waveforms, namely the air flow and the airway pressure -provided by default by all mechanical ventilators- into distinct breaths. A 1-Dimensional Convolutional Neural Network (1D-CNN) classifier is then employed, on each distinct breath, to infer patients' effort per breath and predict ventilatory over-assistance.

In order to accurately train our system, the level of effort per breath is quantified invasively by a balloon-catheter system that measures the pressure produced by diaphragmatic contraction [1]. Subsequently, the annotated dataset is used to systematically train the 1D CNN. It is worth emphasising that this technique is employed only during the network's training and evaluation phases and that the proposed methodology is non-invasive and designed to be readily applicable to clinical practice without any hardware modification requirement.

The rest of the paper is organised as follows. In Sect. 2 we describe the rationale behind our approach along with an overview of contemporary methods for breath segmentation and classification. Section 3 describes in detail the proposed methodology and the design of the deep learning model. The experimental setup and the evaluation results are described in Sect. 4, followed by a discussion on the paper's findings in Sect. 5.

2 Related Work

It is hypothesised that the level of patients' effort under assisted ventilation in order to prevent both over- and under-assistance should be similar to that of unassisted breathing in healthy persons. The gold standard method to evaluate inspiratory effort is the evaluation of the Pressure-Time Product (PTP) of the transdiaphragmatic pressure (PTP_{Pdi}), which unfortunately is rather complicated and cannot be implemented at the bedside. Thus, several studies have examined alternative methods to quantify inspiratory effort to help titrations of the level of assist [11,19]. Direct measurement of the transdiaphragmatic pressure is feasible, and the swings of the transdiaphragmatic pressure have shown to estimate effort with good accuracy, but is invasive and labour-intensive [21]. Other studies have examined the pressure generated in the airways after a brief, manual, end-expiratory occlusion, and shown that over- or under-assist can be estimated with reasonable accuracy (approximately 80%) [18]. These methods are easily applicable but not suitable for continuous monitoring and smart alarms.

To the best of our knowledge, only one work has proposed a non-invasive method to evaluate a patient's inspiratory effort. Albani et al. [2] have introduced a metric named "Flow index" and demonstrated that it is closely related to diaphragmatic work and that it can be measured non-invasively. Nevertheless, as the authors mention, the validity of their results requires further evaluation to be generalizable as several limitations exist in their study.

Regarding automated breath segmentation, one can find several approaches in contemporary literature. An example of such an approach is the automatic segmentation of respiratory data technique, described in [12]. Wearable sensors are employed to acquire breathing data, which are then segmented and classified into 4 distinct human activities with great success, namely resting, reading, food intake and smoking. In a more recent approach Noto et al. [13] assume a feature extracting technique to directly process and analyse human nasal airflow.

As regards to breath classification, it is part of the broader field of Time-Series Classification (TSC) that has been extensively studied. Guerts et al. [5] compared standard machine learning algorithms, such as Decision Trees, Decision Tree Boosting and 1-Nearest Neighbour across several TSC problems. Recently, Deep Learning techniques, such as LSTM networks [16], have been successfully applied on TSC tasks, while, Fawaz et al. [4] conducted an exhaustive study on Deep Neural Networks for TSC and concluded that end-to-end deep learning architectures, such as Convolutional Neural Networks (CNNs) and Residual Networks, can achieve state-of-the-art performance. Although 2D CNNs have been repeatedly used for image classification in recent research demonstrating compelling results [9], when dealing with 1-dimensional data, 1D CNNs have been shown to provide analogous results [10] with significantly lower complexity.

3 Methodology

The level of a patient's diaphragmatic effort, which is needed to infer whether the patient is under- or over-assisted, is typically provided by invasive techniques, which are unsuitable when dealing with ICU patients. To address this, our work is developed around the hypothesis that the breathing signals, provided by default by the mechanical ventilator, i.e. without requiring invasive techniques or ventilator modifications, are deemed to provide information on whether a patient is under- or over-assisted. We exploit the latter to develop a decision support system that will operate along with the mechanical ventilator to help the clinician recognize over-assistance and avert diaphragmatic weakness.

The proposed method is depicted in Fig. 1. Initially, a wavelet-based approach is applied on the patient's respiratory recordings to automatically segment distinct breaths, which are then fed to the 1D-CNN classifier to infer possible over-assistance and alert the clinician. During the Network's learning and evaluation phase, segmented breaths are automatically labelled, based on ground truth data acquired from 38 ICU patients.

3.1 Data Acquisition and Filtering

The analysis was performed on anonymous respiratory recordings obtained by ICU physicians as part of the clinical practice, mainly to titrate the level of ventilatory assistance. Acquired data consist of:

- *Flow* signal, namely Air Flow; the flow of air that goes in and out of the patient.
- *Paw* signal, namely Airway Pressure; the pressure that develops in the airway as air enters the lungs.

The above data are provided by default by the mechanical ventilator. For network training and evaluation purposes only, we exploit three additional signals, acquired using a balloon-catheter system connected to pressure transducers to measure the pressure produced by diaphragmatic contraction [1]:

- *Pes* signal, namely Esophageal Pressure.
- *Pga* signal, namely Gastric (stomach) Pressure.
- *Pdi* signal, namely Transdiaphragmatic Pressure; the pressure generated by the contraction of the diaphragm, as the difference between the pressure in the stomach (Pga) minus the pressure in the esophagus (*Pes*).

Due to the fact that the acquired waveforms are generated by the human lungs and muscles, emphasis is given on the analysis of lower, physiologic frequency ranges (typically less than 10 Hz) that are most sensitive to normal physical processes as well as pathologic structural alterations [8].

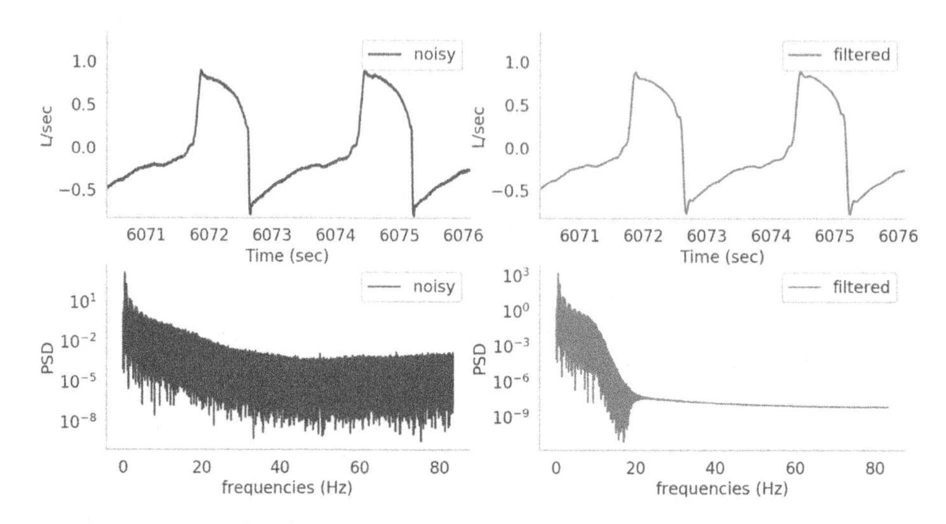

Fig. 2. Plots of the respiratory signal flow before and after the filtering are presented along with the Power Spectral Density (PSD). As indicated by the PSD, the filter eliminated the high frequency component caused by the electronic noise.

To exclude unwanted residual electronic noise that is unrelated to the patient, such as measurement disturbance in an electrical signal, the acquired signals must be filtered. A 5th-order Butterworth low-pass filter with a cut-off frequency 10 Hz is used twice (to achieve zero-phase digital filtering). In this way the high-frequency component is removed, while the low-frequency component of the signals, caused by breathing and movements of the diaphragm, is retained (see Fig. 2). After denoising, respiratory signals go through a processing pipeline to achieve automated individual breath segmentation and labeling.

3.2 Automatic Breath Segmentation

Breaths are automatically segmented based on a 2-step procedure (Fig. 3). Initially, extrema on the *Flow* signal are detected, in order to provide valid reference points for distinct breath segments. Wavelet transformation on the *Paw* signal points out inhale onset candidate points, in the vicinity of the identified breath reference points, which are then filtered out according to the ventilator's "trigger variable".

Extrema Detection. We designed a method to accurately identify extremas, on the *Flow* signal, using a sliding window voting system. Initially, based on the plausible assumption that maxima have adjacent points that are of lower

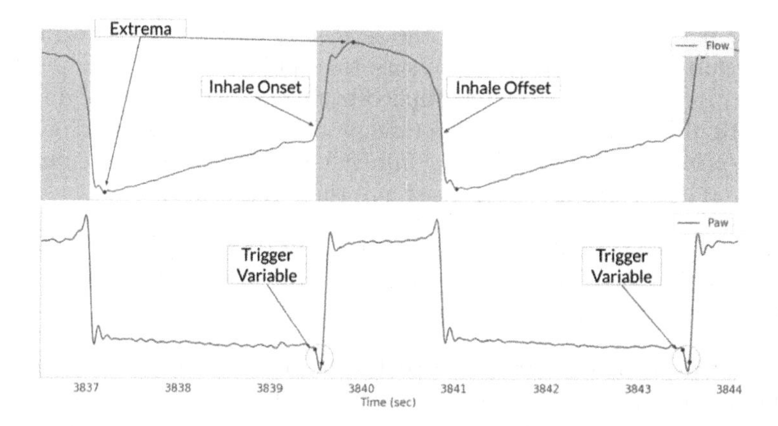

Fig. 3. Extrema on the *Flow* signal (Top) are used as breath reference points. Trigger Variable candidates are identified on the *Paw* signal (Bottom) based on the proposed wavelet-based approach, which are then refined to provide for the inhale's (green area) onset and offset.

(or higher in the case of minima) values, we implemented an overlapping sliding window that voted the possible extrema. The window slides over the flow waveform and in each iteration votes possible extrema based on the aforementioned assumption. The less voted candidates are, then, identified and rejected.

Since respiratory waveforms consist of iterations of inhales and exhales, it is obvious that every inhale maxima should be both followed and preceded by an exhale minima. Thus, when adjacent peaks (or valleys) are found, only the highest (or lowest) of them is kept. This results to a set of points that consists of all pairs of peaks and valleys in the signal, that is one pair for each breath, that will be used for the identification of each inhale's onset.

Inhale Onset Detection and Refinement. The initiation of a patient's inspiratory effort (i.e. the inhale onset) is marked by the contraction of the diaphragm which causes a small decrease in the value of *Paw*. This effect, called "trigger variable" [15], is sensed by the ventilator, which subsequently delivers the predetermined pressure. Accordingly, inhale onsets were set to be at the onset of the trigger variable.

A Mexican-hat Continuous Wavelet Transformation is applied on the *Paw* signal to detect "trigger variable" candidates, close to the initial breath reference points, which are then slid backwards on the *Flow* signal until it met the onset of the trigger variable. Eventually, each inhale offset was set at the point where the *Flow* signal crosses the value of its corresponding inhale onset.

3.3 Automatic Breath Labeling

The pressure time product of the Pdi (PTP_{Pdi}), that has already been used for quantifying the loading of the diaphragm in mechanical ventilation [17], is also used in our work for labeling the segmented breaths. By integrating the *Pdi* waveform we calculate the pressure time product of the *Pdi* per breath (PTP_{Pdi}/b) [14], which is then multiplied by 60 and divided by the duration of the breath, to compute the pressure time product of the diaphragm per minute PTP_{Pdi}/min. Based on the PTP_{Pdi}/min value, and according to contemporary literature [17], breaths are categorised into three classes:

- "Over-assisted", for $PTP_{Pdi}/min < 50\ cmH_2O/min$
- "Normal", for $50\ cmH_2O/min \leq PTP_{Pdi}/min \leq 150\ cmH_2O/min$
- "Under-assisted", for $PTP_{Pdi}/min > 150\ cmH_2O/min$

As stated previously, the proposed breath labeling approach is completely automatic. It requires an invasive system only during the network's training, whereas the method's general applicability refers to any ICU patient.

The above-mentioned three classes comprise the "classes of interest" from an ICU point of view. However, the "Over-assisted" class is by far the most interesting to capture, given that it is the one with no apparent symptoms and, at the same time, the class that dictates action by the ICU personnel. Consequently, accurate detection of ventilatory over-assistance, besides being challenging, greatly facilitates clinicians decision, on level of support titration, leading to reduced risk of ventilatory complications.

Erroneous Breath Detection and Deletion. Some samples happen to provide inaccurate information regarding the diaphragmatic effort, that is, the value of the Pressure-Time Product of the *Pdi* per minute (PTP_{Pdi}/min). These artifacts occur because of contractions of the esophagus. When the aforementioned samples occur, they are distinguished by the unusual long spikes formed in the *Pes* and *Pdi* signals. In order to automatically detect and delete those regions all peaks of the *Pes* waveform are first identified. Then, using the mean and the standard deviation of the value of all peaks, the z-score (the distance, expressed by the number of standard deviations, of the data point from the mean) [7] for every peak is calculated. Peaks with a z-score higher than a predefined threshold are declared as outliers, and the corresponding breath is rejected.

3.4 Breath Classification

In this work a 1D CNN classifier is used as shown in Fig. 4. The mentioned network consists of the input layer which is a passive one that receives the 2-channel 1D signal, i.e. the *Flow* and *Paw* channels that correspond to each breath. Subsequently, 3 convolution blocks follow with 2 1D convolution layers, 1 dropout layer and 1 Gaussian Noise layer each. The 1D convolution layers in the first convolution block have filters with kernels of size 40. The second and the third convolution blocks utilise filters with kernels of size 20 and 10, respectively. The use of dropout and Gaussian Noise within each convolution block was found to be essential for the model to be robust and generalise across different patients. After each convolution block, a subsampling (pooling) operation takes place

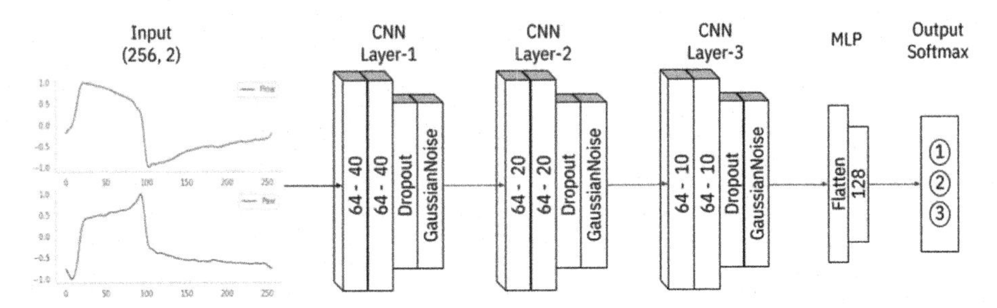

Fig. 4. The configuration of the 1D CNN used in this work. The network consists of 3 1D convolution layers and 1 densely-connected layer

with a subsampling factor of 2. Finally, the output layer is a softmax layer that produces the probability distribution over the output classes. The above-mentioned network parameters have been fine-tuned and set experimentally.

4 Experimental Results

In the current section we provide results and assessment that regards the automatic breath segmentation and classification. The former is empirically assessed with the assistance of trained respirologists, whereas for the latter quantitative assessment is applied.

4.1 Experimental Setup

The respiratory dataset, used in our analysis, consists of 40 anonymous recordings from 38 ICU patients of the General University Hospital of Heraklion. As described above, each recording has five channels of continuous respiratory waveforms, namely *Flow*, *Paw*, *Pes*, *Pdi* and *Pga*, as described in Sect. 3.1. After automatic breath segmentation and artifact removal, the dataset consisted of 76,595 distinct breaths. From those, 34,515 (45.06%) were classified as Over-assisted, 27,887 (36.41%) as Normal and 14,193 (18.53%) as Under-assisted.

The 1D CNN was trained and evaluated on different groups of patients. Accordingly, the dataset was split into two subsets, namely training and testing ones. The training set was used for designing and training the model and consisted of 28 patients and a total of 53,123 breaths (Over-assisted: 24,714–46.52%; Normal: 18,717–35.23%; Under-assisted: 9,692–18.24%). The test set was used to produce the final results and consisted of 10 patients and 23,472 breaths (Over-assisted: 9,801–41.76%; Normal: 9,170–39.07%; Under-assisted: 4,501–19.18%).

The CNN classifier was developed using Python 3 and the TensorFlow 2 platform. All experiments were conducted on a GTX 1050 Ti GPU with 16 GB of ram memory. Neural networks were trained with Adam optimizer for 10 epochs with a learning rate of 0.001. The loss function employed is sparse categorical cross entropy.

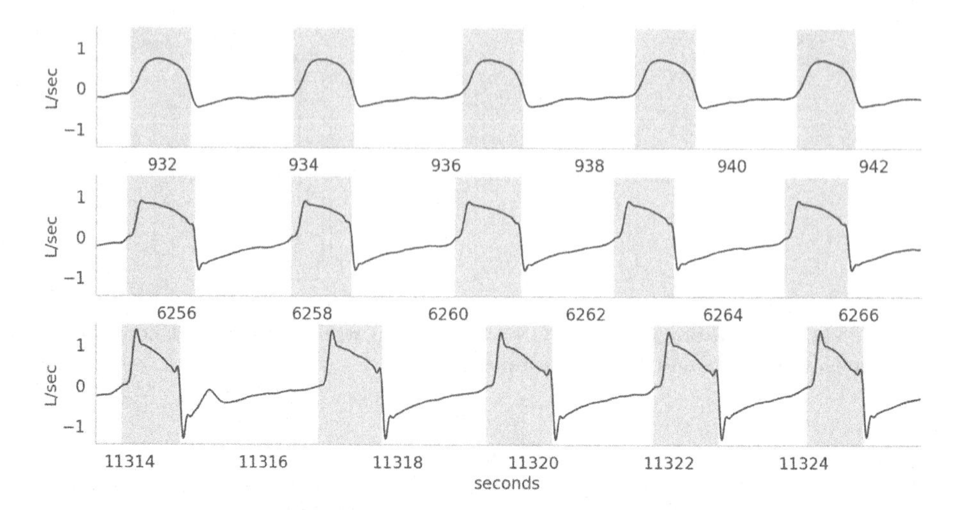

Fig. 5. The result of the automatic segmentation. Breaths from all classes are shown. From top to bottom: over-assisted, normal, under-assisted.

4.2 Breath Segmentation Evaluation

To evaluate the segmentation process a user interface was designed for respirologists to examine the inhale onsets and offsets produced by the algorithm. Out of the 76,595 breaths in total, a sample set of 22,136 breaths (28.9%) was carefully examined, and empirically assessed by means of breath segmentation accuracy, to produce the following results:

- 22,075 breaths (99.72%) were marked as correctly segmented.
- 61 breaths (0.28%) were marked as falsely segmented.

Overall, the performance of the proposed segmentation is qualitatively illustrated in Fig. 5.

4.3 Classification Assessment

Although accuracy is the most intuitive performance measure as it is simply the ratio of correctly predicted observations to the total observations, it can be misleading when dealing with imbalanced datasets. Therefore, several auxiliary metrics were used for the evaluation of classification performance, specifically a confusion matrix as well as precision, recall and F1-score per class.

A **confusion matrix** is a table layout that allows visualisation of the performance of an algorithm. The samples in an actual class are represented by the rows of the matrix, whereas the samples in a predicted class are represented by its columns. In our case (see Fig. 6) the number of predictions per class is normalised according to the total number of samples in that class.

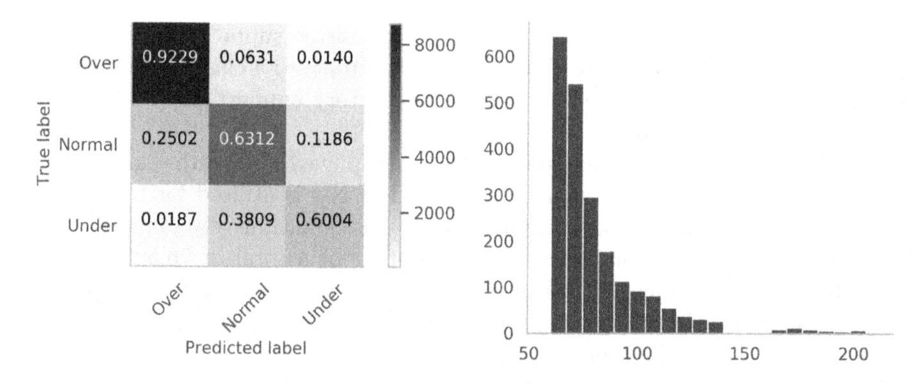

Fig. 6. The results of the evaluation of the final model. Left: Confusion matrix; Right: the distribution of the false positives of the over-assisted class.

Table 1. Precision, Recall and F1-score of all classes.

	Precision	Recall	F1-score
Over-assisted	0.801	0.923	0.858
Normal	0.720	0.631	0.673
Under-assisted	0.672	0.600	0.634

Precision is a ratio of correctly predicted positive (i.e. breath classified as Class X and being Class X) observations to the total positive predicted observations. Intuitively, the question this metric answers is: Of all breaths that are predicted of Class X, how many actually belong to X.

Recall, or "Sensitivity", is a ratio of correctly predicted positive observations to the number of positive observations. Again intuitively, the question this metric answers is: Of all breaths that belong to Class X, how many were identified.

F1-score is the harmonic mean of precision and recall. Intuitively, it is not as easy to understand as accuracy, however it is superior at describing a model when fitted on data with an uneven class distribution.

As observed in Table 1, the classifier successfully identified 92.3% of the cases in which the patients were over-assisted (see left part of Fig. 6), hence resulting in diaphragmatic weakness. Still, approximately 20% of the "Over-assist" alarms are False Positives (FPs). An examination on the FPs of the Over-assisted class reveals that the majority of FPs belong to the Normal class's low levels of diaphragmatic effort (see right part of Fig. 6). In particular 77,38% of FPs are breaths where the effort is in the low-normal range (below 90 PTP_{Pdi}/min) and therefore a decrease in assist would not have adverse effects on the patient.

5 Discussion and Future Work

In the current work we presented an autonomous classification methodology for labeling breath patterns in ventilatory supported patients. Contemporary

ICU research has revealed that in cases of over-assisted support, diaphragmatic weakness can effectively arise. Towards this, we proposed a classification system to aid ICU clinicians titrate the level of respiratory support and, thus, avoid ventilatory complications.

A generalizable wavelet-based algorithm is employed for breath segmentation over continuous respiratory signals, while a 1D CNN is utilised for the classification of each segmented breath. Our system was quantitatively evaluated over a dataset of 40 respiratory recordings consisting of a total of 76,595 breaths. Despite the given difficulty in distinguishing breath classes without employing invasive methods, the proposed approach greatly succeeded in detecting the most important class, i.e. the over-assisted one.

Classification accuracy is strongly dependent on the precision of the segmentation process. Although the employed onset identification was found to provide significantly good segmentation results, further improvement in breath delineation will have a beneficial impact on ventilator support titration. In addition, anomaly detection algorithms for detection and elimination of breath outlier patterns may prove particularly beneficial for enhancing the accuracy and robustness of the proposed methodology.

The obtained results should be considered as a rigorous proof of concept, demonstrating that state-of-the-art deep learning algorithms can thrive against urgent medical complications and provide readily applicable solutions. We acknowledge that the employed dataset may not be sufficiently diverse and possibly additional evaluation could be beneficial. Towards this, we aim at (i) intensifying our collaboration with respirologists and ICU clinicians to obtain larger and more diverse datasets, and (ii) studying methods for automatic reproduction of realistic synthetic data (e.g. Adaptable GAN encoders).

On the other hand, in order to enhance accuracy and alleviate the constraints imposed by the number of classes, it could be worth addressing the problem from different perspectives, e.g. regression rather than classification, in order to directly predict the value of PTP_{Pdi}/min. Nevertheless, our methodology provides a generic approach and design, and, therefore, is inherently scalable so as to support and lead further research in the sector.

References

1. Akoumianaki, E., et al.: The application of esophageal pressure measurement in patients with respiratory failure. Am. J. Respir. Crit. Care Med. **189**(5), 520–531 (2014)
2. Albani, F., et al.: Flow index accurately identifies breaths with low or high inspiratory effort during pressure support ventilation. Crit. Care **25**(1), 1–11 (2021)
3. Dres, M., Goligher, E.C., Heunks, L.M., Brochard, L.J.: Critical illness-associated diaphragm weakness. Intensive Care Med. **43**(10), 1441–1452 (2017). https://doi.org/10.1007/s00134-017-4928-4
4. Ismail Fawaz, H., Forestier, G., Weber, J., Idoumghar, L., Muller, P.-A.: Deep learning for time series classification: a review. Data Min. Knowl. Discov. **33**(4), 917–963 (2019). https://doi.org/10.1007/s10618-019-00619-1

5. Geurts, P.: Pattern extraction for time series classification. In: De Raedt, L., Siebes, A. (eds.) PKDD 2001. LNCS (LNAI), vol. 2168, pp. 115–127. Springer, Heidelberg (2001). https://doi.org/10.1007/3-540-44794-6_10
6. Goligher, E.C., et al.: Mechanical ventilation-induced diaphragm atrophy strongly impacts clinical outcomes. Am. J. Respir. Crit. Care Med. **197**(2), 204–213 (2018)
7. Ilyas, I.F., Chu, X.: Data Cleaning. Morgan & Claypool (2019)
8. Kaczka, D., Dellacá, R.L.: Oscillation mechanics of the respiratory system: applications to lung disease. Crit. Rev. Biomed. Eng. **39**(4) (2011)
9. Khan, A., Sohail, A., Zahoora, U., Qureshi, A.S.: A survey of the recent architectures of deep convolutional neural networks. Artif. Intell. Rev. **53**(8), 5455–5516 (2020). https://doi.org/10.1007/s10462-020-09825-6
10. Kiranyaz, S., et al.: 1D convolutional neural networks and applications: a survey. Mech. Syst. Signal Process. **151**, 107398 (2021)
11. Lassola, S., et al.: Central venous pressure swing outperforms diaphragm ultrasound as a measure of inspiratory effort during pressure support ventilation in COVID-19 patients. J. Clin. Monit. Comput., 1–11 (2021)
12. Lopez-Meyer, P., Sazonov, E.: Automatic breathing segmentation from wearable respiration sensors. In: Fifth International Conference on Sensing Technology. IEEE (2011)
13. Noto, T., Zhou, G., Schuele, S., Templer, J., Zelano, C.: Automated analysis of breathing waveforms using breathmetrics: a respiratory signal processing toolbox. Chem. Senses **43**(8), 583–597 (2018)
14. Ranieri, M.V., et al.: Effects of proportional assist ventilation on inspiratory muscle effort in patients with chronic obstructive pulmonary disease and acute respiratory failure. J. Am. Soc. Anesthesiol. **86**(1), 79–91 (1997)
15. Sassoon, C.S.: Triggering of the ventilator in patient-ventilator interactions. Respir. Care **56**(1), 39–51 (2011)
16. Smirnov, D., Nguifo, E.M.: Time series classification with recurrent neural networks. In: Advanced Analytics and Learning on Temporal Data 8 (2018)
17. Spadaro, S., et al.: Impact of prolonged assisted ventilation on diaphragmatic efficiency: NAVA versus PSV. Crit. Care **20**(1), 1–12 (2015)
18. Telias, I., et al.: Airway occlusion pressure as an estimate of respiratory drive and inspiratory effort during assisted ventilation. Am. J. Respir. Crit. Care Med. **201**(9), 1086–1098 (2020)
19. Umbrello, M., et al.: Oesophageal pressure and respiratory muscle ultrasonographic measurements indicate inspiratory effort during pressure support ventilation. Br. J. Anaesth. **125**(1), e148–e157 (2020)
20. Vaporidi, K.: NAVA and PAV+ for lung and diaphragm protection. Curr. Opin. Crit. Care **26**(1), 41–46 (2020)
21. Vaporidi, K., et al.: Esophageal and transdiaphragmatic pressure swings as indices of inspiratory effort. Respir. Physiol. Neurobiol. **284**, 103561 (2021)

Author Index

Printed in the United States